Urban Economics and Public Policy

Second Edition

JAMES HEILBRUN
FORDHAM UNIVERSITY

ST. MARTIN'S PRESS NEW YORK

For Carol

ACKNOWLEDGMENTS

p. 73, Figure 4.1: Adapted from figure 6, p. 86, in William Alonso, "Location Theory," reprinted from *Regional Development and Planning* by John Friedman and William Alonso, eds., by permission of the MIT Press, Cambridge, Mass. © 1964 by the Massachusetts Institute of Technology.

p. 115, Table 5.5: Changes in the hierarchy of trade centers in Saskatchewan, 1941–61. Data from Gerald Hodge, "The Prediction of Trade Center Viability in the Great Plains," *Papers* of the Regional Science Association, vol. xv, table 2, p. 95.

p. 138, Figure 6.5: Adapted from William Alonso, *Location and Land Use* (Cambridge, Mass.: Harvard University Press, 1964), figure 32, p. 112.

Preface

The very favorable reception accorded *Urban Economics and Public Policy* has encouraged me to prepare this second edition. As I sought to emphasize in the first edition, the urban-metropolitan system develops and changes profoundly through time. That truth was brought home to me once again as I undertook this revision. Not only have cities themselves changed since the first edition was completed in 1973, but also the national economic environment in which they operate has altered.

Three contextual changes stand out. First, a strong regional pattern has developed in the U.S. economy that weakens the older cities of the Northeast and North Central regions while strengthening those of the South and West. Second, the repeated escalation of fuel prices since 1973 has increased the relative cost of transportation and, through that key variable, may have important long-run effects on urban form and structure. Third, the national mood of fiscal restraint that became evident in the late 1970's has altered the prospects for many urban-oriented government programs. I have taken care to ensure that the second edition fully reflects these important changes in the economic environment. Consequently, revising the book has required not simply bringing its statistical content up to date but also analyzing new problems, reporting new insights, and describing new policies in the areas of urban transportation, poverty, housing and neighborhood development, and public finance. To do that while simultaneously incorporating suggestions from users of the first edition, I have rewritten fully half the book and added three chapters, including two entirely new ones on urban transportation.

In this volume, as in the first edition, I have tried to bring together three elements essential to an understanding of the present economic situation of cities. The first of these is a sense of where we are now and how we got there. Thus, following the Introduction, Chapters 2 and 3 of this book provide an economic explanation of the growth of cities and metropolitan areas. They emphasize the forces of technological change that first built up great cities during the Industrial Revolution and later brought about the massive dispersion of jobs and population into the metropolitan suburbs that is still going on. In this new edition, I have added a major section to Chapter 3 analyzing the deceleration of metro-politan growth and the unexpected development of a migratory flow from metropolitan to nonmetropolitan areas that occurred after 1970.

The second essential element is an understanding of the forces that determine the location, form, and economic structure of cities. Chapters 4 through 7, which cover the fundamentals of urban economic theory, deal with these topics. The theoretical analysis in these chapters is buttressed with factual evidence at many points. In the second edition these chapters, while largely unaltered, have been expanded to include analysis of the possible effects of rising energy prices on individual and business location decisions and consequently on urban growth and form. In addition, the theoretical analysis of intrametropolitan land-use patterns in Chapter 6 has been substantially extended.

As the Introduction to this book points out, the analysis of urban size, growth, form, and structure is vital to an understanding of urban economic problems precisely because these problems are significantly affected by the spatial organization of the city. Consequently, Chapters 2 through 7 are not only interesting in their own right but also provide the foundation for an understanding of the third part of the book, which examines four major urban problems: transportation, poverty, housing and neighborhood development, and the organization and financing of the metropolitan public sector. In order to deal with these four problems in their full complexity, I have devoted two chapters to each of these topics.

Since transportation is a crucial determinant of urban form and also an important policy area in its own right, the two new chapters on trans-portation provide an appropriate bridge between the earlier sections on form and structure and the later ones on urban social and economic problems. Chapter 8 deals with the economics of urban transportation, including the theory of optimal short-run pricing and long-run investment, while transportation policy issues are discussed in Chapter 9.

All chapters on public policy are thoroughly up-to-date in covering legislative changes, recent empirical studies, and new analytical insights. For example, the chapter on antipoverty policies includes an expanded section on the problem of work incentives under welfare programs and presents evidence on that question from the federal government's income maintenance experiments that was not available for the first edition. The chapters on urban housing include new sections on neighborhood deterioration and on the results of the experimental housing allowance program.

Analysis of the metropolitan public sector has been greatly expanded and divided into two chapters. The subject is developed with a good deal more applied microeconomic theory than was employed in the first edition. Chapter 14 includes a wholly new section on the property tax which explains both the "old" and the "new" views of the incidence and effects of this preeminently important urban levy. In Chapter 15, the theory of intergovernmental grants is developed in detail and integrated with the discussion of actual grant and revenue sharing programs. Both chapters also have new sections on recent events: the movement to limit taxing and spending is taken up in Chapter 14, while Chapter 15 contains a new section on urban fiscal distress and on what cities can do to improve their own economic and fiscal performance. The volume concludes with a chapter on the outlook for revival in the older central cities.

The book as a whole will be easily intelligible to anyone who has had an introductory semester of economic principles. Except for a bit of high-school algebra employed in Chapter 7, the approach is entirely nonmathematical. Nevertheless, the economic arguments are, I believe, rigorously developed and carefully qualified. While the book is intended primarily as a text for an introductory course in urban economics or urban economic policy, the chapters on transportation, poverty, housing, and public finance will also prove useful as supplementary reading for courses in urban sociology and politics or in urban planning.

My own experience in teaching urban economics suggests that the book contains a good deal more material than can be effectively conveyed in a single semester. Indeed, with the addition of a modest number of supplementary readings it provides enough matter for two semesters of study. Instructors limited to one semester might consider the following alternatives. If they prefer to emphasize urban economic theory, they can use Chapters 1 through 6, continue with 8 and 9, and conclude with 7. Chapters 6, 7, 8, and 9 contain enough policy analysis to bring home to students the applicability of the theory to current urban problems. On the other hand, instructors who prefer to emphasize policy can set up a sufficient theoretical foundation with Chapters 1, 2, 3, and 6 and then take up some or all of the policy issues covered in Chapters 8 through 16.

As in the first edition, the reader will find, both in the body of the text and in the footnotes, numerous references to the names and the works of other urban economists. These have been inserted, in part to indicate my intellectual debts but, more importantly, to provide students with a bibliography of the major writers on urban economics keyed to the topics on which I have found their works most relevant and useful. From these clues inquisitive readers will easily find their way to the major works in any part of the discipline. In order to familiarize students with major sources of information and help them to begin their own empirical work, I also provide detailed sources for most statistical data. The footnotes thus comprise my list of "suggested further readings." I hope it may be said that they are as valuable as any other part of this book.

I am indebted to many people for indispensable assistance in completing this work. The manuscript of the first edition was reviewed in its entirety by Professors Benjamin Chinitz, then of Brown University, and John F. Kain of Harvard, both of whom made innumerable helpful comments and suggestions. Professors George F. Break of the University of California at Berkeley and William G. Grigsby of the University of Pennsylvania provided most helpful reviews of the first edition chapters on public finance and housing, respectively. The chapters on transportation, written for the second edition, were reviewed by Professors Charles Clotfelter of Duke University, George W. Hilton of the University of California at Los Angeles, Herbert Mohring of the University of Minnesota, Roger F. Riefler of the University of Nebraska, and Kay Unger of the University of Montana as well as by Michael A. Kemp of The Urban Institute. Professor Riefler and Dr. Kemp also reviewed other sections of the second edition. The comments and suggestions of all these reviewers were most helpful and are gratefully acknowledged. Of course, none of them should be held responsible for the views I have expressed or for any errors of fact or logic that may remain in the text.

In tracking down elusive facts and publications, I relied on the advice and help of many people, some of them personal friends. I wish particularly to acknowledge the help of Diane De Are of the U.S. Bureau of the Census; Frank Kristof, President of the Rent Stabilization Association, New York City; Allan Mendelowitz of the U.S. General Accounting Office; and Seymour Sacks of the Department of Economics, Syracuse University. For research assistance on the second edition, I am grateful to Julie Ross, Wayne Estey, Frank Altieri, and, especially, Robert Heilbrun.

I wish to thank Bertrand Lummus and Michael Weber of St. Martin's Press for their genial cooperation in preparing the second edition, Gail Goldey for admirably copy editing the second edition, as she did the first, and Edith Flanders for typing the manuscript, often under great pressure, but always impeccably.

Above all, I am again grateful to my wife, to whom this book is dedicated, not only for her patience and support, but also for taking time from her own busy professional life to help with the long task of revision, and for remaining, like me, a lover of cities.

February 1981   James Heilbrun

Contents

ONE
Introduction 1

The Scope of Urban Economics 2
    Spatial Aspects of Urban Problems 3
The Criteria of Efficiency and Equity 4
The Theme and Outline of the Book 5

TWO
The Economics of Urbanization 7

Specialization, Trade, and Urban Growth Before the
    Industrial Revolution 8
The Impact of the Industrial Revolution 10
The Agglomeration of Economic Activity 13
Economies of Agglomeration 16
Diseconomies of Agglomeration 19
Is There An Optimum City Size? 20

THREE
The Growth of Cities and Metropolitan Areas 23

Some Definitions 23
    "City" 23

"Metropolitan Area"   24
"Urban" and "Rural"   26
"Central Business District"   28
"Suburb" and "Satellite City"   28
The Urbanization of the United States   29
The Growth and Decentralization of Metropolitan Areas   31
The Impact of Successive Revolutions in Transportation Technology   34
    Railroads   34
    Skyscrapers   35
    Streetcars and Subways   35
The Mononuclear City   36
Decentralization: The Overflow Effects   37
    Influence of City Age   39
Decentralization: The Automobile Effect   42
Decentralization of Jobs   43
    Changes in Work Trip Patterns   48
Decentralization of Population   48
    Evidence of the Automobile Effect   49
    The Influence of Rising Living Standards and Changes
        in Consumer Preferences   49
    The Influence of Public Policy   51
Migration and Metropolitan Growth   52
    Patterns of Migration by Race   55
Decreasing Concentration After 1970   55
    Effect of Metropolitan Size and of Region   58
    The Question of Metropolitan "Spillover"   59
Migration and Economic Opportunity   61
    Income, Well-being, and City Size   64
Higher Energy Prices and the Pattern of Settlement   66

FOUR
The Location of Economic Activity and the Location of Cities   67

Effects of Transport Costs on Choice of Location   68
    Materials Orientation Versus Market Orientation   70
    The Mathematics of Rates, Weights, and Distances   71
    Effect of Terminal Costs and Declining Rates   72
    Transport Advantages and Urban Growth   74
Locational Effects of Production-Cost Differentials   76

Production-Cost and Transport-Cost Orientations Compared   77
Types of Production-Cost Orientation   79
Summary of Locational Orientation   80
Changes in the Determinants of Location   82
Energy Costs and Locational Choice   82
Limitations of the Analysis   85
What Location Theory Contributes to an Understanding of
Urban Growth   85

FIVE
The System of Cities and the Urban Hierarchy   87

Central Place Theory   87
The Economic Basis for a Central Place   88
A Network of Central Places for a Single Service   90
Determinants of Characteristic Market Size   92
A Hierarchy of Central Places   93
Systematic Exceptions to the Hierarchical Order   95
The Problem of Empirical Verification   96
Two Case Studies: Washington and Saskatchewan   97
Defining a City's "Hinterland"   100
How the System of Cities Develops and Changes Through Time   102
Effect of a Rise in Population or Income   105
The Effect of Increased Economies of Scale   106
Effect of a Change in Transportation Costs   108
Transportation Costs and the Scale of Social Organization   110
The Energy Crisis and the Central Place System   111
Economic Development and the Impact of "Latent"
Central Services   112
Evidence for the Effects of Growth and Development   113
Intrametropolitan Patterns Are Not Explained by
Central Place Theory   116

SIX
Site Rent, Land-Use Patterns, and the Form of the City   117

A Simple Model: Residential Land Use   118
The Economic Character of Site Rent   121
Limitations of the Simple Model   121

A Model That Generates Systematic Variation in
       Density of Development   122
The Effect of Competing Land Uses on Urban Form   128
    Interdependence Through Competition for Sites   132
    The Doctrine of "Highest and Best Use"   134
Externalities and Land-Use Zoning   134
Introducing the Effects of Change and Growth   136
    The Effect of an Improvement in Transportation Technology   137
    The Effect of an Increase in Population   139
    The Effect of an Increase in Income   139
    Income and Travel Cost   143
    An Alternative Explanation of the Spatial Income Pattern   144
    Policy Implications of Alternative Theories   145
    Recapitulation: The "Automobile Effect," the "Overflow Effect,"
        and the "Income Effect"   146
    The Effect of Higher Fuel Costs   147
Toward Greater Realism: Transportation Corridors, Interpenetration
       of Uses, and the Decline of Mononuclearity   147
Empirical Evidence of Land-Value Changes Over Time   149
The Role of Site Rent Under Dynamic Conditions   150
Transportation Planning and Land Use   152

SEVEN
The Urban Economic Base and Economic Policy 153

The Basic-Nonbasic Theory   154
    Location Quotients As Export Allocators   157
    Measuring Indirect Exports   160
The Foreign-Trade Multiplier Approach   160
    The Similarity of the Keynesian and Basic-Nonbasic Multipliers   165
A Critique of the Basic-Nonbasic Method   166
    Excessive Aggregation   166
    The Instability of the Multiplier in the Short Run   167
    Changes in the Multiplier over the Long Run   168
Input-Output Analysis   170
    The Relationship Between the Structural Matrix and
       the Final Demand Sector   174
    The Simple Mathematics of Input-Output Analysis   175
    The Advantages of a Disaggregated Model   176

Input-Output Multipliers   179
The Limitations of a Static Model   181
Urban and Regional Simulation Models   182
Studying the "Supply Side" of the Local Economy   184
Growth as an Objective   185
Local Economic Policy and National Welfare   186
Subsidizing Industrial Relocation   188
Repelling Low Income Migrants   189
Local "Growth Control"   191
Pollution Control   191
Policies to Improve the Local Economic Environment   192

EIGHT
The Economics of Urban Transportation   195

Interdependence of Transportation and Land Use   195
Outline of Chapters 8 and 9   196
The Urban Transportation System   197
Mass Transit Versus the Automobile   200
Analysis of Modal Choice   201
Time as a Cost of Travel   202
Income, Value of Time, and Modal Choice   203
Income, Automobile Ownership, and Modal Choice   206
Elasticity of Demand for Transportation   207
Policy Implications of Inelastic Transit Demand   209
Fuel Prices and Modal Choice   212
Optimum Transportation Pricing in the Short Run   212
Pricing Highway Services in the Short Run   214
Pricing on Congested Roads   214
Pricing on Uncongested Roads   217
Pricing on Roads Subject to "Peaking"   218
Pricing on Urban Mass Transit Systems   218
Optimum Long-Run Adjustment of Transportation Systems   219
Why Aren't All Roads Congested?   222
Pricing with Economies and Diseconomies of Scale   223
Evidence on Transportation Cost   224
Highway Costs   225
An Estimate of Optimum Congestion Tolls   226
Mass Transit Costs   227

NINE
Urban Transportation Policy   231

Transportation Pricing in Practice   231
    Opposition to Congestion Tolls   232
    The Problem of Deficits Under Marginal Cost Pricing   234
    Financial Stress in the Transit Industry   236
    Subsidies for Mass Transit   239
    Income Effects of Mass Transit Subsidies   239
Choosing Among Transportation Systems   242
    Intermodal Cost Comparisons   242
    Pollution and Other External Costs   245
    Benefit-Cost Analysis of Transportation Projects   247
    Transportation Benefits   248
    External Benefits of Mass Transit   250
    The Distribution of Transportation Benefits   250
Government Policy and Transportation Choices   250
    Focus on Highways: 1916 to 1964   251
    Capital Grants for Mass Transit, 1964–   251
    An Evaluation of San Francisco's BART   253
    BART's Financial Record   256
    Demonstration Grants to Test Transit Innovations   258
    The Possibilities of Paratransit   259
Energy Costs, Transportation, and Urban Form   261
    Transportation Policy and the Energy Requirements of
        Alternative Modes   262
    Fuel Cost and Urban Form   263
    Possible Future Patterns   264
    The Rising Cost of Transportation and the System of Cities   266

TEN
The Urbanization of Poverty   269

Defining Poverty   269
The Changing Geography of Poverty   271
Race and Poverty   272
Why Poverty Is Concentrating in the Cities   276
    The Distribution of Poverty Within Metropolitan Areas   277

Shift in Relative Income Level: Central Cities Versus Suburbs   278
City "Age" and Intrametropolitan Income Differentials   280
Growth of the Urban Black Population   281

ELEVEN
Antipoverty Policies   285

Three Types of Employment Policy   286
Training, Education, and Human Capital   286
Job Creation   287
Overcoming Discrimination   288
The Growth of Employment and Training Programs   290
The Comprehensive Employment and Training Act   291
Evaluation of Training Programs   294
Evaluation of Demand-Side Policies: Tight Labor Markets   298
Evaluating Direct Job Creation   299
Accounting for the Relative Increase in Black Incomes   301
The Role of Income Support   302
Scope of Present Programs   304
Impact on the Rate of Poverty   307
Dissatisfaction with the Welfare System   309
Work Incentives in the Current Welfare System   311
A Guaranteed Income Plan   311
Balancing the Objectives of an Income Maintenance Program   316
The Difficulty of Welfare Reform   317
Urban Poverty and Racial Segregation   319
Ghetto Economic Development   320
Cumulative Effects of Development   323
Urban Poverty and Metropolitan Decentralization   325
Evaluating the Case for Dispersion   326
Black Unemployment Rates: Central Cities Versus Suburbs   327
Black Income and Occupational Status: Central Cities
Versus Suburbs   328
The Losses Imposed by Segregation   331
Other Arguments for Dispersion   332
Policies to Encourage Dispersion   333

TWELVE
The Problem of Urban Housing   335

Measuring the Quality of Housing and of Neighborhoods   336
    Neighborhood Quality   338
An "Adaptive" Model of the Housing Market   339
    Varying the Supply of Housing "Quality"   341
    The Demand for Housing Space and Quality   343
    The Effect of Income on the Demand for Housing   343
    The High Cost of New Construction   345
    The "Filtering" Process   347
Trends in U.S. Housing Conditions   349
    Is There Still an Urban Housing Problem?   354
    The Problem of Abandonment   355
    Interpreting Abandonment   357
    The Problem of Neighborhood Quality   358
The Rationale for Subsidizing Housing   359
    Does Housing Confer Indirect Benefits?   361

THIRTEEN
Urban Housing Policy   365

Public Housing   366
    How Good (or Bad) Is Public Housing?   368
    Some Alternatives to Housing in "Projects"   371
Urban Renewal   372
Market Imperfections and the Case for Urban Renewal   373
    The Problem of Site Assembly   377
Land-Use Succession in a Competitive Market   378
    Cost-Benefit Analysis of Subsidized Redevelopment   381
Subsidized Private Housing   382
    Subsidies Under Section 221(d)(3)   383
    Rent Supplements: A "Deeper" Subsidy   384
    Subsidies Under Sections 235 and 236   385
    The National Housing Goals   386
    Housing Subsidies and the Filtering Process   387
    Moving Away from a New Construction Strategy   389
Housing Allowances: A "Demand-Side" Subsidy   391
    Housing Allowances and Code Enforcements   393

Other Arguments for Housing Allowances   394
Section 8: Subsidies for Demand as Well as Supply   396
The Experimental Housing Allowance Program   399
Participation Rates   401
Income and the Demand for Housing   401
Effects on Mobility   402
Improvements in Housing   403
Effects on Housing Prices   403
Cost of the Program   404
Evaluating the Results of the Experiment   405
The Problem of Deteriorating Neighborhoods   406
Segregation and Discrimination in Housing   408
"Opening Up" the Suburbs   410
Exclusionary Zoning   411
Motives for Exclusionary Practices   413
What Would Be Gained by Opening Up the Suburbs?   414
Policies to Encourage Racial and Economic Integration   415
The Consequences of Alternative Policies   419

FOURTEEN
The Metropolitan Public Sector: Functions, Growth, Revenues   421

The Multilevel Public Sector   421
Metropolitan Fiscal Problems   422
The Assignment of Functions to Levels of Government   424
Stabilization of Economic Activity   424
Redistributing Income from Rich to Poor   425
Providing Public Goods and Services   427
An Optimum Division of Responsibility: The Principle of
Fiscal Equivalence   429
Complex Cases and Joint Responsibility   430
Local Government Expenditures   431
Growth of Local Spending   433
Urbanization and the Demand for Public Service   434
Rising Costs per Unit of Service   435
The Effect of Productivity Lag   437
The Effect of Inelastic Demand   437
The Movement to Limit Spending and Taxing   440

Local Government Revenue   442
> Tax Revenue and Economic Growth: The Concept of
> > Tax Base Elasticity   445

The Property Tax   448
> Site Value Taxation   449
> The Tax on Improvements: The Old View   452
> The New View of the Property Tax   455
> "Global" Effects and "Excise" Effects   456
> Comparison of Results: New View Versus Old   459
> Backward Shifting to Land and Labor   459
> Incidence of the Tax on Other Sectors   461
> The Debate over Regressivity   462
> Current Income Versus Permanent Income   464
> The Property Tax from a Local Perspective   466
> The Unique Role of the Property Tax in Local Finance   468

FIFTEEN
Problems of the Metropolitan Public Sector: Inefficiency,
Inequity, Insolvency   471

Haphazard Boundaries: The Problem of Inefficiency   471
> Providing the Optimum Level and Combination of
> > Public Services   472
> Supplying Public Services at Minimum Unit Cost   475
> Political Participation and Accessibility   476
> Planning and Coordination   477

Geographic Disparities: The Problem of Inequity   478
> Disparities in the Distribution of Taxable Resources   479
> Disparities in the Cost of Services   482
> Disparities in Tax Burden   483
> The Effects of Redistributive Local Budgets   485
> Selective Migration and the Erosion of the Central City
> > Tax Base   488
> Do the Suburbs "Exploit" the Central City?   489

Urban Fiscal Distress   491
> Difficulty of Intercity Comparisons   492
> The Causes of Urban Fiscal Distress   493
> Structural Problems of Declining Cities   494
> Political Problems of Budgetmaking in Declining Cities   495

Measuring Urban Distress   497
A Summary of Problems and Proposals   500
The Reassignment of Functions: Proposals to Transfer
          Fiscal Responsibility   500
     Proposals to Increase the Functional Role of the
          Federal Government   501
     Effects on Geographic Disparities and Fiscal Distress   504
     Increasing the Responsibilities of the States:
          The Case of Education   505
Reorganizing the Local Public Sector   506
     Metropolitan Federation   507
     Counties as Metropolitan Governments   508
     Tax Base Sharing   508
     Policies for "Muddling Through"   510
Intergovernmental Grants   511
     Effects of Grants on Fiscal Behavior   513
     Conditional Matching Grants   514
     The Debate over Categorical Grants   517
     Unconditional, Nonmatching Grants   518
     General Revenue Sharing   519
     Redistributive Effects   521
     Effects on Tax Effort   523
     Outlook for General Revenue Sharing   524
     Conditional, Nonmatching Aid: Block Grants   524
     Growth of Federal Aid to Cities   525
What Cities Can Do for Themselves: Improving Economic and
          Fiscal Performance   527
     A Strategy of Private Development and Public Frugality   528
     Economizing   529
     Improving Productivity in Local Government   530

SIXTEEN
Postscript: The Future of Central Cities   533

Outlook for the Older Cities   533
     Demographic Change and the Future of the Inner City   535
Renovation and Revival?   537
     The Problem of Managing Decline   539

Index   541

Introduction

ONE

Since the Industrial Revolution began about two hundred years ago, our way of life has been profoundly altered by the rapid growth of cities and metropolitan areas. The extraordinary pace of urbanization in every part of the world is one of the most striking facts of modern history. Seen in retrospect, the rate of change seems incredible. In 1790 the population of the United States was 5 percent urban and 95 percent rural; by 1970 it was 73 percent urban and only 27 percent rural. In Japan, where the Industrial Revolution began only in the second half of the nineteenth century, the pace of urbanization was even faster: the proportion of population living in urban areas rose from 18 percent in 1920 to 72 percent in 1970. In the underdeveloped nations, too, rapid urban growth is a major fact of modern life.[1]

Yet the history of cities is not simply a story of continuous growth. Old cities may decline while newer ones are still growing. In the United States some of the older, inner cities of metropolitan areas have been losing jobs and population for years. By 1980, decline at the center of the older metropolitan areas had become the rule rather than the exception and brought with it a set of problems that the earlier years of seemingly endless growth had not prepared

1. Japanese data are from Norman J. Glickman, *The Growth and Management of the Japanese Urban System* (New York: Academic Press, 1979), table 2.21, p. 71. For U.S. data, see table 3.1, below. Numerous concise studies of the history of urbanization are available. See, for example, Emrys Jones, *Towns and Cities* (London: Oxford University Press, 1966), ch. 2; and Kingsley Davis, "The Urbanization of the Human Population," in *Cities* (New York: Alfred A. Knopf, 1965), a Scientific American Book, pp. 3–24.

us to deal with. For better or worse, the system of cities in the modern world does not stand still. In whatever country one lives today, many of the most pressing social and economic problems inevitably will be associated with urban and metropolitan development.

THE SCOPE OF URBAN ECONOMICS

It is hardly surprising that in such a world students should be increasingly concerned with matters of urban public policy or that economists should have developed the special branch of their discipline that we now call urban economics. More remarkable, perhaps, is the fact that urban economics became a distinct and recognized specialty only in the last thirty years. It can be defined as a field of study in which we use the analytical tools of economics to explain the spatial and economic organization of cities and metropolitan areas and to deal with their special economic problems.

This definition has the advantage of putting first things first. Students are often impatient to go directly to the "issues." They want to investigate the problems of urban poverty, slum housing, land-use decisions, transportation, the delivery of urban public services, and they are eager to debate the merits of the various public policies that might be used to meet them. But neither the problems nor the policies can be discussed intelligently until one understands the highly complex urban-metropolitan environment in which they occur. Hence we must deal with the spatial and economic organization of the city first, and only then with its problems.

In the definition of urban economics, the word "spatial" deserves particular emphasis. Traditional economic theory omits any reference to the dimensions of space by treating all economic activity as if it took place at a single point. It refers to consumers and producers, firms and industries, but not to distance or contiguity, separation or neighborhood. The fact that population and economic activity are arranged in a spatial as well as a functional order is simply ignored. In recent years the discipline known as "regional economics" has sought to restore the balance. "Regional economics," in Hugh Nourse's apt phrase, "is the study of the neglected spatial order of the economy."[2]

Regions may be areas of any size from neighborhoods to cities, river basins, farm belts, nations, or continents. Urban economics is that subcategory of regional economics that deals with the regions we call cities

---

2. Hugh O. Nourse, *Regional Economics* (New York: McGraw-Hill, 1968), p. 1.

and metropolitan areas. It concentrates on those economic relationships and processes that contribute to the important spatial characteristics of such places, especially to their size, density of settlement, and structure or pattern of land use. And, since cities and metropolitan areas undergo continuous change in all these spatial characteristics, urban economics is also vitally concerned with the forces that attract or repel economic activity and population and thus cause growth or decline, concentration or dispersion, preservation or replacement. It seeks to understand, not only the present spatial order, but the direction of change and development.

Here are a few examples of the sort of question about urban spatial economic organization that this book attempts to answer:

What accounts for the enormous concentration of population and economic activity in cities and metropolitan areas?

Is there an optimum size for cities?

Within metropolitan areas, why has there been such a marked dispersion of jobs and population from the large cities to their suburban rings in recent decades?

Will the dramatic increase in the price of gasoline, by making transportation more costly, bring a halt to dispersion and lead to more compact settlement patterns?

Why is it principally the middle and upper classes that have been attracted to the suburbs, while low-income families continue to live in the central cities?

Can racial segregation within cities be explained by spatial-economic factors such as the location of low-skill jobs and low-income housing, without reference to race prejudice?

Spatial Aspects of Urban Problems

The analysis of urban size, growth, form, and structure is vital to an understanding of the problems of urban transportation, poverty, housing, and public finance precisely because these problems almost always have significant spatial aspects. Transportation policy offers some obvious examples, since transportation and the spatial arrangement of land use are highly interdependent. A rail mass transit system, for example, will be feasible only if trip origins and destinations within a metropolitan area are highly concentrated, while a highway system can operate efficiently only if they are *not* concentrated. Consequently, when deciding whether to recommend the development of a rail mass transit system or the extension of a highway network, planners must look very carefully at the way a city's existing land-use pattern—the spatial distribution of jobs and homes—affects the travel behavior of its residents.

Antipoverty policy, too, has spatial aspects. In metropolitan areas, the poverty population remains heavily concentrated in the core cities, while job growth is most rapid in the suburban ring. When antipoverity policies are framed, this spatial characteristic of the poverty problem must be taken into account. It is important to know, for example, whether the separation of the poor from the areas of most rapid job growth is significantly slowing their rise out of poverty.

Or consider the connection between the housing problem and the pattern of land use. In the United States, decisions as to what will be built, and where, are taken largely in the private market for land and structures. Does this market work efficiently to give us the optimum development of each parcel and neighborhood? Or are there significant defects in the market process that justify public intervention to stimulate the redevelopment of old neighborhoods? These questions can be answered only by a careful study of the way in which the urban land market influences the spatial organization of the city.

The problems of metropolitan public finance, too, have many strongly spatial characteristics. To cite only one: consider the question of jurisdictional boundaries. The typical metropolitan area of the 1980s contains a large core city surrounded by the numerous smaller political units of the suburbs. Jurisdictional boundaries generally were drawn a century or more before the metropolitan area became a highly integrated economic unit. In today's circumstances can this minutely parceled set of local governments be expected to provide the level and assortment of public services that best satisfy the desires of the metropolitan population as a whole, or do local political boundaries now interfere with the efficient and equitable operation of the public sector? If so, what changes are desirable? Urban economic analysis, as we will see, can help to answer such vital policy questions.

THE CRITERIA OF EFFICIENCY AND EQUITY

Efficiency and equity are two of the general criteria to be applied in comparing alternative economic policies. To the economist, efficiency means the most productive use of resources to satisfy competing material wants. The productive resources available in even the most affluent economy are limited. Every use that we decide to make of them has as its real cost the next best opportunity for their use that we had to forego in choosing the one we did. ("Opportunity cost," thus defined, is the fundamental basis of real cost in economics.) If we are to achieve maximum satisfaction of material wants by the application of limited resources, it behooves us not to waste resources by using them in less than the most productive way. In the context of urban economics this often means finding the most efficient spatial arrangements or configurations, as in the examples from land use and public finance policy cited above.

The term "equity" in economics usually refers to fairness in the distribution of income or wealth or, more broadly, "welfare." When we evaluate a particular public policy (such as urban renewal or subsidies for low-income housing) or a private policy (such as discrimination in housing or employment), we usually try to apply some standard of equity to the policy's outcome: Which groups does it help? On whom does it impose burdens? Are these results desirable?

The ultimate question—desirability—cannot be answered on strictly economic grounds. It requires an explicit ethical judgment, and economists, in their professional capacity, have no special claim to ethical authority. Nevertheless, their work is indispensable as a precondition for informed judgment of economic policies. Since we judge policies by their consequences, accurate judgment requires a clear understanding of what those consequences are. Unfortunately, causes and consequences in economics are not very easily identified. The economy is a complex network of markets that connects all persons, institutions, functions, and regions and that transmits impulses among them in ways that are not always obvious. Careful analysis, however, can help us to understand how the system works so that the results of past or present policies can be deciphered, even if imperfectly, and the likely consequences of proposed future programs foreseen. By contributing to such an understanding the economist lays a foundation upon which others can then base their own judgment about the desirability of the various alternatives.

THE THEME AND OUTLINE OF THE BOOK

Broadly speaking, this book moves from a historical description and economic explanation of the growth of cities in Chapters 2 and 3, through a theoretical analysis of their location, form, and economic structure in Chapters 4 through 7, to the investigation of current urban economic problems in Chapters 8 through 16. Two chapters are devoted to problems and policy issues in each of four areas: transportation, poverty, housing and land use, and the operation of the public sector.

Running through the entire book is a connecting theme: the influence of economic growth and development, as they have actually been experienced in the United States, on the spatial organization of cities and metropolitan areas and on the major economic problems they face. Growth and development result partly from technological change, so we shall be looking closely at the effect on the urban pattern of such major technical innovations as the railroad, the truck and the automobile. In the United

States, economic development has been accompanied by rapid population increase and a high level of internal migration, so we shall examine systematically the urban consequences of those forces as well. For the individual and the family, economic development has produced a long-run rise in living standards, so we shall also look carefully at the way in which rising real income influences the urban pattern through its effect on consumer behavior. Finally, worldwide economic development has produced rapidly increasing fuel prices and a growing recognition that the age of energy abundance is over. We shall therefore analyze the probable effects of more costly energy, especially on transportation costs and, through transportation costs, on the form and organization of the entire urban-metropolitan system.

To speak of innovation and growth is obviously to suggest that cities change through time. Yet there is a sense in which they are also imprisoned in their own past. For they cannot be built anew to adopt the technology and suit the needs of each new era. Although the grand designs, the structures, and the boundaries laid down at an earlier date are often inappropriate to the present, they can be changed only at great expense of money, or effort, or disruption—and therefore only very slowly. It is precisely this tension between the needs of the present and the legacy of the past that makes the subject matter of urban economics so unusually challenging and endlessly absorbing.

The Economics of Urbanization

TWO

Economics has always been a major force determining the pattern of human settlement. Man cannot live by bread alone, but neither can he live without bread. From the earliest age, when our ancestors at the margin of historical time settled in the fertile river valleys to live by farming, to our own century, in which the rural poor migrate to the city in search of higher wages, man has moved over the surface of the earth in search, perhaps not of El Dorado, but, at least, of a place where the living was easier.

Cities are themselves evidence that an economy has reached a certain stage of development. Since city dwellers do not grow food, they can survive only if someone else in the economic system produces a food surplus. As long as agriculture is relatively unproductive, most men necessarily are tied to the soil. In a society in which 90 farmers can produce enough food and fiber for only 90 families, all men must remain farmers. If agriculture improves to the point where 90 farmers can feed and clothe 100 families, then one-tenth of the population can move off the land.

This obvious proposition enables us to characterize three major phases in the history of human settlement. The first is a society in which either agriculture is unknown and men live by hunting and fishing or agriculture is so primitive that it yields almost no surplus for the support of nonagricultural workers. In such a society farming and fishing villages, of course, exist, but they remain very small and contain at most only a few people, such as a priestly class, who are not food producers.

The second phase is a society not yet industrialized, in which agriculture becomes productive enough to yield persistently a small surplus beyond bare subsistence. This surplus enters into trade and can support a limited urban population. True towns and cities now arise in which men specialize in nonagricultural activity. The limit to such urbanization in most areas before the Industrial Revolution appears to have been around 10 percent of total population, although we lack anything like adequate statistics on the question. Something like that ratio probably prevailed in the Mediterranean civilization of the Roman Empire. Despite the existence of a few great cities—Rome itself may, at its zenith, have reached a population of a million or more—society remained predominantly rural.

The third phase, and the only one in which we find substantially urbanized societies, occurs with and after what we may loosely call the Industrial Revolution—loosely, because a necessary condition for industrialization is a rise in output per farm worker, either in the industrializing country itself or in an area with which it trades, to support the growing industrial population. Such a rise in farm productivity in turn requires the application of scientific and mechanical techniques to farming and so may itself be treated as an aspect of industrial revolution. In the third phase we do not know what the limit to urbanization may be. Suffice it to say that the United States is today 73 percent urbanized, that most of the rural population is no longer engaged in farming, and that the nation nevertheless continues to be a net food exporter.

This chapter explains the economics of urbanization and illustrates its principles by very briefly tracing the history of cities from ancient times to our own. Chapter 3 examines in much greater detail the development of cities, suburbs, and metropolitan areas in the nineteenth and twentieth centuries.

SPECIALIZATION, TRADE, AND URBAN GROWTH BEFORE THE INDUSTRIAL REVOLUTION

Wherever cities have existed, the city dweller lives by exporting something in exchange for the produce of the countryside. Clearly, trade and its necessary correlate, the geographic division of labor, are intimately bound up with people's pattern of settlement. The great metropolis of ancient times, however, was, as Scott Greer has pointed out, engaged principally, not in the export of goods, but in the export of "order."[1] Cities dominated society not because they were centers of economic activity but because they were centers of government. The "order" they "exported"

1. Scott Greer, *Governing the Metropolis* (New York: John Wiley & Sons, 1962), pp. 4–6.

to the rural territory of their state consisted of defense, of law, and of a system of communication. In exchange for these services the city collected taxes from the countryside, and the tax revenues in turn became the means of paying for the agricultural imports upon which the city depended for survival. Trade, except for the import of food, was limited in volume by two factors: first, the high cost of transport and, second, the fact that the city could produce little that could not be produced equally well in the peasant village.

However limited the volume of trade may have been in late antiquity, it was sufficient to feed and clothe a considerable population in the urban centers of the Roman Empire. The later decline of the cities of Western Europe—say, from about the seventh to the tenth centuries—has been attributed not only to the breakup of the Empire but also, in Henri Pirenne's famous thesis, to the closing of the Mediterranean to European trade by the "abrupt entry of Islam" and its "conquest of the eastern, southern and western shores of the great European lake."[2] Western Europeans were thrown back upon the self-sufficient manor, or estate, as the fundamental economic unit. The territorial division of labor, trade, and consequently urban population all declined in a self-reinforcing spiral.

Just as the decline of the cities followed the decline of trade, their revival accompanied, and in turn reinforced, the restoration of commerce that took place at about the beginning of the eleventh century, when Western Europeans, led by the energetic and thoroughly commercial Venetians, once more extended their influence across the Mediterranean. Indeed, from the eleventh century onward, the rise of the towns is one of the major themes in medieval history, with implications going far beyond the mere economics to which we are here confined.

What had been a declining spiral of city life now became a rising one. The growth of urban population led to increased demand for the commodities needed to support it. Hence trade increased further, and more and more workmen were drawn into the specialized occupations of craft and commerce, further increasing the demand for trade. Centuries later Adam Smith observed that the division of labor depends upon the extent of the market: the growing urban-rural interdependence of the late Middle Ages was, in fact, a form of territorial division of labor, within which major division the ever finer specialization by trade and craft proceeded in its turn.

Then, as now, the process was a complex one: the goods and services a town exported in order to pay for its necessary imports accounted for only a fraction of its total employment. Much urban labor has always

2. Henri Pirenne, *Economic and Social History of Medieval Europe* (New York: Harcourt Brace Jovanovich, 1961), a Harvest Book, pp. 1–7, 39–40.

consisted of what we now call "service employment." Every medieval clerk, every apprentice working for a tradesman, required the goods of other trades and the services of other clerks, and so the population of the towns must always have far exceeded the number of those engaged directly in trade or service to other regions.

The expansion of European influence and settlement, the growth of trade, and the rise of urban population continued down to the end of the thirteenth century. With the opening of the fourteenth century, Europe's forward motion apparently ceased. A time of troubles set in. Trade and population seem to have leveled off even before the Black Death of 1347–50 reduced Europe's population by perhaps one-third. The end of the thirteenth and the beginning of the fourteenth centuries is thus, in a sense, the high-water mark of medieval European civilization. By that date the towns had been growing for some three hundred years. How large had they grown? Not very big by today's standard. Pirenne estimates that at the beginning of the fourteenth century only a few of the largest cities had attained a population of 50,000 to 100,000. Florence in 1339 numbered perhaps 90,000 inhabitants. Venice at that period probably exceeded 100,000, while Paris may have had as many as 200,000.[3]

Europe's trade and population surged ahead once more from the mid-fifteenth century onward. The age of exploration opened up new trade routes by sea. Banking, insurance, and trading enterprises were now undertaken on a truly grand scale. The cities of Europe began to expand once again. By 1800 London, by far Europe's largest city, contained more than 950,000 people. Yet because the techniques of agricultural production had improved but little, the bulk of European population remained tied to the soil. Kingsley Davis has pointed out that "urbanization" properly means, not simply the growth of urban population, but its growth relative to rural and hence to total numbers. In the three centuries before the Industrial Revolution Europe's cities grew considerably, but their margin of growth over that of the rural sector was slight indeed. Hence, as Davis points out, "On the eve of the industrial revolution Europe was still an overwhelmingly agrarian region."[4]

THE IMPACT OF THE INDUSTRIAL REVOLUTION

Why did the Industrial Revolution suddenly cause mankind to congregate in cities and towns? Why couldn't it have taken a different course, leaving workers in their rural surroundings and spreading industrial facili-

3. Ibid., pp. 170–71.
4. Kingsley Davis, "The Urbanization of the Human Population," in *Cities* (New York: Alfred A. Knopf, 1965), a Scientific American Book, p. 8.

ties thinly over the countryside? The answer emerges if we consider its effects in greater detail. Let us first note that the Industrial Revolution comprised (at least) three radical developments: a manufacturing revolution, a transportation revolution, and an agricultural revolution.

The last has already been described as the application of scientific and mechanical techniques to farming to bring about a sharp increase in farm output per worker. Its effect was to make possible a shift of population from agricultural to nonagricultural pursuits, but in no respect did it *require* the urbanization of those released from farming.

The transportation revolution, on the other hand, certainly encouraged urban agglomeration. Cities have, throughout history, tended to locate at economical transport points: at seaports, on navigable lakes and rivers, or at junctures of important overland trade routes. The transportation revolution of the nineteenth century consisted chiefly in the improvement in water-borne transport following the development of canals and the invention of the steamship and the even more radical change in overland transport made possible by steam railroads. These developments combined to increase enormously the transportation advantages of those points they served as compared with all other points. Both modes of transport operated, not ubiquitously, but along lines of movement that formed rather coarse-meshed networks. The point of service for the steamship network was the port—and the number of good ports is limited by topography. The canal and later the railroad system, on the other hand, could serve many points. Despite the topographical constraints, many possible routes existed, and the choice among them was sometimes determined by noneconomic factors. Once the system was built, however, those points it served obtained decisive cost advantages over all other places, for overland travel apart from the railroad remained in the horse-and-buggy stage throughout the nineteenth century. Thus ports and points along the railroads and canals powerfully attracted industry and often became manufacturing towns or cities.

Indeed, so effectively did the railroad encourage villages to grow into towns and towns into cities that it proved to be the most powerful agglomerative invention of all time. To enjoy its benefits, one had to build directly along the right of way or on a short siding. Hence nineteenth-century factories huddled next to one another in the familiar railside industrial districts still visible in every manufacturing town. Moreover, the railroad was relatively more efficient for long than for short hauls. It was miraculously economical for intercity movement of both goods and people, but until the invention of the electric railway it did little to improve intra-urban transport. Thus the workers in their turn lived as close as possible to the factories, and the nineteenth-century city grew up at an extraordinarily high level of density.

That it could also grow to encompass an immense population was another effect of the transportation revolution. Since long-distance haulage had become relatively cheap, it was now possible to feed huge populations concentrated at any point on the transport network by bringing food from distant agricultural zones, which, incidentally, the railroad had often helped open up. Without such a network, even if cities could have obtained sufficient food from nearby farm areas, they would have run a grave risk of famine whenever the local crop was deficient. Indeed, the wide chronological fluctuations in local death rates that occurred in, say, medieval Europe were due partly to local famines, which a better transport network could have mitigated.[5]

The manufacturing revolution consisted essentially of the development of factory methods of production incorporating power-driven machinery in place of the hand-tool system of production that had prevailed for thousands of years. This encouraged urbanization for several reasons. First, the optimum scale for a single plant, even in the early days of the Industrial Revolution, was likely to be large enough to form the economic nucleus for a small town. Second, and perhaps more important, commercial activities show a marked tendency to locate where other commercial activities already exist, and it is this process of agglomeration we now wish to examine in detail.

It is important to note that economic activity displayed agglomerative tendencies long before the Industrial Revolution. We have already mentioned the obvious point that banking and financial services concentrated in the great ports and trading centers of Renaissance Europe. At the same period handicraft trades, such as the Flemish cloth-weaving complex, were geographically concentrated even though still organized as cottage industries. The economic basis of agglomeration, which we will analyze below, was not much different then than now. But one of the profound effects of the Industrial Revolution was vastly to increase specialization through increased division of labor. Before the Industrial Revolution most production was carried on within the home—do it yourself was the rule in those days—and homes were mostly rural, located wherever farming was possible. The Industrial Revolution split off more and more of these domestic activities, converted them into full-time occupations within factories, and freed them to find their optimum location, no longer bound to home and farm. Thus it vastly increased the possibilities of agglomeration.

In a capitalist economy entrepreneurs will build their plants at the location where they think they can maximize profits. Precisely where on the map that will turn out to be depends on a number of discoverable

5. Carlo Cipolla, *The Economic History of World Population* (Baltimore: Penguin Books, 1962), a Pelican Book, pp. 77–80.

factors, including the location of sources of supply and geographic differentials in transport costs, in wage rates, and in market potential. These factors are handled systematically in what is usually called "the theory of the location of industry," which will be taken up in Chapter 4. At this point, however, we will examine the matter from a different perspective, focusing on why economic activities in an industrial society generally tend to agglomerate rather than on the somewhat different question of why they tend to locate at particular points on the map, such as Buffalo, New York, or Peoria, Illinois.

Implicit in most analyses of urban growth, including perhaps the argument of this chapter, is the assumption that one must, so to speak, account for the fact that people move from a natural rural life to a somehow unnatural urban one. The argument need not proceed that way, however. R. M. Haig, in a notable tour de force, shrewdly reversed matters and suggested that "the question is changed from 'Why live in the City?' to 'Why not live in the City?' "[6] He took as his starting point the observation that the economically most efficient pattern for the production and distribution of goods would assign to metropolitan areas everyone except those needed to farm the land or extract minerals plus those needed to transport such raw materials. According to this logic, what requires explanation is not the tendency of the population to concentrate in cities but the fact that it is not *all* concentrated there.

One might also draw upon the authority of the philosophers for this point of view: man, the social animal described by Aristotle, fulfills his nature only in association with his fellows. Or, in the current phrase, people want to go where the action is. Thus, one might argue, social as well as economic drives make the city the natural destination of men and women. Urbanism as a way of life then requires no special justification, and no apologies.

THE AGGLOMERATION
OF ECONOMIC ACTIVITY

The locational pattern of economic activity reveals a complex system of interrelationships among firms. One soon realizes that the location of any particular economic unit depends upon the location of all the others. No matter where we begin the analysis we are quite likely to find the argument running in circles. But we must cut into it somewhere. Let us

6. R. M. Haig, "Some Speculations Regarding the Economic Basis of Urban Concentration," *Quarterly Journal of Economics*, February 1926, pp. 179–208; the quotation is from p. 188.

start, therefore, by adopting Raymond Vernon's distinction between "local-market activities, . . . which generate goods and services of the sort which are typically consumed in the area where they are produced," and "national-market activities . . . devoted to the generation of goods and services which characteristically are 'exported' over broad market areas."[7] Local market activities, as Vernon explains, "respond largely to changes which go on inside the region." Therefore, if we can explain the tendency for national market activities to concentrate at a certain place, we will also have explained the tendency of local market activities to do so: the latter expand wherever the local market expands, and the local market expands wherever the growth of national market activities stimulates local employment and income.

Within the category of national market activities, agglomeration is the result partly of a kind of inverted pyramiding. One industry—say, shipping—locates at a place because it has a good natural harbor. That activity then attracts others linked to it—say, banking, insurance, inland transport. The concentration of those industries in turn attracts others linked to them—say, a stock market, a commodity exchange, a printing and publishing industry, a university. And, of course, all these build up a large demand for local market products—that is, for the services of retail traders, bakers, dentists, plumbers, policemen, bus drivers, school teachers, and all the other members of the local market sector, who provide services both to those in the national sector and to other local market producers.

The linkages of which we speak consist of a need for either communication or the movement of goods between firms and individuals doing business with one another. Linkage, however, need not itself imply proximity: firms have links both to their suppliers and to their customers, and proximity to both is not always possible. The locational pull exerted by such connections depends on numerous factors including the technology of communication and transport, the functions performed by the firm, and the locations of its suppliers and customers. The pull varies directly both with the need for communication and with the unit cost of accomplishing it. Since improvements in technology have reduced the relative cost of communication and transport in recent years, distance has become relatively less expensive, and some of the linkages that formerly pulled economic activity into the urban core have grown weaker. Before one can gauge correctly the effects of such changes, however, it is necessary to understand the relationship between linkages and the functions and organization of the firm.

Haig pointed out that what we call the "firm" actually comprises a

7. Raymond Vernon, *Metropolis 1985* (New York: Doubleday, 1963), an Anchor Book, p. 25.

"packet of functions," which may not all have the same communication and transportation needs.[8] If these functions are spatially separable, then the ideal solution for the firm might be to place each at a different location. The separability of functions is in fact dependent on the state of technology. One important result of the reduced cost of communication and transportation has been to make possible increased spatial separation of functions within firms. In principle this might either increase or decrease the tendency of economic activity to agglomerate. A corporation that formerly located both its manufacturing plant and head office in a low-wage small town might now move its head office to a large city. A firm that formerly operated a department store and warehouse in the central business district might now move the warehouse out to a lower rent area, still within the city. A book publisher that formerly maintained its head office downtown and its storage and shipping departments in a nearby warehouse might now locate the last two in a distant suburb.

In fact, if we mean by agglomeration not just the tendency of activities to concentrate in central cities but their tendency to concentrate in metropolitan areas, then the displacement of a warehousing operation from downtown to the suburbs is not deglomerating. It represents a loosening up, a spreading out of the structure of the metropolis rather than a dispersion of activity into nonmetropolitan areas. A genuine dispersion, ending at the point where urban and rural densities of activity converge and become indistinguishable, is a conceivable but still distant possibility. But this anticipates later discussion. Suffice it to say at this point that despite the telephone, the airplane, and the automobile, certain activities find their links to the center still strong enough to hold them. Many of these are industries that Vernon has characterized as requiring face-to-face contact with either customers or suppliers in the daily conduct of business. Such industries, he points out, generally combine two characteristics: their activities are nonroutine, and speed is crucial to their success. He calls these industries "communication oriented" in their choice of location.[9] A list of them would certainly include at least some parts of banking and finance, law, government, advertising, publishing, and broadcasting. For these activities the letter and the telephone are not adequate substitutes for face-to-face contact; their personnel, or at the very least their management personnel, must remain close to the center.

Some kinds of manufacturing certainly fall within this category, too. In a telling illustration, Vernon contrasts two cases: first, the producer of standardized goods, whose communications needs do not dictate an urban

8. R. M. Haig, "The Assignment of Activities to Areas in Urban Regions," *Quarterly Journal of Economics*, May 1926, pp. 402–34.

9. Vernon, pp. 105–06, 139–43.

location because he can probably use the telephone to order raw materials or parts by giving the catalogue number or standard specification to his supplier; second, the manufacturer of the unique or the highly styled product, such as ladies' dresses, who has to locate close to his suppliers because day in, day out, he must see and compare various combinations of color, quality, and design before he can decide what materials to buy.

ECONOMIES OF AGGLOMERATION

For a fuller understanding of the causes of the geographic concentration of industry we must go beyond the concept of linkages, even the face-to-face variety, to a discussion of what have sometimes been called "economies of agglomeration." When they operate on the input side such economies have generally been known as "external economies of scale," where the word "external" stands for "external to the firm." These are the economies (i.e., the unit cost savings) that depend not upon the size of the firm but upon the size of the industry. Stigler explains the matter succinctly: "When one component is made on a small scale it may be unprofitable to employ specialized machines and labor; when the industry grows, the individual firms will cease making this component on a small scale and a new firm will specialize in its production on a large scale. . . . The progressive specialism of firms is the major source of external economies."[10] What has this to do with urban agglomeration? Stigler goes on to explain: "Many of the functions which an industry can delegate to auxiliary and complementary industries must be performed in fairly close proximity, and this is a powerful factor making for the geographic concentration of industries."

When external economies of agglomeration are possible, individual firms will enjoy lower costs when the industry is geographically concentrated than if it were geographically dispersed. A classic case is, once again, the concentration of the ladies' garment industry in New York City, more specifically in midtown Manhattan. The industry in New York is large enough to provide a profitable local market for a host of specialized suppliers. Thus, without incurring the risks and costs of carrying large inventories, the garment manufacturer who locates in New York gains ready access to a full line of the inputs needed in a trade where style requirements change rapidly and speed and flexibility are crucial. This advantage is not confined to material inputs but applies equally to the

10. George Stigler, *The Theory of Price*, rev. ed. (New York: Macmillan, 1952), p. 146.

labor supply: with access to a common pool of trained labor, the manufacturer can vary his work force without having to bear the expense of training or, alternatively, of carrying idle workers.

One must not suppose that the cost savings resulting from external economies are merely savings to one firm or industry at the expense of others; on the contrary, they are true social economies, reductions in the real cost of output to society. Thus urban agglomeration is economically beneficial.

The garment industry provides an example also of the advantages of agglomeration on the output, or sales, side: by locating in New York the manufacturer places his showroom in the major national market to which buyers regularly come from stores all over the country. He could not reach nearly as many potential customers if the showroom were in, say, Chicago. (Of course, this suggests that only the showroom, not the whole operation, need be in New York. Moreover, it may well pay to have a showroom in Chicago as well.)

Does this instance also yield social benefits, or is it merely a case of one manufacturer gaining sales at the expense of another? Again, society is clearly the gainer: the expenses incurred by the buyer in canvassing the market—expenses involving real costs of time and travel, which must be recouped from customers—are minimized when markets are geographically concentrated. Moreover, similar gains accrue through geographic concentration of like stores at the micro-scale of the neighborhood: the consumer bent on comparative shopping saves time and money when stores are close together.

E. M. Hoover has pointed out that the external economies of scale that influence geographic concentration of production can be divided into two classes: "localization economies," which result when firms of the same industry congregate at a given place, and "urbanization economies," which result when firms of different industries locate in the same place.[11] This distinction would be more useful if "industry" were a less ambiguous term. One may observe, nevertheless, that the concentration of the garment industry in New York unambiguously produces localization economies. On the other hand, New York City also unquestionably offers urbanization economies. For example, the local labor market is so large that it can offer not merely a large number of employment agencies but a large number that specialize in finding particular kinds of personnel. It has not only many banks but banks large enough to maintain highly specialized departments for a wide variety of functions. Thus the concentration of industries,

---

11. Edgar M. Hoover, *Location Theory and the Shoe and Leather Industries* (Cambridge, Mass.: Harvard University Press, 1937), pp. 90–91.

even though they be unlike industries, makes possible an efficient specialization of service firms, and these latter are the source of external economies for the congregating firms that made them profitable.

The concentration of corporate head offices in New York City testifies to the importance of urbanization economies. A.T.&T., Exxon, and General Motors have their head offices in New York not so much because they do business with one another as because they all want to do business with New York banks and investment houses, with Wall Street law firms, and with Madison Avenue advertising agencies. Just as in the case of localization economies, the advantage to be gained is essentially that of easy access to highly specialized services.

We spoke earlier of the fact that the location of any one economic unit depends upon the location of all the others. The complex interrelatedness of the forces that have produced agglomeration should by now be clear: within the national market sector one industry attracted other, related activities to its locality; this increased agglomeration produced external economies that attracted still more firms and produced still more external economies. As employment and income rose, local market industries also expanded, and this expansion too was potent for the creation of further economies of agglomeration and further urban growth.

In order to explain the growth of cities we have thus far emphasized the advantages of large communities as places of production. The primary importance of production advantages, however, should not lead us to overlook other factors associated with community size. As Chinitz points out, large communities also afford superior opportunities for consumption.[12] The basic necessities of food, clothing, and shelter can be purchased anywhere, but the more specialized forms of consumption goods—the "luxuries" that people turn to increasingly as their income rises—are more readily available in the larger centers. In general, the range of types of goods and services offered to the consumer increases as community size increases. Some items, such as opera performances or major league baseball games, are found only in the largest cities.

The large community also offers important advantages to the worker. Obviously, the range of job choice increases with community size. Wage levels, too, are higher in the larger centers. Within specific occupational categories there is a fairly regular pattern of rising wages as one moves from smaller to larger metropolitan areas.[13] We return to the question of income and city size in Chapter 3.

---

12. Benjamin Chinitz, ed., *City and Suburb* (Englewood Cliffs, N.J.: Prentice-Hall, 1964), editor's intro., pp. 10–12.
13. See data in Edgar M. Hoover, *An Introduction to Regional Economics* 2nd ed. (New York: Alfred A. Knopf, 1975), pp. 170–71.

DISECONOMIES OF AGGLOMERATION

Economies of agglomeration in production and consumption make up only one side of the urban ledger. Diseconomies of agglomeration—the negative effects of size that cumulate as cities grow—make up the other. Indeed, the growth of cities is influenced simultaneously by both forces, the positive economies of agglomeration inducing growth, while the negative diseconomies discourage it. We have thus far concentrated on the positive effects because they have predominated in the modern period, producing rapid urban growth and cities of great size. Yet urban growth has probably always had negative effects as well. Let us examine them briefly.

Diseconomies of agglomeration occur when the concentration of population or of economic activity in one place either raises the real cost of production by requiring more inputs per unit of output or reduces the real standard of living by increasing the level of physical or social disamenities.[14] In many cases, a single diseconomy has both effects. Air pollution and crime are good examples. Both increase with city size. The presence of air pollution raises production costs for some businesses and cleaning and health costs for households. Yet even after these costs are paid, the physical disamenity of a polluted atmosphere remains. Similarly, higher crime rates impose increased security and insurance costs on households and firms, but a residual disamenity remains, since protection is never complete. Thus pollution and crime simultaneously raise the cost and reduce the pleasure of living in cities.

Transportation requirements are the source of another diseconomy of agglomeration. Average trip length, and therefore the time spent traveling to work, increase with city size. Since time is a resource to which we all attach some value, this introduces another element of cost that increases with urban scale. Traffic congestion, too, is often alleged to be a diseconomy of agglomeration, imposing increased travel time on both businesses and households as city size increases. The fact of such congestion is not in question. As Richardson points out, however, it may reflect not a diseconomy of scale but simply a failure to expand the capacity of the local transportation system to its optimum size.[15] (See the discussion of optimum transportation investment in Chapter 8, below.)

---

14. Evidence of diseconomies is presented by Irving Hoch in "Income and City Size," *Urban Studies*, October 1972, pp. 299–328, and in "Variations in the Quality of Urban Life Among Cities and Regions," in Lowdon Wingo and Alan Evans, eds., *Public Economics and the Quality of Life* (Baltimore: Johns Hopkins University Press, 1977), pp. 28–65; and in Harry W. Richardson, *The Economics of Urban Size* (Lexington, Mass.: D. C. Heath, Lexington Books, 1973), chs. 3 and 8.

15. Richardson, pp. 25–27.

IS THERE AN OPTIMUM CITY SIZE?

The fact that as cities grow there are productivity gains in certain functions and losses in others has suggested to some students of urbanism the naive hope that we might be able to determine from a comparison of economies and diseconomies of urban scale exactly what the optimum size for a city is.[16] In that case, man's ancient search for utopia could at last be conducted on scientific principles. For example, according to this view, the optimum size city from the perspective of its residents would be that size at which the value of economies of agglomeration per capita most exceeds the value of diseconomies of agglomeration, similarly measured. Net economies of size accruing to each resident would thus be maximized.[17] From the local point of view, a welfare optimum would be achieved.

Such a formulation is naive for many reasons. To begin with, it is difficult to measure the value of economies and diseconomies of agglomeration with the precision that would be needed to determine optimum size. Next, we would expect changes in technology and income greatly to alter such values as time passed. Widespread use of automobiles, trucks, and buses, for example, added substantially to the cost of air pollution (a diseconomy of agglomeration) during the middle decades of the twentieth century. At the same time, those improvements in transportation plus others in communications probably reduced the benefits obtained by producers from proximity to suppliers and customers (an economy of agglomeration). Income changes also systematically affect the value of economies and diseconomies of agglomeration. For example, as their incomes rise, people are willing to pay more for such amenities as clean air, so that the perceived damage from air pollution—a diseconomy of agglomeration—probably rises with living standards. In the real world changes in technology and income occur endlessly. As a result, even if we could calculate optimum city size at a moment in time, we would have to revise the goal continually and, given the slow pace at which cities adapt, would never reach it. In short, optimum city size is a static notion that has little meaning in a dynamic world.

Most important of all, the concept of optimum size is naive because it overlooks the need in every society for a variety of cities performing

16. For a review of the theory and the evidence on optimum city size see William Alonso, "The Economics of Urban Size," *Papers of the Regional Science Association,* 26 (1971), 67–83; and Richardson. Both authors are critical of naive versions of the theory.

17. The existence of a point at which net economies are maximized, of course, requires that the curves representing economies and diseconomies of size have the appropriate shapes. See Richardson, pp. 11–12.

different functions and therefore differing systematically in size. As we shall see in Chapter 5, the cities in any nation form an interdependent network, or system, in which the size and character of any one place is conditioned by the size, character, and location of other places in the system. In search of the ideal, therefore, one would have to conceive, not of a single optimum size applicable to all cities, but of an optimum set of cities in which each city has the optimum size to perform its expected functions. No one could hope to define such a system for the dynamic society in which we now live.

In any analysis of "city" size, the relevant urban unit is the metropolitan area, to be defined in the next chapter. Until 1970 it was almost unheard of that a major U.S. metropolitan area should stop growing. Since 1970, many have done so. In Chapter 3 we shall analyze their growth and decline in some detail. In the meantime, let us note that although the notion of optimum size may be a will o' the wisp, cities do grow and decline in response to the positive and negative forces of economies and diseconomies of agglomeration. What is more, these forces are themselves constantly in flux as a result of underlying changes in the economy. Consequently, the urban system never reaches a state of equilibrium, and, for better or worse, city dwellers are fated to live continually under the stress of change.

The Growth of Cities
and Metropolitan Areas

THREE

When Mark Twain informs the reader of *Huckleberry Finn* that he has painstakingly incorporated seven different dialects into the book, he excuses his explanation by saying that "without it many readers would suppose that all these characters were trying to talk alike and not succeeding." Unless a similar warning is issued here, the unwary reader may assume that "urban," "metropolitan," and "central city" are terms that sound different but have the same meaning, or that "rural," "suburban," and "nonmetropolitan" are nothing more than synonyms used to ward off fatigue. In short, the time has come for some definitions. And since to define is also to understand, the labor of definition will provide the reader with a kind of spatial paradigm, a map of the essential elements of urban and metropolitan structure.

SOME DEFINITIONS

"City"

Let us begin with "city," the easiest of the essential terms to define. "City" is often used loosely as a generic term for all kinds of large or dense settlements. When used with precision, however, as in classifying population data, it simply denotes the area contained within the political boundaries of a large incorporated municipality. We will make frequent use of the term "central city" in this book. A central city is the principal city (defined as above) around which some larger unit—say, a standard metropolitan statistical area—is formed.

23

The definition of "city" and "central city" by political boundaries has two important consequences. First, the area of a city, and hence its population, is partly the result of historical accident. If a city is originally incorporated with a large geographic area or is able to grow by annexing neighboring towns as its population expands, then it will become larger than another city, equally prosperous and attractive, which either starts with a relatively small area or is unable, for political reasons, to gain much territory or population through annexation. Consider the contrast between Boston and Baltimore. In 1970 the population of the "Boston urbanized area" exceeded that of the "Baltimore urbanized area" by almost 1.1 million, yet the city of Baltimore contained 265,000 more people than did the city of Boston. Baltimore city accounted for 57 percent of the population and covered 34 percent of the land in the Baltimore urbanized area. The figures for Boston were, respectively, only 24 percent and 13 percent.

Since cities can expand by annexation, the second consequence of the use of political boundaries to define cities is that historical comparisons of population size (or other measures) can be misleading if care is not taken to adjust for boundary changes. The place on the map defined as Indianapolis, Indiana, increased in area from 71.2 square miles in 1960 to 379.4 square miles ten years later. During the same period its population rose from 476,258 to 744,624. Without all that annexation, Indianapolis would actually have lost population over the decade: the 1970 population within the 1960 boundaries was only 437,892—8 percent less than in 1960. Which figure is the relevant one depends, of course, on the problem at hand.

"Metropolitan Area"

Students of urbanism have long recognized that every city is the center of a larger socioeconomic system organized around it and often extending far beyond its politically defined boundaries. The term "metropolitan area" describes the territory over which such a system extends. In order to gather data concerning metropolitan populations on a uniform and consistent basis, the government developed the concept of the "Standard Metropolitan Area" and introduced it into the 1950 census. Since then the definition has several times been slightly modified, and for the 1960 census the name was changed to "Standard Metropolitan Statistical Area," or, for convenience, SMSA.[1]

1. The rules for defining SMSA's, the official list of such areas, and the precise geographic definition of each are published periodically by the federal government. See Executive Office of the President, Office of Management and Budget, *Standard Metropolitan Statistical Areas, 1975*. Responsibility for defining SMSA's was subsequently transferred from OMB to the Department of Commerce, Office of Federal Statistical Policy and Standards.

As we shall see, the metropolitan population of the United States has grown enormously since 1950. Consequently both the number of SMSA's and the geographic size of the individual units has regularly increased. For the 1970 census, the government recognized 243 SMSA's in the United States and 4 in Puerto Rico. By the end of 1979, the total number in the United States had reached 281. Many of these now cover a far larger area than they did when first defined. To cite an extreme example, the Atlanta, Georgia, SMSA, which included only 3 counties in 1950, now comprises 15.

Except in New England, SMSA's are built up of units not smaller than whole counties. This has the practical advantage of making data collected for SMSA's readily comparable with local business or government information assembled on a county basis. The SMSA is fundamentally an economic unit. It defines the metropolis largely, though not entirely, by its character of being an integrated, nonagricultural labor market. An integrated labor market might, for our purposes, be described as the smallest area that is large enough to contain the workplaces of most of the people who reside in it and the residences of most of the people who work in it. In a major metropolitan region, such as the one centered on Philadelphia, for example, the smallest area that will answer such a definition is large indeed. The Philadelphia SMSA includes the city of Philadelphia plus four counties in Pennsylvania and three in New Jersey. As we shall see, the Census Bureau definition treats the web of journeys from home to workplace as primary evidence that the regional population forms "an integrated social and economic system"—a metropolitan system, in truth, about which it is exceedingly useful to collect statistics.

The definition of a standard metropolitan statistical area starts with the concept of a central city, which, with minor exceptions, must be a place of at least 50,000 inhabitants.

An SMSA then consists of the following elements:

1. The county or counties containing the central city
2. All contiguous counties that are (a) metropolitan in character, and (b) socially and economically integrated with the county or counties containing the central city

The labor market emphasis of this definition emerges clearly if we examine the specific standards employed with it. The primary criterion of metropolitan character for a contiguous county is that at least 75 percent of its resident workers be in the nonagricultural labor force. The primary criterion of integration for such a county is that at least 30 percent of the employed workers living in it work in the central county or counties.

When the Census Bureau publishes SMSA data it generally subdivides them into "inside central city" and "outside central city." The latter category, which is simply the SMSA total minus the central city total, is often referred to as "the ring," since it comprises the ring of counties that commonly surround the central city and lie within the SMSA. Thus the Philadelphia SMSA consists of the central city of Philadelphia and a ring of seven contiguous counties. In some cases an SMSA may be defined as having more than one central city. If so, the additional city's name is included in the SMSA title (for example, San Francisco-Oakland) and the "inside central cities" category includes both places.

As a metropolitan area grows and spreads out, it may flow into other nearby SMSA's, giving rise to a larger metropolitan mass than can be accommodated within the SMSA definition. When such supermetropoli are sufficiently large and economically integrated and display a pattern of unbroken urbanization, they are recognized by the Census Bureau for statistical purposes as "Standard Consolidated Statistical Areas," or SCSA's. By 1979 there were thirteen SCSA's, covering such regions as the San Francisco Bay area, Chicago–northwestern Indiana and New York–northern New Jersey–southwestern Connecticut. Just as SMSA's are built up out of whole county units, so SCSA's consist of two or more whole SMSA's.

Since counties are often large and contain diverse kinds of settlement, parts of the counties included in an SMSA may be thinly settled and essentially rural rather than urban. The people living in these rural areas within SMSA's may or may not be part of the region's integrated nonagricultural labor market. In either case, the fact we are confronted with is that if "metropolitan" can include "rural" then "metropolitan" does not equal "urban." What, then, do we mean by "urban" and what by "rural"?

"Urban" and "Rural"

Urban and rural have, indeed, proven difficult for social scientists to define. Economists offer no help here: apparently economic science has been able to get along without empirically meaningful definitions of these categories. Sociologists, however, to whom the concept of community is central, have given the matter a good deal of attention. The urban community, they find, displays social characteristics different from those of rural society, but they are not always in agreement as to the extent of the differences or the inferences to be drawn from them. Consequently there is no definition of urban and rural universally accepted among sociologists. Moreover, it is highly improbable, as Duncan has argued, that any single, scalable characteristic can provide an adequate system of classification for all purposes.[2] Hatt and Reiss, however, point out that

2. Otis Dudley Duncan, "Community Size and the Rural-Urban Continuum," in Paul K. Hatt and Albert J. Reiss, Jr., eds., *Cities and Society, The Revised Reader in Urban Sociology* (Glencoe, Ill.: Free Press, 1957), pp. 35–45.

A growing number of sociologists appear to share the point of view that the formal criteria of a scientific definition of urban phenomena is satisfactorily met by defining communities solely in terms of their demographic uniqueness—the variables of population and area. "Urban" usually is defined, then, as a function of absolute population size and density of settlement. Most so-called urban variables then are considered causal consequences of variation in size and density of settlements.[3]

A definition of urban in terms of population size and density is, in fact, what the U.S. Bureau of the Census has adopted for compiling statistics on urbanization. The economist will have no trouble accepting this. He is likely to be much more directly interested in the population characteristics of communities than in sociological variables such as degree of kinship solidarity or incidence of deviant behavior, the correlation of which with the population variables used to define urban may be doubtful. Hence he will not be disturbed at the choice of demographic features themselves as the sole criteria.

By common consent, however, any dichotomous definition—that is, any definition that divides all places into two mutually exclusive groups labeled "urban" and "rural"—is bound to be arbitrary. Between the polar cases of rural and urban, along whatever scale we choose, there lie many intermediate situations. There is no obvious point at which to draw the line and say "all places larger and more densely settled than this one are urban, and the rest are rural." Yet a simple, two-way classification is so convenient that it continues to predominate in statistical studies.

The Bureau of the Census adopted its present definition of urban for the 1950 census. Included as urban are three kinds of places:

1. All incorporated municipalities having a population of 2,500 or more
2. The densely settled urban fringe, whether or not incorporated as municipalities, around cities of 50,000 or more
3. Unincorporated places of 2,500 or more population outside any urban fringe area

The Census Bureau also publishes data for an important subcategory of urban places to which it gives the name "urbanized areas." An urbanized area is a city of 50,000 or more plus its densely settled contiguous urban fringe. With a few exceptions, there is one urbanized area within each SMSA. Data are collected on this basis in order to sort out the population living at urban densities (i.e., those living in the central city and its urban fringe) from the population of the usually larger SMSA, which

3. Hatt and Reiss, p. 20.

may, as a result of its definition in terms of whole counties, contain extensive, low density, rural areas.

All places not defined as urban in the census are counted as rural and further subdivided into rural-farm and rural-nonfarm. The neophyte should be warned not to confuse farm–nonfarm with rural–urban.

The new criteria adopted in 1950 met the requirements of an up-to-date definition of urbanism about as well as possible. One must note, however, that changes in the technology of communication and transportation during the twentieth century have made the distinction between urban and rural less clear and perhaps less meaningful than it had been. Down to the end of the nineteenth century urban settlement was typically quite dense, while rural areas were settled at the low density appropriate to farming. Rural life, built around horse-and-buggy transport for short journeys, was still relatively isolated from the influence of cities. Today the urban-rural distinction is less clear: urban settlement has spread out at a much lower density than before; rural life is increasingly tied to the country towns and the larger cities by rapid communication and transport, and it has lost most of the characteristics attributable to its isolation and relative self-sufficiency.

"Central Business District"

A few terms that do not have formal Census Bureau definitions remain to be mentioned. "Central business district," commonly abbreviated as CBD, refers to the commercial center of a large city. There are no precise rules for defining a CBD according to which we could delineate comparable areas in various large cities. Thus, when the term is encountered in the literature it may quite properly mean simply what the analyst wants it to mean, or it may be defined according to local usage for a particular city. In New York, for example, CBD conventionally refers to Manhattan south of 60th Street. The steady migration of workplaces up the island now threatens this traditional dividing line with extinction. CBD's are anything but static.

"Suburb" and "Satellite City"

"Suburb" and "satellite city" are likewise terms usually defined *ad hoc*. In general, these two kinds of settlement make up the ring area of an SMSA. Suburbs are primarily "bedroom communities" containing relatively few places of employment; they may be either urban or rural. Satellite cities are urban localities within the SMSA that are places of employment and centers of commerce in their own right. As Margolis has shown in a study of the San Francisco Bay area, a set of formal definitions can be based on the ratio of local jobs to resident labor force. When the ratio was below .75, he defined the place as a "dormitory city" (i.e., suburb). When it fell between .75 and 1.25, he classified the municipality as a "balanced city" (i.e., satellite city). If the ratio exceeded 1.25 he considered the place an "industrial enclave."[4] Of course, the precise dividing lines between these categories, or others one might wish to interpose, are likely to be arbitrary. Especially since the rise of auto and truck transport, residential suburbs have increasingly sought or permitted the construction of light industry and of research and office enterprises, while satellite cities may have growing residential districts the inhabitants of which commute to jobs elsewhere in the region.

So much for terminology. A useful device for making all these spatial distinctions concrete and fixing them in the reader's mind is the schematic map of Figure 3.1. It shows how SMSA, central city, urbanized area, urban fringe, urban place, and rural area might be related spatially within a typical metropolitan region.

THE URBANIZATION OF THE UNITED STATES

Table 3.1 summarizes the history of urban and metropolitan development in the United States. At the earliest census, in 1790, only 5 percent of the whole population lived in cities of 2,500 or more—the definition of urban used until the 1950 census. If we take "urbanization" to mean a rise in the proportion of population living in urban areas, and "urban growth" to mean an absolute increase in urban population, then the United States has been experiencing both processes almost continuously since 1790. Urbanization obviously occurs whenever urban growth exceeds rural growth, and that condition has been fulfilled in every decade of our history except 1810–20. In the decades between 1790 and 1840, with that one exception, the urban population grew at an average rate almost twice that of the rural population. But because cities were so small at the beginning of the period—there were only twenty-four in all, of which only five exceeded the 10,000 mark—it took a long time for these high growth rates to urbanize very many people. As late as 1840 the country was still 89 percent rural and only 11 percent urban.

By the 1840s, according to most students of the subject, the Industrial Revolution was well under way in the United States, and all the economic forces making for agglomeration were unleashed. Thereafter the ratio of urban to rural growth increased markedly, and the pace of

4. Julius Margolis, "Municipal Fiscal Structure in a Metropolitan Region," in Ronald E. Grieson, ed., *Urban Economics, Readings and Analysis* (Boston: Little, Brown, 1973), pp. 379–95.

FIGURE 3.1
Schematic Map of an Urban-Metropolitan Area

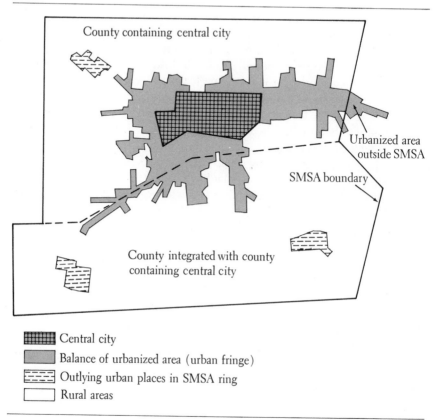

Central city
Balance of urbanized area (urban fringe)
Outlying urban places in SMSA ring
Rural areas

Source: Adapted from Donald J. Bogue, *Population Growth in Standard Metropolitan Areas, 1900–1950*, Housing and Home Finance Agency, December 1953, fig. 1, p. 8.

urbanization quickened. Immigration from abroad contributed to the trend, since a disproportionate number of immigrants to the United States have always stopped in the cities. The urban portion of the population reached 20 percent in 1860 and 40 percent in 1900. Sometime between 1910 and 1920 the nation passed the historic milestone of a population half urban and half rural: by 1920, 51 percent of the population was urban. Indeed, the decade of 1910–20 was marked by an unusually high ratio of urban to rural growth. Economic mobilization for war attracted labor from the farms to the cities. The urban population grew 29 percent, while rural numbers rose only 3 percent.

Urban growth slowed drastically during the Great Depression, since

TABLE 3.1
Growth of Urban and Metropolitan Population in the United States

DATE	PERCENTAGE OF TOTAL POPULATION		PERCENTAGE OF TOTAL POPULATION	
	Urban[a]	Rural[a]	Metro-politan[b]	Nonmetro-politan[b]
1790	5.1%	94.9%	—	—
1840	10.8	89.2	—	—
1900	39.6	60.4	31.7%	68.3%
1910	45.6	54.4	37.5	62.5
1920	51.2	48.8	43.7	56.3
1930	56.1	43.9	49.8	50.2
1940	56.5	43.5	51.1	48.9
1950	64.0	36.0	56.8	43.2
1960	69.9	30.1	63.0	37.0
1970	73.5	26.5	68.6	31.4

[a] Revised definition for 1950 and later. Using the older definition, proportions for 1950 would have been: urban, 59.6 percent, rural, 40.4 percent.
[b] Data for 1900 through 1950 refer to the areas that would have qualified as SMSA's at the given dates according to the 1950 definition, as estimated by Bogue. Data for 1960 and 1970 refer to SMSA's as defined at those census dates. "Nonmetropolitan" comprises all areas outside SMSA's
Sources: Donald J. Bogue, *Population Growth in Standard Metropolitan Areas, 1900–1950*, Housing and Home Finance Agency, December 1953; and U.S. Bureau of the Census, *Census of Population, 1960* and *1970*.

there were now no job openings to attract migrants out of the country-side. However, the industrial mobilization accompanying the Second World War stimulated urbanization once again, and it continued unabated down to 1970. By that date 73.5 percent of the U.S. population was urban. Later data on urban versus rural population growth will not be available until results of the 1980 census have been published.

THE GROWTH AND DECENTRALIZATION OF METROPOLITAN AREAS

We turn next to the metropolitan areas themselves, to look both at the rise of total metropolitan population and at the profoundly important changes in spatial organization that have been taking place *within* metropolitan areas during the twentieth century. Systematic collection of metropolitan area statistics began only with the census of 1950. At that time, however, Bogue was able to estimate population data for metropolitan areas retrospectively to 1900.[5] (See Tables 3.1 and 3.2.) His figures refer to those areas that would have qualified as SMSA's if the 1950 definition had been in effect at the earlier dates. The number of such areas diminishes as one moves back in time because populations grow smaller.

The history of metropolitan settlement in this century is best explained in terms of four trends, concentration and deconcentration, which refer to the ratio of metropolitan population to total U.S. population, and centralization and decentralization, which refer to the ratio of central city to ring area population *within* metropolitan areas. Let us briefly define these trends and see how they combined over time before investigating the powerful forces that lay behind them.

1. *Increasing concentration.* From the nineteenth century to the late 1960s, U.S. population was increasingly concentrated into metropolitan areas. Evidence for this is shown in Table 3.1. In 1900 areas outside SMA's contained 68 percent of our total population, while SMSA's contained only 32 percent. By 1970 these figures had been almost exactly reversed; SMSA's accounted for 69 percent of the national population, nonmetropolitan areas for only 31 percent.

Increasing concentration necessarily occurs whenever the metropolitan population grows faster than the nonmetropolitan. As Table 3.2 shows, that pattern prevailed from the earliest period for which we have estimates down to about 1970.

2. *Decreasing concentration.* Around 1970 the historic trend toward increased concentration, which had so long dominated our thinking about urban phenomena, came to a rather unexpected halt, to be replaced by a tendency toward deconcentration. Table 3.6 (later in this chapter) shows that from 1970 through 1978, the nonmetropolitan population grew 10.3 percent, while metropolitan areas gained only 6.2 percent. The difference in those numbers may seem small, but, as we shall see below, they do mark an important break with the past.

3. *Increasing centralization.* We define centralization as a rise in the proportion of metropolitan population living in central cities. It necessarily occurs whenever the population of central cities is rising faster than that of the suburban ring. Table 3.2 shows that this was, in fact, the case from the time of the earliest available data down to about 1920.

4. *Increasing decentralization.* In the 1920s suburban population began to grow faster than that of central cities: decentralization succeeded centralization. Table 3.2 shows that it has continued ever since.

At the opening of the century the central cities of the SMSA's were growing at a remarkable pace. Table 3.2 shows that from 1900 to 1910,

5. Donald J. Bogue, *Population Growth in Standard Metropolitan Areas, 1900–1950*, Housing and Home Finance Agency, December 1953.

TABLE 3.2
Rate of Population Growth in Central Cities, Metropolitan Rings, and Nonmetropolitan Areas of the United States

DATE	Number of SMSA's[a]	SMSA Total	Central Cities of SMSA's	Ring Areas of SMSA's	Nonmetro-politan Areas
		RATE OF GROWTH DURING PRECEDING DECADE (PERCENT)[a]			
1910	71	32.6%	35.3%	27.6%	15.0%
1920	94	25.2	26.7	22.4	8.1
1930	115	27.0	23.3	34.2	7.1
1940	125	8.3	5.1	13.8	6.2
1950	162	21.8	13.9	34.7	6.0
1960	212	26.4	10.7	48.6	7.1
1970	243	16.6	6.4	26.8	6.8

[a] Data for 1910 through 1950 refer to the areas that would have qualified as SMA's at the given dates according to the 1950 definition, as estimated by Bogue. Data for 1960 and 1970 refer to SMSA's, central cities, and rings as defined at those census dates. "Nonmetropolitan" comprises all areas outside SMSA's.

Sources: Donald J. Bogue, *Population Growth in Standard Metropolitan Areas, 1900–1950*, Housing and Home Finance Agency, December 1953; and U.S. Bureau of the Census, *Census of Population*, 1960 and 1970.

their population rose 35 percent, while that of the ring areas of SMSA's grew 28 percent and the population outside SMSA's increased only 15 percent. In the next decade relatively the same pattern persisted. After 1920, however, a dramatic reversal occurred: in every decade since that date the population of ring areas has grown faster than that of the central cities, and the margin between the rates of growth has greatly increased. So far did the reversal of trend go that in the 1950s and 1960s many of the older central cities for the first time actually lost population.

In 1960 there were twenty-one U.S. cities with a population above 500,000. Fifteen of them lost population during the next decade, and the losses ranged as high as 14 percent for Cleveland and 17 percent for St. Louis. Yet, while these two cities were losing population, their suburban rings were gaining 27 percent and 29 percent, respectively. By the 1970s, central cities in the aggregate were losing population. Between 1970 and 1979 their population dropped 3.7 percent, while ring areas showed a 14.3 percent gain.[6] New York City lost substantial population for the first time, and even Los Angeles registered a slight decline.

6. U.S. Bureau of the Census, *Current Population Reports*, series P-20, no. 350, May 1980, table 15. Data refer to the 243 SMSA's recognized in the 1970 census.

Defining Three Periods of Metropolitan Development

Combining the trends of concentration-deconcentration and central-ization-decentralization as they overlap in time, we can divide the history of metropolitan development into three distinct and well-defined periods (dates, of course, are approximate):

1. *Period I* (to 1920), increasing concentration and increasing centralization
2. *Period II* (1920 to 1970), increasing concentration and decreasing centralization
3. *Period III* (1970 to date), decreasing concentration and decreasing centralization

A fourth period may well be in the offing as a result of higher energy and transportation costs. We take up that question at the end of this chapter and in Chapter 9.

THE IMPACT OF SUCCESSIVE REVOLUTIONS IN TRANSPORTATION TECHNOLOGY

Railroads

Behind the changing patterns of settlement revealed in Tables 3.1 and 3.2 lie the successive revolutions in transportation during the nineteenth and twentieth centuries. The Industrial Revolution began with water but soon switched to steam, and the cities of the nineteenth century grew up on a pattern influenced largely by the strengths and limitations of steam transport. As we pointed out in Chapter 2, the steam railroad revolutionized long distance, intercity haulage, thus making possible great concentrations of urban population at favorable points on the rail network. Steam railroads, however, did little to improve transportation within cities, since they were not efficient for short hauls that involved frequent starting and stopping of their ponderous equipment. Indeed, mass transit in the age of steam was accomplished mostly on foot, while harnessed animal power helped to move local freight. Limited to such ancient modes of intraurban transport, the "hoof-and-foot city," as Blumenfeld has called it, could not extend over great distances. Factories crowded in close to the waterfront and the railroad lines, and workers' homes huddled as close as possible to the factories. Since distance within the city was costly to overcome, proximity was at a premium. And, since proximity was at a premium, close-in land was in great demand, brought high prices, and had to be used intensively. The nineteenth-century city therefore grew up at an extraordinarily high level of density.

Skyscrapers

In the second half of the century the introduction of the skyscraper made possible still greater intensity of land use. The skyscraper, in turn, was the product of two interdependent innovations, the passenger elevator and the iron and steel frame method of building construction. The passenger elevator, a revolutionary means of urban transportation in the previously unexploited vertical dimension, was first perfected by Elisha Graves Otis, who personally demonstrated it at the Crystal Palace Exposition in New York in 1853. First use of the fully developed iron and steel frame in a tall building is credited to the architect William LeBaron Jenney in the famous ten story "skyscraper" he completed for the Home Insurance Company of Chicago in 1885. Within a few years the steel frame largely replaced masonry construction; the race toward the modern skyscraper was under way.

Meanwhile, escape outward from the crowded center was reserved for those who could afford, if they wished, to commute to the city on steam railroads. Toward the end of the century commuters' suburbs grew up around the stations along the railroad lines leaving the principal cities. These suburbs were compact in form. Since local transportation was still by horse and buggy, commuters could not live far from the railroad station. Hence commuting towns were strung out like beads along the railroad lines that radiated from the city. By 1898 *Harper's Weekly* reported that more than 118,000 people arrived daily at New York City's Grand Central Terminal from Westchester and Connecticut alone.[7]

Streetcars and Subways

Between 1870 and 1900 the "hoof-and-foot city" was rapidly transformed into the "city of the streetcar." In various ways rail transportation was adapted to serve urban needs. Horsedrawn streetcars had been in use since the middle of the nineteenth century. They were not fast enough or large enough, however, to influence urban size and form. Although the cable car was introduced in 1872, its construction was expensive, and it remained for the electric streetcar, first operated on a large scale in the late 1880s, to alter matters by radically extending the distances city dwellers could conveniently travel to their workplaces. By the first decade of the twentieth century a web of streetcar lines crisscrossed every major city and made it possible for residential neighborhoods to spread far out from the old centers. Sometimes the new neighborhoods were more spacious than the old; sometimes they repeated the old high densities. In

7. Reported by John A. Kouwenhoven in *Columbia Historical Portrait of New York* (New York: Doubleday, 1953), p. 422.

either case, vast new areas became accessible for housing, and cities were able to grow to unprecedented size.

In the largest cities the age of the streetcar also became the age of the elevated train and the subway. New York City began to build elevated intraurban railroads in the 1870s and possessed an extensive network by 1890. Steam engines were used at first, but the lines were soon electrified. In 1900 the city began construction of its first subway, and service started in 1904. Boston had begun service on a small section of subway in the late 1890s.

THE MONONUCLEAR CITY

Rapid transit by subway or elevated train extended the feasible journey to work or to shop and thus reinforced the effect of the streetcar in stimulating the growth of great cities. Even more than the streetcar lines, however, the rapid transit systems were laid out like the spokes of a wheel. They were intended to move people from outlying residential areas to a central business and shopping district and back again to their homes. Such a system did little to improve communication between points in outlying areas. It was intended to serve a mononuclear city, and once in place it provided formidable economic support for the mononuclear structure. Only in the central business district could the large insurance companies, banks, and other office enterprises daily assemble the thousands of clerks and bookkeepers they required. Centrality was equally crucial to the large department stores. Located at the hub of the transport network, they could serve not only the downtown work force but the crowds of shoppers the system funneled toward them from all parts of the city.

During those years in which the streetcar and the subway were radically improving urban passenger transport, no similar improvement occurred in the transportation of goods. Within cities freight was still moved by horse and wagon, often on unpaved streets. Consequently, as Alex Anas and Leon Moses point out, "The cost of moving goods inside cities . . . was high relative to the cost of moving people," and close-in locations therefore remained attractive for manufacturing.[8] By moving farther out (but still within the city) manufacturing firms could have reduced their costs of land and labor, but those savings would have been less than the increased expense of freight movement to and from outlying locations. Manufacturing, like other economic activity, therefore remained highly centralized in the early twentieth-century city.

8. Alex Anas and Leon N. Moses, "Transportation and Land Use in the Mature Metropolis," in Charles L. Leven, ed., *The Mature Metropolis* (Lexington, Mass.: D. C. Heath, Lexington Books, 1978), pp. 150–51.

Supported by the great transportation innovations of railroad, street-car, subway, and elevator, central cities reached what might be called their demographic zenith in the early years of the twentieth century. Between 1900 and 1920 the population of central cities grew considerably faster than that of their ring areas and incomparably faster than the nation's nonmetropolitan population.

We have already indicated the reversal of this pattern when, after 1920, ring areas of SMSA's began to gain population faster than central cities. For this reversal we can supply two principal explanations; the first might be termed the overflow effect and the second the automobile effect.

DECENTRALIZATION: THE OVERFLOW EFFECT

The overflow effect is easily described. If a central city with fixed boundaries enjoys continuous growth of numbers, vacant land will eventually be used up, and, even though growth continues in the form of higher density, additional metropolitan population will tend increasingly to spill over into the suburbs. Before the outward-moving margin of continuous development reaches the central city boundaries, suburban ring development will be relatively slight, based upon the growth of scattered suburbs and satellite cities. After the margin of development passes those boundaries, however, suburban population will rise at an incomparably faster pace than before and will certainly outstrip the growth rate of the central city.

Statistical evidence of the overflow effect can be obtained if we restate the relationship as follows: the greater the density of population per square mile in the central city, the greater the proportion of SMSA population growth that will be accounted for by the ring. Figure 3.2 demonstrates the existence of such a relationship. Its horizontal scale measures central city population per square mile in 1960. Its vertical scale measures percentage of total SMSA population growth between 1960 and 1970 accounted for by the ring area of the SMSA. Plotted on the diagram are points showing the central city density and ring proportion of SMSA growth for twelve SMSA's: the six largest (in 1978) in the North and East (marked by stars) and the six largest in the South and West (shown by circles). The SMSA's were selected on a regional basis in order to bring out the contrast—which we will have occasion to illustrate along many socioeconomic scales—between the older, more densely settled SMSA's of the former group and the newer, more spread out metropolitan areas of the latter.

The diagram shows clearly that the proportion of growth accounted for by the ring increases as central city density rises. With one exception,

FIGURE 3.2
Relationship Between Central City Density and Suburban Population Growth

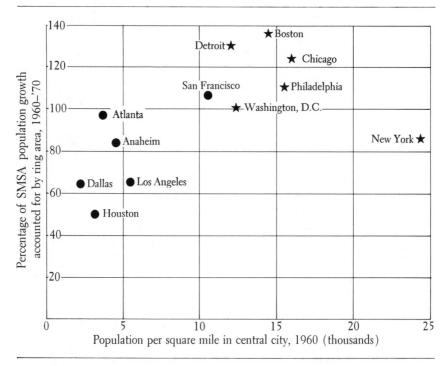

Notes: Data refer to the 1960 areas of SMSA's, central cities and ring areas. The two groups of SMSA's are:

NORTH AND EAST (SHOWN BY ★)

New York, N.Y.
Chicago, Ill.
Philadelphia, Pa.–N.J.
Detroit, Mich.
Washington, D.C., Md.–Va.
Boston, Mass.

SOUTH AND WEST (SHOWN BY ●)

Los Angeles-Long Beach, Calif.
San Francisco-Oakland, Calif.
Houston, Texas
Dallas, Texas
Atlanta, Ga.
Anaheim-Santa Ana-Garden Grove, Calif.

Orange County was deducted from the Los Angeles–Long Beach SMSA data for 1960, since that county was subsequently recognized as the independent Anaheim–Santa Ana–Garden Grove SMSA.

Source: U.S. Bureau of the Census, *Census of Population, 1960 and 1970.*

all the cities having a density above 6,000 persons per square mile in 1960 lost population in the next decade. In the SMSA's centered on those cities, the ring therefore necessarily accounted for more than 100 percent of SMSA population growth. The one exception was New York City. Although its population density is approximately double that of the other large central cities of the North and East, it nevertheless registered a small population gain during the 1960s, and began to lose population only in the 1970s. (See Table 3.3, below.) One must keep in mind, however, that New York City, as the highest order city in the hierarchy of U.S. urban centers, is literally a unique case. It may therefore display a relationship between density and overflow different than do other large U.S. cities. (We will explore the notion of urban hierarchy in Chapter 5.)

Influence of City Age

Figure 3.2 shows a dramatic contrast between the large central cities of the North and East and those of the South and West. With the single exception of San Francisco–Oakland, the central cities of the South and West are grouped at the low end of the density scale; without exception those of the North and East fall at the high end. This striking difference is a function primarily of central city age. As we have already pointed out, cities that achieved their major growth before the automobile era typically developed to very high densities; these are the old central cities of the North and East. On the other hand, as we will explain below, cities that grew rapidly after 1920 were laid out to be served by the automobile and truck and typically show a dispersed, low density pattern; such are the newer cities of the South and West.

The age of an SMSA has often been measured by the census date at which it first would have qualified as a metropolitan area according to our present definition. Such a procedure, however, fails to draw the distinction intended here. The definition of an SMSA requires a central city of at least 50,000 population, but almost all the very large SMSA's of 1970 had central cities of 50,000 or more well before the automobile era. An age measure capable of distinguishing development before from development after the automobile era would have to be based on a different criterion than simply a 50,000 population size. One might, for example, assign as the age of a central city the census date at which it reached half its maximum size. Such a measure enables one to distinguish those cities that enjoyed half or more of their growth before the automobile age from those that did not. Applying that criterion, we find that all six of the northern and eastern cities in Figure 3.2 had achieved at least half their maximum size by 1920, and four had done so by 1910 or earlier. According to this measure, the western and southern cities are much

TABLE 3.3

Population Inside and Outside Central Cities of Selected Metropolitan
Areas, 1978, and Percentage Change in Population, 1960–70 and 1970–78

SIX LARGEST SMSA'S IN NORTH AND EAST[b]	POPULATION 1978	PERCENTAGE CHANGE[a] 1970–78	1960–70
New York, N.Y.–N.J.	9,221,800	−7.5%	4.6%
New York City	7,134,542	−9.6	1.5
Outside central city	2,087,258	0.4	18.2
Chicago, Ill.	7,029,600	0.7	12.2
Chicago city	3,049,479	−9.5	−5.1
Outside central city	3,980,121	10.3	35.1
Philadelphia, Pa.–N.J.	4,770,400	−1.1	11.1
Philadelphia city	1,754,829	−10.0	−2.6
Outside central city	3,015,571	4.9	22.8
Detroit, Mich.	4,386,400	−1.1	12.3
Detroit city	1,257,879	−16.9	−9.3
Outside central city	3,128,521	7.1	28.1
Boston–Lowell–Brockton–Lawrence–Haverhill, Mass.–N.H.	3,887,800	1.0	11.3
Inside central cities	885,148	−5.6	−4.3
Outside central cities	3,002,652	3.1	17.5
Washington, D.C.–Md.–Va.	3,016,900	3.7	38.0
Washington city (D.C.)	671,001	−11.3	−0.9
Outside central city	2,345,899	8.9	60.1
Aggregate of six SMSA's in North and East	32,312,900	−2.0	11.3
Inside central cities	14,752,878	−10.1	−1.9
Outside central cities	17,560,022	6.1	28.6

newer. Four achieved half their maximum population only by 1940 or later. Atlanta achieved it in 1930 and San Francisco–Oakland in 1920. As Figure 3.2 demonstrates, the California pair display density and growth characteristics similar to cities of the North and East rather than those of the South and West, just as one would expect from their similarity in age.

As the older central cities in Figure 3.2 lose population, their population per square mile will diminish, and they will move leftward on the density diagram. As the newer central cities gain population, they will move to the right. Thus the two groups, now so widely separated, are gradually converging along the density scale. It seems unlikely, however, that they will meet in the foreseeable future. The newer cities, built on the principle of automobile transportation, cannot develop to anything like the densities achieved in the older cities, with their mass transit frame-

SIX LARGEST SMSA'S IN SOUTH AND WEST[c]	POPULATION[a]	PERCENTAGE CHANGE[a]	
	1978	1970–78	1960–70
Los Angeles–Long Beach, Calif.	7,080,900	0.6%	16.6%
Inside central cities	3,126,805	−1.5	12.4
Outside central cities	3,954,095	2.2	20.3
San Francisco–Oakland, Calif.	3,183,800	2.4	17.4
Inside central cities	981,562	−8.9	−2.8
Outside central cities	2,202,238	8.4	31.9
Dallas–Fort Worth, Tex.	2,719,900	14.4	36.8
Inside central cities	1,214,852	−2.3	20.0
Outside central cities	1,505,048	32.6	61.6
Houston, Tex.	2,595,400	29.8	39.8
Houston city	1,572,981	20.0	36.7
Outside central city	1,022,419	48.5	45.7
Atlanta, Ga.	1,851,500	16.0	36.5
Atlanta city	405,437	−18.1	1.6
Outside central city	1,446,063	31.4	61.5
Anaheim–Santa Ana–Garden Grove, Calif.	1,833,000	29.0	101.9
Inside central cities	514,911	16.2	53.5
Outside central cities	1,318,089	34.8	135.6
Aggregate of six SMSA's in South and West	19,264,500	9.8	27.8
Inside central cities	7,816,548	1.0	15.8
Outside central cities	11,447,952	16.8	39.1

[a] For each SMSA as a whole, population in 1978 and percentage changes from earlier years are based on constant (1978) SMSA boundaries. In calculating percentage changes for central cities (and outside central cities), 1970 population was adjusted to 1978 boundaries, but 1960 population could not be so adjusted.

[b] Corresponds to Northeast and North Central census regions plus Maryland and Washington, D.C.

[c] Corresponds to South and West census regions less Maryland and Washington, D.C.

Sources: U.S. Bureau of the Census, *Current Population Reports*, series P-25, no. 873, February 1980, table 1; unpublished Census Bureau data; and *Census of Population, 1960.*

work. Indeed, some of the denser new cities of the South and West appear already to have reached, or may be close to reaching, their maximum population size.

Data on the present size and recent growth of population in the twelve metropolitan areas discussed above are given in Table 3.3. From

1960 to 1970 the aggregate population of the new SMSA's of the South and West grew at more than twice the rate shown by the old areas of the North and East. The central cities in the former group gained 16 percent in aggregate population, while those in the latter lost 2 percent. Ring areas grew rapidly in both regions, but more rapidly in the new SMSA's than in the old. Decentralization continued unabated in the 1970s. In addition, Table 3.3 displays some of the evidence for the beginning of deconcentration. Three of the six SMSA's in the North and East actually lost population in the 1970s. In the South and West the Los Angeles and San Francisco SMSA's, which had grown rapidly in the previous decade, registered almost no further gain. We return to the question of deconcentration at the end of this chapter.

DECENTRALIZATION: THE AUTOMOBILE EFFECT

The high ratio of ring to central city population growth in metropolitan areas with central city densities as low as those of Dallas, Houston, and Anaheim–Santa Ana–Garden Grove is strong evidence that the automobile effect as well as the overflow effect has been an important cause of the rapid development of suburbs since 1920. In addition, the overflow effect, acting alone, could never account for the decline in population experienced by so many central cities in recent years. With the automobile effect we come to the last revolutionary change in transportation technology that has shaped the geographic pattern of metropolitan settlement in our times.

Until the automobile and the truck came into widespread use, rail transport (including street railways) was the only rapid and efficient system of overland movement both for men and for goods. Rail transport, however, has important limitations. Obviously service is restricted to points along the right of way. Yet the number of rights of way that can be operated economically is limited because high fixed costs impose a need for heavy traffic. Within cities, population density was sufficient to support a rather fine-grained network of streetcar lines, but a highly articulated network of commuter railroads, even around the largest cities, was never feasible. Instead the commuter was restricted to a few lines radiating from the central city. Suburban streetcar service, if it existed at all, was subject to the same sort of constraint at its own scale of operation. One could not profitably operate streetcar lines through thinly settled residential districts. Before the advent of the automobile commuters therefore had to live near the railroad stations. Vast areas between the radiating spokes of the railroad system, if they were outside the range of the central city streetcar or subway lines, were too inaccessible for suburban settlement.

Industrial and commercial activities were similarly restricted in their choice of location. Manufacturing plants could and did locate outside the central cities along existing railroad lines. Indeed, many satellite cities thrived and grew on such an economic base during the nineteenth century. But even the lightest of industries could not move away from the railroad lines on which they depended for the movement of goods. Nor could they have assembled a daily work force at any suburban point outside the satellite towns.

Large clerical enterprises were even more restricted. Nowhere but at the hub of the central city could they find a labor supply large enough for their needs. Retailing, too, was centralized. Highly specialized stores of all sorts could find enough customers only in the central city, and often only in its central business district. Department stores grew up in satellite towns as well as in central cities, but the suburban "shopping center" in open country was not yet even an inspired land developer's dream.

Thus, because rail transport could best serve a centralized metropolis, metropolitan areas grew up centralized. Indeed, centralization was a self-reinforcing process: the greater the concentration of employment in the central business district, the more it thrived as a center for specialized retail and business services; and the more it developed such services, the greater its attraction as a place of business and employment. Congestion could act as an automatic brake on centralization, but, contrary to our fantasies about the ultimate traffic jam, congestion limits but does not reverse concentration at the center.

Only a radical improvement in our ability to overcome what Haig called the "friction of space" could break up this historic drive toward centralization. The automobile and the truck provided that improvement by freeing people from the need to live and work close to the fixed lines of the railroad, the subway, and the streetcar. Beginning about 1920 a vast loosening up took place within the metropolis, and, as it proceeded, the self-reinforcing tide of centralization halted and was succeeded by an equally powerful process of decentralization.

What followed has sometimes been called the "suburbanization" of metropolitan America. That term may be misleading, however, if it connotes simply the rise of commuting suburbs, for the process of decentralization has involved jobs as much as residences.

DECENTRALIZATION OF JOBS

Job decentralization within metropolitan areas need not mean that firms close up shop within the central city, pack their movables into vans, and unload at new sites in the suburbs. Such moves can and do take place.

But decentralization occurs also as a result of differential rates of expansion of existing firms and differential rates of formation of new establishments as between areas. In fact, these sources of decentralization cannot be disentangled except through painstaking case by case study of individual firms in each area.

We know, however, that the development of trucking made it possible for many firms to cut their ties to railroads and ports. Simultaneously, the widespread ownership of automobiles enabled them to break away from mass-transit-oriented urban labor markets. The need for more ground space often provided the impetus either to move old plants or, when expansion was desirable, to establish new ones at suburban locations. In order to take advantage of assembly line techniques and modern methods of materials handling, manufacturers and distributors needed extended single-story plants rather than the traditional multistory mills of the nineteenth century. Space to build such plants was far too expensive in the old urban locations but was readily available in the ring areas of the metropolis. Hence many firms, whose face-to-face contact requirements with other industries in the central city were not overriding, either moved to the suburbs or opened new plants there. They acquired space without sacrificing effective proximity to either their suppliers or their customers in the metropolitan market.

The extent to which new manufacturing plants were truck rather than rail oriented has been documented by Hoover and Vernon in their study of the New York metropolitan region. One of their surveys revealed that the proportion of plants served by railroad sidings fell from 63 percent for sites acquired before 1920 to 40 percent for sites acquired between 1946 and 1956. Hoover and Vernon also show the extent to which modern production and materials-handling techniques have steadily increased the land requirements of factories and thus encouraged suburban rather than central city location. They found that plants built outside the central and old satellite cities of the region before 1922 occupied an average of 1,040 square feet of land per worker, while those built between 1922 and 1945 occupied 2,000 square feet per worker, and those built after 1945 took up an average of 4,550 square feet per worker, or almost as much as a small suburban housing lot.[9]

In an economy built on specialization and interdependence, one new job at a particular place gives rise to others. As the manufacturers, the distributors, and the research laboratories moved out into the suburban rings, suburban employment in complementary service trades increased, too. The rise in job opportunities, of course, attracted population, and the

---

9. Edgar M. Hoover and Raymond Vernon, *Anatomy of a Metropolis* (Cambridge, Mass.: Harvard University Press, 1959), pp. 31 and 37.

increased population in turn enlarged the market for consumer services, creating still further job opportunities. In short, suburban areas were launched on a continuous round of self-reinforcing economic and demographic growth.

The decentralization of manufacturing within metropolitan areas in the period before World War II has been documented by Kitigawa and Bogue. They found that the proportion of metropolitan area production workers within central cities declined from 67 percent in 1929 to 63 percent in 1939, while the proportion in ring areas rose from 33 percent to 37 percent. Despite the enormous increase in manufacturing production that took place during the war, these aggregate ratios did not show further change by 1947.[10] Since that date, however, decentralization has resumed, and its pace has quickened. Table 3.4 shows the decentralization of manufacturing, retail, wholesale, and selected service employment that took place within our twelve major SMSA's between 1948 and 1972. In both the older and the newer groups every category of activity shows marked decentralization, as indicated by the rise in the ring share and the fall in the central city share of the industry total.

It is interesting to note that in every industrial category the older metropolitan areas were more centralized in 1948 than were the newer areas. This is just what we would have expected, since the newer areas tended to develop during the age of the automobile, while the older areas were products of the railroad age. For the same reason, we would expect the older areas to decentralize more rapidly than the newer ones: they had, so to speak, more adapting to do under the pressure of technological change. Table 3.4 shows that this was, indeed, the case. From 1948 to 1972 the central city share of aggregate employment (righthand panel of table) fell 26 points in the older SMSA's, while it declined only 17 points in the newer ones. Especially striking is the accelerated decentralization of jobs in the older SMSA's after 1967. The central city job share fell 8 points in the short space of five years after 1967, as compared with 18 points in the nineteen years preceding that date. No such acceleration occurred in the six SMSA's of the South and West. (The speed-up of job decentralization in the older SMSA's was accompanied, of course, by the rapid decentralization of population already depicted in Table 3.3.)

In the North and East, decentralization has involved an actual decline in the number of jobs in central cities. As the lefthand panel of Table 3.4 shows, only the service sector has registered an absolute increase since 1948, and that was insufficient to offset losses in manufacturing,

10. Evelyn M. Kitigawa and Donald J. Bogue, *Suburbanization of Manufacturing Activity Within Standard Metropolitan Areas* (Oxford, Ohio: Scripps Foundation, 1955), table II–3, p. 22.

TABLE 3.4

Decentralization of Jobs and Population in
Selected Metropolitan Areas

SIX LARGEST SMSA'S IN NORTH AND EAST[a]	PERCENTAGE CHANGE IN JOBS[b]		PERCENTAGE DISTRIBUTION OF JOBS BETWEEN CENTRAL CITIES AND RING AREAS		
	1948–67	*1967–72*	*1948*	*1967*	*1972*
Manufacturing					
Central city	−16.1%	−28.0%	72%	55%	47%
Outside central city	73.7	−0.6	28	45	53
Retail					
Central city	−14.1	−6.7	77	55	46
Outside central city	132.5	30.0	23	45	54
Wholesale					
Central city	−5.4	−18.9	92	71	60
Outside central city	352.1	32.2	8	29	40
Selected services					
Central city	33.6	1.8	87	73	63
Outside central city	213.2	66.7	13	27	37
Total, four industries					
Central city	−8.7	−17.3	77	59	51
Outside central city	105.8	16.0	23	41	49

	PERCENTAGE CHANGE IN POPULATION		PERCENTAGE DISTRIBUTION OF POPULATION		
	1950–70	*1970–78*	*1950*	*1970*	*1978*
Population[c]					
Central city	−5.2	−10.1	67	50	46
Outside central city	94.1	6.1	33	50	54

retailing, and wholesaling. In the South and West, on the other hand, despite decentralization, the number of jobs in central cities rose in all categories through 1967. Thereafter, the number declined in manufacturing but continued to increase in other categories. Overall, the six central cities in the South and West continued to gain jobs even in the most recent period.

As we shall see in later chapters, job loss in the older cities of the North and East has important consequences for many aspects of public policy. For example, it clearly makes more difficult the relief of inner city poverty. Job loss is also an important cause of city government fiscal stress, since tax revenues fall when the number of local jobs declines.

Two cautions are necessary in the interpretation of Table 3.4. First, one must note the effects of annexation. SMSA boundaries have been held constant in Table 3.4 at the definitions that obtained in 1972. It was

SIX LARGEST SMSA'S IN SOUTH AND WEST[a]	PERCENTAGE CHANGE IN JOBS[b]		PERCENTAGE DISTRIBUTION OF JOBS BETWEEN CENTRAL CITIES AND RING AREAS		
	1948–67	1967–72	1948	1967	1972
Manufacturing					
Central cities	67.6%	−7.3%	61%	48%	47%
Outside central cities	179.3	16.5	39	52	53
Retail					
Central cities	31.3	9.7	71	55	50
Outside central cities	157.6	35.6	29	45	50
Wholesale					
Central cities	31.4	3.5	87	55	59
Outside central cities	377.4	35.0	13	35	41
Selected services					
Central cities	142.9	31.4	77	68	63
Outside central cities	297.0	63.0	23	32	37
Total, four industries					
Central cities	58.8	5.4	69	55	52
Outside central cities	193.2	16.5	31	45	48
	PERCENTAGE CHANGE IN POPULATION		PERCENTAGE DISTRIBUTION OF POPULATION		
	1950–70	1970–78	1950	1970	1978
Population[c]					
Central cities	51.8	1.0	53	44	41
Outside central cities	120.9	16.8	47	56	59

[a] As defined in Table 3.3.

[b] With minor exceptions it was possible to gather 1948 and 1967 employment data on the basis of 1972 SMSA boundaries. Thus SMSA boundaries are held virtually constant. No adjustment is made, however, for annexation of territory by central cities, which, in some cases, took a substantial number of jobs away from ring areas between 1948 and 1972. Manufacturing data are for 1947 rather than 1948.

[c] Population data are consistent with those in Table 3.3. See footnote (a) of that table.

Sources: U.S. Bureau of the Census, *Census of Manufactures*, 1947, 1967, and 1972; *Census of Business*, 1948, 1967, and 1972; *Census of Population*, 1950 and 1970. Population data for 1978 are from Table 3.3, above.

not feasible however to correct the data for annexations of suburban territory by central cities during the period covered. Such annexations were negligible in the older areas but quite substantial in the newer ones, where they added automatically to the central city share of economic activity at the expense of the share reported for the ring. In the absence of such annexation, decentralization of jobs in the SMSA's of the South and West would have been more rapid than Table 3.4 indicates. Second, the table does not account for all jobs. Data were not available for such categories as government and nonprofit institutions. These are probably more centralized than the four private sector categories included in the table. Conseqeuntly, the table probably understates to some extent the level of centralization for jobs as a whole in both the older and the newer SMSA's.

Changes in Work Trip Patterns

Influenced by recollections of an earlier period, some residents of the older central cities are inclined to think of "suburbanite" and "commuter" as interchangeable terms. Table 3.4 indicates that such an interpretation is increasingly inappropriate. The four rows at the bottom of the table show that jobs in the aggregate have been decentralizing even faster than population. It necessarily follows that as the suburbs have grown, the proportion of suburbanites who also work in the suburbs has steadily increased, while the proportion who commute to the central city has steadily diminished. Anas and Moses analyzed the work trip pattern in six "mature SMSA's" in 1960 and 1970. The level of commuting to the central city was roughly stable. On the other hand, the number of suburbanites holding jobs in the suburbs increased substantially. By 1970 they outnumbered commuters by a ratio that varied from better than 2 to 1 to more than 3 to 1. The fastest growing categories of jobholders, though not the largest in absolute terms, were "reverse commuters," those who lived in the central city and traveled outward to jobs in the suburbs and those who lived in the suburbs and held jobs entirely outside the SMSA.[11]

We see, then, that as jobs and residences have dispersed in the pattern we have called decentralization, the web of work trips has become increasingly complex and certainly less and less focused on the inner city. We shall explore the implications of decentralization for urban transportation policy in Chapter 9.

DECENTRALIZATION OF POPULATION

We have yet to examine in detail the forces that led to the decentralization of metropolitan population in the twentieth century. Obviously this movement has depended on some of the same technological forces—especially the automobile effect—that led to the decentralization of jobs.

11. Anas and Moses, table 8.1, p. 158.

Nevertheless, the change in residential patterns also depended on other factors and is important enough to warrant separate analysis.

For the resident of the metropolis, the automobile made possible a home in the previously inaccessible areas between the spokes of the railroad lines radiating from the central city. The commuting towns, which had once appeared as compact beads strung out along the railroad lines, began to spread out. Wholly new residential settlements were built in what had been rural areas, miles from the nearest railroad station. By the 1970s, after more than fifty years of "automobilization," the suburban rings around major cities were not yet "filled up," but open space was fast disappearing.

Evidence of the Automobile Effect

Population statistics dramatically illustrate the abrupt change in pattern that occurred in the age of the automobile. In every decade up to 1930, urban places in the ring—the satellite cities and the compact, rail-oriented commuter towns—had gained population far faster than had the rural ring areas. Even during the 1920s, when automobiles were coming into widespread use, the rates of growth were 48 percent for urban ring places and only 19 percent for rural ring areas. But with the decade of the 1930s the relationship suddenly reversed. Thereafter, rural parts of the ring gained residents far faster than urban ring places. In the 1940s the rates of growth were 41 percent and 29 percent, respectively.[12]

It is important to note that the change in pattern from faster ring-urban to faster ring-rural growth took place at the same date in all size classes of metropolitan area (except the very smallest).[13] This coincidence in time reinforces the belief that the change relates to the nationwide impact of the automobile on patterns of settlement rather than to factors associated with the size or stage of development of individual metropolitan areas.

The Influence of Rising Living Standards and Changes in Consumer Preferences

The advent of the automobile and the truck was a necessary condition for the rise of suburbia in its present low density pattern. Even in conjunction with the overflow effect, however, it was not a sufficient force to produce the degree of suburbanization we find in metropolitan America today. Rising living standards are another factor that deserves mention.

12. Bogue, table 1, p. 13.
13. Ibid., table 16, p. 31.

In the technical language of economics, living space is a "superior good" —that is to say, a good people want more of as their incomes rise. To be sure, they can obtain more space by moving into larger quarters in the city. But there is reason to believe that many who lived in the city while they were poor will choose more space in the suburbs rather than more space in the city as they grow wealthier. That reason lies in the peculiarly fixed nature of commuting costs. A poor family might just possibly find inexpensive housing in the suburbs. But for any given location, commuting costs are fixed: it will cost a poor person as much to ride a train from Tarrytown to New York City as it costs any of the Rockefellers. A low income family will find that cost simply prohibitive. As income rises, however, the barrier of fixed commuting costs looms less and less large, and eventually the family surmounts it. Thus many who chose the city when they were poor will be found to choose the suburbs as their income rises, just as many who drove used cars when they were poor will buy new cars when their fortunes improve. It is their income, not their taste, that changes. The steady rise of living standards generates a flow of migration from city to suburb quite independently of any change in consumer tastes or in the cost of satisfying them. (The effect of higher income on locational choice is a complex matter that is dealt with at greater length in Chapter 6. See Figure 6.6 and the related text.)

Yet consumer preferences, or tastes, do change as well. Images of the good life are difficult (before the age of the sociological questionnaire one might have said impossible) to measure and quantify. It does seem likely, however, that the suburban life style—informal, fecund, child centered—exercised a more powerful appeal after the end of the Second World War than it had before the war, even for those who could then have afforded it. If this change in the underlying preferences of the population did, indeed, occur, it simply worked to reinforce a process of suburbanization that would have occurred, in any case, without it.

Quite clearly, the pendulum is now swinging in the other direction. The recent sharp drop in the birth rate, the increase in the number of two-worker households, the rise of the new feminism, the increasing questioning of the desirability of the traditional nuclear family, all suggest that at least some Americans are now moving away from the values that have hitherto been the foundation of suburban life. A rapidly growing segment of the population is a new class of young adults, including a fast increasing number of working women, who are either unmarried or, if married, do not intend to raise large families. These men and women are more likely to be attracted to the inner city than were the generation that produced the postwar baby boom, and when they share two incomes they can often afford to live in convenient downtown neighborhoods. It is not clear that they will be numerous enough to halt the recent population declines of our older central cities, but they are already having an impact on inner city housing markets.[14] We will take a closer look at this new wave of urban settlers in the concluding chapter.

The Influence of Public Policy

The growth of the suburbs has, in the main, been a natural consequence of changes in technology and rising living standards. However, we should not overlook the fact that public policy has been an indirect influence. It has stimulated suburban as opposed to central city development by favoring home ownership, typical of suburban living, over home rental, which is largely a city phenomenon. This bias is manifold and coincides in time with the impact of the automobile.

First of all, the federal income tax, which was introduced in 1913 and reached the mass of Americans beginning with the Second World War, treats homeowners more favorably than home renters. Suppose that a woman, now living in a rented house, inherits some capital. On the one hand, she can invest the inheritance in stocks and continue to live in a rented house. In that case the investment earns dividends on which she must pay income tax. On the other hand, if she invests the inheritance in a house and occupies it herself, she pays no rent, and the investment yields no taxable income under U.S. law. An economically neutral tax system would add to the income of the owner-occupant an estimate of the gross rental value of the house and allow her to deduct interest, property taxes, maintenance, and depreciation as expenses of earning that income. The difference between these amounts is the imputed net income the owner could have earned had she leased the house to someone else at the going market price instead of occupying it herself. U.S. tax law favors homeowners twice over. It does *not* tax them on the imputed net rental value of their homes, yet it *does* allow them to deduct the interest and property tax costs of producing that income. Because taxable income is being understated, the tax saving is greater the higher the homeowner's marginal tax bracket.[15] Consequently, U.S. tax law not only favors home-ownership, it stimulates home-ownership by the rich more than by the poor and there-

14. For a wide-ranging examination of the probable effects of the declining birth rate and changing household arrangements on urban phenomena, see William Alonso, "The Population Factor and Urban Structure," in Arthur P. Solomon, ed., *The Prospective City* (Cambridge, Mass.: The MIT Press, 1980), p. 32.

15. For detailed estimates, see Henry J. Aaron, *Shelter and Subsidies* (Washington, D.C.: Brookings Institution, 1972), ch. 4. Aaron also examines depreciation provisions under the income tax that favor rental rather than owner-occupied housing. He suggests that under the most probable assumptions the value of these depreciation benefits to rental housing is much smaller than the value of the special treatment accorded to owner occupants (p. 68).

fore encourages the segregation of the rich in the suburbs and the poor in the central cities.

The notion that the imputed rental value of housing ought to be counted as income is not, incidentally, as far-fetched as it may appear to the reader whose concept of income is based on conventional rather than logically consistent reasoning: the Department of Commerce, in measuring national income and gross national product, has always included an estimate of imputed annual home rental in the grand aggregate.

A second source of bias in public policy is the long-standing federal policy of intervening in the mortgage market to encourage home-ownership. Since the Great Depression this intervention has taken many forms, of which the most important was and is the Federal Housing Administration's program of home mortgage insurance. The FHA has been startlingly successful in achieving its purpose of reducing both the down payments and the monthly carrying costs on new owner-occupied housing, and that is all to the good. But for many years its program was administered so as to favor ownership in new suburban areas, and it failed to develop equally powerful institutional supports for the construction of new urban rental housing. By and large the FHA, from the inception of its mortgage insurance program, underwrote the advertising man's version of the good American life as requiring a Cape Cod cottage, surrounded by a hedge and a well-cropped lawn, and filled with new home appliances. Since the Second World War policies to aid urban as well as suburban housing have gradually gained momentum. But for about twenty-five years—say, from the early 1930s until the late 1950s—the net effect of federal intervention was surely to hasten the flight to the suburbs.

To summarize briefly, we have now cited five forces that contributed to the rapid growth of suburban relative to central city population during the twentieth century: the overflow effect, the effects of technological innovations, the rise in living standards, a probable change in consumer preferences among life styles, and, finally, the effects of biases in public policy. Each of these can be thought of as a separate force that would have acted even in the absence of the others. Acting together, they provided a remarkably powerful stimulus for change. (In Chapter 6 we will reexamine the first three in the tighter theoretical framework of an urban land-use model.)

MIGRATION AND METROPOLITAN GROWTH

Where did the people come from who filled the cities and suburbs of twentieth-century America? There are only two possible sources of local population growth: natural increase, which occurs when local births exceed local deaths, and migration from other places. Until recently the rate of natural increase was probably higher outside than inside metropolitan areas. Hence, in the absence of migration, nonmetropolitan population would have grown faster. Since, on the contrary, metropolitan population increased more rapidly than nonmetropolitan, we know that migration from nonmetropolitan areas and/or from overseas into SMSA's has long been taking place. (This abstracts from the relatively minor complication that nonmetropolitan places, after sufficient growth, are reclassified as metropolitan for statistical purposes.)

As we pointed out earlier, foreign immigrants into the United States have always moved disproportionately to urban destinations. Immigration from abroad was therefore a major source of urban growth down to the mid-1920s. Then restrictive quotas, and later the Great Depression, sharply reduced the inflow. Since 1950 it has gained in significance once again. More important, however, in explaining urban and metropolitan development is the internal migration that has probably been going on at least since the early nineteenth century. According to Shannon, farmers' sons who moved to the city outnumbered those who became owners of new farms by ten to one.[16] While aggregate earlier data are unavailable, figures for 1920 through 1954 show that during those thirty-five years the *net* migration from farms to urban areas totaled 24 million. For the sake of comparison, the *net* migration of aliens into the United States during the twenty-four years 1907 through 1930, while immigration was still at a relatively high level, amounted to only 8.4 million.[17] The farm sector in the United States is now so small, however, that it cannot continue to be a major source of population for the rest of the country.

Estimates of the flows of net migration from nonmetropolitan to metropolitan areas between 1940 and 1970 are shown in Table 3.5. (The post-1970 pattern is displayed separately in Table 3.6.) Net migration into a given area is estimated as a residual by applying the formula: net change in population — change through natural increase = net migration. The first term is easily calculated from successive census reports. Natural increase is estimated as the difference between local births and deaths. Net migration necessarily accounts for any remaining population change. It must be emphasized that figures derived in this way represent only the *net* flows—that is, the difference between the number of people who moved into an area and the number who moved out during a given period. A

16. Fred A. Shannon, "A Post-Mortem on the Labor-Safety-Valve Theory," *Agricultural History*, vol. 19 (1945), pp. 31–37, cited in Conrad Taeuber and Irene B. Taeuber, *The Changing Population of the United States* (New York: John Wiley & Sons, for the Social Science Research Council and the U.S. Bureau of the Census, 1958), p. 106.
17. Taeuber and Taeuber, pp. 54 and 107.

TABLE 3.5

Estimates of Net Migration: Metropolitan and Nonmetropolitan Areas of the United States, by Race

| | NET MIGRATION[a] | | | |
| | METROPOLITAN AREAS | | NONMETROPOLITAN AREAS | |
	Number	Rate	Number	Rate
1940–50 (147 SMA's)				
Total civilian[b]	6,397,125	9.2%	−5,808,275	−9.3%
White	4,423,523	−	−	−
Nonwhite	1,605,631	−	−	−
1950–60 (212 SMSA's)				
Total[c]	8,125,354	9.1	−5,460,266	−8.8
White	6,489,380	8.1	−3,813,274	−7.0
Nonwhite	1,636,046	18.2	−1,646,992	−22.9
1960–70 (243 SMSA's)				
Total[d]	5,307,000	4.4	−2,306,000	−3.9
White	3,169,000	3.0	−885,000	−1.7
Nonwhite	2,138,000	15.5	−1,421,000	−21.2

[a] Minus sign indicates net out-migration. Rates calculated as net migration divided by population in base year. Migration of aliens accounts for difference between nonmetropolitan out-migration and metropolitan in-migration.

[b] Civilian population only. Because of differences in estimating procedures, white and nonwhite do not add to total. *Source:* Donald J. Bogue, *Components of Population Change, 1940–50* (Oxford, Ohio: Scripps Foundation, 1957), table II–A and III–B.

[c] Includes military as well as civilian population. *Source:* Gladys K. Bowles and James D. Tarver, *Net Migration of the Population by Age, Sex and Color, 1950–60,* U.S. Department of Agriculture, Economic Research Service, November 1965, table 4. Rates have been recalculated on 1950 population base to conform with footnote (a) above.

[d] Includes military as well as civilian population. State Economic Areas are substituted for the SMSA's of New England. *Source:* U.S. Bureau of the Census, *Census of Population and Housing, 1970,* U.S. Summary, PHC(2)-1, table 7.

small net flow may be the result of much larger but mutually offsetting movements in both directions. Rates of net migration are usually calculated as the flow during a period divided by the population at the period's starting date.

Table 3.5 shows that both the amount and the rate of net migration out of nonmetropolitan areas were highest during the 1940s, helped along, no doubt, by the attraction of wartime jobs in the cities. The *rate* of net migration into metropolitan areas was also at its highest level in the 1940s. However, the absolute level of net in-migration rose rather than fell during the 1950s. This asymmetry is made possible by net immigration from abroad, which accounts for the difference between the net outflow from nonmetropolitan areas and the net inflow to SMSA's. Obviously, net immigration from abroad rose sharply after the Second World War.

During the 1960s net migration out of nonmetropolitan areas fell to less than half the level of the 1950s, and there was a corresponding absolute drop in the flow into metropolitan areas. The net inflow of foreign immigrants—almost all bound for urban areas—amounted to about 3 million, so it is apparent that during the 1960s immigration from abroad actually outweighed internal migration as a source of metropolitan population growth.

Of course, this emphasis of migration should not lead us to overlook the importance of natural increase. During the 1960s metropolitan areas gained 20.2 million in population. Natural increases accounted for 14.9 million, or almost three-fourths of that total.

Patterns of Migration by Race

Table 3.5 shows a significant breakdown of net migration by race. Nonwhites (principally blacks moving out of the nonmetropolitan South) have provided a substantial proportion of the net migration to metropolitan areas in recent decades, accounting for 40 percent of the net inflow during the 1960s. However, the data in Table 3.5 are at a level of aggregation that conceals major differences between central cities and the ring areas of SMSA's. Most of the black migration into SMSA's down to 1970 was destined for central cities. This inflow was offset, or more than offset by heavy out-migration of whites from central cities to suburbs. The suburbs also received substantial white in-migration from nonmetropolitan areas. Largely as a result of these flows, the black proportion of central city population increased rapidly, while the suburbs remained very nearly all white. Since blacks moving into central cities often had low incomes, while whites moving to the suburbs were mostly from the middle class, racial change had substantial economic consequences for central cities. (Race, migration, and urban poverty will be discussed in greater detail in Chapter 10.)

DECREASING CONCENTRATION AFTER 1970

Students of urbanism had become so thoroughly accustomed to the long-established trend of concentration into metropolitan areas, that it came as something of a shock when, in the early 1970s, annual population estimates by the Census Bureau began to indicate a change of direction:

TABLE 3.6

Growth and Net Migration, Metropolitan and Nonmetropolitan Places, by Size and Region, 1970–78

	POPULATION		NET MIGRATION	
	1978	Percentage Change 1970–78	Number	Rate
All SMSA's	160,040,100	6.2%	731,500	0.5
3,000,000 or more	39,560,700	−1.6	−2,449,400	−6.1
1,000,000 to 3,000,000	48,654,800	8.9	1,087,900	2.4
500,000 to 1,000,000	27,631,900	7.6	419,000	1.6
250,000 to 500,000	23,531,400	10.5	818,800	3.8
Under 250,000	20,661,440	11.9	855,200	4.6
Nonmetropolitan areas	58,022,600	10.3	2,709,500	5.1
Northeast				
SMSA's	41,885,100	−1.4	−1,944,100	−4.6
Nonmetropolitan areas	7,196,200	9.4	376,400	5.7
North Central				
SMSA's	40,853,900	2.0	−1,601,700	−4.0
Nonmetropolitan areas	17,397,100	5.2	233,200	1.4
South				
SMSA's	45,419,000	13.5	2,554,300	6.4
Nonmetropolitan areas	25,207,600	10.6	1,165,700	5.1
West				
SMSA's	31,882,200	13.4	1,723,000	6.1
Nonmetropolitan areas	8,221,700	22.3	934,300	13.9

[a] Foreign migration is included. In its absence SMSA's in the aggregate would show negative net migration.

Source: U.S. Bureau of the Census, Current Population Reports, series P-25, no. 873, February 1980, tables 5, 6, and 7.

the nonmetropolitan areas of the United States were now growing faster than the SMSA's. As Table 3.6 indicates, the population of nonmetropolitan areas increased 10.3 percent between 1970 and 1978, well above the 6.2 percent gain estimated for metropolitan areas. Taken at face value, these figures tell us that a new period in the history of metropolitan settlement has begun, a period of decreasing concentration and decreasing centralization.

The pattern of change now taking place is a complex one, and must be interpreted cautiously. Decreasing concentration does not mean, for example, that Americans have at last given up on the metropolitan way of life; metropolitan areas in the aggregate continue to grow, far more of them are growing than declining, and some continue to grow very rapidly. Nor does it mean that we are witnessing a massive back-to-the-soil movement. As we shall see, a number of rather diverse factors accounts for the recent increase in nonmetropolitan population. Among these, a romantic return to the simplicities of rural life is probably one of the least important.

Nevertheless, the change in trend has several dramatic aspects. Until 1970 it was almost unheard of for a major metropolitan area to lose population. Only one of the 24 SMSA's whose population exceeded 1 million in 1960 failed to grow in the following decade, and that one—the Pittsburgh SMSA—lost only trivial numbers. On the other hand, 8 of the 35 metropolitan areas whose population exceeded 1 million in 1970 registered losses by 1978, certainly a dramatic increase.[18]

Equally significant was a reversal in the direction of net migratory flow. Except perhaps during periods of severe depression, the direction of flow had always been from rural and nonmetropolitan America to the cities and metropolitan areas. Yet this historic trend reversed after 1970. If immigration from abroad is excluded, the net flow within the United States is now from SMSA's to nonmetropolitan areas; the former have thus become a source of population growth for the latter.[19] When foreign migration into the United States is included, SMSA's in the aggregate still register a very small positive inflow, but the rate of in-migration to nonmetropolitan areas is far higher. (See Table 3.6 and compare with Table 3.5.)

Decreasing concentration is taking place against a background of other forces that are important to examine at the outset. The first of these is a shift in regional patterns of migration. For many years the dominant pattern had been one of net migration out of the South and into the Northeastern, North Central, and Western regions.[20] This changed gradually in the 1960s as the South began to attract a small net inflow. During the 1970s the trickle to the South became a flood. The Northeast and North Central regions now lost substantial numbers through out-migration, while the South and West were large gainers in a pattern that has been widely described as "sunbelt versus snowbelt." These strong regional movements must be thought of as underlying whatever pattern of metropolitan

18. U.S. Bureau of the Census, *Current Population Reports*, series P-25, no. 873, February 1980, table 4.

19. See William Alonso, "The Current Halt in the Metropolitan Phenomenon," in Leven, fig. 2–1, p. 29.

20. These are the four regions into which the Census Bureau divides the continental United States. For a summary of interregional migration patterns from 1950 to 1975, see U.S. Bureau of the Census, *Current Population Reports*, series P-25, no. 64, November 1976, table B. The same report explains in detail the bureau's method of estimating population change and migration at dates between the decennial censuses.

area growth and decline we can discern. For example, all of the SMSA's with population greater than 1 million that lost numbers between 1970 and 1978 were located in the Northeast or North Central regions; most of the same group that gained population were located in the South or West. The comparison between the six largest SMSA's in the North and East and the six largest in the South and West presented in Tables 3.3 and 3.4 (and which recurs elsewhere in this book) should remind the reader not only of the contrast between old and new metropolitan areas but also of the importance of the regional dimension of U.S. urban development.

A second noteworthy factor operating in the background is the reduced rate of national population growth. The birth rate in the United States declined from almost 24 per 1,000 population in 1960 to about 15 per 1,000 in the late 1970s. Consequently, the rate of natural increase in population has fallen sharply. Some metropolitan areas have been sources of net out-migration for a good many years. When birth rates were high, these losses were more than offset by the high rate of natural increase and attracted little notice, but now that natural increase has fallen off, net out-migration often results in population loss. Alonso, in fact, finds that the low rate of national population increase is a more important cause of the recent slowdown in metropolitan population growth than is the admittedly dramatic reversal in direction of migratory flows.[21]

A third background factor is the sluggish performance of the U.S. economy during much of the 1970s. Traditionally, metropolitan areas have been most attractive to in-migrants during periods of rapid national economic growth, when an abundance of jobs at high wages drew young workers from small town and rural America to "the big city." The first signs of deconcentration during the 1970s coincided with the very severe recession, accompanied by high rates of unemployment, that began in 1973–74. Indeed, some observers believed that deconcentration would be a passing phenomenon, coming to an end when the national economy revived. Instead, as Kevin McCarthy and Peter Morrison point out, deconcentration continued into the recovery phase of that cycle.[22] Nevertheless, it is probably true that the state of the national economy exerts some influence on the rate of deconcentration.

Effect of Metropolitan Size and of Region

Table 3.6 shows that the recent trend of deconcentration is related to metropolitan area size. In the aggregate, only the largest SMSA's—those

21. Alonso, "The Current Halt," p. 27.
22. Kevin F. McCarthy and Peter A. Morrison, "The Changing Demographic and Economic Structure of Nonmetropolitan Areas in the United States," *International Regional Science Review*, Winter 1977, p. 125.

with 3 million or more residents in 1970—lost population between 1970 and 1978. Each of the smaller size classes displayed continued growth. The smallest size group was the fastest growing and, in fact, grew virtually as fast in the 1970s as it had in the previous decade. (We shall return below to the question of why the larger SMSA's have lost their once great power of attraction.) Nonmetropolitan areas in the aggregate grew rapidly, but not quite as fast as the smaller SMSA's.

Net migration, not surprisingly, shows a relationship to SMSA size similar to that of growth. It was substantially negative for the largest size class and increasingly positive for smaller metropolitan areas. Nonmetropolitan areas, however, had a higher rate of in-migration than any class of SMSA's.

Table 3.6 also shows a clear regional pattern. In the Northeast and North Central regions metropolitan population growth came virtually to a halt in the 1970s. In the South and West, on the other hand, SMSA's continued to grow briskly. This outcome resulted in part from substantial movement between metropolitan areas of the four regions, with the dominant flow being from SMSA's in the North and East to those of the South and West, in other words from the cities of the snowbelt to those of the sunbelt. At the same time, nonmetropolitan areas in all regions except the North Central displayed relatively high rates of net inflow.

The Question of Metropolitan "Spillover"

Whatever rule one chooses for drawing the boundaries of a metropolitan area, there will always be places just beyond the line that are in some degree functionally related to the metropolis by means of high-speed transportation and communications, but not sufficiently so to be included within its boundaries. When the statistical fact of deconcentration was first noticed in the mid-1970s, analysts wondered how much of it could be explained as the expansion of settlement into such adjacent areas. Perhaps the "functional field" of the SMSA had simply been expanding faster than its officially recognized boundaries. On this matter numerous studies have now reached a common conclusion: the population of counties just outside the borders of SMSA's is, indeed, growing very rapidly, yet that is by no means a complete account of deconcentration, since the population of counties remote from any metropolitan influence has suddenly begun growing, too.[23] Indeed, the turnabout is the more impressive the farther one moves from metropolitan influence.

23. See Alonso, "The Current Halt"; Calvin L. Beale, "The Recent Shift of United States Population to Nonmetropolitan Areas, 1970–75," *International Regional Science Review*, Winter 1977, pp. 113–22; McCarthy and Morrison; and Peter A. Morrison, *Current Demographic Change in Regions of the United States*, doc. no. P-6000 (Santa Monica, Calif.: Rand Corporation, November 1977).

TABLE 3.7
Growth and Net Migration in Nonmetropolitan Counties, 1960 to 1978

| | AVERAGE ANNUAL PERCENTAGE CHANGE | | | |
| | POPULATION GROWTH | | NET MIGRATION | |
	1970–78	1960–70	1970–78	1960–70
Nonmetropolitan counties by percent commuting to metropolitan areas				
20 percent or more	1.7%	0.9%	1.2%	0.1%
10 to 19 percent	1.2	0.6	0.7	−0.2
3 to 9 percent	1.1	0.5	0.6	−0.5
less than 3 percent	1.1	0.2	0.5	−0.9
All nonmetropolitan counties	1.2	0.4	0.6	−0.6
All SMSA counties	0.7	1.6	0.1	0.5

Source: U.S. Bureau of the Census, *Current Population Reports*, series P-20, no. 350, May 1980, table 14.

Evidence on this point is presented in Table 3.7. Nonmetropolitan counties are grouped according to the extent of their attachment to an SMSA as measured by the percentage of their resident workers who commute to jobs in a metropolitan area. As the figures in column one show, the rate of population growth in nonmetropolitan counties is higher the more closely they are integrated with a metropolitan labor market. Thus adjacency does affect growth. But it is also true that even the most remote counties, in which commuting is below 3 percent (fourth row of table), have been growing far faster than the aggregate of metropolitan counties (sixth row of table). Furthermore, a comparison between columns one and two shows that from the 1960s to the 1970s by far the sharper *increase* in growth rates took place in the remote counties, rather than in the adjacent ones.

Data on net migration tell the same story (see columns three and four): the closer the connection to a metropolitan area, the higher is the rate of in-migration, but the increase in the rate has been sharpest in the most remote counties. Clearly deconcentration is more than just metropolitan spillover.

For the student of urbanism, however, a further question remains. What accounts for the sudden, rapid growth of the more remote nonmetropolitan areas? Recent studies concur on the significance of two factors: recreation activities and retirement communities.[24] Both are important "growth" industries; they are frequently found in the same place,

24. See Beale, pp. 117–22; and McCarthy and Morrison, pp. 132–36.

since both are highly dependent on physical amenities; and their presence undoubtedly stimulates the development of ancillary services to meet the needs of the population they attract. In addition, employment connected with the extraction of energy (especially coal) accounts for rapid growth in some nonmetropolitan counties, as does the dispersion of manufacturing from large metropolitan centers into small cities where wages are lower. But neither of these factors appears to be statistically significant as a nationwide explanation of nonmetropolitan growth.[25] Indeed, after all the diverse factors that might plausibly be thought of as causes have been appealed to, much about the current trend toward a more dispersed pattern of settlement remains to be accounted for.

MIGRATION AND ECONOMIC OPPORTUNITY

The classic explanation of migration has always been that men and women move in search of economic opportunity. We expect them to leave places where incomes are low or job opportunities are scarce and move to places where incomes are higher or jobs more plentiful. Just as one would expect migration to flow in the direction of higher income, so one would also expect the result of migration to be a gradual decline in the geographic income differentials that initially gave rise to it. This follows from the influence of migration on the local labor supply. In areas experiencing out-migration the labor supply is reduced, which tends to raise wages. On the other hand, areas to which migrants move enjoy an increase in the labor supply, which tends to hold wages down. The combined effect should be to reduce interarea differentials.

Moreover, we would expect capital to migrate in the opposite direction from labor, and to contribute further to the reduction of interarea wage and income differentials. This expectation is based on marginal productivity analysis. Low per capita regional income usually results from (among other things) a scarcity of capital relative to labor. Because the ratio of capital to labor is low, the average worker has relatively little capital to work with, the marginal product of labor is low, and wages, which depend on marginal productivity, are also low. But it is a corollary proposition that when capital is scarce relative to labor, so that the marginal product of labor is *low*, the marginal product of capital, and therefore the return to capital, will be *high*. Thus we would expect that capital, searching out areas of low wages and high returns, would migrate in just the opposite direction from labor. This would tend to reduce interarea wage differentials because the inflow of capital stimulates the demand for labor in the low income area by creating additional jobs. As

25. McCarthy and Morrison, table 5, p. 135.

the demand for labor rises relative to its supply, wages, and hence incomes, will tend to rise, and interarea differentials will be further diminished.

Down to 1970, experience in the United States broadly conformed to these expectations. We have already seen that net migration was then flowing from nonmetropolitan areas to SMSA's. Table 3.8 shows that this was in the direction of higher income. In 1959, for all races, median family income was 40 percent higher in SMSA's than in nonmetropolitan areas. For blacks it was more than twice as high. No wonder, then, that blacks made up such a substantial portion of net migration to metropolitan areas. If this emphasis on money income differences as determinants of the flow of migration seems unduly materialistic, one can readily broaden the concept of income to take account of the value of the greater degree of choice offered by the metropolis—greater choice among jobs, among social groups, among the specialized forms of material goods themselves.

TABLE 3.8

Median Family Income by Place of Residence and Race

	MEDIAN FAMILY INCOME IN 1979 DOLLARS[a]		INCOME RATIO: METRO/ NONMETRO
	Metropolitan Areas	*Nonmetro- politan Areas*	
1959			
All races	$15,594	$11,174	1.40
White	16,223	11,826	1.37
Black	9,436	4,258	2.22
1969			
All races	20,460	15,212	1.34
White	21,144	15,817	1.34
Black	13,140	7,847	1.67
1979			
All races	21,100	16,687	1.26
White	22,104	17,564	1.26
Black	12,357	9,263	1.33

[a] Income in 1959, 1969, and 1979 for families by place of residence in 1960, 1970, and 1980.

Sources: Data for 1959: U.S. Bureau of the Census, *Current Population Reports,* series P–23, no. 37, June 24, 1971, table 7. Data for 1969: *Current Population Reports,* series P–23, no. 75, November 1978, table 17. Data for 1979: *Current Population Reports,* series P–60, no. 125, October 1980, table 1.

Until recently the pattern of interregional movement also conformed to expectations. Incomes were substantially lower in the South than elsewhere, and, as we have already noted, the predominant flow of net migration was from the South to other regions. Regional, metropolitan, and racial patterns of migration were, of course, interrelated. Rural blacks in the South earned incomes even lower than the southern average. The movement of blacks out of the nonmetropolitan South into the central cities of the Northeast and North Central regions made up a substantial part of national migratory flow before 1970.

As expected, too, these flows were accompanied by a reduction of income differentials between areas. Table 3.8 shows that the metropolitan-nonmetropolitan differential declined from 1959 to 1969. In fact, convergence can be demonstrated from as far back as we have data. Commerce Department figures indicate that per capita income in SMSA counties was 131 percent higher than in non-SMSA counties in 1929. By 1950 the margin had been cut by more than half to only 60 percent.[26] Interregional differences have diminished, too, as per capita income in the South rose toward the level in other sections of the United States. As expected, capital flowing from the North helped finance the very rapid industrialization of the South, multiplying the number of jobs there and pushing wages and incomes up.

It is clear that migratory flows in the United States down to about 1970 are easily explained by conventional economic analysis. What is much more difficult to account for is the change in those flows since 1970. We have seen that when foreign immigration is excluded, the net flow is now from metropolitan to nonmetropolitan areas. Yet Table 3.8 shows that the income advantage of the former over the latter, though diminishing, remains substantial. Economists find this puzzling. Just as they do not expect water to flow uphill, so economists are surprised when men and women migrate from areas of higher income and wider job choice to places that appear to rank lower on both scales.

The post-1970 pattern is still imperfectly understood. Calvin L. Beale's study of nonmetropolitan counties reveals the expected highly regular relationship of migration to county income level during the 1960s: the rate of net in-migration was strongly negative for low income counties and increased to moderately positive for high income counties. However, Beale's figures show that the relationship virtually disappeared in the 1970s. He concludes that "on the average, people are simply not moving to or between nonmetropolitan counties in a manner associated with the

26. "Metropolitan Area Income in 1967," *Survey of Current Business*, May 1969, table 2, p. 26.

income levels of areas, suggesting that many of them are not moving for monetary motivations."[27]

Kevin F. McCarthy and Peter A. Morrison reach a similar conclusion. After controlling for other county characteristics, such as region and specialization in recreation or retirement activities, they found that in the early 1970s the rate of in-migration increased faster in counties where earnings were *lower*.[28] Like Beale's results, these seem to indicate that the search for economic opportunity is no longer the dominant motive for migration. Yet it would be premature to conclude that economic motives no longer matter. Instead, perhaps it is our way of comparing the level of economic well-being in different localities that is at fault.

With this in mind, consider a second puzzling aspect of the post–1970 pattern of migration and metropolitan development: Table 3.6 shows that *within* the metropolitan sector the rate of growth and in-migration is *highest* in the *smallest* SMSA's and lowest in the largest ones. Yet per capita income is generally *higher*, the *larger* the metropolitan area.[29] We must ask, however, whether money income is truly an accurate measure of local welfare.

Income, Well-being, and City Size

One obvious problem in using per capita money income to compare well-being among metropolitan areas is the fact that living costs vary with city size. Making use of what little cost of living data is available for individual cities, Irving Hoch found that living costs increase significantly as size of place increases. (The principal cause is probably that land rent and transportation costs are higher in large cities, as we shall see in Chapter 6.) Hoch was then able to adjust data on local money income for differences in living costs, to produce an index showing the variation of *deflated* income by size of place. He found that in every U.S. region this adjusted measure of income rises with city size (although only about half as fast as the *un*adjusted measure does).[30]

As we have already argued, economists expect migration to reduce intercity differences in income, producing an equilibrium when workers

27. Beale, table 1 and p. 116.
28. McCarthy and Morrison, p. 138.
29. See Victor R. Fuchs, *Differentials in Hourly Earnings by Region and City Size, 1959*, occasional paper 101 (New York: National Bureau of Economic Research, 1967).
30. Irving Hoch, "Income and City Size," *Urban Studies*, October 1972, tables 2, 3, and 4, pp. 310–11. Also see Hoch, "Variations in the Quality of Urban Life Among Cities and Regions," in Lowdon Wingo and Alan Evans, eds., *Public Economics and the Quality of Life* (Baltimore: Johns Hopkins University Press, 1977), pp. 50–53.

of equal skill earn equal cost-of-living adjusted incomes in all cities. Instead, we find that in the United States such differences still exist, and are not growing narrower, yet net migration to the larger, higher income SMSA's has, in fact, already ceased. What can account for the persistence of these disparities in adjusted income? Hoch suggests an interesting explanation. He hypothesizes that the *non*pecuniary returns to urban living are, on balance, negative, and that these net costs also increase with city size. If that is so, then income differences by city size that remain after adjustment for differences in the cost of living can be interpreted as "compensatory payments" to city workers needed to offset the net, nonpecuniary disadvantages of urban living, which increase with city size.[31]

How can producers in large cities afford to pay the higher wages needed to cover both higher living costs and (if they exist) compensatory payments? The answer is that the economies of scale and agglomeration discussed in Chapter 2 add enough to factor productivity as city size increases to finance such payments. (That does *not* mean, however, that labor appropriates the whole gain from economies of agglomeration. As we shall see in Chapter 6, a major portion probably goes to landowners in the form of rent.)

When it comes to naming nonpecuniary disadvantages of urban living, each of us will have his or her own list. Certain disadvantages, however, are widely perceived as important. Some of these have already been pointed out in the discussion of diseconomies of agglomeration in Chapter 2. There is strong evidence that environmental degradation, as measured for example by air and noise pollution, increases with city size; crime rates, too, are higher in larger cities.[32] On the other hand, larger city size also confers nonpecuniary advantages, principally wider choice among jobs and a wider variety of consumer goods and of cultural activities. It must be emphasized that in the present state of our knowledge we cannot demonstrate by direct measurement that the nonpecuniary "bads" of living in large cities outweigh these nonpecuniary "goods." Rather, that conclusion is inferred by Hoch from the persistence of money income differentials for which he finds no other plausible explanation. It gains support, however, from our observation that the direction of migratory flow is now *out* of larger metropolitan areas and *into* smaller ones.

It is interesting to note that this reversal in the direction of net migratory flow is not found only in the United States. Daniel R. Vining and Thomas Kontuly show that in many of the more developed countries internal migration into the core metropolitan area either fell sharply or

31. Hoch, "Income and City Size," p. 302, and "Variations in the Quality of Urban Life," p. 28.
32. See Hoch, "Income and City Size," pp. 318–24.

reversed from positive to negative in the late 1960s and early 1970s.[33] Consistent with Hoch's reasoning, they speculate that this pattern might be explained by the appearance of diseconomies of agglomeration in the large metropolitan areas of countries that have reached an advanced stage of development.[34] They do not attempt to measure such diseconomies, however.

HIGHER ENERGY PRICES
AND THE PATTERN OF SETTLEMENT

Earlier in this chapter we argued that the decentralization of metropolitan areas, dating from early in this century, depended importantly on radical improvements in transportation and communication and especially on the introduction of the truck and the automobile. It can plausibly be argued that the very recent trend toward deconcentration of population, marked by resurgent growth in *non*metropolitan areas, results largely from the same improvements. Today, men and women who wish to enjoy the advantages of living in nonmetropolitan areas can do so while still remaining in relatively close touch with large urban centers.[35] Those who want to combine a rural lifestyle with a metropolitan area job can settle in an adjacent county and commute into the SMSA to work. Others may choose both to live and to work in more remote areas. They can nevertheless keep in touch with any metropolitan center by telephone or reach it quickly by air. Cheaper and faster transportation and communication have allowed many people to indulge preferences for locations that they would once have found too costly in terms either of money spent for those two functions or of urban opportunities forgone.

But if the long decline in transportation costs helped produce deconcentration, then it is possible that a prolonged rise in those costs may bring it to an end. Such a reversal could well occur as a result of the world "energy crisis." If fuel prices continue to increase, as seems very likely, then transportation costs will also continue to rise, and the dispersed pattern of settlement which we have described as "decreasing concentration and decreasing centralization" may be modified in the direction of one that requires less expenditure on transportation. For example, increased concentration into small and medium-sized metropolitan areas—a pattern that has been described as "dispersed concentration"—would have such an effect.[36] We return to these speculations at the end of Chapter 9.

33. Daniel R. Vining, Jr., and Thomas Kontuly, "Population Dispersal from Major Metropolitan Regions: an International Comparison," *International Regional Science Review*, Fall 1978, pp. 49–73.
34. Ibid., p. 68.
35. McCarthy and Morrison, p. 140.
36. Vining and Kontuly, p. 66, quoting M. Tachi.

The Location of Economic Activity and the Location of Cities

FOUR

The rise of cities at particular places in an industrialized society depends largely on those forces that determine the location of economic activity. In Chapter 2 we explained that economic activity tends to concentrate geographically because external economies of agglomeration have the effect of reducing costs or increasing sales for many types of industry. A description of the external economies of agglomeration, however, is by no means a complete account of the forces affecting the location of firms or of people. In particular, it tells us nothing about *where* agglomeration is likely to occur. We must now look into the matter more systematically.

Traditional Anglo-American economic theory has been called "spaceless." As Isard puts it, "Transport costs and other costs involved in movement within a 'market' are assumed to be zero. In this sense the factor of space is repudiated, everything within the economy is in effect compressed to a point, and all spatial resistance disappears."[1] Even international trade theories have sometimes abstracted entirely from the elements of space and distance. Students of urban phenomena, however, generally have sought to incorporate in their theories as many regularities in spatial relationships as they could discover or accommodate. This and the following chapter deal with the interurban aspects of space. In this chapter we start with the individual location decisions of firms, explaining why firms locate in one place rather than another, and consequently account for the fact that cities of a particular kind and size are where they are in-

1. Walter Isard, *Location and Space-Economy* (New York: John Wiley & Sons and M.I.T. Press, 1956), p. 26.

stead of someplace else. Chapter 5, adopting a somewhat different but complementary point of view, looks at the spatial relationships between cities and explains why it makes sense to speak of a "system of cities" or of an "urban hierarchy." In Chapter 6 we will take up the problem of intraurban location: why firms and people locate in one part of the city rather than another and why cities consequently display a certain regularity of form.

EFFECTS OF TRANSPORT COSTS ON CHOICE OF LOCATION

Isard has suggested that the forces affecting a given business firm's choice of location can be classified conveniently into three groups: (1) transport costs, the distinguishing feature of which is that they vary systematically with distance; (2) other input costs, which, if they vary at all from place to place, do so in what is, from the spatial point of view, a haphazard manner; (3) economies and diseconomies of agglomeration, which are a function not of geographic position but of the magnitude of activity gathered in one place, wherever it may be.[2]

It is convenient to begin by examining the influence on the location of a single firm of transport costs considered in isolation. To do so we must postulate a radically simplified world. It will suffice to assume the following:

1. The firm in question is so small in relation to the relevant markets that its activities have no perceptible effect on the prices of the goods it buys or sells and no effect on the location of other economic units.
2. The prices of land, labor, and capital are everywhere equal. Raw materials that are not ubiquitous are priced f.o.b. the source.
3. There are no economies or diseconomies of scale or of agglomeration.
4. The market for the product of the firm is concentrated at a point rather than geographically extensive. (This assumption is *not* necessary in order to isolate the effect of transport costs, but it helps to simplify the argument.)

The profit-maximizing firm will obviously seek out the profit-maximizing location. Under the conditions we have postulated, production costs are everywhere equal. The location at which profits are maximized

2. Ibid., pp. 138–39.

will therefore be the one at which transport costs per unit of output are minimized.

The transport costs in question are the costs of transporting raw materials from their point of origin to the manufacturing plant and the costs of transporting finished goods from the plant to the customer. Using Alonso's terminology, we may call the former "assembly costs" and the latter "distribution costs."[3]

If the customer instead of the manufacturer were to bear the cost of transport from the plant it would make no difference; under our assumptions the price of the final good is already established at the market. If a firm required customers to pay for transportation, they would refuse to buy unless price at the plant were below the established market price by the amount of the required transport costs. Hence, it is in the interest of the producer to minimize total transport costs per unit of output, including cost of delivery to the market, no matter who actually pays the carrier.

If the firm used only ubiquitous raw materials, like air, it is obvious that production at the market would minimize transport costs and maximize profits. It is only because indispensable raw materials are not ubiquitous that a manufacturing firm in our radically simplified world might find it desirable to locate close to materials sources rather than the market.

To begin with the simplest case, consider a firm that requires only a single raw material: a sawmill manufacturing finished lumber. Suppose that logs are available from a forest at point M and the firm wishes to manufacture lumber to be sold in a market at C. Points M and C are connected by a railroad. The railroad charges the same rate per ton-mile to haul logs or to haul finished lumber. Should the lumber mill locate at M, at C, or at some point between?

The answer can be seen at once. If the raw materials that have to be assembled at the plant weigh more than the finished product they yield, it pays to locate the plant at the source of the materials and pay transport charges only on the lighter product. On the other hand, if the finished product weighs more than the raw materials that must be assembled, it pays to locate the plant at the market and pay transport charges only on the lighter raw materials.

The former case is called a "weight-losing" process, the latter a "weight-ganing" one. Clearly lumber milling is a weight-losing process: the finished boards weigh less than the logs. Consequently the firm would build at M, where the logs originate, rather than at C.

3. William Alonso, "Location Theory," in John Friedmann and William Alonso, eds., *Regional Development and Planning, A Reader* (Cambridge, Mass.: M.I.T. Press, 1964), p. 83.

Materials Orientation Versus Market Orientation

Since, other things being equal, weight-losing processes tend to locate near their source of raw materials, they are often called "materials oriented." Prominent examples, in addition to sawmilling, are steelmaking, smelting of other ores, and raw materials processing in general.

Weight-gaining processes, on the other hand, since they tend to locate near their markets, have been called "market oriented." One may well wonder, given the principle of the conservation of matter, how any process could be "weight gaining." The answer found in the traditional literature on location theory is that some processes use ubiquitous materials, such as air and water, whose weight has thus far been left out of account. Soda bottling, for example, results in a large weight gain if one does not count the water on the input side. The argument has traditionally been that since water is available everywhere it doesn't have to be transported and so may be left out of transport cost calculations. For the soda bottling industry this may be a supportable oversimplification. Water does, in fact, have to be transported, but the cost of moving it is so low in relation to the value of the soda produced that the bottler can afford to ignore geographic differentials in the cost of "assembling water." As a general rule, however, it is no longer safe to treat water as a ubiquity in the United States. Increasingly, it is becoming a scarce resource, exerting a locational pull of its own.

An effect similar to weight gain occurs when a finished good, though not heavier than the materials that go into it, nevertheless gains in bulk, fragility, or perishability and so takes a higher transport rate per ton-mile than do its constituent materials. Such a rise in transport rate has the same locational effect as a gain in weight, pulling the plant toward its market and away from its source of (nonubiquitous) materials. The automobile industry provides a good example of this sort of thing. The assembled car weighs no more than the parts that go into it. Nevertheless, the large multiplant firms build their assembly plants near important markets because it is cheaper to ship the constituent parts to an assembly plant than to ship the bulky, and in its own way fragile, finished vehicle to the market.

Broadly speaking, the early stages in a production process are likely to be materials oriented, since they frequently result in great weight loss in the refining of raw materials. The later stages, however, are often market oriented, since as a product approaches the final form in which it is to be consumed it is likely to gain in fragility or perishability.

The Mathematics of Rates, Weights, and Distances

It is worthwhile recasting what has been said so far in a simple mathematical statement.[4] We will employ the following symbols:

w_m = tons of material m needed to make one unit of final product

w_c = weight of one unit of final product in tons

r_m = rate per ton-mile to transport material m

r_c = rate per ton-mile to transport final product c

t = rail distance in miles between M and C

K = transport cost per unit of output

Then transport cost per unit of output for location at M can be expressed as the cost of delivering the finished good to market, or

$$K_m = w_c \cdot r_c \cdot t$$

and for location at C as the cost of assembling the raw materials at the market, or

$$K_c = w_m \cdot r_m \cdot t$$

It follows that if

$$w_m \cdot r_m > w_c \cdot r_c$$

the firm will prefer location at M to location at C, and if

$$w_m \cdot r_m < w_c \cdot r_c$$

the firm will prefer location at C to location at M.

The product of rate times weight is what Alfred Weber, in his seminal book on location theory, called the "ideal weight" of the material or product in question.[5] In the one-material–one-market case we are dealing with, the firm will locate at the materials source if the ideal weight of the material is greater and at the market if the ideal weight of the product is greater. The reader can see by reference to these ideal weights the locational choice that is optimal in case of weight gain, weight loss, differences in transport rate on account of bulk, perishability, and the like, or some combination of these.

Thus far, however, we have dealt only with end-point locations. How do we know that transport costs will not be minimized at some intermediate point along the railroad line? The answer can be deduced as follows.

---

4. Adapted from ibid., pp. 83–84 and 99.
5. Written in German and published in 1909, the book was translated into English by Carl J. Friedrich under the title *Alfred Weber's Theory of the Location of Industries* (Chicago: University of Chicago Press, 1929).

For each mile that the firm shifts its location from M toward C, it adds $w_m r_m$ to its assembly costs and subtracts $w_c r_c$ from its distribution costs. The net change in total unit transport costs is therefore $w_m r_m - w_c r_c$ for each mile the firm moves from M toward C. If this difference is positive, transport costs rise continually as the firm moves from M toward C; hence no intermediate point can be as desirable as M. The firm is materials oriented. If the difference is negative, transport costs fall continuously as the firm moves from M to C, and no intermediate point can be as desirable as C. The firm is market oriented. Only if the ideal weights of material and product are equal could an intermediate location be as attractive as an end point.

Effect of Teminal Costs and Declining Rates

The likelihood of an end-point location is increased by two characteristic features of the structure of transport costs that we have thus far neglected. These are, first, the fact that the movement of goods involves terminal costs as well as ton-mile carrying charges and, second, the fact that ton-mile carrying charges themselves generally decline as the distance to be covered increases.

Terminal costs arise if the shipper has to bring goods to the loading point of the carrier at one end of the journey and take them away from the unloading point at the other end. For example, if shipment is by rail or water it will be necessary to haul the goods by truck to and from the freight terminal or pier. In addition, the shipper will bear administrative expenses in the form of supervision and paperwork.

We may speak of loading and unloading expenses as constituting one set of terminal costs. Terminal costs vary according to the mode of carriage. They are generally lower for truck than for rail and for rail than for water shipment. Since terminal costs do not vary with the length of the haul, they have the effect of making long hauls cheaper per ton-mile than short hauls, even if the carrier charges ton-mile rates that are constant for all distances.

In practice, however, carriers do *not* charge constant ton-mile rates. In general, the rate per ton-mile declines as distance increases because the carrier can spread fixed expenses per shipment over a larger number of miles. Thus the charge for a single shipment of 1,000 miles will generally be far less than for five similar shipments of 200 miles.[6]

How do terminal costs and rates that decline with distance reinforce

---

6. For further discussion of "the structure of transfer costs," see Edgar M. Hoover, *An Introduction to Regional Economics*, 2nd ed. (New York: Alfred A. Knopf, 1975), pp. 37–59.

the likelihood of an end-point location? Consider the consequences if the lumbermilling firm should choose to build at some point, call it *L*, along the railroad line between *M* and *C*. The firm would now have to pay two sets of terminal costs: one set for loading at *M* and unloading at *L*; a second set for loading at *L* and unloading at *C*. If located at *M* or at *C*, however, the firm would have to pay only one set, clearly an advantage. Furthermore, the rate structure would generally penalize location at *L*: the two short hauls, *M* to *L* and *L* to *C*, would cost more per ton-mile than a single long haul from *M* to *C*.

Figure 4.1, adapted from Alonso, summarizes the problem of choosing a minimum-transport-cost location exactly as we have discussed it so far. The diagram is drawn with one corner at *M*, another at *C*. The hori-

FIGURE 4.1

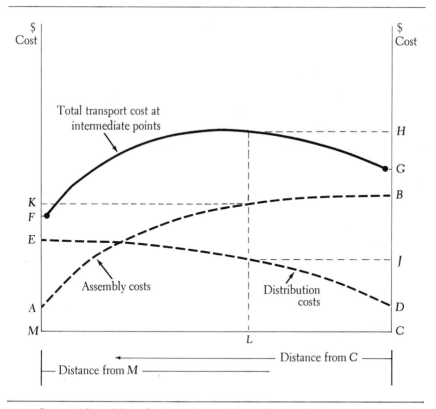

Source: Adapted from fig. 6, p. 86, in William Alonso, "Location Theory," in John Friedman and William Alonso, eds., *Regional Development and Planning* (Cambridge, Mass.: M.I.T. Press, 1964).

zontal axis measures, in one direction, distance from M, and, in the other direction, distance from C. The vertical axis measures transport costs.

The curve MAB shows how the cost of transporting a unit of raw material weighing w_m increases as plant location moves away from M toward C. Terminal costs of loading and unloading the material are indicated by the segment MA. If transport rates per ton-mile charged by the carrier were invariant with distance the segment AB would be an inclined straight line, its constant slope indicating the constant marginal rate. As drawn here the curve flattens out. Its diminishing slope indicates a diminishing marginal transport rate as distance increases. If the plant locates at C, assembly costs rise to CB per unit of material, while distribution costs are zero.

If the plant locates at M, assembly costs are zero, but now the firm must pay distribution costs of carrying the product all the way to C. These costs are indicated by the curve CDE, where CD is the terminal cost and the curve DE indicates the way cost of carriage to C rises as the plant moves away from C toward M. If the plant locates at M, distribution costs total ME per unit of product. Since ME < CB it is clear that in this case location at M is preferable to location at C.

The curve FG shows transport costs for all intermediate points. FG is nothing but the vertical sum of the curves of assembly cost and distribution cost. At an intermediate point, such as L, the firm would pay assembly costs of MK for a unit of raw materials coming from M and distribution costs of CJ for a unit of product sent to C. The sums of these costs is CH, indicated by the height of the curve of total transport costs at L.

For any intermediate location the extra set of terminal costs incurred is shown by segment EF or BG. The disadvantage of making two short hauls instead of one long one is indicated by the fact that FG is higher in the middle than at either end. The diagram shows how these effects combine to reinforce the attractiveness of end-point locations.

Transport Advantages and Urban Growth

We can now begin to see how the transportation advantages of certain locations explain why they become great centers of economic activity. Let us start with a very simple case: raw materials deposits attract materials-oriented industry, industry creates markets for intermediate goods used in production and for consumer goods for its employees, and these markets in turn attract market-oriented industry. Thus, great urban industrial complexes grow up in regions that are rich in raw materials: one thinks immediately of the Pittsburgh region in Pennsylvania or the Ruhr Valley in Germany, in both of which proximity to coal deposits (plus accessibility to other complementary materials) explains the subsequent growth of industry.

Yet we know that proximity to raw materials is only a small part of the story. New York, Chicago, Buffalo, and many other important manufacturing centers are not cheek-by-jowl with great raw materials deposits. These cities do, indeed, owe their unusual growth to transport factors, but of a sort different from those we have considered so far. Let us extend the analysis.

Returning to our original scheme of materials at *M*, market at *C*, and an intermediate point at *L*, we can imagine that *M* and *L* are on opposite shores of a body of water. (Figure 4.1 no longer applies.) Transportation is therefore by ship from *M* to *L* and by rail from *L* to *C*. Point *L* may now be a feasible location for industry. A manufacturer or processor who set up at *L* would no longer pay the penalty of extra terminal costs and higher transport rates. Terminal costs are incurred at *L* in any case, since the mode of transport changes there. For the same reason, two short hauls rather than a single long one are required whether one locates at *L*, *M*, or *C*. In this fashion, any point at which a break in the transport network requires transshipment of goods gains important advantages. Of course, an end-point location might still be preferable if there were a significant difference between the ideal weight of the materials ($w_m r_m$) and the ideal weight of the finished product ($w_c r_c$), but it would no longer be virtually dictated by the structure of transport charges.

The choice of a minimum-transport-cost location becomes more complicated when firms have multiple materials sources or markets. In some cases location at one market or at the source of one material will still be preferable—as, for example, when the ideal weight of one material or market is greater than the sum of all the others. When such a "dominant weight," to use Weber's term, is not present, the minimum-transport-cost location, taking account of terminal costs, may turn out to be at a materials source, at a market, or at an intermediate route junction.

Probably the most often cited case of a city that has attracted industry because it is a transshipment point is Buffalo. An enormous flour-milling industry developed there because grain could be carried inexpensively across the Great Lakes from the grain belt of the North Central states, unloaded at Buffalo, the easternmost port that could be reached before the St. Lawrence Seaway was built, there milled into flour, and then shipped by rail to the large East Coast markets. But there are many other examples. Port cities in the East receive crude oil by water, refine it, and then ship it out by other modes of transport to eastern markets. New York and Boston both refine sugar received by the shipload in crude form from overseas and then distribute it to regional markets by rail or truck.

In most cases port cities, in addition to being transshipment points, gain the further advantage of nodality. To return to our hypothetical example, the port L would be likely to develop shipping connections with other materials sources or markets in addition to M and would become a railhead for lines radiating to other points besides C. If a manufacturer required bulky materials from several sources or wished to be in close contact with several markets, a junction point such as a port, though not itself either a market or a materials source, might well be the best location. Of course, a junction has this advantage even when it does not connect unlike modes of transport but joins only different routes on a rail or road network.

In addition, as Hoover has pointed out, ports and other modal interchange points are apt to offer the advantage of economies of scale in terminal operations and will generally "be better provided than most other points with specialized facilities for goods handling and storage."[7] In short, economies of scale and of agglomeration in freight handling give major transportation centers an advantage that helps explain why they attract industrial activity.

Moreover, as new modes develop in competition with old ones, the transportation advantages of major centers tend to be self-perpetuating. For example, with the growth of air transportation in the United States, New York and Chicago, which had been the nation's leading port and railroad center, became the principal nodes in its air traffic network, a position that undoubtedly helps to sustain their economic importance.

LOCATIONAL EFFECTS OF PRODUCTION–
COST DIFFERENTIALS

Up to this point we have restricted the analysis to cases of pure transport orientation by assuming (1) that the prices of land, labor, and capital are everywhere equal and (2) that there are no economies or diseconomies of scale or agglomeration (other than those associated with transportation). These two assumptions ensure that production costs will be everywhere equal and consequently that the firm will choose its location by reference to transport costs alone. Let us now relax these assumptions and see what effects geographic product-cost differentials might have.

Returning to our hypothetical example, suppose that we are dealing with a weight-losing process for which M is the minimum-transport-cost location. Suppose also that production costs are everywhere equal except that at L the prevailing wage rate for the same quality of labor is lower

7. Ibid., p. 57.

than elsewhere. A firm would locate at L instead of at M if the saving on production costs per unit of output at L exceeded the loss due to higher transport costs per unit as compared with M. The same sort of calculus applies in the case of any geographic difference in input prices.

Note that L's advantage is measured in terms of reduced *production* costs per unit of output rather than reduced labor costs per unit of output. This is necessary because a firm producing at L would tend to use a more labor-intensive technique than a firm located elsewhere—it would substitute labor for other factors of production. Only by comparing all production costs per unit of output at L and M can we take account of the fact that as a result of substitution, the producer at L uses a different mixture of inputs than the producer at M.

Indeed, substitution is pervasive in economic processes. Isard has shown that location theory itself can be handled within the substitution framework of the traditional theory of production.[8] For example, we have assumed that transport costs per unit of output are higher at L than at M, while wages, and therefore production costs, are lower at L. Thus, in moving from M to L a firm would, in Isard's terminology, substitute dollar outlays on transport for dollar outlays on production, while at the same time substituting physical inputs of one factor of production, labor, for physical inputs of the others.

Production-Cost and Transport-Cost Orientations Compared

Industries for which geographic differentials in production cost are more important than geographic differentials in transport cost are said to be "production-cost oriented" rather than "transport-cost oriented." No precise classification is possible, however, since an industry may be significantly affected by both factors. In general—and again this is no more than a rough rule—an industry will be transport-cost oriented if the ratio of bulk to value in its manufacturing process is high and production-cost oriented if the ratio of bulk to value is low.

The iron and steel industry illustrates the first case. At the input end of the process, between 3 and 3½ tons of raw material are required to produce one ton of crude steel, a ratio which insures that the transportation cost of obtaining materials will account for a significant fraction of total cost. At the output end, finished steel products sell for an average of $375 to $400 a ton, or 19¢ to 20¢ a pound. The low value of finished steel in relation to its bulk means that the cost of transporting it to market is bound to be high relative to its price. Thus, transportation costs

8. Isard, *passim*.

are important at both ends of the process, and the iron and steel industry is highly transport-cost oriented.[9]

Steel mills tend to locate where the combined transportation cost of assembling the materials and delivering the product to market is minimized. Since the two principal materials—coal and iron ore—can be obtained from a number of sources, but not usually side by side, many locations for mills are feasible in the United States. For example, mills at Pittsburgh enjoy very low transportation costs for coal, which is mined nearby, but pay relatively high charges to obtain ore from Minnesota. Mills at the Great Lakes ports, on the other hand, can bring in ore relatively economically by water from Minnesota but pay higher transportation costs per ton of coal. Mills along the Atlantic coast in Maryland and Pennsylvania pay relatively low shipping costs to bring in ore by sea from eastern Canada, Brazil, and Venezuela but bear higher costs than do Pittsburgh mills to obtain coal. All of these locations are relatively close to major market areas.[10]

Over the years the tonnage of material required to produce steel has been gradually reduced. Today's figure of 3 to 3½ tons of material per ton of crude steel can be compared with a range of 4½ to 5 tons in the late 1930's.[11] The reduction of input requirements has gradually made the industry less materials oriented and more market oriented. It bears repeating, however, that both of these are types of transport-cost orientation.

The cotton textile industry offers a good example of production-cost orientation. Originally concentrated in New England, the industry moved south beginning in the late nineteenth century, in order to take advantage of the lower wage level there. Cotton textiles illustrate the general rule that an industry will tend to be production-cost oriented if the ratio of bulk to value in its processes is low. At the input end, weight-loss in the production process is negligible—a 480 pound bale of cotton lint will yield enough yarn to weave about 450 pounds of cotton print cloth. This is not quite comparable to the weight-loss figure cited for steel since it ignores fuel consumption, but it suffices to show that textile production is not a heavily weight-losing process. Neither is it a fragility- or perishability-gaining process. Hence it is not materials oriented. At the output end, a cotton print cloth in its gray or unfinished state sells for about 65¢ a yard and runs about 4 yards to the pound, indicating a value of about $2.60 per

9. Current figures are estimated by Professor William T. Hogan, S.J., Fordham University. On changes in the technology, materials sources, and locational pattern of the industry, see his *Economic History of the Iron and Steel Industry in the United States* (Lexington, Mass.: D. C. Heath, 1971).

10. See data in Walter Isard, *Methods of Regional Analysis* (New York: John Wiley & Sons and M.I.T. Press, 1960), table 4, p. 351.

11. Edgar M. Hoover, *The Location of Economic Activity*, paperback ed. (New York: McGraw-Hill, 1963), table 3.1, p. 43.

pound.[12] This high value in relation to bulk means that the cost of transportation to market is a relatively small part of total cost, and the industry therefore feels little pressure to locate close to its markets. We see at once why the steel industry is far more sensitive to intersite transport-cost differentials than the textile industry: transport costs are an important part of the whole in the case of steel but only a very small part in the case of textiles.

Types of Production-Cost Orientation

Production-cost orientation is sometimes further subdivided according to the sort of input involved. One can distinguish "labor orientation" (e.g., textiles), "power orientation" (e.g., aluminum refining), or "amenity orientation" (e.g., research and development laboratories).

Amenity orientation is increasingly important in the United States. It means simply locating the plant in a place where the firm's most specialized, highly paid employees would particularly like to live. Research scientists and engineers, for example, seem to have a strong preference for areas with good schools for their children and interesting recreation for their leisure time. Consequently research laboratories are attracted to areas such as southern California or the suburbs of New York or Boston, where, apparently, good schools and good living are found together.

Logically, amenity orientation is really a subclass of labor orientation: there must be some salary differential that would induce scientists to leave Santa Monica by the thousands and take up research employment on the plains of North Dakota. But as long as Santa Monica offers free sunshine and ocean sports there is no reason why the laboratory should not take advantage of them and acquire for itself a contented scientific staff at no premium in salary.

The concentration of research and development in certain areas cannot, of course, be accounted for solely by amenities of the physical and social environment. Economies of agglomeration probably play an important part, as well. Nevertheless, amenity orientation should not be dismissed as a mere curiosum. As the work week shrinks, leisure time grows; as living standards rise, people can afford increasingly complex and expensive forms of recreation and will increasingly wish to live where these are available. The income elasticity of demand for yachts is high. In the long run it is bound to influence the location of economic activity.

To complete the list of types of production-cost orientation, we must return briefly to the subject of agglomeration. When we analyzed the

12. Data on cotton supplied by courtesy of L. B. Gatewood, Economic and Market Research Service, the National Cotton Council of America, Memphis, Tenn.

causes of industrial agglomeration in Chapter 2 we found two different forces at work. First, some industries are attracted to cities because of a special need for face-to-face contact with customers or suppliers. These are conveniently classified as "communication oriented." Second, we described the external economies of agglomeration and explained how these result in lower costs and so attract industries that can take advantage of them.

Both these forces can now be incorporated in a general analysis of the location of the firm. External economies of agglomeration usually result in lower costs.[13] Hence external-economy orientation can be treated as a subclass of production-cost orientation. Communication orientation also can be seen as a way of minimizing production cost. A firm that needs face-to-face contact with customers or suppliers at C could conceivably locate at M and maintain contact by having the appropriate personnel travel back and forth between M and C. But this would entail large travel outlays and would require a larger staff on account of the time lost traveling. If it is cheaper to operate at C than to locate elsewhere and pay the cost of maintaining contact with C, then we would say this as a "communication-oriented" firm. The choice we have suggested is not a fanciful one. Many firms do regularly maintain contact with other places by sending their personnel on expensive travels. (Of course, if one chooses to classify business travel expense as a subclass of transportation outlay, then communication orientation is a form of transportation-cost rather than production-cost orientation.)

Occasionally in the literature on the economics of location one encounters the term "footloose" or "foot-free." Sometimes this is used as a catchall for industries that locate without reference to any identifiable influence. As Alonso has pointed out, however, this usage might suggest erroneously "that one place is as good as any other," which is surely not the case.[14] It is better to describe as footloose those industries for which transport costs are relatively unimportant and which are therefore free to use some other criterion in choosing a location.

SUMMARY OF LOCATIONAL ORIENTATION

Table 4.1 summarizes our analysis of the locational orientation of the firm. Necessarily, it omits much detail and many qualifications. The table, and indeed the analysis up to this point, may be misleading if it

13. "Usually" because in some cases the advantage may be greater sales rather than lower costs. The same qualification applies in the case of communication-oriented firms. (See ch. 2.)
14. Alonso, p. 101.

TABLE 4.1
Types of Locational Orientation of Industry

ORIENTATION	DECISIVE CHARACTERISTIC	OPTIMUM LOCATION	EXAMPLES
Transport-cost oriented	High bulk-to-value ratio, hence transport inputs relatively important		
Materials oriented	Weight- or perishability-losing process	Close to materials sources	Ore refining, steel, fruit and vegetable canning
Market oriented	Weight-, perishability-, or fragility-gaining process	Close to market	Brewing, baking, automobile assembly
Production-cost oriented	Low bulk-to-value ratio, hence transport inputs relatively unimportant		
Labor oriented	Labor-intensive process	Low wage area[a]	Textiles
Power oriented	Power-intensive process	Cheap power area	Aluminum refining
Amenity oriented	Employs high proportion of specialized, highly paid personnel	Attractive physical and social environment	Research and development
Communication oriented	Need for face-to-face contact with customers or suppliers	Close to customers or suppliers	Corporate head offices, advertising, law, investment banking
External-economy oriented	Need for specialized ancillary services	A city of appropriate size or specialized character	Apparel manufacturing, broadcasting

[a] For labor of the required skill level.

suggests that every firm can be classified according to a single factor that dominates its choice of location. Quite probably the optimum location will be determined by a combination of factors. For example, the decisive attraction may be a complex mixture of external economies and opportunities for face-to-face contact, two factors difficult to distinguish in practice. Or again, the optimum location may be one that offers neither the lowest transport costs *nor* the lowest production costs but the lowest combination of these. In short, the table simplifies a complex world.

CHANGES IN THE DETERMINANTS OF LOCATION

As the U.S. economy developed, technological change and rising living standards gradually modified the economic forces that determine the location of industry. Until the energy crisis that began in the 1970s sharply increased the price of fuels, technological progress appeared to be bringing about a persistent decline in the importance of transport-cost orientation. Alonso offered three cogent reasons for believing that it was declining.[15] Foremost was the long-run tendency for transportation to become cheaper, quicker, and more efficient. (It is this tendency that higher fuel prices now bring into question.) Second, one of the fruits of technical progress is a gradual reduction in the quantity of raw material used to produce a unit of a given product. (This has already been described in the case of steel smelting.) Third, products have been gradually improved through ever more complex fabrication, so that value per unit of weight increases. (As the advertising copywriter might put it, "There's a lot more car in today's car.") Each of these tendencies reduced the ratio of transport outlays to total costs and therefore also reduced the likelihood that geographic differences in transport costs would dominate location decisions.

Simultaneously, two other changes were occurring. First, as we showed in Chapter 3, the internal migration of labor and capital was gradually reducing differences in wage levels among regions and between metropolitan and nonmetropolitan areas, thus weakening the locational pull of geographic labor-cost differentials. Second, as explained in the previous section, rising living standards have increased the average citizen's interest in local amenities, thus strengthening the pull of geographic differences in amenities. These changes, combined with the decline in the relative importance of transport costs, brought about what might be called a "gradual revolution" in the location of population and industry: men, women, and social institutions were increasingly free to move away from the old transport-determined points of production and start over again in an environment of their own choosing.

Energy Costs and Locational Choice

Will the higher cost of energy now modify this trend? Probably yes, but it is impossible to predict how far. With fuel costs rising, and continued increases likely, transportation services are now becoming relatively more expensive rather than cheaper. This is likely to affect the residential location choices of households in ways that we explore at the end of

15. Ibid.

Chapter 9. Its probable consequences for industrial location are less clear, since the other factors that have been working to reduce transport-cost orientation will continue to operate, thus offsetting the effect of rising fuel costs, at least in part. Even so, transportation factors are likely to assume greater importance in future location decisions, if only because firms will seek to protect themselves against uncertain future cost increases.

Higher energy costs can also be expected to affect locational choices of firms in ways unconnected with transportation. First, a given firm's energy needs, in physical units, are likely to vary geographically. For example, more energy is required for heating, but less for airconditioning in a northern as compared with a southern location. In addition, both the price of fuel and the available mix of fuels vary geographically. On balance, all of these factors appear to favor the sunbelt over the snowbelt: energy requirements tend to be less, prices lower, and the mix of available sources more favorable there.

To be sure, analysis at the regional level conceals structural differences between metropolitan areas that also affect fuel consumption. The metropolitan areas of the sunbelt, since they are newer, rely largely on the fuel hungry automobile for local transportation. (See discussion of city "age" in Chapter 3.) By contrast, in the older metropolitan areas of the North, mass transportation is often well developed and provides an alternative to driving (see Table 8.1). The resulting saving in fuel costs, however, is apparently not sufficient to offset the other energy disadvantages of the snowbelt.

The magnitude of regional energy-cost differences in the United States is best illustrated by per capita data for households rather than data for all sectors, including industry. This is so because it is plausible to assume that household preferences are reasonably uniform geographically and that regional differences in the physical consumption of energy per capita can therefore be attributed largely to differences in climate. Industrial production, on the other hand, is geographically diverse. Energy intensive industries tend to locate in regions with ample fuel resources, thus driving up the level of per capita energy consumption in those regions.

Table 4.2 presents data on household energy use by region from Hoch's massive study of energy consumption in the United States.[16] Column one shows an index of combined energy prices in each region

16. Irving Hoch, *Energy Use in the United States by State and Region*, research paper R-9 (Washington, D.C.: Resources for the Future, 1978). The regions employed by Hoch and shown in Table 4.2 correspond to the Census Bureau's nine geographic divisions. They are subdivisions of the four census regions: Northeast, North Central, South, and West. For a map of the regions and divisions, see *Statistical Abstract of the United States, 1979*, fig. 1.

TABLE 4.2

Per Capita Energy Consumption of Households, by Region, 1972

REGION[a]	ENERGY PRICE INDEX	PER CAPITA ENERGY CONSUMPTION	
		Million BTU's	Expenditure
New England	113.7	116.1	$297.0
Middle Atlantic	109.6	103.2	256.7
East North Central	97.4	112.5	256.6
West North Central	96.0	104.4	244.9
South Atlantic	101.4	82.4	238.1
East South Central	92.6	85.1	223.7
West South Central	89.5	88.6	222.9
Rocky Mountain	98.6	95.5	232.0
Pacific	97.3	86.9	211.5
U.S. average	100.0	97.7	243.0

[a] See footnote 16 for explanation.

Source: Irving Hoch, Energy Use in the United States by State and Region, research paper R-9 (Washington, D.C.: Resources for the Future, 1978), p. 27.

relative to the U.S. average. Household consumption of energy in BTU's per capita is given in column two. Column three shows expenditure on energy in dollars per capita. The general pattern is clear: both prices and physical consumption per capita tend to be higher in the snowbelt (Northeast and North Central regions) than in the sunbelt (South and West regions). The average household in New England spent $297 per capita on energy, or 40 percent more than the $212 spent by the average household in the Pacific West. At the state level, the variation is even greater. The states with the highest household energy expenditure per capita were Vermont ($354) and New Hampshire ($320), while those with the lowest were Louisiana and West Virginia (both $197).[17]

These figures are for 1972, one year before OPEC began the rapid escalation of oil prices, which subsequently touched off price increases in coal and electricity as well. With the general level of energy prices rising, later figures will undoubtedly show larger absolute (though not necessarily larger relative) cost differences among regions. Geographic differences in energy costs are therefore likely to increase relative to other cost differences, and firms, in choosing a location, will give greater weight than previously to energy considerations.

17. Hoch, table 23, p. 83.

LIMITATIONS OF THE ANALYSIS

Throughout this chapter we have used the method of partial equilibrium analysis, or, as it has sometimes been called, "one-thing-at-a-time" analysis. The method proceeds by asking, in effect, if all other things except the location of one firm are held constant, where will that one firm locate? We set the scene for this sort of analysis when we explicitly assumed that "the firm in question is so small in relation to the relevant markets that its activities have no perceptible effect on the prices of the goods it buys or sells and no effect on the location of other economic units." We thus assumed away the possibility that our one firm's decisions would in fact alter the prices, costs, and other magnitudes we had specified as given. We could then find the equilibrium location for a single firm in a world of given markets, prices, and costs.

Suppose, however, that we are dealing with a firm so large in relation to its economic environment that it must in fact have an impact on local markets, prices, and costs. In that case the method of partial equilibrium analysis breaks down. For example, our analysis of transport orientation takes as given a market of a certain size and production costs of a certain level at C. But if a large firm decides to locate at C instead of M, won't that perhaps increase employment, wage rates, production costs, incomes, and market size at C, thus altering all the determinants of location not only for this firm but for others both at C and elsewhere? Clearly, there are limits to the valid use of the partial equilibrium method.

In contrast to this approach, the method of general equilibrium attempts to reveal simultaneously the equilibrium locations for all firms. To do this, it must, of course, also simultaneously yield equilibrium prices and quantities for goods and services in all markets. Needless to say, such an analysis is complex and difficult to carry through, but for certain problems such as planning a new city that will maximize some specified value, or calculating the impact of a proposed new urban transit facility on citywide real estate values, it would appear to be indispensable.

WHAT LOCATION THEORY CONTRIBUTES
TO AN UNDERSTANDING OF URBAN GROWTH

In this chapter, we have attempted to explain why economic activities locate in particular places—for example, why a large flour-milling industry developed at Buffalo rather than Albany, or why textile mills are concentrated in North Carolina rather than northern New Jersey. The explanation has turned out to depend almost entirely on the existence of irregularities in space, including variations in the physical configuration of the land, discontinuities in the means of transportation, and the facts that resources are localized rather than ubiquitous and climate is not spatially uniform. Because of these irregularities and discontinuities, the business firm's costs of production or transportation are potentially lower at some places than at others. Places offering lower costs attract economic activity, become centers of production, and therefore increase in market size and attract market-oriented activity, which contributes to further growth. As they grow they offer increasingly important economies of agglomeration, which then reinforce their initial locational advantage. By these processes the railroad junction or the little river port of 1850 becomes the large city of 1900 and the great metropolitan area of 1980. An entire urban-metropolitan economy grows from the small seed of initial locational advantage.

The next chapter continues the discussion of location theory. However, the focus shifts: instead of examining the question of why cities grow up at particular places, we will be investigating the spatial relationships *between* cities. The theories offered in the two chapters are entirely complementary. A full account of urban reality must recognize that there are not just individual urban places whose character, development, and location can be studied. Rather, there is a "system of cities," and this system is marked by important spatial-economic regularities.

The System of Cities and the Urban Hierarchy

FIVE

It is meaningful to speak of a "system of cities" because the size and character of any one urban place, or in dynamic terms its power to attract activity, is conditioned by the size, character, and location of other, related places. The nature of this system is dealt with in a branch of urban study known as "central place theory," which began with work done by Walter Christaller in the 1930's and was subsequently extended and systematized by August Lösch.[1] Central place theory is, in fact, an integral part of the theory of the location of economic activity. The link between the two is provided by market area analysis, as will emerge shortly.

CENTRAL PLACE THEORY

The analysis in the preceding chapter realistically assumed a world of differentiated topography, discontinuous transportation facilities, and nonubiquitous resources. Central place theory, on the other hand, is best expounded by assuming just the opposite sort of world. Instead of explaining the location of activity in terms of the

1. Christaller's work was published in German. For an English translation see Carlisle W. Baskin, *Central Places in Southern Germany* (Englewood Cliffs, N.J.: Prentice-Hall, 1966). An early, concise description of it is Edward Ullman's well-known article "A Theory of Location for Cities," reprinted in William H. Leahy, David L. McKee, and Robert D. Dean, eds., *Urban Economics* (New York: Free Press, 1970), pp. 105–15.

Lösch's major work, published in German in 1941, appeared in an English translation by W. H. Woglom and W. F. Stolper as *The Economics of Location* (New Haven: Yale University Press, 1954).

unique features of particular places, it begins by assuming away all unique features. It postulates a perfectly uniform physical world, consisting of a featureless plane on which transportation is equally efficient in any direction and resources are evenly distributed.

J. H. von Thunen had first postulated a uniform land surface as early as 1826, in his explanation of the formation of concentric agricultural belts around a market city. (See Chapter 6, footnote 1.) Central place theory shows us how, in a similar environment, a regular network of urban places would be expected to form to provide various services to an evenly distributed, homogeneous rural population.

The Economic Basis for a Central Place

In explaining the development of central places, Lösch begins by assuming that self-sufficient farms are the only producing units on the uniform transport surface. He then asks whether, if one of the farmers decides to produce a surplus of some commodity and offer it for sale, he will be able to do so. The answer, fundamental to all analysis of market areas, is that "he will be helped by the economies of large scale production, and handicapped by costs of transportation."[2]

In a much simplified version of Lösch's argument, let us assume that farmer *F* has decided to produce a surplus of bread to sell to his neighbors. They will be willing to buy it from him if he can deliver it to their farms at a price below what it would cost them to make it themselves. Farmer *F* will be able to deliver at such a price only if the cost he saves by baking in larger quantities outweighs the expense of delivery. Otherwise the potential customers would be better off continuing to bake at home.

The situation is illustrated in Figure 5.1. Farmer *F* is located at point *O*. Distances from *O* are measured along the horizontal scale and unit costs along the vertical. The average unit cost of producing bread at home is *OA*. Farmer *F*, however, produces on a larger scale and therefore at lower cost. Suppose that he finds he can maximize profits by setting an f.o.b. price of *OB*.[3] His customers must also bear the cost of transportation, which rises with distance from *O* as indicated by the line *BC*. The delivered price at any given distance is shown by the height of *BC* above the horizontal at that distance from *O*. Thus a customer at point *D* would pay a delivered price of *OG* per unit, of which *BG* is the cost of transportation and *OB* the price at the source. Under the monopolistic conditions assumed, farmer *F* would serve a circular market with a radius of *OE*

2. August Lösch, "The Nature of Economic Regions," in John Friedmann and William Alonso, eds., *Regional Development and Planning, A Reader* (Cambridge, Mass.: M.I.T. Press, 1964), pp. 107–15.

3. "F.o.b." stands for "free on board." The "f.o.b. price" is the charge at the source for goods that the seller places on board a carrier provided by the purchaser.

FIGURE 5.1

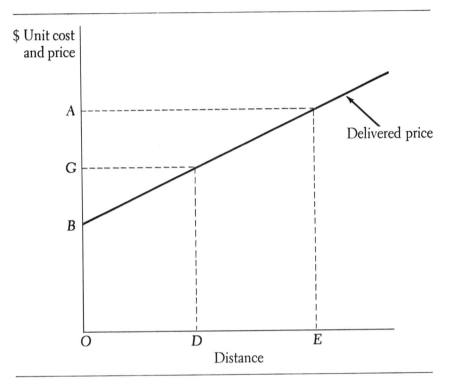

miles. Beyond that distance his delivered price would exceed the cost to potential customers of producing at home; sales would be zero. (Throughout the following analysis matters are greatly simplified if we continue to assume that the producer sells to all customers at a uniform f.o.b. mill price. Buyers pay all delivery costs. The seller engages in neither price discrimination nor freight absorption.)

A more extended analysis of farmer *F*'s situation would show explicitly the relationship between price, market area, quantity sold, cost of production, and total profit. Such a detailed picture, however, is not necessary for our purposes. It suffices, as in the general case for monopolists, to say that the price, *OB*, at which he maximizes profits must be that price at which the marginal revenue from sales just equals the marginal cost of production. The spatial-monopoly situation analyzed here differs from the standard, textbook monopoly case only in this respect: in the spatial setting it can be shown explicitly that a reduction in price results in a greater quantity being sold both because existing customers buy more *and* because a lower price extends the boundary of the market outward to take in additional customers.

FIGURE 5.2(a)
Network of Circular Markets Leaves Some Areas Unserved

Market radius = OE miles   Shading indicates unserved areas

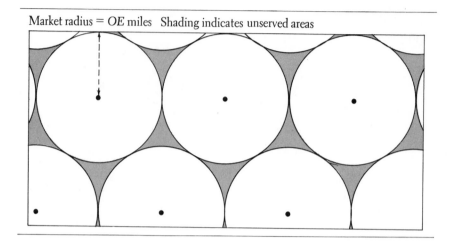

A Network of Central Places for a Single Service

Let us now assume that other farmers can set up bakeries under the same cost conditions enjoyed by farmer *F*. To maximize profits each would locate away from other producers in order to sell as a monopolist to a circular market of optimum size (i.e., the same size as farmer *F*'s). If the whole region were to be filled up by such sellers, a map of their markets would show a series of tangent circular areas, each having a radius of OE miles as in Figure 5.2(a). Since each bakery would be earning monopoly profits, however, there is no reason to assume that this situation would persist. On the contrary, one would expect additional firms to be attracted by the high profits. The newcomers would locate between the existing producers, and by their competition reduce the market areas of the former monopolists.

The situation would now take on the characteristics of monopolistic competition as defined by E. H. Chamberlin.[4] We assume that bread is an undifferentiated product, so each customer buys from the nearest supplier. Producers are differentiated in the eyes of their customers not by differences in their product but by differences in their location. The effect is the same, however: instead of facing the horizontal demand curve of perfect competition, each firm faces a negatively sloped demand curve:

---

4. E. H. Chamberlin, *The Theory of Monopolistic Competition*, 8th ed. (Cambridge, Mass.: Harvard University Press, 1965), ch. 5.

FIGURE 5.2(b)
Network of Hexagonal Markets Serves All Areas

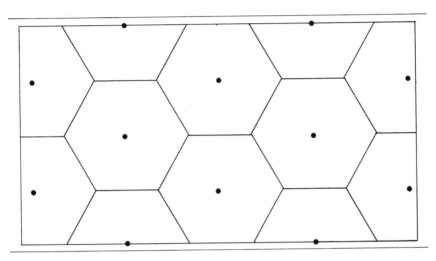

as it reduces the f.o.b. price, sales to existing customers increase, and also the radius of the market is extended to take in new customers at the geographic margin. The competition of new firms pressing in to fill the terrain, however, ensures that no producer can take advantage of a spatial monopoly (with its negatively sloped demand curve) to earn monopoly profits. When competition is fully effective, each firm will find that its market area has been so compressed by the entry of other firms that the most profitable nondiscriminatory price level it can establish will yield only the normal rate of return (i.e., its demand curve will be tangent to the average cost curve at that price level; it is assumed that average cost includes an allowance for "normal profit").

Since we assume that all firms produce under similar cost conditions and that population and effective demand are spread uniformly over the region, it follows that f.o.b. prices will be the same in all markets and that all markets will be the same size. As Lösch points out, this size will also be the minimum threshold size for a firm producing the given service.

The geometrical shape to be expected theoretically for such markets in a system that has reached equilibrium has been a matter of debate. The early central place theorists realized that if markets were circular, as in Figure 5.2(a), unserved areas would remain between the points of tangency of the circles. They argued that this could not be an equilibrium scheme and concluded that the most efficient arrangement that would leave no place unserved would be a network of regular hexagons, with a central place at the center of each, as shown in Figure 5.2(b). A more recent analysis, however, has shown that other outcomes are possible.[5]

The hypothetical scheme of monopolistic competition in space outlined above for a single good can readily be extended to take in any number of products or services. Let us call the goods so distributed "central services." Each such service would develop market areas of a characteristic size. The economy would thus contain not a single net of markets but a system of nets overlaid upon each other, each net delineating markets for a different good or service.

Determinants of Characteristic Market Size

The forces that determine the characteristic market size for each central service are a matter of great interest, since, as we will see below, they also determine the dimensions of the entire central place system. For each service, then, market size depends on three factors:

1. The extent of economies of scale in production of the service. Market areas will tend to be larger when economies of scale are attainable, since large-scale firms will then be able to produce at lower unit cost than smaller firms and will be able to drive the latter out of business. The survivors will necessarily have markets large enough to support large-scale output.

2. The density of demand for the service. The greater the demand for a service per unit of land area, the smaller the area needed to support a producing firm of optimum size. Demand per unit of land area is a function not only of price but of population density and income level per head of population. Therefore the greater the population density and/or the average income level in a region, the smaller the characteristic market areas for given services in that region will be.

3. The cost of transporting the good or service. At first glance it would appear that the lower the cost of transportation, the larger the typical market area would be. In Figure 5.1 the cost of transport per unit of output per mile is shown by the slope of the gradient BC. If transport were cheaper and this slope consequently were flatter, it would appear that farmer F's market could extend farther before his delivered price rose to the level of the home-production cost, OA. As we will see below, however, the case is more complicated than that. While transportation costs certainly affect market size, one cannot assume a priori that lower rates will always make for larger markets.

5. Edwin S. Mills and Michael R. Lav, "A Model of Market Areas with Free Entry," *Journal of Political Economy*, June 1964, pp. 278–88.

A HIERARCHY OF CENTRAL PLACES

The fact of wide variation in the characteristic market size for different central services implies the existence of a hierarchy of central places or, as it is sometimes called, an "urban hierarchy." In an economy of fixed extent, the number of individual markets necessary to handle the distribution of a given good, such as haircuts, over the entire economy would be inversely proportional to the characteristic area of a haircut market. Some goods, including haircuts, would in fact be distributed through many small markets; others, say finished lumber or television broadcasts, through a smaller number of larger markets. In order to take advantage of economies of agglomeration in both production and marketing, firms selling these various services will tend to cluster in villages, towns, and cities instead of seeking isolated locations. But, if there are fewer television stations than lumberyards and fewer lumberyards than barber shops, it is apparent that many towns will have only barber shops, while a smaller number will have barber shops and lumberyards, and still fewer will offer all three central services. Thus we could describe a central place hierarchy by classifying places according to the number and types of central services they offer. We would find that size of city increased and number of cities decreased as we moved up the scale from first order places (those offering the fewest services) to the highest order place (which offers the most services).

It is worth noting that higher order places offer not only more services but services of an entirely different sort than lower order places. A major center, for example, not only contains more kinds of retail stores than does a small town, but provides services like wholesaling and transshipment that are entirely absent in the smaller place.

Indeed, as Philbrick has shown, one can define a hierarchy of places in terms of the level or nature of the functions performed rather than by their sheer number. Using economic functions only, he suggests a sevenfold hierarchy in which the seven levels of function from lowest to highest order are: consumption (i.e., the household function), retail, wholesale, transshipment, exchange, control, and leadership.[6]

Philbrick's scheme emphasizes the fact that a developed economy is highly specialized by function, that specialization requires exchange of goods and of information by means of flows along well-defined paths, that cities are focal places in the organization of such flows, and that their rank in the hierarchy is defined by the stage in the process of production and distribution for which they serve as a focal place.

6. Allen K. Philbrick, "Areal Functional Organization in Regional Geography," *Papers* of the Regional Science Association, vol. III, 1957, pp. 87–98.

Thus a town with a retail store is a focal place for the activities of a group of household consumption units, a city containing a wholesale establishment is a focal place for the activities of a group of towns containing retail stores, and so forth up the table of organization to the highest order place, which provides leadership to the economy as a whole.

Such an organization is not unlike the plan of a telephone network. Each subscriber cannot have a direct line to every other; instead, each is connected to a local exchange, which in turn is connected to other focal points through a long-distance network. As Philbrick has pointed out, this sort of scheme can be used to describe the hierarchy of political and social as well as economic functions.

As the discussion to this point indicates, theoretical models of central place systems display a high degree of internal regularity. For example, at each level of the hierarchy all the towns serve market areas of the same size and shape. Each town is at the center of its market area, and the markets do not overlap. Consequently towns of each hierarchical order are uniformly spaced. The number of towns decreases as we move up the hierarchy, and, necessarily, the average distance between them increases at successively higher levels. At 'each level we could map out a perfectly regular set of mutually exclusive market areas that would exhaust the space of the economy. Each would contain a town of appropriate size at its center. Each city of a higher order would provide services to the same number of towns of the next lower order. In addition, each would provide

FIGURE 5.3
Schematic Diagram of an Urban Hierarchy

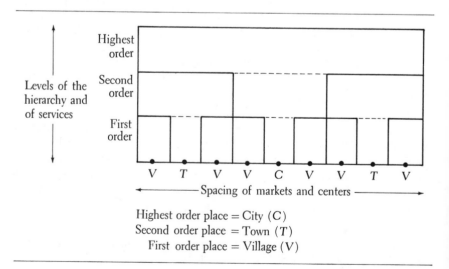

Highest order place = City (C)
Second order place = Town (T)
First order place = Village (V)

for itself all the services performed for themselves by all places lower in the hierarchy. Figure 5.3 is a diagram of such a system containing three levels. The number of market areas decreases by a factor of three as we move up from level to level of this hypothetical system.

Systematic Exceptions to the Hierarchical Order

No central place theorist would expect to find in the real world a hierarchy of places as perfectly ordered as the one depicted in Figure 5.3. First of all, resources and population are not spread evenly over the earth as central place models usually assume. Extractive industries necessarily concentrate where the resources are and attract population to such regions. Topographical irregularities, too, obviously interfere with the uniform spacing of economic activity, both directly and through their influence on the transport network. Thus ports and navigable rivers attract concentrations of activity and population. Climate and other natural amenities also strongly influence the location of people and of industry. And if population and industry are unevenly distributed over the map, then, obviously, central places will also be unevenly distributed: their size and spacing will not display the regularity to be found in theoretical models of central place systems.

So far as manufacturing is concerned, the scheme applies, even roughly, only to those industries such as baking that are locationally consumer-market oriented. Manufacturing industries that are materials oriented locate near materials sources, and if the sources are not evenly distributed, they, like the extractive industries, will concentrate in a few favored areas from which they serve the entire economy. The geographic concentration of the coal, iron, and steel industries is a good example. In similar fashion, manufacturing firms that are production-cost oriented frequently breach the scheme by competing for the entire national market from a single plant, perhaps in some relatively small town that otherwise performs only the lowest order functions.

Large cities, too, may develop disproportionately in the sense that they perform one higher order function without performing others to the expected degree. Thus Pittsburgh, clearly not a highest order metropolis, nevertheless ranked fourth in the United States in nonlocal banking activity in 1960, ahead of Philadelphia, Boston, Los Angeles, and Cleveland, all larger cities and in many respects more "metropolitan."[7]

Central place theory best applies in two cases: consumer-market oriented manufacturing and the general run of service industries. Even for

7. Otis Dudley Duncan, et al., *Metropolis and Region* (Baltimore: John Hopkins University Press, 1960), pp. 116–17.

these, however, there is an important qualification to the deductive model: the market areas of individual suppliers are rarely mutually exclusive. Since most products and services are differentiated either by brand names, like loaves of bread, or by the personal qualities of the supplier, like automotive repair services, consumers do *not* always purchase from the nearest source. This alone would make for interpenetration of markets. In addition, however, many producers employ pricing practices such as freight absorption in a deliberate effort to foster sales to distant customers. Though usually mentioned in connection with industries serving national markets, freight absorption is equally important locally. Retail distributors of home heating oil or bottled gas, for example, do not charge for delivery. In such cases nearby customers are, in effect, subsidizing distant ones. The customer has no incentive to seek out the closest supplier. We must allow for a great deal of cross-hauling, both of goods going to customers and of customers shopping for goods.

THE PROBLEM OF EMPIRICAL VERIFICATION

A large number of empirical studies have sought evidence in the real world of economic geography for the regularities that central place theory predicts will exist. Most of these have examined relatively thinly settled agricultural regions, such as the farm belt of the American Midwest and Canada, where central place theory's assumption of an even distribution of population and resources is approximately realized. In such areas (and in many parts of the world) the central place system has, indeed, been found to display a high degree of regularity.[8]

At this point the alert reader may detect a problem in scientific methodology: is there really an urban hierarchy containing classes of cities with demonstrably different characteristics, or is there merely a continuum of cities from small to large on which we have arbitrarily imposed the character of hierarchy? For if we take the cities and towns of a given region and array them by size we will, of course, find that there are more small than large towns and more large towns than cities. Average market area size and average distance between places will therefore necessarily increase as we go up the scale from small to large places. We will also certainly find that the number of establishments performing central services and the number of different services performed typically increases as population size of centers increases. A town of 200 might have only 4

8. Much of the empirical work is reviewed in Brian J. L. Berry, *Geography of Market Centers and Retail Distribution* (Englewood Cliffs, N.J.: Prentice-Hall, 1967). Also see the many studies of central place systems published in the annual volumes of *Papers* of the Regional Science Association.

establishments providing 2 or 3 different services, while a town of 1,000 in the same region has 30 establishments covering 24 functions, and a town of 3,000 has 100 establishments in 40 service categories. Yet the plain fact is that we could use an arbitrary rule to partition an array of towns into a number of size classes, and no matter where we drew the lines we would certainly find those kinds of regularity. Consequently, such a finding would not demonstrate the existence of a hierarchy. In Berry and Garrison's phrase, the analyst would merely have "used an arbitrary division and then proved what he had in fact assumed."

Two Case Studies: Washington and Saskatchewan

Berry and Garrison set out to test the hypothesis that the central places in Snohomish County, Washington, form an observable hierarchy rather than merely a continuum from small to large.[9] They concluded that a hierarchy was indeed observable. Their procedure need not be described here in detail. In summary, they found that the towns in their study area could be "arranged into three types . . . defined on the basis of the presence of urban functions . . . in varying degrees." They then demonstrated that "these center types differ more one from another than they differ within types."[10] By using appropriate statistical tests they were able to show that their classification of types was not arbitrary but, instead, led to statistically significant groupings. Moreover, the three groups, or types, of central places differed significantly from one another not only in number of functions performed but in types of function.

Table 5.1 summarizes the dimensions of the hierarchy revealed in Berry and Garrison's study. Obviously, the mean population size of central places increases as we move up the scale from hamlets to villages to towns. So also does the average number of establishments per place and the average number of different functions performed. Since the former increases faster than the latter, the number of establishments per function also increases as we move up the hierarchy. The individual hamlets rarely have more than one or two establishments of a single type. A town, on the other hand, might easily have six or more establishments in categories such as food stores, restaurants, churches, or filling stations.

9. Brian J. L. Berry and William L. Garrison, "The Functional Bases of the Central-Place Hierarchy," *Economic Geography*, April 1958, pp. 145–54, reprinted in Harold M. Mayer and Clyde F. Kohn, eds., *Readings in Urban Geography* (Chicago: University of Chicago Press, 1959), pp. 218–27.
   For a later test that verifies the existence of an observable central place hierarchy over a much larger region of the Pacific Northwest, see Richard E. Preston "The Structure of Central Place Systems," reprinted in L. S. Bourne and J. W. Simmons, eds., *Systems of Cities* (New York: Oxford University Press, 1978), pp. 185–206.
10. Berry and Garrison, p. 220.

TABLE 5.1

Characteristics of the Central Place Hierarchy in Snohomish
County, Washington

	CLASSES OF CENTRAL PLACES		
	Hamlets	Villages	Towns
Number of places in class	20	9	4
Average population per place	417	948	2,433
Total number of establishments in class of places	138	490	596
Average number of establishments per place	6.9	54.4	149
Total number of functions in class of places	118	289	239
Average number of functions per place	5.9	32.1	59.8
Average number of establishments per function	1.2	1.7	2.5

Source: Brian J. L. Berry and William Garrison, "The Functional Bases
of the Central-Place Hierarchy," Economic Geography, April 1958, pp.
145–54.

A different perspective on the system is presented in Table 5.2,
which measures the prevalence of selected functions in the three classes
of central place. The functions are ranked down the table from most common (filling stations) to least common (public accountants) on the basis
of Berry and Garrison's estimates of minimum threshold population size
for each. Almost without exception, all four towns in the study area had
at least one establishment in every functional class. The nine villages without exception offered all of the more common functions, but halfway
down the table they showed a pronounced falling off. Fewer than half of
the villages are represented in the selected functions with the largest
threshold sizes. As for the hamlets, they drop out almost completely when
we reach central services with a population threshold larger than an elementary school. It is interesting to note this inference from Table 5.2:
with very few exceptions, the central place hierarchy of Snohomish County
possesses the characteristic (predicted by the theory) that places of a higher
order provide for themselves all services that are found in places lower in
the hierarchy.

A hierarchy is by definition a systematic arrangement of the classes
of an object. Central place theory emphasizes especially the systematic
nature of the spatial arrangement of centers. The best analogy is to a
planetary system in which the units are held in place by the gravitational
forces between them. Thus central place theory purports to show that
each particular urban settlement is, so to speak, held in place within a

TABLE 5.2
*Prevalence of Selected Functions in Central Places of Snohomish
County, Washington*

TYPE OF FUNCTION[a]	NUMBERS OF PLACES IN CLASS HAVING AT LEAST ONE ESTABLISHMENT		
	Hamlets, 20	*Villages, 9*	*Towns, 4*
Filling stations	17	9	4
Food stores	7	9	4
Churches	8	9	4
Restaurants	6	9	4
Elementary schools	13	9	4
Physicians	0	6	4
Appliance stores	0	8	4
Barber shops	5	9	4
Insurance agencies	0	5	3
Drug stores	2	9	4
Lawyers	0	5	4
Apparel stores	0	6	4
Banks	2	7	4
Dry cleaners	1	4	4
Jewelry stores	0	4	4
Department stores	1	3	4
Hospitals and clinics	0	1	3
Public accountants	0	1	3

[a] Functions are ranked from smallest to largest by estimated minimum
threshold population size.
Source: Brian J. L. Berry and William L. Garrison, "The Functional Bases
of the Central-Place Hierarchy," *Economic Geography*, April 1958, pp.
145–54.

system of cities; it suggests that the development of each is affected in a
predictable way by its position within the system.

Gerald Hodge's study of central places in Saskatchewan verifies this
characteristic of the system.[11] Hodge distinguished seven classes of trade
center in Saskatchewan and studied changes in the relative importance
of each of these classes in the system as a whole between 1941 and 1961.
A given trade center was said to have "declined" during the period if it
either shifted downward one or more classes in the hierarchy or disappeared altogether as a center. Central place theory would predict that,
other things being equal, at any given level in the hierarchy, towns that
are nearer than the average to centers of like character will be more likely

11. Gerald Hodge, "The Prediction of Trade Center Viability in the Great
Plains," *Papers* of the Regional Science Association, vol. XV, 1965, pp. 87–115.

to decline than the average in their class, for they will be too near their competitors. Hodge's study showed just such a result. He found: "Of hamlets thus situated [i.e., closer than average to other hamlets], 66 percent declined from 1941–61 compared to 46 percent for all hamlets in the same period. Similar differentials of decline were found for the other types of centers studied."[12] Here is direct evidence that central places behave not as independent entities but as parts of a coherent "system of cities."

DEFINING A CITY'S "HINTERLAND"

Sociologists have long spoken of cities as having "hinterlands" over which, in the language of that discipline, they extend their "dominance." By dominance is meant the power of exerting "an organizing influence upon the economic and social structure of the communities in their hinterlands."[13] In analyzing the central place system we have concentrated attention on the market areas served from central places. These market areas for outputs provide one means of defining hinterlands—but not a simple means, since all but the smallest central places produce a multiplicity of services, and the market areas for these services will typically differ widely in size. Moreover, outputs require inputs, and therefore each central place also has a set of supply areas from which it draws the resources that feed its production processes. These supply areas provide another and equally important contribution to the definition of a city's hinterland. For example, the SMSA around each major central city, as delineated by the Census Bureau, is in effect defined by its character of being a labor market area. Roughly speaking, it is the area from which the metropolis daily draws its supply of workers—the labor supply hinterland of the metropolis. It is almost always far smaller in extent than the hinterland of that same metropolis as defined by the market area of its highest order services. In the discussion that follows, we propose to simplify matters by focusing on the market area definition of hinterland. Even so, we will find more than enough ambiguities and complications.

In an urban hierarchy the highest, or "nth order," city has the entire nation as its hinterland, since the entire nation depends upon it for nth order services. Each city below that level has as its hinterland all the cities to which *it* supplies central services plus all *their* hinterlands. In a descrip-

12. Ibid., p. 101.
13. Rupert B. Vance and Sara Smith, "Metropolitan Dominance and Integration," reprinted in Paul K. Hatt and Albert J. Reiss, Jr., eds., *Cities and Society, The Revised Reader in Urban Sociology* (Glencoe, Ill.: Free Press, 1957), p. 103.

tion of U.S. cities New York is likely to rank as the nth order place (although it lacks federal government functions found in Washington). Boston would probably rank as a city of $n - 1$ order. Thus Boston is within New York's hinterland for nth order services. But for services of the $n - 1$ order, each has its own hinterland.

In the perfectly ordered hierarchy of central place theory as we have defined it, these hinterlands at the $n - 1$ level would not overlap: one would be able to draw a line somewhere between New York and Boston that would unambiguously divide them. We have argued, however, that hierarchies in the real world are not perfectly ordered. Hinterlands, for example, are not mutually exclusive. Here is some interesting evidence of how they overlap. Park and Newcomb in 1933 delineated regions around major cities by mapping the circulation of the leading morning newspaper of each. They defined the region of each city as consisting of those places in which its newspaper was the dominant one. By that definition Hartford, Connecticut, fell within the Boston region, while New London, Connecticut, and Newport, Rhode Island, came within New York's. Whatever else may be said about this classification, it should not be permitted to obscure the fact that many people in Hartford read the *New York Times*, and some in Newport and New London read the *Boston Globe*. Clearly the influence of one central place does not stop where the influence of another starts.

Since market areas inevitably overlap, hinterland boundaries can be drawn only by devising some rational rule of the sort used by Park and Newcomb. However, the boundary will vary greatly depending both on the rule and on the kind of central service it refers to. In 1955 Howard L. Green compared Park and Newcomb's findings with other attempts to locate the hinterland boundary between New York and Boston.[14] He showed that Dickinson's 1934 study using different service components had exactly reversed Park and Newcomb's findings by placing Hartford in New York's region and New London and Newport in Boston's. Green then made his own delineation of the hinterland boundary by taking the median of seven different functional indicators. The extent to which these seven give contradictory delineations of the regional boundary is indicated in Table 5.3, which shows how five cities close to the median borderline are classified according to the separate criteria. Green's composite, or median, line places Springfield, Providence, and Newport in New York's region, Holyoke and Pittsfield in Boston's. The table, however, shows that none of these cities fell unambiguously to one side or the other. In every case the indicators were split 5 to 2 or 4 to 3. Green recognized the

14. Howard L. Green, "Hinterland Boundaries of New York City and Boston in Southern New England," in Mayer and Kohn, pp. 185–201.

TABLE 5.3
How Regional Classification of Cities Varies with Choice of Indicator

	REGIONAL CLASSIFICATION OF CITY				
INDICATOR OF REGION	*Springfield*	*Providence*	*Newport*	*Pittsfield*	*Holyoke*
Railroad coach ticket purchases	New York	Boston	New York	Boston	On the borderline
Estimated truck freight movement	New York	New York	New York	New York	New York
Metropolitan newspaper circulation	Boston	Boston	Boston	Boston	Boston
Long-distance telephone calls	Boston	Boston	Boston	Boston	Boston
Metropolitan origin of vacationers	Boston	New York	New York	New York	Boston
Business addresses of directors for major industrial firms	New York	New York	New York	New York	New York
Metropolitan correspondents for hinterland banks	On the borderline	New York	New York	Boston	Boston
Composite of indicators	New York	New York	New York	Boston	Boston

Source: Based on Howard L. Green, "Hinterland Boundaries of New York City and Boston in Southern New England," in Harold M. Mayer and Clyde F. Kohn, eds., *Readings in Urban Geography* (Chicago: University of Chicago Press, 1959), pp. 185–201.

existence of a broad band of hinterland overlap and placed all five of the above cities within it.

The overlapping of regions, the interpenetration of central place influences, obviously makes it impossible to map out a single exhaustive and unambiguous set of central place hinterlands for the United States. More important, it should remind us that the appropriate definition of a city's hinterland will depend upon the subject and purpose of the analysis.

HOW THE SYSTEM OF CITIES DEVELOPS AND CHANGES THROUGH TIME

Probably the most interesting contribution of central place theory is the help it provides in understanding the historical trend of changes within the system of cities. Under the impact of technological innovation and economic development, profound alterations occur in the pattern of urban settlement, the size distribution of cities, and the division of functions among cities at various levels of the hierarchy. Central place theory helps to illuminate these complex changes.

We have already shown that the various dimensions of the central place system (number, size, and spacing of cities; number and location of functions and of establishments; etc.) depend largely on the size of the characteristic market areas for central services. Therefore, the obvious point of entry for an analysis of change in those dimensions is to consider what might cause the typical market area to alter in size.[15] It was pointed out earlier that market area size for any central service depends on three factors: the extent of economies of scale in its production; the level of demand for the service per unit of area; and the cost of transporting it. We must now examine the effects of technological change and economic growth on these three factors. Five types of change will be analyzed:

1. Growth of population
2. Rise in living standards (i.e., increased per capita income)
3. Innovation leading to the development of greater economies of scale in production
4. Innovation leading to a reduction in transport costs
5. Rise in fuel prices leading to increased transport costs

To keep the discussion within bounds we will use retail trade as the illustrative case and derive conclusions from it that are applicable to central services in general. Figure 5.4 depicts three spatially separated competing retail outlets, A, B, and C. As before, we measure distance along the horizontal scale, average unit cost of production and unit delivery cost along the vertical.

Assume initially that the outlets are old-fashioned general stores, selling a variety of goods such as groceries, housewares and the like. The unit cost of this merchandise, measured on the vertical axis, is the cost of a composite of those items which a typical consumer might buy and carry home on a single shopping trip. Since the buyer carries the goods home, delivery cost is to be interpreted as the cost of making a round trip from home to store and back. This consists of two elements: first, the money cost of the trip and, second, a nonmonetary cost, consisting of the disutility of the trip in terms of time lost and discomfort undergone. The disutility of the trip can, in principle, be given a money equivalent: the amount the shopper would pay not to have to undergo it. Thus the

---

15. For a more complex analysis that relates arithmetically the number and population size of centers at each level of the hierarchy to the population of the market areas they serve, see Hugh O. Nourse, *Regional Economics* (New York: McGraw-Hill, 1968), pp. 40–44 and 209–18.

FIGURE 5.4

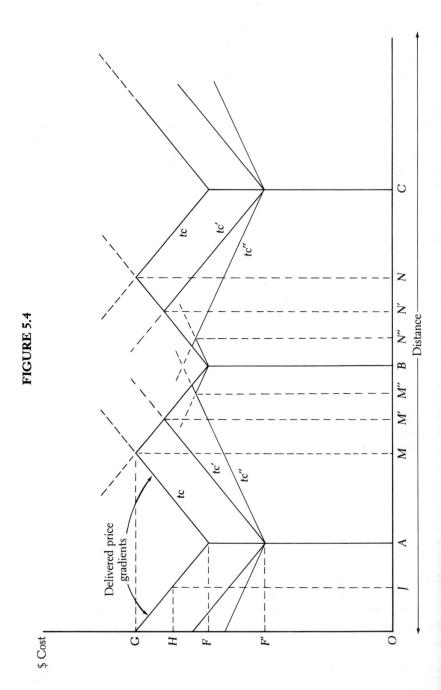

two costs can be combined into a single money equivalent, which, for a given route and mode of transport, can be expressed as a cost of so many cents per mile. Now in the ordinary case in which the nonmonetary disutility of a journey is positive, the faster the mode of transport, the less the disutility of covering a given distance and the lower, therefore, the nonmonetary cost per mile.

In Figure 5.4, then, we start with three general stores located at villages A, B, and C along a line that represents geographic space. The villages are of equal size. Rural population is spread uniformly in the space between them at residential locations that are assumed to remain fixed. We also assume that more such stores are located at regular intervals to the left and right of the segment we are looking at. Initially these spatial competitors are in equilibrium. Each has a store of optimum size and can just manage to earn a normal return by supplying a unit of goods at an f.o.b. price of OF. The absence of monopolistic profits indicates that stores have been "packed in" as closely as is consistent with long-run equilibrium.

Shoppers who do not live in a village travel to market by automobile. Their round-trip travel costs, a combination of monetary and nonmonetary elements, are a linear function of their distance from the store. Each buys in that store for which the sum of f.o.b. price plus travel costs is least. Thus sum, which we may call the "delivered price," is shown for any point of residence by the height above the horizontal at that point of the delivered price gradient from the supplier. The slope of the gradient equals round-trip travel cost per unit of distance. Initially, the relevant gradients are those labeled tc. Thus a customer living at J would pay OF for a unit of merchandise and incur travel costs of FH in going from home at J to the store at A and returning. For this customer, total cost per unit is therefore OH. The market boundary between stores A and B is at point M, where the delivered price gradients of these two suppliers intersect. A customer at M would incur a cost OG per unit when buying from either A or B. Similarly, N marks the boundary between the markets of B and C.

Effect of a Rise in Population or Income

We examine first the effect of a geographically uniform increase in the region's population. A rise in population, with income per capita remaining constant, would clearly increase the level of demand for general store services per unit of area. Store owners at A, B, and C would find demand for their output rising and would begin to earn above-normal profits. These profits would attract new firms to the industry. New points of service would spring up between previously existing centers, and the markets of store owners at A, B, and C would be compressed by this competition.

At the higher level of demand density, a store of optimum size could earn normal returns with a smaller market area. The end result would be an increase in the number of firms and in the number of central places and a decrease in the characteristic size of market areas for general stores. The distance between centers would decrease.

Let us assume that these general stores and the villages at which they are located make up the lowest order of the central place hierarchy. We can see that the changes taking place at this level would have their counterparts at higher levels, too. The number of higher order firms and centers would also increase (for example, more wholesalers would be needed to service the larger number of general stores), their market areas would grow smaller, and the distance between higher order centers would also diminish.

Berry has amply documented these and other effects of varying population density by comparing the central place systems in Iowa with those in much more thinly populated South Dakota.[16] To be sure, this approach is cross-sectional rather than longitudinal: it examines areas having unequal densities at a single point in time instead of observing a single area as its population density changes through the years. Such a cross-sectional method, however, has the great advantage that it holds constant other crucial variables, such as the technology of transportation, which could not be held constant in a study running through time. With "other things remaining the same" one can isolate more successfully the effect of the single factor of population density.

The general effect of a rise in per capita income with population held constant would be much the same as the effect of a rise in population with per capita income held constant, since in both cases the areal density of demand increases. Consequently, we need not repeat the argument for the case in which income rises.

The Effect of Increased Economies of Scale

In order to examine the effect of a technological innovation leading to increased economies of scale in production, let us assume that the owner of store A "invents" the principle of the self-service supermarket. This innovation allows average unit cost to be reduced, provided that the scale of operation can be sufficiently enlarged. The owner of store A calculates that by creating a supermarket she can achieve economies of scale such that she will maximize profits by reducing the f.o.b. price from OF to OF'. With this lower price owner A can expect to increase sales for two reasons: first, if the demand of individual consumers is elastic, she will

16. Berry, *Geography of Market Centers*, ch. 2.

sell more to her present customers; second, if her competitors do not also build supermarkets she will capture their outlying customers. For example, when A lowers her price to OF', the delivered price gradient shifts to tc' (parallel to tc, since transportation cost is unchanged). If B does not respond in kind, A's market boundary now moves out to point M'.

If owner C also builds a supermarket, B's market area will be squeezed from both sides, contracting from MN to M'N'. Initially, B was earning a normal return. Now his return will fall, and he may decide to close up, leaving his customers to be divided between supermarkets A and C. This, of course, is precisely what has happened since the advent of the supermarket: many small stores have disappeared. But suppose B had also attempted to open a supermarket? In that case none of the firms could have expanded its market area. Unless demand were so elastic that lower prices permitted considerably enlarged sales within fixed market boundaries, not all the supermarkets could survive. Some suppliers would be forced out until those remaining could earn normal returns by enlarging their market areas. This seems the most likely outcome provided that population, income, and transportation costs remain constant.

Granted that increased economies of scale will probably lead to a reduction in the number of establishments providing the given service, what effect will that have on the number and spacing of central places? The answer depends on the situation from which one starts. In Figure 5.4 we assume that general store retailing is the only service provided by villages, which are the lowest order places in the hierarchy, and that there is only one store per village. In that case, a reduction in the number of firms necessarily means a reduction in the number of villages and an increase in their spacing.

Of course, other possibilities abound. Initially, for example, villages A, B, and C might have provided several central services in addition to general store goods. In that case, B could continue supplying other central services even though supermarkets at A and C had eliminated its general store. Economies of scale would then have reduced the number of central service establishments in the system as a whole but not the number of centers, although some centers would have been weakened relative to others.

If we assume, however, that economies of scale increase substantially in the production of many types of central services rather than in only one, then it seems highly probable that some of the smallest centers will be eliminated entirely as services are gradually concentrated into larger towns. Within the category of retail services, such consolidation is also affected by the importance of economies of agglomeration in shopping. Other things being equal, the retail customer will prefer to shop at the center where more needs can be satisfied on a single trip. If villages A and *B* provided the same services, the customer midway between them would be indifferent as to where he shopped. But if *A* provided more services than *B*, he would probably prefer shopping at *A* even for those goods also available at *B*. Thus the existence of agglomeration economies in shopping accelerates a process of consolidation that may begin with the development of scale economies in a particular service: each function lost at a small center weakens those that remain.

Effect of a Change in Transportation Costs

We come last to the question of transportation costs. How would a change in transport costs per mile affect the central place system? This is both the most interesting and the most complex question we can ask about the response of the system to the forces of economic change. Two cases will be examined. The first is a technological innovation that reduces transport costs. The historical reality we here attempt to capture in simplified form is the impact of the automobile, and the improved highways that were built for it, on the twentieth-century central place system. The second case is the effect of higher fuel prices on transport costs. Here we look forward, rather than back, to anticipate the way in which the energy crisis might affect the central place system in the future.

Let us first examine a situation such as was described initially in Figure 5.4. Producers at competing centers operate under identical cost conditions. Their market areas are identical in extent and just large enough to afford each a normal rate of return from a plant of optimum size. Analyzing this case, Hoover has argued that a reduction in transport costs has two distinguishable effects: an output effect (or, as he calls it, an "income effect") and a substitution effect.[17] Since the output effect of reduced transportation costs makes market areas smaller, while the substitution effect makes them larger, one cannot say, without knowing the details of each case, what the net effect will be.

This situation is a familiar one in the economic theory of production. For example, if a firm uses two production inputs, labor and machinery, and the relative price of machinery falls, the firm will tend to substitute machinery for labor in its production process. The substitution effect clearly will be to use more machinery and less labor to produce a given quantity of goods. But there will also be an output effect: since the cost of one of the firm's inputs has fallen, it will be able to sell at lower prices and therefore in larger quantities. Output will rise above its previous level, and the output effect will cause the firm to purchase more of both

17. Edgar M. Hoover, "Transport Costs and the Spacing of Central Places," *Papers of the Regional Science Association*, vol. XXV, 1970, pp. 255–74.

labor and machinery. Purchases of machinery will certainly rise, since both effects make for that result. But purchases of labor may either rise or fall, since the substitution effect reduces labor inputs, while the output effect increases them.

Using Isard's method of treating transport as an input to the production process that is substitutable for other inputs, Hoover shows how the output and substitution effects operate in the case of declining transportation costs. The ouput effect works as follows. When transport costs per mile are reduced, the delivered price of each supplier of a central service falls for all customers not located at the very center of the market. Consequently, at whatever f.o.b. price he chooses, each supplier can now sell more than he previously did to customers within his existing market area. His profits therefore rise above the normal rate of return he had previously been earning. This is the ouput effect of the fall in transport rates. It makes for smaller market areas because new firms are attracted to the production of the central service by the existence of above normal profits. They press in upon the previously existing firms. Market areas are compressed, the number of centers increases, and the distance between them falls.

The substitution effect, Hoover argues, works in the opposite direction. As transport becomes relatively cheaper, profit-maximizing producers increase the use of transport inputs relative to other inputs by delivering the service to greater distances. Market areas become larger, centers fewer and farther apart. Since the substitution and output effects work in opposite directions, the net effect of reduced transport costs is theoretically uncertain.

It is most important, however, to note the stringent initial assumption of this analysis that all firms operate with identical production costs. The outcome is quite different where production costs are *not* assumed to be equal for all suppliers. Moreover, the latter case is probably much the more significant in explaining the impact of economic change on the central place system. To illustrate it, let us return to the situation depicted in Figure 5.4.

Suppose that owners A and C have installed supermarkets but owner B has decided to continue running his general store, even though his market has been cut down to size $M'N'$. (This can be made more plausible if we recognize that in reality points A, B, and C may initially have had not one but two or three stores each and that the construction of supermarkets at A and C would then result in a reduction in the number of stores at all points. In that case a lone survivor at B could well continue to earn normal returns.) Now suppose that with the passage of time a technological improvement, in the form of better roads, speeds up travel, thus reducing transport costs. On the diagram this appears as a flattening of the delivered price gradients from *tc'* to *tc"*. Even though *B*'s gradients flatten out as much as the others, his market boundaries move inward from *M'* and *N'* to *M"* and *N"*. Thus *A* and *C* once again expand their territory at his expense. Indeed, *B* may well be forced out of business.

Why does *B* lose market ground to *A* and *C* when transportation costs drop uniformly in all three markets and the f.o.b. price differential between them does not change? The answer is that the lower transport costs per mile drop, the more miles a consumer will travel to save a price differential of given magnitude. An analogous principle was shown to be at work in connection with problems of industrial location: if, as a result of technological improvements, transport costs drop relative to other costs, industries tend to become less transport oriented and more production-cost oriented.

We have already argued that an increase in economies of scale in production interacts with economies of agglomeration in shopping to strengthen larger retail centers at the expense of smaller ones. Precisely the same interaction occurs when a reduction in transport costs eliminates high cost suppliers while extending the markets of low cost firms. To the extent that economies of agglomeration exist, either in shopping or in production, the centers at which low cost suppliers are concentrated will find themselves gaining cumulative advantages over the smaller centers at which functions are being eliminated. The smaller centers will suffer progressive loss through what might be called "the diseconomies of deglomeration."

Transportation Costs and the Scale of Social Organization

The general principle that for any given industry a reduction in transport costs benefits low cost and large scale producers at the expense of high cost and small scale producers is of the greatest importance in spatial economics. It helps to explain why the scale of organization throughout society is steadily increasing. It lies at the root of Hoover's observation: "Other things being equal, high transport costs mean scattered local production, and cheap transport means localized (i.e., concentrated) production."[18]

With a little imagination the reader can change the terms employed

18. Edgar M. Hoover, *Location Theory and the Shoe and Leather Industries* (Cambridge, Mass.: Harvard University Press, 1937), p. 20. More recently Hoover has added a caveat, however. He notes that some interlocal variation in production costs may itself be related to transport costs insofar as the latter affect the cost of transported inputs or cause factor immobilities. "Consequently," he concludes, "cheaper transport might well be expected to narrow such cost differentials . . . and thus run against the tendency for the cheaper locations to eliminate the more expensive ones" ("Transport Costs and the Spacing of Central Places," p. 271). However, this reservation does not apply to cost differentials based on economies of scale.

in our example and see that it is a paradigm for a large number of cases. For instance, in the public rather than the private sector, it explains why the "scale" of local schools and their districts increased and the number of schools diminished when a faster form of transportation—the school bus—replaced a slower one—shank's mare. The change in organizational scale of the school system is easily verified from national data. Between 1930 and 1977, the number of public elementary and secondary schools in the United States diminished from 262,000 to 88,000, while enrollments increased from 25.7 million to 44.3 million.[19] Average enrollment per school—a good measure of scale—consequently soared from 98 to 504. If we substitute cost and ease of communication for cost and ease of transportation, we can understand how technological improvements have enabled all kinds of economic and social institutions to expand from a local to a regional scale of operation or from a regional to a national or international scale.

The Energy Crisis and the Central Place System

The cost of fuel has increased sharply since the energy crisis first loomed in 1973–74, and it is reasonable to expect substantial further increases in the foreseeable future. Rising fuel prices obviously increase the cost of transportation. In principal, the effect on the central place system will simply be the reverse of that attributed to a decline in transportation costs. Thus, as transportation cost per mile *rises*, the distance consumers will travel to obtain a given f.o.b. price differential will *decline*. Therefore, higher cost, local suppliers will begin to gain customers at the expense of lower cost, more distant ones. The further consequences of this should by now be clear: smaller centers will gain strength at the expense of larger ones and may become more numerous, the distance between centers will decline, and so on.

This is not to suggest, however, that rising fuel costs will reverse the revolution wrought by the automobile and the highway. That invention and those public facilities now exist and will continue to be used for their convenience even if fuel prices go on rising sharply. Moreover, in the case of personal transportation, the impact of rising fuel prices on trip cost is less dramatic than the casual observer might expect. The marginal cost of a trip for an automobile user is the sum of operating costs, parking charges, the cost of time in transit, and the cost of any other disutility of travel. As we explain in Chapter 8 (see Table 8.4) the equivalent money cost of travel time typically equals or outweighs operating cost in the commuter's calculus, and fuel cost is only a fraction of operat-

19. *Statistical Abstract of the United States, 1972,* tables 152 and 154, and *1979,* tables 211 and 213.

ing outlays. On that basis, doubling gasoline prices would increase marginal trip cost by 25 percent, at most. For the average commuter, the increase might be a good deal less. This contrasts with the case of the transportation innovation analyzed above. The effect of introducing the automobile was precisely to speed up travel, thus reducing time cost, and simultaneously to increase comfort, which reduced other elements of disutility, as well. We should not assume that the energy crisis will have as dramatic an effect in raising the cost of personal transportation as the introduction of the automobile had in lowering it.

In addition, it must be emphasized that the situation depicted in Figure 5.4 and the argument based on it include some special assumptions made to facilitate the exposition of central place theory. For example, it was assumed that population is spread evenly over rural areas and that residential locations of households remain fixed, while their shopping patterns and, therefore, the market areas of their suppliers, adjust to changes in the cost of transportation. In fact, as transportation costs change, some households are likely to change their location. We speculate on the probable consequences of such moves for the system of cities as a whole at the end of Chapter 9.

Finally, the general increase in the scale of social organization, as it is reflected in the central place system, owes as much to improvements in communication as it does to those in transportation, and such improvements will not be adversely affected by rising fuel costs. On the contrary, we should expect a substantial increase in transportation costs to encourage the development and use of ever more sophisticated communication techniques, since communication can often serve as a substitute for personal transportation.[20]

Economic Development and the Impact of "Latent" Central Services

A complicating factor, largely ignored in the literature of central place theory, remains to be mentioned. The analysis to this point assumed implicitly that despite the impact of economic change and growth, the number of central services to be performed in the region remained constant. But this helpful simplification is wholly unrealistic. There are at all times and in any region "latent" central services that might be brought to the threshold of feasibility by either an increase in demand density or a decrease in transportation cost. For example, a given population with a given average level of income might have a desire to see motion pictures,

20. For a stimulating, if somewhat fanciful, assessment of the possible impact of further improvements in communication, see Norman Macrae, "Tomorrow's Agglomeration Economies," in Charles L. Leven, ed., *The Mature Metropolis* (Lexington, Mass.: D. C. Heath, Lexington Books, 1978), pp. 131–45.

but because local transportation is so costly it is impossible to collect enough customers at any one point to make even the smallest sort of establishment pay. Suppose that the nearest motion picture theater is fifty miles away. When transportation becomes cheaper the probable result is not that local residents now make a hundred-mile round trip to the movies, thus extending the market area of the distant producer. Rather, a local theater now becomes feasible because the cost of reaching it has fallen. A central service new to the region comes into existence. A like effect, of course, occurs when rising population or per capita income lifts demand for some latent central service to the threshold at which it becomes commercially feasible to produce it.

It is clear, then, that economic growth and declining transportation costs increase the number of central functions actually provided. The impact of such an increase on the central place system, however, cannot be determined a priori. It might seem probable, for example, that an increase in the number of functions would reinforce the tendency of rising population and income to increase the number of centers and reduce their spacing. Such an outcome, however, cannot be taken for granted. If the new services are subject to significant economies of scale in production (as bowling alleys or movie theaters are, for example) they will tend to locate in the larger centers and, by adding to agglomeration economies at those points, further erode the position of smaller centers. Each new service, however, will have its own characteristics. There appears to be no general principle upon which to predict the impact of new services on the system as a whole.

EVIDENCE FOR THE EFFECTS
OF GROWTH AND DEVELOPMENT

We have now analyzed the impact on the central place system of five factors associated with economic growth and development. Four of these factors—increased population and real income, economies of scale in production, and reduced transportation cost—have operated simultaneously and powerfully throughout this century. The fifth—higher fuel costs —has yet to make its influence clear and so can hardly be subjected to empirical test. What evidence can be found to test the effects of the other four? These effects can be summarized as follows. Either rising population or increased income per capita would lead to smaller market areas and a larger number and closer spacing of centers. On the other hand, increased economies of scale in the output of central services would, under the most probable circumstances, reduce the number of very small centers and strengthen the larger ones. The impact of reduced transport costs is uncertain when all suppliers have identical costs of production but favors large, low cost suppliers when there are interfirm cost differentials. This almost certainly leads to a cumulative strengthening of large at the expense of small centers—and probably to the elimination of some of the latter. Thus the four factors associated with economic growth prior to the onset of the energy crisis, must have had offsetting effects on the development of the central place system.

Although we analyzed these factors one by one, they were, in fact, operating on the central place system simultaneously, which makes it difficult to verify their individual impacts. We can, however, observe the net effect on the central place system of all of them operating together. Among the lower order places in the United States and Canada during the twentieth century the pattern of change is quite clear: towns and small cities have been growing in number relative to villages and hamlets. In recent years the very smallest places have declined not only in relative importance but in absolute number.

Two sets of data indicate this tendency. Table 5.4 shows how the number of places in the United States, classified by population size, has changed during the twentieth century. The table reveals that the rate of

TABLE 5.4

*Changes in the Number of Places by Size
in the United States, 1900–70*

	NUMBER OF PLACES			PERCENTAGE INCREASE
SIZE AND TYPE OF PLACE	*1970*	*1930*	*1900*	*1900–70*
Total, all places, urban and rural	20,768	16,643	10,673	95%
Urban, total	7,062	3,179	1,740	306
25,000–50,000	520	185	83	527
10,000–25,000	1,385	607	281	393
5,000–10,000	1,839	853	465	296
2,500–5,000	2,295	1,342	833	176
Less than 2,500[a]	627	—	—	—
Rural, total	13,706	13,464	8,933	53
1,000–2,500	4,191	3,107	2,130	97
Less than 1,000	9,515	10,357	6,803	40
Urban and rural, less than 2,500	14,333	13,464	8,933	60

[a] Definition of "urban" changed in 1950. Previous to that date, all places with population under 2,500 were classified as rural.

Source: U.S. Bureau of the Census, *Census of Population, 1970,* U.S. Summary, PC(1)A-1, table 7.

growth in the number of places per size class increases steadily as size class increases for all classes from the smallest up to 50,000 population. Thus the number of places with population under 1,000 increased only 40 percent between 1900 and 1970, while the number of places with a population of 10,000 to 25,000 increased 393 percent, and the number in the 25,000 to 50,000 class rose 527 percent. Places with a population of less than 2,500 made up 84 percent of all places in 1900 but only 69 percent in 1970.

Precisely because they cover the whole United States, however, it may be objected that the data in Table 5.4 are too highly aggregated to be really satisfactory. In each size class places located in growing regions and declining regions, in metropolitan areas and nonmetropolitan areas, are lumped together. In addition, the census definition of "place" changes over the interval covered and, in any case, does not correspond with the definition of "central place" employed in central place theory.

These objections, however, cannot be raised against the data in Table 5.5, which are drawn from Hodge's study of the central place system in the southern part of Saskatchewan. Hodge identified seven orders of central place in the study area, which is a relatively homogeneous farming region. The total number of such places declined from 906 in 1941 to 892 in 1951 and 779 in 1961. The number of places in the four highest

TABLE 5.5
Changes in the Hierarchy of Trade Centers in Saskatchewan, 1941–61

	1941		1951		1961	
	Num-	Per-	Num-	Per-	Num-	Per-
CLASS OF TRADE CENTER	ber	centage	ber	centage	ber	centage
Primary wholesale-retail	2	0.2	2	0.2	2	0.2
Secondary wholesale-retail	5	0.6	8	0.9	9	1.2
Complete shopping	26	2.9	23	2.6	29	3.7
Partial shopping	57	6.3	66	7.4	85	10.9
Full convenience	171	18.9	169	18.9	100	12.7
Minimum convenience	287	31.8	191	21.4	150	19.4
Hamlet	358	39.3	433	48.6	404	51.8
All trade centers	906	100.0	892	100.0	779	100.0
Four highest orders	90	9.9	99	11.1	125	16.1
Three lowest orders	816	90.1	793	88.9	654	83.9

Source: Gerald Hodge, "The Prediction of Trade Center Viability in the Great Plains," *Papers* of the Regional Science Association, XV, 1965, table 2, p. 95.

orders increased from 90 in 1941 to 125 in 1961, while the number in the three lowest orders fell from 816 to 654. The three lowest orders made up 90 percent of all places in 1941, but only 84 percent in 1961.[21] Studies by Berry and others of central place systems in farming areas of the U.S. Midwest reveal similar tendencies there.[22] These patterns of development are quite similar to the one suggested by the aggregate data for the United States in Table 5.4: under the impact of economic change and growth, central service functions have been gradually concentrating into fewer and larger places.

INTRAMETROPOLITAN PATTERNS ARE NOT EXPLAINED BY CENTRAL PLACE THEORY

It is no accident that this discussion of central place theory has focused on villages, towns, and small cities rather than on the great urban centers or metropolitan areas of the nation. True, we can observe hierarchical differences among large cities as well as among smaller places. Major cities and metropolitan areas can be differentiated into hierarchical classes by the order of services they provide and the regions for which they are the dominant provider. Thus they, as well as the smallest towns, are a part of the "system of cities," and our insight into urban phenomena is greatly enhanced by understanding that. Yet within metropolitan areas themselves it is not easy to discern the hierarchical pattern of market areas (and of centers) for the distribution of goods and services that is described in classical central place theory. Population is so dense and travel relatively so easy that shoppers habitually visit many suppliers, and the market areas of suppliers cease to be even approximately exclusive. Under these conditions, as Berry has pointed out, the locational pattern of central service firms becomes a complex of "ribbons" and "specialized areas" as well as of "centers."[23]

In the face of this complexity economists have, after the manner of their kind, looked for some underlying, simplifying principle that would explain the essence of the whole intrametropolitan pattern of location. They have employed as their point of departure a model that does not break the metropolis up into a hierarchically related system of submarkets but assumes instead that it is a single market area, organized into specialized districts around a single, unchallenged center. It is to this model that we turn in the next chapter.

21. Hodge, table 2, p. 95.
22. See Berry, *Geography of Market Centers*, pp. 114–17, and references cited therein.
23. Ibid., pp. 44–58 and 117–24.

Site Rent, Land-Use Patterns, and the Form of the City

SIX

Just as transport costs influence the location of producers and therefore of cities, so, too, they systematically affect locational patterns within the city itself. We are all conscious of the general form of the city: concentrated activity and development at the center; a gradual decline of intensity as one moves out toward the edge. This characteristic form is constantly impressed on us by the clusters of tall buildings and the dense crowds of people and vehicles we see at the center, so dramatically different from the lower skyline and the smaller crowds we find at the periphery.

It is not difficult to construct economic models that will generate this easily observed pattern as a function of transport cost and the need for accessibility. Although these relatively simple models do not account for the full complexity of land-use arrangements that are found in the city, they do explain successfully the general pattern of land use, land value, and density of development. In addition, they are vitally important because they illuminate the process by which the real estate market sorts out potential occupants of land, allowing those who can make the most productive use of central sites to obtain them and pushing those less dependent on centrality out toward the edge. From an understanding of this process much can be gained. The city planner learns the strengths and weaknesses of a free market in land as a rational allocator of scarce central sites. Students of housing and urban renewal gain insight into the economics of "land-use succession," the process by which "renewal" occurs (or fails to occur) in a freely functioning market. The transportation analyst learns the interdependence of land values, land use, and the transportation network.

117

In all such models of land use, the price of urban land at various sites plays a crucial role. This price can be expressed either as the capital value of a site or as its annual rental value. Although land is more commonly sold than rented in the United States, it is usually more convenient for purposes of analysis to use annual rent rather than capital value as the measure of price. The relationship between the two concepts is, in any case, simple enough: the capital or market value of a site is the present value of the stream of net returns it is expected to yield in the future. Since land in uses other than agriculture does not "wear out," its expected future life is infinitely long. If, then, its yield is expected to be constant per year, the expression for its present capital value reduces to the formula for evaluating the worth of a perpetual income: capital value equals the expected perpetual annual net return divided by the interest rate appropriate for capitalizing an income of that degree of risk.

A SIMPLE MODEL: RESIDENTIAL LAND USE

Let us start with a drastically simplified model based on the following assumptions: (1) a city has sprung up on a flat plain, or transport surface, of the sort assumed in the explanation of central place theory in the preceding chapter; (2) all production and distribution activity in this city takes place at a single point at its center; (3) the populace consists of families of uniform size, taste, and income who must live in rented single family homes of uniform house and lot dimensions ranged around the central production and distribution point; (4) the cost of building and maintaining houses (site rent excluded) is constant throughout the city.[1] Since housing costs other than site rent are spatially invariant, differences in total rent paid by tenants at two different sites clearly represent differences in the site-rent component of the total. "Site rent" itself we define as the rent paid for a site less the rent it could command in an agricultural use.

Under these assumptions it can be shown that site rent for residential lots will be highest adjacent to the business center, will decline along any

1. The land-use model that we here apply to the city had its origin in J. H. von Thünen's work *Der isolierte Staat*, published in 1826. Von Thünen made use of the featureless plain and the need for access to a market center to explain the pattern of agricultural land uses that typically formed around a market town. In the twentieth century, urban economists have relied almost exclusively on a similar model to explain the pattern of urban land use. For a summary of twentieth-century theories of the economics of urban land use down to 1960, see William Alonso, *Location and Land Use* (Cambridge, Mass.: Harvard University Press, 1964), ch. 1. The heart of Alonso's book is a model, far more elaborate than the one attempted here, that comprehends residential, business, and agricultural land uses within the now familiar von Thünen framework.

FIGURE 6.1(a)

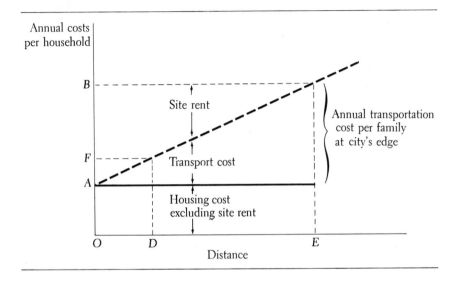

FIGURE 6.1(b)

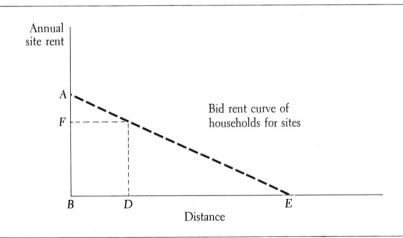

radial from that point, and will fall to zero at the periphery. Beyond the periphery land will command agricultural rent only.

In Figure 6.1(a) we place the center of the city at O and measure distance from the center along the horizontal axis to the right. The vertical axis measures costs per family unit on an annual basis. Let us assume that for a given population and lot size and with no vacancies, the area needed to accommodate all families is provided when the city extends as far out as point E on the horizontal axis.

The vertical distance OA on the cost axis represents the annual cost of housing per unit, exclusive of site rent. This cost is equal for all locations, as indicated by the horizontal line at height OA. Since jobs and all consumer services are concentrated at the center, each household must bear an annual transportation bill for trips to the center and back. The annual cost of these trips increases with the household's distance from O and is shown by the rising transportation cost curve. Transport costs per family rise from zero at the city center to a maximum of AB for households located at the city's edge.

We can now show how site rent would arise as a payment for the saving in transport cost that could be obtained by living at any particular site. Consider, for example, a site adjacent to the city center. The owner of such a parcel could ask an occupant to pay as much as AB in site rent. If all houses are occupied, a householder would be willing to pay that much site rent to locate at the center, since the alternative would be to move just beyond the present edge of the city, where site rent would be zero but it would be necessary to bear transportation costs equal to AB.

Under the usual assumptions about competition of occupants for houses and of landowners for maximum rent, the same argument can be extended to all sites: at any point within the city, occupants would be willing to pay as site rent the difference between transportation costs at that site and the higher transportation costs that would be incurred if they moved to the city's edge. Under these conditions the combined cost of housing plus transportation plus site rent is the same at all sites and equals OB in Figure 6.1(a).

In Figure 6.1(b) site rent itself is plotted against distance from the center. (We have simply inverted the site-rent triangle of Figure 6.1(a), while retaining its dimensions and labels.) Rent declines from BA at the center to zero at the edge. Thus our simple model approximates observed reality, in which land values are highest downtown and fall off with some consistency as one moves out to the metropolitan periphery.

The declining line in Figure 6.1(b) is usually described as a "bid-rent curve," since it shows the maximum site rent that households would willingly bid at each location. Since by assumption in this model no other land users compete with households for urban sites, the bid-rent curve of households becomes in fact the "rent gradient" for the city. Later, when introducing other land uses, we will show that the actual rent gradient in a city is produced from competition among uses and can be depicted by graphically combining their several bid-rent curves.

The Economic Character of Site Rent

The very simplicity of the model employed so far is a virtue, since it enables us to see clearly many of the important characteristics of rent in general and of site rent in particular. "Economic rent" is defined by economists as a payment to a factor of production in excess of its opportunity cost (for which reason it is also called an "economic surplus"). The opportunity cost of a factor in a given use is the payment it could command in its next best employment. The next best employment for urban sites is as agricultural land. Since site rent is a payment in excess of this opportunity cost for urban sites, it clearly conforms with the general definition of economic rent.

Factors of production command an economic rent only to the extent that they are "scarce," and they are scarce in the long run only to the extent that they are nonreproducible. Again urban sites illustrate the general case. While land on which to build is plentiful, land with accessibility to economic centers is scarce; it is the scarce attribute of accessibility that gives rise to site rent. In our simplified model sites can be added indefinitely by extending the edges of the city, but each incremental ring of sites has less accessibility than the adjacent ring closer to the center and commands correspondingly less rent. Accessibility to a given center cannot be reproduced, though it can be altered by changes in the technology of transportation.

Although rent is a payment in excess of opportunity cost and can therefore be described as an economic surplus, it is nevertheless a payment equal in value to the margainal product of the factor to which it accrues. Site-rent payments are therefore consistent in every respect with the marginal productivity theory of distribution and, as we will see, perform an essential function in bringing about an efficient allocation of land among competing uses. That site rent equals the marginal product of the site can easily be seen from Figure 6.1(a). Compare, for example, site D with site E. The rent at E is zero; at D rent equals FB. Suppose the site at D were vacant and a family moved there from E. At E the family would have borne transportation costs equal to AB, as compared with transportation costs of AF at D. The reduction in transportation costs brought about by the move is given by $AB - AF = FB$. This reduction is a saving in real resource costs, and this saving is precisely the marginal product of the occupied site at D. It is also precisely the competitive site rent payable at D. Hence under competitive conditions rent equals marginal product.

Limitations of the Simple Model

The model developed above yields results that are unrealistic in several respects. First of all, numerous studies have been made in recent years of actual urban site-rent gradients. Most of these have concluded that the gradients are not linear—that is, they do not have a constant slope as in Figure 6.1(b). Instead they tend to be steepest at the center and to flatten out toward the edge, a shape that is often best approximated by a negative exponential curve.[2] Such a curve has the characteristic of declining at a constant *relative* rate, instead of at the constant *absolute* rate of a linear gradient. Along a negative exponential curve, site rent would decline by the same percentage for each mile of movement away from the center. It should be added that the rate of decline of the rent gradient appears to vary widely from city to city.

Our initial site-rent model is unrealistic in a second respect. We know from casual observation that density of urban settlement is not spatially uniform, as the model requires, but instead is much greater at the center. Again, statistical studies have verified the pattern. Like the gradient of site rent, the gradient of population density in modern cities has usually been best approximated by a negative exponential curve.[3]

Finally, greater population density at the center is associated with greater density of improvements—that is, with more cubic feet of building per acre. The visible evidence of this is, of course, the higher skyline we observe at the center, not just for office buildings, but for apartment structures as well.

Figure 6.2 shows the gradient of land value per square foot on the west side of Manhattan. The curve traces values along a ray extending from the edge of the central business district at Sixty-second Street to the northern tip of the island. It displays the diminishing slope with movement away from the center that is typical of large modern cities. In the next section we show how such a gradient can be generated by our residential model if we relax some of its initial simplifying assumptions.

A MODEL THAT GENERATES SYSTEMATIC VARIATION IN DENSITY OF DEVELOPMENT

In constructing a more realistic model, we retain the assumption of a mononuclear city built on a transport surface with all commercial activity

2. See Edwin S. Mills, "The Value of Urban Land," in Harvey S. Perloff, ed., *The Quality of the Urban Environment* (Washington, D.C.: Resources for the Future, 1969). In addition to reporting his own findings (which are discussed at length later in this chapter), Mills summarizes the work of several other investigators.

3. See, for example, Colin Clark, *Population Growth and Land Use* (New York: St. Martin's Press, 1969), ch. 9; Richard Muth, *Cities and Housing* (Chicago: University of Chicago Press, 1969), ch. 7; Edwin S. Mills, "Urban Density Gradients," *Urban Studies*, February 1970, pp. 5–20; and Brian J. L. Berry and Frank E. Horton, *Geographic Perspectives on Urban Systems* (Englewood Cliffs, N.J.: Prentice-Hall, 1970), ch. 9.

FIGURE 6.2
Gradient of Land Value on the West Side of Manhattan Island, 1970[a]

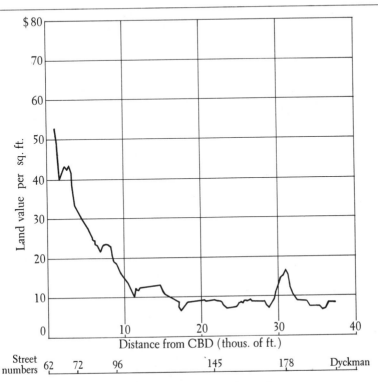

[a] Five-block moving average of land value per square foot

Source: "The Empirical Investigation of a Residential Land Value Model," unpublished doctoral dissertation by Joseph E. Earley, Fordham University, 1974.

concentrated at a point in the center. Under these conditions, the transport-cost gradient remains as in Figure 6.1(a)—a linear function, rising as distance from the center increases. We continue to assume that families are uniform in size, taste, and income and that they occupy units of standard size. However, the requirement of uniform density of housing per acre is abandoned. Instead, we allow developers to pile units up on a given lot by building vertically. It is assumed that building developers do not own the sites on which they build but lease them from site owners. Tenants, in turn, rent space in buildings from the developers. Thus the market has three tiers: site owners, building owners, tenants. This institutional arrangement is used only occasionally in the United States, but it

FIGURE 6.3

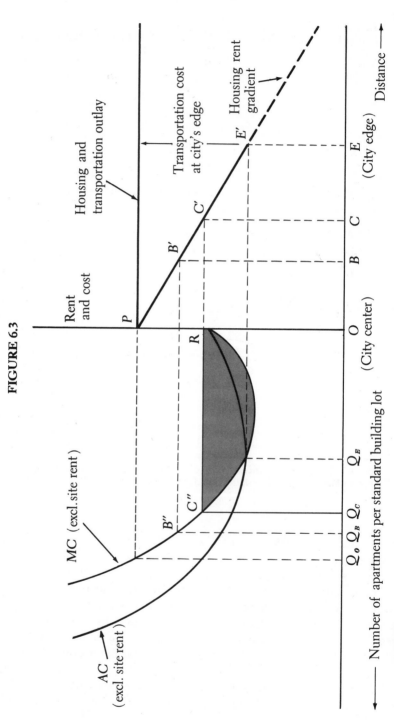

is quite common in England. It is assumed here only as a convenience, and does not affect the outcome of the analysis.

The new model is depicted in Figure 6.3. The right-hand panel shows transport costs and housing rent per family at various distances from the city center at *O*. The left-hand panel shows annualized costs to developers of building and operating standard size apartment units in multiple dwellings of varying heights.

Let us first examine the right-hand panel. Rent per apartment and transport cost per family are measured on the vertical scale between the two panels. To simplify the argument, we assume that all families arrange their budgets so as to pay a constant sum (equal for all families) for the combination of housing plus transportation. This outlay equals *OP* along the vertical scale, and the horizontal line through *P* indicates that the outlay is constant for all families regardless of location. At the center, transportation cost per family is zero, so *OP* is available as rent per apartment. Since transportation costs per family increase with mileage from the center, the sum available for rent decreases with distance and is shown by the housing-rent gradient, which declines from *P* at the center to *E'* at the city's edge. Transportation costs at any site away from the center are shown by the vertical distance between the horizontal line through *P* and the declining housing rent gradient.

The left-hand panel is a mirror image of the conventional diagram of the long-run cost curves of a business firm, in which *AC* represents average cost and *MC*, marginal cost. In this instance the curves measure annual long-run average and marginal cost, per apartment, of building and operating apartment structures of varying heights on lots of standard size. Cost includes normal profit but, unlike the conventional case, excludes site rent. The horizontal scale shows number of apartments per structure, increasing in the leftward direction. Moving leftward from the vertical axis at the center, there is an initial stage of declining average cost (i.e., *increasing* returns) as structure size increases from zero. This decline reflects the fact that construction and operating cost per square foot diminishes as floor area size increases, if other dimensions are held constant.[4] Thus a very small building on the standard lot would probably cost more per unit than a building that made maximum permissible use of the ground area. However, as more stories are added, the increasing cost of building higher eventually offsets this initial gain. Diminishing returns to the use of land set in for buildings larger than Q_E. Marginal and average costs per apartment rise, beyond a certain structure height, because the construction cost per apartment of adding additional stories

4. See John J. Costonis, *Space Adrift* (Urbana, Ill.: University of Illinois Press, 1974), pp. 95 and 101–02.

begins to rise as the building grows taller. The rise in cost has two sources: first, the need for heavier foundations and structural elements and, second, the shrinkage of rentable interior space per story as height rises, on account of required building setbacks and the need for additional space-using elevator shafts.[5]

Taken together, the two panels of Figure 6.3 show the intensity of development that will occur and the site rent that will be generated at any distance out from the center. For example, at site *C*, tenants will be willing to pay *CC'* in housing rent. We assume that builder-operators behave as perfect competitors, treating the going rent level at any distance from the center as if it were independent of their own decision to build. Builders at distance *OC* from the center will be guided by rent level *CC'* in determining how intensively to develop their sites. They will build structures to the height at which the last story adds apartments whose marginal cost just equals the rent offer *CC'*. In other words, they follow the conventional rule for the perfect competitor, which is to extend output to the point at which marginal cost just equals price. Price at site *C* is shown by the horizontal line extending left from *C'*. This intersects the marginal cost curve at *C''*. The builder at *C* therefore puts up a structure containing Q_C apartments.

What about site rent, which is not included in the cost curves depicted in Figure 6.3? The maximum annual site rent that a builder could pay at any site is the difference between total annual housing rent and total annual cost (excluding site rent) for an optimum size structure at that distance from the center. Total housing rent that could be realized in a building at site *C* containing Q_C apartments equals the product of the rent per unit times the number of units, which is shown by the area of the rectangle $OQ_CC''R$. Total cost (excluding site rent) equals the sum of all marginal costs and is shown, for site *C*, by the area under the marginal cost curve up to the quantity Q_C. Maximum site rent is the difference between these two areas, shown by the saucer-shaped shaded area on the left-hand panel. Since builders are competing to obtain scarce sites, actual site rent will in the long run tend to equal the indicated maximum.

Our example illustrates the fact that site rent arises as a residual in the pricing process. Out of the proceeds from the sale of output (in this instance, housing services) producers must pay the going market price for whatever reproducible inputs they employ, including capital. The owners of nonreproducible scarce factors, such as urban sites, can then command as the price for the use of such factors whatever residual remains when all other inputs have been paid for by producers. The size of this

5. Concerning these increasing costs see Ralph Turvey, *The Economics of Real Property* (London: Allen and Unwin, 1957), pp. 15–16; and Costonis, pp. 95–97 and 101–02.

residual depends on the price producers can obtain for their products and, therefore, on the level of demand. It is for this reason that rent is usually said to be "price determined" rather than "price determining."

We can now use Figure 6.3 to demonstrate two points. First, as we move toward the city center, say from site C to site B, the intensity of development increases. Builders at B can obtain higher rents per unit than builders at C. They therefore carry development on the site farther before reaching the point at which MC = rent: Q_B is to the left of Q_C, indicating that buildings at B are taller than those at C.

Second, it is easily seen that site rent is higher at B than at C, since the saucer-shaped site-rent area grows larger as rent per apartment rises to BB' and the number of apartments increases from Q_C to Q_B. But we can say more: the increase in site rent per mile of movement toward the center is greater for each successive mile. This means that the bid-rent curve for housing sites that could be derived from the left-hand panel of Figure 6.3 does not have the constant slope displayed by the simpler model in Figure 6.1. Rather, the increased intensity of development as we move toward the center generates increasingly large increments to site rent, so the bid-rent curve for sites grows steadily steeper as it nears the center. This result can easily be deduced from the shape of the site-rent area. Each mile of movement toward the center in the right-hand panel generates a constant increase in housing rent per apartment equal to the transportation cost saved by locating one mile nearer the center; apartment rent rises along a gradient of constant slope. But these successive, equal-per-mile increments to apartment rent, which could be measured along the vertical center scale, generate *increasing* increments to site rent, as demonstrated by the fact that the layers added to the saucer-shaped site-rent area are successively longer as they pile up in the vertical direction. These layers are longer only because intensity of development increases as we move toward the city center.[6]

Intensity of development at the city's edge equals Q_E apartments per building lot. At that location, housing rent just covers average unit cost at the lowest level at which a developer could break even. Nothing is available for site rent, which is therefore zero. Tenants need not pay

6. Edgar M. Hoover used a price line and a rising marginal cost function to derive a site-rent gradient of increasing slope for agricultural land uses in *Location Theory and the Shoe and Leather Industries* (Cambridge, Mass.: Harvard University Press, 1937), pp. 24–26. The model in fig. 6.3 applies his argument to the urban case. It is interesting to note, however, that the entire argument of this section (and the following one on competing land uses) could equally well have been derived from the work of Alfred Marshall. See his *Principles of Economics*, 8th ed. (London: Macmillan, 1930), pp. 447–50.

For a somewhat different derivation of an increasingly sloped urban site-rent gradient, see Harold Brodsky, "Residential Land and Improvement Values in a Central City," *Land Economics*, August 1970, pp. 229–47.

site rent to live in housing at the city's edge, since they have the alternative of building on adjacent vacant land for which site rent is zero. At the city's center, development reaches a density of Q_0 apartments per building lot and site rent (the saucer-shaped area above the marginal cost curve) is at a maximum.

We have shown that the model in Figure 6.3 generates a skyline that rises higher and a bid-rent curve for housing sites that grows steeper as we approach the center of the city. Since the model assumes housing to be the only land use, the bid-rent curve for housing sites is by assumption also the site-rent gradient for the city. It displays the characteristic shape found in empirical studies of land value in major cities.

THE EFFECT OF COMPETING
LAND USES ON URBAN FORM

The analysis developed above can now be modified to cope with something closer to the full complexity of land uses in a typical city. Although in principle the argument could be extended to any number of uses, let us for convenience combine city functions into three major groups and see how competition among them for sites will establish a land-use pattern and site-rent gradient for the city. The first group, which we will call "central office functions," includes such activities as corporate headquarters offices, banks and other financial institutions, and law and accounting firms, all of which are complementary in providing high level business services that require frequent daily contact between firms. The second group, which we will call "ancillary services," includes such categories as office equipment, parts and supply houses, printing shops, maintenance and repair firms, and telephone exchanges, whose function is to provide routine rather than high level services to the central office sector. The third category is housing.

We assume that each of the business sectors operates under conditions of perfect competition. We continue to posit a city on a flat transport surface so that movement is equally costly per mile in any direction. Within this city, central office functions and ancillary services, since they require frequent contact between firms, will exert a mutual attraction and will therefore locate close together rather than occupying scattered sites. It follows that the city will have a well-defined business district and that the center of this district will be the point offering greatest accessibility to other firms. The question to be answered is: How will the three kinds of land use locate in relation to this central point? The answer turns out to be that when various uses are competing for sites, the one that can pay the highest site rent at each particular location will come into possession here. Consequently the first point to investigate is: What determines the spatial pattern of demand for sites by each use?

To simplify the argument we make these additional assumptions: first, as in the housing case analyzed above, buildings are constructed and operated by developers who rent sites from landowners and in turn lease shelter space to tenants. Second, all structural types have similar cost characteristics. More specifically, all display identically increasing marginal and average cost per unit of floor space per year for building and operating structures of increasing height on lots of standard size. Thus the left-hand panel of Figure 6.4 shows cost curves resembling those of Figure 6.3. However, the horizontal scale to the left now measures quantity in square feet of floor space per structure rather than in number of apartments. As before, increased quantity (i.e., increased output per site) is obtained by building higher.

In the right-hand panel of Figure 6.3 we drew a bid-rent curve of households for apartments, showing the maximum price that would be paid at each location as a decreasing function of distance from the center. The curve represented utility-indifferent positions for individual households. In the same fashion, bid-rent curves can be drawn for floor space to be occupied by each of the other types of activity, and each of these will show the maximum rent that can be paid consistent with earning a normal competitive return. This rent will decrease with distance from the city center.

First consider central office functions. Each firm in this group is heavily dependent on daily face-to-face contact between its own executives and their counterparts in firms with which it deals. The closer each firm can come to location at the center of the business district, the less costly to it in time and transportation outlay will be the task of maintaining contact with other firms. Thus a central location will reduce the firm's own costs (other than rent). For the same reason it will reduce the cost to others of maintaining contact with that firm. Hence a central location will also increase the firm's sales volume. Thus the rent per unit of floor space that a central office firm can pay while still earning a normal return will increase with proximity to the center both because transportation and communication costs will be decreasing and because sales will be increasing as distance from the center diminishes.

Much the same argument applies to the group of ancillary services. Firms in this group are in business to supply services to the central office firms (and to one another). They, too, will find costs (except rent) decreasing and sales increasing as distance from the center diminishes. Thus the rent they can pay per unit of floor space while still earning normal returns will also rise with proximity to the center.

Would the bid-rent curve for floor space be steeper for central office

FIGURE 6.4

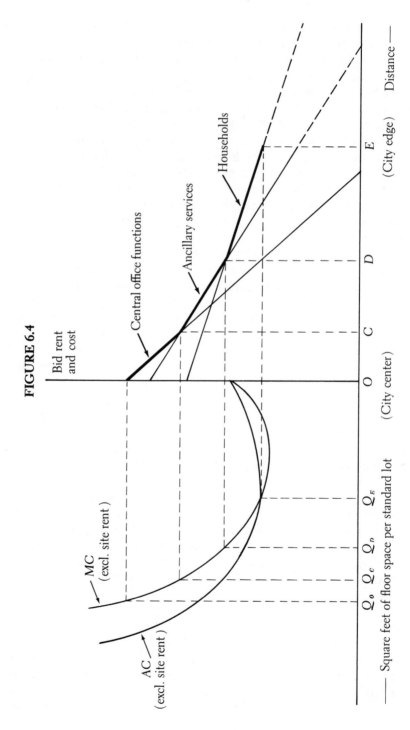

functions or for ancillary services? What determines its steepness in either case? Three factors can be distinguished. First, its steepness is greater, the greater the cost per unit of output of maintaining contact with the center. Second, its steepness is greater, the larger the number of units of output the firm produces per square foot of floor space occupied. Third, it is steeper, the less readily other inputs can be substituted for floor space in the production process as the price of floor space rises.[7]

It seems probable that central office functions would have a steeper bid-rent curve than ancillary services. First, since they are less routine and standardized than ancillary services, they are likely to require more frequent personal contact between firms. In addition, since contact by central office firms frequently involves highest echelon executives, while contact for ancillary service is more apt to be carried out by lower-salaried personnel such as salesmen, truck drivers, or repairmen, it is probable that travel time would be valued far more highly for the former group than for the latter. Second, the quantity of output per unit of floor space is likely to be larger for a central office function than for an ancillary service. Comparable units of "output" are difficult to conceive of in this instance, but the point is that central office functions are, in some sense, able to make more intensive use of space than are ancillary services.

We show the bid-rent curve for households as the least steep of the three. The household typically has less need for central location than do business firms. Whereas the firm wishes to facilitate numerous daily contacts with customers and suppliers, the household need make only one daily journey to the center for each working member. (We have not introduced shopping activity into the model.) To shorten these daily trips, households are willing to pay higher rent, as shown by a bid-rent curve that rises toward the center, but they are not willing to pay as much for centrality as do business firms. Thus the household curve lies below the inner (more central) portions of the other two.

The spatial distribution of the three land uses within the city is determined by the relationships among their bid-rent curves. At each location building owners, in order to maximize net income, rent space to the highest bidder. Hence the use with the highest bid-rent curve takes over occupancy at each point. In Figure 6.4, central office functions occupy the segment from O to C, ancillary services locate between C and D, and households occupy the segment from D to the edge of the city at E. Thus the highest portions of the three bid-rent curves (as indicated by the heavier line) become the rent gradient for the city. In this instance the gradient refers to rent per square foot of shelter space, but, as we have

7. For a more extended discussion of these factors see Hugh O. Nourse, *Regional Economics* (New York: McGraw-Hill, 1968), pp. 96–110.

argued above, a unique land-rent gradient is, under the assumed conditions, associated with it. Both gradients become steeper as they approach the center. If we rotate either one about the city center we generate a corresponding rent surface. Looking down at such a surface from above we would see that the city is circular, that central office functions occupy the center and that the other land uses are ranged thereabout in concentric rings.

Interdependence Through Competition for Sites

The arrangement of land uses produced by the model depicted in Figure 6.4 forms an interdependent system. Not only are the several activities related to one another through the usual linkages of complementarity and substitution; they are related also by their competition for sites. In a more elaborate model that comes closer to articulating the general equilibrium nature of the problem, one would link the demand for sites by each activity to the quantity of output of each that could be sold in the markets served. In such a model the values of all supply and demand variables would have to be solved for simultaneously, since the site area occupied by each activity influences its output from the supply side, while at the same time the area that can be occupied by a given activity in competition with other uses depends on the demand for its output, the supply of complementary factors, and so on. The partial equilibrium model employed here can suggest the nature of these interdependencies, although it does not incorporate them explicitly.

For example, the outcome shown in Figure 6.4 was assumed to be an equilibrium division of land uses. In arriving at that division it was assumed implicitly that the quantity of central office functions that could be produced in the circular area of radius OC was just that quantity which could fetch a price sufficient to enable central office firms to exert the demand for space represented by their depicted bid-rent curve. Analogous assumptions held for the other land uses. Now suppose that an exogenous increase in the demand for central office services occurs. The price of such services would rise, and producers would seek to increase output. Their demand for sites—which is a "derived demand" based on the demand for their output—would increase. We could represent that increase by shifting their bid-rent curve up and to the right, which would cause the point of intersection of their bid-rent curve and that of ancillary services to move rightward. The immediate result would be an increase in the area occupied by central office functions at the expense of the ancillary service area.

But the chain of effects does not end there. If the area occupied by ancillary services shrank, output would fall and prices would rise. At higher prices for output, this industry, too, could bid more for sites. Hence the bid-rent curve of the ancillary service group would also move up and to the right (and thus would have an analogous effect on household demand for sites). The final equilibrium of the system would show that the margin of the central office area had moved out, but by less than would have occurred if the bid-rent curve of ancillary services had not thereby been forced up. Likewise the margin of the latter ring would have moved out, but by less than would have occurred had the household curve remained fixed. Finally, the upward shift of the household curve would have pushed the edge of the city farther from the center. All these effects are the result of direct competition between uses in the land market. We need not here trace out the effects of additional interdependencies, such as the increased demand for ancillary services when central office functions expand or the increased population that would be attracted into the household sector by these expanding industries.

We see, then, that a change in one part of the system causes a spreading wave of effects that in some degree alters the entire land-use pattern. Just as central place theory explains how cities are held in place, so to speak, by the location of all other cities, so, too, a fully developed model of intraurban land use would have to explain how the whole array of urban activities is mutually held in place by intraurban forces of attraction and repulsion operating through competitive land markets.

One might well ask whether our manner of combining the bid-rent curves in the model depicted in Figure 6.4 is not simply arbitrary. Why, for example, do the flatter bid-rent curves necessarily lie below the steeper ones at the center? The answer is that no other arrangement provides a stable equilibrium. If we were dealing with linear bid-rent curves for shelter space (i.e., each with constant slope throughout) and the curve that was highest at the center were also flattest, then it would be higher than all other curves throughout its length, and the city would be entirely devoted to that single land use. This is true a fortiori if the bid-rent curves are concave upward. But suppose one of them were concave downward? Then it might be higher but also flatter than the others at the center. This case can be ruled out, however, since it implies that the cost per mile of transportation to the center increases with the length of the journey, whereas the general tendency in transportation is for cost per mile to remain constant or else decrease with distance covered.

If these arguments seem to lean too heavily on mere geometry, consider the economic logic that lies behind them. The slope of a bid-rent curve measures the benefit that accessibility confers on a given activity: the greater their need for accessibility in terms of reduced cost or increased sales, the more firms of a particular type are willing to pay in higher rent to move one mile closer to the center. The more they are willing to pay per mile, the steeper their bid-rent curves. The slope of the bid-rent curve of a particular activity, therefore, measures the benefit that accessibility confers on it. Industries that can benefit the most from accessibility have the steepest curves and occupy the center. Hence the model behaves efficiently in the economic sense: it allocates the scarce resource of accessibility to those who can make the most productive use of it.

The Doctrine of "Highest and Best Use"

Consistent with the foregoing argument, it is often said that a competitive real estate market allocates urban sites to their "highest and best use." Competition puts sites in the hands of the highest bidder. The highest bidder is the one who can make the most economically productive use of the site. The market operates so as to maximize rent from each site. We have already shown that site rent equals the marginal product of land. Hence the market also maximizes the contribution (i.e., marginal product) that each site adds to total output. It is in that sense that "highest" is also "best" from the viewpoint of society as a whole.

As we will see in Chapter 13, however, the process by which one use *succeeds* another on a given site is far more complicated than the above passage suggests. If a cleared site is thrown on the market it will obviously be sold to the highest bidder, who will then construct a building on it that represents the highest and best use of the site. If, however, a site has an old building on it that is still capable of rendering service, that old use may be sufficiently profitable to persist on the site even though it is not the kind of building that anyone would now construct if the site were already cleared. Frequently observed examples of this sort are the old four-story commercial buildings that stand cheek-by-jowl with skyscrapers in the CBD or the small, walk-up apartment houses scattered among tall, modern elevator structures in a residential district. These cases are not exceptions to the doctrine of highest and best use. Properly interpreted, the doctrine comprehends them. However, the matter will not be taken up in detail until we analyze the economics of land-use succession in Chapter 13.

EXTERNALITIES AND LAND-USE ZONING

A major qualification to the argument that competitive land markets operate efficiently in the assignment of sites must now be introduced. We have treated land uses as though they were independent of one another except for those connections made through market transactions. Thus we have ignored external, or neighborhood, effects. These arise when activity at one site confers benefits or imposes costs on the occupant of another

:e for which no fee can be charged or no recompense collected. For
ample, a beautiful garden in front of one house produces a free aesthetic
:nefit for neighbors and passers-by, while the noise and fumes from a
iiler factory impose unrequited damages on the occupants of nearby sites.
ich effects are especially likely to occur in densely built-up urban areas.

If the owners of the boiler factory could somehow be made to bear
; external costs, they would either contrive to reduce the output of noise
d fumes or else move to a more remote location where such emissions
iuld cause less offense. Land-use zoning arose as an attempt to meet
is problem, not by inducing occupants of sites to internalize the costs
ey impose on others, but by direct regulation of land use. Although
ime forms of land-use regulation appeared earlier, comprehensive zoning
the United States is usually dated from the adoption of a zoning
iolution by New York City in 1916.[8] Zoning was intended to minimize
hat we now call "externalities" in two ways. First, incompatible uses
:re to be kept from impinging on one another. Second, regulation was
prevent overintensive development of one site from imposing burdens
its neighbors. Incompatible uses could be kept apart by zoning certain
:as for residential development to the exclusion of all industry and
hers for residential, commercial, and light industrial uses, while con-
iing truly "noxious" activities, such as boiler factories or stockyards to
:ripheral locations. The same zoning ordinance could prevent individual
iprovements from blocking the light and air of their neighbors or im-
•sing other burdens on them by regulating the height and bulk of build-
gs or requiring open space along lot boundaries.

Land-use zoning was quickly accepted in the United States after the
ipreme Court in 1926 upheld its constitutionality in the *Euclid* case.
•ning ordinances are adopted and administered by local government,
der authority granted to them by state law. The preparation and
:riodic review of such ordinances is often one of the principal functions
a city planning commission.[9] Exceptions (known as "variances") to the
ecific requirements of an ordinance are usually provided for preexisting
:es that do not conform, and additional variances can generally be
anted by a board of standards and appeals.

In recent years, many economists have begun to question whether
•ning, as it is practiced in the United States, is either an efficient or an
iuitable way of regulating land use. Examining the issue of efficiency,

8. See John Delafons, *Land Use Controls in the United States* (Cambridge,
ass.: M.I.T. Press, 1969), pp. 16–31.
9. For a description of zoning from the viewpoint of the city planner, see
ithony J. Catanese and James C. Snyder, eds., *Introduction to Urban Planning*
Jew York: McGraw-Hill, 1979), ch. 10; and Richard F. Babcock, "Zoning," in Frank
So, et al., eds., *The Practice of Local Government Planning* (Washington, D.C.:
:ernational City Managers' Association, 1979), pp. 416–43.

Mills, for example, points out that land-use zoning purports to contr
nuisances such as noise pollution when, in fact, it merely moves the
about. While not opposing some degree of use separation through zonin
Mills argues that antipollution policies aimed directly at externaliti
would often be more effective and would render some traditional zonii
controls redundant. Appropriate policies would include greater relian
on such devices as effluent fees or other charges that encourage econoi
ically efficient marginal adjustments in the behavior of firms and inc
viduals, in place of the all-or-nothing system of toleration or prohibitic
through zoning.[10]

The all-or-nothing structure of zoning not only prevents efficiei
marginal adjustments but also contributes to the politicization of tl
zoning process. Whenever a particular use for which there is strong mark
demand has been forbidden by zoning—say the construction of apa
ment houses in a neighborhood zoned exclusively for single family hom
—a powerful incentive is created for an aggressive developer to profit l
obtaining a zoning variance that breaks the restriction. Political forc
are brought into play. Zoning then becomes a game in which the prize
the potential private gain from changing the initial rules.

The most frequently voiced objection to zoning on grounds of equit
however, is not that the zoning process itself is highly political, but rath
that it can be used by one class of citizens to the disadvantage of anothe
For example, by manipulating zoning regulations, well-to-do suburb;
towns can effectively prevent families of low or moderate income fro
moving in. This sort of "exclusionary zoning" will be examined in det;
in connection with housing policy in Chapter 13.

INTRODUCING THE EFFECTS
OF CHANGE AND GROWTH

The land-use model depicted in Figure 6.4 is wholly static. Ignorii
time and change, it shows us what the equilibrium pattern would be if
city were suddenly to be built *de novo* under given conditions. It does n
tell us how land-use patterns evolve as cities age or as the things assum(
constant in the model—especially population, income level, and techn(
ogy—change through time. It leaves out of account all the dynamic forc

10. Edwin S. Mills, "Economic Analysis of Urban Land-Use Controls" in Pe
Mieszkowski and Mahlon Straszheim, eds., *Current Issues in Urban Economics* (Ba
more: Johns Hopkins University Press, 1979), pp. 511–41. The article includes
useful bibliography. For a more extended economic analysis see David E. Ervin, et ;
Land Use Control: Evaluating Economic and Political Effects (Cambridge, Mas
Ballinger, 1977).

of urban evolution that for better or worse prevent the achievement of any final equilibrium. Because structures and—even more so—the underlying framework of streets and utilities are long lived, the pattern of land uses that exists at any actual time is never the same as the optimal pattern that could be produced by a wholly fresh start at that moment. The aging of structures and the process of land-use succession on given sites will be examined in detail in Chapter 13. At this point we wish to analyze the general, or macrolocational, effects on land use of changes in transportation cost, population, and income.

The consequences of such changes have been worked out very clearly by Alonso, and the following discussion is based largely on his work.[11] Although Alonso's study covers business and agricultural as well as residential patterns, he simplifies the formal analysis of the effect of changes in technology and the like by restricting it to the latter sector. (The results are fundamentally the same for urban business uses as well.) Alonso's model, like the highly simplified one used above, assumes a transport surface and a mononuclear city. It is far more complex, however. Among other things, it explicitly rejects the assumption of constant residential lot size. Rather, lot size is one of the variables to be solved for. What follows below is not the Alonso model itself but one of its applications.

The Effect of an Improvement in Transportation Technology

Figure 6.5 shows the bid-rent curve of households for land (or, as Alonso calls it, the price structure for residential land) in a metropolis with its business and employment center at O. The land units in terms of which price is expressed may be square feet, acres, or what have you. Initially, the price structure is given by line AB. OA equals rent at the center, and point B marks the edge of urban settlement. Now suppose that an improvement in technology takes place that reduces the time and/or money cost of transportation from the outlying areas to the center. Rent at the center is based on the saving in transportation cost obtained by locating there instead of at the city's edge. Accordingly, rent at the center will be reduced by the technological improvement, other things remaining the same. More specifically, if lot size were held constant the outer edge of settlement would remain at B and the bid-rent curve would fall to A'B. But with the price of land reduced, lot size will *not* remain constant. Alonso's model incorporates the important fact that to the householder space is a consumer good as well as an impediment to access. Other things being equal, if the price of land drops, householders will increase their consumption of it: lot size will increase. That, in turn, means that the area needed to

11. Alonso, pp. 105–16.

FIGURE 6.5

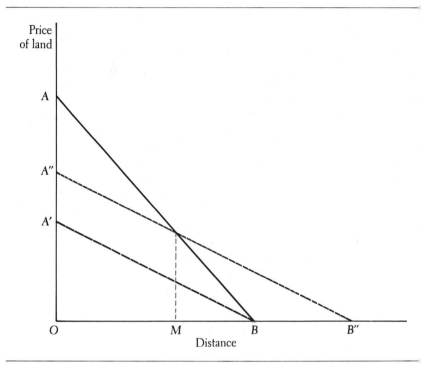

Source: Adapted from William Alonso, *Location and Land Use* (Cambridge, Mass.: Harvard University Press, 1964), fig. 32, p. 112.

house a given population will also increase. The margin of settlement will move out—say, to B". Instead of falling to A'B, the bid-rent curve will shift to a position such as A"B".

We know that A" must be above A'—in other words, that rent at the center falls less than it would have if lot size had remained constant—because when the city's edge moves from B out to B", the transportation cost saved at a central location increases, and therefore so does rent at the center. It is interesting to note that although the new bid-rent curve A"B" shows rents lower than before at the center, it also shows them to have increased beyond some point, M. Why should households beyond M be paying higher rents after the improvement in transportation than they paid before? The answer is that people living farther out than M could pay more rent than before and still be better off than they were because the technological change has allowed them to gain utility through reduction in the time and/or money cost of transportation.

The Effect of an Increase in Population

The effects of population change also are easily deduced from Alonso's model. An increase in population will increase the demand for residential sites. In order to accommodate the new households, the margin of the city will move outward. As it does so, the cost of transportation from the edge to the center will increase, and the bid-rent curve will shift upward and to the right. For example, an increase in population, while transportation technology and income remain unchanged, will cause the bid-rent curve to rise from a position such as *A'B* in Figure 6.5 to something like *A"B"*. The result will be higher land costs for all households and a tendency to reduce lot size. Hence the city's area will increase less than in proportion to the increase in population. Thus, as Alonso points out, a rise in population, other things being equal, will cause an increase in both land prices and density of settlement as well as in the physical extent of the urban area.

Figure 6.5 also enables us to compare expected land costs in cities that differ in population size. The diagram predicts that land prices, and therefore housing costs, will generally be higher in large than in small cities, and that is, indeed, the case. As we pointed out in Chapter 3, these higher costs, in turn, help to explain why the cost of living rises with city size. (See the section on "Income, Well-being and City Size.")

The Effect of an Increase in Income

We next examine the impact of changes in average household income. Alonso deals with the effect of differences in income among households rather than with the effect of a change in its average level. Once the former effect is established, however, we can easily transform the argument to describe the latter.

The facts are not in doubt. In U.S. cities wealthier families tend to settle near the periphery, while poorer households remain close to the center. Thus the gradient of income rises with distance from the center. This is crudely verified, later, in Tables 10.5 and 11.7. Within SMSA's median family income is lower in the central city than in the suburbs. (It is equally clear that the U.S. pattern is not a universal norm. In many cities of Latin America, for example, the well-to-do live near the center, while the poor occupy peripheral sites.[12])

As we shall see, there are two alternative explanations of the U.S. pattern. Both are plausible, but they have very different implications for

12. See Leo F. Schnore, "On the Spatial Structure of Cities in the Two Americas," in Philip M. Hauser and Leo F. Schnore, eds., *The Study of Urbanization* (New York: John Wiley, 1965), pp. 347–98.

housing and renewal policy in the central city. In what follows, both are examined in detail.

Alonso argues that higher income, in and of itself, can lead families to choose suburban rather than central city locations. By close theoretical reasoning he shows that wealthy families will tend to have bid-rent curves less steep than those of poor families and therefore settle on large lots of relatively cheap land toward the city's edge, while the poor tend to occupy very small portions of higher priced land near the center. The argument is complex. An important factor in it, however, is the cost of commuting. Assume to begin with that the cost of commuting increases directly with distance but does not vary with income. (We will reconsider this assumption in a moment.) On the other hand, the cost of housing per square foot declines with distance because the land component becomes cheaper with movement away from the center. Households therefore face the following choice: at locations close to the center commuting costs are low but the unit costs of land and housing are high; at locations farther out commuting costs are high, but the unit costs of land and housing are low. For the poor family, the increase in commuting costs as distance increases will diminish rapidly the small fund of income available for housing. Consequently the poor cannot bid much for locations where commuting is expensive. On the other hand, since commuting costs are invariant with income or quantity of land occupied, the rich, who desire ample housing space and are prepared to spend large sums on housing, find the barrier of commuting costs rather inconsequential and can bid higher prices than the poor for land at distant locations. In choosing such locations the rich gain more by consuming larger quantities of cheaper housing than they lose by paying additional transportation costs. (Of course, Alonso recognizes that individual tastes are not uniform. Some wealthy families with a strong aversion to commuting and a weak preference for added space will always continue to live in luxury housing near the center.)

Figure 6.6 may help the reader to visualize the outcome just described. Consistent with the above explanation and with the earlier treatment of housing and transportation outlays in Figure 6.3, it illustrates the way in which income influences household locational choices.[13] In this interpretation households regard commuting outlays as part of the cost of occupying housing. At all levels of income they are assumed to budget 20 percent of income for housing and commuting costs combined. This implies that the income elasticity of demand for housing is 1.0, since housing expenditures always rise in proportion with rising income. Each

13. Figure 6.6 is an interpretation of the income-distance effect that does not appear in Alonso.

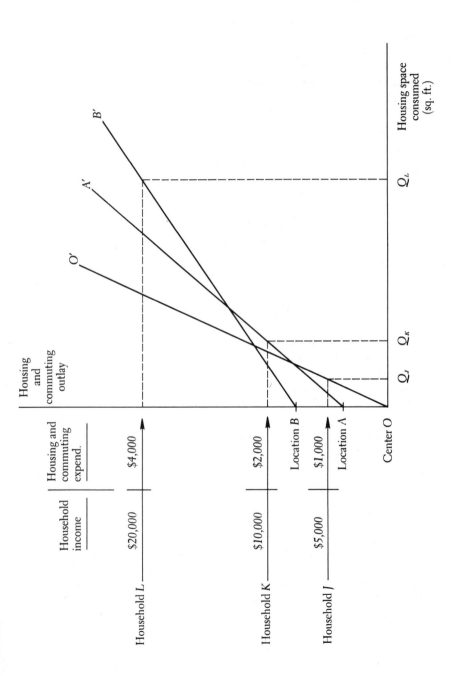

household seeks the location at which it can obtain the largest quantity of housing space for the outlay budgeted. Thus households do not have preferences among locations as such but choose solely on the basis of housing cost per unit of space.

In Figure 6.6 quantity of housing consumed per household is measured in square feet along the horizontal axis. The vertical axis measures annual dollar outlays for housing and commuting. Cost curves relating outlay to square feet consumed are shown for three locations. The commuting cost at each location is given by the intercept of the cost curve on the vertical axis. Thus annual commuting cost to the center of the city from location A is OA and the curve AA' relates housing outlay to square feet occupied at A. Likewise, OB is the cost of commuting at location B, which is farther out than A, and the slope of BB' measures the cost of housing at B. The slope of OO' indicates housing cost at the center, where commuting costs are zero. Since commuting costs are directly proportional to distance, intercepts on the vertical axis can be read to indicate relative distance of each location from the center. As indicated by the diminished slopes of successive curves, cost per unit of housing space declines as distance increases because land costs fall with distance.

Figure 6.6 illustrates locational choices for households at three income levels. The outcome for each household is read on the diagram by following that household's horizontal income line to the right and finding its intersection with the housing cost curve that lies farthest out along the quantity scale. Household J with an income of $5,000 budgets $1,000 a year for housing and commuting. At that level of spending the largest number of square feet is obtained by living at the center of the city, where commuting costs are zero. Household K, with a budget of $2,000 for housing and commuting, finds that location A offers the most space, while household L, spending $4,000 per year, settles still farther out at B. If housing cost curves for all locations within commuting range of the center were plotted, the successive portions that lie farthest to the right would generate something approaching a smooth curve from which one could read the location that would be optimal for households at every income level. Under the conditions assumed here, household choices would yield an income gradient rising continuously with distance from the center. The forces producing that result can be observed in Figure 6.6. Housing outlays double as we move up the income scale from J to K and from K to L. Likewise distance doubles from A to B. But for each doubling of income or distance, the market offers more than twice the quantity of housing space: Q_K is more than double Q_J, and Q_L more than double Q_K.

This interpretation of Alonso's argument can readily be extended to cover the effect of an increase in the average level of income as well as the effect of income differences among households. As the income of American households increases over time, they move gradually up the vertical scale of Figure 6.6. Consequently, the proportion of the population that chooses to take up suburban living increases. This means that even if population, tastes, and the technology of transportation were constant, rising living standards alone would suffice to increase the suburban population and diminish that of the inner cities. This process would also produce the trend in geographic income differentials that we do in fact observe and will discuss at length in later chapters: average family income is rising far faster in the suburbs than in the central cities.

Income and Travel Cost

The results obtained from Figure 6.6 are unambiguous because it was assumed explicitly that commuting cost is a function of distance but not of income. This was a convenient simplifying assumption that must now be given up. As already explained in Chapter 5, travel cost in general consists of two parts: first, the money cost of making a trip; second, the nonmonetary cost comprising the value of time lost and of discomfort undergone. It is reasonable to assume that the money cost is proportional to distance—that is, so many cents per mile—and that it does not vary with income. The time cost of travel, however, is a different matter. As we shall explain in Chapter 8, empirical studies indicate that individuals value travel time at some fraction of their wage rate. The perceived time cost of covering a given distance will therefore rise with income, although not necessarily in proportion to it.

In models of the Alonso type the effect of income on the locational choices of households depends upon whether the demand for space or the marginal cost of travel increases faster with income. If the income elasticity of demand for space is greater than the income elasticity of the marginal cost of travel, then the rich will tend to locate farther out than the poor. This is the case depicted in Figure 6.6, where the former elasticity is assumed to be fairly high, while the latter is assumed to be zero. If, however, the latter elasticity were to exceed the former, the burden of distance would increase faster with income than would its advantages. The income-distance pattern would then be reversed, with the rich living at the center and the poor toward the edge.

Alonso, Muth, and others, who argue that higher income per se explains the peripheral location of the well-to-do in U.S. cities, do so from a belief that in the United States the income elasticity of demand for space exceeds the income elasticity of the marginal cost of travel. This belief gains plausibility from the fact that the total cost of travel for any individual will always be less responsive to income than the time cost, because the total includes a money cost component that depends only on distance.[14]

Recent work by Wheaton, however, questions whether what he calls the Alonso-Muth spatial income effect is really an important determinant of residential location. Using data for a sample of households in the San Francisco Bay area, he estimated the effect of income on locational choice. He concluded that it was relatively weak because the estimated income elasticities of land consumption and of travel cost proved to be very similar in magnitude.[15] Further empirical work will be required, however, before this issue can be resolved.

If the income effect per se is as weak as Wheaton's findings suggest, then the suburbanization of middle and upper income families in the United States must, of course, have had other causes. Which causes, in fact, produced the present pattern is an important question, since the answer has implications for policies intended to stimulate central city revival.

An Alternative Explanation of the Spatial Income Pattern

The principal alternative to the Alonso-Muth explanation is the view that the outward movement of the middle and upper classes is the result of the growth, development, and aging of the central city over time. Based on observations in Chicago, this theory was first put forward by the sociologist Ernest W. Burgess in the 1920s and has been highly influential.[16] It holds that the wealthier classes, who originally lived in fashionable districts near the city center, moved outward for two reasons. First, the expansion of the CBD as the city grew encroached on their close-in residential zone, destroying its amenities. Second, since the close-in housing was the oldest, it was also the first to become obsolete. Because it is easier to build new on vacant land than in built-up districts, the wealthy tended to move to the periphery to construct another round of up-to-date housing. Older housing was abandoned to poorer classes, and the oldest of all (adjacent to the CBD) to the immigrants whose arrival fed the city's growth.

This theory of city form has come to be known as the "concentric

14. Muth, p. 31.
15. William C. Wheaton, "Income and Urban Residence: An Analysis of Consumer Demand for Location," *American Economic Review*, September 1977, pp. 620–31.
16. Ernest W. Burgess, "The Growth of the City," in Robert E. Park, Ernest W. Burgess, and Roderick D. McKenzie, *The City* (Chicago: University of Chicago Press, 1925).

zone theory," because Burgess described four distinct types of housing, which he believed were grouped in concentric rings around the CBD. He identified the zones and their residents as follows (moving from the center outward):

1. The Central Business District (in Chicago, "The Loop")
2. The Zone in Transition: as the CBD grows, business and light manufacturing encroach on old slums and rooming houses, making this the least desirable residential area
3. The Zone of Workingmen's Homes: inhabited by laborers who have escaped from the deterioration of Zone 2 but wish to live close to their central workplaces
4. The Residential Zone: a restricted or exclusive district consisting of high-class apartments and single family homes for the middle and upper classes
5. The Commuters' Zone: suburban areas and satellite cities, outside the city limits but within commuting distance of the CBD

Burgess's view that the spatial arrangement of urban social classes is explained by the growth and aging of the city can easily be brought up to date. European immigrants were replaced by poor ethnic minorities in the deteriorating housing at the city's core. Racial tensions in the inner city grew, and poverty brought crime and fiscal distress, further encouraging the exodus of the white middle class, which sought relief from such problems in suburban communities segregated by income class as well as by race. In Wheaton's concise summary this view holds that "the suburbanization of America's middle and upper classes is a response to housing market externalities and the fiscal incentives of municipal fragmentation."[17] (These fiscal incentives will be carefully examined in Chapter 15.)

Policy Implications of Alternative Theories

Alternative explanations of the suburbanization of the middle and upper classes clearly have different policy implications. For example, if housing obsolescence at the core is an original cause of the exodus, then policies that stimulate inner city housing renewal might stem and eventually reverse the outflow and thus encourage general central city revival. This argument was used to support federal subsidies for urban renewal projects, including the construction of new luxury housing at the center, in the 1950s and 1960s. (See Chapter 13.) The case is entirely different, however, if the preference of households for space-consuming

17. Wheaton, p. 631.

suburban living increases directly with income. In that event, the outward movement of the wealthy is simply the result of their rising living standards, and urban renewal in the older central cities will be relatively ineffective in stemming their outward migration or attracting a return flow.

Much the same reasoning applies to a diverse group of other policies that attempt to overcome structural obsolescence or race and class antagonism in the central city. These policies may be desirable for other reasons, but they are less likely to have the additional effect of attracting the middle and upper classes back to the city if the spatial income effect described by Alonso and Muth has, indeed, been a major cause of their suburbanization.

Recapitulation: The "Automobile Effect," the "Overflow Effect," and the "Income Effect"

It is worth noting that with regard to the causes of dispersion within metropolitan areas, the inferences drawn from Alonso's formal land-rent model coincide with those cited in the essentially descriptive-historical analysis of the same process we presented in Chapter 3. Referring back to Figure 6.5, assume for convenience that M marks the fixed boundary between a central city and its suburbs. Formal theoretical analysis then supports the following conclusions:

1. An improvement in transportation, other things remaining the same, allows the margin of urban settlement to move out. If total population remains constant this causes population to rise in the suburbs and fall in the central city. This is the "automobile effect" of Chapter 3.

2. An increase in total metropolitan population, other things remaining the same, also pushes the margin of settlement out. It leads, by way of reduced lot size, to greater density and therefore to a larger population in the central city as well as in the suburbs. However, since the suburbs start with a smaller population base, the percentage increase recorded there will be greater than in the central city. This is the essence of the "overflow effect" cited in Chapter 3.

3. An increase in the average standard of living, other things constant, reduces the demand for central sites and increases the demand for more distant ones. Average lot size increases, and again the margin of settlement moves out. With no change in total numbers, this means a smaller population in the central city and a larger one in the suburbs. This is the "income effect" of Chapter 3.

We see then that each of the three effects, taken separately, leads to increased suburban population, while two reduce and one—the population effect—increases central city numbers. Since early in the twentieth century all three have operated simultaneously. What were the consequences for the pattern of settlement? As we showed in Table 3.2, the growth rate of central city population was at its height in the first decade of the century. It slowed down more or less steadily thereafter and turned negative for some of the older central cities in the 1950s and 1960s. It thus appears that for a long time the strength of the population effect was sufficient to maintain some central city growth despite the strong impetus to dispersal from improved transportation and rising living standards. As metropolitan population growth slowed down, however, it was less and less able to offset the other two effects, which continued to make for dispersion throughout the 1970s. Consequently, central cities as a whole began to lose population after 1970.

The Effect of Higher Fuel Costs

Will the rising cost of energy now slow, or reverse, the long established trend of decentralization? In principle, higher fuel costs leading to increased costs of transportation would be expected to have the opposite effect to that illustrated in Figure 6.5 for an improvement in transportation technology. In a mononuclear city, site rent at the center is based on the saving in transportation cost gained by living there instead of at the edge. Accordingly, if transportation costs rise, rent at the center will increase and the rent gradient will become steeper, producing proportionate rent increases at all locations. But this will not be an equilibrium configuration. At higher land prices households will choose to consume less land. The edge of the city will move in. With density increasing, the population of the central city will rise. Assuming total population to be constant, the population of the suburbs therefore must fall. Thus in the model depicted in Figure 6.5, a rise in transportation costs, all other things remaining the same, would be expected to cause increased centralization within metropolitan areas.

However, it is necessary to add at once that reality differs significantly from the world depicted in Figure 6.5. Consequently, as we shall see in the next section, if centralization resumes as a result of higher fuel costs, it is likely to take quite a different form than would be suggested by that diagram.

TOWARD GREATER REALISM: TRANSPORTATION CORRIDORS, INTERPENETRATION OF USES, AND THE DECLINE OF MONONUCLEARITY

The model illustrated in Figure 6.5 is unrealistic in a number of respects. We have employed it because its basic implications are valid and important, but we must now recognize some real-world complications.

It must be admitted, first of all, that cities are not built on feature-less transport surfaces. Topographical irregularities abound. Differences in elevation, view, wind direction, or proximity to natural features such as lakes, beaches, or mountains have an effect on locational choice. Equally important, transportation itself is not ubiquitous but is always channeled into corridors. These corridors themselves are often distorted by topographical irregularities, and the modes of transport vary according to corridor and purpose. Since major corridors offer superior accessibility along their own length, they generally command higher rents than minor streets or roads. Corridors, in effect, become centers.

Second, land uses are not arranged by the market into mutually exclusive districts, whether of concentric rings or any other shape. Not only are types of business intermixed within the CBD, but business and residential uses interpenetrate in both the central city and the suburbs. Retailing, for example, is found in all parts of the metropolis. This, how-ever, is only the most obvious exception; other types of business, too, survive and prosper at a wide variety of locations.

Third, and most important of all, the dispersion of business activity has made metropolitan areas increasingly multinuclear. As we stressed in Chapter 3, urban evolution, driven by the force of changes in the tech-nology of transportation, has moved steadily away from the nineteenth-century pattern of business activity concentrated at the center toward a much more decentralized arrangement. It was shown in this chapter that an improvement in transportation causes the city's residential zone to spread out, its population dispersing into a pattern of lower density settlement. The results are similar for business firms. Cheaper transport allows them to both obtain from suppliers and offer to customers as much accessibility as before in terms of time and money cost at a greater dis-tance out from the center, where they can afford larger sites. Some firms, at least, will be induced by this change to move outward. The greater the possibility of substituting space for other inputs in the production process, the more likely they are to move. Thus automotive assembly plants or wholesale food distributors are more likely to disperse than are corporation law offices or advertising firms.

It should be emphasized that the business dispersion described here is not the spreading out of a discrete central business district at the heart of the city. Rather it is the dispersion of activity from that center toward the periphery; in other words, the suburbanization of industry. In the process new subcenters are created in the ring area. (To be sure, "satellite cities" already existed there.) These new centers often arise at inter-sections on the transport grid. Each exerts its own attraction for certain functions and emerges as a lesser peak on the urban rent surface.

Table 3.4 showed the extent of decentralization in twelve major

SMSA's after 1948. The analysis in Chapter 3 and the population data in Table 3.4 also made it clear that the outward movement of jobs encourages, and in turn is encouraged by, the simultaneous outward movement of population. Since jobs are moving outward simultaneously with people, it follows that the suburbanization of population does not imply an increase in commuting. (See Chapter 3, section on "Changes in Work Trip Patterns.")

If renewed centralization now takes place under the pressure of higher fuel prices and rising transportation costs, it will occur in the context of metropolitan areas that have become distinctly multinuclear. In that setting, increased centralization is more likely to take the form of increased density in and around the new subcenters of the suburban ring than to appear as a substantial movement back into the old inner city. (For a more detailed analysis, see the concluding section of Chapter 9.)

EMPIRICAL EVIDENCE OF
LAND-VALUE CHANGES OVER TIME

Empirical studies of changes in urban land-value gradients over time show that they have changed in the way our model would suggest under the impact of urban growth and decentralization. Mills estimated land-value gradients for Chicago from data gathered by Homer Hoyt for 1836, 1857, 1873, 1910, and 1928.[18] Mills' technique was to regress land value on distance from the CBD. He tested three forms of relationship at each date: linear in both variables, which fit poorly at all dates; log of land value against arithmetic distance—the equation for a gradient of the negative exponential type; and log of land value against log of distance. Since the negative exponential form fitted as well as any, we use it as the basis for this discussion.

Mills found that between 1836 and 1857 the slope of the land-value gradient increased moderately. The coefficient of determination, R^2, of the line of regression also increased, indicating that the negative exponential curve provided an increasingly good fit to the data. From 1857 to 1928, however, both the slope of the gradient and the value of R^2 gradually diminished. The flattening of the gradient is just what theory would have led us to expect as a result of successive improvements in the technology of intrametropolitan transportation. Moreover, Berry and Horton, building on Mills' analysis, have shown that the decline in the slope of Chicago's land-value gradient over that period is paralleled by a decline in

18. Mills, "The Value of Urban Land."

the slope of the population-density gradient—again, just the combination that theory would predict.[19]

Mills' analysis also shows that while the slope of the land-value gradient was diminishing, its height at the center was steadily rising, so the whole gradient at each later date lay above its position at each earlier time. This rise in the level of the gradient is precisely what the mononuclear model would predict as a result of the vast increase in population during the period.

The decline in the value of the coefficient of determination, R^2, for the fitted gradients between 1857 and 1928 suggests, as Mills himself points out, that the mononuclear model has become less valid with the passage of time. As a result of the dispersion of business activity and the growth of other centers, distance from the CBD is gradually losing its once commanding power to explain intrametropolitan variation in site value. Economists are now developing more sophisticated approaches to the problem of intrametropolitan location, primarily through the use of computerized urban simulation models. The need for these complex techniques, however, does not render the simpler mononuclear theories useless as explanatory devices. Even in more advanced models the fundamental logic of business location decisions depicted in this chapter remains essentially intact: firms locate where they expect to maximize profits and are strongly influenced in so doing by the trade-off between accessibility to customers and suppliers on the one hand and the site rent they must pay to obtain that accessibility on the other. Despite the complexities of real-world location patterns, each class of urban activity does display a characteristic, measurable locational tendency. The observed complexity, in fact, is simply evidence that for most functions there remains a sufficiently wide range of feasible locations at going rent levels to produce considerable overlapping in spatial distribution.

THE ROLE OF SITE RENT
UNDER DYNAMIC CONDITIONS

Whatever their differences in either structure or complexity, theories of intraurban location do not disagree on the crucial role of site rent as the free market's allocator of land among alternative uses. We opened this chapter with the analysis of rent as an allocator under static conditions. It is appropriate now to examine the role of rent under the impact of change and development.

19. Berry and Horton, p. 302 and fig. 9.18. Chapter 9 of their volume reviews the extensive empirical work that has been done on population-density gradients and their change over time.

Consider the situation in a city with a rapidly growing population. Land value per acre in such a city will generally be rising, just as theory suggests. The rise in value and the growth of population stem from a single source: the economic advantages that the city offers in terms of individual income and business profit as compared with other places. To the extent that a given site confers valuable access to these gains, its owner can appropriate a share of the city's net advantages in the form of urban site rent. These net advantages, as we explained in Chapter 2, consist of the difference between the economies and the *dis*economies of agglomeration. Assuming perfect competition in factor markets and full geographic mobility of all nonland factors of production, landowners as a group would, in the long run, be able to appropriate the entire value of the city's net locational advantages. This would equal the difference between the aggregate returns that the nonland factors of production can earn when used in the city (net of any payments to compensate them for bearing the diseconomies of agglomeration) and the returns they could obtain if employed at a place where urban site rent was zero. The aggregate of site rent in a city is thus one measure of the net economies of location and agglomeration that the city offers.[20]

To the individual business that must rent space, high site costs per se are, of course, a *dis*advantage. As the city grows, some firms that found it profitable to locate there when rents were low may find it unprofitable to remain as they rise and will choose to move away. But the fact that site rents are rising (by which we mean rising relative to the general level of prices) in itself is sufficient evidence that the city's net advantages to land users as a whole have increased. Were it otherwise, bidders would not be pushing site rents up. Thus, from the point of view of society as a whole, high site rents should not be regarded as one of the "diseconomies of agglomeration." On the contrary, they measure the extent of the positive economies of agglomeration and location to be found there.

In practice the spatial redistribution of activity that occurs under the pressure of rising site rents may take forms other than the movement of whole firms. Haig long ago pointed out that business firms actually comprise many distinct functions that need not all be carried on at the same place.[21] As site rents in the CBD rise, firms often separate out those functions that do not require centrality—manufacturing, warehousing, and

20. For an empirical study of the relation between aggregate land value (assumed to measure net economies of agglomeration) and city population size, see Matthew Edel, "Land Values and the Costs of Urban Congestion: Measurement and Distribution," *Social Science Information*, vol. 10, no. 6, pp. 7–36.

21. R. M. Haig, "The Assignment of Activities to Areas in Urban Regions," *Quarterly Journal of Economics*, May 1926, pp. 402–34.

record-keeping, for example—and move them to less costly areas on the periphery or even to points outside the metropolis. In the end perhaps only the head office will remain in the CBD. A prominent recent example of this has been the tendency of book publishers, who are still heavily concentrated in New York, to move their distribution, storage, and billing operations to localities on the outskirts of the metropolitan area, where rent is lower, while retaining head office, editorial, and sales functions in New York City.

TRANSPORTATION PLANNING AND LAND USE

The argument of this chapter has focused exclusively on the way the private land market determines patterns of urban land use. No mention has been made of public planning or intervention, apart from zoning. This was deliberate but also unrealistic, for the land-use pattern in any city results from a combination of private and public decisions. In choosing where to locate, households and firms (the private sector) have to trade off the value of greater accessibility against the cost of obtaining it. In the real world, however, as opposed to the world of the "transport surface" assumed at the beginning of this chapter, the accessibility of any point is determined not only by its distance from the city center but also by its relationship to an existing transport network, and transport networks, including streets, highways, and the mass transit system (if any), are planned and paid for by the public sector. The actual urban land-use pattern thus results from interaction between the private sector, in which individual location decisions are made, and the public sector, which plans and develops a transport network that inevitably influences subsequent private decisions. In this chapter we have dealt only with the private side. In Chapters 8 and 9, which deal specifically with the economics of transportation, we will tell the other half of the story when we examine the impact of public policy on transportation and, through transportation, on urban form.

The Urban Economic Base and Economic Policy

SEVEN

The economics of location have dominated the first six chapters of this book. We have examined, both historically and theoretically, the forces that draw industry and population together to form cities and metropolitan areas and, within those places, distribute them into orderly patterns of settlement. We have examined linkages among industries and between industries and population in a spatial context, emphasizing the way the technology of transportation and communications establishes physical connections between activities and determines the distance at which they can best locate with respect to one another. This chapter brings a change of perspective. We will look at the urban community as a functioning economic unit, examining the employment- and income-creating relationships between activities instead of their spatial relationships, which can now be taken for granted.

The employment- and income-generating activities of the city have often been called "the urban economic base." We now wish to examine the structure and behavior of that base and to see especially how its internal characteristics interact with external forces to determine the level, stability, and growth of local income and output. When those relationships have been made clear, we will move on to the problem of local economic policy, explaining the methods by which local authorities try to influence the level of income and output and examining the implications of these methods for both local and national welfare.

It is well to start with the distinctions between internal structure and external relationships. At any moment in time the city possesses a stock of useful resources in the form of labor skills, land, capital, enterpreneurship. These are the available factors of production. When they are fully and efficiently employed, the city is producing as much as it can. These factors of production and the relationships among them make up the internal economic structure.

It is obvious, however, that a city is very much an "open economy." It does not produce everything it consumes; nor does it consume everything it produces. Even if a great city could turn out all the manufactured goods its residents wanted, it could never be the source of all the necessary food and raw materials. These goods, at least, must be imported, and to pay for them the city must send exports to the rest of the world. Trade is not merely incidental to the city's life; it is absolutely indispensable. Thus, even if there were no migration of the factors of production between areas, trade would suffice to open up the city to the influence of exogenous forces—that is to say, forces arising outside its boundaries.

All the methods that have been devised to analyze the urban economic base recognize the fundamental openness of the urban economy and therefore stress the importance of its relationships with the outside world. They differ, however, in the extent to which they simplify the complex reality of the city's internal structure and therefore of its external relationships. The three principal methods that have been used, in ascending order of complexity, are the basic-nonbasic approach, the foreign-trade multiplier method, and input-output analysis. They will be taken up in that order. The purpose of so doing is not so much to elucidate the methods themselves—although that is important—as to provide an understanding of how the urban economy functions, and the simplifications these methods impose on reality, both when they are tenable and when they are not, are the best means we have to that understanding. Indeed, the weaknesses of these theories are often as instructive as their strengths, and we will show that despite some very important differences they share a common logical structure and therefore common weaknesses and limitations.

THE BASIC-NONBASIC THEORY

The basic-nonbasic theory derives its odd name from the causal significance it attaches to exports as compared with other local activity. (Strictly speaking, it is a "theory" rather than a "method" precisely because it does postulate a particular causal relationship between the variables it deals with.) According to this theory, a city's export industries are its economic foundation, its source of growth, and therefore rightly called "basic." Other industries are said to live by servicing these basic industries (and one another) and are therefore called "nonbasic." If there is a

TABLE 7.1
Employment Forecast for a Hypothetical City

	ACTUAL EMPLOYMENT 1980	PREDICTED EMPLOYMENT 1990
Basic emplyoment (exports)	20,000	30,000
Nonbasic employment (service)	40,000	60,000
Total employment	60,000	90,000
Ratio of nonbasic to basic	2	2
Ratio of total to basic ("the multiplier")	3	3

change in the level of employment, or of activity measured in some other way, in the basic (i.e., export) sector, it will lead automatically to a change in the same direction in the nonbasic (i.e., service) sector. The theory holds that the ratio of nonbasic to basic employment (or activity) can be measured and is sufficiently stable so that future changes in total employment can be derived from forecasts of basic employment. And from future total employment it is but one step further to a prediction of future population.

The basic-nonbasic theory was first worked out in full by Homer Hoyt in the 1930s.[1] As an economist with the Federal Housing Administration in Washington, he needed a simple model of urban economic performance in order to assess the economic prospects of a multitude of cities. Thus from the very beginning simplicity has been an intended feature of the basic-nonbasic theory. And despite subsequent refinements, when the theory is compared with other methods, simplicity remains its leading virtue today.

Table 7.1 illustrates an application of the theory using hypothetical data. Suppose that in 1980 total employment in a certain city was 60,000, of which 20,000 was basic employment and 40,000 was nonbasic. The ratio

1. For an account of the origin of the basic-nonbasic theory, see Richard B. Andrews, "Mechanics of the Urban Economic Base: Historical Development of the Base Concept," reprinted in R. W. Pfouts, ed., *The Techniques of Urban Economic Analysis* (West Trenton, N.J.: Chandler-Davis Publishing, 1960), pp. 5–17. Andrews points out reference to an export-versus-service dichotomy in the pathbreaking *Regional Survey of New York and Its Environs*, I (1928), directed by Robert M. Haig for the Regional Plan Association.

Subsequently, Max R. Bloom came upon an anonymous article in *The Monthly Magazine*, an English journal dated February 1, 1811, that now stands as the earliest statement of the basic-nonbasic relationship. See "Economic Base and City Size: an 1811 Commentary on London," reprinted in L. S. Bourne and J. W. Simmons, eds., *Systems of Cities* (New York: Oxford University Press, 1978), pp. 441–44.

of total to basic employment was therefore 3:1 in 1980. The analyst is asked to predict total employment in 1990. The basic-nonbasic theory (at least in its simplest form) holds that the total-to-basic ratio will remain constant over time. Therefore if the analyst can predict employment in the basic sector the problem is solved. Total employment in 1990 will simply be three times basic employment. In the hypothetical case the analyst predicts that basic employment will rise to 30,000. It follows that nonbasic will increase to 60,000 and total to 90,000. As this example makes clear, the total-to-basic ratio is, in effect, an employment "multiplier." The change in basic employment times the multiplier yields the change in total employment.

The multiplier in the table is stated in terms of an average relationship, and the example shows that this average relationship is expected to be maintained over time. As a city grows, however, the ratio of total to basic employment typically increases (for reasons we will explain below). If this is the case, then the ratio of total to basic employment for changes at the margin must be greater than the average ratio. When there is reason to believe that the marginal ratio differs from the average, the analyst will prefer to use the marginal multiplier, which equals the ratio of change in total employment to change in basic employment. Stated that way, the relationship takes on a strong resemblance to some forms of the Keynesian multiplier. Later, when describing the foreign-trade multiplier method, we will show that the Keynesian and the basic-nonbasic multipliers are, in fact, formally equivalent. It is interesting to note, however, that the latter was developed quite independently of the Keynesian analysis.

The operational simplicity of the basic-nonbasic method derives from several factors. First of all, instead of having to predict changes in each industry, the analyst need be concerned only with the export trades. In any city these are a minor fraction of the whole. In addition, they often have the added virtue of being characterized by large firms. The time and effort needed to make predictions are thus minimized. Second, the method makes use of the most easily available local data, those on employment. True, the basic-nonbasic theory could be stated instead in terms of total payrolls or value added. Indeed, value added might be theoretically the soundest unit of account. But employment is an acceptable proxy for value added, and the data are easier to come by.

Lack of data on economic activity in cities is an acute problem and frequently dictates the form that a study of the urban economic base must take. In particular, although measurement of the relationship between the local economy and the nation as a whole is important in any such study, no data are regularly collected by any statistical agency on the flow of goods or capital funds into or out of even the largest cities. Unless the analyst can pay the cost of a sample survey to measure the size of such flows, it will be necessary to fall back on some form of approximation. Here again, the basic-nonbasic method has the advantage of simplicity. It requires information only about the volume of local and export activity. Imports and capital flows are ignored. In the absence of direct data, the technique of approximation most frequently used to estimate export activity is the location quotient method.

Location Quotients As Export Allocators

The "location quotient" is a statistical device that measures, usually in terms of employment, the degree to which a given industry is concentrated in a given place. Quite apart from its role in estimating the level of exports, it is an extremely useful descriptive measure in urban studies. It is defined as the percentage of local employment accounted for by a given industry divided by the percentage of national employment in that industry. Suppose that in our hypothetical city shoe production makes up 2.5 percent of all employment, while in the United States as a whole it accounts for 2.0 percent. Then the location quotient for shoe production in the hypothetical city is .025 ÷ .020 = 1.25. When the value of the quotient is exactly unity the industry in question is present at the given place just to the same extent as in the whole nation. When it is above unity the industry is relatively concentrated at that place; when below unity, relatively scarce.

Now let us see how this device can be used to estimate the level of export activity. It will be convenient to use the following terms:

e_i = local employment in the ith industry

e = total local employment

E_i = national employment in the ith industry

E = total national employment

Then the location quotient for the ith industry is

$$\frac{e_i/e}{E_i/E}$$

To use this coefficient as the basis for estimating export activity, we must make the three following assumptions: (1) patterns of consumption do not vary geographically; (2) labor productivity does not vary geographically; (3) each industry produces a single, perfectly homogeneous good. Suppose that we are dealing once again with the shoe industry in our hypothetical city. Given the assumed uniformity of consumption patterns, local residents will wish to buy the same quantity of shoes per capita as does the nation as a whole. Barring international trade, the nation as a whole obtains the desired quantity of shoes when E_i/E percent of the national labor force is devoted to shoe production. Given the assumption of uniform labor productivity, it follows that the local demand for shoes can be satisfied from local production when $e_i/e = E_i/E$, which occurs when the location quotient for shoe production equals one. In short, when the location quotient for a particular industry is unity, local consumption can just be satisfied by local production. There will be neither exports nor imports. It follows that when the quotient exceeds unity, the city will be exporting, and when it falls short of unity, importing. The amount of employment in each industry that can be assumed to serve the export sector is precisely the amount that, so to speak, pushes the location quotient above one. This may be written algebraically as follows: let

$$X_i = \text{export employment in the } i\text{th industry}$$

Using terms previously defined,

$\dfrac{E_i}{E} =$ the percentage of local employment that would have to be devoted to production of the ith good to supply local demand

$\dfrac{e_i}{e} =$ the actual percentage of local employment devoted to such production

Then

$$X_i = \left(\frac{e_i}{e} - \frac{E_i}{E}\right) \cdot e$$

If the two terms inside the brackets are equal, the location quotient equals one, and export employment in the ith industry is zero.

In the hypothetical city described earlier, total local employment in 1980 was 60,000. For shoe production we gave the following: $e_i/e = .025$, $E_i/E = .020$. In that case we can calculate export employment in the shoe industry as follows:

$$X_i = (.025 - .020) \cdot 60,000 = 300$$

If we make a similar calculation for every local industry for which the location quotient exceeds one and sum the results, we obtain an estimate of total basic employment in the city. All other employment can then be classified as nonbasic. Thus the location quotient method allows us to estimate the size of the basic (or export) sector even though we have no direct observations of goods flows.

Unfortunately, such an estimate is open to question because the three assumptions on which the analysis rests are in varying degrees doubtful. The assumption of geographically uniform consumption patterns is not strictly valid. Climate in particular causes variation in the consumption of such things as clothing and heating fuels and equipment. Nor is the assumption of uniform productivity entirely accurate. These are minor shortcomings, however. The real difficulty lies in the third assumption: that each industry, taken over the whole nation, produces a single homogeneous good. Unless this is true, there is simply no warrant for assuming that when the location quotient equals one, local production will be entirely absorbed by local consumption, leaving nothing for export.

Suppose, for example, that the location quotient for book publishing in Boston were equal to unity. The analysis requires us then to believe that the literary public in Boston reads only books published there and that no books published there are read in other places. The assumption of homogeneous goods is, in most cases, obviously wrong. What we call an "industry," even at the finest level of classification in the U.S. Office of Management and Budget's Standard Industrial Classification system, contains a multitude of firms that more often than not make differentiated products. Consequently there is a great deal of geographic cross-hauling of goods within given "industries." Boston's books are read in San Francisco and San Francisco's in Boston. Since this effect is systematically present in our economy, estimates of the amount of basic (or export) employment arrived at by the location quotient method are systematically biased downward. That means, in turn, that the multiplier, which equals total employment divided by basic employment, is biased upward.

TABLE 7.2
Estimates of Export Percentages Based on Surveys
and on Location Quotients, 1955–56

	DECATUR		INDIANAPOLIS	
MANUFACTURING INDUSTRIES	*Survey*	*Location Quotient*	*Survey*	*Location Quotient*
Food	87%	71%	63%	24%
Chemicals	98	44	100	50
Printing	—	—	51	24
Primary metals	97	20	99	0
Fabricated metals	—	—	98	11
Nonelectrical machinery	97	74	98	38
Electrical machinery	—	—	100	67
Transportation equipment	100	45	100	68

Source: Charles M. Tiebout, *The Community Economic Base Study* (New York: Committee for Economic Development, December 1962), Supplementary Paper 16, table 10, p. 49.

A questionnaire survey is probably the most accurate method of estimating exports. Charles M. Tiebout, who wrote extensively on economic base studies, compared export percentages estimated by survey techniques with those arrived at by the location quotient method.[2] His figures for Indianapolis and Decatur are reproduced in Table 7.2. Clearly, the downward bias imparted by the location quotient method is not trivial.

Measuring Indirect Exports

Tiebout concluded that despite its shortcomings the location quotient method should not be rejected out of hand, since it does cope, even if imperfectly, with the tricky question of indirect exports. This problem deserves careful attention. Suppose that in order to measure the export sector of a city the analyst surveyed all local firms to find out how many workers they employed and what percentage of their sales were made to purchasers outside the city. It would then be possible to divide each firm's labor force between export and local employment by using the export percentage revealed in the survey. Summing for all industries would yield a figure for total export employment. But this would be a measure of "direct exports" only. In leaving out "indirect exports," it would understate the true size of the local export sector.

Indirect exports occur whenever one local firm sells to another that in turn ships its products outside the city. Any local firm that supplies a local exporter is thus producing indirect exports. Its dependence on the export market is just as real as that of the direct exporter and must be appropriately taken into account. Does the location quotient method do so? To some extent, yes. For example, if the shoe manufacturing industry has a high location quotient in a given city, then activities that specialize in direct service to the shoe industry are likely to have high location quotients, too, and will therefore also appear as exporters. As we will see, however, this is not the best way of taking the indirect effects of exports into account. Only the input-output method comes close to representing the true interrelatedness of industries in the local economy. We will take up that method after examining foreign-trade multiplier analysis.

THE FOREIGN-TRADE MULTIPLIER APPROACH

The fundamental relationship posited by the basic-nonbasic theory is the dependence of total local employment on the level of employment

2. Charles M. Tiebout, *The Community Economic Base Study* (New York: Committee for Economic Development, December 1962), Supplementary Paper 16. Data originally supplied by the Federal Reserve Bank of Chicago.

 the export sector. The foreign-trade multiplier method, which developed
ut of Keynesian income-determination theory during the 1930s and
940s, allows us to examine the same relationship at a much higher level
f sophistication. This method has not been used widely in empirical
 udies of urban areas because it requires data on local income and the
ow of trade into and out of local areas that are not ordinarily available.
 merits attention, nonetheless, for the insights it provides into the be-
avior of the urban economy. The following version is necessarily highly
 breviated.

In the Keynesian system the aggregate income generated in an econ-
my during a given period is shown to be equal to the aggregate of spend-
 g on final goods during that period. In a "closed economy"—that is, an
 onomy with no foreign trade—spending on final goods comprises private
 nsumption, private investment, and government spending on goods and
 rvices. This closed economy model is the one ordinarily dealt with in
 tail in a first course in principles of economics. Foreign trade can be
 troduced into it quite easily, however, to cover the case of an "open
 onomy." The model including foreign trade was, of course, originally
 eveloped to deal with national economies, but since urban areas are also
 gaged in trade with places outside their own boundaries it applies with
 qual logic to them.

Exports, since they represent foreign spending to buy domestic final
 ods, make up a part of the aggregate spending on those goods just as
 o domestic consumption, investment, and government spending. By the
 me token, however, imports, which represent domestic consumption or
 vestment that pays for foreign goods, are a subtraction from the demand
 r domestic output. Introducing foreign trade into the model, therefore,
 quires adding exports to and subtracting imports from the aggregate
f spending that creates domestic income.

To simplify matters, let us make the following assumptions:

1. We are dealing with an urban economy in which there is no public
   sector. Therefore, all spending is either for private consumption
   or private investment.

2. All business income is paid out to individuals (i.e., there are no
   retained corporate profits). Therefore net national product and
   personal income are identical.

3. Imports are entirely for consumption, never for investment.

4. The level of investment spending is determined autonomously
   (i.e., is not dependent on the level of local income). For the purposes of this analysis it will be assumed constant.

The usual symbols for the components of aggregate spending are the following:

Y = net national product generated in the local area (by assumption equal to personal income)

C = spending on local consumption goods (including imports)

I = net spending on local investment (above depreciation allowances)

E = exports

M = imports (assumed to be only for consumption)

The relationship between income and spending is then expressed by the following identity (it is written as an identity because it is necessarily true by definition of its components):

$$Y \equiv C + I + E - M$$

While consumption is one of the components of aggregate spending that generate income, its level is also determined by the level of income generated. The dependence of consumption on income can be expressed by the following equation (or "consumption function"):

$$C = a + mpcY$$

where a is a positive constant and mpc is the marginal propensity to consume. The marginal propensity to consume expresses the relationship between increments of income received by consumers in the aggregate and the amount by which they increase consumption out of that increment. Empirical studies demonstrate that its value is positive but less than one—i.e., some income is saved. The above equation is written on the assumption that its value is also constant as income changes.

Imports are entirely for consumption, of which they form a part. We will assume that, like consumption, they are dependent on the level of income, that the marginal propensity to import (mpm) is positive but less than one and constant as income changes.

Personal income is either spent on consumption or saved. Since consumption varies with the level of income, it follows that saving must do so as well. In fact, the marginal propensity to save (mps) equals one minus the marginal propensity to consume.

Since imports are entirely for consumption, we can obtain the level of spending for locally produced consumption goods by subtracting imports from total consumption. The same relationship holds for incremental changes: the marginal propensity to consume local goods ($mpcl$) equals the marginal propensity to consume minus the marginal propensity to import.

We can write the marginal relationships in the system as follows:

$$\text{marginal propensity to consume} = mpc = \frac{\Delta C}{\Delta Y}$$

$$\text{marginal propensity to import} = mpm = \frac{\Delta M}{\Delta Y}$$

$$\text{marginal propensity to save} = mps = 1 - mpc$$

$$\text{marginal propensity to consume local goods} = mpcl = mpc - mpm$$

Using the fundamental income identity and the terms defined above we can now derive an equation for the "foreign-trade multiplier." This multiplier shows how much local income will change for a given change in the level of exports. If we use the symbol K for the multiplier, then we may define it as

$$K = \frac{\Delta Y}{\Delta E}$$

The fundamental income identity tells us that $Y \equiv C + I + E - M$. It follows that any change in Y must equal the sum of changes in the terms on the right side of the identity. Thus we can write

$$\Delta Y \equiv \Delta C + \Delta I + \Delta E - \Delta M$$

However,

$$\Delta C = mpc \, \Delta Y \quad \text{and} \quad \Delta M = mpm \, \Delta Y$$

Substituting these expressions into the preceding equation and rearranging the order of the terms, we obtain

$$\Delta Y = mpc \, \Delta Y - mpm \, \Delta Y + \Delta I + \Delta E$$

This can be rewritten as

$$\Delta Y = \Delta Y \, (mpc - mpm) + \Delta I + \Delta E$$

Transposing the first term on the right to the left side, we obtain

$$\Delta Y - \Delta Y \, (mpc - mpm) = \Delta I + \Delta E$$

After factoring, this becomes

$$\Delta Y[1 - (mpc - mpm)] = \Delta I + \Delta E$$

Whence

$$\Delta Y = \frac{1}{1 - (mpc - mpm)}(\Delta I + \Delta E)$$

Assuming $\Delta I = 0$ and recalling that $K = \dfrac{\Delta Y}{\Delta E}$ we find

$$K = \frac{1}{1 - (mpc - mpm)}$$

This can be stated in many equivalent forms. For example, since $mpc - mpm$ has been defined as the marginal propensity to consume local goods, or $mpcl$, we can also write

$$K = \frac{1}{1 - mpcl}$$

Thus any change in local exports, ΔE, will lead to a change in local income, ΔY, that is K times as great, where the value of K is given by either of the above expressions. Strictly speaking, this version of the multiplier is only a first approximation, a sort of partial equilibrium statement that ignores interregional feedback effects. A version that sought to capture all the effects of a change in one area's exports would take into account the following sequence for two regions trading with each other: a rise in region A's exports to region B leads to an increase in A's income and hence in its imports from B. These imports are region B's exports and induce a rise in region B's income, which leads to a further rise in B's imports, which are A's exports, and so on in diminishing series. If, however, we are analyzing an urban area that is relatively small in relation to the national economy with which it trades, these repercussions may safely be ignored.

As the derivation above illustrates, the same multiplier effect occurs if the level of investment spending rather than the level of exports changes, or if both change simultaneously. Indeed, for any autonomous change in spending, including government spending on goods and services (which would be included in a more complete model), or a shift in the consumption function, the same multiplier operates.

Some of the characteristics of the multiplier can be read directly from its formula. We know that its value must be positive and greater than one from the following argument: If there is any local service sector at all, the marginal propensity to consume local goods will almost certainly be greater than zero. If there is any foreign trade at all, it will almost certainly be less than one. Consequently the denominator of the multiplier must also be positive but less than one. The multiplier itself must therefore have a value that is positive and greater than one. Moreover, this value will be greater, the larger is the marginal propensity to consume and the smaller is the marginal propensity to import.

The Similarity of the Keynesian and Basic-Nonbasic Multipliers

The resemblance between the Keynesian multiplier and the basic-nonbasic multiplier, mentioned earlier, goes beyond the fact that both relate increases or decreases in total local employment to increases or decreases in export employment. In addition, there is a strong formal similarity between the two formulas. The marginal form of the basic-nonbasic multiplier has already been given (in units of employment) as:

$$K = \Delta \text{ total}/\Delta \text{ basic}$$

Since

$$\Delta \text{ basic} = \Delta \text{ total} - \Delta \text{ nonbasic}$$

we can also write the multiplier as

$$K = \Delta \text{ total}/(\Delta \text{ total} - \Delta \text{ nonbasic})$$

which can readily be transformed into

$$K = \cfrac{1}{1 - \cfrac{\Delta \text{ nonbasic}}{\Delta \text{ total}}}$$

The basic-nonbasic theory is usually stated in terms of employment units. However, as we noted, this is done largely for statistical convenience since employment data are the most readily available. The theory could equally well be posed in terms of factor income arising in each of the sectors, with sector employment regarded simply as an acceptable proxy for that measure in applying the theory. If the multiplier were stated in terms of income arising in each sector it would read:

$$K = \cfrac{1}{1 - \cfrac{\text{nonbasic sector income}}{\text{total income}}}$$

Now compare that formulation with the Keynesian multiplier, where

$$K = \cfrac{1}{1 - mpcl}$$

The term *mpcl* in the Keynesian version is the marginal propensity to consume locally produced goods. The term "Δ nonbasic sector income ÷ Δ total income" in the basic-nonbasic multiplier is analogous to that. Nonbasic sector income is income arising from sales within the local community. Although imports are sold locally, their consumption, as Nourse points out, does not give rise to local employment or income.[3] Any change in nonbasic sector income that occurs must therefore be the result of the consumption of locally produced goods. When such a change is divided by the change in total income that causes it we have a ratio that is equivalent to the marginal propensity to consume locally produced goods in the Keynesian multiplier. Hence the two multipliers are essentially the same

The analogy, should not be pressed too far, however. The basic-nonbasic theory makes no distinction between employment to produce consumption goods and employment to produce investment goods. Ordinarily the nonbasic sector will include some investment activity—for example, via employment in the local construction industry, which builds investment goods such as houses and factories for local use. It may be convenient to assume that the investment component of nonbasic activity responds to changes in the export sector via precisely the same multiplier that determines the level of other nonbasic activity. The assumption is tenuous, however, since local investment is often influenced not only by the level of local exports but by other forces, both internal and external, that are not specified in the model. It is precisely in this regard that the Keynesian multiplier analysis is conceptually superior to the basic-nonbasic: it introduces investment as an explicit category of spending and allows the relationship of investment to income and to other variables in the system to be handled in a variety of ways. We will not trace out these variations, however, because, despite its conceptual superiority, the Keynesian analysis has rarely been applied to urban areas. As we have already pointed out, the necessary data are simply too difficult to obtain at the local level.

A CRITIQUE OF THE BASIC-NONBASIC METHOD

Because its data requirements were so much easier to meet than those of the foreign-trade multiplier model, the basic-nonbasic method was frequently used for empirical studies in the 1940s and 1950s. Unfortunately, the method suffers from so many serious defects, both in theory and practice, that few economists today would endorse its use. It will suffice here to mention just a few of these difficulties.

Excessive Aggregation

First of all, the model loses a great deal in being so highly aggregated. The division of activity into only two classes is too gross to capture the complex interindustry relations of an urban economy. This is not merely

3. Hugh O. Nourse, *Regional Economics* (New York: McGraw-Hill, 1968), p. 161.

matter of theoretical nicety. It also reduces the accuracy with which the
odel does its job of prediction. The basic-nonbasic multiplier represents
ie average response of the whole nonbasic sector to a change in the level
all exports. If only one industry's exports were to increase there is no
ason to assume that nonbasic activity would respond in this average
ay. For example, an export industry that relies heavily on imported com-
inents and materials will certainly transmit weaker impulses to the
inbasic sector than will an export industry that buys heavily from local
ppliers. Hence predictions made by the model about the level of total
tivity are likely to be wrong unless all exports are expected to change
nultaneously by the same percentage.

This problem can be looked at in another way. One of the purposes
economic base analysis is to predict the impact on the local economy
expected changes in the export sector. For example, a city with a large
fense plant wants to know what will happen if a policy of disarmament
ises that plant down. Not only will the basic-nonbasic model probably
edict the wrong overall impact for the reasons just given, but also it will
: unable to say which parts of the nonbasic sector will suffer more and
hich less. Such details would be far more useful than a simple statement
iout the average impact, even if it were correct. As we will see, the diffi-
lties that result from excessive aggregation can be overcome by using
e more complex input-output method.

The Instability of the Multiplier in the Short Run

A second series of difficulties centers around the time dimensions
the basic-nonbasic model. The analysis may be thought of as dealing
her with the short run or the long run. A typical short-run problem
iuld be a defense-industry impact study of the sort just described or a
ediction of the consequences for the local community of an expected
ing in the national business cycle. The method assumes that impulses
im the export sector have a multiplied effect on the local economy as a
iole, that the size of the multiplier can be calculated, and that its value
ll be sufficiently stable over the short run to warrant using it to predict
e extent of the local economy's response to exogenous change. Un-
ippily the multiplier has not proven to be stable in the short run and is
nsequently unreliable as a tool for short-run prediction.[4]

The instability of the multiplier in the short run can probably be
cribed to lagged adjustment. Let us grant that for a city with a given

4. See evidence cited in Walter Isard, *Methods of Regional Analysis* (New
irk: John Wiley & Sons and the Technology Press of Massachusetts Institute of
chnology, 1960), p. 201. The book offers a detailed analysis of the basic-nonbasic
thod at pp. 189–205.

population, economic structure, and location, at a given time in econom
history, there is a "true" or equilibrium ratio of service to basic activit
If the level of basic activity changes, the response of service activity w
not occur instantly and may well be drawn out over many years. Indee
if its export sales are continually in flux, a city may be always moving t
ward its "true" ratio without ever reaching it. Under these circumstanc
the difficulty of determining the "true" ratio or of deciding what oth
ratio to use and how to allow for time lags in making short-run forecas
is obviously enormous. Given the other weakness of the basic-nonbas
method this sort of refinement has not seemed worth undertaking.

Changes in the Multiplier over the Long Run

Even if the basic-nonbasic analysis is ineffective for short-run pi
diction, might it still be reliable for long-run forecasts? Here the objecti
would be to predict the long-run growth of employment and populatic
in a metropolitan area on the basis of the long-run prospects for its expor
Will the method perhaps work better in the long run when fluctuatio
in the multiplier can somehow be averaged out to determine its true val
and the usual adjustment lags will no longer matter? The answer is clea
"no," for in the long run all the variables of taste, technology, populatic
size, and economic structure that must be held constant in order even
conceive of a "true" or equilibrium ratio are free to vary. If there is a tr
ratio it will almost certainly change as time passes. Once again, the effo
that would be required to overcome the difficulty—for example, by es
mating long-run changes in the multiplier for a particular city—is simp
not justified, given the other limitations of the basic-nonbasic method.
One source of long-run change in the ratio of basic to nonbas
activity is the growth of a city's population. Central place analysis, alrea
presented in Chapter 5, tells us that the larger the market in a communi
the more services that community will provide for itself and the fewer
will have to import from other centers, for as a city grows in populatic
it will pass successive "threshold" levels at which local provision of add
tional services becomes profitable. Translated into basic-nonbasic tern
nology, this means that the ratio of nonbasic to basic activity will rise
a city grows and that the multiplier, which equals the ratio of total
basic activity, will also rise. Not surprisingly, population growth has tl
same implications when the multiplier is expressed in Keynesian term
As the city's economy grows, its average propensity to import will fall.
lower marginal propensity to import is likely to be associated with tl
lower average propensity. The Keynesian multiplier increases in size as tl
marginal propensity to import falls. Consequently the value of the Keyn
ian multiplier will also increase as a city's economy grows.

Empirical studies do confirm the tendency of the nonbasic sector to grow relative to the basic as a city's population rises through time. For example, Britton Harris calculated values of the basic-nonbasic multiplier for 67 Standard Metropolitan Areas in 1940 and 1950.[5] Population increased in each of these metropolitan areas over that interval. The nonbasic-to-basic ratio—which necessarily equals the multiplier minus one—rose in 57 of the 67 cases. Its failure to increase in the remaining 10 cases might well be evidence of the lagged adjustment process mentioned above.

The same tendency can be observed if we compare the nonbasic-to-basic ratios of large and small cities at a given moment in time. Table 7.3, derived from Harris's data, compares the ratios for 1950 in the six metropolitan areas with population above 2 million and the six metropolitan areas in his sample having the smallest population. The nonbasic-basic ratio averaged 4.02 in the largest areas but only 2.77 in the smallest ones.

To be sure, empirical studies also show that the relationship between size and the nonbasic-to-basic ratio is a far from perfect one. Cities of the same size vary widely in economic structure. For example, Table 7.3 shows that Detroit has a much smaller nonbasic sector than the average metropolitan area of its size. Indeed, Detroit is known to be a not very metropolitan metropolis, and the economic data confirm this.

Undoubtedly, as central place analysis would suggest, the location of a given city in relation to competing centers affects the relative size of its nonbasic sector. We would expect a small city that is close to a large metropolis to have fewer local service activities than a city of equal size that is geographically isolated. Table 7.3 perhaps illustrates the point. South Bend, which is less than 100 miles from Chicago, has a nonbasic-to-basic ratio of only 1.84, while El Paso, a small metropolitan area that is many hundreds of miles from any large center, has a ratio of 3.42.

The inability of simple two-sector models adequately to depict urban economic structure has been amply demonstrated. In recent years most students of the urban economic base have therefore favored the multisector approach known as input-output analysis. This method, as we will see, enables one to lay bare both the internal and the external relationships of an urban economy in great detail. In this respect it overcomes many of the defects of the simpler methods, especially for purposes of short-run analysis. So far as long-run applications are concerned, however, input-output analysis does not in itself offer a solution to the problem of predicting growth and change. We will return to this problem below.

5. Britton Harris, "Comment on Pfouts' Test of the Base Theory," *Journal of the American Institute of Planners*, November 1958, p. 236. Harris's calculations are based on data from the *Census of Population*.

TABLE 7.3

Ratios of Nonbasic to Basic Activity in Large and Small Metropolitan Areas, 1950

STANDARD METROPOLITAN AREA	POPULATION[a]	NONBASIC EMPLOY-MENT ÷ BASIC EMPLOYMENT
Six areas with largest population[b]		
New York-Northeast New Jersey	10,232,039	4.03
Chicago	4,285,902	3.65
Los Angeles	3,405,797	4.15
Philadelphia	2,848,698	5.99
Detroit	2,269,725	2.19
Boston-Lawrence-Lowell	2,049,947	4.13
Mean—largest areas		4.02
Six areas with smallest population[c]		
Erie	163,850	2.37
South Bend	155,535	1.84
Charlotte	144,579	3.33
Fort Wayne	138,110	2.88
El Paso	137,221	3.42
Evansville	120,695	2.75
Mean—smallest areas		2.77

[a] Population data based on 1950 definitions of Standard Metropolitan Areas.

[b] The six largest SMA's in Harris's samples were also the six largest in the nation.

[c] These were the six smallest SMA's in Harris's sample, though not the smallest in the nation.

Source: Britton Harris, "Comment on Pfouts' Test of the Base Theory," *Journal of the American Institute of Planners*, November 1958, p. 236.

INPUT-OUTPUT ANALYSIS

Input-output analysis was developed by Wassily W. Leontief at Harvard, beginning in the 1930s. Inspired by Walras's theory of general equilibrium, which depicted the interrelationship of each economic sector with every other, Leontief sought a scheme in which those interrelationships could be quantified to yield an actual working model of the economy. The result was input-output analysis, a method specifically designed to portray in great detail the actual interindustry relationships of a real economy. The method was first applied to the national economy of the

TABLE 7.4
Input-Output Table for a Hypothetical City
(Flows expressed in millions of dollars)

SECTOR PURCHASING / SECTOR PRODUCING	PROCESSING SECTOR			FINAL DEMAND SECTOR	ROW TOTALS
	1 *Manufac-turing*	2 *Services*	3 *House-holds*	4 *Exports*	*(Output)*
1. Manufacturing (X_m)	—	10	40	50	100
2. Services (X_s)	30	—	60	10	100
3. Households (X_h)	30	70	—	—	100
4. Imports	40	20	—	—	60
Column totals (inputs)	100	100	100	60	360

United States. In the 1950s economists began to adapt it for regional and urban use.[6]

Although input-output analysis can become highly complex, its analytical framework is based on a simple accounting identity that can be stated as follows: for each sector or industry the sum of all outputs (sold to other sectors or industries) must equal the sum of all inputs (purchased from other sectors or industries), provided we take care not to omit any transactions. This is equivalent to the accounting identity for an individual firm, which states that total receipts must equal total costs plus profit. If such an identity holds for each industry and sector separately it must also be true in the aggregate: total inputs to the economy equal its total output.

The full array of input-output relationships for an economy can be shown conveniently in a two-way table or matrix such as Table 7.4. Down the left-hand side are listed the sectors or industries producing outputs. Across the top the same sectors or industries are listed as purchasers of inputs from the sectors at the left.

A crucial assumption is introduced in order to simplify the relationships between the sectors: the assumption that all production processes have fixed technical coefficients. This means that no matter what the level of production in a given industry, it is assumed that inputs are required in fixed proportions to output. For example, the same number of tons of coal will be required to produce a ton of steel whether steel output is high

6. For a more detailed account of input-output analysis in a regional setting (but one that is nevertheless comprehensible to the beginning student) see Isard, ch. 8. William H. Miernyk's *The Elements of Input-Output Analysis* (New York: Random House, 1965) also provides an excellent introduction to the subject.

or low, and the same number of yards of cloth and hours of labor will be needed to make a suit of clothes whether clothing production is up or down.

As a further simplification, the input-output method states the input coefficients not in physical units but in cents worth of input per dollar of output. Thus the input of electric power needed to produce aluminum would be stated, not as kilowatts per ton, but as cents worth of electricity per dollar's worth of aluminum output. An input-output model is generally employed to analyze change through time rather than simply to describe a perfectly static situation. In that case, the use of constant input coefficients expressed in monetary units implies an assumption that as the level or composition of output changes through time the relative prices of all goods will remain as they were in the base year.

Table 7.4 shows a highly compressed version of an input-output table for a hypothetical city. The unit of measurement is millions of dollars per year. To simplify matters it is assumed that labor and management are the only factors of production. Since capital is not employed, all transactions are on current account, and it is unnecessary to have a heading for capital transactions. The government, if there is one, exists without levying taxes or spending money, so no government sector appears in the table.

Of course, this example contains nothing like the detail that would be incorporated in an actual input-output study. In addition to including separate sectors for government and capital transactions, such studies attempt to divide industry into relatively fine classes. The degree of detail achieved depends on the time and money available for the study. Generally it varies from 20 or 30 sectors to the nearly 600 used in the Philadeliphia Region Input-Output Study directed by Walter Isard.[7]

In this highly compressed version, industry is divided into only two types—manufacturing and service. In addition, the table shows a household sector and a foreign trade sector. Moving across each row one reads the sales by the industry or sector named at the left to the industries and sectors named across the top. For simplicity it is assumed that there are no sales within sectors (an assumption that is not made in actual studies). Thus the first column in the first row is blank. Reading to the right across the first row shows that manufacturers sell $10 million of output per year to the service sector and $40 million to households and that they ship $50 million of exports to purchasers outside the area. The sum of these sales is total manufacturing output of $100 million shown in the right-hand column. Output and sales by the service industry are shown in row 2.

    7. Walter Isard, E. Romanoff, and T. W. Langford, Jr., *Working Papers, Philadelphia Region Input-Output Study* (Philadelphia: Regional Science Research Institute, 1967).

Household "output," recorded in row 3, consists of labor and management compensated by wages and salaries. The table indicates that each year households sell $30 million worth of labor and management to manufacturing and $70 million worth to service industries. The total value of this output—$100 million, as shown in the last column—is also total household income.

Just as each row shows sales by the sector listed at the left, so each column shows purchases by the sector named at the top. The entry at the bottom of each column is the sum of that sector's purchases. Because inputs equal outputs for each sector, the figure for total purchases at the bottom of each sector's column equals the figure for total sales at the end of that sector's row. Since the table shows the sales of each local sector to every other as well as the transactions of each with the outside world, it offers a complete and logically consistent picture of economic activity in the area under study.

This highly simplified model, unrealistic though it may be, is convenient for showing how input-output analysis works. The logical starting point for such an explanation, however, is not Table 7.4 but Table 7.5. The latter shows the same industries and sectors as the former, but instead of presenting sales and purchases it records the value of the various input coefficients for industries in our hypothetical city. For example, column 1 indicates that the manufacturing industry requires 30 cents worth of service inputs, 30 cents worth of household inputs (i.e., labor and management), and 40 cents worth of imports for each dollar of output. A somewhat different set of coefficients appears in the service industry column: the service industry uses more labor and less imports per dollar of output than does manufacturing. The input coefficients for households, while analogous to those for industry, might better be thought of as repre-

TABLE 7.5
Input Coefficients of Industries in a Hypothetical City

INPUTS PURCHASED FROM:	DOLLARS WORTH OF INPUTS PER DOLLAR OF OUTPUT IN:		
	1 *Manufacturing*	2 *Services*	3 *Households*
1. Manufacturing	—	.10	.40
2. Services	.30	—	.60
3. Households	.30	.70	—
4. Imports	.40	.20	—
Sum of coefficients	1.00	1.00	1.00

senting the division of household purchases between locally produced manufactures (40 percent) and locally produced services (60 percent). Households import nothing directly. The input coefficients in every column add up to unity.

The Relationship Between the Structural Matrix and the Final Demand Sector

In any application of the input-output method industries or sectors must be divided into two groups, one called collectively the "final demand sector," the other collectively the "processing sector" or "structural matrix." The division will vary according to the scope and purpose of the analysis. It is intended to reflect in each case a distinction between those "outside" (exogenous) sectors in which the level of activity is autonomously determined and those "inside" (endogenous) sectors in which the level of activity can be explained by the model. The former group make up the final demand sector, the latter group the processing sector. The entire analysis rests on the premise that the autonomous "outside" forces to which the processing sector responds are those issuing from the final demand sector. The level and composition of final demand thus determine the level and composition of activity inside the structural matrix. The relationship can be expressed another way. The industries within the structural matrix are regarded as a set of "processors" whose output goes to satisfy the requirements of the final demand sector. Once the dollar value of those final demand requirements is specified, the value of all the inputs and outputs necessary to supply it is automatically determined.

The manner in which industries within the structural matrix respond to demands put upon them from the outside is controlled entirely by the input coefficients that establish relationships within the matrix. The logic of input-output analysis therefore reduces to this: calculate input coefficients to delineate the processing sector, confront that sector with a set of final demands, and it follows that the output of every industry, its transactions with every other industry, and the output of the system as a whole will be fully determined.

In the hypothetical urban economy shown in Tables 7.4 and 7.5, the final demand sector consists only of exports. Manufacturing, services, and households are placed within the structural matrix. Thus the model posits that the level of activity in the two local industries and the income of households, which depends on that level, are determined entirely by the demand of the outside world for the city's exports. In a more complex and realistic analysis the final demand group would also include the government and capital-formation sectors omitted here. These sectors would be placed in the category of final demand because the levels of activity within them cannot reasonably be explained by means of fixed coefficients relating their output to the level of activity in the industries within the structural matrix. Instead, the dollar value of government activity and of capital formation is assumed to be autonomously determined.

The Simple Mathematics of Input-Output Analysis

The relationship between the parts of an input-output table can best be understood by means of some simple mathematics. Each row of the table of input coefficients can be read as part of an equation for the total output of the industry named at the left end of that row. Let us employ the following terms:

$$X_m = \text{total manufacturing output}$$
$$X_s = \text{total service output}$$
$$X_h = \text{total household output}$$

Using the input coefficients given in Table 7.5, we can show that the equations for these outputs are

$$X_m = .1X_s + .4X_h + \text{exports}$$
$$X_s = .3X_m + .6X_h + \text{exports}$$
$$X_h = .3X_m + .7X_s + \text{exports}$$

What the first equation states is that total manufacturing output must be sufficient to supply the required manufacturing exports (i.e., final demand) and to supply in addition the other two processing sectors with the manufacturing inputs that *they* need. What the other sectors require is given to us by the table of input coefficients. We know that the service industry needs 10 cents worth of manufacturing inputs for every dollar of its output. Its output will be X_s. Therefore the service industry will require $.1X_s$ of manufacturing inputs. This is the first term in the equation for required manufacturing output. Similarly the table of input coefficients tells us that households will require 40 cents worth of manufacturing inputs for every dollar of their output. Therefore the second term in the equation for manufacturing output is $.4X_h$. The equations for service output and household output are similarly constructed.

We have written three equations, which appear to contain six unknowns: X_m, X_s, X_h, and the level of exports for each of the three sectors. Exports, however, are not an unknown to be solved for in the analysis. Rather they are the "final demands" that the local economy responds to. Their value is determined outside the system. Let us assume that the manufacturing sector must produce $50 million of exports, the service sector $10 million, and the household sector none. The three equations thus become

$$X_m = .1X_s + .4X_h + 50$$
$$X_s = .3X_m + .6X_h + 10$$
$$X_h = .3X_m + .7X_s + 0$$

Since the three equations now contain only three unknowns, a solution must exist, and anyone who recalls high school algebra can find it by the usual method for solving "simultaneous equations." (In actual practice, input-output tables contain far too many sectors and therefore too many simultaneous equations to permit solution by simple hand methods. The job can be done, however, by using matrix algebra and a computer.) In this instance the solution has already been given in Table 7.4. Total output of each of the processing sectors will be $100 million, which, as the input-output table shows, will enable each sector to supply the required exports plus the inputs simultaneously needed by each of the other sectors. Since total inputs equal total output for each sector, imports into each can be calculated by subtracting all other inputs from total output. The total income generated by the local economy is the sum of all returns to local factors of production. Since the factors of production—in this case labor and management—are provided by households, locally generated income equals household receipts of $100 million.

The Advantages of a Disaggregated Model

Input-output analysis is flexible enough to serve many purposes. The simplest of these is straightforward description. A detailed input-output table is a unique map of an economy as it functions in a particular year, showing the flows of goods and services among all the local sectors and between each of them and the outside world. More interesting, however, is the way in which the method can be used to answer questions about the effects of predicted changes. Because it is so much more highly disaggregated than the basic-nonbasic or foreign-trade multiplier models, it answers questions not only in greater detail but, in all likelihood, with far greater accuracy.

Suppose, for example, that we wish to know what the effect on the local economy will be of a predicted change in the level of exports. Both of the other methods use an aggregate multiplier that is averaged over all the export sectors. Therefore the predicted effect of, say, a $10 million increase in exports will be the same no matter which exporting industry enjoys the increase. Not so with input-output analysis, as the following example will demonstrate.

Let us assume that the situation in the base year is represented in Table 7.4. Exports total $60 million, of which $50 million is from the manufacturing and $10 million from the service sector. Local income equals $100 million per year. Now compare the effects of a $10 million increase in exports alternatively of the manufacturing sector and of the service sector. The results are shown in Table 7.6, which contains two entries in each cell of the input-output table. The upper entry in each cell shows the outcome when manufacturing exports rise from $50 to $60 million while service exports remain at $10 million. The lower entry

TABLE 7.6
Results of Export Expansion in a Hypothetical City: Two Cases[a]
(Flows expressed in millions of dollars)

SECTOR PRODUCING	SECTOR PURCHASING	PROCESSING SECTOR			FINAL DEMAND SECTOR	ROW TOTALS
		1 Manufac-turing	2 Services	3 House-holds	4 Exports	(Output)
Manufacturing	1st case	—	11.5	46.2	60.0	117.7
	2nd case	—	12.7	48.9	50.0	111.6
Services	1st case	35.3	—	69.4	10.0	114.7
	2nd case	33.5	—	73.4	20.0	126.9
Households	1st case	35.3	80.3	—	—	115.6
	2nd case	33.5	88.8	—	—	122.3
Imports	1st case	47.1	22.9	—	—	70.0
	2nd case	44.6	25.4	—	—	70.0
Column totals (inputs)	1st case	117.7	114.7	115.6	70.0	418.0
	2nd case	111.6	126.9	122.3	70.0	430.9

[a] The two cases are: 1st case—manufacturing exports = $60 million, service exports = $10 million
2nd case—manufacturing exports = $50 million, service exports = $20 million

shows the results when service exports rise from $10 to $20 million while manufacturing exports are held constant at $50 million.

The outcome is entirely different in the two cases. Most notably, household income rises to $122.3 million when service exports increase by $10 million but reaches only $115.6 million when manufacturing exports rise by that amount. Why should service exports have so much stronger an effect, dollar for dollar, on local income? The answer can be deduced from an examination of the input coefficients in Table 7.5. The manufacturing sector uses 40 cents worth of imports per dollar of production, while the service sector uses only 20 cents worth. Consequently a dollar increase in service exports involves much less leakage of spending outside the economy in the form of increased imports than does a dollar increase in exports of the manufacturing sector. Less leakage means a larger increase in the demand for local output and hence a greater ultimate expansion of local output and income.

The expansion process can be viewed as a round by round series of increments. When manufacturing exports rise by $10 million, the input coefficients in column 1 of Table 7.5 show that the direct requirements to produce that output are $3 million of service inputs, $3 million of household inputs, and $4 million of imported goods. But that is only the first round of requirements, since those inputs themselves must be produced, giving rise to a second round of expansion. Specifically, in order to produce that $3 million of output sold to the manufacturing sector, the service sector requires $2.1 million of household inputs, $.3 million of manufacturing inputs, and $.6 million of imported goods. Likewise, the household sector receiving $3 million of additional income from sales to the manufacturing sector will buy (as, so to speak, its additional inputs) $1.2 million of manufactured goods and $1.8 million of services. These requirements comprise the second round of the expansion. Since they, too, must be produced there is a third round, and so on in diminishing series. The final expansion, as shown in Table 7.6, is the sum of this infinite series of rounds. We can now see that a $10 million increase in service exports leads to a greater expansion of local income than a similar increase in manufacturing exports primarily because on the first round of service industry expansion $8 million of spending remains within the community, while for an equal increase in manufacturing exports only $6 million of first-round spending would do so. And if the first round is smaller, subsequent rounds based on it will be reduced, too.

This illustration suggests another of the many uses for input-output analysis: it can show precisely what the total direct and indirect input requirements would be for an expected increase in output for final demand by a particular sector. Information of that kind might be crucial to city planners—for example, in anticipating the requirements for indirect services such as housing and transportation that would accompany a projected expansion of a major local industry. Or, if the trend is reversed and cutbacks are expected in a major local industry—say, a defense plant—the analysis will tell, not just the aggregate output reduction to be expected as the sum of direct plus indirect effects, but also precisely which sectors will suffer how much of a decline in activity.

Input-Output Multipliers

The expansion or contraction of a local economy in response to a change in final demand as explained by input-output analysis is as much a multipler process as were the expansions previously described by means of the other two models. This is one ground for stating, as we did earlier, that the three models are fundamentally similar in their logical structure. A second ground is the division of the economy in all three cases into an outside, or exogenously oriented, sector in which the level of activity is autonomously determined and an inside, or endogenous, sector that responds passively to the stimulus transmitted from the other. A third is the mathematically similar character of the three multiplier relationships. In each case the multiplier is based on one or more system coefficients that are assumed to be fixed, at least in the short run: the basic-nonbasic ratio, the marginal propensity to import, and, finally, the set of technical input coefficients.

As we have shown, however, the value of the multiplier under input-output analysis varies according to which sector receives the initial impulse. Conceptually a variety of multipliers can be distinguished in an input-output model.[8] We have been discussing one that can be defined as the change in income divided by the change in exports. For our hypothetical city, the different values this multiplier takes—depending on the composition of the change in exports—are shown in Table 7.7. The first two rows have already been explained. The third represents the special case of a uniform expansion of exports: each sector's exports increase by the same ratio, in this case one-sixth. The resulting rise in income is $16.7 million. Initial income was $100 million, and $16.7 \div 100 = \frac{1}{6}$. Thus income has increased by the same proportion that exports increased. The case illustrates a basic property of the input-output model: if every element in the final demand sector increases by a given percentage, the entire transactions matrix expands by the same percentage. In short, it "blows up" uniformly. This characteristic results from the assumption that input co-

8. See Miernyk, pp. 42–55.

TABLE 7.7

Variation in Multiplier Effect Depending on Which Sector Expands Exports

	CHANGE IN EXPORTS ($ MILLIONS)	CHANGE IN INCOME	MULTIPLIER
	(ΔE)	(ΔY)	$\Delta Y/\Delta E$
1st case: manufacturing exports rise by $10 million	10	15.6	1.56
2nd case: service exports rise by $10 million	10	22.3	2.23
3rd case: each export category rises by ⅙ (manufacturing rises $8.33 million; service rises $1.67 million)	10	16.7	1.67

NOTE: In each case the total increase in exports = $10 million. All changes are measured from initial equilibrium shown in Table 7.4. Full results for the first two cases, but not the third, are shown in Table 7.6.

efficients remain constant as the economy expands, which means, in effect, that marginal relationships and average relationships are equal. If this equality were assumed in either of the other two models it would have precisely the same results: an increase of k percent in exports (or, in the Keynesian model, in exports plus other autonomous components of spending) would lead to an increase of k percent in output and income.

The theoretical superiority of input-output analysis to other methods of analyzing the urban economic base is abundantly clear. Unfortunately, there are severe data problems. It is difficult enough to gather the numbers required for an input-output table for the United States as a whole. It is even more difficult for smaller regions, since in general the smaller the area, the less statistical detail is available in published sources. Basically there are two alternatives: conduct an independent interview and questionnaire survey of the local area, or use the technical coefficients already calculated by the Department of Commerce for national input-output tables. The second alternative, though widely adopted, runs the risk of throwing away just those special features of the local economy that may have suggested the need for a study in the first place and that, in any event, it is risky to suppress. Therefore the first is preferable.[9]

9. The task of surveying a moderate-size local economy is not prohibitively difficult. See, for example, Patrick McGuire, *A Simulation Model of the Rochester, New York, Region*, unpublished doctoral dissertation, Fordham University, 1973.

The Limitations of a Static Model

The input-output model discussed up to this point is essentially a static one. Fundamentally, it is a highly detailed map of the interindustry relationships in an economy *at a moment in time.* Such a model is highly effective for analyzing short-run problems such as the impact of an anticipated change in final demand on the level and composition of local activity and income. A static model, however, cannot cope with the long-run problems of urban change and growth. Economic development and urbanization are processes in which crucial relationships are continually changing. They cannot even be approximated by the linear expansion of a system whose internal relationships are fixed. The assumption of fixed input coefficients is not tenable over the long run.

As numerous students of input-output analysis have pointed out, fixed coefficients of production and fixed relative prices are unlikely to prevail in the long run for a variety of reasons. Most basic of these is the pervasive influence of technological innovation, which consists precisely either of changes in the way inputs are combined to produce given outputs or in the development of entire ranges of new products that render old goods and the methods of producing them obsolete. The revolutionary effect of the automobile and truck suggests how profound these influences can be over a period of a few decades. They not only made other modes of transportation obsolete for certain purposes but rendered obsolete the physical layout of the older central cities themselves.

Technological change affects relative input prices directly. Quite apart from that, however, differential price changes among inputs or, for a given input, among regions may occur either because resource supplies are limited or because the demand for various resources changes differentially over time. And we know that as relative input prices change, producers will substitute those that are becoming relatively cheaper for those that are not. In recent years, for example, homeowners and builders have been using more insulation and less heating oil to produce housing services because the price of oil has risen relative to the cost of insulation. In the face of such changes, input coefficients will not remain fixed.

In the long run, local growth itself is bound to affect local input coefficients. First of all, growth fosters economies of agglomeration. These, by their very definition, are increases in the technical efficiency of certain inputs as city size increases. Second, there are the central place effects of growth operating through market size. As an urban market grows, it becomes profitable to produce locally services that were formerly imported. Thus, increasing urban size inevitably means change in urban economic structure.

Changes in local population characteristics, especially as a result of migration, are also likely to have important effects over the long run. Population change might affect both supply conditions, via changes in labor productivity, and demand conditions through shifts in the pattern of consumption.

There is no need to extend the list. Most of what we see currently as major urban problems have been caused by the long-run, dynamic forces of technological change, economic growth, and population movement. Can input-ouput analysis be made to handle these dynamic forces? The best answer, perhaps, is that its proponents believe it can, and they are trying. Fundamental technological innovations are unpredictable, but the rate at which existing technical improvements will be adopted by industry can be estimated. Long-run trends in relative prices can be measured. One can also estimate the effects of local market growth in bringing about the substitution of local production for imports. As Miernyk has shown, the probable results of these changes can be incorporated in a new set of local input coefficients to be used when making long-run projections based on input-output analysis.[10] The application of these dynamic adjustments, depending heavily as it does on the judgment of the analyst, is still far from an exact science. Nevertheless, it appears to offer the only real hope we presently have for obtaining useful long-run projections of local economic activity.

URBAN AND REGIONAL SIMULATION MODELS

In recent years economists and city planners, spurred by the capacity of computers to operate with large systems of equations, have used computer simulation techniques in an attempt to create dynamic models of the urban economy that are even more comprehensive than an input-output analysis. What these models "simulate" is the movement of a city's or a region's economic system through time. Prescott and Mullendore, for example, constructed a simulation model for the eight-county region centered on Des Moines, Iowa.[11] The model contains five subsectors, labeled demographic, employment, output, final demand, and capital. The last three actually constitute an input-output model made dynamic by the inclusion of a sector linking net capital formation with the expansion of output. Thus the system as a whole is actually a dynamic input-output model with two additional sectors included to explain the

10. Miernyk, ch. 6.
11. James R. Prescott and Walter Mullendore, "A Simulation Model for Multi-County Planning," *Proceedings of the American Real Estate and Urban Economics Association,* IV (1969), 183–207.

growth of employment and population in a way that is consistent with the growth of output.

The following simplified explanation suggests how the parts of such a model are put together. The rate of growth of local output depends on the growth of exogenous demand and also on population growth determined in the demographic sector of the model and investment demand determined in its capital sector. Employment growth depends on the growth of output, moderated by an assumed trend in labor productivity. Employment provides a link between the output sector of the model and the demographic sector. To convey the sense of how simulation models work, let us examine the latter in somewhat more detail. The size and age distribution of the population and the local birth, death, and labor-force participation rates are found or estimated for the base period. From this data the natural annual increase in the labor force is calculated. Migration is then made to depend on the difference between job growth and natural increase in the labor force. When the model runs through time, in-migration occurs if job growth exceeds natural labor force growth, out-migration if vice versa. Migration plus natural increase yields change in total population. The effects of population change are continuously fed back into the input-output sector of the model via changes in household demand and in outlays by the state, local, and federal governments, which are assumed to rest on a per capita basis.

The accuracy of such a model can be tested by seeing how closely it reproduces actual changes over some observed past period. If it fits the facts reasonably well it can be used to predict the future course of the economy, given various assumptions about future changes in demand, productivity, fertility, and so on. That it fits the past data from which its parameters were estimated does not, of course, ensure that it will accurately predict future trends. Because simulation models are so recent a development, their predictive accuracy can scarcely be said to have been established. If they prove successful, however, they will become an indispensable tool for urban and regional planning.

The sort of simulation model just described is a nonspatial one. Although it generates a level of business activity, employment, and population for a region, it makes no attempt to specify the location of these activities within the study area. Spatial concerns are simply omitted. We have used that particular sort of model as an illustration both because it is relatively simple and because its aims are similar to those of the other methods of economic base analysis dealt with in this chapter. In principle, however, simulation models can be developed to reproduce the movement of any social or physical system through time. Urban economists have now developed models that simulate the spatial form and land-use pattern of an actual metropolis. These models attempt to reproduce spatial reality by assigning population and business activity to specific sites within the metropolitan area. They deal, at a high level of sophistication, with the whole range of topics in intra-urban location that were introduced in Chapter 6, as well as with aspects of housing market economics to be taken up in Chapter 12. Like other simulation models, they are intended to be used as tools for policy planning and evaluation.[12]

STUDYING THE "SUPPLY SIDE" OF THE LOCAL ECONOMY

Traditional methods of studying the urban economic base have long been criticized for overemphasizing the role of demand in determining the level and rate of growth of local economic activity. In a widely cited article Chinitz wrote that "our efforts so far have been almost exclusively devoted to the demand dimensions of interdependence. The supply side has been virtually ignored."[13]

This comment applies with as much force to input-output and simulation methods as it does to the simpler basic-nonbasic and foreign-trade multiplier models. The fact that the input-output and simulation methods depict the flows of goods and services between the sectors of local industry in great detail is all to the good but does not bear on this point. Chinitz argues that we must look not only at the flows between local industries but at the way in which the structure of local industry affects factor supply prices, production costs, and entrepreneurial behavior within the local economy. He suggests, for example, that the supply of entrepreneurship and risk capital for launching new ventures may be significantly greater in a city where the industrial structure is largely competitive than in one that is dominated by a few very large firms. Thus the organizational structure of local industry may in the long run affect the way the local economy responds to opportunities for growth and diversification.

As Tiebout put it, a study of the supply side "deals with the nature

12. See, for example, David L. Birch et al., *The Community Analysis Model,* HUD–PDR–363–2, U.S. Department of Housing and Urban Development, January 1979; John F. Kain and William C. Apgar, Jr., "Simulation of Housing Market Dynamics," *Journal of the American Real Estate and Urban Economics Association,* Winter 1979, pp. 505–38; and Gregory K. Ingram, John F. Kain, and J. Royce Ginn, *The Detroit Prototype of the NBER Urban Simulation Model* (New York: National Bureau of Economic Research, 1972). An earlier influential intra-urban location model was developed by Ira S. Lowry. See his *A Model of Metropolis* (Santa Monica, California: RAND Corporation, 1964).

13. Benjamin Chinitz, "Contrasts in Agglomeration: New York and Pittsburgh," reprinted in Ronald E. Grieson, ed., *Urban Economics: Readings and Analysis* (Boston: Little, Brown, 1973), pp. 26–37.

of the local economy as an economic environment."[14] An examination of the supply side would attempt to uncover the strengths and weaknesses of the community as a place in which to live and to conduct business. Once these were known, local policymakers could set about using its strengths and ameliorating its weaknesses in order to increase the area's productivity and attractiveness and help to ensure the long-run growth of its output and living standards.

It is a limitation, if not a defect, of the methods of economic base analysis reviewed above that (with some modification in the case of simulation models) they ascribe changes in the level of local activity entirely to changes in the level of an exogenously determined final demand. As John F. Kain has pointed out in another context, this way of looking at the local economy inevitably focuses attention on matters over which local authorities have no control—the exogenously determined components of final demand—while distracting attention from the very thing they *can* influence—the nature and attractiveness of the local economic environment.[15] It is well to recognize that in the short run, local activity will fluctuate in response to shifts in outside demand, but that is no reason to neglect the importance of internal supply factors in determining the course of events over the long run.

Precisely what can be done to take the supply side into account? First of all, location or feasibility studies can be made to discover what industries can best make use of the area's physical location and economic advantages. Second, the city can examine its local supply of labor, land, capital, and entrepreneurship to see whether these can be marshaled more effectively for economic growth. Third, the city can survey its public "infrastructure" of transportation facilities, schools, public services, and recreation areas—indeed, its whole "physical and social plan"—to see whether they are attractive, well balanced, and efficient or inadequate, uncoordinated, and stultifying.

Growth as an Objective

The argument up to this point suggests an implicit assumption that the aim of local economic policy is to promote local economic growth or to combat local economic decline if that is occurring. The objective of growth would, at one time, have been taken for granted everywhere. Then in the late 1960s concern about environmental degradation, combined perhaps with less high-minded exclusionary motives, led some communities, especially in the more distant suburbs or in nonmetropolitan areas,

14. Tiebout, p. 18.
15. See Kain's review of Wilbur R. Thompson's *A Preface to Urban Economics* in *Journal of the American Institute of Planners,* May 1966, pp. 186–88.

to adopt policies of trying to slow down or halt the expansion of population, even if that meant slowing economic growth as well. In most cities, however, the desire to maintain growth, or to limit decline, remains strong.

Growth undoubtedly serves the special interests of the individual class of local "boosters" who typically own real estate that will appreciate in value or commercial firms whose profits will rise if the local economy expands. However, there are likely to be losers as well as gainers from any local policy that promotes economic expansion. One example is that of elderly retirees living on fixed incomes in rented housing, who are likely to find their living standard going down as growth pushes rents up. What the distribtuion of gains and losses would be, or whether a policy of stimulating growth would produce an increase in the average level of local well-being are questions so complex that in the present state of our knowledge categorical answers are probably not possible.

The case in favor of growth can be made on the following grounds. First, economic expansion is likely to bring increased economies of agglomeration, which will benefit local workers, businessmen, and consumers, as well as local landowners. Second, wages will tend to be higher and job preferences easier to satisfy in the "tight" labor market of a growing area than in the "easy" labor market of a static or declining one. This, however, is a one-time rather than a cumulative effect. If we assume that the local wage level is connected to the national level by the force of migration, then wages in a growing area can be higher than wages in a declining area by whatever differential is required to induce migration from the latter to the former. A similar argument applies to the return on local capital.

More generally, we can argue that policies to improve the local environment as a place to live and conduct business, and which thereby attract business and population, are in their very nature policies that increase both material productivity and population well-being. However, the suggestion that population and activity might be attracted from another place raises an issue that is often overlooked in discussing local economic policy: What happens in the other place? Any statement about the welfare effects of a policy requires a definition of the relevant population. Since local economic policy often affects people living outside the specific jurisdiction, it is necessary to investigate the connection between local policy and national welfare.

LOCAL ECONOMIC POLICY AND NATIONAL WELFARE

Suppose that a city adopts a policy of stimulating economic growth, but that the resulting growth occurs mainly in very low wage industries and attracts an influx of low-skilled population. In such a case the growth of the local economy might reduce rather than increase the average level of local family income. Has welfare increased or decreased? The answer depends upon whose welfare one takes into account. The preexisting local population may be worse off after the low income population increases, if the newcomers cost the locality more via increased public expenditure than they contribute in additional tax revenue.[16] On the other hand, the low-skilled in-migrants are presumably better off in the town to which they moved than in the place from which they came; they would not otherwise have migrated (barring ignorance and uncertainty). If we somehow aggregate the well-being of both groups, welfare may be found to increase as a result of in-migration. If we count only the welfare of the preexisting population, it may decrease. A full account of the welfare effects of a local policy would have to go even further and look not only at changes in the welfare of the preexisting local population and of the potential in-migrants, but at effects on the rest of the nation. If we fail to examine this last element, we run the danger of advocating policies that benefit a local area while harming the nation as a whole. In short, the relevant welfare universe for discussing the effects of local economic policy is not the local population, either before or after the policy takes effect, but the entire nation. Where does this lead us?

To simplify matters, let us assume that localities will not knowingly pursue policies harmful to themselves and that all policies that are beneficial locally will either be neutral toward other areas in the nation or else impose some loss on them. In that case we can say that for any local policy, the net effect on national welfare must be equal to the local gain less the losses (if any) elsewhere. For the nation as a whole it would be desirable (if it were possible) to insist that localities act not to maximize local gain but to maximize national welfare. This is not quite the same thing as saying "maximize local gain subject to the condition that local gains exceed outside losses." For under the latter rule localities might adopt policies that would lead to large local gain at the expense of large outside loss when from the national point of view it would have been better for them to choose alternative policies that entail moderate local gain at the cost of much smaller losses elsewhere.

We see, then, that consideration of the nation's welfare requires, not that localities avoid policies that hurt other localities, but only that losses elsewhere be properly taken into account. Of course, this proposition is, in the present state of economic knowledge, quite impossible to put into

16. This should not be taken to imply that the tax-expenditure calculus gives an adequate account of changes in individual welfare. On this point see Julius Margolis, "On Municipal Land Policy for Fiscal Gains," *National Tax Journal*, September 1956, pp. 247–57.

effect. It requires some way of quantifying welfare for various populations so that gains and losses can be compared along a common scale. Economists are not hopeful of discovering the "social welfare function" (or formula) that would make such comparisons possible. Even if we were to retreat from welfare to income as the relevant unit of account, the rule is presently impracticable because the effects of alternative policies on local income and, even more so, on outside income are extraordinarily difficult to measure.

Subsidizing Industrial Relocation

Despite the absence of reliable ways of measuring welfare, the above argument does help in judging some real policy questions. Consider, for example, local subsidies intended to influence the location of industry. Many cities that want to promote economic growth or stem decline try to attract new industry (and the jobs that go with it) by offering subsidies in the form of low cost leases, industrial development loans, tax abatements, and the like. Consistent with the conclusions of the basic-nonbasic theory, new industries that can export to the rest of the nation are seen as a way of strengthening the city's "economic base."

Careful analysis, however, demonstrates that a policy of attracting new industry by means of subsidies violates the welfare rule proposed in the previous section. Let gains and losses be measured simply in terms of net changes in local income. Now suppose that the town of West Greenbush, suffering from unemployment, attracts a textile mill from some other location by means of a subsidy sufficient to overcome the higher transportation costs from West Greenbush to the market. The mill's output and exports, we may assume, are the same in West Greenbush as they were at the previous location. The factor incomes added by the mill at its new location will therefore just equal the incomes lost by its leaving the other place. In effect, West Greenbush exports its unemployment. From a welfare point of view, however, the situation is not a stand-off, because the net income gain to West Greenbush equals the rise in factor incomes *less* the locally financed subsidy needed to attract the mill from its preferred location. Hence the net gains at West Greenbush must be less than the losses at the old location by the amount of the annual subsidy.

Since we do not assume *general* unemployment, the added transportation costs cannot be counted as net increases in factor incomes. They measure only the opportunity cost of factors transferred from some other employment into transportation. The added transportation cost—or its equivalent, the reduced output in other industries from which factors were shifted into transportation—equals the net annual loss to society as a whole from this method of attracting export industry. (To this must be added the once-over loss equal to the cost of moving the firm.)

Repelling Low Income Migrants

The important issue of low-income population movement is another question on which the proposed welfare rule casts much light. High income suburbs all over the United States quite correctly see that their own self-interest is served by keeping low income populations out. Even our great central cities that have always contained large numbers of the poor now wonder if they should make themselves less open to new arrivals. It should be obvious, however, that local policies to exclude the poverty-stricken do not diminish the total number of the poor in the nation. Indeed, by denying full mobility and therefore maximum choice of occupation and environment to the poor, such policies probably interfere with progress toward reducing poverty. At the very least this is an area where policies that maximize local welfare are unlikely to be in the national interest. Yet we know that local voters and local politicians will always be tempted to serve local self-interest. If the national interest is to prevail it will have to be asserted via state and national policies that limit local discretion to control the variables of housing, zoning, and welfare benefits through which localities currently influence the movement of the poor.

These conclusions may seem painfully obvious. Unfortunately they are easily lost sight of when attention is focused on solving intense local problems. A stunning example of this occurs in Jay Forrester's influential study entitled *Urban Dynamics*.[17] Forrester wished to examine the effects of alternative public policies in combating the stagnation and decay of the older central cities. To do this he devised a simulation model, calibrated it with hypothetical "data," and ran it through centuries of time. He deliberately set his hypothetical city in what he described as a "limitless environment." The connections between the city and the environment he put in the form of "attractiveness for migration multipliers," the size of which depended upon the values of key variables within the city. For example, the attractiveness for migration multiplier that affected the influx of low income workers was made to depend in part upon the vacancy rate in the city's low rent housing. The multiplier would rise as the vacancy rate increased. As the model ran through time it showed that a rise in the city's low income population either caused or exacerbated a great many problems and was a principal factor in the city's stagnation and decay.

17. Jay W. Forrester, *Urban Dynamics* (Cambridge, Mass.: M.I.T. Press, 1969).

Forrester "tested" the effects of various public policies on the city's economic health by building them into the model and running it through time. One of these policies was a subsidy for low income housing. He found that even if the subsidy cost were paid entirely from sources outside the city, a policy of building low income subsidized housing would have deleterious effects on the city's economic health because it would attract a larger number of the poor. The reader was left to draw the conclusion that subsidies to low income housing must be avoided if we wish to rescue our older cities from decay.[18] Surely one must ask whether that is the right way to view the problem.

The issue is not whether low income populations create problems for cities—quite obviously they do. The point is, rather, that Forrester's framework is wholly inappropriate for judging the welfare consequences of alternative policies. In his model, everything outside the city is part of the "limitless environment." It could better be described as a limitless void, since we do not know what goes on out there. Given this void, the model can tell us nothing about the national welfare effects of either local or national urban policies. It is capable of registering nothing but the local gains or losses from local policies. Forrester concludes that a policy of low income housing subsidies is bad because it attracts low income families. This overlooks two crucial points: first, if low income housing were equally subsidized everywhere, the subsidy would have *no* effect on migration. Consequently, if the heavy concentration of low income populations in large cities is undesirable, the solution is not necessarily to do away with housing subsidies but rather to use state or national policy to achieve a more desirable spatial distribution of the poor. Second, the low income population may be better off in Forrester's central city than in the place from which it came. A model that considers only one city is simply incapable of addressing this important welfare question.[19]

---

18. *Ibid.*, pp. 65–70.
19. Forrester does attempt, in a two-paragraph afterthought, to meet the criticism that his model overlooks effects on the outside world. He writes (ibid., p. 116):

> The policies for controlling population balance that the city must establish are not antisocial. No purpose is served by operating a city so that it is a drain on the economy of the country and a disappointment and frustration to its occupants. An urban area that maintains effective internal balance can absorb poor people from other areas at a faster rate than can one that is operating in deep stagnation.

Indeed, this may be so. But the Forrester model is certainly incapable of demonstrating it. The inadequacy of Forrester's single-city model as a basis for testing national policies is developed at greater length by Leo P. Kadanoff in "From Simulation Model to Public Policy," *American Scientist*, January–February 1972, pp. 74–79. Also see the penetrating critique by Gregory K. Ingram in his review of *Urban Dynamics* in *Journal of the American Institute of Planners*, May 1970, pp. 206–08.

Local "Growth Control"

The arguments used in judging the welfare effects of a policy of repelling low income migrants can also be applied to a local policy of "growth control." In recent years many towns, especially in the exurban fringe of metropolitan areas, have sought to limit population growth by means of exclusionary zoning, limitations on the annual number of building permits issued, or other forms of control over development. (These policies are examined in greater detail in Chapter 13.) Such policies may, in fact, promote the welfare of the people already living in the town. But they are clearly against the interests of those who would move in if not thus prevented. As Alonso has pointed out, from a national perspective these are not growth control policies at all, since they do nothing to influence the size of the national population. Rather, they are "distribution" policies, affecting "not whether these people and their children shall exist, but where and how."[20]

Like a policy of repelling low income migrants, these so-called growth controls operate on the principle of "beggar-thy-neighbor." Since the population in question must go somewhere, whatever gain accrues in localities where population is held down is presumably offset by losses in towns where it finally settles. There remains a net loss to the nation as a whole because freedom of movement is curtailed. Individuals are deprived of the freedom to choose a residential location that an unrestricted market would provide. The resulting land use pattern may be wasteful of resources (including gasoline!) since those whose locational choices are restricted probably cannot make the optimal adjustment of residence to workplace and are therefore likely to travel farther to work than they otherwise would.

Pollution Control

Pollution control is another area in which self-interested local policy may conflict with national welfare objectives. Here again the motive may be a desire to offer location inducements to industry. An industrial town may fear that if it raises its antipollution standards it will drive industry away. Taking account only of their own welfare, the local citizens may correctly prefer to suffer the consequences of pollution rather than lose their jobs. In so deciding, however, they overlook the pollution costs

20. William Alonso, "Urban Zero Population Growth," in Mancur Olson and Hans H. Landsberg, eds., *The No-Growth Society* (New York: W. W. Norton, 1973), pp. 191–206. Also see Richard F. Babcock, "The Spatial Impact of Land-Use and Environmental Controls," in Arthur P. Solomon, ed., *The Prospective City* (Cambridge, Mass.: MIT Press, 1980), pp. 267–70.

thrown off by local industry onto neighboring towns whose interests they have not consulted. This is the familiar problem of external costs. Local industry is, in effect, being subsidized to stay put, and the subsidy is paid partly by those living outside the benefiting jurisdiction, who bear some of the pollution costs. The solution here, as in the somewhat different case of low income housing policy, is to raise the decision-making power to a higher level of government: a pollution-control jurisdiction must be found or created that is large enough to capture most of the externalities. Efficient pollution control requires a combination of regional and national standards.

Policies to Improve the Local Economic Environment

There are, of course, many ways in which localities can attract or hold industry that do not violate a national welfare rule. We have already described them above in the discussion of taking the supply side into account. These, by and large, are policies that would improve the local economy as an economic environment. As the environment becomes more productive for industry and more desirable for residents it will attract additional industry on its own merits, and growth will be achieved without special subsidies. While competition among cities to attract industry by means of subsidy is, as we have shown, necessarily harmful from the point of view of the nation as a whole, competition that takes the form of creating more attractive environments can hardly fail to be generally beneficial. True, not all places would prosper under such a regime, but it would not be difficult to show that the national welfare would be enhanced. Of course, the question of subsidy is not so easily put aside as the above statement may seem to suggest. We have already pointed out that location subsidies may take an indirect form, as in the case of low pollution-control standards. "Fair competition" would likewise rule out attracting industry by reducing business taxes to the point where firms receive local services at less than cost.

In a classic article criticizing the basic-nonbasic theory for its irrational export bias, Hans Blumenfeld performed the *tour de force* of turning the theory upside down. He pointed out that the great metropolitan areas of modern times are centers of production that have shown remarkable persistence in the face of economic change and concluded with this passage:

> The bases of this amazing stability are the business and consumer services and other industries supplying the local market. They are the permanent and constant element, while the "export" industries are variable, subject to incessant change and replacement. While the existence of a sufficient number of such industries is indispen-

sable for the continued existence of the metropolis, each individual "export" industry is expendable and replaceable.

In any commonsense use of the term, it is the "service" industries of the metropolis that are "basic" and "primary" while the "export" industries are "secondary" and "ancillary." The economic base of the metropolis consists in the activities by which its inhabitants supply each other.[21]

In this sense the service sector is essentially the "economic environment" of the city, and the appropriate aim of local economic policy is to render that environment efficient and attractive by means that are consistent with the objectives of national policy.

21. Hans Blumenfeld, "The Economic Base of the Metropolis," reprinted in Fouts, pp. 229–77.

The Economics of Urban Transportation

EIGHT

Cities exist to facilitate human interaction. If transportation were instantaneous and costless we would not need cities; we could have as much interaction as we wished while living at the four corners of the globe. However, what Haig called "the friction of space" cannot be overcome costlessly. We invest substantial time and quantities of resources in moving people and products from place to place. The relationship between transportation costs and the spatial and economic organization of cities has been analyzed in detail in previous chapters. We saw in Chapter 4 that cities grow up at locations possessing transportation advantages and in Chapter 5 that transportation costs are an important determinant of the dimensions of the urban hierarchy. The land use model developed in Chapter 6 showed that, within cities, higher rent is paid for the privilege of occupying more accessible sites because, at such locations, the need for transportation outlays is reduced. Throughout those chapters we emphasized the way in which changes in transportation technology, by altering the cost of accessibility, profoundly affect both the system of cities and the form of the metropolis.

INTERDEPENDENCE OF TRANSPORTATION AND LAND USE

Chapter 6 explained how a competitive land market determines the pattern of urban land use through a process in which individual land users adapt to a given system of transportation. In this and the following chapter we shall see that government decisions concerning transportation also profoundly affect land use patterns because they establish the frame of reference within which individual location decisions are made.

The relationship between transportation systems and land use is a reciprocal one. The land use pattern depends upon the character of the transportation network, while the viability of the transportation network depends upon the land use pattern. To some extent new transportation links, whether urban expressways or additional transit lines, are built in response to visible traffic demand generated by private locational decisions. But causality runs the other way, too. A major traffic facility, once in place, exerts a powerful influence on subsequent private market development. This is obvious at the microlocational scale. For example, commercial development inevitably springs up around subway stations, highway interchanges, and airports.

More important, however, are the macrolocational effects of transportation systems as a whole. The transportation framework a city installs profoundly influences its future development. Cities that depend heavily on mass transit, like New York or Chicago, tend to become highly centralized and densely developed. On the other hand, if a city relies mainly on highway transportation as it grows, it develops into a decentralized, low density metropolis such as Los Angeles or Houston. (These tendencies have already been described in Chapter 3. Figure 3.2 shows how greatly auto-oriented differ from transit-oriented cities in population per square mile.) Once an urban expressway system has been built, the decentralized, low-density land use pattern that develops cannot be served effectively by a mass transit system. The latter requires concentrated origins and destinations to operate economically; the former operates economically only when destinations are *not* concentrated. Hoover has pointed out that since each system tends to promote the pattern of settlement that it can serve efficiently, the choice of a transportation system is to some extent self-justifying.[1] Because it plays such a crucial role in determining the spatial-economic organization of cities, transportation itself deserves a closer look.

OUTLINE OF CHAPTERS 8 AND 9

A great many public policy issues arise in connection with urban transportation. Before addressing them, however, it is necessary to understand the economic character of the transportation system itself. Conse-

1. Edgar M. Hoover, *An Introduction to Regional Economics*, 2nd ed. (New York: Alfred A. Knopf, 1975), pp. 384–85.

quently, we divide the discussion into two parts. The economics of urban transportation—how the system works—is explained in this chapter, while public policy issues, with a few exceptions, are reserved for Chapter 9.

We begin with a brief description of the modes of transportation available in metropolitan areas and then analyze the way consumers choose among those modes—in effect, an analysis of consumer demand for urban trips. The second half of this chapter deals with the supply (or cost) side of urban transportation. Applying the standard concepts of microeconomics, we look at the nature of transportation costs in both the short and the long run. The point of view is normative, in that the analysis of cost is used to develop rules for the most efficient operation of the system. The normative question in the short run is: "Given the nature of short-run costs, what prices should be charged for the use of an existing transportation system if it is to operate with maximum efficiency?" In the long run the existing system can be altered by investment. The normative question then becomes: "Given the nature of long-run costs, what is the optimum transportation investment policy?" The chapter closes with a review of some empirical cost studies that put statistical flesh on these bare bones of theory.

Local government is inevitably involved both in planning and developing an urban transportation network and in regulating its use by the public. The federal government is heavily involved in financing these local efforts. Chapter 9 will focus on urban transportation policy at both levels of government.

THE URBAN TRANSPORTATION SYSTEM

The argument in Chapter 6 was greatly simplified by assuming that the city had sprung up on a "transport surface," a featureless plain on which transportation required no improved right-of-way and was equally efficient in any direction. Transportation was thus reduced to a technologically determined transport cost per mile, uniform throughout the city. We had eliminated by assumption all the complicating features of any real transportation system, among them the following:

Channels and networks. Far from being equally easy in any direction, transportation moves along rights-of-way that form channels into which traffic is concentrated. A transportation system is a network of channels. Sites along such channels, and especially at nodes in the network, have greater accessibility than sites not so located.

Alternative modes. The transportation system serving a metropolitan area usually consists of several modes of transportation differing from one another in cost, speed, comfort, and convenience. For some journeys the modes are complementary; in many cases they are competitive.

Segmentation. Commuting trips from the suburbs to the CBD must accomplish three functions, which have been described as residential collection, line-haul (along a corridor to the center), and downtown distribution.[2] In some cases the three functions are accomplished door-to-door in a single vehicle. Often they are segmented among different modes or involve transferring from vehicle to vehicle on a single mode. There may be a walking segment at either end or between modes.

If we leave aside bicycle and shoe leather, then automobile, bus, trolley, streetcar, subway, and elevated train make up the list of alternative modes of urban passenger transportation. The important distinction between "private" and "public" modes places autos in the private category and all the others in the public. It is worth noting that the classification is based not on ownership but on the general public's right of access. For example, although the buses in a transit system may be owned and operated by a private firm, they provide "public" transportation because any member of the public may use them. Likewise, automobiles are classified as "private," not because they are privately owned—after all, the streets and highways they require are *publicly* owned—but because they are not individually open to public use.

The proportions in which public and private modes are used varies greatly from place to place, but the variation is highly systematic. In Table 8.1 the transportation mix in metropolitan areas is measured by looking at data on the type of transportation workers choose to reach their jobs. Obviously, public transportation is used much more frequently in central cities than in suburbs. In metropolitan areas as a whole in 1975, residents of central cities employed public modes for 14 percent of their journeys to work, as compared with only 4 percent for suburban residents. Use of public transportation also increases with SMSA size and city age. Public transportation accounts for 57 percent of work trips by New York City residents, by far the highest proportion for any city, just as New York is by far the largest city and SMSA. In small metropolitan areas (not shown in the table) public transportation is almost nonexistent.

When size is held constant, public transportation is far more important in old central cities than in new ones. This follows from the fact, already emphasized in Chapter 3, that the older cities of the North and East were built to exploit the advantages of mass transit, while the newer ones of the South and West were laid out to accommodate widespread use of the automobile. The effect can be seen in Table 8.1 by

2. J. R. Meyer, J. F. Kain, and M. Wohl, *The Urban Transportation Problem* (Cambridge, Mass.: Harvard University Press, 1965), p. 171.

TABLE 8.1

Mode of Transportation in Metropolitan Areas, 1975–1978[a]

| | | JOURNEYS-TO-WORK (PERCENT)[c] | | | |
| | | AUTO OR TRUCK | | PUBLIC TRANSPORTATION | |
METROPOLITAN AREAS[b]	SMSA 1970 POPULATION (MILLIONS)[b]	Central City Resi-dents	Suburb Resi-dents	Central City Resi-dents	Suburb Resi-dents
U.S. total	—	77.1	88.6	14.0	4.4
New York, N.Y.	11.6	27.6	73.9	56.5	14.1
Los Angeles– Long Beach, Calif.	7.0	84.1	89.3	7.5	2.9
Chicago, Ill.	7.0	60.5	84.3	30.5	9.7
Philadelphia, Pa.–N. J.	4.8	58.7	85.4	30.4	7.2
Cleveland, Ohio	2.1	62.4	80.4	18.5	6.6
Houston, Texas	2.0	85.0	91.6	5.5	0.6
Cincinnati, Ohio	1.4	79.0	91.2	13.3	3.7
Denver, Colo.	1.2	75.0	88.4	10.2	2.6
Riverside–San Bernardino– Ontario, Calif.	1.1	92.0	91.2	0.9	0.4

[a] Dates vary as follows: U.S. total, 1975; Chicago, Cincinnati, Philadelphia, Riverside, 1975–76; Cleveland, Denver, Houston, New York, 1976–77; Los Angeles, 1977–78.

[b] Areas as defined for the 1970 Census were used in these sample surveys.

[c] Percentage of all workers surveyed. Not shown are the following categories, which bring totals to 100%: bicycle, motorcycle, walk only, work at home, other means, and not reported.

Sources: U.S. total: U.S. Bureau of the Census, *Current Population Reports,* series P-23, no. 99, July 1979, table F. Selected cities: U.S. Bureau of Census, *Current Population Reports,* series P-23, nos. 86, 87, 94, 95, August-October 1979, and unpublished data from the Travel-to-Work Supplement to the Annual Housing Survey.

looking at old and new SMSA's of equal population size. For example, compare the use of public modes in the relatively old central city of Chicago (31 percent) and in much newer Los Angeles (8 percent), or in relatively old Cleveland (19 percent) and much newer Houston (6 percent), or relatively old Cincinnati (13 percent), relatively new Denver (10 percent), and even newer San Bernardino (0.9 percent).

It has been estimated that in 1970 the automobile accounted for 94 percent of all passenger miles traveled in urban areas.[3] One can infer

3. U.S. Department of Transportation, 1972 *National Transportation Report,* July 1972, table VI-1, p. 189.

from Table 8.1 that public transportation today has an important shar
of the market *only* in very large and relatively old cities. Table 8.2
however, shows that it was not always so.

Mass Transit Versus the Automobile

Public transportation has become less important over time, in par
because the automobile predominates in the suburbs and in the newe
central cities, where population growth has been fastest, but also becaus
even in the old, transit-oriented core cities transit use has fallei
precipitously as residents have switched to automobiles. Ridership b
type of transit since 1950 is displayed in Table 8.2, which also show
vehicle miles traveled by passenger cars in urban areas during the sam
period.

Transit ridership reached its peak just after World War II. It the
declined steadily until 1972. Since that date it has recovered slightly
helped along by massive federal subsidies and, after 1973, by risin
gasoline prices and intermittent fuel shortages. Nevertheless, in 197
transit ridership remained 57 percent below its 1950 level. Urban aut
use nearly quadrupled in the same interval. It must be borne in mind tha
the numbers in Table 8.2 are not adjusted to a per capita basis. If the
were, transit use would be seen to decline even more sharply, becaus
urban population has increased markedly since 1950, while the numbe
of passengers was declining.

TABLE 8.2
Trends in Urban Transportation Use

| | PASSENGER CARS: VEHICLE MILES IN URBAN AREAS (BILLIONS) | TRANSIT (MILLIONS OF REVENUE PASSENGERS CARRIED) | | | | |
		Total	*Subway and el.*	*Street-car*	*Trolley Coach*	*Motor Bus*
1950	182.5	13,845	2,113	2,790	1,261	7,681
1960	284.8	7,521	1,670	335	447	5,069
1972	567.5	5,253	1,446	147	100	3,561
1978	693.6	5,963	1,415	80	51	4,406
Percentage change 1950–1978	+280	−57	−33	−97	−96	−43

Sources: Federal Highway Administration, *Highway Statistics*, various years;
American Public Transit Association, *Transit Fact Book*, 1978–1979,
table 9.

As this chapter and the next will make clear, the rivalry between mass transit and the automobile has been an important component in a wide range of urban public policy debates. Given the great difference in their effects on both urban form and the urban environment, it could hardly be otherwise. At stake is something fundamental: the physical nature of the city itself as a place to live and work. On this matter city planners especially are apt to have strongly held convictions, which give the debates over transportation policy at times an almost ideological intensity.

The data in Table 8.2 tell us that when offered a choice, on the terms that prevail almost everywhere, users have been choosing the automobile rather than public modes of transportation with a high degree of regularity. Before we can analyze urban transportation policies that are apt to depend on altering urban travel behavior, we had better understand how such choices are made. The analysis of modal choice is thus an essential preliminary to the investigation of urban transportation policy.

ANALYSIS OF MODAL CHOICE

Faced with alternative modes of transportation, the consumer selects among them on the basis of money cost, time cost, comfort, carrying capacity, and convenience. To simplify the analysis, we assume only two modes, the automobile and public transportation. First, consider their money cost. In the case of public transportation, money cost is simply the fare. Most commonly it does not vary with distance, provided the rider stays on the same vehicle. Transferring to a vehicle on an intersecting route usually entails paying another full fare. The money cost of automobile travel is far more complex. It includes both operating costs, such as gasoline, repairs, parking, and tolls, and ownership costs, such as depreciation, garaging, and insurance. An estimate of these costs over the normal life of an automobile, divided by the number of miles expected to be driven, produces a figure for average cost per mile. Table 8.3 shows that cost per mile over the life of an automobile was estimated at 24.58 cents in 1979. Operating costs account for about half the total.

The quality we call "comfort" when analyzing competing modes needs no explanation in theory, though it is difficult to quantify in practice. "Convenience" refers to scheduling and proximity. The automobile has the great advantage of allowing self-scheduling by the user, as contrasted with public transportation in which the user must either adhere to a known schedule or else allow for average waiting time between vehicles. Moreover, journeys by public transit often require one or more transfers, each of which potentially adds waiting time or complicated

TABLE 8.3

Estimated Cost of Owning and Operating an Automobile

	CENTS PER MILE 10-YEAR AVERAGE[a]
Depreciation	6.26
Gasoline, incl. taxes	6.00
Repairs and maintenance	4.80
Insurance	2.44
Garaging	2.40
Parking and tolls	.80
Other	1.88
Total	24.58
Ownership costs	13.36
Operating costs	11.22

[a] Assumes standard-size 4-door sedan, 10-year lifespan, 100,000 miles driven.

Source: Federal Highway Administration, *Cost of Owning and Operating Automobiles and Vans,* 1979, table 2.

scheduling. Proximity often favors the auto, too. At the home end of the journey, at least in low-density neighborhoods, the car owner has service right at the door, whatever the situation may be at the other end of the trip. For shopping the automobile also has the advantage of far greater package-carrying capacity. On the other hand, the automobile may incur parking charges. On trips into the CBD such charges can easily outweigh other money costs.

Time as a Cost of Travel

Transportation analysts recognize that time cost as well as money cost enters into modal choice.[4] Consumers often select a high speed, high cost mode in preference to a low speed, low cost one. The obvious explanation of this behavior (leaving aside possible differences in comfort and convenience) is that savings in time cost outweigh the higher money cost of the more expensive mode.

As we shall see in Chapter 9, the time cost of travel also enters importantly into transportation investment analysis. Reduced travel time is usually one of the expected benefits of an improvement in the trans-

4. See, for example, Donald Dewees, "Travel Cost, Transit, and Urban Motoring," *Public Policy*, Winter 1976, pp. 59–79 and references cited in his note 2, p. 61.

portation system. Such time savings, however, must be given a dollar value before they can be entered into the investment calculus. The question "How much is an hour of travel time worth?" has not been easy to answer. For example, there is evidence that commuters place a higher value on waiting time and walking time than they do on in-vehicle travel time.[5] In what follows, we shall ignore this complication and treat travel time as homogeneous.

Opportunity cost is the basis of all real cost in economics. If time spent traveling is thought of as time that might have been devoted to working, then the opportunity cost of travel time is the individual's wage rate net of marginal income taxes. Although the results of statistical studies vary, it appears that in practice individuals value travel time at not more than half their wage rate.[6] Most people are not, after all, free to set their own work schedules so that they can work a little longer if they travel a little less. Even allowing for wide variation in the statistical estimates, however, it is clear that the value of time is a very important component of urban travel cost. Moreover, as long as the value individuals attach to it is positively related to income, we would expect the well-to-do to value time more highly than the poor, and that is what statistical studies have found.

Income, Value of Time, and Modal Choice

These relationships are illustrated in Table 8.4, which compares the journey-to-work decisions of two hypothetical individuals: White, a middle class commuter who values travel time at $6.00 an hour, and Green, a working class commuter who values it at $3.00 an hour. Both work in the business district of the central city and must decide whether to commute by car or public transportation. To simplify matters we assume that considerations of comfort and convenience cancel out for the two modes—the convenience of self-scheduling enjoyed in using a car is offset by the greater effort of driving as compared with riding in a public conveyance.

How the money cost of driving a car should be measured depends on the assumed circumstances. If neither White nor Green owns a car and would consider buying one only to commute, then the full cost per mile, including both operating and ownership costs, would be the relevant figure. If both already own cars, then the decision whether to use it would logically seem to depend only on operating cost per mile, which is about

5. Ibid., p. 61.
6. See M. E. Beesley, *Urban Transport: Studies in Economic Policy* (London: Butterworths, 1973), pp. 160, 179.

TABLE 8.4

Modal Choice for the Journey to Work

| | MS. WHITE: MIDDLE CLASS COMMUTER | | MR. GREEN: WORKING CLASS COMMUTER | | | |
| | | | Inbound | | Outbound | |
	Auto	Transit	Auto	Transit	Auto	Transit
One-way trip length						
miles	10	10	5	5	10	10
minutes	25	50	20	30	25	50
Cost, round trip						
Operating						
@ 12¢/mile	2.40	—	1.20	—	2.40	—
Transit fare						
@ 50¢ per segment	—	2.00	—	1.00	—	2.00
Parking	2.00	—	2.00	—	—	—
Time cost						
@ $6/hour	5.00	10.00	—	—	—	—
$3/hour	—	—	2.00	3.00	2.50	5.00
Total cost (dollars)	9.40	12.00	5.20	4.00	4.90	7.00

half the full cost. There is a third possibility. It is sometimes argued that in making trip choices, owners perceive only "out-of-pocket" costs such as gasoline, tolls, and parking, while ignoring all other operating costs. Out-of-pocket costs would be only about half of operating costs or a quarter of full costs per mile. In Table 8.4 we assume that both parties already own cars, and that they base their commuting decisions on operating rather than out-of-pocket costs. As suggested by the data in Table 8.3, these are calculated at 12¢ per mile.

White lives in a suburb ten miles out. Commuter rail service is not available. She can reach her job either by driving at a cost of 12¢ a mile and parking at a daily cost of $2.00, or by taking a bus and then the subway at 50¢ apiece for a total fare cost of $1.00 each way. The trip, including walking and waiting time, takes 25 minutes by auto or 50 by public transportation. Travel time therefore costs $2.50 each way by auto or $5.00 each way by public transportation. The total round-trip cost by auto, including parking, is $9.40. Since a round trip by public transportation would cost $12.00, White uses her car. (Incidentally, she would do so even if the decision to drive to work entailed buying a second car and taking into account its full cost of 24¢ per mile.)

Green, whose income is much lower than White's, lives in a working class neighborhood five miles from the center of the city and a short walk from the subway. He can be at his job in 30 minutes by public transportation at a fare of 50¢ and a time cost of $1.50, or he can drive to work in 20 minutes, incurring $1.00 in time costs, 60¢ in operating expense and $2.00 in parking fees. The round-trip via transit costs $4.00 as compared with $5.20 when driving. Green will therefore prefer to ride the subway, even though he owns a car. His evaluation of time cost would have to rise to $6.60 an hour before driving would appear as attractive as public transportation.

If White lived at Green's location she would not drive to work despite her higher valuation of travel time. Her choice would be influenced, among other things, by the fact that in our hypothetical example (as in the real world) the relative speed advantage of the automobile as compared with public transportation, is less at the close-in location. For the suburban commuter the automobile cuts travel time in half. For the resident at Green's location it reduces it only 33 percent.

It is interesting to note that if Green lived in the central city and worked in the suburbs, he would probably drive to work, even though his workplace could be reached by public transportation. The right hand panel of Table 8.4 shows hypothetical data for a "reverse commuter" at Green's income level, who faces transportation choices in commuting outward that are essentially the same as those facing White for the inward journey to work. Since suburban employers usually provide free parking, automobile cost does not include parking charges, and the round-trip total amounts to only $4.90, far less than the $7.00 cost via public transportation.

Indeed, reverse commuters are a fast-growing segment of the metropolitan labor force. Car-pooling is common among these workers so that even if Green did *not* own his own car he might very well make the reverse commuting trip via automobile. This probability is reinforced by the fact that routes and schedules of public transportation systems are generally arranged to accommodate the inbound rather than the outbound commuter. (See the discussion in Chapter 9.) It is unlikely that, as we have assumed in Table 8.4, Green would have outbound public transportation choices as favorable as those available to White for the inbound journey.

An advantage similar to car-pooling occurs when a family owns a car. If they use public transportation, each member pays a fare. When they ride together in a car, cost per person drops as the number of passengers rises. Coupled with the fact that operating costs are far lower than full costs per mile (and *perceived* costs may be lower still), this effect heavily favors the use of the automobile, once it is owned, even where good public transportation is available. For example, members of the Green family may use public transportation to reach downtown jobs. But since the family owns a car they are very likely to use it as well for evening recreation or for shopping within the metropolitan area. Instead of riding on public transportation to shop or go to the movies "downtown," they may now drive out to nearby suburban shopping or entertainment centers.

This example helps to explain why the sharpest drop in mass transit ridership has occurred in the off-peak rather than the rush hours. It also illustrates the interdependence of land use and transportation. The introduction of the automobile does not mean simply that people make the same trips in automobiles that they formerly made via public transportation. Often it means that they substitute new destinations for old, thereby encouraging or reinforcing change in metropolitan land use patterns.

Income, Automobile Ownership, and Modal Choice

We have seen that income influences modal choice indirectly through its effect on time value. Even though Green owns a car he is more likely than White to choose transit for the journey to work because his income is lower and he therefore places a lower value on time savings. However, income also affects modal choice through its influence on automobile ownership. The connection between income, car ownership, and modal choice is demonstrated in Table 8.5, which draws on Kain and Fauth's study of journey-to-work mode choices. The upper panel shows that automobile ownership rises sharply with income, the lower panel

TABLE 8.5
Family Income, Car Ownership and Modal Choice, 1970[a]

	FAMILY INCOME PER YEAR		
NUMBER OF CARS	$2,000– 4,000	$6,000– 8,000	$15,000– 25,000
	PROPORTION OWNING		
0	.23	.10	.01
1	.49	.60	.25
2+	.28	.30	.75
	PROPORTION DRIVING TO WORK		
0	.06	.13	.29
1	.72	.78	.67
2+	.83	.91	.90

[a] Single-worker households residing in the 125 largest SMSA's (4-person family, age of head 35–65 years).
Source: John F. Kain and Gary R. Fauth, *The Effects of Urban Structure on Household Auto Ownership Decisions and Journey to Work Mode Choices,* Harvard University, Department of City and Regional Planning, Research Paper R 76–1, May 1976, tables 3–2, 3–3, 3–4, 3–7.

that auto ownership, in turn, is closely related to the choice of mode at all levels of income. In short, the poor are less likely than the rich to own a car and therefore are less likely to drive to work.

Income also affects modal choice *indirectly* through its influence on residential location. We have shown in Chapter 6 that residential location depends in part on income: as their incomes rise, families tend to move out to the suburbs to indulge their appetite for living space. But public transportation is generally less available and convenient in the suburbs than in the central city. Hence the higher its income, the less likely a family is to live where public transportation is an attractive alternative to the private car.

For a variety of reasons then, consumers buy less public transportation as their incomes rise.[7] No doubt this helps to explain the long-run decline in transit ridership shown in Table 8.2. It also necessarily has a chilling effect on plans for expansion of the nation's mass transportation system. We generally take it for granted that living standards will continue to rise in the future. But unless other conditions change in offsetting fashion, rising incomes could mean that demand for rides on public transit will continue to shift down, jeopardizing new and old facilities alike.

Elasticity of Demand for Transportation

The responsiveness of travel behavior to changes in one or more components of travel cost depends on the elasticity of demand for transportation services. Elasticity in this case can be defined as the ratio of the percentage change in the number of trips taken to the percentage change in trip cost that brings it about. Since travel demand depends on both time and money cost, which can be manipulated independently by policymakers, it is generally useful to measure elasticity of demand separately for each of these costs.

It should be recalled that price elasticities carry a negative sign because the quantity purchased always changes in the opposite direction to the price. A value between 0 and −1 indicates an *inelastic* demand relationship, one in which price changes bring about *less* than proportional changes in quantity demanded. If a price change induces a *more* than proportional change in quantity taken, price elasticity exceeds −1 and the demand relationship is an *elastic* one.

Statistical studies indicate that commuting behavior is not very responsive to changes in money price, whether these occur via alteration of transit fares or of automobile operating costs. A word of caution may

7. For additional evidence, see *1972 National Transportation Report*, p. 191 and table VI–4, p. 254.

be warranted, however. The studies cited below refer to short-run price elasticity. In the longer run, when they have had time to adapt, consumers may be more responsive to price changes than these figures suggest. Consequently, there is some risk involved in using short-run elasticities to guide long-run policies.

Michael Kemp summarizes the available evidence by pointing out that estimates of the fare elasticity of transit demand in the developed countries of Europe and North America fall in the range of −0.1 to −0.7. He adds that in very large cities and at peak hours when the alternatives to transit are most costly, elasticities usually fall in the lower end of that range.[8] Indeed, it has become a kind of rule of thumb among transit operators, when they adjust fares, to expect a percentage change in ridership about one-third the size of any percentage change in fares, which implies an expected price elasticity of −.33.

Table 8.6 presents a set of travel demand elasticities estimated by Domencich, Kraft, and Valette for the Boston metropolitan area. It includes estimates for auto as well as transit demand, for time cost as well as fare cost, and it separates journey-to-work trips from shopping trips. Transit money and time costs are divided into a line-haul and an access component. The latter covers all costs except those incurred on the principal travel mode, which is the "line-haul." Auto money costs are divided into a "line-haul" component, which covers operating but not ownership costs per trip, and an out-of-pocket component, which covers tolls and parking charges. Auto time costs per trip are divided into in-vehicle and out-of-vehicle components.

The results in Table 8.6 conform closely with a priori expectations. Transit fare elasticity is very low, though slightly higher for shopping than for work trips. Auto money cost elasticity is also low for journey-to-work trips, though not as low as transit elasticity.

For both modes, elasticity is considerably higher with respect to time cost than money cost. This is consistent with the fact, illustrated in Table 8.4, that the time cost of travel often outweighs its money cost. Consequently, a reduction of X percent in time cost will have a greater impact on total trip cost than a reduction of the same proportion in money cost.

Within the time category, elasticity is much higher for access time than for line-haul time of transit trips and for out-of-vehicle than for in-vehicle time of auto trips. This would seem to confirm that travelers find walking and waiting time more onerous than time spent riding or driving.

8. Michael A. Kemp, "Some Evidence of Transit Demand Elasticities," *Transportation* 2 (1973), p. 25.

TABLE 8.6
Elasticity of Demand for Urban Transportation

	AUTO TRIPS	
	Line-Haul Cost[a]	*Toll and Parking Cost*
Money Cost Elasticity		
Work trips	−.494	−.071
Shopping trips	−.878	−1.65
	In-Vehicle Time	*Out-of-Vehicle Time*
Time Cost Elasticity		
Work trips	−.82	−1.437
Shopping trips	−1.02	−1.440

	TRANSIT TRIPS		
	Line-Haul Cost[b]		*Access (feeder-line) Cost*[c]
Money Cost Elasticity			
Work trips	−.09		−.10
Shopping trips		−.323[d]	
	Line-Haul Time		*Access Time*
Time Cost Elasticity			
Work trips	−.39		−.709
Shopping trips		−.593[d]	

[a] Includes operating cost from origin to destination. Ownership costs are excluded.
[b] Includes fare paid on principal transit mode. Fares on feeder lines at either end of line-haul are excluded.
[c] Includes cost of access from origin to principal mode, plus cost of travel from that mode to destination.
[d] Transit shopping sample too small to permit disaggregation of components.
Source: T. A. Domencich, G. Kraft, and J. P. Valette, "Estimation of Urban Passenger Travel Behavior: An Economic Demand Model," *Highway Research Record*, no. 238 (1968), reprinted in M. Edel and J. Rothenberg, eds., *Readings in Urban Economics* (New York: Macmillan, 1972), pp. 464–65.

Policy Implications of Inelastic Transit Demand

A policy of "free transit" has often been advocated as a dramatic step to improve the economic health of the older central cities. It has been argued that free transit would help to revive fading central business districts, reduce the diseconomies of highway congestion and air pollution, and improve job access for ghetto-bound minorities. Kraft and Domencich used the data summarized in Table 8.6 to evaluate these claims. The low elasticities shown there mean that free transit would produce only very modest increases in ridership, and therefore at best would have slight effect in reaching the intended objectives. The authors concluded that other policies were available to do the job far more effectively, and without entirely discarding the rationalizing influence of market prices (to which we return below).[9]

While it is true that low transit fare elasticities make it difficult to increase ridership by *reducing* transit charges, the other side of the coin (or, in some cities, token) is that low elasticities also mean ridership will decline very little if fares are *increased*. Hence higher fares will generally produce higher revenues, a lesson well known to both public and private transit operators.

Since the time elasticities in Table 8.6 are much higher than the fare elasticities, Kraft and Domencich inferred from the data that faster and more frequent service would do more than lower fares to encourage transit ridership. Moreover, time elasticities are higher for access time than for line-haul, from which they inferred that service improvements in the residential collection and downtown distribution systems would be more effective in attracting riders than would attempts to speed up the main-line service.

Perhaps because the fare level is such a politically potent symbol of concern with urban problems, transit pricing policies often run directly counter to these inferences. When the object is to promote ridership, operating authorities usually reduce the fare instead of improving service. Or, if they are under pressure to cut financial losses without raising fares, they economize by reducing the frequency of service, thus losing customers (and revenues) by increasing the time cost of using the system.

However, even if the elasticity of demand is higher with respect to transit service than transit fare, it cannot be assumed that service improvements will be so attractive as to be self-financing. After surveying the evidence from a number of demonstration projects, Kemp concludes that "service improvements . . . can significantly improve ridership, but rarely to the extent of recovering the full incremental cost of the improvements."[10] If it were otherwise, of course, an "urban transportation problem" would not exist: we could have mass transit systems in our

9. Gerald Kraft and Thomas A. Domencich, "Free Transit," in Matthew Edel and Jerome Rothenberg, eds., *Readings In Urban Economics* (New York: Macmillan, 1972), pp. 459–80.
10. Kemp, p. 38.

large cities that offered high quality service and were also self-financing. Transit operators, though much criticized, cannot be so incompetent as to have missed that sort of opportunity.

The difficulty that policymakers face in trying to influence urban travel patterns can also be illustrated by referring back to modal choice data for hypothetical commuters Green and White. Suppose, for example, that the government wished to discourage commuting by automobile in order to reduce air pollution or encourage fuel saving. What would the transit fare have to be to lure well-to-do commuter White out of her private car? Table 8.4 shows that even if transit were free she would continue to drive. The government would have to pay her fare and add a cash bonus of at least 60¢ for every round trip into town to induce her to commute by transit. This outcome reflects the fact that time costs "dominate" White's decision. Even substantial percentage changes in other costs are insufficient to change the outcome.

In Green's case it is only the considerable cost of parking—obviously reflecting high land values in the CBD—that would discourage him from driving to work if his job were located centrally. Were he to become a reverse commuter with a job in the suburbs, we have already seen that he would drive to work. Even free transit would not suffice to divert him from the highway. He would require a small bonus in addition.

These results are not entirely fanciful. Leon Moses and Harold Williamson, Jr., in a well-known 1963 study based on a survey of Chicago automobile commuters, estimated the transit fares that would be required to divert commuters from automobiles to their "best alternative" mode. They found, for example, that of those auto users who listed "el-subway" as the best alternative, only 18 percent would be diverted to that mode even if it were free. It would have required an additional bonus (or "negative price") of 40¢ to 50¢ per one-way ride to induce as many as half of such commuters to use the el-subway system. The authors concluded that "If our results are at all reasonable, the possibility of significantly reducing auto congestion by reasonable reductions in the price of public transportation appears slight."[11]

Substitute "air pollution" for "congestion" and the statement is equally relevant to that problem. Metropolitan air pollution and automobile use are directly related. Pollution could be reduced if commuters were diverted from private automobiles to mass transportation, provided —and this is an important qualification—that the level of demand is high enough so that transit vehicles are reasonably well-filled. However,

11. Leon N. Moses and Harold F. Williamson, Jr., "Value of Time, Choice of Mode, and the Subsidy Issue in Urban Transportation," *Journal of Political Economy*, June 1963, p. 262.

the Moses and Williamson study shows that even in a transit-oriented city such as Chicago it would be impossible to achieve much diversion by manipulating transit fares unless the price were pushed well below zero.

Fuel Prices and Modal Choice

What about the effect of higher fuel prices on travel demand? Won't the rise in the price of gasoline associated with the "energy crisis" divert commuters back to public transportation, thus reducing both fuel consumption and air pollution? There is not much evidence of diversion so far, and the hypothetical numbers in Table 8.4 suggest why. The effect of rising fuel prices on travel behavior is moderated by the fact that time costs—and, in the case of journeys to the CBD, parking charges—make up so much of the full cost of a trip. In the hypothetical world of Table 8.4, the cost of gasoline, including taxes, comes to about 6¢ a mile. At that level it accounts for only 13 percent of White's commuting costs and about 25 percent of Green's (as a reverse commuter). The cost of gasoline would have to rise above 16½¢ a mile to divert the outward-bound Green to public transportation and above 19¢ a mile to divert White. The effect of rising fuel prices on modal choice is also moderated by the fact that auto users tend to purchase smaller, more fuel-efficient cars as fuel prices rise. Consequently, cost per mile for the average driver does not increase as fast as cost per gallon.

Though modal choice for commuting may respond little to higher fuel prices, other aspects of travel behavior are much more likely to be affected. We would certainly expect consumers to rely less on the automobile for long-distance travel. In the longer run, choice of residential or job locations is also likely to be affected. That is a question to which we return at the end of Chapter 9.

Up to this point we have concentrated on the demand side of the market for urban transportation. We turn next to the supply side, examining highway costs in the short run in order to develop rational pricing rules for operating an existing transportation network.

OPTIMUM TRANSPORTATION PRICING
IN THE SHORT RUN

It is an important objective in any society to make efficient use of productive resources. The student of economics learns in the elementary course that an optimum, or "efficient," allocation of resources could be achieved if all goods were produced and sold under conditions of perfect competition and no externalities occurred in production or consumption.

Under perfect competition, the price of every good sold would equal the marginal private cost of producing it. In the absence of externalities, marginal social cost could not exceed marginal private cost. Thus the price charged in the marketplace would cover the full cost to society of producing the marginal unit of every commodity. No one could consume any commodity for which he or she was not willing to repay the full social cost. At the same time, competition among producers would guarantee that the sales price of a commodity could never *exceed* its marginal cost. Consumers would be assured of receiving all goods for which they were willing to pay at least the full social cost. "Marginal cost pricing" would thus lead automatically to optimum resource use in the short run.

Unhappily, no such automatic optimization can be expected in the urban transportation sector, which departs from the ideal in several crucial respects.

1. Instead of perfect competition with its many sellers, we find competition among a few modes, each of which is typically operated by a public or private monopolist. Consequently, regulated prices are the rule rather than the exception.
2. In many cases the "decreasing cost" nature of production makes the usual "marginal cost equal to price" solution peculiarly difficult to attain.
3. Finally, externalities in the form of congestion, air pollution, noise, and other disamenities abound in the urban transportation sector, so that the private cost of a mile of urban travel is often significantly less than its full social cost.

Transportation is a multidimensional service. The number of trips per hour over a given route is usually taken as the measure of output, but, ideally, the output measure should also reflect both degree of comfort and reliability of service. So far as urban mass transit is concerned, the cost of producing a unit of output depends very much on how the service is organized. How frequent is it? How many scheduled stops are made per mile? How fast are the vehicles? These and many more factors affect cost and output. Herbert Mohring's economic model of an urban bus route contains no fewer than thirteen variables.[12]

Transportation analysts usually begin by examining the highway case, since it is somewhat simpler than urban mass transit and serves to illustrate the main issues in optimum pricing policy. Once these have been clarified, application of the analysis to urban mass transit systems is quite straightforward. We begin with the analysis of highway pricing in the

12. Herbert Mohring, *Transportation Economics* (Cambridge, Mass.: Ballinger Publishing Co., 1976), pp. 149–50.

short run, when the set of facilities can be taken as fixed. Optimum short-run pricing is essential if society is to use existing facilities efficiently.[13] It also provides a crucial link to optimum long-run investment policy, which will be taken up subsequently.

Pricing Highway Services in the Short Run

Let us assume that a network of roads exists by virtue of past public investment. The existing roads are owned and operated by a public authority. On what terms should that authority make them available to individual users?

In the short run, efficient pricing requires that road users make payments for each trip equal to the cost of all the resources used up as a result of that trip.[14] These resource costs can be classified as follows:

1. Highway maintenance costs dependent upon use, borne by the highway authority
2. Automobile operating and time costs, borne by the trip-maker
3. External costs, borne by neither the trip-maker nor the highway authority
    a. congestion costs, borne by other highway users
    b. environmental costs (air pollution, noise, etc.), borne by the adjacent population

If the auto trip-maker can be made to bear all of the above costs, then he or she will undertake only those trips the utility of which is at least equal to their full incremental cost. As long as the trip-maker is not charged *more* than the sum of these costs, then he or she will make *all* trips that yield utility greater than cost. Society will be making optimum use of the existing highway network.

Pricing on Congested Roads

Since the cost of travel, especially in urban areas, often is affected by congestion, we begin with the problem of optimal pricing when

13. One of the earliest advocates of marginal cost pricing for urban transportation facilities was William S. Vickrey. See his 1963 article, "Pricing in Urban and Suburban Transport," reprinted in Ronald E. Grieson, ed., *Urban Economics: Readings and Analysis* (Boston: Little, Brown: 1973), pp. 106–18, which contains many illustrative applications.

14. The following analysis draws heavily on A. A. Walters, *The Economics of Road User Charges* (Baltimore: Johns Hopkins Press, 1968), chs. II and III.

FIGURE 8.1

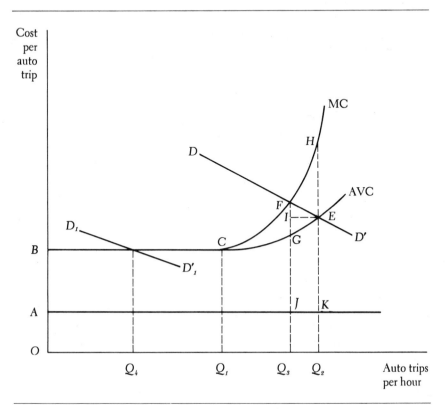

Source: Adapted from A. A. Walters, *The Economics of Road User Charges* (Baltimore: The Johns Hopkins University Press, 1968), fig. 2, p. 24.

congestion is present. Figure 8.1 will help to clarify the relationship between trip cost and the level of highway use. It depicts the components of cost for journeys along a given stretch of highway. The horizontal axis measures number of auto trips per hour along the highway segment. The traffic flow increases as we move to the right. The vertical axis measures cost per trip, including components 1, 2, and 3-a of the above list. (To simplify the argument we assume, at this point, that environmental pollution costs are zero.)

A part of highway maintenance cost depends on weather and the passage of time, but part also depends on the number of vehicles using the highway. Walters calls the latter "variable maintenance costs," since they vary directly with the number of vehicles using the road. In Figure 8.1 the amount of these costs *per vehicle* is OA. The variable maintenance cost curve, *AJK*, is a horizontal line because the amount *OA* per vehicle remains constant over a wide range of traffic volumes.[15]

The distance *AB* measures automobile operating and time costs per trip when traffic on the highway segment is light. These costs remain constant up to traffic volume Q_1. At that point congestion sets in: the traffic flow becomes heavy enough so that cars begin to get in one another's way and average speed drops. Because trips now take longer, their time cost increases. The curve *BCGE* begins to rise. Its height above *B* at any point to the right of Q_1 shows the extent to which an individual driver bears the cost of congestion as a private cost at that level of traffic. Its height above the horizontal axis measures the average variable cost of a trip—including road maintenance, vehicle operation, and driver time costs—at each level of traffic. Hence it is labeled AVC.

Congestion is a social as well as a private problem. Suppose traffic is at level Q_1 per hour. If an additional driver—call him Smith—then enters the flow, congestion begins. Not only Smith but every other traveler then on the road finds the going slower. Smith bears the cost of congestion only in so far as it increases his own travel time. But by entering the traffic stream he has imposed a like cost on every other traveler. Thus congestion costs are a form of externality: the action of one individual imposes costs on others in addition to those he bears himself. The external costs of congestion are shown by the curve *CFH*, which rises above *BCGE* once congestion sets in. The external cost that a single additional vehicle entering the stream at any given level of traffic flow will impose on all other drivers is measured by the vertical distance between the two curves. For example, if the traffic flow equals Q_2, an additional driver entering the stream imposes congestion costs of *HE* on the aggregate of other drivers already on the road. *CFH* shows the increment to total social cost occasioned by one additional trip. Since it measures the increment to total cost, it is a marginal cost curve in the usual meaning of that term and is labeled MC.

The demand for the use of the road segment analyzed in Figure 8.1 is shown by *DD'*. Demand is depicted as fairly elastic because there are presumably other routes that drivers could choose between the points served by this segment.

Let us assume that the highway authority charges each driver a toll equal to *OA*, thus covering those maintenance expenditures attributable to use of the road. Then the curve *BCGE* represents the cost to each driver of using the highway segment. *BCGE* becomes, in effect, a supply curve, showing the price at which journeys can be obtained, for any level of traffic flow. The demand curve *DD'* shows how many trips drivers will

15. Ibid., p. 23.

wish to make at any given price. The traffic flow will actually settle at level Q_2, corresponding to the intersection of the supply and demand curves at point E. At that level each driver will pay a maintenance toll of OA and, in addition, bear private costs of KE per journey.

Q_2, however, is not the optimal traffic level because the pricing system thus far assumed ignores the external costs of congestion. The full cost of the Q_2th journey is not $OA + KE$, as paid by the marginal road user, but $OA + KE + EH$, where EH measures the increment to aggregate congestion costs attributable to the marginal journey. In order to achieve optimum road use the highway authority, in addition to charging maintenance toll OA, must levy a congestion toll equal to the external cost of congestion. That cost varies with the level of traffic and equals the vertical distance between curves BGE and CFH. If such a congestion toll were charged, the supply curve of journeys would effectively be shifted to $BCFH$. Intersection with the demand curve would then occur at point F, and the flow of traffic would be reduced from Q_2 per hour to Q_3.

It can easily be shown that Q_3 is the optimum flow. At traffic level Q_3 the marginal traveler places a dollar value of $OA + JF$ on his journey, as shown by the height of the demand curve at F. This just offsets the full social cost of the trip, shown by the height of the full cost curve CFH at F. To the right of Q_3 the demand curve drops below the full cost curve. The marginal traveler would be consuming journeys that were worth less to him than their full cost. To the left of Q_3 the demand curve lies above the full cost curve. Travelers would be foregoing journeys that were worth more to them than their full social cost. In either case, resource use would be less than optimal.

Note that the optimum solution at Q_3 does not eliminate all congestion. As much congestion remains as travelers are willing to pay for. Of course, it must be borne in mind that we are dealing here only with the short run in which, by definition, the stock of highways is fixed. As we shall see below, a sufficiently high level of congestion tolls would be taken as a signal that more highways should be built. Even in the long run, however, when society has obtained an optimum network of roads, there would continue to be congestion at many points. We shall return to this question below. In the meantime, it must be added that no variable congestion tolls yet exist in the United States. The theoretical, practical, and political objections to them will be taken up subsequently.

Pricing on Uncongested Roads

Suppose that in Figure 8.1 the demand for trips were shown by D_1D_1' instead of DD'. With less demand for trips, the road would be uncongested, since the intersection of D_1D_1' with the supply curve $BCGE$ occurs to the left of point C, where congestion begins. In that case the appropriate toll would be only OA, a charge sufficient to cover variable maintenance costs. In addition, drivers would bear their own operating and time costs, AB.

Pricing on Roads Subject to "Peaking"

It cannot have escaped the reader's attention that in urban areas the journey to work (and back) often generates morning and evening traffic jams. Radial highways connecting large-city CBD's with the suburban ring are particularly subject to such congestion. This sort of "peak loading" greatly complicates the problem of urban transportation, including, in the short run, the achievement of optimal pricing.

Referring again to Figure 8.1, imagine that DD' represents demand during the peak morning and evening hours while D_1D_1' shows demand at other times. In that case, the theory of road pricing suggests that a congestion toll should be charged only during the "rush hours," since the road is not otherwise congested. Thus, the highway authority would be called upon to vary its charges according to time of day and direction of flow. During rush hours, highway space becomes a relatively scarce commodity. By charging a price for its use the highway authority allocates it to those who value that use most highly. During non-rush hours, if the road is not congested, highway space is not scarce and need not be rationed. Users are then charged only the cost of the wear and tear they impose on the facility, a toll of OA. An empirical estimate of optimum peak and off-peak congestion tolls for the San Francisco Bay area is presented in Table 8.7 on page 227.

Pricing on Urban Mass Transit Systems

If we are willing to accept a certain degree of abstraction from the complexity of actual bus or subway operations, Figure 8.1 can also be taken to represent short-run costs in urban mass transit. The quantity on the horizontal axis becomes hourly flow of passengers past a given point on the particular line in question. Fixed costs are not shown. The curve $BCGE$ represents average variable costs. As Martin Wohl has suggested, such a curve begins to rise beyond a certain flow level for reasons analogous to those that explain rising costs in the highway case.[16] First, increased passenger crowding on vehicles eventually leads to discomfort

16. Martin Wohl, "Congestion Toll Pricing for Public Transport Facilities," in Selma Mushkin, ed., *Public Prices for Public Products* (Washington, D.C.: The Urban Institute, 1972), pp. 245–46.

(for example, lack of seating), which adds to the perceived cost of a trip. Second, congestion eventually reduces average vehicle speed, thus increasing the time-cost of a trip (for example, when the number of riders increases, buses and trains take longer at each stop to discharge and board them). The segment *CGE* shows how these congestion costs are borne by the individual user. As in the case of highways, when the external costs each additional user imposes on all others are added to individual costs, we obtain the curve *CFH*. The height of *CFH* above *CGE* measures these externalities at each level of traffic.

Using rational pricing principles, an urban transit authority would charge the following prices: during nonrush hours, charge a toll just sufficient to cover the marginal cost to the authority of an incremental passenger; during rush hours, cover the marginal cost to the authority *plus* the congestion cost that the marginal passenger imposes on the riding public at the rush-hour traffic level.

OPTIMUM LONG-RUN ADJUSTMENT OF TRANSPORTATION SYSTEMS

Congestion tolls provide the link between the optimum short-run operation and the optimum long-run adjustment of a transportation network. If congestion tolls on a given highway segment appear sufficient to cover the cost of an increase in capacity, it seems intuitively correct to argue that capacity should be expanded. (Indeed, one of the strongest arguments for charging congestion tolls is that they would provide valuable information about when and where to invest in expansion.)

The logical connection between tolls and expansion can be shown most readily if we adopt a useful simplifying assumption suggested by A. A. Walters. Let us suppose, for the moment, that roads are made of "pure putty."[17] In that case, Walters points out, roads could be expanded quickly and by very small fractions: one would simply add to, or stretch, or squeeze the putty. Awkward discontinuities such as the jump from two lanes to three, or from unlimited to limited access, would be eliminated because "pure putty" roads would be infinitely malleable. Let us further assume that under these conditions expansion could be carried out at a constant cost per additional unit of capacity. We can show that it would then be desirable to expand each road as long as the congestion tolls collected from the users exceeded the cost of expanding capacity sufficiently to accommodate one more vehicle at a given level of congestion.

17. Walters, pp. 31–32.

FIGURE 8.2

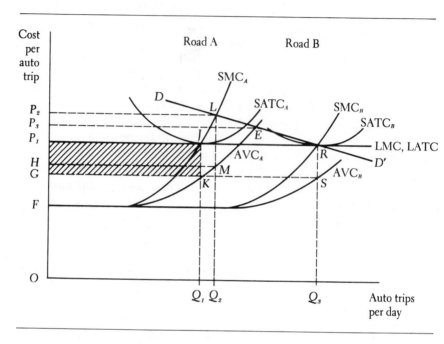

The case of constant cost is illustrated in Figure 8.2. This diagram is similar to Figure 8.1, but in addition to the relationships shown there, it displays short-run average total cost (SATC), long-run average total cost (LATC), and long-run marginal cost (LMC). As in Figure 8.1, average variable cost (AVC) includes road maintenance, vehicle operating, and driver time costs, while short-run marginal cost (SMC) shows the increment to total cost, including the cost of congestion, occasioned by one additional trip.

Figure 8.2 shows a road at two different capacity levels, A and B. The peak-load problem is eliminated by assumption: we assume that traffic flow is the same at all times of day. The horizontal axis therefore measures daily vehicle trips. Because the road can be expanded at constant cost per unit of additional capacity, the long-run average total cost curve is a horizontal line. Moreover, it is an elementary proposition in microeconomic theory that if long-run average total cost is constant, then long-run marginal cost is also constant and equal to it. Hence on the diagram LMC corresponds with LATC.

By definition, average fixed cost equals average total cost minus average variable cost. In Figure 8.2, when Q_1 vehicles per day use Highway A, average fixed cost per day is therefore given by JK, which also equals P_1G. This means that a toll of P_1G collected daily from Q_1 users will provide sufficient revenue over the life of the highway to finance the construction cost of Highway A. This daily revenue of $Q_1 \times (P_1G)$ is shown by the area of the shaded rectangle P_1JKG. In order to expand this constant cost highway by a single unit of capacity, it would be sufficient to collect the toll of P_1G from a single additional trip-maker each day. (Another way of putting it is that P_1G equals the daily cost of borrowing the capital needed to expand the capacity of the highway by one unit. If the same toll (P_1G) were collected daily from Q_3 users, the additional revenue $(P_1G) \times (Q_3 - Q_1)$ would pay for the expansion of capacity from Q_1 to Q_3. Thus the constant cost of expansion per unit of capacity is P_1G per day, collected over the life of the highway.

Highway A is the optimum size road to carry a daily flow of Q_1 vehicles, because the short-run average total cost of Highway A ($SATC_A$) reaches its minimum point at flow Q_1. However, it is *not* the optimum size road in the situation depicted in Figure 8.2. The demand for trips is shown by DD'. If Highway A is the existing road and the Highway Authority employs optimum short-run pricing it will limit traffic to the flow Q_2 indicated by the intersection of the short-run marginal social cost curve (SMC_A) and the demand curve, doing so by charging a congestion toll of LM. However, Highway A is not the optimum size for traffic flows greater than Q_1. This is demonstrated by the fact that $SATC_A$ rises above LATC to the right of Q_1. For larger flows, a larger road would be desirable. Moreover, the revenue generated by congestion toll LM collected from Q_2 users (the area of rectangle P_2LMH) exceeds the revenue needed to finance the fixed costs of A (the area of rectangle P_1JKG). We can be certain of that because both dimensions of the former rectangle are larger than those of the latter. Since we assume there are no discontinuities in highway construction, expansion of A is clearly warranted.

Given the demand for trips indicated by DD', the highway should be expanded from scale A to scale B. Figure 8.2 shows that the latter is the optimum size road to cope with existing demand. To the left of Q_3 the demand curve lies above the long-run marginal cost curve, which means that users are willing to pay more for additional trips than the full incremental cost to society of producing them (including increments to fixed as well as variable cost). Too little highway capacity is being supplied. To the right of Q_3, the situation reverses. DD' falls below LMC, indicating that users are not willing to pay the full cost of trips beyond level Q_3. Highway capacity is being oversupplied.

However, when Highway B is in place we find that users are just willing to pay a price (OP_1) that equals both long- and short-run marginal cost. That means that in constructing B, the Highway Authority reaches both a long- and a short-run optimum: long run because they are supplying that amount of capacity for which users are just willing to pay the full cost; short run because they are allowing every consumer to use the road who is willing to pay the full marginal cost (including the congestion cost) of an additional trip.

It is important to note that the expansion in scale from A to B is self-financing. The increment to fixed cost per day necessary to pay for expansion is the area of the rectangle *KJRS*. But this is also precisely the amount added to daily toll revenue when journeys increase from Q_1 to Q_3 per day.

The theory of highway pricing, then, leads to a clear set of rules for both short- and long-run operation. These have been summarized by Mohring as follows: "Given constant returns to scale . . . (1) Establish short-run marginal cost prices for the use of each link. Doing so would require levying tolls equal to the difference between the short-run marginal and average variable costs of trips. And (2) alter the size of each link to the point where the toll revenues generated by it equal the costs to the authority of providing that link . . . ."[18] Following these simple rules, we would have the best of all possible road systems: a self-financing highway network of optimum size, with every link operating at the optimum level of traffic flow. Moreover, if urban mass transit systems displayed constant returns to scale, the same rules would apply to them, with the same happy consequences.

If matters were truly that simple, of course, there would be no transportation problem, urban or otherwise. Much of the next chapter will be devoted to reintroducing "real-world" complications into the analysis.

Why Aren't All Roads Congested?

The theory of road pricing just expounded leads to the curious conclusion that if we had an optimum road network operating under conditions of long-run equilibrium, every part of it would be congested: witness optimum-size Road B of Figure 8.2, on which congestion tolls of *RS* are collected from each user. According to the theory, any road segment with zero congestion (for example, Road B if traffic flow were only Q_2) is too large for the level of traffic it serves. The reader, recalling that by far the greater part of the United States' road system is *not* congested, may wonder whether it is the theory or the road system that is at fault.

18. Mohring, p. 21.

The answer would appear to be that there are economies of scale in the construction and operation of highways at the small end of the size spectrum such that it is uneconomical to build and operate very small roads. For example, one-lane roads require extremely low operating speeds and cause great difficulty in passing, both features that add enormously to the time cost of a trip. Consequently, it pays to build two-lane roads, even though in rural areas most of these will never be congested.[19] The theory of road pricing can accommodate these aspects of reality. Let us abandon the assumption of long-run constant cost that is incorporated in Figure 8.2 and introduce economies and diseconomies of scale.

Pricing with Economies and Diseconomies of Scale

If a large highway can be constructed or operated at a lower average cost per vehicle trip than a small highway, then we say that highways are subject to economies of scale, or, what is the same thing, that highway services display decreasing long-run cost. The optimum pricing policy under these conditions is the same as before. In the short run the Highway Authority should charge tolls that equate the price to users with the short-run marginal cost (including congestion cost) of a trip. In the long run facilities should be expanded (or contracted) until the price, equal to short-run marginal cost, also equals the long-run marginal cost of providing journeys.

Although the "pricing rule" is the same as before, the result differs in one important respect: when marginal cost pricing is employed under conditions of long-run decreasing cost, revenues from optimum-size facilities necessarily fall short of covering full costs. Highways will no longer be self-financing. This outcome is explained as follows. In the case of a decreasing cost facility, the long-run marginal cost curve (LMC) lies below the long-run average total cost curve (LATC). Now suppose the highway authority, employing the pricing and investment rules explained above, expands the facility up to the point where the demand curve intersects LMC. This point necessarily lies below LATC. Consequently, when tolls are charged based upon marginal cost, a deficit results equal to the excess of average over marginal cost per journey.

A simplified version of the decreasing cost case is shown in Chapter 9, Figure 9.1. Referring ahead to that diagram (and reinterpreting it to represent a highway rather than mass transit) the reader will see that the optimum size facility is indicated by the intersection of DD

19. See Walters, pp. 36–41, 83–84.

and LMC at point A. On a facility of that size, if the Highway Authority employs marginal cost pricing and the level of traffic is Q_A per day, a daily deficit will occur equal to the area $P_A P_B BA$.

It is a standard proposition in microeconomic theory that decreasing cost firms employing marginal cost pricing will run deficits. In the presence of decreasing costs, marginal cost pricing can be adopted only if firms are subsidized or an additional special charge is levied. Whether marginal cost pricing continues to be desirable under those circumstances and how subsidies or special charges should be arranged, are subjects to which we return in Chapter 9.

Suppose roads are subject not to decreasing but to increasing long-run costs? In that case marginal cost pricing on the optimum-size road results, not in a deficit, but in a surplus. In the case of increasing costs the long-run marginal cost curve lies *above* the long-run average total cost curve. When marginal cost pricing is employed on an optimum-size facility, the intersection of the demand curve with LMC will therefore occur at a level *above* rather than below LATC. Surplus revenues will be generated equal to the excess of marginal cost over average total cost per journey.[20]

To summarize the economic theory of transportation in the long run, we can clearly define three cases that apply to mass transit as well as to highway systems:

> *Constant cost.* If facilities can be expanded at constant cost, marginal cost pricing on optimum-size facilities will yield revenues that just equal full costs. Transportation will be self-financing.
>
> *Decreasing cost.* If cost decreases as facilities are expanded, marginal cost pricing will fail to cover the full cost of optimum-size facilities. Transportation will operate at a deficit.
>
> *Increasing cost.* If expansion entails increased unit cost, marginal cost pricing on optimum-size facilities will yield revenues in excess of costs. Transportation will yield a surplus.

EVIDENCE ON TRANSPORTATION COST

We have reviewed the theory of optimum transportation pricing in the long run and found that the outcome depends importantly on the behavior of costs. What, in fact, do empirical studies tell us about transportation costs in the long run?

20. The case is depicted in Wohl, fig. 10.7, p. 259.

Highway Costs

Whether highway services are produced under conditions of constant, increasing, or decreasing long-run cost is not an easy matter to sort out. The answer depends, not only on how construction cost per lane-mile varies as the number of lanes increases, but also on how much traffic flow each additional lane adds to the carrying capacity of a highway. Moreover (and this is especially the case when the subject is urban highways), these costs should be measured, not along isolated strips of roadway, but in the context of a network of intersecting, interconnected roads.

It has already been pointed out that economies of scale exist at the low end of the road-size spectrum. Consequently, we build two-lane rather than one-lane roads in rural areas except where the traffic level is extraordinarily low. These economies of scale result from the fact that a two-lane road allows much higher operating speeds than a one-lane road. Engineering studies of the U.S. Bureau of Public Roads indicate that vehicle capacity per lane continues to increase up through the fourth lane (when there are two lanes in each direction) to a maximum sustainable flow of about 2,000 passenger vehicles per lane per hour. Capacity per lane levels off thereafter. A four-lane highway has a total capacity of about 8,000 vehicles per hour, while a two-lane highway (one in each direction) has a total capacity of only about 2,000 per hour.[21]

The behavior of construction cost as highway width increases has been a matter of some debate.[22] Analysis is complicated by the fact that costs per mile depend not only on the scale of a highway but also on the extent of urbanization in the area through which it runs. Urbanization increases highway costs, because both the price of land and the number of interchanges, overpasses, etc., that must be provided increase with population density. These matters are scarcely in doubt. Since, however, highway width and degree of urbanization tend to be associated, the effect of urbanization becomes confounded with that of width.

In a recent study of highway costs and service levels in the San Francisco Bay Area, Theodore E. Keeler and his associates assembled information on 57 road segments in nine counties for the purpose of making cost comparisons on the evidence of consistent data. Based on an analysis in which they controlled statistically for the effects of urbanization, they concluded that the evidence is "consistent with the hypothesis

21. Highway Research Board, *Special Report 87: Highway Capacity Manual* (Washington, D.C.: Highway Research Board of the National Academy of Sciences—National Research Council, 1965), pp. 75–76.
22. See, for example, Meyer, Kain, and Wohl, pp. 199–208; Mohring, pp. 140–45; Walters, pp. 183–84.

of constant returns" in the construction of highways.[23] In other words, there are neither economies nor diseconomies of scale in construction, costs per lane mile do not vary as the number of lanes increases.

An Estimate of Optimum Congestion Tolls

With constant returns to scale, an optimal system of congestion and maintenance tolls will just cover the full cost of each segment of a highway. However, since cost per segment rises sharply with degree of urbanization, optimal tolls and congestion levels will be much higher in central cities than in rural or suburban areas. Where there is a peaking problem, as in most metropolitan highway systems, tolls will also be much higher in peak than in off-peak periods. Keeler and his associates calculated optimal peak and off-peak tolls based on their data for the San Francisco Bay Area and using alternative assumptions concerning the rate of interest and the average value of travel time. It should be noted that these are optimum *long-run* tolls in which the cost of long-run expansion as well as short-run congestion is taken into account (as in Figure 8.2). A summary of Keeler's results is shown in Table 8.7. All calculations are in terms of 1972 dollars.

At an assumed interest rate of 6 percent, optimal peak period tolls were estimated to rise from about 3¢ per vehicle mile in outlying areas to 15¢ per vehicle mile in Oakland and San Francisco. Daytime, off-peak tolls were less than 1¢ in all areas. When interest rates are assumed to be 12 percent, the range of peak period tolls approximately doubles. Off-peak tolls are far less sensitive to the interest rate. The connection between interest rates and tolls is straightforward. A higher rate of interest implies a higher cost of borrowing the capital that is embodied in the highway and therefore higher total costs to be covered by tolls.

The relationship of time value to tolls is more complex. Calculations were carried out for alternative values of $4.50 and $2.25 an hour. Since the cost of congestion is principally a time cost, one would expect, as Keeler points out, that "a lower value of time would lead to lower toll." That turns out to be true in the off-peak but not in the peak hours. An optimal road segment will have fewer lanes if time values are lower. Such a road might then become more congested during peak hours than the wider road that would be built if time values were higher.[24] However, Table 8.7 shows that optimal congestion tolls, especially at the peak period, are not very sensitive to variation in the assumed average value of time.

23. Theodore E. Keeler and Kenneth A. Small, "Optimal Peak-Load Pricing, Investment and Service Levels on Urban Expressways," *Journal of Political Economy*, February 1977, p. 7.
24. Ibid., p. 17.

TABLE 8.7

Optimal Congestion Tolls, San Francisco Bay Area, 1972

	CENTS PER VEHICLE MILE			
	Peak		Daytime Off-Peak	
HIGHWAY LOCATION	$i = 6\%$	$i = 12\%$	$i = 6\%$	$i = 12\%$
Rural-Suburban				
V = 4.50	2.7	5.3	.6	.8
V = 2.25	3.1	6.9	.4	.4
Urban, Outside Central City				
V = 4.50	3.3	7.0	.7	.8
V = 2.25	4.2	9.1	.4	.5
Central City				
V = 4.50	14.5	31.0	.9	.9
V = 2.25	17.4	34.3	.5	.5

i = assumed interest rate.

V = assumed time value in dollars per hour.

Source: Theodore E. Keeler and Kenneth A. Small, "Optimal Peak-Load Pricing, Investment and Service Levels on Urban Expressways," *Journal of Political Economy*, February 1977, table 5, p. 18.

Mass Transit Costs

Cost studies of rail and bus transit systems are less numerous than those of highways. Mohring has studied urban bus transit.[25] Meyer, Kain, and Wohl undertook a first, pathbreaking comparison of costs on all three modes in their volume on *The Urban Transportation Problem.* Boyd, Asher, and Wetzler later compared rail and bus costs in the urban commuter market.[26] Keeler and his associates also examined rail and bus transit, together with highways, in their more recent San Francisco Bay Area study.[27]

Unlike later investigators, Meyer, Kain, and Wohl did not include the value of time as a cost in trip-making. Despite this and other differences in method, the results of the three intermodal cost comparisons are strikingly similar. Keeler's findings are summarized in Figure 8.3,

25. See his *Transportation Economics*, pp. 147–57, and "Optimization and Scale Economies in Urban Bus Transportation," *American Economic Review*, September 1972, pp. 591–604.

26. Meyer, Kain, and Wohl, chs. 8–11; J. Hayden Boyd, Norman J. Asher, and Elliot S. Wetzler, *Evaluation of Rail Rapid Transit and Express Bus Service in the Urban Commuter Market*, prepared for the U.S. Department of Transportation (Washington, D.C.: U.S. Government Printing Office, October 1973).

27. Theodore E. Keeler, Kenneth A. Small, et al., *The Full Costs of Urban Transport*, part III, "Automobile Costs and Final Intermodal Cost Comparisons," monograph 21 (Berkeley: Institute of Urban and Regional Development, University of California, July 1975).

FIGURE 8.3

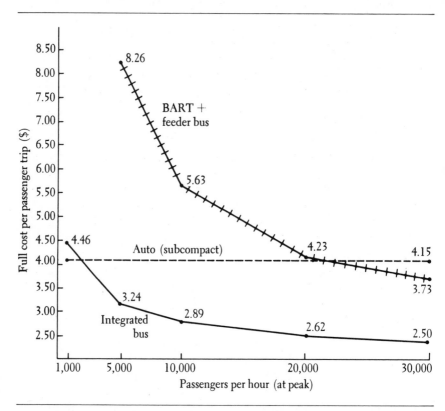

Source: Adapted from Theodore E. Keeler and Kenneth A. Small, *The Full Costs of Urban Transport*, part III, Monograph 21 (Berkeley: Institute of Urban and Regional Development, University of California, July 1975), fig. 4, p. 128 .

which shows the full cost of a trip from a residential suburb to the CBD on each mode, as a function of the peak hourly traffic in a single corridor. Since peak traffic volume, plotted on the horizontal axis, is a measure of output quantity, the relationships depicted in Figure 8.3 are, in effect, long-run average cost curves.

Following Meyer, Kain, and Wohl, Keeler defines the complete work trip as consisting of three segments: residential collection, line haul, and downtown distribution. If the trip is by auto, the commuter completes the three segments in a single vehicle and parks it downtown. For the bus trip, too, the commuter is assumed to use a single vehicle, which collects passengers on a trip through a residential neighborhood, then runs as an express along a freeway to reach the CBD, where it enters city streets to accomplish downtown distribution. The rail transit trip is assumed to be a combination of feeder bus for residential collection, followed by line haul and downtown distribution on San Francisco's BART system. For each type of trip the authors calculate the combination of inputs that would minimize total costs, including time costs of users. Calculations are for peak hour traffic levels varying from 1,000 to 30,000 passengers per corridor in the major direction. Dividing total cost by traffic volume yields the estimates of average cost shown in Figure 8.3. Because the optimum factor combination has been chosen to produce each level of output, these are the minimum long-run average costs for each level of traffic.

Long-run average cost declines for both bus and rail mass transit as systems are expanded to accommodate larger volumes of traffic. We have previously shown that if transportation is produced under conditions of decreasing cost, marginal cost pricing will fail to cover the long-run cost of optimum-size facilities. Thus bus or rail transit systems employing marginal-cost pricing and expanded to their optimum size in all likelihood would not be self-financing. (We will return to intermodal cost comparisons in Chapter 9.)

The definition of costs employed in Figure 8.3 is a broad one. It covers both the costs incurred by the user (including the value of time spent traveling) and the costs borne by the agency that builds and operates the facility. In the case of mass transit, economies of scale apparently occur with respect to both kinds of cost. Mohring studied urban bus transportation, using data from the Twin Cities, Minneapolis and St. Paul, to calibrate a model of a city bus route. His results, summarized in Table 8.8 for one of several cases he examined, indicate that with optimum long-run adjustment, both average agency cost and average user time cost decline as the number of users rises. Marginal cost is therefore below average cost. If marginal cost pricing were used, riders would pay fares in the neighborhood of 17¢ for a three mile trip at peak hours and between 9¢ and 12¢ at the off-peak (not shown in table). These charges are far below the level of agency costs, requiring the payment of subsidies that vary from about 31¢ per ride at low levels of patronage to about 5¢ at very high levels.

The decline in average agency costs as ridership increases can be explained by the fact that it costs little more to run a full bus than an empty one. User time cost declines because, as ridership increases, service is more frequent and average waiting time is reduced.

The same factors operate for rail mass transit. In the rail case, however, the decline in average cost is greater and extends over a wider range of traffic. This reflects the additional influence of indivisible fixed costs for the construction of rail trackage: a two-track line is both the

TABLE 8.8

Economies of Scale in Urban Bus Service[a]

NUMBER OF USERS	AVERAGE AGENCY OPERATING COST	AVERAGE USER TIME COST	FULL AVERAGE COST	FULL MARGINAL COST	MARGINAL COST FARE	SUBSIDY PER USER
9	47¢	55¢	102¢	71¢	16¢	31¢
21	36	45	81	62	17	19
45	29	40	69	57	17	12
90	25	37	62	55	18	8
150	23	36	59	54	18	5

[a] Costs are for a three mile trip, 16 stops allowed per mile, peak period conditions, with optimum adjustment of service level.

Explanation of terms (figures may not add due to rounding)

Col. 1: Average number of passengers per mile per hour

Col. 2: Agency operating cost = marginal cost fare (col. 6) plus subsidy per user (col. 7)

Col. 3: Value of time supplied by average user

Col. 4: Full average cost = average user time cost (col. 3) plus agency operating cost (col. 2)

Col. 5: Full marginal cost includes both user time and agency operating cost

Col. 6: Marginal cost fare = full marginal cost (col. 5) minus cost of user-supplied time (col. 3)

Col. 7: Subsidy per user = full average cost (col. 4) minus full marginal cost (col. 5)

Source: Herbert Mohring, *Transportation Economics* (Cambridge, Mass.: Ballinger, 1976), tables 12–2, 12–3, pp. 153–54.

minimum and the maximum needed for most traffic densities.[28] Heavy fixed trackage costs make the average cost of a trip very high at low traffic levels, but since these expenses do not rise with traffic density, average cost falls markedly as patronage increases.

In this chapter we have examined the economics of urban transportation, focusing on the analysis of modal choice and on the theory of optimum short-run pricing and long-run investment. The chapter closed with a brief review of empirical evidence on transportation cost. In Chapter 9 we take up the problems of urban transportation policy.

28. Keeler and Small, *The Full Costs of Urban Transport*, Part III, p. 126.

Urban
Transportation Policy

NINE

Transportation systems are largely planned, built, financed, and operated by governments. In this chapter we analyze urban transportation
policy: what government does, or could do, to develop transportation
systems that operate both efficiently and equitably. Short-run questions are covered first. Under what pricing policies are existing
systems actually operated? What financial problems do they face,
and how have these been dealt with? What effects do transportation
subsidies have on the distribution of income?

The second part of the chapter, "Choosing Among Transportation Systems," deals with problems of the longer run. What are the
costs and benefits of alternative transportation systems? How can
cities make rational decisions to invest in new facilities?

A third major section covers "Government Policy and Transportation Choices." The chapter closes with a discussion of the
possible impact of rising energy prices on transportation behavior,
residential location, and, ultimately, urban form.

TRANSPORTATION PRICING IN PRACTICE

The gap between theory and practice in transportation pricing
is considerable. Historically both highway and transit charges have
been based on average cost calculations rather than on the marginal
cost principles explained in the previous chapter. Although serious
transit deficits have developed, they certainly cannot be blamed on
marginal cost pricing, since that system has rarely been used in
transit operations.

In the case of highways, tolls are charged only on major bridge. tunnels, and a few heavily traveled turnpikes. Even in those cases, the toll are almost always flat rates that do not vary, as a marginal cost based tol would, according to the degree of congestion. The major charges paid b highway users are the state and federal gasoline taxes; federal excise taxe on trucks and buses, tires, parts and accessories; and state registration an license fees. These are, indeed, "user charges." The conventional wisdon has it that the aggregate of these revenues approximately covers the annua cost of building, maintaining, and servicing highways in the United State: if we do not count indirect or external costs such as accidents or pollution However, a recent study that takes a broader view of highway-associate governmental costs finds that between 1956 and 1975 total expenditure exceeded user payments by 10 percent.[2] Whether or not they accept tha conclusion, most analysts of highway economics would probably agre that extensive cross-subsidies are being paid within the system: some part of the network are clearly subsidizing others. The system is not efficient a the micro level.

Opposition to Congestion Tolls

Keeler reports that "the typical auto in the Bay Area in 1972 pai user charges of 1.15 cents per vehicle-mile," a level far below the peak-hou congestion tolls in Table 8.7.[3] Raising tolls to the levels indicated woul surely arouse opposition among highway users. Reservations about th desirability of congestion tolls, however, have also been voiced by a re spectable number of transportation economists.

One objection is based on short-run welfare considerations. Th theory of short-run congestion tolls was illustrated in Figure 8.1. Exan ining such a case, Wohl points out that in the short run all users of th road segment are made worse off by the imposition of congestion tolls The reduction in trips from Q_2 to Q_3 results from the fact that thos drivers who decline to pay the new charges are "tolled off" the road. The must be worse off than before because they have given up trips (at leas by this route) that formerly were desirable. The drivers who continue t use the road after imposition of a toll are also worse off. Congestion i

1. See, for example, the data on total current revenue and total expenditures o highways in *Facts and Figures on Government Finance*, 20th ed. (New York: Tl Tax Foundation, 1979), table 133, p. 162.

2. Kiran Bhatt, Michael Beesley, and Kevin Neels, *An Analysis of Road E penditures and Payments by Vehicle Class (1956–1975)* (Washington, D.C.: Tl Urban Institute, March 1977), table 1, p. 18.

3. Theodore E. Keeler and Kenneth A. Small, "Optimal Peak-Load Pricin Investment and Service Levels on Urban Expressways," *Journal of Political Econom* February 1977, p. 21.

4. Martin Wohl, "Congestion Toll Pricing for Public Transport Facilities," Selma Mushkin, ed., *Public Prices for Public Products* (Washington, D.C.: The Urba Institute, 1972), pp. 245–47.

reduced, so that each driver's private costs fall from KE to JG. The saving in private cost amount to GI. But to save GI in congestion cost, each driver pays a toll of GF and therefore suffers a net loss of $GF - GI = IF$. We reach the seemingly paradoxical conclusion that an optimal short-run pricing policy leaves all users of the road worse off.

But there is no paradox. Before imposition of higher tolls, users may have been paying less than the full cost of the road. They are receiving an unjustified subsidy, which is now taken away. No harm in that. If the higher tolls lead to a surplus of revenue above full cost, then (assuming constant long-run cost) the road should be expanded until tolls just cover average long-run costs. Users will then benefit by the provision of a highway developed to optimal capacity.

Indeed, it can be shown that users paying an optimal congestion toll on the expanded road will be better off than they were on the smaller facility before congestion tolls were imposed. Referring back to Figure 8.2, suppose that Road A were operated without congestion tolls. Equilibrium would occur at E, where the driver's average variable cost curve, AVC_A, intersects the demand curve DD'. Cost per trip would be OP_3, with no congestion toll being paid. (This corresponds to the solution at point E on Figure 8.1.) If, now, congestion tolls are imposed and the highway is expanded to its optimum size (Road B), equilibrium occurs at R. Cost per trip falls to OP_1, which is less than OP_2, even though OP_1 includes a congestion toll and OP_3 does not. Each driver benefits because the saving in congestion costs to each vehicle (GP_3) exceeds the required congestion toll on the expanded road (RS).

A second objection to congestion tolls is based on the cost of implementing a highly articulated toll system in which charges could vary by direction, time of day, and position on an entire road network. Not only are there costs of collection, but also, if toll booths are used, drivers will bear time costs, since toll collection reduces average trip speed. This problem has spawned some interesting proposals that would use sophisticated technology in place of the toll booth. For use in city streets, Vickrey has described a computerized electronic tracking system that could plot the course of every vehicle passing through congested areas, compute appropriate tolls, and render monthly bills to vehicle owners. Much less complex and less precise in their impact are proposed licensing systems that would simply require those driving into designated congestion-prone areas to display a special license for which they would pay an appropriate fee.[5]

5. See William S. Vickrey, "Pricing in Urban and Suburban Transport," reprinted in Ronald E. Grieson, ed., *Urban Economics: Readings and Analysis* (Boston: Little, Brown, 1973), pp. 111–13; and the discussion in Michael A. Kemp and Melvyn D. Cheslow, "Transportation," in William Gorham and Nathan Glazer, eds., *The Urban Predicament* (Washington, D.C.: The Urban Institute, 1976), pp. 321–24.

A third objection concerns differential effects by income class. Since individual evaluations of time vary directly with wages, the poor tend to have lower time values. It has sometimes been argued that congestion tolls based on "average" evaluations of time will therefore be a bargain for the rich and a burden for the poor. Given the paucity of data about the incomes of those who drive through congested areas in peak hours, the question has been a difficult one to resolve.[6] In any case, a standard reply to this objection is that congestion tolls are part of a general price system necessary to achieve efficient resource use and should not be manipulated with an eye to their effects on income distribution.

No doubt there is strong political opposition to the introduction of highway congestion tolls. Users are opposed because, as a group, they will be made worse off, at least in the short run. The poor believe that they will be disadvantaged as compared to the rich. In addition, there is the force of habit: drivers do not object to paying tolls on bridges or roads that were built as toll facilities, but they are outraged at proposals to institute tolls on previously free facilities. And there may be a deeper force at work, as well. Perhaps people (and especially Americans) feel, although they do not articulate it, that they have a fundamental, almost constitutional right to movement, which the government ought not to infringe by anything that looks like a tax on mobility. Keeler recognizes that "there may be political obstacles to such tolls" but concludes that "the more general understanding there is of the benefits . . . the more feasible they will be."[7]

The Problem of Deficits Under Marginal Cost Pricing

We explained in Chapter 8 that under declining cost conditions, marginal cost pricing will generate deficits. Figure 9.1 displays declining long-run average and marginal costs such as might obtain in mass transit. To focus on financial deficits, user time costs are now ignored. The curves show agency costs only, and, to avoid clutter, short-run cost curves are omitted. When demand is given by DD, equilibrium under marginal cost pricing is at A, where the marginal cost curve intersects the demand curve. The transit authority charges a fare of P_A, and traffic flow is Q_A trips per day. However, the average cost of a trip is P_B, well in excess of P_A. The transit authority runs a daily deficit shown by the shaded rectangle $P_A P_B BA$.

Average cost pricing would lead to equilibrium at C, where price, given by the demand curve, just covers agency cost as indicated by the

6. One of the most elaborate studies is Damian J. Kulash, *Income Distributional Consequences of Roadway Pricing* (Washington, D.C.: The Urban Institute, 1974).
7. Keeler and Small, p. 24.

FIGURE 9.1

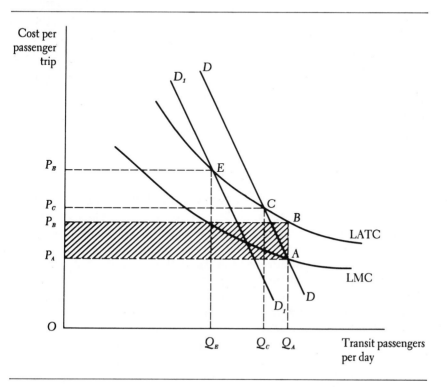

average cost curve. There would be no deficit. However, the average cost solution is economically inefficient because $Q_A - Q_C$ customers are denied the use of the system even though they would be willing to pay prices (indicated by the demand curve between points C and A) in excess of the marginal costs they impose.

Economists have long debated the question of how deficits generated by marginal cost pricing should be covered. One solution would call for subsidies to be paid out of tax revenue. But taxes levied for that purpose might have harmful effects elsewhere that would offset the efficiency advantages of marginal cost as compared with average cost pricing.

Another proposal is the so-called two-part tariff. Users would be charged the marginal-cost price for each unit of service taken. In addition, in order to qualify as a user, each consumer would have to pay a flat annual fee. These fees, equivalent to membership dues, would be used to cover the deficit from marginal cost pricing. Though not perfect, such an arrangement would probably cause less inefficiency in resource use than the alternative of average cost pricing.[8] It also has the advantage of ensuring that users themselves defray the full cost of the facilities that serve them instead of relying on the general taxpayer to share their burden.

Musgrave and Musgrave point out that where the facility in question produces a local service, a general local tax to cover the deficit "may be viewed as the flat-charge component of the two part tariff, since participation in the service hinges on local residence."[9] Thus economic theory provides an argument for the use of local tax revenues to subsidize local transit deficits. In practice, however, urban transit operators, may be giving us the worst of both worlds by running deficits *without* simultaneously offering the advantage of marginal cost pricing.

Financial Stress in the Transit Industry

The U.S. transit industry as a whole has been running at a deficit since 1963. By 1978 the aggregate annual operating loss amounted to $2.3 billion, or about 39 cents for each passenger who actually paid a fare. Operating revenues covered only 50 percent of expenses. These and other industry statistics are summarized in Table 9.1. Since the transit industry generally shuns marginal cost pricing, what accounts for its large operating deficit? The simple answer is the decline in demand, shown in the top line of the table. The number of revenue passengers fell 62 percent from 1950 to the low point reached in 1972. Ridership recovered slightly thereafter but by 1978 was still 57 percent below its 1950 level. We have seen that transit service benefits from economies of scale as demand increases. Unfortunately that means it suffers from *dis*economies if demand moves the other way: cost per trip rises as demand falls.

As illustrated in Figure 9.1, an urban transit operator might traditionally have charged an average cost fare and broken even at point C. However, with the rise of automobile ownership and the decline of central city population, the demand for trips shifts steadily to the left and average cost rises. Nevertheless, as long as the demand curve continues to intersect the average cost curve at all, the point of intersection indicates a fare at which the operating authority could meet its costs out of fare revenues.

Conceivably demand could shift so far to the left that no intersection occurs and deficits become unavoidable. Kemp and Cheslow, however, find little evidence that such a disjunction has actually occurred. Rather, they explain the rapid growth of deficits in the following terms.[10]

8. This point is more fully developed in Richard A. Musgrave and Peggy B. Musgrave, *Public Finance in Theory and Practice*, 3rd ed. (New York: McGraw-Hill, 1980), pp. 745–46.
9. Ibid., p. 746, n. 3.
10. Kemp and Cheslow, pp. 331–34.

Fares have, in fact, increased very rapidly for several decades, but not fast enough to keep up with rising costs. From 1950 to 1970 the average fare rose more than 175 percent, while consumer prices as a whole increased only 61 percent. Transit fares are a highly visible charge. With the rise of public transit ownership they have also become a major political issue. Elected officials frequently run on a "save the fare" plank. They try to avoid fare increases until every alternative has been exhausted. One alternative is to reduce service frequency, which has less political impact. Unfortunately, since ridership is more sensitive to service levels than to fare levels, it contributes strongly to the further decline of patronage.

Rising labor costs have also aggravated transit's financial woes. The industry is labor intensive: labor accounts for about two-thirds of operating costs. Transit provides a classic example of the "productivity lag" problem that afflicts many local government services (see Chapter 14). Transit wages must rise at more or less the same rate as do private industrial wages. But labor productivity (i.e., output per man-hour) in the transit industry is not only lagging behind the increases registered by private industry, it is actually falling. From 1972 through 1978 vehicle miles per employee fell 3 percent, and revenue passengers per employee declined by 5 percent. Earnings per employee rose 58 percent in the same interval (see Table 9.1). Unit labor cost equals wages per worker divided by output per worker. With wages rising and output per worker falling, unit labor cost in the transit industry has increased sharply in recent years.

At least until a fiscal crisis overtook U.S. cities in 1975, transit wages had been rising considerably faster than the cost of living. Strong unions played a part in this outcome. For a variety of reasons public involvement in operating and subsidizing transit has probably strengthened the position of the unions and accelerated the rise in labor costs.[11] However, even if transit wages in the new era of austerity do no more than keep up with the cost of living, "productivity lag" makes the outlook for transit finances decidedly grim.

Grimmest of all is the outlook in declining older cities that have rail mass transit systems. Since rail mass transit displays marked economies of scale, it also suffers pronounced *dis*economies when population and therefore patronage fall off. Once such an interconnected system is built one cannot economize by abandoning portions of it. There is no way to cut the cost of operating and maintaining the system except by reducing service frequency, and that, as we have already argued, is likely to lower patronage even further and certainly imposes severe waiting costs on remaining users.

11. Ibid., p. 333 and n. 85.

TABLE 9.1
Transit Industry Revenues and Costs[a]

	1950	1965	1972	1978	PERCENTAGE CHANGE 1972 TO 1978
Output					
Revenue passenger rides (millions)	13,845	6,798	5,253	5,963	13.5
Vehicle miles operated (millions)	3,008	2,008	1,756	2,028	15.4
Operating results					
Operating revenues ($ millions)	1,452	1,444	1,729	2,381	37.7
Operating expenses ($ millions)	1,386	1,454	2,242	4,712	110.2
Operating surplus or (deficit) ($ millions)	66	(10)	(513)	(2,331)	354.5
Average fare (cents)	10.0	19.7	31.4	38.1	21.3
Average oper. deficit per passenger (cents)	—	0.1	9.8	39.1	299.0
Financial assistance					
Total operating assistance ($ millions)	[b]	[b]	[b]	2,232	—
Local				978	—
State				564	—
Federal				690	—
Federal capital grant approvals ($ millions)	—	50.7	510.9	2,037	298.7
Labor costs					
Average annual earnings per employee ($)	3,479	6,645	10,515	16,569	57.6
Number of employees	240,000	145,000	138,420	165,400	19.4
Vehicle miles per employee	12,533	13,848	12,686	12,261	-3.3
Revenue passengers per employee	57,688	46,883	37,950	36,052	-5.0

[a] Includes rail transit, trolley coach and motor bus.

[b] Data not available.

Source: American Public Transit Association, *Transit Fact Book, 1978–79*

Subsidies for Mass Transit

Public subsidy is, of course, the only possible source of funds to cover transit deficits. Since most mass transit systems are now owned by local public authorities, deficits are the responsibility primarily of local governments. In some cases, states bear some of the burden, and since 1974 the federal government has also contributed operating subsidies through the Urban Mass Transportation Administration. (See data in Table 9.1.)

In 1978, federal operating subsidies amounted to $690 million and covered about 30 percent of operating deficits. Federal funds are distributed by a formula heavily weighted by population. Since large cities have a much higher proportion of transit users than small cities, they receive a systematically smaller subsidy per user. This strikes many observers as perverse. Mahlon Straszheim points out that such a formula is intended "to avoid the disincentives associated with basing assistance on the size of the operating deficit."[12] Probably it also reflects a need to spread aid widely among congressional districts if it is to muster enough political support for passage.

Income Effects of Mass Transit Subsidies

What effect do mass transit subsidies have on the distribution of income? The answer will vary with local circumstances and may sometimes come as a surprise. The conventional view, in all probability, is that a mass transit subsidy is bound to help the poor and the working classes since they are presumed to be frequent users of public transportation. Yet economists have found that in some cases, and especially for rail mass transit systems recently built or now under construction, that may be just the opposite of the truth.

Consider the impact of San Francisco's BART. The system was built with the intention of reducing the Bay Area's dependence on the automobile by offering commuters a rail route from relatively distant suburbs to the central business districts of Oakland and San Francisco. This orientation is indicated by the fact that only 13 of the system's 34 stations are within those two cities.[13] We know that the gradient of income in U.S. metropolitan areas rises with distance from the central city. Consequently there is a presumption that passengers on a transit system built

---

12. Mahlon R. Straszheim, "Assessing the Social Costs of Urban Transportation Technologies," in Peter Mieszkowski and Mahlon Straszheim, eds., *Current Issues in Urban Economics* (Baltimore: Johns Hopkins University Press, 1979), p. 227.

13. Regarding BART's strong orientation toward serving the suburb-to-CBD commuter, see Andrew Marshall Hamer, *The Selling of Rail Rapid Transit* (Lexington, Mass.: D. C. Heath, Lexington Books, 1976), pp. 61–67, 75–77.

to carry suburbanites to the central city to work, shop, or engage in cultural activities will have incomes well above the regional average.

One might ask, however, why a system that connects the central city with the suburbs cannot carry central city workers to suburban jobs as readily at it transports suburban commuters to jobs in town. The answer can be deduced from what we know about the pattern of metropolitan job locations. The job destinations of the inbound commuter are typically concentrated in the CBD (as a result of nineteenth century centralization). Those of the reverse commuter are typically scattered throughout the suburbs (as a result of twentieth century *de*centralization). Thus for inbound journeys the system connects scattered suburban residential points with concentrated downtown job locations, while for outbound journeys it must connect scattered central city residential points with even more scattered suburban job locations. This asymmetry strongly affects user convenience.

The inbound commuter, using a system such as BART, either drives a car or takes a feeder bus to the transit line, then rides the train to a CBD station that is within a short walk of his or her place of work. Disregarding the final walk, there are only two segments to the journey. The outbound commuter takes a bus to an inner city transit station (which in the case of new systems like BART that have few stops inside the city is not likely to be within walking distance of home) and then rides the train to the suburbs. That makes two legs already, but the worst is yet to come. The job is not likely to be close to a suburban rail station, since radial transit lines diverge to wide spacing in the suburbs and jobs are not concentrated near them. The reverse commuter, however, has no car waiting at the suburban station but must rely on bus service. If such a connection exists, it makes a third leg to the journey. (Often it does not exist, and reverse commutation can be accomplished only by auto.) For the sake of parity, we disregard a possible final walk from bus to job. Even so, the outbound commuter's journey, if, indeed, it can be accomplished using public transportation, requires one leg more than that of the inbound commuter, with all that implies for extra waiting time and additional scheduling problems.

BART's ridership reflects its suburb-to-central-city orientation. E. G. Hoachlander has studied the distribution of BART's benefits and costs among income classes and ethnic groups. He reports that a survey of riders in 1975 found that over 48 percent had incomes above $15,000. In the 1970 Census, however, the proportion with such incomes in the general population of the Bay area was only 25 percent. Ethnic class confirmed the story. Whites constituted 77 percent of BART riders in 1975 but only 68 percent of the 1970 general population. On the other hand, black and

Spanish minorities accounted for only 12.5 percent of BART riders, although they made up 25 percent of the area's population.[14] If who rides is a good proxy for who benefits, it is clear that BART's benefits are distributed progressively with respect to income.

Who, on the other hand, pays the taxes that finance local subsidies to BART? To support both capital expenses and operating subsidies the Bay Area Rapid Transit District levies property and sales taxes in the three counties served by the system. Passenger revenues cover only 30 to 39 percent of operating costs and less than a fifth of total costs including debt service.[15] Consequently, there is a large deficit to be met out of local tax revenues and state and federal financial assistance.

While there is some dispute about details, most economists would agree that the sales tax is moderately regressive to income. There is less agreement about the property tax. (See discussion in Chapter 14.) According to the "old view," that portion of the tax levied on residential property is borne by tenants and owner occupants in proportion to rent and is therefore thought to be fairly regressive with respect to current income. The "new view" of the property tax calls this into question so far as the national average rate of tax is concerned. However, differences between the local rate of tax and the national average are still thought to be distributed more or less as in the old view. Consequently, if a particular locality raises its property tax rate it is probably imposing an additional burden on residents that is regressive with respect to their current income.

If this reasoning is accepted, the local taxes supporting subsidies to BART are taking a higher proportion of income from the poor than the rich. Since BART's benefits flow disproportionately to the rich, the "inescapable conclusion," in Hoachlander's words, is that "the wealthy ride BART and the poor pay for it."[16]

The BART benefit/subsidy combination is especially regressive because BART's benefits are so strongly oriented toward well-to-do suburban commuters. In that respect it resembles other new rail transit systems in the United States. On the other hand, the older rail transit networks, such as New York's, and the bus systems of the typical large city, are oriented toward serving a broad spectrum of the population, and in small and medium-sized cities, where the automobile dominates personal transportation, buses tend to serve a below-average income class. Even in the

14. Data from E. Garreth Hoachlander, "Bay Area Rapid Transit: Who Pays and Who Benefits?" Working Paper no. 267 (Berkeley: Institute of Urban and Regional Development, University of California, July 1976), tables VIII and IX, pp. 31–32.
15. See table 9.3 and the accompanying discussion below.
16. Hoachlander, p. 35.

more favorable cases, however, the regressive nature of the taxes used to finance local assistance severely limits the net benefit that present across-the-board subsidies provide to the poor.

Nor should we lose sight of the classic problem of the trade-off in economics between the goals of efficiency and equity. Economists usually argue that it is best, where possible, to let the pricing system do its work of allocating resources efficiently and then, if income adjustments are desirable, to make them by direct transfers that interfere as little as possible with efficient pricing. In that spirit, Kemp and Cheslow suggest that if we wish to help the "transportation disadvantaged" through subsidies, we might develop programs that would specifically select them out to ride at lower cost, while "setting fares to the rest of the population . . . solely on the basis of making the urban transportation system work most efficiently."[17]

CHOOSING AMONG TRANSPORTATION SYSTEMS

Because the choice of a transportation system strongly influences a city's land-use pattern and therefore its very life style, decisions about transportation investment are recognized by the public, by city planners, and by politicians as having paramount importance. True, the existence of structures inherited from the past makes it a rare occasion when a city can choose to develop a whole new system. But decisions must frequently be made to expand or contract, to maintain or to abandon what already exists. Localities must make choices about how to use not only their own monies but also funds of the state and federal governments. To make rational transportation investment decisions, one must know both the costs and the benefits of alternative modes. Let us look first at costs.

Intermodal Cost Comparisons

The results of Keeler's intermodal cost comparison for a suburb-to-CBD commuter trip were presented in Figure 8.3. Costs comprise both agency outlays and the value of user inputs, including time. Although the results of intermodal cost comparisons depend on particular assumptions as to interest rates, time values, and trip lengths, Keeler's findings are broadly consistent with those of earlier studies.[18] For the suburb-to-CBD trip, integrated bus is by far the least costly mode, except at very low traffic densities. Even at the highest assumed volume of 30,000 peak hour passengers in the major direction in a single corridor, the full cost (not

17. Kemp and Cheslow, p. 342.
18. See studies cited in ch. 8, n. 26 and 27.

just the fare) of a one-way, six-mile, BART plus feeder bus trip is $3.73, almost 50 percent more than a trip by integrated bus. As traffic volume drops below 30,000, the cost advantage of bus over rail increases markedly.

In terms of cost, auto is competitive with bus at low traffic volumes. More surprising, it is significantly cheaper than BART until a volume of 20,000 per corridor per hour is reached. Even at a traffic level of 30,000, it is only 11 percent more costly than BART. For a 12-mile trip, rather than the six miles assumed in Figure 8.3, auto would be a few cents cheaper than BART, even at the highest traffic volumes.

Since the average cost of public transit depends heavily on traffic volume, it is important to know what the actual range of volumes is. For years around 1960, Table 9.2 gives the approximate volume of peak hour traffic per corridor leaving the CBD in selected U.S. cities. New York was far ahead of any other city, with a volume averaging above 60,000 persons. Chicago was next, with 30,000 to 40,000. Philadelphia, Boston, and Washington averaged between 20,000 and 30,000, Los Angeles and San Francisco between 13,000 and 20,000. Cities as large as Cincinnati, Seattle, and Kansas City ranged below 6,000 per hour.

No other U.S. city is ever likely to approach the peak hour traffic volume generated in New York City. What Keeler's study and other recent intermodal comparisons indicate is that at the maximum traffic densities existing elsewhere, and under today's construction and operating cost conditions, integrated express bus offers a far cheaper ride than rail mass transit. Indeed, the above figures suggest that at the traffic levels generated in most cities, even the private automobile is cheaper than rail.

Five of the older large cities—New York, Chicago, Philadelphia, Boston, and Cleveland—have had rail mass transit for many years. In those cities the cost of construction has long been properly treated as a sunk cost, not relevant for any current decisions, which should be based only on the cost of continuing to operate existing systems as compared with the cost of providing alternatives. In such comparisons rail undoubtedly continues to be the least costly alternative. Other cities—including San Francisco, Washington, Atlanta, Baltimore, and Buffalo—have recently completed or are now building rail transit systems. For these cities, too, much of construction is now a sunk cost. Except in the case of San Francisco, however, the cost disadvantage of rail as compared with bus was already under discussion at the time they began building, as a result of Meyer, Kain, and Wohl's work. The recent studies cited here merely confirmed it. Why new systems were built despite their cost disadvantage is a matter we return to below.

It is important to remember, however, that cost minimization is not an objective in economics except when it can be said that all other things are equal. That is certainly not the case with respect to urban trip-making.

TABLE 9.2

Peak Hour Traffic Leaving CBD per Corridor, Selected U.S. Cities (years around 1960)

	APPROXIMATE NUMBER OF PERSONS LEAVING CBD PER CORRIDOR, IN PEAK EVENING HOUR
New York City	Above 60,000
Chicago	30,000 to 40,000
Philadelphia Boston Washington	20,000 to 30,000
Los Angeles San Francisco	13,000 to 20,000
Cleveland Detroit Atlanta Baltimore	9,000 to 13,000
Dallas Minneapolis Milwaukee	6,000 to 9,000
Cincinnati Seattle Kansas City	Below 6,000

Source: Data selected from J. R. Meyer, J. F. Kain, and M. Wohl, *The Urban Transportation Problem* (Cambridge, Mass.: Harvard University Press, 1965), table 25, p. 86.

Even apart from differences in time and money cost, few riders will judge trips by auto, bus, and rail to be perfectly equivalent in other respects. The average rider appears to regard the automobile as superior in both comfort and convenience to either of the public modes.

The high cost of a new rail system like BART is partly attributable to a decision to provide a ride that could compete with the automobile in speed and comfort. Buses are often thought of as less comfortable and attractive than modern rail transit. But Fisher and Viton report that more luxurious buses can be operated on commuter routes at very little extra cost per rider.[19] If this is so, then buses could compete with high speed rail on comfort without giving up much of their large cost advantage.

19. Peter Fisher and Philip Viton, *The Full Costs of Urban Transport*, Part I, Economic Efficiency in Bus Operations; Preliminary Intermodal Cost Comparisons and Policy Implications, Monograph no. 19 (Berkeley: Institute of Urban and Regional Development, December 1974), pp. 134–35.

In the comparison between modes, flexibility must also be taken into account. Rail mass transit is extraordinarily *in*flexible. Once the lines have been built, they cannot be moved. If they are built underground, even minor alterations become very costly. If they turn out to have been built in the wrong place, a great deal of capital will have been wasted. Physical inflexibility thus leads to a considerable risk of making costly mistakes through a failure accurately to predict local growth patterns.

Bus systems, on the other hand, are highly flexible. Capital costs account for only a small part of the cost per ride, if we make the reasonable assumption that buses do not have to bear the cost of highway construction. Old bus routes can be contracted or abandoned and new routes developed using the same equipment. The only construction costs involved (and risked) would be for reserved entry and exit ramps or special traffic controls used in developing express bus service. Failure to predict traffic demand accurately in a changing world thus involves much less risk in the case of buses than of a fixed rail system.

Pollution and Other External Costs

The full social cost of transportation includes, not only those costs borne by the individual user and by the operating agency, but also external costs caused by transportation but thrown off onto third parties. It must be emphasized at the outset that these external costs are extraordinarily difficult to measure. Data are generally inadequate, and results are highly sensitive to assumptions made by the analyst. The art of measuring "full social costs" is still in its infancy.

We have already analyzed congestion costs as a form of externality. This and several other externalities are included, though not shown separately, in Keeler's estimates of the full costs of urban trips in Figure 8.3. However, since the cost of pollution and other externalities, especially those due to the automobile, is a public issue in its own right, it merits separate attention. A list of external costs (other than congestion) attributable to the automobile would include the following:

Air pollution. Automobile emissions are acknowledged to be an important source of air pollution. However, the damage costs that an automobile produces per vehicle mile vary greatly according to the age of the car, which determines what sort of emission controls it has, and the location in which it is driven, which determines how likely emissions are to accumulate locally. Natural air movement provides every locality with some capacity to disperse pollutants—a capacity that varies with local topography. However, the number of automobiles and other sources of pollution rises as population per square mile increases. Therefore, the larger the metropolitan area, the less able are natural air movements to disperse the resulting pollutants. Consequently damage cost per vehicle mile rises with population size and density.

Given the difficulties of measurement and the extent of local variability, economists recognize that their estimates of automobile air pollution costs are highly tentative. Keeler placed the cost at about .5¢ per vehicle mile in the Bay Area in 1972.[20] Straszheim, using a different approach, estimated a value of about 1.3¢ per vehicle mile for urban areas as of 1975.[21]

Noise, smell, aesthetic loss. It is generally agreed that major highways create undesirable noise and smell and diminish aesthetic values for adjacent properties. Keeler evaluated Bay Area noise pollution at .1¢ per vehicle mile. Straszheim, using noise as a proxy for all such proximity effects, estimated the cost at .6¢ along urban freeways. He then added another .3¢ for property losses in the form of inadequate compensation to owners whose property is acquired for a highway right-of-way after the foreknowledge of construction has already reduced its value.

Disruption of communities. In addition to the losses highways impose on nearby property owners, they may cause wider damage to entire communities. When a limited access highway is built through a city it often permanently obstructs access between the neighborhoods on either side, adding to the communication costs of individuals and weakening or destroying social organizations that depend on a community base. This form of externality, however, has not been measured.

Government service costs. The operation of a highway system entails public sector costs for planning, administration, traffic control, and police service that are not included in conventional calculations of highway costs, nor reimbursed out of highway-related revenues. These are, in a broad sense, external costs thrown off by highway beneficiaries onto the public sector. Keeler estimates their value at .5¢ per vehicle mile. Straszheim does not count them.

The costs tallied by Keeler come to 1.1¢ per vehicle mile. Figure 8.4 shows that he estimated the full cost of a six-mile auto trip (including.

20. See Theodore E. Keeler, Kenneth A. Small, et al., *The Full Costs of Urban Transport*, part III, "Automobile Costs and Final Intermodal Cost Comparisons," monograph 21 (Berkeley: Institute of Urban and Regional Development, University of California, July 1975), pp. 51–54, for estimates of this and other automobile externality costs.

21. Straszheim, table 7.5, p. 214. This is the sum of pollution abatement costs (.77¢) and residual (unabated) pollution damage (.50¢). Straszheim's estimates of other automobile costs appear in the same table.

the value of time and the cost of parking) at $4.15. Pollution costs apparently account for only 7¢ out of that total—not enough to affect intermodal cost comparisons significantly.

According to Straszheim's estimate, externalities other than congestion amounted to 2.2¢ per vehicle mile for urban areas in 1975. Exclusive of externalities (and excluding the value of time and the cost of parking), he calculated the private cost of operating an automobile plus the public cost of providing roadways at 14.5¢ per vehicle mile in the same year. Including externalities would add 15 percent to that narrower cost figure. Seen in that light, the external costs of automobile pollution are far from trivial.

Benefit-Cost Analysis of Transportation Projects

In principle, transportation investment decisions ought to be made on the basis of a benefit-cost analysis of alternatives.[22] For each alternative, a complete accounting should be made in money terms of all benefits and costs, both direct and external, estimated over the useful life of the project. Next, both the benefit stream and the cost stream should be discounted to obtain present values.[23] The aggregate present value of benefits should then be compared with that of costs and the excess of benefits over costs calculated for each alternative. This excess, or net benefit, measures the net gain to society as a whole from undertaking a given project.

The appropriate decision rule to follow when using benefit-cost analysis depends on such circumstances as whether or not the projects under consideration are mutually exclusive and whether or not budgetary constraints exist. In the case of transportation projects, the alternatives usually *are* mutually exclusive—one builds either a large bridge or a small one, but not both. In such cases, the public authority should choose the alternative that yields the largest excess of benefits over costs within the budget constraint, if there is one.

There is a strong formal similarity between the benefit-cost calculus prescribed for investment decisions in the public sector and the profit-maximizing calculus of the ordinary private investor. Net benefit in the former is the excess of benefits over costs, including the cost of capital. Economic profit in the latter is the excess of revenues over costs, including

22. For an introduction to the theory and practice of cost-benefit analysis that contains numerous citations to its use in connection with transportation investment, see A. R. Prest and R. Turvey, "Cost-Benefit Analysis: A Survey" in International Economic Association, *Surveys of Economic Theory*, vol. III (New York: St. Martin's Press, 1966), pp. 155–207.
23. For an explanation of the meaning of present value and of its importance in comparing cost and benefit streams, see Musgrave and Musgrave, 3rd ed., pp. 184–86, or some other standard text on public finance.

the cost of capital. The appropriate decision-making rules are the same in both sectors if the circumstances are similar.

In one respect, however, the benefit-cost calculus is superior to its private-sector counterpart. At least in principle, benefit-cost analysis takes external costs and benefits systematically into account, while the private sector almost always ignores them.[24] Admittedly, the measurement of externalities is fraught with difficulty, but it is not impossible, as the previous section demonstrated.

Unfortunately, the benefit-cost approach to evaluating investment alternatives cannot readily be applied to whole transportation systems. Its analytical method assumes a given economic context, or state of the world, in which the benefits and costs of alternatives can be measured. Entire alternative systems, however, are likely to produce environments so different as to render quantitative comparison between them virtually impossible. On the other hand, benefit-cost analysis has proved useful in dealing with increments to existing networks. As we shall see in the next section, however, the impact of a new facility on an existing transportation system can be very complicated to measure. Quantitative results must be regarded as approximate, at best.

Transportation Benefits

In their well-known benefit-cost study of the Victoria Line, a proposed addition to the London Underground, C. D. Foster and M. E. Beesley traced out systemwide benefits according to the scheme outlined below.[25] Although developed for the analysis of a mass transportation project, these benefit categories apply equally well to improvements in an urban highway system.

Benefits to diverted traffic. When a new link is added to a transit system it will attract some riders who previously made the trip by a different mode or route. These passengers are diverted to the new line because it offers a superior alternative to the means used previously. Their

24. Since the publication of R. H. Coase's classic article on "The Problem of Social Cost" (*Journal of Law and Economics*, October 1960, pp. 1–44), it has generally been agreed that if the private sector parties concerned are few enough in number, we should expect them to arrive through bargaining at a solution in which externalities are fully (and optimally) taken into account. In practice, however, the parties are usually too numerous to permit such a "market solution" to the problem of externalities.

25. "Estimating the Social Benefit of Constructing an Underground Railway in London," reprinted as ch. 1 in M. E. Beesley, *Urban Transport: Studies in Economic Policy* (London: Butterworths, 1973). Foster and Beesley's study was originally published in 1962; the Victoria Line was built subsequently and completed in 1969.

net benefits may take the form of time savings, greater comfort due to reduced crowding, or, if they had previously used an automobile, savings in vehicle operating costs.

Benefits to undiverted traffic. The diversion of traffic to a new link reduces congestion or discomfort on other transit routes or on city streets, thereby spreading benefits systemwide. Those continuing to use other routes or modes make gains in the form of improved comfort, greater speed, or both. In addition, there may be cost savings to the transit authority in operating fewer vehicles on the preexisting network. Foster and Beesley estimated that net benefits to undiverted traffic would account for 52 percent of total net benefits of the Victoria Line. The size of this component underscores the importance of looking at systemwide effects when evaluating transportation improvements.

Benefits to generated traffic. A new facility, by improving the accessibility of certain destinations, will induce people to make additional trips. The value to be attributed to these generated trips is probably the most uncertain calculation of all. As a first approximation, it can be measured by the fares that riders willingly pay for them.

Foster and Beesley estimated the value of the expected benefits of the Victoria Line under each of the above headings. The aggregate present value of benefits over the life of the project far exceeded expected costs. Consequently, the study showed that building the Victoria Line would produce a substantial net gain for society. The authors did not estimate the external costs or benefits of the line because the necessary information was not available at the time. They were convinced, however, that the omitted externalities would have provided additional net benefits.

The expected rate of return provides another perspective on the desirability of an investment project. Foster and Beesley estimated that the internal rate of return on the Victoria Line project would be about 10.5 percent. This number is calculated as the rate of discount that will make the present value of all expected benefits equal to the present value of all expected costs. When the internal rate of return is higher than the opportunity cost of capital, a project is held to be worth undertaking. The private market rate of interest is one possible measure of the opportunity cost of capital, but whether it is the most appropriate measure has been a matter for extended debate among economists.[26] In any case, a return of 10.5 percent in 1962 was well in excess of any then current measure of the opportunity cost of capital. Hence the Victoria Line

26. See Musgrave and Musgrave, 3rd ed., pp. 186–89.

looked like a socially profitable undertaking. However, since benefit-cost studies were not conducted simultaneously for alternative projects, one could not be certain that it was the most desirable of all possible ways to improve London's transportation.

External Benefits of Mass Transit

Since the automobile is a major source of air pollution and other environmental damage, it can be argued that substitution of mass transit for the automobile, when traffic levels are sufficiently high, will tend to reduce environmental damage. Such reduction can legitimately be counted as an external benefit of mass transportation. However, since we have already treated these environmental effects as external *costs* of automobile transportation it is not necessary to repeat the discussion, and it would in fact be double-counting were we also to reckon their removal as an external *benefit* of mass transit in an intermodal benefit-cost comparison.

The Distribution of Transportation Benefits

The direct benefits of a passenger transportation system are those that accrue to its users. The characteristics of users, and hence the distribution of benefits, vary systematically by mode. A highway-passenger automobile system, for example, cannot be used by the young, the old, the infirm, or those too poor to own a car. These groups, sometimes referred to as the transportation disadvantaged, are more dependent than the rest of the population on the use of public transportation. As our earlier discussion of transit pricing and subsidies suggests, the question of how the benefits of new projects or policies will be distributed among social and economic classes has received increased attention in recent years. We return to it below in sections dealing with transit innovations and "paratransit."

GOVERNMENT POLICY AND TRANSPORTATION CHOICES

The consumer is the ultimate judge of transportation systems. The rise of the automobile and the decline of public transportation no doubt reflect fundamental shifts in demand as consumers' incomes increase and as technological change offers them new choices. Yet transportation choices are also influenced by decisions of government. Urban transportation is not supplied under conditions of competition in which one might assume a sort of automatic, incremental response of supply to the dictates of demand. On the contrary, investment is "lumpy" rather than incremental, service is usually in the hands of a monopolist, and the hands are frequently those of government. Consequently, public policy does matter. Federal policy is particularly important, not only because of the federal government's superior financial capability, but also because it can and does use its financial strength to influence state and local policy by attaching conditions to its grants. In keeping with the developmental perspective employed throughout this book, it is appropriate to describe the broad trends in federal transportation policy as they have affected the development of urban and metropolitan areas.

Focus on Highways: 1916 to 1964

Federal aid to the states for highway construction began in 1916 and increased almost yearly thereafter. In 1956 the Highway Trust Fund was established to finance the new federal interstate highway system out of receipts from federal excise taxes on vehicles, gasoline, and tires. By 1965 federal aid to state and local governments for highway programs (including Trust Fund payments) had reached $4 billion per annum. Yet that was the first year in which mass transit received substantial federal support.

Furthermore, federal money for the interstate system was available on a 90-10 matching basis: local officials could obtain 90¢ of outside funds by putting up 10¢ from their own taxpayers. That is an offer difficult to refuse, especially when one considers that new roads bring not only transportation benefits but also the local economic stimulus and political leverage that come from expensive construction projects. There can be little doubt that the 90-10 highway formula distorted local choices away from alternative transportation investments and led to the construction of some roads that local users would never have agreed to pay for on their own.

For fifty years, then, federal policy facilitated the financing of highways, and consequently the suburbanization of metropolitan America, while steadily ignoring the problems of public transportation. Even if highways were not being subsidized (and we have seen that there is some disagreement about that), it was important that an institutional arrangement had been developed to finance highways out of user charges, while no such financial mechanism was devised for public modes.

Capital Grants for Mass Transit, 1964–

In the early 1960s there began a revival of interest in rail mass transit, in cities that previously lacked it, as an alternative to continued expansion of urban highway systems. Many influences converged to bring this about, among them the rising concern with air pollution, to which automobiles are a major contributor; dissatisfaction with the traffic congestion associated with urban growth; and, perhaps most important of all, the increasingly effective opposition to the destructive effects of major highways on the aesthetic character and daily life of urban neighborhoods.[27] (Somewhat later the energy crisis, with its suggestion that we may come to regret an exclusive commitment to the fuel-hungry automobile, added an additional argument for reconsidering mass transit.)

With these forces operating, a second period in the development of federal policy began. The Urban Mass Transportation Act of 1964 authorized the first substantial federal grants to support urban public transit. In 1966 the U.S. Department of Transportation was established, and in 1968 the Urban Mass Transportation Administration (UMTA) was created within the department to coordinate its urban efforts.

During its first ten years, the federal assistance program emphasized grants for capital improvements and for demonstration projects. The economic reasoning behind this was spelled out in a study by Lyle Fitch, William S. Vickrey, and others entitled *Urban Transportation and Public Policy*. This study had originally been prepared as a report to the government, and it strongly influenced the 1964 legislation.

Fitch, et al., argued that it was important "to put competing forms of urban transportation—private automobile and public transportation—on an equal footing with regard to support from external tax funds . . . to foster experimentation with and development of new urban transportation systems, technology . . . to prevent premature demise and abandonment of existing public-transportation facilities."[28] They recommended that federal support take the form of capital grants rather than subsidies for service improvements because the latter would be difficult to administer and might "be dissipated by labor demands and by wasteful management practices." Capital grants, on the other hand, could be used both for modernization of old facilities and for construction of new ones. The authors held out the hope that many transit systems could "be given a new lease on life with the application of modern, low-operating-cost, efficient technology."[29] Finally, they urged that these benefits be sought within a framework of regionally planned transportation systems.

This line of reasoning led the federal government to an early emphasis on capital grants for rail mass transit. Existing systems were extended in the old cities of the North and East, and new systems built or

27. See Kemp and Cheslow, pp. 299–308, for an extended discussion of "discontent with the automobile."
28. Lyle Fitch and Associates, *Urban Transportation and Public Policy* (San Francisco: Chandler Publishing, 1964), p. 209.
29. Ibid., p. 210.

planned in Washington, Atlanta, Baltimore, and elsewhere. The matching ratio was 2:1 until 1973, when it was increased to 4:1. The economic rationale for favoring rail systems was the belief that modernized, comfortable, high-speed rail transit would prove able to compete effectively with the automobile if only someone would give it a trial. Political pressures also supported rail transit as opposed to such alternatives as modernized express bus systems. What mayor would not prefer to run for reelection as builder of an elaborate new subway line rather than as sponsor of a possibly more efficient but certainly less visible express bus system?

Politics also influenced the configuration of the new rail systems. In order to marshal financial support from well-to-do suburbs, sponsors of proposed new systems tended to choose route layouts that maximized the suburban catchment area while slighting intra-central city service.[30] New rail systems like BART were consciously designed to take on the automobile in head-to-head competition for the suburb-to-central-city work trip. Existing systems were extended into the suburbs for the same purpose. The outcome, as we shall see, was generally disappointing to the sponsors of rail.

An Evaluation of San Francisco's BART

Although the Bay Area Rapid Transit system eventually met about 18 percent of its capital cost with federal grants, it was begun before federal aid was contemplated, with funds raised through a local bond issue. Because it was the first of the post-World War II systems in the United States to have been completed—partial service began in 1972 and full service in 1974—BART offers the longest record on which to judge performance. Consequently, evaluating the Bay Area system is the best way to illustrate the difficulties new U.S. rail transit facilities have faced or are likely to encounter.[31]

BART's performance is generally described as disappointing for one very simple reason: the system has manifestly failed to attract the expected number of riders. This failure, in turn, causes three others. First, BART has diverted far less traffic from highways than was anticipated. Second, passenger revenues are lower and the system's operating deficit larger than predicted. Third, with ridership low, agency cost per trip is far higher than expected.

When the proposal for bonds to finance construction of BART was

---

30. See the discussion in Kemp and Cheslow, pp. 309–11.

31. The following section draws heavily on Melvin M. Webber's comprehensive article, "The BART Experience—What Have We Learned?" in *The Public Interest*, Fall 1976, pp. 79–108. Webber's data, however, ran only through mid-1976. They have been brought up to date, where possible.

TABLE 9.3
Bay Area Rapid Transit System: Actual Performance Compared with Forecasts

ACTUAL RESULTS FOR FISCAL YEARS	AVERAGE DAILY PATRONAGE (JUNE)	NET OPERATING REVENUE ($ THOUSANDS)	TOTAL OPERATING EXPENSE ($ THOUSANDS)	OPERATING SURPLUS OR (DEFICIT) ($ THOUSANDS)	REVENUE AS PERCENTAGE OF OPERATING EXPENSE
1975	121,337	16,157	49,822	(33,665)	32%
1976	131,466	23,222	60,168	(36,946)	39
1978	144,885	29,898	78,204	(48,306)	38
1980	164,558	29,760[a]	88,581[a]	(58,821)[a]	30[a]
FORECASTS					
1962 forecast of 1975	258,496	24,500	13,500	11,000	181
1971 forecast of 1975	191,150	38,200	27,500	10,700	139

[a] Revenues and expenses in fiscal 1980 were reduced by a 12-week strike beginning September 1, 1979.

Sources: Actual patronage, revenues, and expenses from Bay Area Rapid Transit District, *Statistical Summary for Month of June,* 1975–80. Forecast, 1962, from Webber, "The BART Experience—What Have We Learned?" tables I and II, pp. 85, 92. Forecast, 1971, from Bay Area Rapid Transit District, BART *Interstation Fare Schedule Report,* May 18, 1971, as follows: patronage, table 1, p. 6; revenue, table 6, p. 36; expenses, table 9, p. 43.

put before the voters in 1962, its sponsors publicized a set of detailed traffic estimates for the year 1975, by which date the system was expected to be in full operation. According to these estimates, the system would carry an average of 258,500 passengers per weekday, of whom 157,400, or 61 percent were expected to be diverted from automobiles. With so many commuters switching to BART, traffic congestion on streets and highways was expected to be noticeably reduced. BART's sponsors were also optimistic about the system's finances. They estimated that by fiscal 1975–76, it would be generating a substantial operating surplus that could be used to help defray capital costs.

Table 9.3 compares the levels of activity forecast for 1975 with actual results for that and subsequent years. Full weekday service began only late in 1974, and the system was plagued with mechanical failures that may have discouraged ridership in the early years. Consequently, 1975 patronage is not a fair test of BART's drawing powers. Even by 1980, however, the system was attracting only 164,558 riders on an average weekday, or 36 percent less than the 1962 forecast. Nor does the modest upward trend suggest that the expected figure will soon be reached.

Diversion from automobiles is far less than predicted, not only in absolute but also in relative terms. Webber reports that in a 1976 survey, only about 44,000 daily BART users were recorded as previously making the trip by car, instead of the predicted 157,000. Diversion from automobiles thus accounted for only about 35 percent of BART trips, as compared with a forecast of 61 percent. Unexpectedly, about 50,000 BART riders, and as much as half of BART's transbay traffic, were diverted from that other form of mass transportation—the motor bus.

Webber rates the overall impact of BART on Bay Area road traffic as, at most, "a small net reduction in auto traffic volume."[32] When full BART service began, diversion of riders from autos and buses temporarily reduced vehicle numbers and increased driving speeds on some routes that closely parallel its tracks. However, normal road traffic growth often resumed thereafter, so that these gains may be very short-lived. Webber concludes that "BART has not effected a significant change in automobile-use habits."

To be sure, BART has added to the Bay Area's transportation capacity. People are now traveling more than they would have in BART's absence, without (so far) increasing congestion. That is a valid measure of system-wide benefits. Unfortunately, these benefits were purchased at a very high cost per trip. Looked at as an investment intended to provide a marginal increase in transportation capacity, BART has proven to be an extraordinarily expensive choice.

32. Ibid., p. 86.

BART's Financial Record

The shortfall in BART patronage obviously implies a similar shortfall in revenues and a corresponding increase in the operating deficit. General price inflation makes it difficult to compare current revenues and costs with predictions made in the early 1960s. The relationship between revenues and costs for any given year is not similarly affected, however. Hence the deficit figures are revealing. The 1962 study predicted a substantial operating surplus when the system was fully operational. Instead, as Table 9.3 illustrates, substantial deficits exist: operating revenues have never covered more than 39 percent of operating costs in the years since full service was begun. Although BART was designed as a highly automated system in which intensive use of capital would produce low operating costs, it has not worked out that way. BART's fare-to-operating-cost ratio of between 30 and 39 percent is far below the 48 to 56 percent ratios reported for the older, less automated rail mass transit systems of New York, Chicago, Philadelphia, and Cleveland. Among the older systems, only Boston, at 27 percent, has a lower ratio.[33] According to Webber's calculations as of 1976, even if BART had then been carrying the full 258,500 daily passengers originally predicted, it still would have covered less than three-fourths of its *then current* operating costs (and costs would, in fact, have been higher if traffic increased that much.) BART's deficits are covered by revenues from a combination of sources. Earmarked local sales and property taxes make up most of the deficit but are supplemented by state and federal operating assistance.

The above comparisons do not include BART's capital costs. Webber estimates annualized capital costs in 1975–76 at $82.4 million, somewhat higher than the level of operating costs in that year, which he calculated at $64.0 million. Total financial costs thus came to $146.4 million. Dividing by the number of trips taken produced an agency cost per trip of $4.48. Since fares averaged only 72¢, the average user was being subsidized by about $3.76 per ride, a figure that must be doubled for a round-trip commuter.

BART's financial costs per ride at current levels of patronage are far above those of public bus alternatives. Webber calculated in 1976 that "the costs of buying a whole fleet of new buses sufficient to carry all BART's passengers projected to 1980 would be under $40 million."[34] BART's capital costs were $1,600 million, or 40 times the cost of such buses. Since BART's operating costs per passenger mile are also higher than those of local bus systems (15.7¢ as compared with 13.6¢ in 1975–76), they do nothing to offset its high capital costs.

33. These ratios are from Straszheim, table 7.2, p. 202.
34. Webber, p. 104.

So far, we have discussed *money* costs only, rather than full costs including the value of time and of externalities, as shown in Figure 8.3. That figure can be used to estimate the full cost of a trip on BART and the bus and automobile alternatives, provided we know the peak-hour volume in the corridor in question. Through 1976, the peak volume on BART's transbay tube was only 8,000 passengers per hour, far below the 20,000 figure at which BART would become competitive with a subcompact car or the 30,000 volume at which (for long trips) it would cost no more than a bus. At a volume of only 8,000, Figure 8.5 indicates that the full cost of a BART trip is about $6.20, approximately double the cost by express bus and about 50 percent more than the cost of using a private car.

Cost by itself, is, of course, not a valid criterion. If a trip on BART were so far superior to the alternatives that riders were willing to pay for its high cost, then there would be no ground for objection. But, of course, riders have *not* been paying its high cost. They ride at a better than five-to-one subsidy.

Great as BART's capital costs may appear, they look like bargain prices compared to costs of systems constructed more recently, for BART's costs were incurred before the rapid inflation of the 1970s. To that extent, the more recent systems are likely to face even greater financial stress than BART has endured.

BART's fundamental error, in Webber's view, lay in its design. Its promoters believed that "high speed, high comfort, high style and downtown delivery were the attributes that matter most to motorists; and BART was then designed to outdo the car on those four counts."[35] BART's management delivered a system that has exactly the qualities its designers sought. Why haven't auto users flocked to it? The answer is that to achieve those attributes BART's designers gave up others that are even more important to motorists. For example, to maximize line-haul speed from suburb to central city they chose rail, with wide spacing between stations. The high capacity and high cost of a rail corridor, in turn, dictated that there be only a few lines radiating into the suburbs. The combination of wide station-spacing and few lines inevitably meant that most commuters would live far from the nearest BART station. Consequently, much time and effort would be required just getting to (and from) the rail line. Here came the unkindest cut of all. Studies of travel behavior (unfortunately, carried out *after* BART was conceived) repeatedly show that trip-makers find time spent walking or waiting to make connections about three times as onerous as in-vehicle time. Thus BART's design minimized time spent on the pleasantest part of the journey—and

35. Ibid., p. 99.

riding on a BART train is, indeed, very pleasant—while making the un
pleasant part as time-consuming as possible. Webber concludes that th
"fundamental mistake" in design explains BART's inability to diver
motorists.

It is probably fair to say that most transportation economists no
regard BART as a beautiful but costly mistake. Its failure to attract any
thing like the expected patronage appears to confirm the opinion some c
them voiced even before it was built, that a well-planned express bu
system, using limited access highways, could deliver as good service t
far more people at a much lower cost and with far greater long-ru
flexibility.

Demonstration Grants to Test
Transit Innovations

In addition to authorizing capital grants for new construction an
new equipment, the Urban Mass Transportation Act of 1964 provide
federal support for demonstration projects in which local transit author
ties could experiment with new technology or with new techniques fo
scheduling and routing.

The American people's faith in the possibilities of high technolog
reached its peak in the late 1960s with the dramatic landing of astronaut
on the moon. The success of our space program led to a conviction tha
if we put our minds and resources to work we could also use technologica
means to "solve" such earthly difficulties as urban traffic congestion. En
couragement came from the supply side, too, since many high technolog
corporations were eager to develop a market in urban mass transit equip
ment as a successor to the dwindling space program.

The results of experiments with new technology were almost entirel
disappointing. In a detailed evaluation of the Urban Mass Transportatio
Assistance Program completed in 1974, George W. Hilton found no suc
cesses among the grants to develop such innovative technologies as hove
craft, tracked air cushion vehicles, or "people-movers," using automate
vehicles on fixed guideways.[36] Nor was UMTA's cooperative venture wit
BART to develop fully automated train controls successful. Repeate
failures of the computerized system seriously delayed the introduction o
service between San Francisco and the East Bay portions of BART. Ult
mately, plans for full automation were abandoned.

Demonstration projects testing new techniques for scheduling an

36. George W. Hilton, *Federal Transit Subsidies* (Washington, D.C.: America
Enterprise Institute, 1974). A shorter version entitled "The Urban Mass Transportatio
Assistance Program" appeared in *Perspectives on Federal Transportation Policy*, e
by James C. Miller III, issued by the same publisher in 1975.

outing produced mixed results. A large number of these involved urban
ous transit and were, in all probability, intended to help overcome the
notorious inertia of local transit operators in the United States in respond-
ng to urban change. Reviewing the evidence in 1975, Hilton found that
experiments with express bus operation had been "markedly successful."
In general these involved creating reserved lanes on expressways for buses
o the CBD, providing such buses with exclusive on and off ramps to the
expressway and, in one case, using ramp traffic lights to restrain automobile access to a level compatible with "free-running" traffic, thus permitting much higher bus speeds. These innovations significantly reduced
running time, enabling buses to divert a considerable number of automobile commuters.[37] On the basis of evidence from UMTA demonstra-
ion programs, Kain in 1972 advocated an express bus "freeway rapid
ransit system" for Atlanta, arguing that it could be built at a capital cost
of between one fifteenth and one hundredth of Atlanta's proposed rail
ransit system, while covering more route miles, offering lower door-to-
door travel times, and preserving far greater flexibility.[38]

UMTA's other demonstration bus programs appeared to be far less
successful than its experiments with express systems. Many of the other
experiments had their origins in the War on Poverty. Following the urban
riots of the mid-1960s, it was observed that inner city ghettos frequently
lacked public transportation connections to places of employment growth
and job opportunity, especially those in the suburbs. UMTA subsidized
numerous experimental bus routes intended to overcome this isolation by
providing outward mobility. Only a few of these attracted substantial
ridership, all were very costly per passenger, and many were subsequently
terminated. Ironically, these projects were inherently self-destructive: the
ghetto worker, upon finding steady employment, immediately bought a
car and abandoned public transit. Nor were UMTA's experiments with
subscription bus services, dial-a-ride minibus systems, and other demand-
sensitive innovations generally successful.[39]

The Possibilities of Paratransit

Although a number of UMTA's demonstration projects failed, many
transportation analysts continue to believe that relatively inexpensive or
even costless reforms such as improved management or selective deregu-

37. Hilton, *Federal Transit Subsidies*, pp. 18–19.
38. John F. Kain, "The Unexpected Potential of Freeway Transit in Regional
Transportation Planning: An Atlanta Case Study," in Andrew Hamer, ed., *Unorthodox
Approaches to Urban Transportation: The Emerging Challenge to Conventional Planning* (Atlanta: Georgia State University, 1973), pp. 38–53.
39. Hilton, *Federal Transit Subsidies*, pp. 21–24, 25–28.

lation could significantly improve the performance of urban transportation systems. Despite the vast locational shifts that have occurred in this century in both place of work and place of residence, many city buses continue to follow routes identical to those of the streetcar franchises that they replaced forty or fifty years ago. Monopolistic conditions typically contribute to this inflexibility, for no matter how unresponsive the operating agency, there are no competitors to take business away. In addition, residents acquire a vested interest in the continued operation of ancient lines that makes it politically hazardous for an operating authority to abandon old routes in order to reallocate resources to new ones.

Paratransit and selective deregulation are often suggested as solutions to this dilemma.[40] We have created an artificial situation, it is asserted, in which the urban transportation market is dominated by two modes that lie at opposite ends of a spectrum. The public mode (usually bus) operates as a tradition-bound, unresponsive monopoly. The principal alternative, opposite in every respect to the public mode, is the highly flexible, rather expensive, and completely private automobile. Between these two extremes, so the argument runs, there is not only room but, in fact, real need for an intermediate type, combining some features of each. The generic name paratransit has been coined for this intermediate mode.

Paratransit comprises those forms of transportation that combine some of the convenience and flexibility of the private car with some of the economy inherent in public transportation. Included are such traditional modes as taxicabs, rental cars, and carpools, as well as such innovative arrangements as dial-a-ride, subscription bus, and organized vanpool. These modes provide personalized service, usually picking up the customer at a prearranged time at the point of origin. Yet, given the quality of the service, they are relatively economical as compared with the private car because their cost is shared among many users.

If taxis are a form of paratransit, however, why do we need any others? Obviously, taxis have long provided a service blending the virtues of public and private transportation. They provide it, moreover, on a surprisingly large scale: Wohl reports that *fleet* taxicabs alone "now handle almost 40 percent *more* passengers than do all U.S. rapid transit systems combined, and carry about 60 percent as many passengers as all bus transit systems."[41] Unfortunately, however, the taxi industry is almost everywhere heavily and irrationally regulated. Such regulation usually prevents

40. See Ronald F. Kirby, K. U. Bhatt, M. A. Kemp, et al., *Para-transit Neglected Options for Urban Mobility* (Washington, D.C.: The Urban Institute 1975).

41. Martin Wohl, "The Taxi's Role in Urban America: Today and Tomorrow," *Transportation*, June 1975, p. 150.

operators from offering the variety of services that the mode is inherently capable of. For example, casual cab sharing is generally outlawed, and taxis cannot legally operate as carpools, although both services would be very useful to consumers. Regulation also frequently involves severe restrictions on entry to the industry. A form of monopoly is thus created artificially, the supply of cabs is reduced, fares are higher and vehicles less readily available than they would otherwise be.

Advocates of paratransit believe that it can produce high quality, economical service on routes or in neighborhoods where demand is not sufficiently dense to support regular public transportation. It may also be the most humane and effective way to provide mobility for the elderly and the handicapped, who are severely disadvantaged by the decline or disappearance of public transportation, which, in any case, does not serve them very comfortably.

Whether or not sophisticated new forms of paratransit prove viable, a strong argument remains for less restrictive regulation of taxis in order to allow the public to take advantage of the inherent flexibility of that mode. As Wohl points out, "taxicabs are the only form of public transportation service (a few private bus firms aside) that must and does pay its own way (inclusive of both capital and operating costs)."[42] Consumers have shown that they are willing to pay for the comfort and convenience of the taxi. As incomes rise over the long run, the market for this superior service is bound to increase. It is time we took seriously its potential contribution to urban mobility, instead of making it into a petty monopoly ineptly regulated to the detriment of the public interest.

ENERGY COSTS, TRANSPORTATION, AND URBAN FORM

Transportation policy today is increasingly bound up with, even dominated by, national concern with the energy problem. Each short-run "energy crisis" interrupts established patterns of travel behavior and stimulates discussion of less fuel-intensive life styles than those we have become accustomed to in the United States.

In this section we take up two questions related to the energy crisis. First, which modes of urban transportation should be encouraged in the interest of saving fuel? Second, what effects are rising fuel prices likely to have on urban and metropolitan form?

42. Ibid., p. 151.

Transportation Policy and
the Energy Requirements of Alternative Modes

It is well known that a bus or rail transit vehicle with an average
passenger load uses far less energy per passenger mile than does an auto
mobile carrying its typical 1.4 occupants. Transportation policies to con
serve fuel therefore aim at substituting other modes that are less fue
intensive for the passenger car. A thoroughgoing intermodal comparison
of energy use, however, must calculate much more than just the fue
consumption of transportation vehicles themselves. A study by the Con
gressional Budget Office shows that the following factors also must be
taken into account:[43]

1. The energy required to manufacture the vehicles and to construct
   maintain, and operate the right-of-way.
2. The energy consumed by users in gaining access to the mode in
   question. For example, commuters using a new rail transit system
   such as BART, typically drive to and from the transit station
   using substantial quantities of fuel in the process.
3. The energy *saving* that can be achieved by promoting a particula
   mode. To estimate net savings it is necessary to allow for the fue
   that new patrons of a given mode would have used under previou
   arrangements. For example, to the extent that a new rail transi
   system attracts former car drivers, net fuel savings are likely to
   result; to the extent that it attracts former bus riders there wil
   probably be a net *increase* in fuel consumption. There is also a
   net increase if a transportation improvement generates new traffic

The authors of the study wisely avoid claiming an unrealistic degree
of precision for their results. Instead, they estimate high, low, and middle
values for potential energy savings by allowing for a wide range of vari
ation in such underlying factors as number of occupants per vehicle o
the means used to gain access to public transportation. Here are thei
principal findings:

1. Among the available urban transportation alternatives, vanpoo
   and carpool promise the largest fuel savings because they usuall
   operate to capacity and draw patrons primarily from the highl
   fuel intensive private automobile. However, government polic
   can do little to encourage use of these arrangements.
2. The new rail transit systems of the 1970s and 1980s probabl
   increase rather than reduce the use of energy. These systems draw

43. Congressional Budget Office, *Urban Transportation and Energy: the Potentia
Savings of Different Modes*, December 1977.

more of their patrons from buses (which use less energy), than they do from automobiles (which use more), and a large majority of those using them reach the transit stations by car. Access is therefore very fuel intensive.

3. Express buses rank highest among the conventional modes of transportation as probable sources of fuel saving. The advantage of express bus service is that a substantial fraction of its patronage is drawn from among former automobile commuters and without requiring them to drive long distances to make the connection. It must be emphasized, however, that bus service is not energy efficient if patronage is low. Energy will be wasted rather than saved if bus service is introduced in situations where it cannot attract a substantial number of riders.

Fuel Cost and Urban Form

The Congressional Budget Office study took as "given" the present rm of the metropolis, with its highly dispersed pattern of residential and ɔ location. In that context, urban transportation policy can, at best, ve only a limited effect in reducing energy consumption. We can obably take it for granted, however, that the real cost of energy will ntinue to rise substantially into the foreseeable future. It is interesting speculate, therefore, about the possibility that rising fuel costs them- ves will eventually alter metropolitan form.

Analytically, it is useful to think of the effects of a radical increase fuel prices or of possible gasoline rationing as consisting of two inter- ated parts. First, taking the existing location of economic activity and transportation facilities as given, consumers in the short run will alter eir behavior by traveling less or choosing different modes or different stinations. Second, a radical increase in energy costs is likely, in the ìger run, to cause changes in the location of jobs and residences— anges in the form of the metropolis itself—that will further alter pat- ns of travel behavior.

The energy crises of 1973–74 and 1979 did bring about short-run luctions in driving and temporary increases in transit patronage. Indeed, e long established year-to-year decline in transit ridership reached bottom 1972. Over the next six years, patronage increased 13.5 percent. (See ible 9.1.) But it is far from certain that this change in trend, if it can called that, was a consequence of the energy crisis. Transit patronage ay have been leveling off anyway, after its prolonged decline, and large ıblic subsidies were beginning to stimulate the extension and improve- ent of service. Nor do the temporary declines in driving that occurred ıring those crises tell us much about the effects of rising gasoline prices

on consumer behavior. Rather, they reflect such factors as the physic
unavailability of gasoline, distaste for waiting on line, and fear of bei
stranded in mid-journey, as well, perhaps, as an initial willingness
answer the call of civic duty by conserving fuel.

The response of consumers to price changes is conventional
measured in economics by the price elasticity of demand, defined as t
percentage change in the quantity purchased as the result of a change
price, divided by the percentage change in price that brings it abor
Elasticities are normally expected to be higher in the long run than in tl
short run, because it will usually take some time for consumers to fi
substitutes or otherwise adjust their habitual behavior. Reviewing a bro
range of elasticity studies, Alex Anas and Leon Moses find that the ela
ticity of demand for motor fuel does fit the normal pattern. In the Unit
States the short-run elasticity is very low—probably between −0.1 a
−0.3—but the long-run elasticity apparently rises to between −0.65 a
−0.85.[44] If these estimates are valid, higher fuel prices will certainly affe
consumer travel behavior over the long run.

As Anas and Moses also point out, however, elasticity studies do n
throw much light on the locational adjustments households will make
response to changes in the cost of travel. This problem is better address
by urban simulation models in which the location of activity and tl
demand for transportation are determined simultaneously. While su
models are now under development, it is too early to expect them
provide formal answers to the questions posed here. Proceeding, therefo
without the support of formal models, what can we say about the like
long-run effect of increases in the real cost of fuel on the pattern
metropolitan settlement?

Possible Future Patterns

Anas and Moses identify three possible long-run patterns of futu
development. The first is simply a continuation of past trends: dispers
of population and jobs within metropolitan regions, including furth
movement into what are now "exurban" areas. This implies no more th
marginal changes in locational choice. Despite steeply rising energy cos
people would continue to make long daily work and shopping trips. T
second pattern is a drawing back of population and jobs into "areas th
are well located with respect to the main corridors of public transpor

44. Alex Anas and Leon N. Moses, "Transportation and Land Use in the Mat
Metropolis," ch. 8 in C. L. Leven, ed., *The Mature Metropolis* (Lexington, Ma
D.C. Heath, Lexington Books, 1978), p. 163. Also see Burke K. Burright and Jo
H. Enns, *Econometric Models of the Demand for Motor Fuel*, doc. no. R-1561-NS
FEA (Santa Monica, Cal.: Rand Corporation, April 1975).

tion." Riders would return to the old public transit networks. Centralization would resume after a lapse of fifty years, restoring a spatial structure that resembled the city of the early twentieth century. The authors describe the third pattern as "increased multi-nucleation: the formation of distinct and quite dense suburban and exurban centers." Instead of recentralization into the old CBD, we would see increased centralization of activity at a number of ring area locations. Multifamily housing would increase around these suburban nuclei and, as population density rose, better public bus transportation would be provided.[45]

Anas and Moses regard the first pattern as the least likely to prevail because it would involve continued increases in average trip length and would therefore be the most costly of the three. The second and third patterns would allow households to economize on transportation either by increasing their use of public transportation or by reducing average trip length. The second may appeal to public officials in the older central cities who would like to think that radically higher energy prices will suddenly throw the machinery of history into reverse, causing a rebirth of public transit and a large-scale recentralization of population within their borders. But history is not like a home movie in which one can reverse the projector motor and watch the children leap out of the swimming pool and back onto the diving board. With radically higher energy prices, Americans are likely to adjust their travel behavior in many ways—they will buy smaller cars, give up long intercity motor trips, make less profligate use of the automobile locally, and even move closer to work—but they will not give up altogether the amenities they associate with the automobile. Witness the rapid growth of car ownership in Europe, where fuel prices have long been in excess of $1.00 a gallon. Anas and Moses, moreover, point out that recentralization on a massive scale depends on job availability: it will be impossible unless significant numbers of employers move back to the central city, which looks highly improbable. On the other hand, the ability of the suburbs to attract and hold additional jobs is hardly in question.

Multinucleation, therefore, appears to be the most likely of the three alternatives.[46] The attractive power of that pattern lies in the fact that it allows for a systematic shortening of the journey to work, while not forcing households altogether to abandon the automobile. Shopping trips, too, might be expected to grow shorter if, as seems likely, increased residential density supports the growth of neighborhood stores at the expense of more remote regional shopping malls. As already indicated, one would expect bus transportation to improve as increased density makes more frequent

45. Anas and Moses, p. 161.
46. Ibid., pp. 164–65.

service feasible. It should be noted, however, that suburban multinucleation will certainly not create origin-destination densities high enough to
support new rail transit facilities.

Multinucleation has some interesting further implications. Anas and
Moses point out that if job growth continues in the suburbs, while a
majority of the low-income and minority population continue to live in
the central city, reverse commuting by these groups to suburban jobs,
already rapidly increasing, will continue to rise.[47] As higher energy prices
increase the cost of such commuting, we should expect that minority
demands for access to suburban housing will become even stronger than
they are now. (This issue is treated in subsequent chapters on poverty
and housing.) At the same time, the demand by suburbanites for mixed
zoning to allow closer proximity of residences to shopping and recreation
(not to mention jobs) and for greater decentralization of governmental
and educational services is also likely to increase.[48] Under these pressures
patterns of location will shift in such a way as to reduce average trip
distances; the form of the city will gradually adapt to changes in the real
cost of transportation.

The Rising Cost of Transportation and the System of Cities

From well back in the nineteenth century the population of the
United States has been increasingly concentrated into its metropolitan
areas. In Chapter 3 we saw that this long-continued and historically fundamental trend came to a rather unexpected halt around 1970. It was
followed by *de*concentration, defined as a decline in the proportion of
population living in SMSA's, which has been taking place at an admittedly
very modest rate. It now seems possible that deconcentration, as we knew
it in the 1970s, will be a short-lived phase, to be halted eventually under
the pressure of rising transportation costs.

The overall trend of concentration or deconcentration, however,
conceals diverse movements among individual metropolitan areas, which
are in some respects more important than the direction taken by the
nationwide aggregate. For example, an end to aggregate deconcentration
need not mean that the largest metropolitan areas, which have recently
shown absolute population losses, will now begin to grow again, much
less grow as fast as the national population. On the contrary, it seems
likely that increasing transportation costs will reinforce the recent strongly

47. Ibid., pp. 166–67.
48. The last two points are made by Richard H. Shackson in "Transportation
and Energy Futures," a paper prepared for the Aspen Conference on Future Urban
Transportation, June 3–7, 1979.

inverse relationship between SMSA growth and size. Household transportation costs are systematically higher in larger SMSA's because the average journey to work is longer. This disadvantage is presumably offset by other factors favoring larger SMSA's. However, as fuel prices rise, the absolute disadvantage of greater trip lengths will increase. We would expect smaller SMSA's to become more attractive relative to large ones, which would reinforce their recently greater rate of growth. To look at it another way, small SMSA's already offer most of the advantages that Anas and Moses see accruing to the suburbs of large SMSA's through multi-nucleation. Indeed, it seems possible that a household could more easily shorten trip lengths while retaining the advantages of low density suburban living by moving to a small SMSA than by living in a multinucleated suburb. Certainly, if higher fuel prices favor the one we should expect them also to favor the other.

We began Chapter 8 with the observation that cities exist to facilitate interaction and that transportation costs are part of the price we pay to obtain that end. We should not be surprised, then, if substantial changes in the cost of transportation affect not only urban form but also the size distribution of the entire system of cities.

The Urbanization
of Poverty

TEN

Ever since America rediscovered her poor in the early 1960s, the words "poverty" and "city" have been almost automatically linked in our public vocabulary. It was not always so. To an earlier generation, poverty appeared to be mainly a rural phenomenon. As late as 1959 considerably more poor people were living outside metropolitan areas than in them. Since then the proportions have changed dramatically, and the end is not yet in sight. In this chapter we briefly examine definitions of poverty, then investigate recent changes in its geography and explain some of the causes and consequences of those changes. In the chapter that follows we will analyze the great variety of policies that have been either tried or proposed to combat poverty in our cities.

DEFINING POVERTY

Definitions of poverty may be either relative or absolute. An absolute definition specifies some level of purchasing power per person or per family that is deemed sufficient to buy a minimum of life's necessities. Households with incomes below that level are classified as living in poverty. A relative definition, on the other hand, classifies households as living in poverty if their income falls below some fraction of the national median or mean. For example, a family with an income of less than half the national median might be defined as living in poverty.

In compiling "official" poverty statistics for the United States, the federal government employs an absolute definition of a poverty-line income that varies according to family size, sex of family head, and farm versus nonfarm residence and is adjusted annually in step with changes in the cost of living. The poverty-line income in 1979 for a nonfarm family of four was $7,412.[1] In principle most analysts would prefer a poverty band rather than a poverty line when framing an absolute definition, since the choice of a particular line will always convey a degree of precision in both concept and measurement that is entirely unwarranted. As Thurow argues, we should recognize "that there is a band over which definite poverty shades into economic sufficiency. . . ."[2] Responding to this view, the federal government now publishes a limited amount of data on persons with incomes below 125 percent of the poverty line. The full range of poverty statistics, however, is not available on that basis.

When an absolute definition of poverty is retained for a number of years while the average living standard in the nation gradually increases, the incidence of poverty (as defined) is almost certain to diminish. Only if the distribution of income became more unequal as income per capita rose could a reduction in absolute poverty fail to occur. So it should occasion neither surprise nor self-congratulation that, as Table 10.2 shows, the incidence of poverty in the United States, according to the official, absolute definition, has fallen markedly since the late 1950s.

The situation is quite different when a relative definition is used. The extent of poverty then depends entirely on the distribution of income and not at all on its level. A reduction in poverty can occur only if the distribution of income among families is changed in an appropriate fashion; a uniform percentage increase in living standards for all income classes has no effect. According to relative definitions, poverty in the United States has not diminished significantly since the end of World War II. In 1947 the poorest 20 percent of families in the United States received just 5.0 percent of all family income. During the late 1960s their share rose to a peak of 5.6 percent, but it gradually slipped back, falling to 5.3 percent by 1979.[3]

Indeed, it may well be argued that the progress registered under an absolute definition of poverty is in part illusory. Historical experience demonstrates that in a dynamic economy the absolute standard of income sufficiency accepted by the social consensus at one period will no longer seem appropriate at a later date. Thus absolute standards tend periodically to be revised upward by common consent, which washes out some, though

1. U.S. Bureau of the Census, *Current Population Reports*, series P-60, no. 125, October 1980, table 17. For a detailed explanation of the federal definition see *Current Population Reports*, series P-60, no. 124, July 1980, pp. 202–11.
2. Lester C. Thurow, *Poverty and Discrimination* (Washington, D.C.: The Brookings Institution, 1969), p. 21.
3. *Current Population Reports*, series P-60, no. 125, October 1980, table 5.

not all, of the reduction in poverty that seems to accrue during the intervals in which the standards remain fixed. In effect, we do think of poverty as partly a relative matter.

Since it was first introduced in the mid-1960s, however, the federal government's definition of a poverty-line income has not been substantially revised, except to adjust it for changes in the price level. As the years pass, this standard is bound to appear increasingly unrealistic, and sooner or later it will be revised upward. But one must add that no single definition should be expected to serve all purposes. Whatever its limitations in other connections, the federal definition does provide an easily understood, unambiguous standard for measuring the geographic distribution of poverty in the United States. It is to this subject that we now turn.

THE CHANGING GEOGRAPHY OF POVERTY

Table 10.1 shows the percentage distribution of the U.S. poverty population by place of residence beginning in 1959, the earliest year for which poverty statistics using current definitions have been calculated. It clearly documents the increasing concentration of poverty in metropolitan areas. In 1959 the poor living outside metropolitan areas outnumbered those living inside them by a ratio of 5 to 4. During the 1960s and 1970s, however, poverty declined much more sharply outside SMSA's, so by 1979 a considerable majority of the nation's poor were metropolitan residents.

If we turn from the absolute level to the rate or incidence of poverty, we see a somewhat different picture. The rate of poverty for a population class is simply the proportion of that class living below the

TABLE 10.1
Geographic Distribution of Persons Living in Poverty

	PERCENTAGE DISTRIBUTION AMONG AREAS		
PLACE OF RESIDENCE	*1959*	*1969*	*1979*
United States	100.0%	100.0%	100.0%
Metropolitan areas	43.9	54.2	61.9
Central cities	26.9	33.1	37.4
Outside central cities	17.0	21.1	24.6
Nonmetropolitan areas	56.1	45.8	38.1

Source: U.S. Bureau of the Census, *Current Population Reports*, series P-60, no. 124, July 1980, table 4, and no. 125, October 1980, table C.

poverty line. Table 10.2 shows such rates by race and area. In 1959 the rate of poverty was twice as high outside as inside metropolitan areas. It fell rapidly in both areas during the 1960s. In the 1970s the rate continued to fall in nonmetropolitan America but actually *increased* slightly within SMSA's. Although by 1979 the incidence of poverty was still slightly lower in metropolitan than nonmetropolitan areas, the two rates were fast converging.

If we look at the metropolis itself these facts stand out:

1. Within metropolitan areas the incidence of poverty is far higher in the central cities than in the suburban rings.
2. After having declined in the previous decade, the rate of poverty increased substantially in central cities during the 1970s.
3. The rate of poverty is now higher in the central cities of large than of small SMSA's.

The first two points are shown clearly in the upper panel of Table 10.2. For all races combined, the incidence of poverty in the central cities was 18.3 percent in 1959 and 15.6 percent in 1979. In the suburban rings the comparable rates were 12.2 and 7.1 percent. These figures demonstrate both that the rate of poverty is far higher in central cities than in ring areas and that the gap between rates in the two areas has widened dramatically in recent years.

The bottom panel of Table 10.2 demonstrates the third point. In 1959 the rate of poverty was far higher in the central cities of small than of large SMSA's. By 1978 the positions of the two groups had reversed. Moreover, the incidence of poverty was as high in 1978 in central cities of large SMSA's as it had been in 1959. As we shall see, this outcome is at least partly a result of the past pattern of migration.

RACE AND POVERTY

Thus far we have not considered racial differences in either the level or the rate of poverty. Although whites make up almost two-thirds of the nation's poor, Table 10.2 shows that the *rate* of poverty is about three times as high among blacks. In both population groups the table shows that the incidence of poverty fell rapidly in the 1960s but very slowly thereafter. (We shall have more to say about this in the next chapter.) The rate of poverty for blacks in the nation as a whole declined from 55.1 percent in 1959 to 30.9 percent in 1979. Over the same period the national poverty rate for whites fell relatively faster, from 18.1 percent to 8.9 percent.

If we look at blacks by place of residence (in Table 10.2), an

TABLE 10.2
Incidence of Poverty by Area and Race

	PERCENTAGE LIVING BELOW POVERTY LINE		
I. Incidence of poverty among persons by area and race (percentage)	1959	1969	1979
All Races[a]			
United States	22.0%	12.1%	11.6%
Metropolitan areas	15.3	9.5	10.6
Central cities	18.3	12.7	15.6
Outside central cities	12.2	6.8	7.1
Nonmetropolitan areas	33.2	17.9	13.7
White			
United States	18.1	9.5	8.9
Metropolitan areas	12.0	7.4	7.7
Central cities	13.8	9.7	10.5
Outside central cities	10.4	5.8	6.1
Nonmetropolitan areas	28.2	14.1	11.2
Black			
United States	55.1	32.2	30.9
Metropolitan areas	42.8	24.5	28.4
Central cities	40.5	24.3	31.1
Outside central cities	50.9	25.4	21.1
Nonmetropolitan areas	77.7	54.3	39.5
II. Incidence of poverty among families by size of SMSA (percentage) Central cities in SMSA's of 1,000,000 or more	1959	1969	1978
All races	13.8	11.1	13.9
Central cities in SMSA's of less than 1,000,000[b]			
All races	17.0	11.1	11.4

[a] Includes others in addition to black and white.
[b] In 1959, central cities in SMSA's of 250,000 to 1 million.
Sources: U.S. Bureau of the Census, *Current Population Reports*, series P-60, no. 124, July 1980, tables E and 4, and no. 125, October 1980, table 20; series P-23, no. 37, June 24, 1971, table 30.

important distinction appears: from 1969 to 1979 the incidence of poverty among blacks living in central cities rose substantially; in all other areas the rate of black poverty continued to decline. Although urban blacks made up only 18 percent of the nation's poor in 1979, it is clear that their situation is peculiarly difficult and deserves special attention.

The systematic collection of poverty data for persons of Spanish

TABLE 10.3

Ratios of Black and Spanish to White Income

	MEDIAN FAMILY INCOME RATIOS		
	Black and Other Races to White	Black to White	Spanish Origin to White
1950	.54	—	—
1954	.56	—	—
1959	.54	.52	—
1964	.56	.54	—
1969	.63	.61	—
1972	.62	.59	.71
1973	.60	.58	.69
1974	.64	.60	.71
1975	.65	.62	.67
1976	.63	.59	.66
1977	.61	.57	.68
1978	.64	.59	.68
1979	.60	.57	.70

Sources: U.S. Bureau of the Census, Current Population Reports, series P-60, no. 123, June 1980, table 10, and no. 125, October 1980, table 1; series P-23, no. 80, 1979, table 14.

origin began only in the 1970s. Hence this ethnic group is not shown separately in Table 10.2. The national rate of poverty in the population of Spanish origin was 21.6 percent in 1979, about midway between the rates for whites and blacks. In central cities the Spanish-origin poverty rate was 25.3 percent, a good deal closer to the black figure than to the white.[4] Unlike the rate for blacks, however, it does not appear to have increased during the 1970s.

The fact that the incidence of poverty is declining less rapidly among blacks than among whites does not mean that the average level of black income is rising less rapidly. The rate of escape from poverty for each group depends on how income gains are distributed within it, as well as on the average rate of increase of income. Consider the averages first. As Table 10.3 indicates, median black family income as a percentage of white has risen substantially since the 1950s. Income statistics for blacks as a separate category extend back only to 1959. For earlier years we must rely on figures for all nonwhites combined, a series that correlates closely with black income. Taken together, the first two columns of Table 10.3

4. Current Population Reports, series P-60, no. 125, table 20.

indicate that there was considerable fluctuation in the income ratio during the 1950s but no pronounced gain for blacks until the middle of the next decade. Then the black-white income ratio moved up from a range of .52 to .54 to a new plateau in the range of .57 to .62. (The year-to-year fluctuations around these levels are related to movements of the business cycle, a topic we return to in the next chapter.)

Although median black income rose substantially as a percentage of white income during the 1960s, there is evidence of increasing socio-economic divergence within the black population. Black husband-wife families as a group have made rapid strides toward equality with whites, while black families headed by a woman with no husband present have remained far behind. The growing size of this latter group accounts for the increased rate of poverty among urban blacks in the 1970s.

Income divergence within the black population is shown in Table 10.4. Between 1970 and 1979 the median income of black husband-wife families (in dollars of constant purchasing power) rose 16 percent, while

TABLE 10.4

Median Income by Type of Family and Race

TYPE OF FAMILY	1970	1979	PERCENTAGE CHANGE 1970–79
White			
Husband-wife families			
Number (thousands)	41,092	43,982	7.0%
Median income (1979 dollars)	$20,034	$21,841	9.0
Female householder, no husband present,			
Number (thousands)	4,386	5,952	35.7
Median income (1979 dollars)	$10,751	$11,464	6.6
Black			
Husband-wife families			
Number (thousands)	3,235	3,353	3.7
Median income (1979 dollars)	$14,603	$16,896	15.7
Female householder, no husband present			
Number (thousands)	1,506	2,430	61.4
Median income (1979 dollars)	$6,681	$6,907	3.4
Ratios: black to white median income			
Husband-wife families	.73	.77	—
Female householder, no husband present	.62	.60	—

Source: U.S. Bureau of the Census, *Current Population Reports*, series P-20, no. 350, May 1980, table 24, and series P-60, no. 125, October 1980, table 1.

the median for female-headed households, no husband present, rose only 3 percent. The same types of white families made income gains respectively of 9 percent and 7 percent. As a result the black-to-white income ratio for husband-wife families rose from .73 to .77 in the space of nine years, while the ratio for female-headed households fell from .62 to .60.

In recent years the number of families living in female-headed households has increased rapidly among all ethnic groups, but faster among blacks than whites (see Table 10.4). During the 1970s, the poverty rate of these black families changed little, hovering in the neighborhood of 50 percent. It is the increasing *size* of this poverty-ridden component rather than any change in its income level that pushed poverty rates upward for blacks as a whole in the 1970s. By 1978, 82 percent of all poor black families in central cities lived in female-headed households.[5] As we shall see in the next chapter, the increasing concentration of urban poverty in female-headed households has serious implications for anti-poverty policy.[6]

WHY POVERTY IS CONCENTRATING IN THE CITIES

The urbanization of poverty in the United States is not difficult to account for. It is the logical outcome of the changing pattern of settlement that has already been described in earlier chapters. The mechanization of agriculture in the twentieth century caused a massive migration of displaced labor from rural areas and small towns to metropolitan areas. Superimposed on this, so to speak, was a flow of migration from relatively poor regions, such as Appalachia, the South, and Puerto Rico, to relatively prosperous regions, such as the Middle Atlantic, Great Lakes, and Pacific states. Both the poor and the nonpoor migrated. The simple statistical consequence of this massive movement of population was, first, to shift the principal locus of poverty from the countryside to the cities and, second, to slow the reduction in the incidence of poverty in the cities below the rate that otherwise would have obtained.

A recent study of interregional migration, which includes information on the incomes of migrants, confirms the widely accepted view that the South was long a net source of low-income migrants to the rest of the nation. It also shows, however, that when U.S. patterns of migration shifted in the late 1960s and early 1970s (see discussion in Chapter 3)

5. *Current Population Reports*, series P-60, no. 124, table E.
6. For further discussion of the implications of socioeconomic divergence within the black population, see Thomas F. Pettigrew, "Racial Change and the Intrametropolitan Distribution of Black Americans," in Arthur P. Solomon, ed., *The Prospective City* (Cambridge, Mass.: MIT Press, 1980), pp. 54, 66–67, 73.

the direction of low-income migration also changed. After 1971 the South became a net recipient of low-income migrants, while the Northeast and North Central regions became net sources.[7] Whatever their direction, however, current migratory flows are unlikely to have much immediate effect on the average rate of urban poverty. In earlier decades, inter-regional migration contributed to the urbanization of poverty because it included a substantial flow of the poor from rural and nonmetropolitan areas to the urban North and West. Current interregional movements of the poor are more likely to be from city to city than from city to suburb or city to nonmetropolitan area, leaving the average rate of urban poverty more or less unchanged.

The Distribution of Poverty Within Metropolitan Areas

Within metropolitan areas the concentration of poverty in the central cities and its relative absence in the suburban rings can be explained largely as the result of three sets of forces: the process of metropolitan growth and development, the impact of public policy, and the pressure of race prejudice. The process of metropolitan development tends to hold the poor close to the center both because the center is the place with the largest concentration of old, and therefore cheap, housing and because it is the area that provides easiest access to a large number of jobs—especially to the types of casual employment that the unskilled are often forced to rely on. Easier job access at the center, in turn, has two aspects. First, the center contains more jobs than does any single place in the ring. Second, it is usually served by a public transportation network that efficiently connects close-in residential neighborhoods with central city places of employment.

We have described previously the process by which the development of highway transportation, the rise in family incomes, and the force of public policy in home finance and income taxation induced the middle and upper classes to move to the suburbs. These inducements scarcely affected low income families, who could not afford either new suburban housing or the relatively high cost of suburban self-transportation. However, the exodus of the middle class from the central city reinforced its attraction for the poor and the blacks by releasing large quantities of housing in the older neighborhoods that they could afford or that could readily be adapted to their low rent-paying capacity. Here was an example of the "filtering" process in the housing market operating on a huge scale. (Filtering will be examined in detail in Chapter 12.) The process of racial

---

7. See Larry H. Long, *Interregional Migration of the Poor: Some Recent Changes*, U.S. Bureau of the Census, *Current Population Reports*, series P-23, no. 73, November 1978, tables 1 and 2.

and income-class change became a circular, or self-reinforcing, one because racial tensions rose as the black population of central cities increased and provided the white middle and upper classes with an additional impetus to move to the largely white suburbs.

If the "natural" process of metropolitan spatial-economic development and the indirect effects of public policy were the only operative forces, we would expect to find poor whites almost as heavily concentrated in the central cities as poor blacks. Since we do not find an equal concentration of poor whites in the cities, it is difficult to avoid the conclusion that racial factors are also at work. Persuasive evidence on this point has been assembled by Kain and Persky, demonstrating that in large urban-metropolitan areas the residential location pattern of poor whites is strikingly different from that of poor blacks. For example, in the Detroit area in 1960, 45 percent of poor white families lived in the suburbs, compared with only 11 percent of poor black families. Differences of a similar order of magnitude were found in most of the nation's ten largest urban-metropolitan areas.[8] The point is reinforced by data covering U.S. metropolitan areas as a whole. In 1978, 51 percent of poor metropolitan white families lived in the suburban ring, while only 17 percent of poor metropolitan black families did so.[9] To a significant extent, then, the concentration of poverty in the central cities appears to be reinforced by the essentially noneconomic forces of prejudice that prevent the low income black population from dispersing into the suburbs. (We take up the question of race prejudice and housing segregation in Chapter 13.)

SHIFT IN RELATIVE INCOME LEVEL: CENTRAL CITIES VERSUS SUBURBS

As might be expected, the dispersion of the middle and upper classes to the suburbs and the influx of a substantial low income population to the central cities has brought about a historic shift in the relative income levels of the two areas. Scattered evidence from earlier periods indicates that prior to 1950 the level of per capita income was higher in central cities than in the surrounding ring areas. More recently the advantage has lain with the ring areas and has been steadily widening.

For example, in their study of the New York metropolitan region, Hoover and Vernon estimated that per capita personal income in the "core" counties fell from 108 percent of the regional average in 1939 to

8. John F. Kain and Joseph J. Persky, "Alternatives to the Gilded Ghetto," *The Public Interest*, Winter 1969, table 1, p. 76.

9. *Current Population Reports*, series P-60, no. 124, table E.

TABLE 10.5

Income Differentials Between Central Cities and Their Metropolitan Areas

	MEDIAN FAMILY INCOME Ratio of Central City Median to SMSA Median			
	1949	1959	1969	1978
SIX LARGEST SMSA'S IN NORTH AND EAST				
New York, N.Y.	.95	.93	.89	.83
Chicago, Ill.	.97	.92	.86	.72
Philadelphia, Pa.-N.J.	.96	.90	.85	.72
Detroit, Mich.	.99	.89	.83	.79
Washington, D.C.-Md.-Va.	.89	.79	.74	.55
Boston, Mass.	.92	.86	.80	.67
Average of six SMSA's in North and East	.95	.88	.83	.71
SIX LARGEST SMSA'S IN SOUTH AND WEST				
Los Angeles-Long Beach, Calif.[a]	.98	.98	.96	.91
San Francisco-Oakland, Calif.[a]	1.00	.95	.89	.81
Houston, Texas	1.02	.98	.97	.88
Dallas, Texas	1.03	1.01	.96	.95
Atlanta, Ga.	.91	.87	.79	.63[b]
Anaheim-Santa Ana-Garden Grove, Calif.[a]	—	—	.96	.94
Average of six SMSA's in South and West	.99	.96	.92	.85

[a] Except in 1978, ratio is for first-named central city only.
[b] Ratio is for 1977.
Sources: U.S. Bureau of the Census, *Current Population Reports*, series P-60, no. 123, June 1980, table 19; series P-60, no. 118, March 1979, table 19; and *Census of Population, 1950, 1960,* and *1970.*

105 percent in 1947 and 98 percent in 1956, while per capita income in the "inner ring" of suburban counties rose from 88 percent of the regional average in 1939 to 97 percent in 1947 and 111 percent in 1956.[10] Thus the mean income in the suburbs rose from 19 percent below the core county average in 1939 to 13 percent above it in 1956.

Table 10.5 shows a like pattern developing from 1949 through 1978 in the 12 large SMSA's that were examined in detail in Chapter 3. (The same pattern can, of course, be found in U.S. metropolitan areas as a

10. Edgar M. Hoover and Raymond Vernon, *Anatomy of a Metropolis* (Cambridge, Mass.: Harvard University Press, 1959), p. 226.

whole. See Table 11.7, below.) Since separate income data are not available for ring areas in all cases, Table 10.5 measures intrametropolitan disparities by taking the ratio of median family income in the central city to median family income in the SMSA as a whole. A ratio below 1.0 means that family income must be lower in the central city than in the rest of the metropolitan area.

City "Age" and Intrametropolitan Income Differentials

It is interesting to note that the income disadvantage of central cities is larger in the six metropolitan areas of the North and East than in the six of the South and West. This regional pattern is strongly associated with differences in the "age" of the central cities in the four regions.[11] As explained in Chapter 3, the older central cities of the Northeast and North Central regions enjoyed most of their population growth before the age of the automobile. They were built as "mass transit" cities and therefore developed high density levels. It was these older cities that suffered the earliest loss of jobs and of middle and upper income population to the suburbs when the truck and the automobile, coupled with rising living standards, made possible a more dispersed pattern of settlement. As middle class families, in search of low density neighborhoods, moved to new homes in the suburbs, old housing became available at low rents in the inner city to accommodate an influx of low income population. Thus the income and wealth status of the older central cities fell below that of their suburbs as early as the 1950s.

On the other hand, the newer cities of the South and West were built largely after the age of rubber-tired transport had begun. In order to accommodate the automobile, they were laid out at much lower levels of density than the older cities. They are therefore more nearly suburban in physical character. Thus they are less affected by decentralizing forces than are the older central cities. In addition, they often have the advantage of very extensive boundaries and easy annexation of suburban territory. When dispersion does occur, it is therefore more likely to remain within the city limits or be recaptured by annexation. Consequently, their income status relative to suburban areas, although declining, is still fairly high. Moreover, since the structural distinction between central city and suburbs is less marked in the newer metropolitan areas of the South and West, it cannot be assumed that they will ever display

---

11. In a careful statistical study, Leo F. Schnore has shown that age of an urbanized area is a significant predictor of city-suburban income differentials. See his *The Urban Scene* (New York: The Free Press, 1965), pp. 206–09. Schnore measured "age" by the census year in which a central city first reached a population of 50,000. In chapter 3 we applied a somewhat different age measure.

central city–suburban income and wealth disparities as great as those of the older Eastern and Midwestern SMSA's.

The sharp relative decline in income in the older cities of the North and East shown in Table 10.5 has implications for metropolitan public finance that will be examined in Chapter 15.

GROWTH OF THE URBAN BLACK POPULATION

The same internal migration pattern that brought about the urbanization of poverty has, of course, also produced the urbanization of American blacks. Philip Hauser points out that "in 1910, before large migratory streams of Negroes left the South, 73 per cent of the Negroes in the nation, as compared with 52 per cent of the Whites, lived in rural areas. . . . By 1960, the distribution of Negroes by urban-rural residence had become completely reversed, with 73 per cent of the Negro population residing in urban areas. . . . In fact, in 1960, Negroes were more highly urbanized than Whites. . . ."[12] By 1970, 81 percent of the black population was living in places classified by the Census Bureau as urban.

Blacks moving out of the South before 1970 tended to settle in large rather than medium-sized or small metropolitan areas in other parts of the country.[13] Consequently, the black proportion of central city population increases markedly with SMSA size. Given the link between race and poverty, the rapid growth and large size of the black population in central cities of large SMSA's helps to explain why the average poverty rate in those cities has not fallen since 1959. (See Table 10.2.)

Table 10.6 shows that within metropolitan areas the blacks, like the poor, are highly concentrated in the central cities. Racial segregation on a heroic scale is indicated by the fact that in 1979 blacks made up more than 23 percent of total central city population as compared with less than 6 percent of population in the suburban ring. From 1960 to 1970, inequality in the distribution of the black population between central cities and suburbs actually increased, since the black population proportion rose substantially in central cities while remaining virtually constant in the suburbs. However, data for the 1970s do indicate a small degree of recent progress toward desegregation: the black percentage of suburban population was slightly higher in 1979 than in 1970.

12. Philip M. Hauser, "Demographic Factors in the Integration of the Negro," in Talcott Parsons and Kenneth B. Clark, eds., *The Negro American* (Boston: Beacon Press, 1967), p. 75.

13. John F. Kain and Joseph J. Persky, "The North's Stake in Southern Rural Poverty," chapter 17 in *Rural Poverty in the United States: A Report by the President's National Advisory Commission on Rural Poverty*, 1968, pp. 291–92.

TABLE 10.6

Population Growth by Race in Central Cities and Suburbs

RACE AND RESIDENCE	PERCENTAGE CHANGE IN POPULATION		NET MIGRATION (*thousands*)[b]	BLACKS AS PERCENTAGE OF POPULATION		
	1960–70	1970–79	1970–77[b]	1960	1970	1979
Central cities of SMSA's						
All races[a]	6.5%	−3.7%	−10,451	16.4%	20.5%	23.4%
White	0.1	−8.4	−9,533			
Black	33.2	9.6	−653			
SMSA, outside central cities						
All races[a]	26.7	14.3	8,190	4.8	4.6	5.8
White	26.1	11.7	7,122			
Black	26.4	44.5	798			

[a] Includes other races not shown separately.
[b] Excludes net immigration from abroad.

Sources: U.S. Bureau of the Census, *Current Population Reports*, series P-20, no. 350, May 1980, table 15; and series P-23, no. 75, November 1978, table H.

The black proportion of central city population has increased in recent decades as a result of three factors: in-migration of blacks, out-migration of whites, and a higher rate of natural increase among blacks than whites.[14] As Table 10.6 indicates, black in-migration is no longer a factor. From 1970 through 1977, blacks moving out of central cities outnumbered those moving in by a substantial margin. The second and third factors, however, continue to operate. Although fertility rates have been falling for both races, the black rate of natural increase still exceeds the white, and, as Table 10.6 shows, net migration of whites out of central cities continues on a massive scale. Unless black out-migration from central cities to suburbs rises very substantially, we must therefore expect the black proportion of central city population to go on increasing for some time to come.

Many Americans are deeply disturbed by the prospect of a society made up of increasingly black central cities surrounded by rings of largely white suburbs. Consequently, a number of policies have been proposed, and some carried out, to encourage the suburbanization of blacks. These will be discussed in relation to antipoverty policy in Chapter 11 and housing policy in Chapter 13.

14. For a statistical study of the relative importance of each of these factors from 1950 to 1970, see Larry H. Long, "How the Racial Composition of Cities Changes," *Land Economics*, August 1975, pp. 258–67.

Antipoverty Policies

ELEVEN

Broadly speaking, there are three ways of relieving poverty. The first is to give money income to the poor; the second is to provide the poor with goods and services either free or below market price; the third is to help them acquire the skills and find the jobs with which they can earn adequate incomes by their own effort. The first method can be accurately described as "income-support policy." It includes both the existing forms of public aid (or "welfare"), which had their origin in the Social Security Act of 1935, and numerous recent proposals to supplement or replace those programs with a guaranteed minimum income or some other comprehensive system of direct income transfers. The second category, sometimes described as "benefits in kind," includes such programs as medical assistance (Medicaid), food stamps, and housing subsidies. The third category covers a variety of strategies that is difficult to describe with a single phrase; for want of a better term these are usually called "employment policies."

A fourth group, which does not fit easily into this system of classification, comprises policies directed toward specific, geographically identifiable areas. Because these policies (when applied in the urban context) are concerned explicitly with the question of where the poor live within metropolitan areas and what effect location has on their welfare, they are of particular interest to students of urban economics. Included in this category are programs to stimulate economic activity inside urban poverty areas, as well as policies to encourage the dispersion of the poor—out of their central city neighborhoods and into the suburbs.

We will look first at employment policies, then at income-

285

support and benefit-in-kind programs, and finally at policies that are area-oriented. Benefit-in-kind programs will be discussed simultaneously with income-support schemes, since eligibility for them is always linked to the income level of the claimant, and the two types of program are often jointly administered. Housing subsidies for the poor, however, will not be discussed here, since they are treated at length in Chapter 13.

It must be emphasized at this point that employment policies and income-support policies are complementary rather than alternative ways of dealing with the problem of poverty. Obviously, employment policies can help only the employable poor. Those who cannot work, including children, the disabled, and others who are for some reason unemployable; those whom society decides ought not to be forced to work, including the elderly and the single head of household with young children; and those whose earning capacity even after reasonable training leaves them still impoverished will always require some form of income support to raise them out of poverty. Nor can the time dimension be ignored: some, though not all, employment policies operate slowly, whereas income support, once established, can be effective immediately.

THREE TYPES OF EMPLOYMENT POLICY

Employment policies have been heavily emphasized in federal legislation since the early 1960s. The War on Poverty may be said to have begun with the passage of the Economic Opportunity Act in 1964. The very title of that act reveals its commitment to employment: the "opportunity" it sought to open up to the poor was the chance to rise out of poverty by improving their skills and finding decently paid jobs.

Employment policies can be divided into three types according to the point at which they have impact on the labor market. The three types are policies affecting the supply side, policies affecting the demand side, and policies intended to match supply and demand more effectively.[1] We will first describe these three types and then attempt to evaluate them.

Training, Education, and Human Capital

Policies "on the supply side" are those that try to improve the training and education of the poor. Their purpose is to raise individual productivity so that the poor become better qualified to fill existing

1. Sar A. Levitan, *Programs in Aid of the Poor for the 1970's*, Policy Studies in Employment and Welfare, 1 (Baltimore: The Johns Hopkins University Press, 1969), p. 49.

vacancies or to advance out of low-end jobs that leave them still impoverished. These policies operate on the supply side of the labor market because their effect is to increase the supply of productive skill. (Hence they are sometimes called "skill-creation" policies.) By themselves, however, they do not increase the demand for labor in the sense of shifting the employer's demand curve upward.

The provision of training and education can be regarded as a form of investment—investment in human resources, or, as it is now called, "human capital." Human capital is the store of productive knowledge and skill that the individual possesses. Lester Thurow explains the link between human capital and income as follows:

> Human capital . . . is one of the key determinants of the distribution of income. Individuals with little education, training, and skills have low marginal productivities and earn low incomes. With very little human capital they earn poverty incomes. . . . What might be called the productivity approach to the elimination of poverty and low Negro income is thus aimed at improving the quantity and distribution of human capital.[2]

The formal economic analysis of human capital and the quantitative measurement of its importance began only in the early 1960s. Interest in the subject grew rapidly when the battle against poverty became a national concern, and human capital analysis, as we will see, now has much to contribute to our understanding of poverty. At a less formal level, of course, the connection between education, training, and economic welfare has long been understood.

Job Creation

At the other end of the spectrum of employment policies are those that operate on the demand side of the market. These strategies attempt to help the poor by stimulating the demand for labor. In effect, they operate by shifting the demand curve for labor upward and to the right, so that the total number of jobs available at existing wage rates increases. (Hence they are often called "job creation" policies.) They include such programs as providing special jobs in the public sector for unemployed or disadvantaged workers or subsidizing private employment for the long-

2. Lester C. Thurow, *Poverty and Discrimination* (Washington, D.C.: The Brookings Institution, 1969), p. 66. See Thurow's appendix K for an extensive annotated bibliography on the economics of poverty, discrimination, and investment in education and training (i.e., human capital).

term unemployed. Demand-side and supply-side policies can be coordinated, as when workers who take subsidized jobs are simultaneously provided with on-the-job training and counseling or, in the opposite sequence, if workers are first trained and then offered subsidized employment.

Job creation also includes the macroeconomic policy of operating the economy at high pressure in order to hold overall unemployment to a bare minimum. According to the "queuing" theory of the labor market, employers rank the corps of job seekers available to them at any particular moment along a continuum from most to least desirable. This continuum is the "queue" from which employers always hire as near to the front end as possible. The low-skilled, the disadvantaged, the minorities are concentrated at the rear end of the queue. The theory consequently predicts that they will be "last hired, first fired." If nationwide unemployment rises, their rate of unemployment will rise faster than the average; if nationwide unemployment falls, their rate will fall faster than the average. If these propositions are true, then the relative economic position of poor minority groups and the disadvantaged can be improved substantially by macroeconomic policies that maintain tight labor markets.

Overcoming Discrimination

Between the policies that increase supply and those that stimulate demand lies a third group, which attempts to help the poor by overcoming "imperfections" in the labor market itself. Among those imperfections that have serious effects on the poor, the foremost is probably employment discrimination against blacks and other minorities. The problem of discrimination in employment has been attacked by all levels of government through various forms of fair employment practices legislation.

The effects of employment discrimination have been demonstrated repeatedly in studies comparing the returns to education earned by whites with those earned by blacks. Using the human capital approach and nationwide data for 1960, Thurow studied the returns to education and to work experience. He estimated that with 20 years of experience and 8 years of education, white males earned $1,367 more per year than blacks similarly situated. Holding experience constant but increasing education to 12 years raised the white advantage to $1,750. With 16 years of education completed (a college degree), the gap widened to $3,556.[3] As Thurow stresses, not all of this difference can be attributed to employment discrimination against blacks. Many other factors are at work, including

3. Ibid., table 5-2, p. 79.

differences among regions where blacks and whites live and differences among the industries in which they are typically employed. But a part of the difference is undoubtedly caused by discrimination in the sense of lower pay for equal work, restricted access to better-paying jobs, and less opportunity for promotion.

Bennett Harrison's study of residents of poverty areas in 12 large SMSA's in 1966 produced very similar results. He analyzed the effects of education on annual earnings of whites and blacks, while controlling for such factors as age, sex, and industry in which employed. He estimated that a white male resident of a poverty area with a high school diploma earned $394 more than a similarly situated black. A college degree increased the margin of white over black earnings to $1,714.[4] Bearing in mind that all the subjects of this study come from similar areas in large central cities, and that Harrison controlled statistically for the effects of most other factors that affect earnings, it is hard to escape the conclusion that much of the remaining earnings differential is the result of employment discrimination.

The existence of employment discrimination probably has serious effects on individual incentives to acquire education. The human capital approach suggests that individuals invest in their own education at least in part to obtain the higher future incomes that education makes possible. If blacks can look forward to lower levels of earnings than whites with similar educational attainment, then they have less incentive to invest in their own education and might, quite rationally, provide themselves with less of it than do similarly qualified whites. (This effect is not eliminated by the existence of "free" public education, since one of the principal elements of cost in obtaining education for a person old enough to join the labor force is the earnings he or she must forego during the years in school.) Thus, eliminating employment discrimination should have a double impact on the incomes of the disadvantaged. First, it will raise earnings at given levels of training and education. Second, by doing so, it will increase the rate of return to investment in education, and therefore it will encourage people to obtain more education and training, leading to an additional round of improvement in their earnings.

Lack of job and career information is another form of market imperfection that is thought seriously to restrict the earnings of the poor and especially of those living in poverty areas where they are out of the economic mainstream. Counseling and information services have therefore been made an important component of many antipoverty programs.

4. Bennett Harrison, "Education and Underemployment in the Urban Ghetto," *American Economic Review*, December 1972, table 4, p. 805.

THE GROWTH OF EMPLOYMENT
AND TRAINING PROGRAMS

Federally assisted employment and training programs have expanded rapidly since the mid-1960s.[5] In 1964, when the War on Poverty began, federal outlays on employment services, training programs, and miscellaneous manpower aids came to $389 million. By 1970, the total had increased to $1.6 billion and by 1980 to an estimated $10.4 billion. During that interval a diverse array of employment programs was put into operation, tested, or seriously proposed. No attempt will be made here to list them all. Instead, we will try to convey a sense of the whole by outlining the development of antipoverty policy and analyzing some representative programs.[6]

In the 1960s, supply-side policies predominated. The strategy of the War on Poverty was based on a belief that, as Robert Haveman put it, "the poor . . . . could earn their way out of poverty if given additional education and skills."[7] Most antipoverty programs therefore contained a large training component, together with emphasis on counseling, job information, and placement. An example was the Manpower Development and Training Act of 1962. MDTA was the first major employment and training legislation of the 1960s. It was originally conceived as a program to retrain the technologically unemployed. After 1964, however, MDTA programs were redesigned to give greater emphasis to helping the poor. Institutional courses and supporting services were offered to a clientele the majority of whom reported their pre-enrollment earnings to be below the poverty level. As its name indicates, the program aimed primarily at skill creation.

Few of the programs of the 1960s operated on the demand side in the sense of subsidizing specific new positions for the poor or the unemployed. It was widely recognized that training and counseling would be fruitless unless jobs were available at the end of the road. However, the government relied on general macroeconomic stimulation rather than direct job creation through antipoverty initiatives to ensure the necessary demand for labor and keep the job market "tight."

The early 1970s brought a change in emphasis. The policy of maintaining tight labor markets in order to fight poverty ran into trouble. Advocates of that policy always recognized that it would cause some

5. It should be understood that federal aid to elementary, secondary, and higher education is not included under the functional heading of employment and training.

6. For further detail see the annual *Employment and Training Report of the President*, transmitted to the Congress each spring.

7. Robert H. Haveman, "Direct Job Creation," in Eli Ginzberg, ed., *Employing the Unemployed* (New York: Basic Books, 1980), p. 146.

price inflation, perhaps even a higher rate of inflation than most people had previously thought tolerable, but they believed that given the unavoidable trade-off between price stability and full employment, it was desirable to accept some price inflation for the sake of greater success in fighting poverty. After 1970, however, the rate of inflation seemed to be getting out of hand. The federal government shifted toward increasingly restrictive monetary policies in the hope of restraining inflation, even at the price of higher rates of unemployment. Inevitably, the price was paid. The average rate of unemployment for all workers rose from 4.8 percent in the 1960s to 6.2 percent in the 1970s. For whites, it rose from 4.3 percent to 5.6 percent, for blacks and other races from 9.0 percent to 11.0 percent. (It is a standard observation that black unemployment rates are twice those of whites.)

In this context, with the economy suffering simultaneously from inflation and unemployment, antipoverty policy moved increasingly to the demand side, and it did so by putting much greater emphasis on direct job creation. Subsidized jobs, made available directly to the poor and the long-term unemployed could, so it was argued, reduce unemployment and meet the objectives of antipoverty policy without generating much inflationary pressure. Moreover, if the jobs could be created in the local public sector, they would have the additional attraction of allowing communities to expand the output of public services at little local cost.

In 1971 Congress adopted the Public Employment Program (PEP), the first large-scale job creation initiative since those of the Great Depression. PEP provided a federal subsidy of up to 90 percent of the cost of approved new public employment programs in state and local governments. The authorizing legislation required that funds be allotted only for jobs that would not otherwise exist, that 85 percent of all funds go toward employee compensation (thus limiting the amount available for training and supportive services), and that all jobs created be transitional to permanent employment (thus ruling out "leaf-raking" enterprises). The program continued for several years, employing 340,000 workers in transitional jobs and some 300,000 more in summer positions.[8] There were to be more, and even larger, programs of subsidized public employment later in the 1970s.

The Comprehensive Employment and Training Act

In 1973 Congress passed the Comprehensive Employment and Training Act (CETA), establishing the legal framework under which most

8. Ibid., p. 144. For a discussion of the political and economic factors leading to the adoption of PEP, see John L. Palmer, "Employment and Training Assistance," in J. A. Pechman, ed., *Setting National Priorities, The 1978 Budget* (Washington, D.C.: The Brookings Institution, 1977), p. 152.

TABLE 11.1

Programs Under the Comprehensive Employment and Training Act

CETA TITLE[a]	DESCRIPTION OF PROGRAM	COST PER PERSON YEAR OF SERVICE 1976	COST PER PARTICIPANT 1976	FIRST-TIME ENROLLMENTS (THOUSANDS) 1978	FEDERAL OUTLAYS (MILLIONS OF $) 1978
	Total			2,874	$9,533[b]
Title I	Comprehensive employment, training, and counseling programs, administered locally	$3,786	$1,256	965	1,992
Title II	Public service employment	7,226	2,175	101	995
Title III	Nationally administered programs, for categorically defined groups				
	Youth programs, incl. summer	2,380	595	994	1,056
	Migrant worker, native American, and other	n.a.	n.a.	210	301
Title IV	Job Corps (institutional training)	9,321	4,156	49	280
Title VI	Countercyclical public service employment	8,262	3,906	556	4,769

[a] Title numbers and descriptions are prior to 1978 amendments.
[b] Includes other categories not shown.

Sources: Enrollments and outlays, 1978: *Employment and Training Report of the President,* 1979, table 1, p. 32, and table F-1. Costs, 1976: Congressional Budget Office, *Public Employment and Training Assistance,* February 1977, appendix table 1.

employment and training programs now operate.[9] The objective was to simplify and decentralize administration of a vast array of programs by giving state and local governments control over many of the federally funded plans operating within their boundaries. Table 11.1 outlines the major provisions of CETA and provides statistics on the size and cost of its current programs.

CETA Title I authorizes a nationwide program of comprehensive labor services—including training, employment, counseling, and placement—to be coordinated and administered by states and by local governments of 100,000 or more. This program is the successor to diverse training and labor service schemes such as those that had previously been carried on under MDTA.

CETA Title II authorizes a permanent program of public service employment, a descendant of the earlier PEP, while *CETA Title III* covers programs for disadvantaged groups in which the federal government takes a specific interest, including youth, migrant workers, native Americans, and others.

CETA Title IV continues the federal commitment to the Job Corps, a program initiated by the OEO in 1964. The Job Corps, which serves disadvantaged youth, is the only federal undertaking that provides training and counseling in a residential-institutional setting. Despite its name, it aims at skill rather than job creation.

CETA Title VI authorizes a temporary, emergency program of public service employment. Under this title, areas having particularly high rates of unemployment receive larger fund allotments. Special appropriations for emergency public service jobs during recession years made Title VI by far the largest segment of CETA in the late 1970s (see Table 11.1).

Several employment and training programs outside the CETA umbrella deserve mention:

The *Work Incentive Program* (WIN) was first authorized in 1967. WIN focuses exclusively on the welfare population, specifically on persons receiving or applying for Aid to Families with Dependent Children (AFDC). The program is of particular interest because its purpose is to help welfare recipients become self-supporting. All AFDC applicants and recipients who are 16 or older *must* register with WIN unless they are exempt by reason of health, age, incapacity, child-care responsibilities, and the like. The program combines training, counseling, and placement services with access to subsidized employment.

9. See Palmer, pp. 150–51.

Targeted Jobs Tax Credit (TJTC), which took effect in 1979, is a program to subsidize jobs in the private sector for special categories of workers, including disadvantaged youth, the disabled, and welfare recipients. Employers receive a tax credit equal to 50 percent of the first $6,000 of wages paid to qualifying workers during the first year of their employment and 25 percent during the second year. TJTC is an example of what is now called a "tax expenditure." Instead of appropriating funds to pay a subsidy, Congress allows beneficiaries to obtain a subsidy by reducing their tax liability. The "tax cost" of such provisions is estimated each year in the Federal Budget. TJTC was expected to cost $315 million in 1981.[10]

What can we say about the success of employment policies in reducing poverty? Which kinds have worked? How much improvement have they produced? These quite obvious questions can be answered, if at all, only by means of rather complex economic analysis. The effort is justified, however, since careful evaluation of the results of employment policies is important, not only in deciding which should be continued and which should be dropped, but also in developing desirable modifications to ongoing programs.

Evaluation of Training Programs

Training programs are relatively amenable to benefit-cost analysis. Consequently, policies aimed at skill creation have been subject to systematic evaluation far more frequently than other antipoverty efforts. Understanding the logical structure of these evaluations will help to clarify just what the benefits and costs of training policies are thought to be. As we shall see, however, there remains considerable disagreement about the validity of particular results.

In a benefit-cost analysis of a training scheme, benefits are usually defined as the gain in earnings when the earnings of trainees after they have completed the course are compared either with their pre-enrollment level or with the earnings of a control group of nontrainees. Since the studies are generally conducted within a year or two after the program ends, the analyst must supply an estimate of how far into the future the gain in earnings is expected to persist. Usually counted as costs are the costs of instruction and administration and the foregone earnings of trainees while enrolled in the program. The expected benefit stream and

10. See The Budget of the United States Government, Fiscal Year 1981, Special Analyses, table G-1.

the computed costs are then both discounted to obtain present values, and the end result is a comparison between the present value of benefits and that of costs. As long as the former exceeds the latter, undertaking the program will produce a net gain for society. In principle, if budget funds are limited, public authorities should choose the combination of programs that will produce the largest total net gain within the budget constraint.[11]

The first benefit-cost studies of manpower training dealt with programs that were carried out in the early 1960s. For the most part these analyses found that from the point of view of society as a whole the economic benefits of training programs outweighed their economic costs, sometimes by a very wide margin. For example, Einar Hardin reviewed five early benefit-cost studies and recomputed the findings to put them as nearly as possible on a comparable basis. Using rather conservative assumptions, he found that the ratio of benefits to costs for programs as a whole varied from 1.5 upward to 5.9. Benefits were found to be less than costs only for one subgroup of trainees who received an unusually long, and therefore expensive, training course.[12]

It was objected that the studies reviewed by Hardin threw little light on antipoverty programs because they were based on experience in the early 1960s, when federal manpower operations were directed toward the technologically unemployed rather than toward the poor. and the disadvantaged. The implication was that the impoverished, the disadvantaged, and the hard-core unemployed would be less easily retrained, leading to less favorable benefit-cost ratios. Subsequently, however, there have been benefit-cost studies of numerous poverty-oriented manpower programs. For example, David O. Sewell in 1971 published a study of a training effort in North Carolina that was designed to serve severely disadvantaged rural workers. He calculated that the average benefit-cost ratio for all clients was an impressive 3.1.[13]

There are, in fact, a good many unresolved questions about the manner in which benefit-cost analysis should be applied to training

11. A. R. Prest and R. Turvey, "Cost-Benefit Analysis: A Survey," in International Economic Association, *Surveys of Economic Theory*, vol. III (New York: St. Martin's Press, 1966), pp. 105–207, provides an excellent introduction to the theory and practice of cost-benefit analysis. It discusses applications to general education but refers only briefly to manpower training.

12. Einar Hardin, "Benefit-Cost Analyses of Occupational Training Programs: A Comparison of Recent Studies," in G. G. Somers and W. D. Wood, eds., *Cost-Benefit Analyses of Manpower Policies*, Proceedings of a North American Conference (Kingston, Ontario: Industrial Relations Centre, Queen's University, 1969), table 1, p. 113.

13. D. O. Sewell, *Training the Poor* (Kingston, Ontario: Industrial Relations Centre, Queen's University, 1971), table 13, p. 98.

programs.[14] Analysts continue to disagree, therefore, about the validity of many of the existing studies. We will mention only a few of the critical questions here, but they are questions that do illuminate the central issue: what is the economic impact of training programs on society as a whole? First, there is the problem of separating out training effects from job-placement effects. How can we be sure that the higher earnings recorded by trainees are not attributable to the organized job-placement effort that accompanies each training program rather than to the value of the training itself? To take up an allied point, does the training program increase a worker's real productivity or does it just fill a "credentialing function," opening up a better job to a trainee than to a nonparticipant solely because employers use training credentials as a screening device in filling jobs? If training does increase worker productivity and we observe this in the first year after training, how far into the future can we expect the gain to persist, given the rapid obsolescence of specific skills? Until recently, follow-up studies rarely extended beyond the first year, so the probable duration of benefits remained an unresolved question. The analyst had to settle it by assumption, and the assumption was likely to be crucial to the outcome: an assumed ten-year benefit stream almost always produced a favorable benefit-cost verdict; an assumed five-year stream sometimes did not.[15]

It may be possible to resolve this last issue by studying "longitudinal" data—that is to say, data that follow the wage history of particular workers through time. Making use of such information, which is now available from Social Security records, Orley Ashenfelter analyzed the incomes earned through a five-year post-training period by workers who completed an MDTA training course in 1964.[16] Trainee earnings were compared over time with those of a randomly selected control group that had not received training. Ashenfelter estimated that the MDTA courses produced an increase in the earnings of all trainee groups in the period immediately following course completion. The increase for both white and black women was on the order of $300 to $600 per year and did not decline over time. The increase for men was smaller and declined by

14. See Congressional Joint Economic Committee, *The Effectiveness of Manpower Training Programs: A Review of Research on the Impact on the Poor*, Studies in Public Welfare, paper no. 3, November 20, 1972; the papers in Somers and Wood; Thomas I. Ribich, *Education and Poverty* (Washington, D.C.: The Brookings Institution, 1968), ch. 3; and Anthony H. Pascal, "Manpower Training and Jobs," in A. H. Pascal, ed., *Cities in Trouble: An Agenda for Urban Research*, memorandum RM-5603-RC (Santa Monica, Calif.: The Rand Corporation, August 1968), pp. 47–79.
15. *The Effectiveness of Manpower Training Programs*, p. 30.
16. Orley Ashenfelter, "Estimating the Effect of Training Programs on Earnings," *The Review of Economics and Statistics*, February 1978, pp. 47–57. Needless to say, the Social Security data used in studies of this type are made available in a way that does not reveal worker identity.

about half over the five-year period. Ashenfelter did not carry out a benefit-cost analysis, but his rough estimate was that the programs in question probably yielded a very high rate of return over cost for women and an acceptable rate of return over cost for men.[17]

A final source of uncertainty in the evaluation of training programs is the possible existence of indirect benefits. Economists generally recognize that training programs may have socially beneficial indirect effects associated with the increased incomes they produce, such as a reduction in crime and civil disorder or an improvement in family stability or health. These indirect benefits are usually omitted from benefit-cost calculations because it is so difficult to estimate their monetary value. Leaving them out, however, may impart a significant downward bias to measured benefit-cost ratios.

Michael Borus recently surveyed the results of more than two dozen evaluative studies of antipoverty training programs. He limited the survey to studies that had made use of a scientifically selected control group with which to compare trainees' earnings. In each case he examined the estimated first-year increase in trainee earnings measured against those of the control group. As often occurs in social-scientific research, the wide variation in outcomes made it difficult to generalize about the results. Nevertheless, Borus cautiously summarized as follows:

> Classroom, on-the-job, and work experience training programs appear to justify their costs.
>
> Training is not superior for either sex or racial group. Nor does the evidence indicate that the impact of training is higher for any educational, age, or other grouping.
>
> Short classroom training courses and training courses with high completion rates appear to yield significant gains in earnings.[18]

Borus found the Job Corps to yield very low economic returns. The reason is that earnings increases are small, while the cost per trainee, because of the residential-institutional setting, is very high. Short classroom-training courses, on the other hand, generally show up as economically productive, because they yield moderate income gains at relatively low cost per participant. (Compare costs of Title I and Title IV programs in Table 11.1.)

What general conclusions about antipoverty strategy can we reach on the basis of these very numerous evaluations? On the one hand, many of the studies show benefits from training programs that more than

17. Ibid., p. 56.
18. Michael E. Borus, "Assessing the Impact of Training Programs," in Ginzberg, p. 39.

justify their costs. On the other hand, the absolute size of the income gain, as Borus points out, is typically small—usually well under $1,000 a year—and therefore "will not substantially reduce the number of persons in poverty."[19] In short, the programs we have undertaken are worthwhile but have not made much difference. Whether more intensive and costly programs would produce commensurately larger gains is uncertain. On the basis of the evidence currently available, not many poverty analysts are ready to testify that they would.

Evaluation of Demand-Side Policies: Tight Labor Markets

We turn next to the evaluation of demand-side antipoverty policies. One of these is the policy of maintaining tight labor markets by using the tools of monetary and fiscal policy to keep aggregate demand in the economy at an appropriately high level.

We already have pointed out that job creation programs and skill creation programs are complementary. If the demand for labor is weak, graduates of training programs will have difficulty in obtaining jobs. Their training may go to waste. Furthermore, the power of training programs to attract and hold trainees depends on their record of success in leading to employment.

On the other hand, if trainees *do* find jobs while unemployment is widespread, it may be reasonable to assume that they have taken positions that otherwise would have been filled by qualified nontrainees. If one-for-one job displacement occurs, there is no gain to society in the form of increased total output; there is only a transfer of employment achieved at considerable public cost. From such a transfer the disadvantaged may gain, but it will be at the expense of other members of the working class, a doubtful benefit from the point of view of society as a whole and one likely to strengthen political opposition to poverty programs. Thus tight labor markets probably promote the efficient operation of training programs.

Causality runs the other way as well. If labor markets are tight, an opportunity exists for employing the hard-core unemployed or for upgrading some of those presently in low-skill jobs. Without adequate training programs, some of these opportunities may be wasted. The real output of society will remain below its attainable level even though labor markets are tight.

In addition to the fact that it complements training programs, a policy of maintaining tight labor markets also has a direct, positive effect on the relative income status of the disadvantaged. Let us see why. We

19. Ibid., p. 38.

have already pointed out that the unemployment rate of blacks is generally twice the rate for whites. To simplify the argument, suppose that this ratio is constant over the course of the business cycle. In that case, as the economy moves toward full employment, for every decline of 1.0 in the white unemployment rate, the black unemployment rate will fall by 2.0. Relative to the size of their respective labor forces, twice as many blacks as whites will be moving from unemployment into jobs. We would therefore expect black income to rise much faster than white. In a recession, the situation would be reversed. Black unemployment would increase twice as fast as white, and black income would therefore fall much faster.

Thurow verified the existence of such a pattern in a study of fluctuations in the U.S. economy from 1954 through 1966. He found that a 1 percent decline in the aggregate level of employment produced, on the average, a 1.2 percent drop in white income but a 2.4 percent decline in the income of nonwhites.[20] From these relationships it follows that the ratio of nonwhite to white median family income would rise during good times and fall during recessions. In fact, that is just what has occurred. For example, the nonwhite-to-white income ratio fell from .57 during the period of high employment generated by the Korean War in 1952 to .51 in 1958, during a sharp recession. After a brief recovery, it fell again during the economic downswing from 1960 to 1961. It then rose from .53 in 1961, a year of high unemployment, to .60 in 1966, a year of low unemployment. A study by James P. Smith and Finis Welch indicates that the business cycle continued to influence black-white income ratios through 1974. However, they also found that black earnings were less sensitive to the business cycle in the early 1970s than they had been previously.[21]

Evaluating Direct Job Creation

Despite its capacity to raise the relative income status of disadvantaged workers, the policy of maintaining tight labor markets was abandoned in the 1970s because it was contributing to the acceleration of inflation. In place of macroeconomic measures, the federal government turned increasingly to direct job creation as the preferred policy to boost the demand for labor.

Direct job creation operates by subsidizing new positions specifically

20. Thurow, pp. 58–61. The simplification in the text, of course, does not do justice to the complexity of Thurow's argument.
21. James P. Smith and Finis Welch, *Race Differences in Earnings: A Survey and New Evidence,* doc. no. R-2295-NSF (Santa Monica, Cal.: The Rand Corporation, March 1978), pp. 25–26.

for the poor and the unemployed. Proponents of this approach argue that it can produce additional employment with much less inflation than would occur under a policy of general economic stimulation. As Robert Solow explains it, one version of this argument is based on "the premise that the general wage level is really determined in an industrial and occupational core of the economy. This core comprises large firms in major industries . . . employing many highly skilled workers in regular jobs, paying high wages, which have often been determined by collective bargaining." An expansionary policy of tax cuts or increases in government expenditure would immediately stimulate activity in this "core," thereby driving wages up in all sectors and accelerating inflation. In contrast to this, direct job creation can take place in peripheral areas of the economy, "exercising little influence on the general wage level."[22] In addition, job creation can be focused on areas or population groups that have a particularly high rate of unemployment. For these reasons it would be expected to generate more jobs and less inflationary pressure per dollar of expenditure than would general macroeconomic stimulation.

On the other hand, direct job creation brings a good many difficulties of its own. In this discussion we focus on programs in the public sector, since there is relatively little experience as yet with those in the private sector. The following problems are particularly important because they often involve painful conflicts among individually laudable objectives.

Displacement effects. Job creation policies fulfill their purpose only if they cause a net expansion of employment. If the subsidized job simply takes the place of a previously existing *un*subsidized one, then there is displacement rather than expansion—no job creation has taken place.

When CETA funds became available to subsidize local government jobs in the mid-1970s, a great deal of displacement occurred.[23] Local governments shifted many regular employees to the CETA payroll. CETA regulations intended to prevent such transfers were subsequently tightened. However, some degree of displacement may persist to the extent that local governments can use subsidized workers to carry out tasks for which they would otherwise have hired additional employees.

Value of the job and of its output. Unless a subsidized job produces useful output, it is a delusion to weigh it in the same scales as ordinary employment. As Baily and Tobin put it, "Shifting a person from recorded unemployment to employment in a job empty of product and training

22. Robert M. Solow, "Employment Policy in Inflationary Times," in Ginzberg, pp. 136–37.

23. See Haveman, pp. 150–51 and sources cited there.

is useless or worse."[24] Nor do workers themselves wish to be given jobs that are meaningless and unproductive. Yet the desire that subsidized jobs produce useful output clearly conflicts with the need to avoid displacement. The most useful or at least the most "do-able" things are presumably already being done, even by local governments not noted for their efficiency. The jobs that can be done without displacement are therefore unlikely to have highly valued outputs.

Incentives for public sector managers. If the local managers of subsidized workers are expected to produce useful output, they will try to hire the most skilled and experienced workers among those who are eligible for subsidy, rather than the most disadvantaged. In that case there is a fair probability that the workers they hire would otherwise have found an *un*subsidized job. A form of displacement will have occurred. On the other hand, if the managers are told that the objective is just to provide "jobs" for some low-skill workers, they are not likely to make the effort needed to organize useful work.

Without belaboring the point, it should be obvious that organizing useful, subsidized employment in the public sector is a very difficult task. Even its proponents agree that public sector job creation programs large enough to have a major effect on the national rate of unemployment would probably risk being discredited by their own failure to meet minimum standards. On the other hand, programs that are carefully organized on a modest scale can probably make a useful contribution in combating poverty.

Accounting for the Relative Increase in Black Incomes

We pointed out in Chapter 10 that after allowing for the effect of business cycles there does appear to have been a long-run rise in the ratio of black-to-white income. In the early 1960s, the ratio fluctuated between .52 and .54. Since 1969 it has varied in the substantially higher range of .57 to .62. Economists would like to explain precisely what factors caused this increase, since the answer would be helpful in designing an optimum set of antipoverty policies. Sorting out the causes, however, is a complex and difficult task. There remains much disagreement about results.

Migration has certainly been one cause. As we explained in Chapter 10, the movement of blacks from low-income rural areas into cities where

24. Martin Neil Baily and James Tobin, "Inflation-Unemployment Consequences of Job Creation Policies," in John L. Palmer, ed., *Creating Jobs: Public Employment Programs and Wage Subsidies* (Washington, D.C.: The Brookings Institution, 1978), p. 73.

the average income level was usually much higher accounts for part of the relative rise in black income. Smith and Welch agree that migration was a cause, especially in the 1950s and 1960s. But between 1967 and 1974—the most recent period they examined—they assign the greatest weight to increases in the quantity and quality of black education.[25]

What about the effect of antidiscrimination legislation? Black-white income ratios rose most sharply in the years just following passage of the Civil Rights Act of 1964. Title VII of the Act prohibits employment or wage discrimination based on race. The Act also created the Equal Employment Opportunity Commission to oversee compliance with its provisions. It is tempting to attribute the substantial improvement in black status in the late 1960s to these important civil rights initiatives and to the change in public attitudes that accompanied them. That would be incorrect, however, since other factors such as education and migration operated so powerfully at the same time. Although antidiscrimination laws, affirmative action programs, and increased public awareness may well have improved the economic status of the poor, it has thus far proven very difficult to measure their effect convincingly.[26]

In the end we are left with a good deal of uncertainty about the impact on poverty of the training, employment, and antidiscrimination policies of the last two decades. At least for blacks, a major part of the gain in that period apparently must be attributed to migration and education. That does not mean, of course, that training, employment, and antidiscrimination programs were without value.

In the next section we analyze income-support programs as anti-poverty policy. In recent years income transfers have substantially reduced poverty in the United States. No one questions that, but, as we shall see, there is a good deal of debate about the form that income support should take and how far it should be carried.

THE ROLE OF INCOME SUPPORT

No matter how successful employment policies may prove to be, income support in the form of transfer payments from the government is undoubtedly necessary to combat poverty. In any society there is a large number of families whose adult members are outside the labor force either because they have retired or are disabled or because society believes they should not work. If these families have inadequate pensions or other sources of income, they can be raised out of poverty only by some form of

25. Smith and Welch, p. vii.
26. See discussion in ibid., pp. 20–25, 47–50, and works cited therein.

TABLE 11.2
Characteristics of Families Below Poverty Line

FAMILIES BELOW THE POVERTY LINE	1959		1979	
	Number (thousands)	*Percentage of Poverty Families*	*Number (thousands)*	*Percentage of Poverty Families*
Total	8,320	100.0%	5,292	100.0%
With no workers	1,981	23.8	2,189	41.4
With head who worked year round at full-time job	2,617	31.5	864	16.3

Sources: U.S. Bureau of the Census, *Current Population Reports,* series P-60, no. 125, October 1980, table 21.

transfer payment. Another large group consists of families with heads whose earning power is so low that even when they are employed full time, their families remain below the poverty line. Although some of these "working poor" may raise themselves out of poverty by acquiring higher skills or better-paying jobs, others will remain impoverished unless they are relieved by direct cash payments.

Table 11.2 indicates the importance of these two groups. In 1979, 41 percent of all families living in poverty contained no wage earner. In the same year 16 percent of all families living in poverty were headed by a person who worked at a full-time job for the whole year. It is highly significant that the proportion of poor families with no wage earner has increased steadily over time, rising from 24 percent in 1959 to 41 percent twenty years later, while over the same period, the proportion with a family head who worked year round at a full-time job fell from 32 percent to 16 percent. Both of these trends result from the same cause: the general, year-after-year rise in labor productivity. As Thurow points out, "Those who are able to take advantage of better job opportunities or of government programs to increase individual productivity are gradually drawn out of the poverty pool. Those who cannot benefit are left at the bottom of the income distribution and consequently represent an increasing fraction of the poor. . . . The bottom of the income distribution will be increasingly made up of those not in the labor force."[27] Thus, as time passes and the number of families living in poverty declines, we must expect the proportion (though not necessarily the number) who need income support to increase markedly.

27. Thurow, pp. 140–41.

TABLE 11.3

Welfare and Social Insurance Programs[a]

	EXPENDITURE BY ALL LEVELS OF GOVERNMENT		
	1960	1970	1978
	(fiscal years, millions of $)		
Total	$23,408	$71,179	$234,721
Public Aid, total	4,101	16,488	59,620
Aid to families with dependent children (AFDC)	1,001	4,853	10,730
Medicaid and other medical vendor payments	493	5,213	20,095
Supplemental security income (SSI)[b]	—	—	7,194
Food stamps	—	577	5,590
General assistance	322	618	1,205
Other[c]	2,286	5,227	14,806
Social Insurance, total	19,307	54,691	175,101
Old-age, survivors, disability, and health insurance (OASDHI)	11,032	36,835	117,433
Other social insurance	8,274	17,856	57,668

[a] Veterans' programs and housing subsidies are omitted.
[b] Program began in 1974 as successor to Old Age Assistance, Aid to the Blind, and Aid to the Permanently and Totally Disabled, payments under which are included in "Other" prior to 1974.
[c] Includes miscellaneous relief categories plus temporary employment assistance and work experience training programs under the Economic Opportunity Act and the Comprehensive Employment and Training Act.
Sources: Alma W. McMillan and Ann Kallman Bixby, "Social Welfare Expenditures in Fiscal Year 1978," in *Social Security Bulletin*, May 1980, table 1; *Social Security Bulletin*, May 1980, "Current Operating Statistics," table M-33.

Scope of Present Programs

The dimensions of existing income support and benefit-in-kind programs are indicated in Table 11.3.[28] Since 1960 these programs have increased very rapidly. In the aggregate they make up the largest and fastest-growing category in the combined budgets of federal, state, and local governments. In 1960 they amounted to only 4.7 percent of Gross National Product. By 1970 the proportion had risen to 7.4 percent and by 1976, to 11.9 percent. In the late 1970s their growth slowed somewhat, so that by 1978, they equaled 11.5 percent of GNP.

28. Omitted are veterans' programs and housing subsidies. The latter will be discussed in Chapter 13.

Among the programs shown in the table, only those under the heading of "public aid" are really aimed at the relief of poverty. These programs can all be described as means-tested: eligibility depends on income. In a broad sense, they make up the nation's "welfare system." Some of the programs provide cash benefits (AFDC and SSI) and some benefits-in-kind (food stamps, Medicaid).

The social insurance category, which is far larger than public aid, includes old age, survivors, disability, and health insurance (usually referred to as "Social Security"), as well as unemployment insurance, public employee retirement plans, worker's compensation, and so on. While these arrangements provide retirement or other income to a large number of people who would otherwise be poor, they are not properly regarded as antipoverty programs. First of all, benefits are paid for largely (though not entirely) out of funds to which the beneficiaries themselves have contributed. Second, benefit levels are not dependent on the beneficiary's current income. Finally, the fact that many of the beneficiaries of a program such as Social Security would be poor in its absence is not persuasive. If Social Security did not exist many of them would have made other arrangements for retirement.

Public aid programs are supported under a bewildering variety of financial arrangements. Several of the largest federally authorized programs are financed jointly with the states under arrangements that had their origins as far back as the Social Security Act of 1935. Matching formulas vary from program to program. Since the states are given considerable freedom of action within limits set by federal law, benefit levels and the details of eligibility rules vary widely among the states. So, too, does the financial contribution required by the states of their local governments.

In 1978 the federal government paid 69 percent of the total cost of the public aid programs shown in Table 11.3. However, the proportions differ widely by program. Food stamps are paid for entirely by the federal government, general assistance entirely by states and localities. Aid to families with dependent children, Medicaid, and Supplemental Security Income are paid for jointly. In 1978, state and local governments paid 47 percent of Medicaid costs and almost as high a proportion of AFDC. These two categories account for most of their "welfare burden." In a majority of cases this burden is borne entirely by the state, but some states do require substantial local contributions. One estimate placed the local share of all welfare costs in 1975 at about 18 percent of the combined state-local amount.[29]

The individual public aid programs can be very briefly described as

29. George E. Peterson, "Finance," in W. Gorham and N. Glazer, eds., *The Urban Predicament* (Washington, D.C.: The Urban Institute, 1976), table 17.

follows.[30] Supplemental Security Income (SSI) was established in 1974 to provide cash assistance, depending on need, to the aged, the blind, and the disabled. It consolidated three programs that had been established for the same purposes under the Social Security Act in 1935. The federal government pays for benefits at a basic level; but states may voluntarily supplement that, so benefit levels vary geographically.

The largest and one of the fastest growing categories of public assistance is Medicaid. This program was written into the Social Security law in 1965. It pays medical expenses for persons who are on the rolls of AFDC and, in most states, SSI. A majority of states make other categories of the poor eligible, as well, but some restrict Medicaid to those two groups. In that case a considerable part of the poor population—for example, poor, childless couples or single persons under 65, will not be eligible for medical assistance.

Aid to families with dependent children, authorized by the Social Security Act in 1935, is the program commonly referred to as "welfare." Until 1961, families were eligible for AFDC only if one parent was absent or had died. This provision is widely believed to encourage desertion (either real or pretended), a remarkable instance of a social policy rule having perverse, antisocial consequences. The law was amended in 1961 to permit states also to assist families in which the father was present but unemployed, but only a little over half the states have adopted this policy. In any event, the new rule does not eliminate the incentive to desert on the part of the *employed* father: society will assist his family if he leaves but not if he stays. (A Supreme Court decision recently removed the sexist bias in this program by holding that an unemployed mother who is the principal earner in a family is entitled to the same benefits as an unemployed father.)

Benefits paid under AFDC vary greatly from state to state. At the end of 1979 the average monthly payment per recipient (i.e., per family member) in the continental United States ranged from a low of $28.31 in Mississippi to a high of $130.32 in Massachusetts. The nationwide average was $93.09.[31] Moreover, the spread between high and low benefit states actually increased in the 1970s.

The food stamp program was initiated in 1964 and grew very rapidly during the 1970s. Eligibility rules were tightened in 1977 to eliminate

30. For further detail see Congressional Budget Office, *Welfare Reform: Issues, Objectives and Approaches*, background paper, July 1977, ch. II; M. C. Barth, G. J. Carcagno, and J. L. Palmer, *Toward an Effective Income Support System* (Madison, Wisc.: The Institute for Research on Poverty, 1974), ch. 1; and Laurence E. Lynn, Jr., "A Decade of Policy Developments in the Income-Maintenance System," in Robert H. Haveman, ed., *A Decade of Federal Antipoverty Programs* (Madison, Wisc.: The Institute for Research on Poverty, 1977), ch. 2.
31. *Social Security Bulletin*, May 1980, table M-35.

persons whose net income exceeded the poverty line. Benefit levels are tied to income. Food stamps are unique among the major public aid programs in providing benefits that are uniform in the continental United States and available to *all* low income persons rather than only to selected categories of the poor.

Finally, "general assistance" is the name given to whatever aid the states and localities see fit to offer those of the poor who do not qualify for any federally authorized program.

Impact on the Rate of Poverty

The cash transfers and benefits-in-kind shown in Table 11.3 have had a considerable effect in reducing the incidence of poverty. Because of the way the Census Bureau defines income, however, the full effect does not show up in the official poverty statistics, such as those cited in Chapter 10. In calculating the official figures, the Census Bureau counts as family income both social insurance benefits, such as receipts from Social Security, and cash transfers received under public aid programs, such as AFDC. *Not* counted as part of a family's income, however, is the value it receives from benefits-in-kind, such as food stamps and Medicaid. If these values were added to family income, fewer families would be found to have incomes below the poverty line. Since benefit-in-kind payments increased faster than cash transfers in the 1970s, the Census data increasingly understate the impact of the nation's antipoverty program.

To sort this matter out, the Congressional Budget Office estimated what the incidence of poverty among families would have been in 1976 under alternative definitions of family income.[32] Some of their results are presented in Table 11.4. Column A shows the number of families in poverty, and the poverty rate, when income is defined to include social insurance receipts but *not* cash transfers received under public aid programs. Hence the numbers in the first column show how matters would stand in the absence of an antipoverty program of cash transfers and benefits-in-kind: the average incidence of poverty in the United States would have been 15.7 percent in 1976. Column B shows the extent of poverty when money transfers under public aid programs are also counted as income. This approximates the Census Bureau measure. The average incidence of poverty in the United States falls to 13.5 percent. Finally, in column C, benefits-in-kind are also counted as income (at a value

32. Congressional Budget Office, *Poverty Status of Families Under Alternative Definitions of Income,* background paper no. 17 (revised), June 1977. Data used in the study were adjusted for both the under-reporting of income and the under-counting of the poverty population believed to occur in the original source, the Census Bureau's *Current Population Survey.*

TABLE 11.4
Effect of Income Support Programs on Poverty Rate, Fiscal Year 1976

| AREA | FAMILIES IN POVERTY WHEN INCOME IS DEFINED TO INCLUDE: | | |
	(A) Social Insurance	(B) Cash Transfers Plus Social Insurance	(C) Benefits-in-Kind Plus Cash Transfers and Social Insurance
U.S. total			
Number of families in poverty (thousands)	12,454	10,716	6,441
Percent of all families (poverty rate)	15.7	13.5	8.1
Northeast			
Number of families in poverty (thousands)	2,521	2,072	1,005
Percent of all families (poverty rate)	14.0	11.5	5.6
South			
Number of families in poverty (thousands)	4,986	4,552	3,041
Percent of all families (poverty rate)	19.5	17.8	11.9

Source: Congressional Budget Office, *Poverty Status of Families Under Alternative Definitions of Income*, background paper no. 17 (revised), June 1977, tables 3 and 7.

equal to their cost). The poverty rate now falls to 8.1 percent, well below the figure indicated by the official definition of income.

Table 11.4 also illustrates the geographic disparity in poverty reduction that results from interstate differences in the coverage and benefit levels of our highly fragmented welfare system. In the Northeast, where benefit levels tend to be highest, the combined impact of cash transfers and benefits-in-kind reduces the poverty rate by 60 percent, lowering it from 14.0 percent to 5.6 percent. In the South, the region with the lowest benefit levels, antipoverty programs reduce the rate from 19.5 percent to 11.9 percent, a reduction of only 39 percent. Thus the post-transfer rate of poverty is more than twice as high in the South as it is in the Northeast.

The Congressional Budget Office also examined the distribution of poverty program benefits among income classes. They estimated that 62 percent of cash transfers and more than 50 percent of in-kind transfers vent to the lowest fifth of families classified by *pre*-transfer income levels. (By way of comparison, only 32 percent of social insurance payments vent to the lowest fifth.)[33] The reader may wonder why antipoverty benefits cannot be concentrated *100 percent* on the nation's poor. Why should we wastefully distribute benefits to families whose pre-benefit incomes are above the poverty line? The answer, which will be clarified below, is that one cannot cut off benefits at the poverty line without simultaneously discouraging the poor who are "on welfare" from working to enhance their incomes.

Dissatisfaction with the Welfare System

No aspect of American social policy has been more widely criticized in recent years than its "welfare," or public assistance, programs.[34] The multitude of objections refer essentially to four points. The first is that the nation's welfare system is not, in fact, a "system." Over the years we have accumulated a set of programs designed to alleviate certain carefully defined categories of hardship, not to attack poverty across the board. As a result, there are large gaps between programs. Many of the poor—including the "working poor" and childless couples and able-bodied single persons under the age of 65, whether or not they are working—are not covered by any mandatory, nationwide program except food stamps, which provided average monthly benefits of only $26.83 per participant in 1978.[35]

A second major criticism is that U.S. welfare programs lack geographic uniformity. Although poverty in a society open to easy internal migration is essentially a national problem, our public aid programs allow enormous interstate variation in benefit levels and coverage. In addition to the data on AFDC benefits already cited, consider the following. A study of the combined impact of Medicaid, AFDC, SSI, food stamps, and general assistance found that in 1976 the aggregate outlay per poor resident varied from a low of $419 a year in Arizona (the only state without Medicaid) to a high of $2,924 a year in Massachusetts. In the Northeast the average level was $2,428, in the South, only $784.[36]

Large interstate differences in welfare benefits raise serious questions of equity not only in the treatment of beneficiaries but also as between taxpayers. States that undertake seriously to relieve poverty through public assistance must tax themselves heavily to do so. If localities within the

33. Ibid., table 2.
34. In addition to the sources cited in note 30 above, see G. J. Carcagno and W. S. Corson, "Welfare Reform," in Pechman, *Setting National Priorities, the 1978 Budget*, ch. 8.
35. *Statistical Abstract of the United States*, 1979, table 208.
36. Ibid., table 572.

state are required by state law to contribute to local public assistance programs (as is sometimes the case), then a heavy burden is placed on taxpayers in localities having a high proportion of citizens in need of aid.

Interstate differences may also be economically inefficient. From the point of view of society as a whole, it is desirable for the poor to move to areas of better economic opportunity, where they can earn higher incomes on the basis of higher real productivity, but it is certainly *not* desirable that their decision to move should be influenced by interarea differences in the level of transfer payments, since these are not connected with differences in productivity.

Some taxpayers in states with high benefit levels are convinced that their states' relative generosity has attracted an influx of poor people in search of aid. To refute the view that high benefit levels attract the poor, others have cited the fact that very few of those "on welfare" in the high benefit states are recent arrivals. But this counterargument is hardly sufficient: it may be that the availability of high benefit levels holds recent migrants in areas they would otherwise leave when their initial expectations about income and employment are disappointed. Thus, without actually attracting the poor from elsewhere, high local benefit levels might nonetheless cause them, so to speak, to "pile up" locally. Migration to areas of greater economic opportunity may thus be inhibited.[37]

The third major criticism of U.S. welfare programs is that they are unnecessarily cumbersome and expensive to administer. The problem arises from the multiplicity of programs. As one study put it:

> Each program has its own rules and regulations and is separately administered, even though much of the same information is required—often from the same people—to determine eligibility and benefits. This complex and duplicative administrative system is confusing for welfare workers and recipients alike. It may lead to high error rates and opportunities for fraud. For some recipients, the system may delay, distort, or deny benefits. Others consider the varied investigative procedures repressive and demeaning.[38]

Finally, U.S. welfare programs are often criticized on the ground that they have socially undesirable effects on the behavior of beneficiaries. We have already mentioned the possibility that AFDC eligibility rules contribute to the break-up of families. Also important are the possible effects of benefit payments on work incentives.

37. See Larry H. Long, "Poverty Status and Receipt of Welfare Among Migrants and Nonmigrants in Large Cities," in *American Sociological Review*, February 1974, pp. 46–56; and I. N. Fisher and S. W. Purnell, *The Connection Between Migration and Welfare Dependency in the Chicago Metropolitan Area*, doc. no. R-1388-IISP (Santa Monica, Calif.: The Rand Corporation, September 1973).

38. Congressional Budget Office, *Welfare Reform . . .* , pp. 24–25.

Work Incentives in the Current Welfare System

Welfare benefits can affect work incentives in two ways. First, if income earned by those on welfare is taxed at too high a rate, they will be discouraged from working. AFDC provisions have been criticized in this regard. Down to 1967, beneficiaries who worked gave up a dollar of benefits for each dollar earned. In effect they were placed in a 100 percent income tax bracket for their initial earnings, thus facing the ultimate disincentive to work. A 1967 amendment permits beneficiaries to retain $30 a month plus one-third of earnings. But that is still nearly a 67 percent marginal tax rate on earnings, hardly a powerful incentive to work.

The availability of multiple benefits aggravates the problem of marginal tax rates. If a family on AFDC also receives food stamps or lives in subsidized housing, the benefits obtained under those income-conditioned programs will also diminish as earned income rises. Henry Aaron has shown that the marginal tax rate in such cases, taking into account the loss of benefits-in-kind, could rise from 67 percent to as much as 80 percent.[39]

Work incentives under welfare programs depend on the *level* of benefits as well as on the marginal tax rate on earnings. Other things being equal, the higher the benefit level, the less need the beneficiary will feel to work for additional income. Again, the availability of multiple benefit programs must be taken into account. A study based on a large sample of 1974 AFDC cases in New York City found that in-kind transfers such as Medicaid, food stamps, and day care services contributed $2,235 in annual value on top of an average cash grant of $3,393 per year. Among four-person, female-headed AFDC cases, 83 percent received aggregate benefits that placed them above the poverty line, and 95 percent received benefits in excess of what a single worker could have earned, if employed year-round at the minimum wage rate (then $2.00 an hour).[40] Clearly, such high benefit levels, coupled with the stiff tax rate on earnings that is implicit in multiple benefit welfare programs, would leave an unskilled welfare recipient with little incentive to work.

A Guaranteed Income Plan

What can be done to correct the defects in the U.S. welfare system? In recent years much serious thought has been given to welfare reform,

39. Henry J. Aaron, *Why Is Welfare So Hard to Reform?* (Washington, D.C.: The Brookings Institution, 1973), pp. 32–33.
40. David W. Lyon, et al., *Multiple Welfare Benefits in New York City*, doc. no. R-2002-HEW (Santa Monica, Calif.: The Rand Corporation, August 1976), table 4.6 and figure 5.1.

yet no consensus has emerged that would permit more than very marginal adjustments.

In the late 1960s and early 1970s many people favored adopting a universal guaranteed income scheme to replace the existing system. They believed that such a plan would in itself overcome the objections we have discussed. By its universality an income guarantee would eliminate gaps in coverage and provide uniform national benefit standards. By its simplicity it would do away with administrative confusion and waste. Finally, it would provide an opportunity to deal systematically with the problem of work incentives.

We use guaranteed income as a general term to cover proposals known variously as the negative income tax, the credit income tax, or the family assistance plan. Versions of these schemes were proposed to the Congress by President Nixon (the Family Assistance Plan) and President Carter (the Program for Better Jobs and Income). Neither was adopted, and opposition to the idea has probably increased with time. Nevertheless they merit discussion because, by examining them, we can better understand the structural problems inherent in cash transfer plans and throw considerable light on the issues in welfare reform.

All rational guaranteed income proposals call for 100 percent financing by the federal government. Whatever benefits they provide would be paid for entirely out of national tax revenues, with no contribution by state or local governments. The objective is to create a uniform national standard for the relief of poverty, without categorical restrictions of any kind. It would be impossible to accomplish this without federal financing, since the poorer states could never afford to pay benefits at the level deemed appropriate by the nation as a whole.

The technical structure, shared by all income maintenance proposals, consists of three elements. First, a guaranteed minimum income per person or per family, which the government will provide when the beneficiary has no other income. Second, a "take-back rate" at which the government reduces cash payments if the beneficiary does have any earned income. Third, a "break-even level" at which earned income is high enough so that benefit payments under the plan cease.

A simple illustration worked out in Table 11.5 shows how these elements fit together. Suppose that the income guarantee is set at $1,000 per person. A family of four would then receive $4,000 per year if it had no other income. Next, assume that benefits are reduced by $40 for every $100 of income the family earns. The "take-back rate," in other words, is 40 percent. For example, if the family earns $2,000 during the year, benefit payments will be reduced by .40 × $2,000 = 800. The family will receive net benefits of $4,000 − $800 = $3,200. Its total income will be $2,000 + $3,200 = $5,200. (See the second line of the table.)

TABLE 11.5

Hypothetical Guaranteed Income Plan Illustrated for a Family of Four

INCOME GUARANTEE (Y_g) = $1,000 PER PERSON		
TAKE-BACK TAX RATE (t_e) = .40		
1	2	3
Earned Income	Net Benefit Paid to Four-Person Family ($4,000 − .40 × Col. 1)	Total Income Before Income Tax (Col. 1 + Col. 2)
0	$4,000	$ 4,000
$ 2,000	3,200	5,200
4,000	2,400	6,400
6,000	1,600	7,600
8,000	800	8,800
10,000	0	10,000

If the family's earned income rises, its benefits under the plan decrease. When earned income reaches $10,000 a year, net benefits fall to zero, since the take-back rate applied to earned income yields a sum just equal to the initial income guarantee (.40 × $10,000 = $4,000). Thus $10,000 is the break-even level of earned income at which net benefit payments under the plan cease for a four-person family.[41]

The three structural elements of an income-maintenance plan are related by a simple mathematical formula.[42] Let

Y_g = income guarantee per person when earned income is zero

Y_e = earned income

t_e = take-back tax rate on earned income

R = break-even level of earned income

Then the relationship between the three structural elements is given mathematically by

$$R = \frac{Y_g}{t_e}$$

41. In practice, guaranteed income plans have to mesh with the income tax system so that the beneficiary moves smoothly from the former to the latter as earned income rises. The problem is not treated here, but see the discussion in Congressional Budget Office, *Welfare Reform . . .* , pp. 66–73.

42. Christopher Green, *Negative Taxes and the Poverty Problem* (Washington, D.C.: The Brookings Institution, 1967), p. 63.

This equation can be explained as follows: by definition, R is that level of Y_e such that

$$Y_g - t_e Y_e = 0$$

which can be rewritten as

$$Y_e = \frac{Y_g}{t_e}$$

Substituting R for Y_e, we obtain

$$R = \frac{Y_g}{t_e}$$

Putting data from Table 11.5 into the equation we observe that

$$\$10,000 = \frac{\$4,000}{.40}$$

It is apparent that once the values of any two of the three structural elements are specified, the value of the third is mathematically determined. In other words, we can freely choose values for any two of them but not for all three. This is obviously an important constraint on the design of guaranteed income schemes.

Each of the three structural elements described above is related directly to one or more of the major objectives of antipoverty policy. Consider first the objective of eliminating poverty by transferring income: the adequacy of an income maintenance plan to relieve poverty depends directly upon the level chosen for Y_g. In measuring the adequacy of a transfer program to relieve poverty, the concept of a national aggregate "poverty gap" is helpful. This gap is defined as the aggregate sum of money that would have to be transferred to the poor population to raise each poor person just to the poverty line. In 1979 the poverty gap amounted to \$22.6 billion.[43] In the plan described above Y_g is clearly too low to close the poverty gap completely. Poverty line income for a four-person family was calculated to be about \$7,400 in 1979, but the proposed income guarantee to that family is only \$4,000. That still leaves a considerable "gap."

A second objective of antipoverty policy is to encourage (or at least not to discourage) work effort by the poor. As explained in the previous section, one would expect work effort under a welfare plan to vary inversely with both the size of the basic guarantee and the rate at which benefits are reduced as earnings increase. This means that both Y_g and t_e

43. U.S. Bureau of the Census, *Current Population Reports*, series P-60, no. 125, October 1980, table 23.

affect work incentives. The plan described in Table 11.5 has relatively low levels for both factors. Hence it would be expected to have relatively favorable effects on work effort.

Finally, there is the objective of designing a plan that is affordable. The budgetary cost of a guaranteed income plan is strongly influenced by the value of R, the break-even level of earned income. Everyone with earned income less than R receives net cash benefits under a guaranteed income plan. Hence, the higher the level of R, the greater the number of persons receiving benefits and, for any given value of Y_g, the greater the total cost of benefits paid. Antipoverty policy is required by the realities of politics to achieve results at an acceptable cost to those who must pay taxes that support it. Consequently the level of R is a key factor in comparisons between alternative proposals. In 1979 the median income of four-person households in the United States was $22,576. About 13 percent of them had incomes below $10,000, the break-even level for the plan illustrated above.[44] That plan would therefore have paid net benefits to less than one-seventh of all four-person families.

In an attempt to measure scientifically what effect a guaranteed income program would have on work effort, the federal government, beginning in 1968, financed several large-scale experiments with income support. Families in selected urban and rural areas were offered the benefits of a guaranteed income over a period of several years while their work behavior was compared with that of a control group. The principal concern was to see what effect an income guarantee would have on the ordinary working poor who are not usually eligible for "welfare," but who *would* benefit under a plan of universal income support. Therefore, the studies concentrated on intact husband-wife families rather than on the broken families that typically make up the AFDC caseload.

The results of the urban and rural experiments were roughly consistent. Average hours worked by male family heads declined slightly (5 to 6 percent) in urban areas. For the most part this reflected fewer hours worked per week, rather than withdrawal from employment. In rural areas there was essentially no change in hours worked by husbands. Working wives, on the other hand, reduced their effort on the order of 20 to 40 percent in both urban and rural areas. However, since wives did not have high labor force participation rates to begin with, these relatively large declines did not greatly reduce aggregate family work effort.[45]

44. Ibid., table 15.
45. See the editors' "Introduction and Summary" and Albert Rees and Harold W. Watts, "An Overview of the Labor Supply Results," in Joseph A. Pechman and P. Michael Timpane, eds., *Work Incentives and Income Guarantees: The New Jersey Negative Income Tax Experiment* (Washington, D.C.: The Brookings Institution, 1975), pp. 1–14, 60–87; and U.S. Department of Health, Education, and Welfare, *The Rural Income Maintenance Experiment, Summary Report*, SR10, November 1976.

If the results of these experiments are judged to be reliable, they lay to rest the fear that a guaranteed income would cause many low-skilled males either to give up work or sharply curtail their hours.[46] The substantial reduction in the work effort of wives was unforeseen but need not be regarded as undesirable, if work in the home replaces work on the job. Albert Rees and Harold W. Watts concluded that "the burden of proof would now appear to be on those who assert that income maintenance programs for intact families will have very large effects on labor supply."[47]

Balancing the Objectives of an Income Maintenance Program

Let us now examine the trade-offs among major objectives that are implicit in the structural equation for any guaranteed income scheme. We have seen that the plan outlined above might be criticized as inadequate to relieve poverty. Then why not increase the minimum income guarantee for a family of four to $7,000 a year and close the poverty gap almost completely? The obvious answer is that doing so would raise the break-even level from $10,000 to $17,500 and add enormously to the cost of the program. The government would be paying net benefits to almost one-third of all four-person families, some of them living at close to a middle-class standard.

Closing the aggregate national poverty gap by means of income allowances requires large-scale transfers, not because the gap itself is so wide, but because there is no way of closing it, consistent with the other objectives of antipoverty policy, that does not involve a good deal of "excess redistribution." Part of this "excess" goes to raise people from below the poverty line to some point above it (example: the family in Table 11.5 with $4,000 of earned income). Another part goes to supplement the incomes of those who were above the poverty line even before receiving benefits (example: the family with $8,000 of earned income in Table 11.5). The result is an aggregate redistribution that far exceeds the size of the poverty gap itself.

The only way to avoid all "excess redistribution" would be to guarantee everyone a poverty line income while at the same time reducing the benefit payment by one dollar for every dollar of earned income. Under that arrangement no family initially above the poverty line would receive anything, and no family initially below the line would receive net benefits

---

46. However, a number of economists have expressed doubts about their reliability. See the papers by H. J. Aaron and B. S. and W. M. Mahoney in Pechman and Timpane; and John F. Cogan, *Negative Income Taxation and Labor Supply: New Evidence from the New Jersey–Pennsylvania Experiment*, doc. no. R-2155-HEW (Santa Monica, Cal.: The Rand Corporation, February 1978).

47. Rees and Watts, p. 87.

that would raise it so much as a dollar above. But we would be imposing a 100 percent take-back tax rate on the first few thousand dollars of people's earnings. As we have already explained, such a policy seriously reduces work incentives for those whose earning power is low. To avoid this weakening of work incentives the take-back tax rate must be kept down, but doing that builds a good deal of "excess redistribution" into the plan. And the lower the take-back tax rate, the greater the amount of the excess redistribution and the higher the cost.

How much in fact would it cost to establish a guaranteed income plan such as the one depicted in Table 11.5? In 1974 the Department of Health, Education, and Welfare developed a proposal called the "Income Supplement Program." ISP would have provided a single cash benefit to replace the existing AFDC, SSI, and food stamp programs. A family of four with no other income would have received $4,325, about the same amount as provided by the hypothetical plan in Table 11.5. The take-back rate on earned income was to be 50 percent. Hence, the break-even point was $8,650, somewhat below the level depicted in Table 11.5. In 1978, at which point ISP would have provided benefits equal to about two-thirds of poverty line income, the Congressional Budget Office estimated that it would have cost the federal government $10.6 billion more than the AFDC, SSI, and food stamp programs that it replaced. Fiscal relief to states was estimated at $2.1 billion, so the net public cost would have been $8.4 billion.[48] Since the hypothetical plan shown in Table 11.5 has a lower take-back rate and a higher break-even point than ISP, it would presumably cost somewhat more.

The Difficulty of Welfare Reform

The unavoidable trade-off among the essential characteristics of any income guarantee plan has proven frustrating to policy designers. No possible combination of guarantee level, take-back rate, and budgetary cost is likely to satisfy everyone's objectives, and, in practice, compromise of objectives has been difficult to achieve. President Nixon's Family Assistance Plan, twice passed by the House of Representatives, was never approved in the Senate. Some thought it provided inadequate support, while others opposed it as overly generous; some thought it undermined work incentives and others that its incentive structure was too strong.[49]

In 1977, the Carter Administration sent to the Congress a comprehensive welfare reform proposal called the "Program for Better Jobs and Income." It would have replaced AFDC, SSI, and food stamps with a

48. Congressional Budget Office, *Welfare Reform* . . . , table 7 and pp. 67–71.
49. Ibid., pp. 38–39.

national system of cash transfers. The Carter plan differed from earlier proposals in attempting to integrate direct job creation with income support. Able-bodied single persons, childless couples, and others who could be expected to work would be required to seek employment, but if they were unable to find it would be offered special public service jobs together with training. Thus the cost of the proposal included not only its cash benefits but a substantial sum for direct job creation. Tax relief was also provided to low income families. The net cost to the federal government (allowing for the savings on discontinued programs) was estimated by the Administration at $8.8 billion but by the Congressional Budget Office at more than twice that figure.[50] With public sentiment turning increasingly against new spending initiatives, however, Congress took no action on the plan.

Apparently a political majority cannot be mustered to support any version of the guaranteed income plan. Future proposals for welfare reform are therefore likely to shun the strategy of comprehensive change that relies on such proposals. Incremental reform is now the more likely approach. For example, a federally financed minimum standard for AFDC benefits in all states could reduce geographic inequities in the relief of poverty and also provide a degree of fiscal relief to the states. In addition, the federal government could require all states to adopt the AFDC-UP program under which intact families can receive benefits if the principal earner is unemployed. If the new minimum standard were set so that the combination of AFDC payments and food stamp benefits came to 75 percent of poverty level income, it is estimated that (in fiscal year 1978) these reforms would have added only $1.5 billion to total benefit costs. In addition, states would have been relieved of $1.5 billion of the tax burden by higher federal contributions. Setting the national standard at 100 percent of poverty-line income, however, would have greatly increased these numbers.[51]

Direct job creation is also likely to play a role in future reform of the income support system. The Carter Administration's 1977 proposal showed how a work requirement, a job creation program, and income support could be meshed. As Palmer has pointed out, integrating a job program with the cash assistance structure is a way of side-stepping the difficult issue of work incentives.[52] Because the work ethic is deeply honored by Americans, many people still find the question of work incentives

50. Congressional Budget Office, *The Administration's Welfare Reform Proposal: An Analysis of the Program for Better Jobs and Income*, April 1978, table 5.

51. Congressional Budget Office, *Welfare Reform . . .* , pp. 59–61.

52. John L. Palmer, "Employment and Income Security," in J. A. Pechman, ed., *Setting National Priorities, The 1979 Budget* (Washington, D.C.: The Brookings Institution, 1978), p. 68.

troubling. The inclusion of a job component makes income-support programs politically more acceptable: beneficiaries capable of working would have to do so to earn their keep.

URBAN POVERTY AND RACIAL SEGREGATION

We come last to those antipoverty strategies that are oriented toward particular geographic areas. In the urban context these are policies that take specific account of the connections between race, segregation into ghettos, and preponderant poverty. The urban riots of the 1960s, coinciding with the rapid increase in the black population of central cities, inevitably drew the nation's attention to the problems of the ghetto. What would be the most effective public policy to deal with them? Although discussion has tended to concentrate on black poverty, the analysis itself is usually applicable to the situation of other poor urban minorities as well—the Mexican-Americans of the South and West or the Puerto Ricans and other Spanish-origin groups in the North and East.

Debate has focused on three kinds of policy that are distinguished by differences in the way they approach the fact of racial segregation.[53] In the heat of debate, advocates have often spoken as if these three policies were mutually exclusive. We will argue that they are not and that the wisest strategy would probably include elements of all three.

The first has sometimes been called "ghetto economic development." This policy would attempt to relieve poverty by taking advantage of possibilities for direct action within the racial ghetto itself. The second policy, a sort of polar opposite to the first, would attempt to relieve ghetto poverty by helping and encouraging the population of central city ghettos to disperse into the largely white metropolitan suburbs. The third policy, standing logically between the other two, would use the conventional tools of antipoverty policy to integrate urban racial minorities into the central city's economy. Supporters of this policy may not approve of segregation, but they do not usually believe that the ghetto itself is a crucial factor that must be dealt with in antipoverty policy.

53. See Anthony Downs, "Alternative Futures for the American Ghetto," *Daedalus*, Fall 1968, pp. 1331–78; John F. Kain and Joseph J. Persky, "Alternatives to the Gilded Ghetto," *The Public Interest*, Winter 1969, pp. 74–87; Matthew Edel, "Development vs. Dispersal: Approaches to Ghetto Poverty," in Matthew Edel and Jerome Rothenberg, eds., *Readings in Urban Economics* (New York: Macmillan, 1972), pp. 307–25; the papers in part 1 of George M. von Furstenberg, Bennett Harrison, and Ann R. Horowitz, eds., *Patterns of Racial Discrimination*, vol. 1: *Housing* (Lexington, Mass.: D. C. Heath, Lexington Books, 1974), pp. 3–101; and Bennett Harrison, "Ghetto Economic Development," *Journal of Economic Literature*, March 1974, pp. 1–37.

This third, or intermediate, policy relies on the conventional tools of manpower training, job information, and placement services focused intensively on residents of poverty areas. Since we have examined these programs above, nothing more need be said here. However, we will now examine the other two policies—ghetto development and ghetto dispersal—in greater detail.

Ghetto Economic Development

The branch plant strategy. Policies to stimulate the economic development of poverty areas may take numerous forms. One approach would attempt to bring jobs into racially segregated neighborhoods by inducing large employers (primarily major white-owned corporations) to open branches there. Some racial ghettos, such as the Watts district in Los Angeles, are relatively isolated from major centers of employment. Thus, the rationale of this first approach is to improve the ghetto residents' access to jobs, both physically and in terms of informal job information flows.

There have been both successes and failures in such attempts to move jobs to the ghetto. An extensive set of case studies by the Conference Board documents the frequent start-up difficulties of poverty-area plants. It concludes, however, that there is "reassuring evidence" on a number of points about which investors have expressed concern: "1. Outside investment has been well-received in ghetto communities. . . . 2. The disadvantaged have been quick to seek work. . . . 3. The disadvantaged have become reliable, productive workers. . . . 4. White managers have been accepted. . . . 5. The safety of property has not been a problem. . . ."[54]

Nevertheless, it is no simple matter to find large-scale business operations that can be carried on profitably from a ghetto location under a commitment to hire the hard-core unemployed and to pay them competitive wages. Start-up losses on poverty area plants may be tolerated by large corporations or could be systematically subsidized by the government. However, it would be difficult to justify substantial permanent government subsidies to maintain such plants, since that would imply very high costs per additional ghetto job created. Yet if high costs are to be avoided, great care must be taken in choosing projects, and the program will necessarily remain small in relation to the magnitude of the ghetto poverty problem.

The "black capitalist" approach. A second approach to ghetto economic development is to stimulate the growth of minority-owned

54. James K. Brown and Seymour Lusterman, *Business and the Development of Ghetto Enterprise* (New York: The Conference Board, Inc., 1971), pp. 59–60.

private business enterprise. The failure of American blacks to develop the strong business tradition found among many other ethnic minority groups in America has long been recognized. The most recent figures show that in 1972, when blacks made up 11 percent of the population, they owned only 2.7 percent of all business firms excluding corporations, and those firms were much smaller than the average, accounting for only 1.7 percent of all noncorporate business receipts.[55]

The weakness of the black business tradition can readily be explained as the result of a long history of slavery, followed by oppressive economic discrimination. Unfortunately, it deprives the black community of effective economic power and a chance to enjoy what is now often referred to as "a piece of the action." The "action" includes not only current profits but an ownership stake in expected economic growth. The policy of fostering "black capitalism" is intended to make good these deficiencies. Federal action to support the growth of minority-group business ownership comes principally through such agencies as the Small Business Administration and the Commerce Department's Minority Business Development Agency. The SBA has developed special programs to assist minority-owned businesses with direct loans. It also offers guarantees (for a fee) that reduce the risk on loans to small businesses and thus make them more attractive to commercial banks. Minority-group entrepreneurs are often short of experience and expertise as well as capital. The SBA therefore provides a modest amount of management counseling to minority-group loan recipients. Independent councils of business people in many cities have probably contributed an even greater counseling effort, some of it in cooperation with the SBA.

A policy of fostering minority-owned business can contribute to ghetto economic development if it helps to bring new businesses into existence or to expand old ones within the poverty area.[56] The problem is to discover what kinds of business can thrive in the ghetto. Opportunities for expansion in the retail and service sector are severely constrained by the near-poverty level of average local income. Of course, it is possible for blacks to expand their share of local activity either by competitive success or by buying out white-owned retail firms. Either of these outcomes would increase the share of profits going to the black community, but neither would be likely to increase the total number of local jobs. Significant expansion of the ghetto economy can come only with the establishment of

55. U.S. Bureau of the Census, *Current Population Reports*, series P-23, no. 80, 1979, table 59.
56. See James Heilbrun and Stanislaw Wellisz, "An Economic Program for the Ghetto," *Urban Riots: Violence and Social Change*, Proceedings of the Academy of Political Science, July 1968, pp. 72–85.

firms that sell to a wider market than the ghetto—for example, to an entire metropolitan area or to the nation as a whole.[57] Finding such business opportunities is a slow process, however, and usually requires the skills of an experienced entrepreneur.

The rapid expansion of the black business sector is hampered by two shortages—of experienced black entrepreneurs and of venture capital. Unfortunately, experience has shown that a policy of forcing the pace of expansion in the minority-owned sector by means of government subsidized loans leads to a sharp increase in the new-business failure rate and therefore entails high financial cost.[58] That means, not that government financial support is undesirable, but only that it must be given prudently. Finally, it must be kept in mind that new minority owned firms are likely to start small and initially create only a few new jobs. Thus, although the expansion of minority-owned enterprise is a highly desirable long-run goal, it cannot be expected to have much immediate impact on economic well-being in poverty areas.

Community development corporations. A third approach to ghetto economic development calls for the use of "community development corporations." These corporations (known as CDC's) vary considerably in structure and intent.[59] Some of them are "strictly business" and operate through the conventional institutions of private enterprise. They devote themselves to assisting new minority owned firms by providing management counseling and direct loans and by arranging access to banks and other sources of financial assistance and to markets for their products. They aim at nothing more complex than the creation of independent, black owned business firms—in other words, "black capitalism" in the most traditional sense.

Frequently, however, CDC's set themselves more ambitious goals. They substitute a degree of community initiative for reliance on private enterprise by taking an active role in planning, financing, developing, and operating large-scale undertakings such as shopping centers and housing projects. They make housing rehabilitation loans, run training and employ-

57. For evidence of the constraining effect of low neighborhood income, see James Heilbrun, "Jobs in Harlem: A Statistical Analysis," *Papers* of the Regional Science Association, XXV (1970) 181–201.
58. Sar A. Levitan, Garth L. Mangum, and Robert Taggart III, *Economic Opportunity in the Ghetto: The Partnership of Government and Business* (Baltimore: The Johns Hopkins University Press, 1970), pp. 79–80; and Timothy Bates and William Bradford, *Financing Black Economic Development* (New York: Academic Press, 1979), ch. 9.
59. See Levitan, Mangum, and Taggart, pp. 75–79; and Martin Skala, "Inner-City Enterprise: Current Experience," in William F. Haddad and G. Douglas Pugh, eds., The American Assembly, *Black Economic Development* (Englewood Cliffs, N.J.: Prentice-Hall, 1969), pp. 162–70.

ment programs, and provide a variety of other nonprofit community services.

It has generally been the expectation of community groups founding CDC's that profits from their business and financial operations would be available to support their nonprofit services. The goal was to make the community truly self-sufficient. However, creating new businesses in the highly competitive American economy is a risky and difficult undertaking—and certainly riskier and more difficult in the ghetto than elsewhere. CDC business operations have thus far not proven very profitable. Community services have therefore been carried on with the help of outside funding. After a careful evaluation of three of the largest CDC's—the Bedford Stuyvesant Restoration Corporation in Brooklyn, the Woodlawn Organization in Chicago, and the Zion Non-Profit Charitable Trust in Philadelphia—analysts at the Urban Institute reached this conclusion: "Each of the CDC's will require subsidy, over at least the next five to ten years, if even current programs . . . are to be sustained. Relatively few of the potential profit centers within the CDC's are currently profitable. . . ."[60] Realistically, the goal of self-sufficiency may never be realized. Nevertheless, CDC's will probably endure, since they perform many useful functions within their communities. As the Urban Institute report concluded, it is not clear that, in solving difficult problems within poverty areas, either the government or the unaided private market would do a better job.[61]

Cumulative Effects of Development

Advocates of poverty area development policies—including the branch plant strategy, the black capitalist strategy, and the CDC approach—argue that these policies gain strength by mutual reinforcement, that their whole effect is, so to speak, more than the sum of their individual parts. There are several reasons for believing this to be true. First of all, we recognize the existence of external economies of agglomeration at the neighborhood level. Producers are attracted to neighborhoods that can provide supporting services; consumers are more likely to shop in retail centers that offer a wide variety of goods. Thus activity attracts activity, and growth begets growth.

Second, there are local multiplier effects. If we define the neighborhood as the unit of analysis, then there exists a neighborhood income

60. Harvey A. Garn, Nancy L. Tevis, and Carl E. Snead, *Evaluating Community Development Corporations—A Summary Report* (Washington, D.C.: The Urban Institute, March 1976), p. 148.
61. Ibid.

multiplier that is formally identical to the income multiplier for a nation, a region, or a city. In Chapter 7 we showed that this multiplier (k) can be written as

$$K = \frac{1}{1 - mpcl}$$

where *mpcl* stands for the marginal propensity to consume locally produced goods.

Though there is no doubt that local multiplier effects exist, recent studies indicate that their magnitude is likely to be very small. The reason for this is not that poverty area residents fail to spend money in their own neighborhoods: estimates of the proportion of income spent locally vary from 38 percent in the Hough area of Cleveland to 55 percent in Brooklyn's Bedford-Stuyvesant. The reason for the small size of the multiplier is, rather, that a high proportion of the money spent in local stores and service establishments necessarily goes for the purchase of imported goods or factor services.[62] Since the marginal propensity to import is high, a very large proportion of local spending "leaks out" of the neighborhood instead of recirculating to generate more local income.

Finally, local economic development is likely to have favorable social and psychological effects. In communities where deprivation has produced apathy and hopelessness, demonstrations of success either in business or in job-holding will encourage others to emulate the pattern of success. Furthermore, local development opens up opportunities for talented and ambitious residents and encourages them to remain in the poverty area instead of taking their exceptional energies and abilities elsewhere. Thus it helps to prevent poverty areas from being deprived of some of their best human resources. Advocates of local development policy believe that success will attract the talent and create the self-confidence out of which greater success can flow.

Yet we must conclude by recognizing the limitations on poverty area development policy as a means of increasing local incomes. Most residents of minority ghettos work in the larger, outside economy and must continue to do so, for ghetto neighborhoods are essentially residential in character. For example, a study of Harlem, one of the more highly developed black ghettos, estimated that in 1966 the neighborhood contained approximately 19,500 jobs. The number of employed Harlem residents was about five times as large. Thus even if Harlem residents held every local job (which was certainly not the case), no more than one-fifth

62. See William H. Oakland, Frederick T. Sparrow, and H. Louis Stettler III, "Ghetto Multipliers: A Case Study of Hough," *Journal of Regional Science*, December 1971, pp. 337–45.

of them could have worked inside their own community.[63] While many poverty areas could accommodate more work places than they do now, it would be virtually impossible and very probably undesirable to make them over into major centers of employment.

Moreover, as whites have moved to the suburbs and inner city population has declined, the black population has spread far from its sites of earlier concentration, which now often contain large areas of abandoned housing. In the face of so much mobility, the case for focusing economic development on particular inner city neighborhoods loses much of its cogency. Or, to look at the same facts from an opposite perspective, as blacks and the Spanish origin population come to make up a larger and larger proportion of the inner city total, policies that promote the general prosperity of the inner city economy and that strive simultaneously to integrate minorities into its mainstream become increasingly relevant. To support that integration we must continue to make available the conventional tools of education, training, job information, and placement discussed at the beginning of this chapter.

As pointed out earlier, "ghetto dispersal" policies would stress integration in a different locale, by encouraging and even subsidizing the movement of minorities to the suburbs. We examine next the rationale for such a policy.

Urban Poverty and Metropolitan Decentralization

It is one of the ironies of our times that the nation's poor minorities migrated to the cities at the very moment when job opportunities there were threatened by the forces of decentralization. The problem is usually described this way: in recent decades jobs have been dispersing within metropolitan areas. (On this point, see Table 3.4.) Many of the older central cities have actually suffered a loss in total jobs since the late 1940s. The suburbs, on the other hand, have enjoyed enormous job growth. Dispersion is most marked among blue collar jobs in manufacturing, wholesaling, and distribution, least pronounced in white collar jobs and in service industries. The poor are usually better qualified for blue collar than for white collar employment. Hence the inner portions of the central cities, where the poor typically live, are an increasingly disadvantageous base from which to look for work. Not only are blue collar jobs moving steadily away from inner-city poverty areas; they are moving to places that are scarcely accessible by public transportation. (See discussion in Chapter 9.) To the inner-city worker with no automobile, the cost in time and money of reaching a suburban job by commuter

63. Heilbrun, "Jobs in Harlem," pp. 185–86.

railroad and/or multiple bus connections is often prohibitive when compared with his or her low earning capacity. Moreover, the casual, informal sort of employment information on which many job seekers rely also thins out with distance. In short, the inner-city resident, especially when isolated in a racial ghetto, is increasingly out of touch with the labor market.

To be sure, this statement of the problem is somewhat oversimplified. First of all, it leans rather heavily on the assumption that white collar jobs are higher skilled than blue collar jobs, whereas, in fact, many white collar jobs in the central city do not call for particularly high levels of skill. Second, the dispersion of jobs has been accompanied by a dispersion of the resident population (again, see Table 3.4). Jobs as well as housing have been left behind for newcomers to the city. A sort of "job filtering" process is at work, parallel to the process of "housing filtering."

These issues deserve the most careful investigation. For if job dispersion is depriving poor minorities in the central city of opportunities for improvement, the implications for public policy are clear: to help relieve poverty, we must encourage the dispersion of blacks and other minorities into the suburbs.

Evaluating the Case for Dispersion

To evaluate the dispersion argument we must try to answer two rather complex questions. First, how does job availability compare, and, second, how do earnings and occupational status compare, between central cities and suburbs? These questions are difficult to answer for several reasons. First there is the unsatisfactory nature of our statistics. Most of the data we have on employment, type of occupation, and earnings that can be geographically classified refer to the locations where workers live rather than where they work. In strict logic one cannot use such data to compare the characteristics of the suburban and central city "labor markets," since some of the people residing in each place, to whom the data refer, actually work at jobs in the labor market of the other area.

Second, there is the fact that the populations living in the two areas are not identical in their personal characteristics. Blacks living in the suburbs and blacks living in the central city are not random samples of a single black population. Rather they are self-selected groups and may differ significantly in relevant ways. This is, of course, equally true of the white population of the two areas.

What the data we are about to analyze describe, therefore, are the opportunities that would be open to a worker who moved to the suburbs and developed the same skills and journey-to-work patterns that present suburbanites have. With this interpretation in mind (and with reservations to be mentioned as we proceed), let us examine the data.

Black Unemployment Rates: Central Cities Versus Suburbs

If it were possible, we would like first to compare the relative "availability" of jobs in the two areas. Since it is difficult to obtain meaningful data on "job openings," the best that can be done is to infer the relative availability of jobs from a comparison of unemployment rates: the higher the unemployment rate, the lower is job availability. This is not wholly satisfactory—it requires, for example, that we posit an equal willingness to work in the two areas, as measured by job seekers' "reservation wages" (the lowest wages at which they are willing to accept a job)—but no better alternative is available.

Table 11.6 shows that in 1970 the unemployment rate for both races was slightly higher in central cities than in the rings of metropolitan areas. Unemployment rates rose in both areas from 1970 to 1977 as the nation adopted anti-inflationary macroeconomic policies, and the rate of increase was somewhat greater for those living inside central cities. When unemployment rates by area and race are examined, it is clear that the most rapid increase occurred for blacks living in central cities. Black central city males registered the sharpest increase of all. If we assume that the black suburban unemployment rate accurately represents the job

TABLE 11.6
Unemployment Rates by Race and Sex, Inside and Outside Central Cities of SMSA's

	INSIDE CENTRAL CITIES		OUTSIDE CENTRAL CITIES	
	1970	1977	1970	1977
All races, both sexes[a]	4.8%	9.1%	4.0%	7.3%
White, both sexes	4.3	7.6	3.7	7.0
Male	4.0	7.6	3.3	6.3
Female	4.6	7.6	4.5	7.9
Black, both sexes	7.1	15.6	6.7	12.8
Male	6.9	16.4	6.3	12.9
Female	7.3	14.8	7.2	12.8

[a] Includes other races not shown separately.
Source: U.S. Bureau of the Census, *Current Population Reports,* series P-23, no. 75, November 1978, table 11.

328   Urban Economics and Public Policy

TABLE 11.7

Median Family Income by Race, Inside and Outside Central Cities of SMSA's

	MEDIAN FAMILY INCOME IN 1979 DOLLARS[a]			
	1959	1969	1979	Percentage Change 1969–79
CENTRAL CITIES				
All races[b]	$14,681	$18,571	$18,089	−2.6
White	15,599	19,892	19,951	0.3
Black	9,579	12,989	11,597	−10.7
OUTSIDE CENTRAL CITIES				
All races[b]	16,529	21,879	22,942	4.9
White	16,796	22,202	23,323	5.0
Black	8,675	13,700	15,047	9.8

[a] Income in 1959, 1969, and 1979, for families by place of residence in 1960, 1970, and 1980.
[b] Includes other races not shown separately.
Sources: U.S. Bureau of the Census, Current Population Reports, series P-23, no. 37, June 24, 1971, table 7; series P-23, no. 75, November 1978, table 17; and unpublished Census Bureau tabulations.

availability that central city blacks would face if they moved to the suburbs, we must conclude that their job prospects would be improved by the move. Moreover, the indicated advantage of the suburbs is increasing over time.

Black Income and Occupational Status: Central Cities Versus Suburbs

Trends in family income confirm the apparent advantage of the suburbs. Table 11.7 shows that between 1969 and 1979 median family income in constant dollars in central cities was unchanged for whites and declined for blacks, whereas it increased for both races in the suburban ring. In 1969 the median family income of blacks was only 5 percent higher in ring areas than in central cities. By 1979 the gap had increased to 30 percent.

What accounts for the rapid relative increase in black suburban income? Table 11.8 allows us to examine separately the influence of higher occupational status and higher earnings within occupation. In 1960 the proportion of both black men and black women in professional, managerial, and white collar occupations was substantially higher in central cities than in the ring area. By 1974 the situation had reversed, indicating that

TABLE 11.8
Black Occupational Status and Earnings by Sex, Inside and Outside Central Cities of SMSA's

	BLACK MALE				BLACK FEMALE			
	Central Cities		Outside Central Cities		Central Cities		Outside Central Cities	
Occupation of the employed[a] (percentage distribution)	1960	1974	1960	1974	1960	1974	1960	1974
All Occupations	100.0	100.0	100.0	100.0	100.0	100.0	100.0	100.0
Professional, technical, and managerial	5.8	10.8	3.9	14.7	8.1	14.7	7.0	15.2
Clerical and sales	11.9	13.1	5.0	10.3	13.2	30.1	8.6	24.0
Blue collar and service[b]	82.2	76.0	91.2	75.0	78.9	55.2	84.4	60.5
Craftsmen, foremen, and operatives	42.2	34.5	34.7	32.6	17.8	14.5	12.4	17.4
Nonfarm laborers	22.1	13.3	28.5	14.4	.7	1.4	1.0	.6
Service workers	17.6	17.7	20.3	16.7	60.4	27.6	67.0	28.0
Earnings of the employed by occupation[a,c] (in 1973 dollars)	1959	1973	1959	1973	1959	1973	1959	1973
All Occupations	$4,873	$ 7,703	$4,277	$ 7,908	$2,291	$4,744	$1,732	$4,705
Professional, technical, and managerial	6,325	10,339	—	11,674	4,949	7,957	—	8,676
Clerical and sales	5,939	7,518	—	9,801	4,470	4,993	—	4,559
Craftsmen and foremen	5,818	8,725	—	9,208	—	5,211	—	4,514
Operatives	5,350	7,541	4,444	8,094	3,086	4,587	—	4,658
Nonfarm laborers	4,598	6,841	3,737	6,107	—	4,377	—	3,554
Service workers (excl. household)	3,882	6,236	3,550	4,721	1,630	4,047	1,253	3,828

[a] Data refer to all employed persons.
[b] Includes farmers and farm laborers, not shown separately.
[c] Median earnings in 1959; mean earnings in 1973.

Sources: Data for 1959 and 1960, U.S. Bureau of the Census, Current Population Reports, series P-23, no. 37, June 24, 1971, tables 14 and 17; data for 1973 and 1974, unpublished Census Bureau tabulations.

occupational status was improving much more rapidly for blacks living in the suburbs. Obviously, a part of the improvement may be due to the migration of economically successful blacks to the suburbs, whence they commute to high status jobs that they continue to hold in the central city. However, that is unlikely to be the whole explanation. Probably the occupational status of black-held jobs actually located in the suburbs has also improved rapidly.

Table 11.8 also shows that from 1959 to 1973 earnings within occupation increased much faster for blacks living in the suburbs than for central city blacks. This supports the conclusion that the rise in suburban relative to central city income for blacks is not due entirely to the migration to the suburbs of blacks already engaged in high status occupations. It strongly suggests that the rapidly expanding suburban economy provides a more favorable job environment for blacks than does the sluggish or declining economy of the central city. This could be true even if labor market discrimination against blacks is no less a factor in the suburbs than in the central cities.[64]

Studies by Bennett Harrison and Bernard Frieden published in the early 1970s might seem to contradict the results outlined here. Using data from the middle and late 1960s, they found no evidence that economic opportunities were better for blacks in the suburbs.[65] However, their studies were based on data at a moment in time when black income, unemployment rates, and occupational status were about equal in central city and suburb. Because the urban system changes profoundly over time (as almost every chapter of this book has emphasized), one can easily be misled by interarea comparisons that are limited to a single date. Tables 11.7 and 11.8 show that at the beginning of the 1960s black incomes and occupational status were actually inferior in the suburbs. By the late 1960s, as the income data in Table 11.7 suggest, they were approximately equal in the two parts of the SMSA. Both tables show that a modest to substantial suburban advantage has developed since then, which would not have been reflected in Harrison's or Frieden's data.

It bears repeating that, because of data limitations, one cannot be certain how much of the observed "advantage" is the result of superior

---

64. For a recent attempt to measure the extent of racial discrimination in suburban as compared with central city labor markets, see John Vrooman and Stuart Greenfield, "Are Blacks Making It in the Suburbs? Some New Evidence on Intrametropolitan Spatial Segmentation," *Journal of Urban Economics*, March 1980, pp. 155–67.

65. See Bennett Harrison, "The Intrametropolitan Distribution of Minority Economic Welfare," *Journal of Regional Science*, April 1972, pp. 23–43; and Bernard J. Frieden, "Blacks in Suburbia: The Myth of Better Opportunities," in L. Wingo, ed., *Minority Perspectives* (Baltimore: The Johns Hopkins University Press, for Resources for the Future, Inc., 1972), esp. pp. 36–39.

economic opportunity in the suburbs and how much the result of selective black in-migration. As Harrison himself has written, "The definitive analysis awaits the availability of longitudinal data on blacks who have actually *moved* from the central city out to the suburbs."[66] The question deserves much more study.

The opportunities open to the black population in suburbs versus central cities cannot be judged solely in terms of economic measures such as employment, occupational status, and income. There are many other dimensions along which the welfare of black families might plausibly be expected to differ by location, including school quality, school integration, level of nonschool public services, quality of housing, racial integration of neighborhoods, and prevailing crime rate.[67] Limitations of space preclude an examination of most of these. However, we will return in Chapter 13 to the question of suburban housing for blacks and in Chapter 15 to the problem of public service quality in central cities as compared with suburbs.

The Losses Imposed by Segregation

Instead of comparing economic opportunity in central cities and suburbs in an attempt to decide where blacks are most likely to prosper, John F. Kain devised another way of analyzing the connection between racial segregation, job decentralization, and minority-group poverty. Kain concentrated on the effects of housing segregation on job opportunities for minorities and on other indicators of minority-group welfare. In a widely discussed empirical study, he tested the following three interrelated hypotheses: that "racial segregation in the housing markets (1) affects the distribution of Negro employment and (2) reduces Negro job opportunities, and that (3) postwar suburbanization of employment has seriously aggravated the problem."[68] Among the important reasons for expecting housing segregation to affect black employment is the fact that segregation limits workers' freedom to move close to job locations and therefore imposes high travel costs that may discourage them from taking otherwise desirable jobs.

To test his three hypotheses, Kain used data for the metropolitan areas of Chicago and Detroit. He started with two sets of facts for each area: a given segregated pattern of black residence and a given spatial distribution of all jobs in the central city and the suburbs. Using statistical

66. Bennett Harrison, "Discrimination in Space: Suburbanization and Black Unemployment in Cities," in von Furstenberg, Harrison, and Horowitz, vol. 1, p. 32.
67. See Frieden, pp. 39–45.
68. John F. Kain, "Housing Segregation, Negro Employment, and Metropolitan Decentralization," *Quarterly Journal of Economics*, May 1968, p. 176.

techniques, he then examined the effect of the segregated housing pattern on the proportion of blacks in the work force at each job location. Next, he compared the actual level of black employment at each location with an estimate of what its level would be if the black population were distributed evenly over all residential areas instead of being confined to a few ghettos. He found that housing segregation imposed job losses on blacks in both cities. The estimated loss was 22,000 to 24,000 in Chicago and 4,000 to 9,000 in Detroit.

It is but one step from these findings to the argument that the continuing decentralization of jobs within metropolitan areas is likely to reduce black job opportunities still further. Trapped in core city ghettos, blacks will find themselves living at an increasing average distance from the aggregate of job locations. Kain concluded that "the rapid postwar dispersal of employment, accompanied by no reduction and perhaps an increase in housing market segregation, may have placed the Negro job seeker in an even more precarious position."[69]

As Kain has argued elsewhere, the reduction in well-being suffered by blacks as a result of housing segregation goes beyond job losses of the sort estimated above. In addition, those blacks who *do* find employment at outlying job locations are likely to spend more on transportation to work than would be necessary if their housing choices were unrestricted. Finally, the restriction of housing choice imposes a welfare loss on blacks by limiting and distorting their consumption of housing itself.[70] Put very simply, this analysis leads to the conclusion that by limiting freedom of choice segregation cannot help and very probably hurts the segregated minority population. The policy prescription that follows from the analysis is obviously to encourage desegregation, and the appropriate area over which to accomplish desegregation is not just the central city but the entire metropolitan region.

Other Arguments for Dispersion

The case for encouraging voluntary dispersion of minorities gains strength from other considerations as well. In the first place, minorities

69. Ibid., p. 196. Kain's study has been criticized on a number of grounds. See Joseph D. Mooney, "Housing Segregation, Negro Employment . . . An Alternative Perspective," *Quarterly Journal of Economics*, May 1969, pp. 299–311; Paul Offner and Daniel H. Saks, "A Note on Kain's 'Housing Segregation, Negro Employment . . . ,'" *Quarterly Journal of Economics*, February 1971, pp. 147–60; and Kain's reply in von Furstenberg, Harrison, and Horowitz, vol. 1, pp. 5–18.

70. See J. R. Meyer, J. F. Kain, and M. Wohl, *The Urban Transportation Problem* (Cambridge, Mass.: Harvard University Press, 1965), ch. 7; and John F. Kain and John M. Quigley, "Housing Market Discrimination, Homeownership and Savings Behavior," *American Economic Review*, June 1972, pp. 263–77.

certainly ought to enjoy equal access to suburban residence as a matter of right. As we will see in Chapter 13, they are presently denied that right by restrictive zoning and other discriminatory practices. Their outward movement would be encouraged by a program that simply guaranteed them the equal access to which they are justly entitled.

Equally important, the national commitment to the goal of integration requires that we take positive action to stem the development of a society in which most blacks live in central cities and most whites in the suburbs. The extent to which the black population is dispersed within metropolitan areas is indicated by the proportion of all metropolitan blacks who live in the suburbs. In 1960 that proportion stood at 22 percent. By 1970 it had fallen to 21 percent: blacks were becoming less rather than more dispersed. By 1979 the proportion had risen to 26 percent: dispersion was definitely increasing. By way of comparison, however, 64 percent of the white metropolitan population lived in the suburbs in 1979. How many generations will it take for blacks to reach that proportion?

Meanwhile, even though net black in-migration has ended, the absolute size of the black central city population continues to rise as a result of natural increase. In the near future it is unlikely that dispersion can operate fast enough to prevent substantial further growth of the minority population within central cities. That is why dispersion should be thought of, not as an alternative to other policies aimed at the relief of urban poverty, but as complementary to them.

The present pattern of macrosegregation by race and income not only defeats the hope of achieving an integrated society but also weakens the nation's antipoverty program. As we shall see in Chapter 15, local governments help to finance a considerable fraction of all public services, including some that are poverty related. The concentration of poverty within their borders adds to their financial burden while simultaneously weakening the tax base that must bear it. As a result central city residents, including the poor, either receive less in the way of public services or pay higher tax rates to receive the same level than do their counterparts in the suburbs. No one would argue that this outcome is either equitable or consistent with an all-out attack on poverty.

Policies to Encourage Dispersion

A variety of policies have been suggested to encourage the voluntary dispersion of ethnic minorities into the suburbs.[71] Most of these focus on the need to open up the suburbs to low income and lower middle income

71. See Anthony Downs, *Opening Up the Suburbs* (New Haven: Yale University Press, 1973) and the articles by Downs and by Kain and Persky cited in note 53 above.

housing and will be taken up in detail in Chapter 13. Also potentially important are the proposals, outlined in Chapter 15, that call for state assumption of all public education costs and federal assumption of all costs of welfare. These changes would help to reduce the opposition of wealthy suburban communities to low income migrants, who, under present fiscal arrangements, are thought to add more to local expenditure needs than they produce in local tax revenues.

In an often quoted passage, the National Advisory Commission on Civil Disorders in 1968 expressed the view that "our nation is moving toward two societies, one black, one white—separate and unequal." Since that date, to be sure, we have managed a modest reduction in the incidence of poverty, including the poverty of minority groups. Unfortunately, however, the geographic projection of the two societies—the separation into poor, heavily black cities and affluent, largely white suburbs—is still clearly etched on the map of metropolitan America. We cannot fail to recognize the threat that this geographic pattern poses to the institutions of a democratic society; yet to this moment we have hardly begun to deal with the problem.

The Problem of Urban Housing

TWELVE

Since the Industrial Revolution first began to transform Western life, no aspect of society has aroused the passionate concern of reformers more consistently than the condition, and especially the housing condition, of the urban poor. One has only to walk through a slum district in an American city and look inside a few buildings to understand at once the long history of protest and the unending series of proposals for housing reform. Yet despite reform and despite much progress, the slums are still with us. Especially in the older cities of the United States, housing and neighborhood conditions persist that seem to most observers to be wholly unacceptable in a highly affluent society.

The Housing Act of 1949 contained a famous statement of intent: "the Congress hereby declares that the general welfare and security of the Nation and the health and living standards of its people require . . . the realization as soon as feasible of the goal of a decent home and suitable living environment for every American family. . . ." Thereafter, as housing acts followed one another with bewildering frequency, the goal proclaimed in 1949 was sought by means of a continuously changing array of federal programs. Although there was substantial improvement in the condition of the nation's housing, it was not always clear that public policy had helped very much to achieve it. The frequency with which one widely heralded federal program supplemented or replaced another gave rise finally to the suspicion that it was not merely the mechanics but perhaps indeed the very premises of public policy that were mistaken. In the 1980s, although some bad housing and many deteriorating neighborhoods remain, there is a good deal of uncertainty about the direction public policy toward these problems should now take.

We will deal with public policy in Chapter 13. This chapter provides the necessary background. It begins with a discussion of the problem of measuring housing and neighborhood quality. That is followed by a description of the urban housing market, intended to explain why the market might fail to produce "a decent home and suitable living environment for every American family." Both good and bad housing in the United States are largely the products of our system of free enterprise and competitive markets. It is only against the background of private market action that we can sensibly evaluate public policy toward housing.

MEASURING THE QUALITY OF HOUSING AND OF NEIGHBORHOODS

The word "slum" carries with it the sense of an evil environment. Indeed, for the outside observer there is a kind of visceral reaction to the total environment of the "slum" that seems to render systematic analysis unnecessary. Yet rational discussion and effective public policy require that we be able to measure the condition of housing and of neighborhoods on some sort of objective scale.

So far as housing itself is concerned, what we really wish to isolate is the quality of service rendered by a given structure. This quality is exceedingly difficult to measure. It certainly cannot be measured along a unidimensional scale. Ideally the dimensions one would like to consider are the following:

1. The physical condition of the structure. Is it sound or unsound—i.e., well maintained or run down?
2. The extent of utilities and equipment. For example, are electricity and complete plumbing provided?
3. The adequacy of the design. For example, does the unit have sufficient light, air, separation of functions?
4. How crowded is the dwelling? How many rooms or how many square feet of floor space does it contain per person?

In each decennial Census of Housing, a series that began in 1940, the Census Bureau has gathered systematic data on the condition of the nation's housing stock. Of the four dimensions of quality listed above, only the third—adequacy of design—has totally eluded the statisticians. To measure physical condition, the Census of 1950 classified units as either "dilapidated" or "not dilapidated," depending on the seriousness and extent of disrepair observed by the enumerator. The Census of 1960 em-

ployed a three-way classification: "sound," "deteriorating," and "dilapidated." It was up to the Census Bureau's enumerators to judge the
condition of each structure as they made their rounds. However, a post-
Census evaluation revealed that these judgments were quite unreliable.
For that reason, and because the 1970 Census was to be conducted by
mail rather than by enumerators, the topic of overall condition was
dropped from the 1970 questionnaire. Later, responding to protests by
local governments that needed housing condition data, the Census Bureau
conducted a sample survey from which estimates of dilapidation were
calculated for 1970.[1]

To measure adequacy of equipment, the Census records the presence
or absence of a long list of items such as water supply, bathing facilities,
toilet facilities, type of heating equipment, and type of cooking fuel. For
the principal plumbing facilities a further distinction is made between
those shared and those for exclusive use of one dwelling unit. Plumbing
facilities have been singled out as the equipment most relevant to an overall evaluation of housing conditions. By combining information on the
extent of plumbing with information on structural condition, U.S. housing
agencies arrive at a final set of categories to describe the physical aspect
of housing conditions: "standard" housing has been defined as housing
that is not dilapidated and that contains all enumerated plumbing facilities; "substandard" housing comprises all units that are either dilapidated
or lacking one or more of the enumerated plumbing facilities.

To measure crowding, the Census Bureau records the number of
persons and the number of rooms in each dwelling unit and then calculates a persons-per-room ratio. Admittedly, this measure leaves out of
account differences in the size of rooms among various units at any one
date and changes in the average size of rooms over time. However, it does
indicate the extent to which a home provides privacy and separation of
functions, which a floor-space measure would not do. The persons-per-
room ratio can also be faulted for not taking into account "economies of
scale" in the use of rooms. For example, one kitchen will suffice for a
six-person family as easily as for a three-person family, so that six people
in six rooms are probably less "crowded" than three people in three rooms.
But despite these limitations, the persons-per-room ratio is a highly useful
index of crowding. A ratio of 1.01 or more persons per room is taken to
indicate "overcrowding" according to standards now widely accepted in
the United States. (By world standards, 1.01 persons per room would be

---

1. See the discussion in John C. Weicher, "Substandard Housing: the Trend
and Current Situation," in *Housing Delivery System* (Columbus, Ohio: Center for
Real Estate Education and Research, Ohio State University, 1980), pp. 61–62; and
U.S. Bureau of the Census, *Measuring the Quality of Housing*, working paper no.
25, 1967.

regarded as normal or, in many places, luxurious. A United Nations survey found that in the 1960s the average persons-per-room ratio was 2.5 in the less developed nations and 1.1 in Europe and Japan.[2])

A new set of data on housing conditions has been available since 1973. Each year the Annual Housing Survey, conducted by the Census Bureau and the Department of Housing and Urban Development, collects a vast array of information on a nationwide sample of housing units.[3] In addition to data on crowding and on the extent of plumbing, utilities, and equipment comparable to that in the decennial Census, the *Annual Housing Survey* contains questions on equipment breakdowns and on physical conditions such as leaky roofs, holes in floors, and broken plaster. It also elicits subjective data such as the occupant's rating of structure condition on a scale from poor to excellent and the occupant's desire to move. However, no summary measure of structural condition comparable to "dilapidated" is included, so substandard housing, as it was traditionally defined, cannot be directly measured with Annual Housing Survey data.

Neighborhood Quality

To this point we have discussed measures of housing quality that are intended to isolate the quality of service rendered in particular structures. A broader definition would attempt to incorporate neighborhood characteristics as well. When people choose housing they take into account not only the quality of service associated with the particular dwelling unit but the attractiveness of the neighborhood as a place to live. Desirable neighborhood characteristics include such features as adequate park and recreation facilities, good schools, clean streets, and, of particular concern in recent years, freedom from crime.

Observation of housing markets indicates that consumers are willing to pay for the attributes of housing and neighborhood quality that appeal to them. Moreover, what they are willing to pay is one measure of the economic value of such attributes. Kain and Quigley studied a large sample of rental and owner-occupied housing in St. Louis for which they had very detailed information on both housing and neighborhood quality characteristics. They estimated multiple-regression equations to explain the variation in monthly rent (for rental units) or house value (for owner-occupied dwellings). According to these estimates, the quality character-

---

2. See Leland S. Burns and Leo Grebler, *The Housing of Nations* (New York: John Wiley & Sons, 1977), table 1.4.
3. Results for the nationwide sample are published each year in six parts. See U.S. Bureau of the Census, *Current Housing Reports*, series H-150, parts A-F. In addition, 60 individual SMSA's are surveyed in rotation, currently fifteen each year. See *Current Housing Reports*, series H-170, for separate volumes on each SMSA.

istics of a dwelling unit and its immediate physical environment had approximately as much effect on price as did such standard quantitative measures as number of rooms, number of bathrooms, and lot size. Clearly, housing and neighborhood quality do matter.[4]

Until the early 1960s housing analysts, following a tradition that went back to the reforms of the late nineteenth century, concentrated their attention on housing conditions, narrowly defined, and devoted relatively little attention to the characteristics of neighborhoods. However, the urban riots of the 1960s focused attention on the importance of neighborhood to social well-being. Reflecting this growing interest, the Annual Housing Survey (described above) collects data on a wide range of neighborhood conditions. It would be virtually impossible in a nationwide survey to assemble objective data such as local crime rate or extent of street litter for neighborhoods. Consequently, the information collected by the Annual Housing Survey is subjective in nature. Occupants are asked to indicate whether they are dissatisfied with conditions such as street noise and crime or with services such as schools, recreation facilities, and police protection. In short, the Survey indicates how residents feel about their neighborhoods.

Before examining the evidence on housing and neighborhood conditions in American cities, we turn to a description of the urban housing market, since an understanding of that market is essential to the analysis of those conditions.

AN "ADAPTIVE" MODEL OF THE HOUSING MARKET

How does the housing market function to produce the mixture of good and bad housing that is found in every U.S. city? For the sake of simplicity, the following discussion assumes that the market is entirely a rental one. Although only 41 percent of urban housing units are renter occupied, focusing on rental housing is justified by the fact that it contains a majority of the overcrowded and substandard urban units. Intro-

---

4. John F. Kain and John M. Quigley, "Measuring the Value of Housing Quality," *Journal of The American Statistical Association*, June 1970, pp. 532–48. Numerous other studies have estimated the influence of individual housing and neighborhood attributes on rent and price. See, for example, Robert F. Gillingham, *Place-to-Place Rent Comparisons Using Hedonic Quality Adjustment Techniques*, BLS staff paper 8, U.S. Bureau of Labor Statistics, 1975; Mingche M. Li and H. James Brown, "Micro-Neighborhood Externalities and Hedonic Housing Prices," *Land Economics*, May 1980, pp. 125–41; and the review of the literature by A. Myrick Freeman III, "The Hedonic Price Approach to Measuring Demand for Neighborhood Characteristics," in David Segal, ed., *The Economics of Neighborhood* (New York: Academic Press, 1979), pp. 191–217.

ducing an ownership sector would add greatly to the complexity of the analysis while not substantially changing its conclusions.

Rapkin, Winnick, and Blank have pointed out that if we use terms from conventional economic theory, the rental housing market in a large city is probably best thought of as an instance of monopolistic competition among a large number of sellers.[5] Competition cannot be described as "pure," since the units supplied are clearly differentiated by size, quality, and location. On the other hand, the very large number of sellers and the small size of the largest in relation to the whole market ensure that effective competition takes place. There is no possibility of monopoly, no collusion among sellers, no tendency for suppliers to become involved in oligopolistic strategies: each building owner behaves as if the market situation were "given" and assumes that his own decisions have no effect upon it. (To be sure, there are some important imperfections in the urban housing market—most notably the prevalence of racial discrimination. We will not neglect these but rather hold them for consideration together with public policy toward housing in the next chapter.)

Because buildings are expensive, durable, and immovable, the housing market differs in important respects from most other consumer goods markets. From the high cost and durability of shelter it follows that in any one year almost the entire supply of housing services is provided by the standing stock. New construction on the average adds only 2 or 3 percent per year to the housing supply of the nation as a whole, and a part of that goes to offset the annual toll of demolitions. If the adjustment of supply to changes in demand could take place only through new construction, the process would be even more cumbersome, slow, and expensive than, in fact, it is. Fortunately, adjustments on the supply side take place not only through new construction but through a series of complex changes by which the quality of existing units, and therefore their rent level, is "adapted" to the pattern of demand expressed in the market for housing services. For example, if a given class of occupants moves out of a neighborhood, the housing they leave behind is usually too valuable to be demolished, since it is still capable of rendering service. Hence it will generally be adapted by alteration of its quality to meet the needs of another class. Thus the character of the housing stock in a particular place frequently changes under the influence of market forces in ways that neither city planners nor housing policy administrators can readily control. Probably the greatest weakness in U.S. housing policy has been its failure to acknowledge the power (and therefore to anticipate

5. Chester Rapkin, Louis Winnick, and David M. Blank, *Housing Market Analysis*, Housing and Home Finance Agency, 1953, p. 22.

the consequences) of the adaptive process in the urban housing market. We will therefore return to a detailed examination of that process below.

In analyzing any housing market it is well to keep in mind one seemingly obvious but frequently neglected fact: every family has to live somewhere (though not necessarily in a separate dwelling unit). Hence the function of the market is, broadly speaking, to match up the population of families with the existing stock of housing. Since family income is the principal determinant of housing demand, this function reduces essentially to matching up a distribution of families by amount of income with a distribution of housing units by rent level. The market operates like a game of musical chairs—except that each family ordinarily ends up with a chair. Unless the number of separately residing households or the stock of housing changes, each move that fills one vacancy creates another somewhere else. When the stock increases relative to the number of households, each new unit that attracts a tenant creates a vacancy elsewhere; likewise, each demolition that removes a unit fills up a vacancy in some other part of the stock, unless the number of households is diminishing. Obviously, partial equilibrium analysis restricted to one sector of a city's housing market can be very misleading. It is usually necessary to trace out the consequences of any change for the entire stock within a given market.

The phrase "given market," of course, conceals many ambiguities. The poor family living in a central city slum is not in the market for luxury apartments, though these may stand only a few blocks from where it lives. For the middle and upper classes the choice is certainly wider. Though living in a central city apartment, the well-to-do family probably finds the suburban owner-occupied house a closer substitute for its present home than a slum flat would be. Nevertheless, the central city rental market is best treated as a continuum, for there is a distribution of housing over all rent classes and a distribution of families over all income levels. The market thus provides a series of small steps by which a household can move up or down the scale of housing quality. The possibility of families making these small substitutions binds the entire range of housing into one market, since there are no gaps at which one can draw logical dividing lines.

Varying the Supply of Housing "Quality"

Looked at from the supply side, the urban housing market is bound together by the adaptability of structures. Just as tenants can move from one rent class into the next, so owners can "move" their buildings from one rent class to another by remodeling, dividing, or combining units or by changing the level of outlays for operation and maintenance.[6] It is useful to think of the owner not just as an "investor" in real estate but as an entrepreneur who is in the business of operating rental housing. The owner's objective is to maintain and operate a building at the level of quality that will maximize profits. Higher levels of quality of housing service will command higher rents but will also cost more to produce. The owner's task is to find the most profitable combination.

Given the basic structure and layout of a particular building, the quality of housing service produced in it depends on two factors. The first is the annual level of operating outlays incurred by the owner. For example, higher outlays might take the form of increased expenditures for cleaning and painting or for heating fuel, minor repairs, or security against crime. The owner will expand these outlays as long as each dollar of additional expense generates more than a dollar of additional gross income from rents. The most profitable combination occurs at the level of operating expense at which one more dollar of outlay would just return one more dollar of rent. In the conventional terminology of price theory, the owner pushes service output to the point at which marginal revenue equals marginal cost.

The second factor that affects quality in a given structure is the frequency with which deteriorating structural parts or equipment are replaced. In general, major elements of structure or equipment do not suddenly and completely cease to function. Rather they deteriorate gradually, as a plumbing system does, providing less satisfactory service as they grow older. It follows that the shorter the average period over which such elements are replaced, the higher the level of service rendered in the building. But also, the shorter the period of replacement, the higher the annual amount of depreciation that the owner must charge as a cost. Those who wish to enjoy high-quality housing service must be willing to pay a high enough rent premium for new as compared with old equipment to make frequent replacement investment profitable to the owner.

Finally, structures themselves can be altered by investment in re-

6. For further elaboration of this point and for references to earlier literature on the housing market, see James Heilbrun, *Real Estate Taxes and Urban Housing* (New York: Columbia University Press, 1966), chs. 2 and 4. Adaptive models of the housing market have also been formulated by Richard F. Muth in *Cities and Housing* (Chicago: University of Chicago Press, 1969), ch. 6; and Edgar O. Olsen, "A Competitive Theory of the Housing Market," *American Economic Review*, September 1969, pp. 612–22. John F. Kain and William C. Apgar, Jr., describe a simulation model of an urban housing market containing an adaptive mechanism in "Simulation of Housing Market Dynamics," *Journal of the American Real Estate and Urban Economics Association*, Winter 1979, pp. 505–38. A review of recent economic analyses of urban housing markets and an extensive bibliography is provided in John M. Quigley, "What Have We Learned About Urban Housing Markets?" in P. Mieszkowski and M. Straszheim, eds., *Current Issues in Urban Economics* (Baltimore: The Johns Hopkins University Press, 1979), pp. 391–429.

modeling. This is the most obvious way of "moving" a building within the rent distribution to meet changed conditions of demand. Apartments can be divided into smaller units or combined into larger ones, or they can be remodeled to overcome design obsolescence and/or to introduce more up-to-date equipment. The owner will invest in remodeling if the expected return on the required funds exceeds the opportunity cost of capital.

The Demand for Housing Space and Quality

Rental housing units differ from one another in three important respects: location within the city, size, and quality. In general the rent will be higher the more central the location, the larger the number of rooms, and the higher the quality of the apartment. For a given rental outlay a family can obtain a smaller apartment of higher quality or a larger apartment of lower quality. Each family will presumably choose that combination of space and quality which best suits its needs, income, and tastes.

Since quality and space compete for the consumer's housing dollar, it is apparent that given the level of consumer incomes, attempts to raise the quality of housing may, if they require a rise in rents, tend to *increase* the degree of overcrowding. Conversely, overcrowding could be reduced by increasing the supply of *low* quality, low price housing. Thus the two major objectives of public policy toward housing—to increase quality and to reduce overcrowding—are potentially in conflict with each other, given the constraint of a fixed level of consumer income and rent-paying capacity.

The Effect of Income on the Demand for Housing

The principal factors shaping a family's demand for housing are income and family size. The higher its income, the more it will spend on housing. The response of housing expenditures to change in the level of income is measured by the income elasticity of demand, which is defined as percentage change in expenditure ÷ percentage change in income.

The income elasticity of demand for housing has been studied repeatedly and with varying results. In an important theoretical and empirical analysis of urban housing, Muth found that the income elasticities of demand for housing "tend to cluster around a value just slightly greater than +1" in 1950 for a sample of six cities studied individually.[7] Margaret Reid, in another comprehensive analysis, estimated that the income elas-

7. Muth, p. 199.

ticity of consumption of rooms per person was only about one-third as high as the income elasticity of housing consumption.[8] This means that although consumption of space rises as family income goes up, the amount spent on increased space can account for only a minor share of the increase in family housing expenditure that occurs as income rises. The major share must therefore be accounted for by a rise in the quality of the space consumed—i.e., by a rise in rent paid per room. In short, these figures imply that the income elasticity of demand for housing *quality* is quite high. As Reid explains it:

> For several decades high quality housing appears to have been an important feature distinguishing the consumption of the rich from that of the poor. Housing improves markedly as one goes up the economic hierarchy of consumers—much more than does food and clothing and probably even more than automobiles . . . with housing as with food, increase in quality rather than sheer quantity accounts for most of the rise in consumption with normal income.[9]

Muth's findings directly confirm the effects of income on housing quality that are only implied in Reid's study. He measured quality by means of the proportion of housing that was "substandard," using the regular Census definition of that term. In his sample of six cities he found that the income elasticity of substandard housing averaged about -2.5; in other words, a 1 percent *rise* in the level of income would, on the average, bring about a 2.5 percent *decline* in the proportion of housing that was substandard. For the same cities he found that the income elasticity of overcrowding was also about -2.5.[10] These are powerful relationships. They indicate, for example, that a 20 percent increase in real family income, which might occur over a period of one decade, would cause a 50 percent reduction in the incidence of substandard and overcrowded housing (since $2.5 \times .20 = .50$).

Subsequent studies of the income elasticity of demand for housing place its value somewhat below the level estimated by Muth. Recent estimates for renters range from .7 to 1.0, while those for homeowners are usually somewhat higher.[11] Even these lower levels, however, indicate a

8. Margaret G. Reid, *Housing and Income* (Chicago: University of Chicago Press, 1962), pp. 376, 378.
9. Ibid., pp. 377–78.
10. Muth, pp. 199–200.
11. See Frank de Leeuw, "The Demand for Housing: A Review of Cross-Section Evidence," *Review of Economics and Statistics*, February 1971, pp. 1–10; T. H. Lee and C. M. Kong, "Elasticities of Housing Demand," *Southern Economic Journal*, October 1977, pp. 298–305; and A. M. Polinsky and D. T. Ellwood, "An Empirical Reconciliation of Micro and Grouped Estimates of the Demand for Housing," *Review of Economics and Statistics*, May 1979, pp. 199–205. Most recently, considerably lower estimates have been calculated using data from the Experimental Housing Allowance Program. See ch. 13, n. 46.

strongly positive relationship between housing quality and income. As we shall see, this income effect helps to explain the rapid decline in the incidence of substandard housing in the United States over the last 30 years. But there is a darker side, too. The relationship between housing quality and income suggests that substandard housing is likely to persist where poverty persists. Central cities, with their concentrations of low income population, will find it especially difficult to eliminate inadequate housing.

The High Cost of New Construction

For many years one of the major sources of dissatisfaction with the whole enterprise of housing has been the high cost of new construction. Over the years economic progress has greatly reduced the "real cost" of most consumer goods in the United States: historically, per capita income has been rising much faster than the prices of the things people buy, so decade by decade the average family finds its real income, or level of purchasing power, rising. Housing is something of an exception, however. Through most of this century the cost of new residential construction has been rising faster than the general price level.

Figure 12.1 displays price and income trends since 1950. (An earlier starting point would show much the same thing.) From 1950 to 1980 per capita disposable income rose 479 percent. Consumer prices on the average rose 240 percent over the same period. *Real* disposable income per capita (disposable income measured in constant dollars) increased by 86 percent.[12] This last figure means that consumers could, on the average, buy almost twice the quantity of goods and services with their 1980 incomes that they had been able to purchase with their smaller incomes in 1950. Residential construction costs, however, rose 327 percent from 1950 to 1980, far above the rate of increase for consumer prices as a whole. Consequently, for the average consumer, the capacity to purchase new housing has increased far less rapidly than the ability to purchase most other goods. (Admittedly, indexes of construction cost must be used cautiously in analyzing housing problems. First of all, comparisons between widely separated points in time are subject to a degree of error on account of changes in quality and in the mix of physical elements that constitute "housing." Second, the capital cost of housing is only one item among the many that contribute to the annual cost of occupancy—others include maintenance and operating costs, taxes, interest rates on mortgage loans, and insurance.)[13]

12. It should be noted that the Consumer Price Index is *not* the deflator used by the Commerce Department in calculating real per capita income.

13. See U.S. Department of Housing and Urban Development, *Housing in the Seventies*, 1974, ch. 8, "The Cost of Housing."

FIGURE 12.1

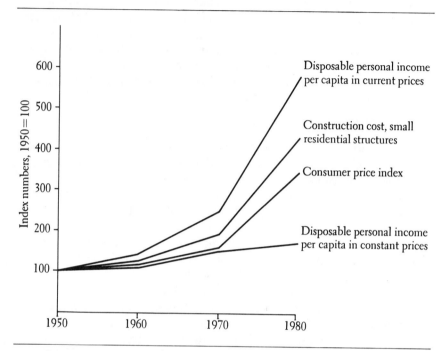

Source: Index numbers have been calculated from the following statistical series: U.S. Department of Commerce series on per capita disposable personal income in current prices and in 1972 prices; E. H. Boeckh and Associates, index of construction costs for small residential structures; Bureau of Labor Statistics, Consumer Price Index.

Our concern at this point, however, is not with the problem of the high cost of housing but rather with the way high construction costs affect the functioning of the housing market: in recent years the construction of dwellings that meet minimum standards in our large cities has been so expensive that only relatively well-to-do families can afford to live in new unsubsidized housing. For example, at a conservative estimate the market rent for a newly-constructed two-bedroom apartment in a large city in the late 1970s was about $500 to $600 a month, or $6,000 to $7,200 a year. To live in such an apartment at a rent-income ratio of .25 (about average for the U.S.) a family would need to earn between $24,000 and $28,800 a year. Yet in 1979 only 23 percent of families in the central cities of large SMSA's earned as much as $25,000, and the median level was only $17,776.[14]

14. U.S. Bureau of the Census, *Current Population Reports,* series P-60, no. 125, October 1980, table 15.

For the great majority of families, new, commercially financed housing in large cities is now clearly out of reach. Apart from the possibility of living in new units subsidized in some way by the government, they are consigned to the second-hand market in housing. Of course, this is not necessarily to be deplored. Most people live in second-hand housing—as Grigsby has remarked, even Queen Elizabeth does. The point is, rather, that the inability of most families to afford new housing does clearly shape the process by which new construction is absorbed into the standing stock: new housing, unless subsidized by the government, enters near the upper end of the rent distribution and triggers a series of adjustments by which older housing then shifts down into lower rent classes. This hand-me-down process is known as "filtering." To be sure, some of the low rent, low quality housing still in use was built for the low end of the market to begin with, at a date when minimum standards, and therefore costs, were lower than they are today. A large portion of it, however, reached the low rent category by "filtering down."

The "Filtering" Process

Grigsby points out that the term "filtering" seems to cause no misunderstanding when used in casual discussion, but that when housing analysts have attempted more precise definitions they find agreement difficult.[15] This is hardly surprising, since the single term "filtering" must bear the burden of describing a large part of the complex process by which adjustments take place in the match-up between the stock of housing units and the tenant population. For our purposes it will suffice to use one of the conventional general definitions and say that filtering takes place when housing once occupied by a higher income group is released by them and becomes available at a lower cost to tenants with lower incomes.

The filtering process gets under way when families in the middle and upper classes move into new housing. The housing thus vacated becomes available to others, to whom it appears better than the dwellings they had. Let us assume no change in population or in the level of family incomes while this process goes on. In that case, when the well-to-do move out of their old housing, its owners quite certainly will have to reduce rents a bit to attract tenants from the next lower income class. The tenants so attracted will vacate other units whose owners will, in turn, reduce rents to attract a still lower income class. Thus a whole chain of moves will take place, made possible by a series of rent reductions. At the

15. William Grigsby, *Housing Markets and Public Policy* (Philadelphia: University of Pennsylvania Press, 1963), pp. 85–86.

end of the chain the poorest families will, presumably, leave the worst housing for something slightly better, and the worst housing will stand vacant or be demolished.

This is a highly schematic explanation, blessedly simplified by the assumption of static population and income. But let us stick to our simplifications a little longer. Why under these circumstances would the upper income classes wish to move into new housing? Numerous motives exist, provided we do not insist on a completely static world. New neighborhoods become fashionable, old buildings become unfashionable or do not offer the latest equipment and conveniences, new modes of housekeeping lead to changes in interior design, architectural styles change, and so on. These can be regarded as various forms of obsolescence.

It is sometimes suggested that age per se leads to physical deterioration of housing and that the well-to-do move out to avoid this. But housing need not deteriorate with age if it is well maintained. In most cases, therefore, physical deterioration should be regarded not as an independent causal factor but as the result of a change in the demand for particular units, which in turn leads to a reduced level of maintenance. As we argued earlier, reducing outlays for maintenance (and for operation, as well) is one of the ways in which owners "move" buildings from one segment of the market to another in response to changes in demand. This view of the matter is supported by the obvious fact that old buildings are often "improved," moved "up" rather than "down," when an old neighborhood becomes suddenly fashionable.

If we introduce the reality of rising living standards, still holding population constant, the filtering process becomes more complicated. If the rich are growing richer, then perhaps they move into new housing because they want something even more opulent than what they had. If the class below them is also growing in wealth perhaps it can move up without a reduction in rent into the housing vacated by the rich. One might then imagine a series of upward moves by all families, while the rents of all occupied housing units remained unchanged. That is too simple, however, since the income classes are not of equal size and cannot fit neatly into the housing vacated by those directly above them. The picture becomes still more complex if we introduce changes in the number, size, and age distribution of households. But there is no need to go further. The details of adjustment will obviously vary with the demands put upon the system. No single description can cover all cases.

Filtering is sometimes defended as the principal way in which we can hope to raise the housing standards of the poor—and often attacked for having failed to do just that. This conflict is correctly resolved by granting that each contention is true in a specifically definable way. In the earlier discussion of the rental housing market it was pointed out that the quality of housing service provided in a given building depends partly on its fixed physical features and equipment and partly on the level of maintenance and operating expenditures applied to them as, so to speak, "variable inputs" by the owner. Filtering *can* raise housing standards insofar as these are concerned with the more or less permanent physical characteristics of buildings; it *cannot* do so insofar as they depend on the owner's inputs of maintenance and operating expense that vary directly with the rent level he is attempting to establish. There are undoubtedly some families now living in standard, filtered-down housing for whom it represents an improvement over what they could have paid for out of the same real income in decades past. The improvement, however, is likely to be not in the level of maintenance or operating services but in the physical features of design and equipment: more light and air, more plumbing, fireproof construction, and so on.

On the debit side, it must be admitted that some of the substandard housing now in use has reached its present disreputable state precisely by the process of filtering down. This is hardly surprising, since low income tenants usually require low rent housing, and low rent housing is often substandard. When the supply of low rent units is insufficient to meet demand, the market is capable of creating more of them either by breaking up larger units or by economizing on maintenance and operating outlays. In the process, additions may be made to the substandard stock. Or, if one thinks in terms of occupancy rather than physical standards, units that filter down may well move into the "overcrowded" category, since lower income tenants economize on rent by using space more intensively. In short, "filtering" is one of the mechanisms by which the adaptive market we have been describing adjusts the services supplied by the housing stock to the demands of the resident population.

Against this background we can now examine recent trends in U.S. housing conditions.

TRENDS IN U.S. HOUSING CONDITIONS

According to all the standard measures, U.S. housing conditions have improved markedly in the last thirty years. Table 12.1 shows separately the incidence of overcrowding (more than 1.0 persons per room) and of substandard housing (units that lack complete plumbing or are dilapidated), as recorded by the Census in 1950, 1960, and 1970 and by the Annual Housing Survey in 1977. Whether one looks at urban or rural areas or at white- or black-occupied units, the trend is the same—there has been a remarkable decline in both overcrowding and substandard conditions.

It comes as no surprise to see in Table 12.1 that the housing con-

TABLE 12.1
Trends in the Condition of Urban and Rural Housing by Race of Occupant, 1950–77[a]

	ALL RACES		WHITE[b]		BLACK[c]	
	Urban	*Rural*	*Urban*	*Rural*	*Urban*	*Rural*
Overcrowded Housing (Percentage of units occupied by 1.01 or more persons per room)						
1950	13.3	20.6	—	—	—	—
1960	10.2	15.1	8.5	12.9	24.7	40.8
1970	7.6	10.1	6.3	8.8	18.1	30.1
1977	4.4	5.0	3.8	4.3	9.6	16.4
Substandard Housing (Percentage of dilapidated or lacking complete plumbing facilities)[d]						
1950	21.9	62.4	18.2	59.1	61.2	96.3
1960	9.6	32.6	7.0	28.0	31.8	85.5
1970	5.5	16.0	4.3	13.7	15.2	65.4
1977	1.3	5.0	1.0	3.6	3.6	27.8

[a] Data refer to combined totals for owner-occupants and renters.

[b] In 1950 and 1960, includes only whites; in 1970 and 1977, includes whites and other races except black.

[c] In 1950 and 1960, includes all nonwhites; in 1970 and 1977, includes only blacks.

[d] Since data on dilapidation were not collected, 1977 figures refer to plumbing condition only.

Sources: U.S. Bureau of the Census, *Census of Population and Housing, 1950, 1960, 1970,* and *Annual Housing Survey: 1977,* Part E; and Housing and Home Finance Agency, *Our Nonwhite Population and Its Housing,* 1963.

dition of blacks is far inferior to that of whites in urban as well as rural areas: the incidence both of overcrowding and of substandard conditions in black-occupied housing averages about three times what it does in units occupied by whites. However, the table also reveals that conditions are improving just as fast in black- as in white-occupied urban housing. Between 1960 and 1977 the incidence of overcrowding declined 61 percent among urban blacks and 55 percent among whites, while the incidence of substandard conditions fell 89 percent among urban blacks as compared with 86 percent for whites.[16]

Since the mid-1970s, the Annual Housing Surveys have made available a wide range of new information on both housing and neighborhood conditions. Table 12.2 shows some of its results for rental housing, when respondents are classified by race, income, and place of residence. Four indicators are presented. Two show the percentage of tenants whose overall rating of their building or neighborhood is "poor"; two indicate the percentage of tenants who wish to move because of structural deficiencies in their building or bothersome neighborhood conditions. Each number in the table can therefore be read as an index of "substantial dissatisfaction." Four conclusions stand out:

1. Both inside and outside central cities, the rate of dissatisfaction with housing and neighborhood conditions is at least twice as high for blacks as for whites and other races.[17]

2. For both racial groups, dissatisfaction is more frequent in central cities than in suburbs, but the difference is not as great as might have been expected.

3. There is considerably more dissatisfaction with condition of neighborhood than with condition of structure. Among whites and other races, the proportion who want to move because of bothersome neighborhood conditions is twice the proportion who want to move because of structural deficiencies. Among blacks, neighborhood conditions produce a desire to move about 50 percent more often than structural deficiencies.

16. It should be recalled that "dilapidation" was not measured in 1977. "Substandard" in that year therefore consists only of units "lacking complete plumbing facilities."

17. It might be questioned whether racial differences in opinion of housing and neighborhood arise from true disparities in circumstance or merely from differences in racial attitudes. A recent study found that more than half the difference in opinion can be accounted for by objectively measurable differences in housing conditions and socioeconomic status. See Stephen C. Casey, "The Effect of Race on Opinions of Housing and Neighborhood Quality," in George Sternlieb and others, *America's Housing, Prospects and Problems* (New Brunswick, N.J.: Center for Urban Policy Research, Rutgers University, 1980), pp. 485–542.

TABLE 12.2
Opinions of Structure and Neighborhood by Race, Location, and Income, Metropolitan Area Rental Housing, 1977

	PERCENTAGE OF HOUSEHOLDS REPORTING EACH OPINION BY INCOME CLASS					
	Less than $5,000	*$5,000 to $10,000*	*$10,000 to $15,000*	*$15,000 to $25,000*	*Over $25,000*	*All Income Classes*
White and other races						
Central cities						
Opinion of structure: poor	6.3%	5.6%	5.9%	4.8%	3.3%	5.6%
Structural deficiencies, want to move	5.3	4.2	4.1	3.1	3.5	4.3
Opinion of neighborhood: poor	8.6	6.2	4.3	3.3	2.7	5.7
Bothersome neighborhood conditions, want to move	8.4	7.1	10.5	8.7	6.8	8.4
Outside central cities						
Opinion of structure: poor	5.0	5.3	4.3	4.5	2.6	3.9
Structural deficiencies, want to move	2.6	2.8	1.9	2.9	1.6	2.5
Opinion of neighborhood: poor	2.6	3.6	2.8	2.4	1.7	2.8
Bothersome neighborhood conditions, want to move	6.5	8.3	6.7	7.2	5.0	7.0
Black						
Central cities						
Opinion of structure: poor	11.9	13.3	13.9	9.4	2.5	12.1
Structural deficiencies, want to move	11.7	11.9	7.5	6.9	8.9	10.5
Opinion of neighborhood: poor	11.2	12.6	7.7	10.0	2.5	10.7
Bothersome neighborhood conditions, want to move	15.6	16.4	18.1	11.9	12.7	15.8
Outside central cities						
Opinion of structure: poor	14.3	10.2	6.9	6.1	4.4	9.9
Structural deficiencies, want to move	13.9	5.4	8.4	3.5	15.6	9.0
Opinion of neighborhood: poor	13.0	7.3	5.3	5.3	6.7	8.4
Bothersome neighborhood conditions, want to move	15.6	11.7	11.5	9.6	17.8	12.9

4. As expected, there is a fairly strong inverse relationship between tenant income and opinion of structure and neighborhood. However, the relationship between the desire to *move* because of unsatisfactory conditions and income appears to be quite irregular.

The relationship of housing condition to income emerges more clearly in a tabulation of deficiencies computed by the Congressional Budget Office from the 1976 Survey. A dwelling unit was classified as "in need of rehabilitation" if it suffered from one or more of a list of major deficiencies. In the nation as a whole 7.8 percent of occupied housing was so classified. However, among households with incomes below $10,000 a year, the rate was 24.9 percent for blacks and 10.6 percent for whites. The rate was less than one-third as high for households of either race with incomes of $20,000 or more.[18]

Table 12.1 shows that, despite great improvement, housing conditions remain far worse for rural than for urban blacks. The surprisingly large percentage of rural black housing that still ranks as substandard is undoubtedly a tribute to the persistence of the rural outhouse. For the black population as a whole, however, the high incidence of substandard and overcrowded housing in rural areas is mitigated by the very rapid decline in the absolute size of the rural black population. That decline came about as a result of the massive migration of blacks from rural to urban areas, and migration, in turn, accounts for much of the improvement in black housing conditions since 1950.

First of all, in migrating, blacks moved from rural areas where housing codes were almost unknown and standards were low to urban areas with relatively stringent housing codes: occupancy of housing without full plumbing facilities is now illegal for families in many large cities. Second, black migration into cities was linked to white out-migration through the filtering process. Blacks were able to move into housing that filtered down to them as whites moved out to the suburbs. Much of that housing had been built to middle class standards of an earlier era and was equipped with full plumbing (and other physical features) to meet the demands of its original higher income occupants. By and large, these physical features remained intact as the units filtered down to lower income occupants. Finally, the rapid decline in overcrowded conditions among urban blacks is also associated with the out-migration of the white population. As whites have moved out, the population of many central cities has declined sharply, leaving room within the housing stock for the black population to spread out, thus reducing the extent of overcrowding.

18. Congressional Budget Office, *Federal Housing Policy: Current Problems and Recurring Issues,* June 1978, tables 1 and 8.

Average black family income has, of course, increased substantially in the last thirty years and undoubtedly played a part in the long-run improvement of black housing conditions. It would be a mistake, however, to overlook the importance of the gross population movements described above. For example, the real income of black families in central cities actually declined during the 1970s (see Table 11.7). Hence, the reduction in overcrowding after 1970 cannot be an effect of higher income; it may well have been an effect of population decline.

Is There Still an Urban Housing Problem?

The persistent and impressive decline in the incidence of substandard and overcrowded urban housing traced in Table 12.1 has brought us to the point where some housing analysts have been asking, "Is there still a housing problem?" Let us try to summarize the present situation.

Despite the general improvement in urban housing conditions, most studies concur in citing these remaining problems:

1. The high cost of housing, and especially its burden on low income households
2. Continuing discrimination in housing markets
3. Concentrations of bad housing in the poverty areas of inner cities
4. The rise of seemingly intractable neighborhood problems in poverty areas

The question of discrimination in housing will be taken up in the next chapter. Within the housing markets of inner cities the other three problems are interconnected, and it is to them that we now turn.

In the United States, the proportion of renter households paying 25 percent or more of their income for housing rose steadily from 31 percent in 1950 to 47 percent in 1976. Among renter households with incomes below $10,000 in 1976, 61 percent had rent-income ratios above .25, and 38 percent had ratios above .35. Nineteen percent paid more than half their income in rent.[19]

We have shown that the median level of real family income in central cities has fallen since 1969, substantially so for black families. (See Table 11.7.) Many of the urban poor lack the rent-paying capacity needed to sustain minimum standard housing in the face of rapidly inflating costs. Frank Kristof has concluded that in cities with large poverty populations "the household budgets of one-quarter to one-third of their households do not permit these households to pay the full cost of proper maintenance

19. Ibid., tables 3 and 4.

of older existing housing."[20] Under these circumstances one would expect landlords in low income neighborhoods to reduce the level of maintenance and operating outlays, bringing about a gradual deterioration in the condition of housing. In fact, that is just what is going on. Much of the housing in low income neighborhoods is not being maintained at a stable, if low, level of quality. Instead, it is being used up, its physical structure literally being consumed rather than maintained. A process of disinvestment is underway that frequently ends in abandonment. In this process measurable housing conditions in the aggregate of occupied buildings may not be found to deteriorate because population decline enables the poor to move on when buildings become uninhabitable. As we shall see, however, the process itself is dangerous and painful and destroys not only buildings but whole neighborhoods as well.

The Problem of Abandonment

The phenomenon known as housing abandonment first came to public attention in the late 1960s. In city after city, owners of rental housing in low income neighborhoods simply "walked away" from their properties. Evidently they had found that their buildings could no longer be operated profitably and could not be sold, since other investors were also trying to withdraw from the low income rental sector. Under the circumstances owners attempted to retrieve some capital by "milking" their properties—continuing to collect rent while withholding maintenance and operating services and failing to pay taxes and mortgage charges. When the building finally became uninhabitable, they abandoned it.

Abandonment has apparently been encouraged by the growth of crime and vandalism. If an apartment in a building in a high crime neighborhood falls vacant, it is often immediately vandalized. Damage to the structure and fear of crime cause other tenants to move out. Vacancies increase. Further vandalism follows, soon leaving the building uninhabitable. Alternatively, if the landlord tries to maximize short-run revenue by eliminating all vacancies, the outcome is likely to be the same: screening processes are dropped, and all prospective tenants are accepted no matter how irresponsible or destructive they are likely to be. Again crime and vandalism ensue, hastening the building's demise. When finally abandoned, the structure often becomes a home for criminal intruders and a scene of fires, thus further contaminating the neighborhood for those

20. Frank S. Kristof, "Federal Housing Policies: Subsidized Production, Filtration and Objectives: Part II," *Land Economics*, May 1973, p. 171. Also see Ira S. Lowry, ed., *Confronting the Crisis*, vol. I of *Rental Housing in New York City* (New York: New York City Rand Institute, February 1970), document no. RM-6190-NYC.

living in buildings that have not yet reached that extreme state. Clearly, abandonment contributes to, and is itself a function of, neighborhood distress.[21]

Analytically one can separate the causes of abandonment into two classes.[22] The first comprises the "normal" forces of demand and supply. On the demand side, abandonment is encouraged by the low rent-paying capacity of impoverished tenants, and the poorest of all are typically the racial minorities in poverty areas where abandonment has been most frequent. On the supply side, the rapidly rising cost of housing service inputs has made it increasingly difficult to maintain and operate low rent housing at an acceptable quality level.

The second class of causes of abandonment includes those special social and institutional factors that seem to exacerbate the housing problem in low income areas: frequent rent skipping and rent delinquency by tenants, the high incidence of crime and vandalism, racial tension between landlords and minority-group tenants, unwillingness of financial institutions to make mortgage loans on low income housing, and, finally, the small scale of operation and minimum competence in management of many rental housing owners in poverty areas.

There is ample reason to believe that both sets of factors have been at work and that their interaction makes matters worse. On the one hand, crime, vandalism, and antisocial behavior raise the maintenance costs of building owners, thus reducing the quality of service that they will—or can—offer at any given rent level. On the other hand, the low rent-paying capacity of the poor in the face of rising costs undoubtedly hastened the withdrawal of private financial institutions from their normal role of supporting investment in the maintenance of the low rent housing stock.

However painful and destructive abandonment has been for both tenants and landlords, it has, at least, forced us to clear away some very unhelpful illusions about low income housing markets. As George Sternlieb points out, we have long subscribed to the folklore that slum landlords

> grow very fat, indeed, on the high rents and low input which their tenants and buildings are subjected to . . . a satisfying illusion

21. For further detail see George Sternlieb and Robert W. Burchell, *Residential Abandonment: The Tenement Landlord Revisited* (New Brunswick, N.J.: Center for Urban Policy Research, Rutgers University, 1973); Kristof, pp. 166–69; U.S. Department of Housing and Urban Development, *The Dynamics of Neighborhood Change,* HUD-PDR-108, 1975; Peter D. Salins, *The Ecology of Housing Destruction* (New York: New York University Press, for the International Center for Economic Policy Studies, 1980); and Michael A. Stegman, *Housing Investment in the Inner City: The Dynamics of Decline* (Cambridge, Mass.: M.I.T. Press, 1972).
22. Philip H. Friedly, "Experimental Approaches to the Amelioration of Housing Abandonment and Neighborhood Decline," *Proceedings* of the American Real Estate and Urban Economics Association, VI (1971) 154.

because it has in turn permitted us the belief that all that is required in low income housing was a repartitioning of an already adequate rent pie. Whether through code enforcement, rent controls, or any of a host of other mechanisms, the problem of good maintenance could be resolved by squeezing some of the excess profits out of the landlord's hands. This process would still leave enough of a residue to maintain his self-interests in the longevity and satisfactory quality of the structure in question. This bit of folklore may have had considerable validity a decade or two ago. It has little relationship to the realities currently.[23]

If it has done nothing else, abandonment has finally dispelled the illusion that slums are highly profitable.

Interpreting Abandonment

Abandonment poses several problems for the housing analyst. First, statistics on the subject must be used cautiously, since it is not always clear what is being measured. Enumerators may find it difficult to distinguish between buildings that have been withdrawn from the market in anticipation of orderly future redevelopment and those from which the owner has definitely "walked away."

Second, the abandonment process itself can be interpreted in diametrically opposite ways. One interpretation would view it as the natural end result of filtering. In many of the cities that have reported high rates of abandonment—St. Louis, Cleveland, and Detroit, for example—population declined substantially during the 1960s and 1970s.[24] These losses resulted from the exodus of middle and upper income families. What followed might be described as "filtering through population decline." In vacating high rent, inner-city housing, the middle and upper classes set in motion a filtering process with precisely the same end result that occurs when population is constant but new construction takes places at the upper end of the rent scale: after a series of moves by tenants, the worst low rent housing is vacated and withdrawn from the market. Thus abandonment could be interpreted as the logical end result of a filtering process that is intrinsically desirable since it brings about a net improvement in housing standards.

Such an optimistic view, however, overlooks the fact that relatively good housing as well as bad is usually engulfed when abandonment sweeps

23. George Sternlieb, "Abandonment and Rehabilitation: What Is to Be Done?" Papers submitted to the Subcommittee on Housing, part 1, U.S. Congress, House Committee on Banking and Currency, June 1971, p. 317.
24. See U.S. General Accounting Office, *Housing Abandonment: A National Problem Needing New Approaches*, doc. no. CED-78-126, August 10, 1978, p. 1. The report contains detailed studies of abandonment in Philadelphia, St. Louis, and Detroit.

a neighborhood. For example, the Rand Institute study of New York City's housing estimated that at least 80 percent of the vast "unrecorded losses" to the housing inventory from 1965 through 1967 were in buildings that had not been classified as dilapidated in a 1965 survey. In a later study, Kristof reports that 64 percent of the housing lost through demolition or abandonment in New York City between 1960 and 1970 was recorded as up to standard (full plumbing and not dilapidated) in 1960.[25]

The pessimistic interpretation of abandonment stresses the gross inefficiency of a process through which the market loses good housing along with bad, the chaotic nature of the process itself, and the sense it conveys of a complete breakdown of the institutional structure of the housing and property markets in low income neighborhoods.

The Problem of Neighborhood Quality

The problem of deteriorating inner city neighborhoods is closely bound up with that of abandonment. When housing units go under, neighborhoods are left with seemingly bombed-out blocks, strewn with rubbish and litter. Gradually the social as well as the physical structure of neighborhood life crumbles. Because population declines, stores go out of business, and shopping choices are reduced; professional services are withdrawn; churches and other community-based organizations wither for lack of membership. As yet no policies have been developed that would guide depopulation in order to minimize these destructive consequences.[26] And, of course, neighborhood problems are not limited to places suffering from abandonment. Crime, vandalism, and litter now seem to be endemic in the inner cities.

We have seen that dissatisfaction with neighborhood conditions in metropolitan areas is now greater than dissatisfaction with housing itself. Since almost everyone living in cities now has full plumbing, and since overcrowding has been drastically reduced, the housing problem, as measured by traditional standards has, indeed, almost disappeared. As Sternlieb puts it, "The old era of absolute housing want has largely come to an end."[27] What remains elusive, especially in the older central cities, is that other goal declared to be a part of the national purpose by the Housing Act of 1949: the provision of a "suitable living environment for every American family."

25. See Lowry, p. 6, for the Rand Institute estimates, and Frank S. Kristof, "Housing and People in New York City," *City Almanac* (published by the Center for New York City Affairs of the New School for Social Research), February 1976, p. 6.

26. See James Heilbrun, "On the Theory and Policy of Neighborhood Consolidation," *Journal of the American Planning Association*, October 1979, pp. 417–27.

27. George Sternlieb, "Epilogue: A Note on Federal Housing Policy," in Sternlieb, et al., *America's Housing . . .*, p. 546.

THE RATIONALE FOR SUBSIDIZING HOUSING

Urban housing policy comprises a great many actual or proposed forms of public intervention in the markets for land and housing. Some are regulatory in nature, such as antidiscrimination laws and zoning ordinances, and are intended to overcome particular imperfections in the housing and land markets. Most forms of intervention, however, are subsidy programs, such as public housing, below-market-interest-rate loans, or rental assistance payments, whose essential purpose is to increase the supply of housing and/or directly reduce its price to consumers. The funds from which these subsidies are paid have alternate uses in either the public or the private sector. What justifies the particular use to which we put them? Why do we subsidize the output or consumption of housing instead of allowing the market to follow its own course in this, as in many other instances?

Over the years, a number of justifications for housing subsidies have been suggested, most of them under one of the following headings:

1. Housing is a "merit want," or "merit good," in the sense first defined by Musgrave.[28] A merit good is something that is better for people than they realize. Consequently, individual consumers, if left to themselves, are likely to consume less of such goods than the amount that would maximize their welfare within the constraints of their income. The concept is easily understood in the reverse case of "demerit goods": we control the use of narcotics on the ground that otherwise many people would use them in ignorance of the harm they cause. In the same fashion, it may be argued that we must subsidize the distribution of, say, education, medical services, or housing because otherwise, largely through ignorance, people would consume less of them than they ought to. Who is to determine the "correct" level of consumption of such merit goods? In a democratic society, that is presumably the function of the well-informed, who must then persuade the majority to adopt the appropriate policies.

2. Poverty, or the unequal distribution of income, prevents some families from obtaining housing that meets a socially desirable minimum standard. In order to bring the poor up to the defined minimum standard, the government provides them with more housing than they can or would pay for out of their low incomes. This argument is actually a variant of the first, for it implies that housing is a merit good. If it were not a merit good, it would be unnecessary to provide housing benefits in kind. One could simply grant cash subsidies to the poor—along the lines of the

28. Richard A. Musgrave, *The Theory of Public Finance* (New York: McGraw-Hill, 1959), ch. 1, and "Policies for Housing Support: Rationale and Instruments," in U.S. Department of Housing and Urban Development, *Housing in the Seventies Working Papers*, vol. 1 (1976) esp. 218–22.

income-maintenance plans discussed in Chapter 11—and rely on them to spend a sufficient portion of the extra cash on housing. Since we do not do that, the argument clearly implies that people do not spend as much of their income on housing as we think they "ought" to—i.e., that housing is a merit good. The only difference between the poverty argument and the merit good argument, then, is that the former suggests, and the latter does not, that above some level of family income we can assume that everyone will voluntarily obtain enough housing.

3. Better housing reduces the cost of providing social services by lowering the incidence of fire, communicable disease, crime, and other social disorders. This is the "external social benefits" argument. If better housing does have these desirable social effects, then individual consumption decisions will result systematically in too little housing being consumed. From the principle of diminishing marginal utility we conclude that the marginal private benefit to the consumer declines as his or her annual consumption of housing increases. Each individual reaches an optimum by consuming up to the point where the (declining) marginal private benefit received from an additional unit of consumption just equals the marginal cost paid for that unit. But this is short of the socially optimal quantity of consumption because the individual ignores the external marginal social benefits generated by his or her act of consumption. Society would be justified in subsidizing housing so that individual consumption of it is carried to the point where the sum of marginal private benefits plus marginal social benefits equals marginal cost. Since marginal social benefit is positive, this equality will occur at a higher level of housing consumption than the individual would choose to pay for in an unsubsidized market.

4. Housing subsidies are an expedient way of redistributing income to the poor. Thus, one might favor such subsidies while remaining skeptical about the merit good or external benefits arguments. Economists generally have agreed that income redistribution is most efficiently accomplished not by making transfers in kind but by making cash transfers, which leave the recipient free to choose whatever additional goods he or she most desires. Yet the "realist" who wishes to redistribute income may believe that it is politically easier to legislate adequate transfers in kind than in cash and that this consideration outweighs the contrary argument based on economic efficiency.

Let us examine some of these contentions in greater detail. We have already shown how the merit good argument serves to justify subsidies. Less obvious is the point that it also justifies the use of housing codes intended to keep housing up to a minimum standard of quality. To be sure, housing codes (other than occupancy standards) may be regarded simply as an effort-saving convenience. Instead of letting each tenant see to it that the landlord maintains decent standards in a building, we agree to let an informed specialized government agency do the job for us. A good many regulatory activities of government can be so justified. But there is probably more to it than that. In a competitive setting such as the urban rental-housing market, given normal vacancies, tenants can enforce standards by refusing to live in substandard buildings. Hence the fact that we adopt housing codes strongly implies a belief that some tenants will not insist on high enough standards, either on account of ignorance or because they cannot "afford" standard housing. Given their low incomes, they prefer substandard or overcrowded housing at low prices to standard or less crowded housing at higher prices. Thus one justification for codes is the merit good argument that at least some consumers fail to realize how important adequate housing is to their own welfare.

Does Housing Confer Indirect Benefits?

What reason can there be for believing that housing is, in fact, better for people than they realize? The answer must lie in the existence of some sort of indirect benefit of which the consumer is not aware, for surely consumers can judge for themselves the direct satisfaction obtained from housing *qua* housing. The indirect benefits to the consuming family would have to be such things as better physical and mental health, higher educational achievement, and less likelihood of family members turning to narcotics, crime, or juvenile delinquency. These same indirect effects— disease, crime, and delinquency—are an important source of the external costs allegedly thrown off upon society at large by bad housing, and therefore they are also a source of the external social benefits attributable to housing improvement. Thus the merit good argument and the external benefit argument turn out to be rooted in the same phenomenon: indirect effects of housing quality on behavior.

What evidence do we have that such effects actually exist? A virtual utopia of indirect benefits has, of course, been alleged. In the 1930s, when slum clearance and public housing first became objectives of national policy, claims for the beneficent effects of good housing were widely accepted. For example, the Court of Appeals of New York, in an important 1936 decision favorable to public housing, held that:

> The public evils, social and economic, of such [slum] conditions are unquestioned and unquestionable. Slum areas are the breeding places of disease which take toll not only from denizens but, by spread, from the inhabitants of the entire city and state. Juvenile delinquency, crime, and immorality are there born, find protection

and flourish. Enormous economic loss results directly from the necessary expenditure of public funds to maintain health . . . and to war against crime and immorality.[29]

Such claims now seem astonishingly naive. The logic, or illogic, upon which they were based has been explained lucidly by John P. Dean:

> In city after city . . . slum areas have been shown to be the areas of poorest health and greatest personal and social disorder. The implication is: "Remove the slums and you remove the social ills!" But it would be just as illogical to say that ills of slum areas are caused not by substandard housing conditions, but by the absence of telephone service, which also correlates with indexes of social disorder.[30]

During the 1930s a good deal of "evidence" was amassed to support the extravagant claims of housing reformers. It might easily be shown, for example, that rates of crime, delinquency, illegitimacy, disease, and death were lower in public housing projects than in the surrounding slum areas from which the tenants were selected. At first it was overlooked that the very process of tenant selection accounted for much of the gain. The old, the criminal, the socially disorganized were systematically excluded in favor of stable working-class families with children. In short, public housing tenants were not a random sample of the slum population.

Valid conclusions about the effects of the dwelling environment can be reached only if the sample of public housing tenants is carefully matched on a variety of socioeconomic characteristics with a selected control group of those remaining in the surrounding slums. A well-known study of the impact of housing on family life conducted in Baltimore in the 1950s employed just that test design.[31] It revealed that public housing is associated with statistically significant improvements in some, but by no means all, of the indexes of health, psychological adjustment, and school performance for which tests were made. The effects of better housing were usually in the expected direction, but the magnitudes of the effects were not very impressive.

More recently the International Housing Productivity Study carried out careful tests of the effects of massive housing improvements on health,

29. Cited in Robert Moore Fisher, *Twenty Years of Public Housing* (New York: Harper & Row, 1959), p. 63.
30. John P. Dean, "The Myths of Housing Reform" (abridged), in Jewel Bellusch and Murray Hausknecht, eds., *Urban Renewal: People, Politics and Planning* (New York: Doubleday, 1967), an Anchor Book, pp. 27–28.
31. Daniel M. Wilner, et al., *The Housing Environment and Family Life: A Longitudinal Study of the Effects of Housing on Morbidity and Mental Health* (Baltimore: The Johns Hopkins University Press, 1962). The volume also contains a useful review of other studies of the effects of housing quality.

worker productivity, education, and social deviance at selected sites in developing countries and in less developed regions of the United States. Statistically significant benefits of housing were found on health at two out of seven sites, on worker productivity at two out of four sites, on education at one of four sites, and on social deviance at the one site where that effect was tested. These results, not unlike those of the Baltimore study, are quite ambiguous. In summarizing the study, Leland Burns and Leo Grebler concluded that "the results of the work reported here do not provide any strong, consistent support for the hypothesis that housing investment yields substantial unperceived internal benefits and externalities. . . . The evidence is mixed."[32]

Even a finding of statistically significant benefits from housing improvements, however, does not provide sufficient grounds for endorsing a subsidy program. In addition, one would have to attach monetary values to the measured indirect benefits of housing and insert them into a benefit-cost study to determine whether they were sufficient to justify the program's cost. As Rothenberg showed in his detailed analysis of urban renewal, this task of quantification has proven very difficult to carry out.[33]

The demand for public intervention in the urban housing market has not proven very sensitive to the validity, or lack of it, of arguments concerning the existence of specific, measurable, indirect housing benefits. Beyond the reach of these arguments there remains a widespread conviction that in some fundamental sense housing *does* matter more than other consumer goods. Housing is, after all, the immediate physical environment of one's life. Apparently we do not want people to live—or, worse, to grow up—in a squalid environment. Whether this is because we find physical squalor morally shocking in an affluent society, or because we believe such squalor is ultimately a threat to the society itself, is perhaps open to question. What cannot be doubted is that housing has long been, and will probably continue to be, an object of special social concern.

32. Burns and Grebler, p. 168. See their ch. 7 for a full analysis of the results and their ch. 6 for a review of the literature on housing externalities. Also see Claude S. Fischer, et al., "Crowding Studies and Urban Life: A Critical Review," *Journal of the American Institute of Planners*, November 1975, pp. 406–18, for a survey of studies dealing specifically with overcrowding; and Stanislav V. Kasl, "Effects of Housing on Mental and Physical Health," in *Housing in the Seventies Working Papers*, vol. 1, pp. 286–304, for a survey of studies on health effects. Both papers include extensive bibliographies.
33. See Jerome Rothenberg, *Economic Evaluation of Urban Renewal* (Washington, D.C.: The Brookings Institution, 1967), chs. 10 and 11, for a review of the conceptual and practical difficulties of measuring the social costs of slum housing.

Urban Housing Policy

THIRTEEN

Public concern with urban housing standards has produced, over the years, a wide range of housing policies and programs. As suggested in Chapter 12, most of these can be classified as either subsidy programs or regulatory policies. Examining them now in greater detail, we will see that subsidy programs can be further subdivided. Historically, the major programs—including such a diverse list as public housing, urban renewal, housing rehabilitation, and interest-rate subsidies—formed a single class in one important respect. In all of these programs, payment of a subsidy was linked either to the construction of specific new dwelling units or to the rehabilitation of specific buildings. The basic purpose of this kind of "new construction," or "supply side," subsidy was to increase the stock of new or high quality dwelling units as directly as possible, in the hope of thus raising urban housing standards for the whole population. In direct contrast to this are some more recent policies that provide cash subsidies in the form of rent assistance to low income families. Such policies operate directly on the demand side, raising the rent-paying capacity of the poor in the belief that the market will then provide them with an adequate supply of decent, standard, older housing. As the chapter proceeds, we will evaluate these alternative subsidy strategies.

We will also discuss regulatory policies that are intended to overcome specific imperfections in the urban housing and land markets, including the enforcement of housing code standards and antidiscrimination laws and the guidance of land use by means of zoning ordinances. Policies aimed directly at neighborhood revitalization will also be analyzed, as will the implications for neighborhood viability of some of the housing programs. The chapter will

365

conclude with a discussion of proposals to "open up" the suburbs to low income housing—proposals that generally call for combining a variety of the forms of public intervention.

Although urban housing policy in the United States has changed frequently over the years, the changes have clearly been evolutionary. Each new program arose, so to speak, from the ashes of its predecessor as government responded to criticism of previous policies or to altered circumstances. Housing programs are taken up chronologically in this chapter in the belief that the logic of each can best be understood in the context of the policies and circumstances from which it evolved.

PUBLIC HOUSING

Public housing is the oldest of all subsidized housing programs in the United States. The term "public housing" refers not to all forms of government assisted housing but only to those units that are owned and operated (or in some cases, leased) by a public housing authority. The federal government had been engaged briefly in building public housing for defense workers in World War I, but its peacetime involvement dates from the Great Depression. Public housing was widely regarded as a radical new departure in the 1930s. It was initiated as an emergency measure to create employment by spending on new construction. In 1933 the Public Works Administration was authorized to include slum clearance projects and the construction or repair of low cost housing among the works that it undertook, and it was neither required nor expected that such housing projects would be self-liquidating. Two and a half years of legislative battling were required, however, before Senator Wagner's United States Housing Act was passed in 1937, putting the public housing program on a permanent basis. Projects built by the PWA had been federally developed and owned. Under the new law, site selection, ownership, and operation were decentralized to the local level, though under federal guidelines, and have remained so ever since. With the exception of wartime housing, initiation of projects has been restricted to local housing authorities. In a sense, the United States has no "national" public housing policy; it has local public housing programs that are federally subsidized and regulated. The role of the federal authorities is limited to setting standards and making loans, contributions, or grants to the appropriate local body. The choice of whether to build or not remains a local one.

As the program has operated ever since 1937, the federal government, in effect, contributes up to 100 percent of the capital cost of a project as a subsidy to keep rents low. Local governments also contribute substantial subsidies by foregoing ordinary property taxes in favor of much lower payments "in lieu of taxes." Since it is a matter of public policy to restrict these large subsidy benefits to the poor, tenants are not accepted for admission unless their incomes fall below a specified limit. Such limits vary locally, but they have been effective in restricting access largely to the poor. As Table 13.2 will show, median family income in 1978 in public housing projects was only $3,718. Poverty line income in that year was $4,396 for a two-person family without children and $6,610 for a four-person family with two children.

Down to the late 1960s, public housing rents were expected to cover operating and maintenance costs plus payments in lieu of property taxes made by the local authority to the municipal government. However, in 1969, Congress limited the rent that could be charged any tenant to 25 percent of income. Since that would hold down housing authority revenue, Congress also for the first time authorized operating subsidies for public housing. During the 1970s operating costs soared as a result of inflation. Tenant incomes did not by any means keep pace. Federal operating subsidies therefore increased rapidly, rising to about 40 percent of operating costs by 1978.[1] Even so, many housing authorities were unable to keep up with necessary maintenance. Physical conditions in some projects deteriorated, often dramatically. Raymond Struyk's 1980 study of Public Housing Authorities in the 29 largest U.S. cities found that five were in the equivalent of bankruptcy and a number of others were in decidedly difficult straits.[2]

From 1950 through 1978, as Table 13.1 shows, the inventory of low rent public housing units under management rose from 201,700 to 1,198,000. Yet at the latter date public housing still accounted for only about 1.4 percent of the nation's total housing stock. The ratio is much higher, however, in many of the larger cities such as New York, Chicago, Washington, and Baltimore.

Political support for public housing probably reached a high point with the passage of the Housing Act of 1949, which authorized construction of 810,000 additional units over a six-year period. During the 1950s, however, congressional appropriations never made possible any such massive program. In the 1960s funds were more plentiful, but by that time the program was running into trouble in the big cities, and available monies were not used to the limit. Local housing authorities were finding it increasingly difficult to obtain politically acceptable project sites. At the same time, earlier enthusiasm by public housing's traditional supporters

1. Congressional Budget Office, *Federal Housing Policy: Current Programs and Recurring Issues*, June 1978, p. 31.
2. Raymond J. Struyk, *A New System for Public Housing* (Washington, D.C.: The Urban Institute, 1980), pp. 8, 70–73.

TABLE 13.1
Growth and Composition of the Public Housing Inventory[a]

| | PUBLIC HOUSING INVENTORY (THOUSANDS) | | TOTAL U.S. HOUSING STOCK (THOUSANDS) | PUBLIC HOUSING AS PERCENTAGE OF TOTAL |
	Under Management	Under Construction		
1950	201.7	31.5	45,983	0.4%
1960	478.2	36.4	58,326	0.8
1970	893.5	126.8	68,672	1.3
1978	1,198.0	65.7	84,000[a]	1.4
Composition of public housing inventory, 1978				
Constructed as public housing[b]	1,045.0	42.2		
Acquired[c]	35.0	9.3		
Leased[d]	118.0	14.2		

[a] Estimated.
[b] Includes conventionally developed public housing and units built for local housing authorities under "turnkey" contracts.
[c] Existing housing acquired by local housing authorities. "Under construction" indicates units undergoing rehabilitation.
[d] Existing housing leased by local housing authorities.
Sources: Statistical Abstract of the United States, 1979, table 1392, and 1972, table 1153; and U.S. Bureau of the Census, Census of Housing, 1970.

was giving way to a rising wave of criticism. During the 1970s many Public Housing Authorities were reluctant to expand even when federal appropriations were available because of the financial difficulty they were having managing their existing projects.

How Good (or Bad) Is Public Housing?

Conventional public housing has come in for increasingly severe criticism on a number of grounds. Public housing in central cities has typically been built in large-scale, multibuilding projects, often covering dozens of acres. These vast "developments" have been criticized widely for their impersonality, institutional atmosphere, uninspired architecture, and inhuman scale. Moreover, their interior amenities suffer from the deliberate imposition of a "no frills" policy. Consequently, it has long been argued that public housing projects, though built at great expense, are destined to be the slums of the future. In some respects they have already taken on the characteristics of slum neighborhoods. Certainly, there are frequent complaints of juvenile delinquency and violent crime within projects.

The social design of public housing policy has been criticized as severely as the physical. Income limits imposed on tenants both for admission and for continued occupancy raise seemingly insoluble problems. On the one hand, such limits seem necessary in order to confine the substantial benefits of public housing to those most in need. On the other hand, they produce a public housing population in which the proportion of tenants "on welfare" is substantial. The high concentration of poverty and distress within the projects may well have destructive effects on individual behavior.

The classic case of public housing failure, resulting apparently from the overconcentration of poverty in a vast development, is the notorious Pruitt-Igoe project in St. Louis. Completed in the mid-1950s, it consisted of 43 buildings on 57 acres near the city's central business district. By 1970 the project was so ridden by crime and vandalism, and so physically deteriorated as a result of the inability of the St. Louis Housing Authority to keep up with maintenance and repairs, that it was virtually untenantable. At first the Authority responded by closing down more than half the buildings. Eventually the entire project was vacated and demolished.

Yet it would be a mistake to take the extreme Pruitt-Igoe case as representative. Because of that fiasco, the vacancy rate in St. Louis public housing in 1967 was a shockingly high 13 percent. But among the 50 largest cities in the United States only 7 others then had public housing vacancy rates above the 5 percent level considered normal in the private rental market. For the 50 cities together, the aggregate public housing vacancy rate was only 2.2 percent. Moreover, the aggregate waiting list for admission numbered 193,072 requests, or 28 times the number of vacancies, an impressive statistic, even allowing for the many persons whose names remained on the list after they were no longer seeking admission.[3] Whatever the critics may say about public housing and however far it may fall short of the expectations with which it was launched in the 1930s, these figures do indicate a considerable degree of tenant satisfaction with the program.

Tenant satisfaction depends in part on how well projects are managed. A statistical study of public housing management performance has shown that authorities located within metropolitan areas do face more difficult problems than those in towns and counties outside SMSA's. For example, vandalism and crime are significantly higher in metropolitan

3. *Building the American City*, Report of the National Commission on Urban Problems (The Douglas Commission), 1969, tables 11 and 12, p. 131.

area projects.[4] Nevertheless, the study found good and bad management performance in both areas, and showed that good management is associated with both lower operating expenses and higher levels of tenant satisfaction.[5]

The design of public housing policy has often been criticized for creating inequities among the very people it is intended to help—the low income population itself. Since the stock of public housing is relatively small (see Table 13.1), only a very few of those who meet the income qualifications are actually admitted. Instead of providing uniform benefits to all who qualify, the program provides costly benefits to a few and nothing for the rest.[6] (By way of analogy, imagine that free public elementary education were available only to a small proportion of families and that pupils were selected from long waiting lists.) The sums involved per family are not trivial: it has been estimated that over the future life of a public housing project initiated in 1980, the full subsidy cost to the government, in 1980 dollars, would range from $2,200 to $2,530 per dwelling unit per year.[7] (Note, however, that when consumption of a particular good is stimulated by a subsidy, it must be presumed that consumers of the good get less than a dollar's worth of benefit for each dollar spent by the government. That is why economists, in principle, prefer cash transfers to subsidies on particular commodities.[8])

A final criticism leveled at the conventional public housing program is that it fosters racial and economic segregation within neighborhoods of central cities. Table 13.2 shows that minorities made up 62 percent of public housing tenantry in 1978, a proportion far higher than their share of the central city poverty population in the same year. Since projects tend to be large, the high proportion of minority tenants in a project automatically establishes a degree of neighborhood segregation. At the same time, efforts to reduce such segregation by scattering smaller projects through white neighborhoods often arouse intense local opposition from whites, who fear the influx of nonwhite population that they know to be typical in public housing. Realistically, however, it seems doubtful that public housing projects have done much to increase segregation within

---

4. Robert Sadacca et al., *Management Performance in Public Housing*, doc. no. 209–5–2 (Washington, D.C.: The Urban Institute, January 1974), p. 28.
5. Ibid., pp. 37–38 and 75.
6. Richard F. Muth, *Public Housing*, Evaluative Studies no. 5 (Washington, D.C.: American Enterprise Institute, 1973), pp. 2–3.
7. Congressional Budget Office, *The Long-Term Costs of Lower Income Housing Assistance Programs*, March 1979, table 12.
8. See John C. Weicher, "Urban Housing Policy," in Peter Mieszkowski and Mahlon Straszheim, eds., *Current Issues in Urban Economics* (Baltimore: The Johns Hopkins University Press, 1979), pp. 494–96.

cities, since most of the minority families now living in projects probably would have lived in segregated neighborhoods in any case.

More important is the possibility that public housing helps to maintain segregation at the macrogeographic scale. Because construction depends on local initiative, a good deal of public housing has been built in central cities, very little in the surrounding suburbs. In effect, the public housing program offers a subsidy to minorities on condition that they remain in the central city. As we will see, many current proposals for housing policy reform take it as a principal objective to undo this link between housing subsidies and intrametropolitan segregation.

Some Alternatives to Housing in "Projects"

Prior to 1965, local housing authorities always owned and operated their own units, and most were built in large-scale, multibuilding projects. As we have pointed out, these were widely criticized for their effects in overconcentrating the poverty population and actually creating segregated neighborhoods. In 1965 Congress authorized local housing authorities to lease units in privately-owned and -operated buildings and sublet them at low rents to the authorities' usual clientele. Under this "Section 23" leasing program, public housing beneficiaries could be scattered among tenants in conventional buildings in existing neighborhoods instead of being concentrated into socially stigmatized "projects." In addition, the full economic cost per unit was calculated to be substantially below the cost for conventional public housing.[9] Finally, the program had the potential advantage of making use of the valuable excess supply of housing that was developing in many older neighborhoods of inner cities as population thinned out. Deterioration of the older stock could actually be arrested through leasing, since rents paid by tenants plus the contributions added by the local housing authority would be sufficient to cover standard maintenance and operating costs.

As indicated in Table 13.1, leased units now account for about 10 percent of the low rent public housing stock. Expansion of activity under Section 23 ended when the program was replaced by Section 8 of the Housing and Community Development Act of 1974. While the Section 8 program (which we return to below) differs in many respects from Section 23, its basic approach is the same: to place subsidized tenants in commercially operated housing rather than in "projects."

9. Frank De Leeuw and Sam H. Leaman, "The Section 23 Leasing Program," in U.S. Congress, Joint Economic Committee, *The Economics of Federal Subsidy Programs*, part 5, October 9, 1972, table 2.

372   *Urban Economics and Public Policy*

URBAN RENEWAL

The Housing Act of 1949, which, as we have seen, authorized a most ambitious public housing program, also gave birth to a new form of government intervention in the housing market that later came to be known as "urban renewal." The unemployment of the 1930s had been succeeded by postwar inflation. Instead of searching for socially acceptable ways to spend money, the government found itself under pressure to cut expenditures in order to check rising prices. Congress sought some means of drawing private investment into the business of improving the nation's housing standards. Urban "renewal," at that time called "redevelopment," was the agreed-upon new program.

Title I of the 1949 Act provided that the federal government would give financial assistance, through local agencies, to make private redevelopment of blighted areas economically feasible. A local redevelopment authority was to select, assemble, and clear a qualified site. It would then resell the site at a loss to a private redeveloper, who presumably could not pay the full cost of acquisition and clearance and still earn any profit. The federal government would make its contribution by paying to the local authority a grant equal to two-thirds of that loss—that is to say, two-thirds of the difference between the sum of site acquisition and clearance cost and the resale price of the land in its new use.

It was not required that the new use be residential, and, in practice, far more sites were residential before than after redevelopment.[10] Moreover, the new housing built on redevelopment and renewal sites was predominantly for the middle and upper income classes, rather than for the poor. It was widely assumed, however, that although the ill-housed would gain little from redevelopment directly, they would eventually benefit by way of filtering. We return to this question below.

The Housing Act of 1954 significantly modified the urban redevelopment program. There had been increasing opposition to the "bulldozer method" used in Title I projects. The method took its name from the fact that whole blocks, and often whole neighborhoods, were leveled to provide sites for Title I housing. The earliest opponents were tenants threatened with dislocation, who could not understand why the power of eminent domain should be employed to destroy their neighborhood and their homes in order to build anew for someone else, at private profit. The 1954 Act—which changed the name of the program to "urban renewal"—sought to reduce reliance on the bulldozer by encouraging a combination of selective rehabilitation and conservation, reserving clearance

10. William Grigsby, *Housing Markets and Public Policy* (Philadelphia: University of Pennsylvania Press, 1963), p. 324.

for those structures or blocks that were beyond a reasonable hope of salvation.

However, the difference between renewal under the 1954 Act and redevelopment under the Act of 1949 was not sufficient to quiet the opposition, for the logic of the programs remained essentially unchanged. The poor continued to be displaced by application of the majestic powers of the state to make way for the middle class. The use of rehabilitation improved matters very little. Like new construction, housing rehabilitated to federal standards was too costly for low income families. Criticism mounted.[11] Sociologists and city planners began to realize that many stable and useful social institutions were going down before the unseeing bulldozer. It became apparent that uprooting the poor in order to clear vast sites for renewal was likely to increase the social disorders associated with poverty while achieving, not the elimination of slums, but simply their removal from one neighborhood to another in the wake of the displaced poor. Moreover, critics continued to point out that the link between urban renewal and slum clearance had the perverse effect of actually reducing the total housing supply, and especially the supply of low cost housing, a result that was bound to be disadvantageous to the poor.

By the late 1960s urban renewal had lost much of its political support. In 1974 it was replaced by the Community Development Block Grant program, to be discussed later in this chapter.

What is the logic of urban renewal as a form of public intervention in the land market? Although the program no longer exists, analysis of it throws light on several crucial aspects of the economics of urban land use, including externalities in the housing market and the process of land use succession. An understanding of these matters is likely to be as important in judging future publicly sponsored redevelopment policies as it is to comprehending those of the past.

MARKET IMPERFECTIONS AND THE CASE FOR URBAN RENEWAL

Because it was so controversial, the urban renewal program stimulated a good deal of inquiry by economists, political scientists, sociologists, and city planners. One of the most influential economic analyses was provided by Otto A. Davis and Andrew B. Whinston in 1961.[12] Their analysis

---

11. The intense debate about the virtues and defects of renewal has been conveniently anthologized by James Q. Wilson in *Urban Renewal: The Record and the Controversy* (Cambridge, Mass.: M.I.T. Press, 1966).

12. Otto A. Davis and Andrew B. Whinston, "The Economics of Urban Renewal," reprinted in Wilson, pp. 50–67.

remains a very useful starting point for looking at possible imperfections in the urban land and housing markets and tracing out their implications for redevelopment policy.

Davis and Whinston suggest a number of reasons for believing that the urban housing market may not function "properly"—in the sense of providing the optimum amount and quality of housing to satisfy consumer wants, given the constraints of cost and of limited incomes. These arguments do not establish the existence of any sort of "exploitation" of tenants by landlords, but, if valid, they do make a case for government intervention.

Two kinds of imperfection may be (not necessarily are) present. The first would result from the strong external effects of one property on the tenants and owner of another. A prospective tenant who thinks about renting an apartment takes into account the attractiveness of the neighborhood, which depends in part on the characteristics of nearby properties. Thus the rent obtainable by one landlord may be affected by the condition in which neighboring landlords keep their properties.

Consider four possible cases that involve this sort of interdependency between two adjacent owners, Smith and Jones.

1. If both owners invest in redeveloping their properties, both can earn a rate of return that makes the additional investment worthwhile. Each benefits from the fact that the other has made improvements, because tenants are willing to pay higher rents for an apartment in an improved neighborhood than in an unimproved one.

2. Owner Smith can obtain higher rents *without* redeveloping, provided that neighbor Jones *does* redevelop. Smith's *rate* of return may even be higher in this case because she can obtain higher rents without investing any additional capital.

3. If neither of the owners redevelops, both will continue to earn a rate of return lower than they could obtain if both had redeveloped, as in the first case.

4. Finally, if Smith were to redevelop her property while Jones did not, Smith's rate of return might actually drop below what it would be if neither she nor Jones undertook redevelopment, as in the third case.

For the sake of illustration, Davis and Whinston assign hypothetical rates of return to the four cases as follows:

	RATE OF RETURN EARNED BY:	
ALTERNATIVE CASES	*Smith*	*Jones*
1. Both invest in redevelopment	7%	7%
2. Jones invests, Smith does not	10	3
3. Neither invests in redevelopment	4	4
4. Smith invests, Jones does not	3	10

It is clear that society benefits most in the first case, where both owners invest in redevelopment. But Davis and Whinston use arguments from game theory (the logic of "the prisoner's dilemma" situation) to show that the actual outcome may well be case 3, where neither property is redeveloped. The argument runs as follows. First examine Smith's situation. When deciding whether to invest in redevelopment she has to consider two possibilities—first, that Jones also redevelops and, second, that Jones does not. Looking at these two possibilities, she sees that in either case she is best off *not* investing. In the first situation, she can earn 10 percent by not investing (case 2) but only 7 percent by investing (case 1). In the second situation she can earn 4 percent by not investing (case 3) but only 3 percent by investing (case 4). Her rational decision is not to invest. Moreover, since Jones as an individual owner is logically in the same position as Smith, he, too, decides not to invest, and no redevelopment occurs, even though such redevelopment would be socially optimal. Here, then, is a case of "market failure" attributable to interdependencies.

Davis and Whinston take as their definition of urban "blight" any case in which the market fails to yield optimum development of the housing stock. They do not equate slums and blight, however, since they recognize that slum neighborhoods may be run down precisely because slum tenants cannot afford anything better. Likewise, "blight" may exist in relatively "nice" neighborhoods, if interdependencies have prevented them from being improved to the optimum extent.

The authors recognize that a suboptimal outcome is due to their assumption of interdependencies that are "sufficiently strong."[13] One can show easily that with interdependencies of a weaker sort, the socially correct outcome will occur. Return to the table and suppose, for example, that we leave cases 1 and 3 as they are but change the outcome of case 2 to Smith earns 6 percent and Jones earns 5 percent; and change case 4 to Smith earns 5 percent and Jones earns 6 percent. We still have interdependency, since one investor's rate of return depends on what the other does. But in this situation it will be rational for Smith individually, and hence for Jones also, to undertake redevelopment.

Interdependencies of the sort described probably exist, but the important question to decide is how strong they may be. The belief that they are strong enough to block redevelopment implies that tenants have substantial demands for housing and neighborhood amenities that go perpetually unfulfilled. The interdependency argument views the tenant as a prisoner of a particular neighborhood, willing and able to pay for a better environment with higher rent but unable to do so because the system fails to produce the desired amenities. However, if the competitive, adaptive

13. Ibid., p. 57, n. 7.

model of the housing market that we described in the previous chapter is accepted as even roughly valid, then the market produces a sufficient variety of housing and neighborhood types and qualities to suit the tastes and rent-paying capacities of a wide variety of consumers. Tenants would consequently be able to select the neighborhood and home in which they live out of a variety of existing neighborhoods and homes because it best suits their needs. We would not then expect tenants in a given neighborhood to nurse latent, unfulfilled demands (which they are able to back with higher rent offers) for something substantially better, if only something better were offered. And if tenants do not have such unfulfilled demands it is unlikely that interdependencies would have the powerful effects on the rate of return hypothesized by Davis and Whinston. The high rates of return from redevelopment hypothesized by Davis and Whinston would occur only if higher income tenants were attracted from other neighborhoods to occupy the redeveloped buildings, but that outcome violates the implicit assumption of their example that it refers to housing for a given population in a given neighborhood.

What little direct evidence we have about tenants in deteriorating neighborhoods supports the notion that they are usually *unwilling* to pay for even moderately costly housing improvements. A survey of families in transitional neighborhoods of New York City in 1969 asked respondents whether they were satisfied with specific features of their housing. Those who said "no" were then asked whether they would be willing to pay $30 a month additional rent to correct the unsatisfactory feature. Of tenants living in units not under rent control, 77 to 78 percent were definitely unwilling to pay the additional rent for those features that would remedy the dissatisfactions they had themselves expressed.[14] While this survey involved too small a sample to be conclusive, its findings are consistent with reports in the daily press of tenants in slum areas who object to proposals to rehabilitate their buildings because they do not wish to pay the higher rent that would be required to finance the job. Given that sort of response, the strong interdependencies hypothesized by Davis and Whinston seem unlikely. The point to be stressed is not that tenants are unaffected by their neighborhoods but only that they are not able or willing to pay very much to alter the effects.

The rise of housing abandonment, with its destructive external effects on neighborhood properties, might seem to strengthen the case for the strong interdependencies of the Davis and Whinston example. Can it be that building owners in a neighborhood that is on the verge of slipping into abandonment are caught in the sort of "prisoner's dilemma"

14. See Ira S. Lowry, Joseph S. De Salvo, and Barbara M. Woodfill, *The Demand for Shelter*, vol. II of *Rental Housing in New York City* (New York: New York City Rand Institute, June 1971), pp. 102–04.

situation they described? If all owners could agree *not* to abandon is it possible that none would choose or be forced to? Housing analysts who claim that abandonment is a "contagious, self-fulfilling prophecy" appear to think so.[15] Yet this argument seems to overlook the force of the most frequently mentioned causes of abandonment, which are inadequate rent-paying capacity, rent delinquency, and high rates of neighborhood crime and vandalism. It may well be doubted whether any agreement by owners to stand fast would succeed in neighborhoods where these forces are at their worst.

The Problem of Site Assembly

The second market imperfection cited by Davis and Whinston has to do with "site assembly." They point out that if interdependencies between properties prevent individual owners from undertaking economically desirable redevelopment, then an incentive exists for a single owner to buy out all the others and make improvements over the entire neighborhood himself. By so doing he can realize the high rate of return hypothesized for the case in which all properties are improved. But now the problem of site assembly rises to plague the developer. In the typical American city, property is held in very small parcels. The entrepreneur wishing to assemble a large site for redevelopment not only must be willing to tie up his capital during the years required to negotiate purchases but must also face the prospect that the last few parcel owners will be able to demand extraordinarily high sums as the price of not blocking the project.

Moreover, the site assembly problem is not confined to cases involving interdependency effects. Suppose that the optimum redevelopment of a given neighborhood requires that a project be planned on a scale far larger than that of the existing small land parcels. The potential developer is again faced with the need to buy out numerous small holders, one by one, in order to achieve the necessary scale. Real estate developers have long recognized site assembly as a major obstacle, which raises the cost of development and presumably prevents some otherwise desirable projects from going ahead.

The site assembly problem is an important market imperfection with direct implications for public policy. The implication drawn by Davis and Whinston is that when properties in a given neighborhood remain underdeveloped either because of interdependencies that the "atomistic" private market cannot cope with or because the difficulty of site assembly

15. See the statements cited by Henry B. Schechter and Marion K. Schlefer in "Housing Needs and National Goals," Papers submitted to the Subcommittee on Housing, part I, House Committee on Banking and Currency, 1971, p. 35.

prevents development at an optimal scale, then public intervention is clearly called for. The government is then justified in using its power of eminent domain to assemble a site by purchasing properties at their fair market value. If interdependencies and site assembly problems were the only obstacles to an otherwise profitable renewal, then all obstacles that prevented private development from moving ahead would have been removed by the government's action. Consequently, the local renewal authority would be able to resell the consolidated site at cost to a private redeveloper who would then complete the project and earn a satisfactory rate of return without benefit of a land-cost write-down or other special subsidy. Market imperfections thus justify public intervention, but not public subsidy, to make renewal feasible.

Behind this piece of analysis lies the traditional argument that a freely competitive market in land tends, by an orderly process of "succession," to bring about the "highest and best use" of each parcel. The concept of highest and best use was introduced in Chapter 6 in explaining how competition between land uses results in an efficient pattern of intra-urban activity location. At that point, however, we did not examine in detail the process of succession by which the highest and best use of a parcel may change over time. If we are to understand fully the general problem of urban change and development (of which "urban renewal" is simply a special case), we must now supply the missing details.

LAND-USE SUCCESSION IN A COMPETITIVE MARKET

In the course of time both buildings and sites pass through a succession of uses. A building constructed originally as a town house may later be converted to commercial occupancy as the business district of the town expands. Or the reverse process may occur—loft buildings in declining commercial areas may be converted to residential uses. These are successions of use within given structures.

Very frequently evolutionary forces in the development of the city make it profitable to tear down existing buildings and replace them with new ones. In that case, we speak of "land-use succession" rather than succession of uses within given structures. With the rapid growth of cities, two of the most obvious forms of land-use succession have been the conversion of agricultural land to residential uses and the conversion of low density areas of single family homes to higher density apartment house neighborhoods. In either case, according to the traditional view, the evolutionary process of development works to bring about the "highest and best use" of land. If the land market is competitive, we can assume that each new building, at the time it is put up, represents the highest and best use of the plot on which it stands.

Succession via the market process can be explained as follows. First, let us define "highest and best" as that use which can pay the most for a given cleared site. In addition, we define the following terms:

V_o = the market value of a given site and the building on it, when the building is of the old type, denoted by the subscript o; this value equals the present worth of the expected future returns (gross of depreciation) from the property in the old use.

V_n = the anticipated market value of the same site and the building on it, when the building is of the new type, n; this value equals the present worth of the expected future returns from the property in the new use. V_n includes an allowance for the developer's normal profit.[16]

D_o = the cost of demolishing use o

C_n = the cost of constructing use n, exclusive of the cost of purchasing and clearing the site

Assume that a building of type o actually stands on the given site. At the time it was constructed, o was presumably the highest and best use for the site, for the developer who constructed o was able to obtain the site by outbidding all other firms for its use. We now wish to see under what conditions the new use, n, would replace o by means of ordinary market operations.

The cost to a developer of acquiring the given site in order to construct use n is V_o, because he has to pay the market price for the old building even though he intends to tear it down. The cost of tearing it down is D_o. Thus, for the new user, we can say that

$$V_o + D_o = \text{cost of acquisition and clearance}$$

On the other hand, the highest price that he can afford to pay for the cleared site and still earn a normal profit by developing use n is given by

$$V_n - C_n = \text{maximum value of cleared site to new user}$$

16. The analysis has been simplified by omitting from both V_o and V_n the present worth of any future uses that might be expected to succeed them. The omitted item is sometimes called the "reversionary value" of the site. For an analysis of succession that specifically allows for reversionary values, see Wallace F. Smith, *Housing: the Social and Economic Elements* (Berkeley and Los Angeles: University of California Press, 1970), pp. 243–50.

It follows that the new user can profitably undertake development on the site only if

$$V_n - C_n \geqq V_o + D_o$$

which is therefore a necessary condition for the new use to succeed the old through ordinary market processes. As a city evolves, this necessary condition may be fulfilled either because the old use becomes increasingly obsolete, making V_o decline, or because the demand for the new use becomes stronger, making the potential value V_n rise, or by a combination of both changes.

The urban renewal program, by means of its land-cost write-down, worked to speed up this process of succession. In order to encourage rebuilding, the renewal authority intervened in situations in which the maximum value of the site to the new user $(V_n - C_n)$ was not yet as large as the cost of acquisition and clearance $(V_o + D_o)$. The government absorbed two-thirds or more of the excess of the latter over the former, thus enabling n to succeed o at a time when it could not have done so by market processes.

To the casual observer this speed-up, which was a principal objective of the renewal program, may seem desirable. To the economist it appears otherwise. If the market functions efficiently, speeding up the process of succession is wasteful, in the sense of unnecessarily destroying economic value. The additional value created by redevelopment of the site from use o to use n is $V_n - V_o$. But the cost of the resources used up in creating the additional value is the sum of $D_o + C_n$. Thus redevelopment adds something to society's total economic output only if

$$V_n - V_o > D_o + C_n$$

But by rearranging terms we see that this is equivalent to the market condition for succession:

$$V_n - C_n > V_o + D_o$$

Employing a subsidy to speed up succession is therefore irrational: the costs incurred for redevelopment exceed the additional economic values created. It is easy to imagine that someone who is concerned about the housing problem might find this conclusion surprising. Walking through a slum neighborhood such a person may think: "These buildings are old, run down and depressing. New housing would be a tremendous improvement. There must be something wrong with a system that allows slums such as these to stand decade after decade when we know how to build so much better." Knowing a little urban economics, our observer might even add: "Surely these slums do not represent the highest and best use of the land. If we were to start over again on this block we certainly wouldn't put up buildings like these."

The economic analysis of succession can explain these supposed anomalies. Certainly, new housing would be a tremendous improvement. But it is very costly to build. Moreover, before a new building can be economically justified, it must be able to absorb, as its site cost, the capital value of the old structure it replaces. In other words, succession will not take place until the old property reaches the point where it is worth more as a site than it is as a building. That moment may be indefinitely delayed because old buildings often continue for a long time to have value based on their ability to render services less expensively than new structures. An old building can continue to be operated as long as rent receipts exceed operating costs, maintenance charges, and taxes, whereas a new building will not be started unless prospective rent receipts will, in addition, allow the builder to recoup the cost of construction. Thus old buildings can survive through many decades at a value less than would justify their being constructed anew but greater than would justify their demolition. During such periods they do *not* represent the highest and best use of the land in the sense employed here, since they would not be reconstructed new if the site were cleared for redevelopment. Yet it would be wasteful to tear them down.

Thus analysis of the economics of succession bears out Davis and Whinston's conclusion that if an otherwise economically desirable redevelopment is blocked only by market imperfections, the government, after intervening to overcome such obstacles, should be able to sell the cleared site to a developer at no loss. Unless additional justification can be found, the policy of subsidizing redevelopment simply to speed up succession is economically irrational.

Cost-Benefit Analysis of Subsidized Redevelopment

It is, of course, possible that the additional justification might be found in a complete cost-benefit analysis of a subsidized redevelopment project, whether under urban renewal or some other program. The market succession calculus described above takes into account only direct, or "on-site," benefits and costs. Perhaps if the indirect, or "off-site," effects were counted as well, the excess of indirect benefits over indirect costs would be sufficient to justify a subsidy. As Jerome Rothenberg's careful conceptual analysis of this problem demonstrated, the indirect effects of a large renewal scheme can be expected to ramify in complex ways through the urban housing and real estate markets.[17] For example, a possible

17. Jerome Rothenberg, *Economic Evaluation of Urban Renewal* (Washington, D.C.: The Brookings Institution, 1967).

indirect benefit from a large project would be an increase in the value of neighboring sites, a spillover effect of the improved environment within the project. Nourse reports that before-and-after studies of site values in the neighborhood of slum clearance and housing projects have found no evidence of such spillovers.[18] But even if it could be demonstrated that adjacent site values increased as a result of a project, it would remain highly uncertain how much of that increase should be counted as a net gain attributable to redevelopment. Subsidized construction may, to an undetermined extent, substitute for construction that would have occurred elsewhere in the city without subsidy, and such unsubsidized construction might also have conferred indirect benefits on adjacent sites.

If a redevelopment project demonstrably reduces the incidence of substandard housing (as urban renewal did *not*), indirect social benefits might also occur in the form of reduced crime, delinquency, or disease. As explained at the end of Chapter 12, however, the evidence for such benefits from improved housing is not strong or consistent, and the task of measuring their value, if, indeed, they exist, is a formidable one.

In principle, cost-benefit analysis is the right technique to use in evaluating redevelopment projects, since it can capture indirect effects that escape the market calculus. In practice, however, it has yet to make a substantial contribution.

SUBSIDIZED PRIVATE HOUSING

As urban renewal declined in favor during the 1960s, Congress enacted a widening array of other subsidy programs that were intended to stimulate new private construction without tying financial aid either to slum clearance or the removal of "blight." For the most part, these programs were designed to reduce rent or ownership costs so that families of moderate or even low income could afford to live in new or rehabilitated standard housing. Because they contained powerful subsidies to private developers, such programs were able to gain important political support from the construction industry. In this instance, unlike the case of public housing during the 1950s, congressional authorization was usually followed by generous appropriations rather than by financial neglect. Some of the programs, therefore, quickly reached very considerable size.

Most of the subsidy programs came to be known, for convenience, by the section number of the particular housing act under which they

18. Hugh O. Nourse, "A Rationale for Government Intervention in Housing . . . ," in U.S. Department of Housing and Urban Development, *Housing in the Seventies Working Papers*, vol. 1 (1976), pp. 245–48.

TABLE 13.2

Federally Subsidized Housing Programs, 1978

	NUMBER OF OCCUPIED UNITS[a]	CHARACTERISTICS OF PARTICIPATING HOUSEHOLDS[b]		
		Median Annual Income	*Median Monthly Rent*	*Minority Percent*
Public Housing	1,100,614	$ 3,718	$ 64	62%
Section 8, New Construction/ Substantial Rehabilitation	92,319	3,660	70	25
Section 8, Existing Housing	489,719	3,690	—	32
Section 236	648,000	6,361	163	30
Section 235, Original Program	287,300	8,085	—	—
Section 235, Revised Program	7,500	11,532	—	23

[a] For Sections 235 and 236, data refer to 1977.
[b] For Section 235, data refer to 1977.
Sources: U.S. Department of Housing and Urban Development, *1978 Statistical Yearbook*, March 1980, tables 54, 87, 89, 94, 95, and 127; Congressional Budget Office, *Federal Housing Policy: Current Programs and Recurring Issues*, June 1978, tables 11 and 12.

were authorized. The most important for urban areas have been the below-market interest rate program (known as Section 221(d)(3) BMIR), the rental housing assistance program (Section 236), the home-ownership assistance program (Section 235), the rent supplement program (not usually referred to by number) and, chronologically the last, Section 8.[19]

Table 13.2 presents data on two aspects of the most recent subsidized private housing programs: first, the size of each program, as indicated by the number of occupied units; second, the characteristics of participating households. Low income public housing is included in the table because its statistics provide a series of reference points to which the other programs can be compared.

Subsidies Under Section 221(d)(3)

Section 221(d)(3) was added to the Housing Act in 1961. Its purpose was to reduce rental costs by means of an interest rate subsidy given to new units built for middle and lower middle income families. Funds

19. For an analysis of the major programs to subsidize private housing down through 1971, see Henry J. Aaron, *Shelter and Subsidies* (Washington, D.C.: Brookings Institution, 1972), ch. 8. Later events are summarized in Congressional Budget Office, *Federal Housing Policy*, ch. 3; and Weicher, pp. 478–83.

were made available at below-market rates of interest to limited profit corporations as well as to cooperatives and other nonprofit sponsors. The Department of Housing and Urban Development (HUD), which administered the program, regulated rent levels and established income limits for admission that varied geographically but generally limited entrance to families that were below the local median income level.

From 1965 onward, the subsidy was provided as follows. A 40-year mortgage loan at 3 percent interest was made initially by a bank or other private lender. The mortgage was then immediately sold at par to a government lending institution: until 1968, the Federal National Mortgage Association (FNMA) and, since then, the Government National Mortgage Association (GNMA). The benefit to the project equaled the difference between capital costs at 3 percent and those at whatever market rate the borrower would otherwise have had to pay for private funds. The direct subsidy cost to the government was considerably less: the difference between 3 percent and the rate at which the government borrowed to subsidize GNMA. For example, if (in the late 1960s) the commercial mortgage rate were 8.5 percent and the government borrowing rate 5 percent, then the government was providing the project a yearly benefit equivalent to 5.5 percent (= 8.5 − 3) at a cost of only 2 percent (= 5 − 3) in its own accounts.

Opposition to 221(d)(3) eventually arose on several grounds. First, it was criticized for being a relatively "shallow" subsidy, not capable of pushing rents down far enough to reach the genuinely poor. Second, subsidies under the program could not be calibrated to the income levels of individual families but were, in effect, passed on as proportional rent reductions to all tenants. Finally, 221(d)(3) had what seemed to federal officials to be an unfortunate time pattern of impact on the federal budget: the full cost of each project appeared as a budget expenditure as soon as GNMA bought the mortgage. Budget makers much preferred a system—similar to the arrangement for financing public housing—in which subsidies could be paid out over the life of a project instead of being charged as a lump sum at the beginning. Most of the later subsidy programs have had just that feature.

Rent Supplements: A "Deeper" Subsidy

The first attempt to remedy the defects of the below-market interest rate program was the "rent supplement" plan authorized by the Housing and Urban Development Act of 1965. On behalf of tenants who qualified by reason of low income, the government would make subsidy payments to a nonprofit or limited-dividend developer of a new building. Bene-

ficiaries were required to pay 25 percent of income in rent. The subsidy
covered the difference between that amount and fair market rent. Thus,
for the first time, the amount of a government housing subsidy was geared
directly to the beneficiary's income level. The higher the family's income,
the less subsidy it would receive in a given housing unit. If income rose
high enough, the subsidy would automatically end, but the tenant would
not have to move. It was hoped that in this way new housing could be
developed that would contain both very low income families and families
that had achieved success and were "on the way up." In short, the plan
was expected to provide socioeconomic integration.

However, what Congress gave with one hand it took away with the
other. Eligibility was limited to those with incomes below the public
housing admission level and who were *also* elderly, handicapped, displaced
by government induced demolition, or previous occupants of substandard
housing. In case these restrictions did not sufficiently limit the program's
scope, Congress concluded the matter by appropriating minimal funds for
its support.

Among the most actively used provisions of the rent supplement
program was one that permitted payments on behalf of tenants admitted
to projects that were also subsidized under other sections of the law. Thus
a double subsidy, or "piggy-back" arrangement, was authorized under
which it became possible to provide a limited number of families with a
very deep subsidy indeed.

Subsidies Under Sections 235 and 236

In 1968 Congress enacted Sections 235 and 236 of the housing law,
a pair of subsidy plans by which 221(d)(3) was eventually replaced. Each
employed a subsidy formula similar in some respects to the provisions of
the rent supplement plan and designed to meet the objections that had
been raised to 221(d)(3). Under the rental assistance provisions of Section 236, HUD contracted with a qualifying sponsor (who developed and
operated the project) to pay a monthly rent subsidy geared to the level
of each eligible tenant's income. In general, eligibility was restricted to
tenants whose income did not exceed the admission limit for public
housing by more than 35 percent. The sponsor obtained a mortgage loan
at the going market interest rate. The tenant was required to pay at least
25 percent of income in rent. The subsidy formula depended on two rent
concepts: (1) "market rent," calculated to cover operating costs plus the
mortgage costs actually incurred; (2) "basic rent," equal to operating
costs plus mortgage costs calculated as if the project had obtained a
mortgage at a 1 percent rate of interest. The government undertook to

make a monthly payment on behalf of each tenant equal to the lesser of the following:

(1) subsidy = market rent − basic rent

(2) subsidy = market rent − 25 percent of tenant's income

As intended, the plan did provide a deeper subsidy than had been achieved under 221(d)(3), and the program therefore reached a somewhat lower income group. However, the double formula soon began to produce perverse effects. It had been expected that under the scheme outlined above, as incomes rose over time, the subsidies required for many tenants would gradually diminish. Instead, inflationary pressures in the early 1970s pushed operating costs up much faster than incomes. Basic rent in many instances came to exceed 25 percent of tenants' incomes. The second formula therefore became irrelevant, and tenants were forced to pay rapidly increasing rents. This was unfortunate in two respects. First, tenants of low to moderate income had been drawn into a situation they were unprepared to cope with. Second, a number of Section 236 buildings were unable to meet mortgage payments and went into default.[20]

The homeownership assistance program, enacted as Section 235, was similar in structure to the rental plan under 236. Families whose incomes fell within the qualifying limits received subsidies to help them meet the monthly carrying cost of a commercially financed mortgage on either a new or existing single-family home. The beneficiary was required to spend at least 20 percent of family income on monthly mortgage payments. The government paid a subsidy equal to the lesser of (1) the difference between the beneficiary's monthly payments and the actual monthly cost, including property taxes and insurance, or (2) the difference between the cost that would obtain with a 1 percent mortgage and the actual monthly cost, *not* including property taxes and insurance. Although renters under Section 236 were required to pay 25 percent of income toward housing, owners under Section 235 paid only 20 percent because they also bore the maintenance and operating costs that are included in rent.

Unlike the rent supplement program, Sections 235 and 236 were supported by generous federal funding and soon produced a large volume of subsidized construction. They became, in fact, the leading subsidy programs employed by the federal government in its effort to achieve the National Housing Goals, beginning in 1969.

The National Housing Goals

In 1968, the same year that it added Sections 235 and 236 to the housing statutes, Congress passed a Housing and Urban Development

20. Congressional Budget Office, *Federal Housing Policy*, pp. 33–34.

Act that included a timetable for achieving "National Housing Goals." For the ten-year period from 1969 through 1978, Congress set a goal of constructing or rehabilitating 26 million housing units, including 6 million subsidized units for low and moderate income families. Its purpose was to redeem the unfulfilled promise of "a decent home and suitable living environment for every American family" that had been set forth in the Housing Act of 1949. The 26 million total figure was based on the assumption that

> the nation's housing problems could be substantially solved in a single decade by producing enough unsubsidized and subsidized housing units to offset expected new family formations, replace substandard housing and losses from the housing stock, increase the vacancy rate and provide income assistance in the form of housing subsidies for families who could not afford the cost of standard housing. . . .[21]

We had, in other words, officially adopted a "new construction strategy" for solving the nation's housing problem.

The announced goal for new construction (excluding mobile homes) came to an average of 2.1 million units per year over a ten-year period—an ambitious undertaking when compared with the annual average of about 1.45 million units actually achieved from 1959 through 1968. However, the housing industry, backed by federal credit and subsidies, was able first to meet and then, in the early 1970s, to surpass the annual production goals set by the President. Subsidized production more than tripled during the first four years of the ten-year goal period, with the Section 235 and 236 programs making up a large share of the total.

Housing Subsidies and the Filtering Process

Subsidies under Sections 235 and 236 were deep enough to reach what might be called the "upper low income population" but not the poorest of the poor. The great bulk of *un*subsidized new housing goes, of course, to middle and upper income families. Clearly, then, the new construction strategy embodied in the national housing goals implied a reliance on filtering to improve housing conditions for those at the bottom of the income distribution. In the preceding chapter we described the filtering process as one in which housing originally built to rent at a higher price to a higher income class gradually "filters down" to a lower rent level and a poorer class of tenants. It has often been argued that subsidies

21. The President of the United States, *Fourth Annual Report on National Housing Goals*, June 29, 1972, p. 27. See chart 9, p. 26, of the report for the estimate of "needs" on which the figure of 26 million was based.

to stimulate the construction of moderate (or even upper) income housing are justified because they encourage this filtering process, which eventually raises housing standards for lower income groups as well as for those better off families who initially move into the subsidized housing. How credible is this argument?[22]

Undoubtedly housing built with the benefit of subsidy can rent for less than unsubsidized new construction of similar quality. As long as there is some price elasticity to housing demand, subsidies are therefore likely to increase the volume of new construction. Consequently, they are also likely to increase the number of already built housing units that filter down to lower rent levels. However, there may well be substantial substitution between housing built with subsidies and new units that would have been put up commercially without such aid. A degree of substitution is certainly to be expected if the subsidized housing is built to rent above the minimum at which new commercially developed construction is feasible.

Given the high cost of new construction, that outcome was unlikely under programs such as 221(d)(3), 235, or 236, in which income limits for eligibility were below the median value for local family income. It may well have occurred, however, under urban renewal, since many of the units built on renewal sites have been "semi-luxury" housing. It is also a strong possibility under locally operated programs that employ real estate tax abatement to stimulate new construction. The point is that one cannot take it for granted that all subsidy programs make a one-for-one contribution to increasing the volume of new construction and, therefore, to accelerating the filtering process.

Granted that subsidies for middle income or lower middle income housing will, under the right conditions, accelerate the filtering process, the question remains: How much is that likely to improve the housing condition of the poor? The answer has already been suggested by the analysis of filtering in the preceding chapter. Insofar as permanent structural characteristics of buildings are concerned—for example, room dimensions, plumbing and heating installations, access to light and air—filtered-down housing can raise standards at the lower end of the rent distribution. Since "complete plumbing" has been a requisite according to the conventional definition of "standard housing," there is no denying that filtering has contributed to improving housing standards as they are conventionally defined.

The situation is quite different for other aspects of housing service, such as expenditures on cleaning, repairing, maintaining, and operating a

22. For a more extended discussion of this issue, see William B. Brueggeman, "An Analysis of the Filtering Process with Special Reference to Housing Subsidies," *Housing in the Seventies Working Papers*, vol. 2, pp. 842–56.

building. In providing variable services of that sort, building owners will adapt to the rent-paying capacity of their tenants. When housing filters down to a lower income class, owners are almost certain to reduce these outlays, thus deliberately moving the building down to a lower quality level. Indeed, structural characteristics, too, may be altered in the process of adaptation: for example, large rooms or large apartments can be subdivided by remodeling. The end result is that good housing may gradually be converted to bad in the process of filtering.

Casual observation suggests that much. Some systematic evidence is provided by Muth's study of housing on Chicago's South Side. Muth employed multiple regression analysis to examine the degree of association between a large number of variables and the incidence of substandard housing in a sample of census tracts. He found that with the level of 1960 income and other variables controlled for, there remained a significant inverse relationship between the proportion of housing classified as substandard in a tract in 1960 and the median income level in that tract in 1950. This is consistent with the hypothesis that housing conditions in 1960 were adapting gradually to income levels that had been established ten years earlier. Muth concluded that "this indicates that if anything, dwelling unit condition adjusts over time to changes in the income level of its inhabitants rather than the reverse."[23]

The use of subsidies to stimulate new construction and accelerate filtering in the hope of raising housing standards for the poor is clearly inappropriate in local markets that are suffering substantial housing abandonment. Abandonment indicates an excess supply of housing at the lower end of the rental market. The poor would gain nothing from efforts to further increase the excess by accelerating filtering.[24] On the contrary, they might even be made worse off, if public policy were to accelerate the chaotic process of abandonment, with all the deprivation of housing services and all the social turmoil that word implies. Indeed, recognition of this fact contributed to the important changes in federal housing policy that occurred in 1973–74.

Moving Away from a New Construction Strategy

Government housing policy during the early 1970s produced a record quantity of new, federally assisted low and moderate income dwelling units. Yet housing programs were again in trouble with their critics, and in 1973 the federal government decreed a moratorium on further subsidy commitments and moved to reexamine the whole array of housing pro-

23. Richard F. Muth, *Cities and Housing* (Chicago: University of Chicago Press, 1969), p. 265.
24. Brueggeman, p. 854.

grams. The immediate cause of the freeze may have been a desire to regain control over federal spending by reining in programs such as 235 and 236 in which modest initial-year outlays led automatically to substantial, though somewhat uncertain, long-run spending commitments. In addition, there were intimations of waste, inefficiency, and scandal. Many of the new homes sold to low income families under Section 235 were badly constructed; many of the old ones were drastically unsound and/or greatly overpriced.[25] Section 236 was criticized as providing overly generous benefits to investors.[26] (Ironically, the objections to Section 236 were reminiscent of those that had been raised against Section 608, the federal government's principal rental housing program of the early postwar years.[27] We seem to have difficulty formulating schemes that can stimulate a large flow of new, moderately priced urban rental housing without at the same time creating substantial windfalls for some investors.)

No doubt, however, the impulse to economize and to avert scandal was reinforced by widely expressed doubts about the fundamental direction taken by urban housing policy in the United States. Housing analysts both inside and outside the government began to question the wisdom of the new construction strategy on which that policy rested.

If we look at the history of urban housing policy from the early postwar years down to 1974, we can discern two major periods, defined by the policy-dictated links connecting slum clearance, subsidized new construction, and the provision of benefits to tenants. The first period began with the birth of urban renewal (then called "redevelopment") in 1949. Urban renewal and the older, low rent public housing program became the principal elements in urban housing policy. These programs shared several characteristics: both provided subsidies that were linked to new construction; both linked new construction in some degree to slum clearance; in both cases the subsidies went initially to the supplier of new housing, whether private or public, rather than to the demander, or occupant.

The second period in housing policy began in the 1960s. The growing unpopularity of urban renewal, and to a lesser extent of public housing, was based partly on their link with slum clearance and the resulting destruction of low income housing and neighborhoods. The new programs of the 1960s—221(d)(3), 235, 236, and rent supplements—severed the

<hr/>

25. See *Interim Report on HUD Investigation of Low- and Moderate-Income Housing Programs*, U.S. Congress, Hearing before the House Committee on Banking and Currency, March 31, 1971.

26. James E. Wallace, "Federal Income Tax Incentives in Low and Moderate Income Rental Housing," in U.S. Congress, Joint Economic Committee, *The Economics of Federal Subsidy Programs*, part 5, pp. 676–705.

27. Ibid., p. 692, n. 15. For a description of the 608 "scandal," see Charles Abrams, *The City Is the Frontier* (New York: Harper & Row, 1965), pp. 87–90.

connection between subsidies and slum clearance. They did not, however, remove the link with new construction; they merely changed its form. In linking benefits for specific income classes to occupancy of specific newly constructed dwelling units, they strongly resembled the conventional public housing program; however much they differed in other respects, both were part of a new construction strategy.

Criticism of U.S. housing policy just before the 1974 moratorium concentrated on precisely that point. It was argued that we should cut the tie between subsidies and the supply of newly constructed units and instead pay "demand-side" subsidies to the poor, to be spent, with only a few restrictions, on old, new, or middle-aged housing at their choice. Of all the policies so far discussed, this is the one most clearly consistent with the adaptive model of the housing market described in Chapter 12. It rests on the assumption that if subsidies bring the demand for housing up to an adequate level, the market process, largely by its own motion, will supply an adequate flow of standard quality housing services.

HOUSING ALLOWANCES: A "DEMAND-SIDE" SUBSIDY

Urban housing market conditions that first developed in the latter half of the 1960s, and have prevailed ever since, have made subsidies for housing demand rather than for supply look particularly attractive. Between 1960 and 1970, 45 percent of all central cities of metropolitan areas lost population. Of the 21 cities that had populations greater than 500,000 in 1960, 15 suffered population decline during the ensuing decade. Population losses continued without let-up in the older central cities during the 1970s. Even at the beginning of that decade, many housing analysts had become convinced that in such cities the existing housing stock, plus the new construction that would take place without subsidy, would make up an ample supply of shelter. The widespread incidence of abandonment provided direct evidence that there was, in fact, an excess supply in many cities. As they saw it, the problem was one not of insufficient quantity but of inadequate quality. To a considerable extent (as we have already argued), the inadequate quality supplied by owners of rental housing is their way of adapting to the low rent-paying capacity of tenants, given the fact of rapidly increasing maintenance and operating costs.

In such circumstances does it make sense to attack the housing problem by means of subsidies to accelerate the pace of costly new construction? Advocates of housing allowances thought not. Instead, they proposed giving subsidies to low income tenants that would enable them to pay the rents needed to cover adequate maintenance and operation of the existing, usable, older housing stock.

It is important to realize that these subsidies would be available on the basis of open enrollment—anyone who qualified by reason of income and family size would become eligible to participate. This would be a radical departure from the usual federal practice of setting up housing subsidy programs in which the number of beneficiaries was strictly limited by the number of "slots" for which funds were appropriated. Partly for that reason, it seemed prudent to test a housing allowance program before deciding whether to adopt it. The federal government was sufficiently interested to carry out an extensive experiment with housing allowances during the 1970s. As we shall see, the results of the experiments were quite unexpected, confirming neither the hopes of those who advocated allowances nor the fears of those who had opposed them.

Before examining those results, however, we must explain the general structure of a housing allowance program. While housing allowance proposals differ from one another in detail, they share an underlying logic that we can conveniently examine in the version developed by Lowry. He explains the core of his proposal as follows:

> In each community a housing assistance agency would determine the rents needed to support full costs of ownership . . . for well-maintained older housing units, a standard amount varying with size of unit. Low-income families would apply to the agency for assistance, providing a Federal income tax return or other evidence of income. Applying a formula or schedule that takes into account income and size of family (and possibly other factors), the agency would determine how much the applicant could afford to contribute toward the cost of his housing. The applicant would be issued a rent certificate whose face value was equal to the difference between that amount and the standard full cost of a housing unit whose size was appropriate for the applicant's family. The certificate would consist of twelve dated coupons, covering a calendar year of rent assistance, each bearing the name of the recipient and the number of family members.
>
> With the additional purchasing power provided by these coupons, the applicant would then seek private rental housing whose location and physical features were congenial to his needs and preferences and whose rent was within his now-augmented budget. Negotiations with the landlord over rent and conditions of occupancy would be solely the responsibility of the applicant; he could and should request evidence that the building was free of violations of the City's housing code. Once accepted as a tenant, he would present his assistance coupon in partial payment of the contracted rent, supplying the balance from his own pocket. Because each dollar of rent above the face value of the coupon would come out of the tenant's pocket he would have a clear incentive to choose

housing within his means and to pay no more than the going market price for the housing he chooses.[28]

The benefit schedule described by Lowry is a version of a "housing gap formula." In its simplest form this can be written as follows:

$$P = R - bY$$

where P is the allowance payment, R is the estimated standard rent of adequate housing, Y is household income, and b is the proportion of income the tenant is required to pay in rent.

For the purpose of illustration, suppose $b = 25$ percent. It can easily be seen that as a household's income rises, the benefit payment diminishes, finally disappearing when the family can pay for standard housing by spending 25 percent of its income.

As Lowry's statement indicates, a housing gap formula has one other important characteristic. It provides benefits based not on *actual* rent paid but on the estimated standard rent for adequate housing. The tenant who can find adequate housing at less than the standard rent "keeps the change"; the tenant who wants housing that rents for more than the standard, pays the difference out of his or her own pocket. At the margin, the tenant is paying the rent and is correspondingly drawn into the market process as an active participant. Thus housing allowances, under this formula, do not create a class of passive tenant beneficiaries, as some welfare housing assistance programs do.

Housing Allowances and Code Enforcement

It is worth examining briefly the interconnection between housing allowances and code enforcement. Most cities have housing codes that require dwelling units to be supplied with specific facilities such as plumbing, heating, and ventilation and to be kept in a state of cleanliness and good repair.[29] In rental buildings it is the responsibility of the landlord to see that essential services are maintained. Periodically it occurs to housing reformers that a "code enforcement drive" with real muscle behind it could force owners of deteriorated slum housing to bring it up to par and keep it there. Such drives are not necessarily useless, but their frequent repetition suggests, at least, that they do not achieve long-lasting improvement. This failure is probably explained by the inability or unwillingness of tenants in slum housing to pay rents that would cover the

28. Ira S. Lowry, "Housing Assistance for Low-Income Urban Families: A Fresh Approach," Papers submitted to the Subcommittee on Housing, part 2, U.S. Congress, House Committee on Banking and Currency, June 1971, p. 505.
29. For a detailed description of housing codes in the United States, see *Building the American City*, part III, ch. 4, "Housing Codes."

cost of operating a violation-free building. For if tenants were willing and able to pay such costs there would seem to be no reason why the landlord would not wish to satisfy them by providing the necessary services. On the other hand, if tenants were not willing and able to pay, landlords would seem likely to resist incurring the extra cost of providing such services.[30]

If this explanation seems unduly simpleminded, consider the case of a well-run middle class apartment house. No one supposes that the owner of such a building keeps it clean and in good repair only because of the threat of housing code penalties. Rather he or she does so because tenants want, and are prepared to pay for, a well-run building. Furthermore, the owner suspects that tenants will move out if they are dissatisfied. Ideally, by providing low income tenants with enough rent-paying capacity to support well-maintained housing, an adequate rent certificate program would make code enforcement as routine and secondary a matter for low income housing as it is today for middle income structures. However, there would probably be a long transitional period following the introduction of housing allowances during which code enforcement would be essential to achieve rapid improvement of the housing stock and to establish a new level of expectations among both tenants and landlords. Hence the emphasis on code enforcement in every housing allowance proposal.

Lowry's plan includes a provision, with teeth in it, for ensuring the maintenance of decent housing standards: rent certificates would be cashed by the housing agency only for owners of buildings that were free of all housing code violations. Thus the power of the tenant to insist on adequate maintenance (which he or she can now afford to pay for) as a condition of continued occupancy would be supported by the power of the housing agency to make the entire building ineligible for rent certificate payments. Landlords catering to a low income clientele would find this a strong incentive to keep their buildings up to full code standards, while the public would be assured that rent subsidies were not being paid for substandard housing.

Other Arguments for Housing Allowances

Proponents of housing allowances believe they have a number of advantages, in addition to those already cited.

Equity. A housing allowance plan is more equitable than a new construction strategy. Under the latter, a relatively small number of families receive very large benefits per household, while the majority of

30. For a more extended argument of this point, see James Heilbrun, *Real Estate Taxes and Urban Housing* (New York: Columbia University Press, 1966), pp. 10–23.

low income families, equally qualified according to eligibility standards, receive nothing. In 1977, according to one estimate, less than 10 percent of the income-eligible population was receiving housing assistance under federal programs.[31] By contrast, a housing allowance plan would provide less ample benefits per family but would be available to all eligible households rather than to a somewhat arbitrarily selected minority. Furthermore, the typical benefit formula under a rent certificate plan provides that assistance payments are gradually reduced to zero as family income rises. Together with universal coverage for low income families, this feature ensures the equitable result that no one receiving assistance is thereby made better off than someone else who is not. Such an outcome is *not* assured under the patchwork arrangement of present housing subsidy programs.

Cost. A housing allowance plan would be far less costly than a new construction strategy per dwelling unit brought up to standard. Lowry estimated that in New York City in 1969 the rent needed to cover the full cost of a well-maintained four-room apartment in an older building ranged from $100 to $150 per month. The equivalent full cost for either new public housing or new Section 236 units was approximately twice as high.[32] Consequently, the subsidy needed to enable a family of a given income class to occupy well-maintained older housing would be far lower than the subsidy needed to put the same family into a newly constructed unit. Data from the Experimental Housing Allowance Program (to be discussed in detail below) placed the average subsidy at about $800 per family, per year, in 1976. Administrative costs would raise that to about $1,000.[33] By way of comparison, consider the cost of two "new construction" programs in 1971–72, when prices were somewhat lower: the full annual subsidy cost per unit of public housing completed in 1971 was estimated at $1,980; the full subsidy cost per unit of housing under Section 236 was $1,901 in 1972.[34] (The latter figure includes the cost of rent supplement payments to make it comparable to a housing allowance or to public housing in reaching the poor.)

Efficiency. It can be argued that a considerable part of the outlay on a new construction strategy ultimately runs to waste so far as raising hous-

31. Congressional Budget Office, *Federal Housing Policy*, p. 12, n.10. The percentage refers to programs administered by the Department of Housing and Urban Development and the Farmers Home Administration.
32. Lowry, pp. 500–01.
33. David B. Carlson and John D. Heinberg, *How Housing Allowances Work*, Integrated Findings from the Experimental Housing Allowance Program, doc. no. 249-3 (Washington, D.C.: The Urban Institute, February 1978), pp. 46–47.
34. De Leeuw and Leaman, table 2, p. 655; U.S. Department of Housing and Urban Development, *Housing in the Seventies*, 1974, table 19, p. 116.

ing standards is concerned. Because low income tenants cannot afford to pay its "upkeep," much of the housing that filters down as a result of subsidized new construction deteriorates into later model slums. Thus the costly new construction program is ultimately futile, much like the efforts of a person who tries to fill up a swimming pool without first mending the leaks in the bottom. Housing allowances are aimed precisely at those leaks. They are designed to prevent filtered-down housing from sinking below acceptable standards.

Consumer choice. As compared with the supply-side subsidies of a new construction strategy, housing allowances have the virtue of greatly increasing the freedom of choice for beneficiaries. If the program were set up nationwide, low income families could obtain equivalent benefits anywhere. Within a given city they would be free to choose any building and neighborhood they could afford, instead of being constrained to live in designated subsidized projects. As between city and city, or city and suburb, they would be free to move, without losing benefits, to any place offering moderate-priced accommodation. Consequently, housing allowances might contribute to achieving a reduction in the degree of racial segregation within cities and between cities and suburbs.

Reduced risk. New construction subsidies tie government obligations to particular buildings in particular locations. A wrong decision can lead to disastrous loss to the government, as in the case of Pruitt-Igoe. Unlike new construction subsidies, housing allowances, because they are geographically mobile, cannot become permanently locked in to the wrong neighborhood or the wrong city, as new construction subsidies may. Instead, they move automatically to wherever people wish, and are able, to spend them. Although this mobility deprives local authorities of some leverage in planning, it also reduces the risk of serious public investment errors.

Before examining in detail the results of the housing allowance experiments conducted during the mid-1970s, it is appropriate to describe the important changes in housing policy that were embodied in the Housing and Community Development Act of 1974.

Section 8: Subsidies for Demand as Well as Supply

The 1973 moratorium on the commitment of additional federal funds for subsidized housing was followed by an intensive reexamination of housing policy, supervised by HUD.[35] As we have pointed out, criticism of the new construction strategy was already commonplace. The weight

35. This "National Housing Policy Review" produced the report, *Housing in the Seventies,* cited in n. 34, above.

of opinion increasingly supported shifting from supply- to demand-side subsidies. The Housing and Community Development Act of 1974 was, in fact, a compromise that included both subsidy types.[36]

Section 8 of the 1974 Act authorized a new program of housing assistance to lower income families, replacing Section 236 and the rent supplement program, commitments for both of which were permanently frozen after the 1973 moratorium. Section 8 also superseded Section 23, which had authorized the leasing of private sector units for use as public housing. Thus Section 8 has been the principal rental housing assistance program of the federal government since 1974. Its dimensions and the characteristics of its beneficiaries are indicated by the data in Table 13.2.

Assistance under Section 8 is made available to tenants in four categories of housing: programs for newly constructed, substantially rehabilitated, and existing units were authorized in 1974. Assistance to moderate rehabilitation was added in 1978. Eligibility is restricted to those whose incomes do not exceed 80 percent of the area median. In addition, at least 30 percent of the beneficiaries must be "very low income families," defined as those whose incomes do not exceed 50 percent of the area median. These requirements have insured that Section 8 payments go to low income families rather than to the moderate-to-low stratum served by Section 236 (compare the median income levels reported for both programs in Table 13.2).

The assistance formula dispenses with the connection to "basic rent" that had caused so much difficulty in the Section 236 program. Under Section 8 there is a single formula: the tenant pays from 15 to 25 percent of income in rent, the fraction depending upon income and family size; a subsidy from HUD makes up the difference between the tenant contribution and what HUD determines to be the allowable rent. Under this formula tenant payments are not automatically forced upward, as they were in the case of Section 236 housing, by rising operating costs. Instead, government contributions increase.

Except for changes in the assistance formula and income limits, the Section 8 programs for new construction and rehabilitation strongly resemble Section 236, which they replaced. HUD enters into multiyear contracts with developers or rehabilitators to pay subsidies on behalf of qualifying tenants in specific buildings. Like the payments under Section 236, these are supply-side subsidies in the sense that they go to designated projects and are intended to stimulate construction and rehabilitation.

The new departure under Section 8 is the provision for paying subsidies to tenants living in existing housing. The "Section 8-existing" pro-

36. See Frank S. Kristof, "The Housing and Community Development Act of 1974," *Journal of Economics and Business*, Winter 1975, pp. 112–21.

gram, as it has come to be called, is a pure demand-side subsidy. It resembles a true housing allowance program except that instead of being open to all who qualify on account of low income, its "slots" are strictly limited by the availability of funds. Apart from that limitation, it would be expected to have most of the advantages already outlined for the housing allowance approach to subsidized shelter.

The program operates as follows. HUD contracts with a state or local housing agency to subsidize a specified number of tenants in existing privately owned rented housing. The agency enrolls qualified beneficiaries and makes payments to their landlords, under the formula described above. Tenants may choose where they wish to live, provided the landlord agrees to participate in the program, the premises meet minimum physical standards, and the rent does not exceed the ceiling established by HUD. The maximum rent rule has been criticized as limiting tenants' freedom of choice and excluding from the program some people, otherwise qualified, who prefer to live in apartments with higher rents.[37] The need for a rent limitation could be avoided if Section 8 benefits were based on the "housing gap formula," previously described. Under such a formula no rent limitation is needed, since government contributions do not depend upon actual rent paid. The advantage gained is that, if the tenant wants to live *above* the program standard and is willing to pay the extra rent, he or she is free to do so.

One of the alleged advantages of demand-side subsidies is that they place beneficiaries in existing housing, where rents, and therefore subsidies, will be far below the level required in newly constructed units. Section 8 provides an excellent test of this proposition, since its existing housing and new construction programs operate under similar rules regarding tenant incomes and benefits. Existing housing does turn out to be much less costly. On the basis of program experience, the Congressional Budget Office estimated that over the future life of contract commitments made in fiscal year 1980, the average subsidy cost for Section 8 existing housing will range from $1,560 to $1,750 per dwelling unit, per year. The comparable range estimated for the new construction/substantial rehabilitation program is $2,490 to $3,510 per unit per year.[38] Taking the mean of those ranges, the existing housing program would appear to be about 45 percent less costly per unit. In other words, a given budgetary outlay would serve almost twice as many beneficiaries in existing housing as in the other program.

Section 8 provides assistance only in rental housing, replacing earlier programs that were halted in 1973. The homeownership assistance pro-

37. James P. Zais, Jeanne E. Goedert, and John W. Trutko, *Modifying Section 8*, doc. no. 240–10 (Washington, D.C.: The Urban Institute, January 1979), pp. 5–23.
38. Congressional Budget Office, *Long-Term Costs . . .* , pp. 43–45.

TABLE 13.3
Federal Expenditure for Housing and Community Development

	FISCAL YEAR	
	1970	1980ª
Federal outlay, millions of dollars		
Housing assistance	$ 499	$5,318
Community development	1,449	4,519
Block grantsᵇ	—	3,500
Other	—	1,019
Percentage of total federal outlay		
Housing assistance	0.3%	0.9%
Community development	0.7	0.8

ª Estimated in source.
ᵇ Program began 1975.
Sources: 1980 data: *Budget of the United States Government,* 1981, pp. 208 and 263. 1970 data: unpublished tabulations, Fiscal Analysis Branch, U.S. Office of Management and Budget.

gram under Section 235 was also suspended in the 1973 moratorium but was not replaced by new legislation. Instead, HUD modified the program and put it back into operation in 1976. Under the new rules, instead of providing a subsidy to push the participant's mortgage interest cost down to 1 percent, the minimum effective rate was raised to 4 percent. Other requirements were tightened up as well, in order to reduce the incidence of default, which had reached an intolerable level under the original program. These changes, necessary though they were, do hold down the rate of activity under the new program and prevent it from reaching families with incomes as low as those previously served. (See Table 13.2.)

Despite the many program changes that took place, total federal outlays for housing assistance rose steadily during the 1970s. Table 13.3 shows that assistance payments multiplied more than ten times over between 1970 and 1980. During the same period, federal outlays for all purposes multiplied by a factor of three. Consequently, the share of housing assistance in the federal budget, while still very small, did rise sharply.

THE EXPERIMENTAL HOUSING ALLOWANCE PROGRAM

In 1970, four years before the Section 8-existing program was enacted, Congress authorized HUD to conduct large-scale tests of the housing allowance concept. Several years were spent in planning the test, which evolved into the Experimental Housing Allowance Program.[39] EHAP consisted of three parts, a Demand Experiment to test the effects of allowances on the behavior of recipients, a Supply Experiment to test effects on entire housing markets, and an Administrative Agency Experiment to test alternative administrative arrangements.

The Demand Experiment was carried out by offering housing allowances, under a variety of formulas, to samples of low income households in Pittsburgh and Phoenix. The Supply Experiment took place in Brown County, Wisconsin (including the city of Green Bay), and St. Joseph County, Indiana (including the city of South Bend), two small but contrasting metropolitan housing markets. At these sites an allowance was made available to any resident who met the income qualifications. Thus the Supply Experiment reproduced locally the opportunities for participation and for the impact of participation on the housing market that would exist nationwide under a full-scale federally financed plan. Enrollments were kept open for five years and participating households allowed to continue in the program for ten years so that the long-run impact of the program could be observed.

A "housing gap" formula was employed for calculating benefits in most phases of the experiment. It should be recalled that under this arrangement, the participant "keeps the change" (or pays it) if actual rent is below (or above) the estimated standard rent for a unit of appropriate size. Hence the tenant who moves to more expensive quarters pays the full extra cost out of his or her own pocket, just as would be the case if there were no allowance.

The results of the housing allowance experiment were surprisingly at odds with the expectations of most observers. In general, the system of allowances produced neither the large benefits its supporters had so confidently expected, nor the harmful outcomes its opponents had feared. In both cases, the cause was the same: the housing market behavior of low income families turned out to be surprisingly resistant to change under the impact of a housing allowance offer.[40]

39. For a description of the background and organization of the experiments, see U.S. Department of Housing and Urban Development, *A Summary Report of Current Findings from the Experimental Housing Allowance Program*, April 1978, appendix I.

40. See ibid.; Marc Bendick, Jr., and James P. Zais, *Incomes and Housing, Lessons From Experiments With Housing Allowances* (Washington, D.C.: The Urban Institute, October 1978); Bernard J. Frieden, "What Have We Learned from the Housing Allowance Experiment?" *Habitat International*, vol. 5, nos. 1/2 (1980), pp. 227–54, published in a shorter version as Frieden, "Housing Allowances: An Experiment That Worked," *The Public Interest*, Spring 1980, pp. 15–35; and Ira S. Lowry, *Housing Allowances: Lessons from the Supply Experiment*, document no. P-6455 (Santa Monica, Calif.: The Rand Corporation, March 1980).

Participation Rates

The inertia of low income housing markets shows up in two findings (themselves interconnected) from which much else follows. First, the participation rate of the eligible population was surprisingly low. Second, participants showed very little inclination to spend more on housing as a result of the subsidy.

In order to receive benefits under a housing allowance plan, a household must live in a unit that meets the program's minimum standards. Some eligible families occupy units of satisfactory quality when they enroll. For them, participation is not difficult. Others, however, live in substandard units. In order to qualify for payments they must either move to a standard unit or upgrade the housing they already occupy. They might consider either of these alternatives too expensive to be worthwhile and therefore never qualify to receive benefits. At the sites of the Demand Experiment, between 80 and 90 percent of those in the sample to whom assistance was offered enrolled in the program, but only 40 to 45 percent satisfied the housing requirement and became recipients.[41] In the Supply Experiment, the participation rate of eligible households at both sites averaged out to 44 percent in the third year of the experiment. In the aggregate, then, less than half the eligible population participated in the experiment at any one time. (Lowry points out, however, that this rate is about in line with findings for other income transfer programs, such as AFDC.[42])

Not only were participation rates relatively low, but also the experiment provided a good deal of evidence that they fall as the required housing standard rises.[43] In other words, the more housing improvement the program requires, the fewer people will participate in it, a result that appears to frustrate the program's major purpose—the improvement of housing conditions.

Income and the Demand for Housing

The relative reluctance of households either to move or to undertake the upgrading of current quarters that would qualify them for benefit payments is connected to the second major finding: although housing allowances augment the income of beneficiaries, relatively little of the additional income is spent on housing. For example, participants in the Demand Experiment at Pittsburgh received an average monthly benefit of

41. U.S. Department of Housing and Urban Development, *A Summary Report*, table 1.
42. Lowry, *Lessons from the Supply Experiment*, table 3 and pp. 6–8.
43. Bendick and Zais, pp. 10–15.

$50, but their expenditure on housing increased by an average of only $13. Comparable figures at Phoenix were $80 and $26.[44] Where did the rest of the money go? The answer is very clear. Participants used the bulk of the subsidy to reduce their own contribution to housing cost. Before participation, the median ratio of gross rent to income ranged from .34 to .53 at the twelve experimental sites. After benefit payments, the median ratio (taking the family's own payments as the numerator) declined to a range of .17 to .30, little more than half of what it had been.[45]

To put the matter in formal terms, participants in the experiment had a very low income elasticity of demand for housing. This elasticity is defined as the percentage change in housing expenditure that accompanies a 1 percent change in household income. As pointed out in Chapter 12, estimates of its value have varied widely, but recent studies generally placed it in the range of .7 to 1.0 for renters and somewhat higher for homeowners. Estimates from EHAP data put it much lower: .45 for owners and .19 for renters participating in the Supply Experiment.[46]

As we shall see, many of the other results of the experiment appear to follow from the combination of low participation rates and low income elasticity of demand.

Effects on Mobility

Because housing allowances—unlike conventional supply-side subsidies—are not tied to specific housing projects, proponents believed that allowances would increase the intrametropolitan mobility of the poor, permitting them to escape from poverty neighborhoods and encouraging socioeconomic and racial integration. Evidence from the experiments, however, indicates that when participants are compared with control groups, the mobility of participants is only slightly higher.[47] Those who did move tended to move to less segregated or more desirable neighborhoods, but there was no indication that the program significantly increased movement to the suburbs.[48]

Marc Bendick and James P. Zais point out that "household moves are primarily associated with changes in needs and circumstances." Very large increases in income are likely to cause movement, since we know

44. Ibid., p. 3.
45. Frieden, "What Have We Learned?" table 7. Also see John E. Mulford, George D. Weiner, and James L. McDowell, *How Allowance Recipients Adjust Housing Consumption*, doc. no. N-1456-HUD (Santa Monica, Calif.: The Rand Corporation, August 1980).
46. John Mulford, *Income Elasticity of Housing Demand*, doc. no. R-2449-HUD (Santa Monica, Calif.: The Rand Corporation, July 1979), p. 33.
47. Bendick and Zais, pp. 16–17.
48. Frieden, "What Have We Learned?" pp. 245–46.

that household location choices *do* vary substantially with income. Thus the experiment might have induced more mobility had benefit levels been substantially higher. The immediate lesson for public policy, however, is that benefits at the level offered by EHAP or other current programs influence location very little and are therefore unlikely to contribute much toward accomplishing desegregation.[49]

Improvements in Housing

Many who enrolled in the experiment were then living in dwellings that did not come up to program standards. In order to qualify for payments they either had to upgrade their units or move. Most of those in the Supply Experiment chose to stay where they were and make or obtain repairs. But these repairs turned out to be surprisingly inexpensive. In many cases tenants themselves supplied the labor. The median cash cost of repairs was only about $10, and three-quarters of all repairs cost less than $30![50] Preliminary results from the Demand Experiment showed approximately the same low costs.

These findings demonstrate that housing allowances *did* improve the quality of housing and did so very economically. But the small cost of the necessary improvements also suggests that they were not very substantial. For all that it increased tenants' rent-paying capacity, the program apparently did not induce massive improvements in the housing stock.

Effects on Housing Prices

Those who were skeptical about housing allowances usually feared that by subsidizing demand, allowances would cause "pure rent inflation" —an increase in the unit cost of housing not accompanied by any improvement in quality as measured by service rendered. Moreover, if rents were thus inflated in submarkets serving participants, *non*participants in the same markets would be hurt: they would have to pay higher prices without benefit of an offsetting subsidy. At issue was the elasticity of supply of housing services. Would landlords readily respond to the increased rent-paying capacity of subsidized tenants by supplying a higher level or quality of service? Advocates of housing allowances clearly believed that they would, a view that is consistent with the adaptive model of the housing market described in Chapter 12. It was a principal purpose of the Supply Experiment to settle this argument by observing rent trends in two markets where a housing allowance program was in full swing.

49. Bendick and Zais, pp. 18–19.
50. Lowry, *Lessons from the Supply Experiment,* table 8.

Factually, the results of the experiment are clear-cut: no perceptible rent inflation occurred at either site.[51] As the discussion of repair costs indicated, it was possible to raise most dwelling units up to standard quality at very little cost. On this test, the supply of housing services appeared to be highly elastic.[52] A skeptic might still argue, however, that this outcome depended importantly on the inertia of consumers. By rough calculation, 20 percent of households were eligible for support, but only half of those were enrolled at any one time, and only 80 percent of the enrolled qualified as participants. Thus about 8 percent of households were receiving allowances at any moment ($.20 \times .5 \times .8 = .08$).[53] If only 8 percent of households were subsidized and those households had a very low propensity for spending additional income on housing, it is not surprising that rents were unaffected.

Cost of the Program

Both supporters and opponents of housing allowances were concerned about the probable cost of a national program. Although the cost per beneficiary was expected to be relatively low, it was generally agreed that the aggregate cost would be high because an allowance scheme, unlike conventional housing programs, would be open to all comers. The unit cost of housing allowances in the experiment was, indeed, low by comparison with costs under alternative policies—only about $1,000 per year in 1976. (This figure, and the per unit costs of other programs, were discussed above.) Surprisingly, the aggregate cost of a national program, estimated on the basis of data from the experiment, also turns out to be quite modest. This occurs not only because unit costs were low, which was expected, but also because the participation rate of the eligible population was only about 40 percent. An Urban Institute study estimated the aggregate cost of a national program, including both administrative and transfer costs, at $7.4 billion a year, in 1976 dollars.[54] That is not much more than the aggregate costs estimated for housing allowance

51. C. Lance Barnett and Ira S. Lowry, *How Housing Allowances Affect Prices,* doc. no. R-2452-HUD (Santa Monica, Calif.: The Rand Corporation, September 1979), pp. 34–35.
52. For other studies of housing supply elasticity, see Frank De Leeuw and Nkanta F. Ekanem, "The Supply of Rental Housing," *American Economic Review,* December 1971, pp. 806–17; James R. Follain, Jr., "The Price Elasticity of the Long-Run Supply of New Housing Construction," *Land Economics,* May 1979, pp. 190–99; and John M. Mason, "The Supply Curve for Housing," *Journal of the American Real Estate and Urban Economics Association,* Fall 1979, pp. 362–77.
53. Frieden, "What Have We Learned?" p. 246.
54. Carlson and Heinberg, pp. 44–47.

programs in the late 1960s, when prices were far lower. However, it is about three times the amount actually spent on housing assistance programs in 1976.

Evaluating the Results of the Experiment

After evaluating the results of the housing allowance experiment, Bernard Frieden called it "an experiment that worked." It worked in the sense of reaching those most in need to a far greater extent than other programs to subsidize private housing had done. It worked in the sense of reaching those groups without requiring, as the public housing program does, that they live in particular, and perhaps undesirable, housing projects. It worked also by allowing its beneficiaries to reduce very sharply the heavy burden of housing expenditure in their budgets.

In Frieden's view it also worked because for the first time the poor were allowed to demonstrate by their own action whether they preferred better housing or more cash to spend on other goods. To a surprising degree, they preferred the cash. As Frieden put it,

> . . . federal officials expected the typical family to move to better accommodations and to spend most of its subsidy for higher rent. The reality was that most families stayed put, made minor repairs if they were required to meet program standards, got marginally adequate housing if they did not have it to begin with, and used most of the payment to free their own funds for nonhousing expenses. As a result, the program had only limited impact on the quality of the housing supply and on mobility; but these were unavoidable consequences of respecting the wishes of families in the program.[55]

While the housing allowance experiment was going on, the federal government introduced the new Section 8 subsidies (previously described). Not unexpectedly, the Section 8-existing program, which has most of the characteristics of a housing allowance, has produced results very similar to those of the housing allowance experiment.[56]

In the light of results from the housing allowance experiment and experience with the Section 8-existing program, urban housing policy faces an as yet unresolved question. On the one hand, it is difficult to make a case for supply-side subsidies under today's circumstances. On the other hand, housing allowances, which were widely supported to replace them, have not produced the anticipated gains. Because the housing demand of

55. Frieden, "What Have We Learned," p. 250.
56. Congressional Budget Office, *Federal Housing Policy*, pp. 31–32.

low income families responds so weakly to subsidies, housing allowances have relatively little impact on what were always thought to be the major housing problems. The strongest effect of demand-side subsidies has been to reduce the income burden of housing for the poor. But if that is to become the major policy objective, it is not clear why it would not be better served by pure income transfers than by transfers tied to the consumption of housing.

Perhaps the participants in the housing allowance experiments were trying to tell us something more. One can interpret the results as evidence that people are no longer greatly dissatisfied with the condition of their housing. Is it possible that citizen discontent with cities no longer arises from bad housing, in the old, conventional sense of that word, but rather from the necessity of living in bad neighborhoods, in environments ridden with crime, vandalism, and juvenile delinquency and pervaded by a general sense of disorder and decay? It is to the problem of neighborhoods that we turn next.

THE PROBLEM OF DETERIORATING NEIGHBORHOODS

While housing conditions for the urban poor have improved greatly in the last 30 years, no one is likely to claim that low income neighborhoods are also measurably improved.[57] Neighborhood data of the sort shown in Table 12.2 do not go back far enough to establish clear trends, but they do show that dissatisfaction with neighborhood on some counts is now greater than dissatisfaction with the condition of housing.

The federal government supports neighborhood rehabilitation through a variety of programs. Outlays under the budgetary title of Community Development, most of which are "neighborhood oriented," totaled $4.5 billion in 1980 (see Table 13.3). Community Development Block Grants accounted for more than three quarters of that amount. These grants, established under the Housing and Community Development Act of 1974, combine into a single allotment the financial aid previously made available under separate, categorical programs for Urban Renewal, Neighborhood Development, Open Space, and other community development activities. Setting up the CDBG system was an important step in the process of "de-categorizing" federal aid to states and localities that will be discussed in Chapter 15. Under a block grant, unlike a categorical grant, the locality is free to use funds according to its own priorities, within a broad range of eligible activities.

As Table 13.3 shows, outlays for community development have only

57. The revival of certain inner city neighborhoods as middle income families move in and restore previously run-down housing will be discussed in ch. 16.

slightly increased their share of the federal budget in recent years. By contrast, outlays for housing assistance grew more than three times as fast as the federal total and, by 1980, exceeded community development outlays by almost $1 billion.

Two fundamental reasons explain why the considerable public effort to improve conditions in low income neighborhoods has had so little effect. First, much of the dissatisfaction with neighborhoods arises not from physical conditions but from such social problems as crime, drug abuse, and juvenile delinquency. These pathologies are not relieved by housing improvements or by neighborhood rehabilitation but, on the other hand, do make such improvements and rehabilitation more difficult to sustain. Second, the physical deterioration of neighborhoods, the problem neighborhood public policy does try to deal with directly, is essentially not controllable with the tools now at hand.[58] We can see why this is so by tracing out the following chain of causes and effects.

The physical deterioration of neighborhoods is bound up with the problem of housing abandonment described at length in the preceding chapter. Housing abandonment has been stimulated by a filtering process set in motion by rapid population decline in the older central cities. Rapid population decline, in turn, resulted, in large measure, from the outmigration of the white middle class to the suburbs. As population decreased, opportunities for movement within the city were opened up to the city's low income residents. Since an influx of the poor was often followed some years later by abandonment as they moved on yet again, whole neighborhoods were often destroyed in the course of these internal migrations.

If the poverty population of a city is continually on the move, public policies aimed at neighborhood rehabilitation are very likely to prove fruitless. What about the possibility that effective housing and neighborhood rehabilitation would have precisely the effect of slowing down population movement and therefore stabilizing neighborhoods? The answer is that, of course, some neighborhoods have been successfully stabilized. For the most part, however, the forces generating movement have simply swamped those making for stability. In areas such as the South Bronx, both public and private investment in rehabilitation have been wiped out in as little as five or six years.[59] It is scarcely an exaggeration to say that neighborhoods disappear even as plans are being made to save them.

58. See Michael A. Stegman, "The Neighborhood Effects of Filtering," *Journal of the American Real Estate and Urban Economics Association*, Summer 1977, pp. 227–41; and Michael A. Stegman and David W. Rasmussen, "Neighborhood Stability in Changing Cities," *American Economic Review*, May 1980, pp. 415–19.

59. See Frank S. Kristof, "Housing Abandonment in New York City," paper presented at Conference on Housing, Georgia State University, May 8, 1978; and *The New York Times*, February 6, p. B-1, and March 9, 1978, p. B-3.

Since population movement plays a crucial role in this sequence, it would appear that we can exercise control over neighborhood deterioration only if we can influence population movement. Two possibilities have been suggested. Michael Stegman points out that we could try to slow the population decline of central cities by deemphasizing federal programs that encourage the production of new housing in the suburbs. He argues that there is an unresolved policy conflict between federal policies to stimulate new construction and those aimed at neighborhood revitalization.[60] Alternatively, or in addition, we could try to develop local policies to guide population decline by designating certain neighborhoods for conservation and others for clearance. The purpose of such a policy would be to ensure that neighborhoods designated for conservation retain enough population to remain viable and attractive.[61] Since there is enormous political opposition to both of these proposals, one has to conclude that uncontrolled depopulation will continue for some time to subvert most efforts to rehabilitate low income neighborhoods.

SEGREGATION AND DISCRIMINATION IN HOUSING

Housing segregation is certainly a major social problem in the United States. Within large cities the increase in black population has not been accompanied by an increase in racial integration.[62] Old black neighborhoods expand outward; new enclaves of black settlement grow until they, too, are large, all-black communities; but few neighborhoods achieve and retain racial balance. As we pointed out in Chapter 11, segregation imposes losses on blacks both because it reduces their employment opportunities and because it limits and distorts their housing choices. In addition, it surely makes school integration difficult, if not impossible, to achieve.

60. Stegman, "Neighborhood Effects of Filtering," pp. 234–39.
61. For a specific proposal see James Heilbrun, "On the Theory and Policy of Neighborhood Consolidation," *Journal of the American Planning Association*, October 1979, pp. 417–27. On strategies for coping with neighborhood deterioration, also see Anthony Downs, "Key Relationships Between Urban Development and Neighborhood Change," ibid., pp. 462–72; and Wilbur R. Thompson, "Land Management Strategies for Central City Depopulation," in U.S. Congress, House Committee on Banking, Finance, and Urban Affairs, Subcommittee on the City, *How Cities Can Grow Old Gracefully*, December 1977, pp. 67–78.
62. See Ann B. Schnare, "Trends in Residential Segregation by Race: 1960–1970," *Journal of Urban Economics*, May 1980, pp. 293–301, and *The Persistence of Racial Segregation in Housing* (Washington, D.C.: The Urban Institute, 1978); and T. L. Van Valey, W. C. Roof, and J. E. Wilcox, "Trends in Residential Segregation: 1960–1970," *American Journal of Sociology*, January 1977, pp. 826–44. The classic study in the field is Karl E. and Alma F. Taeuber, *Negroes in Cities* (Chicago: Aldine Publishing, 1965).

Segregation by race obviously exists in U.S. cities. Is that fact sufficient to prove the existence of racial discrimination in housing markets? Or might the observed degree of racial segregation be explained entirely by economic factors, such as the location of low skill jobs and of old, inexpensive housing, which would cause low income blacks to concentrate in particular neighborhoods? The answer is that economic forces alone cannot explain what we see. Anthony Pascal tested the hypothesis that economic factors could account for racial segregation by estimating multiple regression equations to predict black residential location in Chicago and Detroit. He found that economic variables could "explain" only one-third to one-half of the observed degree of segregation.[63]

But perhaps blacks are so highly segregated because they choose voluntarily to live in predominantly black neighborhoods? After all, other urban ethnic minorities have tended to cluster out of preference for their own culture and kinfolk. Pascal tested this possibility, too. Using data for Chicago, he compared the observed degree of segregation for Italian-Americans—who are reputed to have a strong tendency toward self-segregation—with that of middle to upper income nonwhites. The segregation index for nonwhites was more than five times that for Italian-Americans. Such a difference could hardly be attributed to voluntary self-segregation alone.[64] In any case, the stated preference of most blacks in Pascal's study was for integrated housing.

Although the force of discrimination can be inferred from the extent of housing segregation, it is difficult to prove its existence by direct observation, especially since the Civil Rights Act of 1968 specifically forbids discrimination in the sale or rental of housing. That discrimination nevertheless continues has often been reported on the basis of anecdotal evidence. It has now also been demonstrated by means of a carefully designed survey of market practices carried out by HUD.[65] In 1977 black and white auditors were sent out in matched pairs to shop for housing that had been advertised in newspapers in a large sample of metropolitan areas. Systematic data were collected on the treatment accorded these prospective customers. Analysis revealed a clear pattern of discrimination. To cite just a few examples, agents were more likely to tell blacks than whites that what they wanted was not available and less likely to volunteer information to blacks about waiting lists. When all forms of discriminatory practice regarding rental housing availability were combined, it was estimated

63. Anthony H. Pascal, "The Analysis of Residential Segregation," in John P. Crecine, ed., *Financing the Metropolis* (Beverly Hills, Calif.: Sage Publications, 1970), p. 407.
64. Ibid., pp. 409–10.
65. U.S. Department of Housing and Urban Development, *Measuring Racial Discrimination in American Housing Markets*, April 1979.

that blacks encountered discrimination in 27 percent of their visits to agents. In the market for owner-occupied housing the like figure was 15 percent.[66]

Do segregation and discrimination impose higher housing costs on blacks relative to whites? This important question has been studied frequently in recent years. While results vary, most studies based on data down through 1970 found that blacks were paying prices on the order of 10 to 15 percent higher for housing inside the ghetto than whites were paying for similar units in all-white neighborhoods. Some studies found that blacks also paid more than whites for housing within the same submarkets, including the suburbs.[67] It is, of course, possible that as population declines and blacks spread out within the older cities the adverse inner city price differentials will disappear. However, we would expect that blacks moving into suburban neighborhoods where discrimination exists and housing is not in excess supply would continue to pay differentials.

Antidiscrimination and antisegregation policies are examined from a different perspective in the next section of this chapter, which deals with proposals to "open up" the suburbs to low and moderate income families and to racial minorities.

"OPENING UP" THE SUBURBS

A recurrent topic in this book has been the ongoing process of job and population dispersion within metropolitan areas. We have emphasized the fact that population dispersion has been highly selective rather than uniform by income and race. That fact shapes almost every policy issue raised in this book. In Chapter 10 we showed that poverty is increasingly concentrated in the central cities and that racial segregation as between central cities and suburbs has diminished very little. We argued in Chapter 11 that job decentralization puts the central city poor at an increasing disadvantage in their struggle to improve their condition. In Chapter 12 we showed that the concentration of the poor in the central city has led to a virtual breakdown of private housing institutions in many neighborhoods. We will argue in Chapter 15 that the unequal distribution

---

66. Ibid., table 3, p. 58, and table 26, p. 124.

67. See the excellent summary of research, including his own, in John Yinger, "Prejudice and Discrimination in the Urban Housing Market," in Mieszkowski and Straszheim, pp. 430–68. Studies of price differentials are discussed at pp. 450–57. For a study of racial price differentials that examines suburban as well as central city markets, see Robert Schafer, "Discrimination in the Boston Housing Market," *Journal of Urban Economics*, April 1979, pp. 176–96.

of the poverty population between central cities and suburbs raises serious issues of both equity and efficiency in metropolitan public finance. The increasing disparity in racial composition and income level between central cities and suburbs is at once probably the most difficult, pervasive, and alarming of current "urban problems." Proposals that the suburbs be somehow "opened up" to low income and lower middle income families have therefore received a good deal of attention since the late 1960s. Because these proposals raise questions of housing policy first and foremost, it is appropriate to discuss them in this chapter. Because they relate housing issues to many others in urban economic policy, it is appropriate that they should make up the chapter's concluding section.

In earlier portions of the book we described the complex of forces that accounts for the present pattern of settlement of rich and poor in metropolitan areas. To recapitulate briefly, the poor are attracted to the center for several reasons. First, it has by far the largest concentration of old and therefore cheap housing, which is all that the poor can afford unless they are subsidized. Second, the central city still offers easy access to the largest single concentration of employment. On the other hand, as their incomes rise, the middle and upper classes find it increasingly desirable to pay the price of higher transportation costs in order to buy spacious housing in the suburbs. These "natural" economic forces, acting alone, would probably have sufficed to produce a pattern of richer suburbs and poorer central cities in the course of metropolitan growth. But they have not been acting alone. Rather they have been reinforced by public policy and by class and race prejudice. At the level of national policy, the provisions of the federal income tax favor home ownership over home rental. Since the incentive to ownership becomes more powerful the higher the individual's tax bracket, the middle and upper classes are far more likely than the poor to be influenced by these provisions. Because homeownership has always been much more prevalent in the suburbs than in central cities (and still is, despite the recent growth of condominium ownership of central city apartments), this bias in favor of homeownership for the well-to-do is also a bias in favor of suburban location. Equally important are the exclusionary zoning policies that suburban communities themselves can use to let the well-to-do in while barring the poor and the lower middle class. While there seem to be a number of motives for exclusionary local policies, race and class prejudice are probably important among them.

Exclusionary Zoning

The poor and the lower middle class can be kept out of a suburban community by a few simple provisions in the local zoning ordinance. For example, a community can zone itself for single family housing only. Thus all multiple dwellings, including such relatively inexpensive forms of construction as garden apartments, are effectively banned. If that is not thought to be a sufficient barrier, the zoning ordinance can also require a large building lot for any new home—say, two acres or more—instead of the quarter of an acre lots on which so much suburban housing has been built in the past. With land costs rising rapidly in the suburbs, a large lot requirement adds substantially to the cost of a home. In addition, builders are reluctant to put inexpensive homes on large lots. Thus zoning provisions can be used to raise the minimum cost of a new home high enough to exclude newcomers whose incomes are less than solidly middle class.[68]

It was pointed out in Chapter 6 that zoning originated in the United States as a means of reducing the harmful effects of externalities in land use. Externalities arise when one person's actions impose costs on others and the injured parties are not compensated. For example, a tall, bulky building may block the light and air of neighboring properties, or a noisy night club may disturb the quiet of a residential neighborhood. This kind of imperfection in the land market does, or could, occur frequently when people are living at typical urban densities and, when it occurs, will prevent the market from yielding optimal results. Zoning has long been accepted as a legitimate way of regulating the land market to reduce the potential damage from these imperfections.

Exclusionary zoning in the suburbs is a different matter, however. Its intent is not to correct market failure but to impose restrictions on consumer choice, thus actually restraining free market activity. There would be no objection to a plan under which a town reserved some areas exclusively for single-family homes, while allowing multiple dwellings in others, since zoning can be defended as a way of preserving certain neighborhood amenities. But when we find that a town has been enacting acreage requirements and building codes far more restrictive than those that prevailed during most of its own period of development, we can hardly doubt that the intent is exclusionary.

Under the regime of local autonomy regarding land-use decisions that prevails in the United States, even public housing cannot breach the exclusionary walls of the suburbs. Although the federal government subsidizes low income public housing, it is planned and built by local authorities. If a town does not want any, it simply does not participate in the federal program. Nor can the housing authority of one town undertake

---

68. See *Building the American City*, part III, ch. 1, "Land-Use Controls: Zoning and Subdivision Regulations."

to build or operate units in another. Thus we have in the United States neither federal nor metropolitan agencies empowered to determine the location of subsidized housing.

Motives for Exclusionary Practices

There are at least three important motives for exclusionary practices in the suburbs. The first is a financial motive. Under our multilevel system, local governments are financially responsible for an important share of public services. Despite state and federal aid, a heavy local tax burden remains. As we will demonstrate in Chapter 15, the citizens of any municipality stand to gain financially by excluding those in-migrants who are likely to contribute less to local tax and grant-in-aid revenue than they will add to local service costs. The property tax is the most important source of local revenue. Suburban voters therefore have a strong financial motive for trying to ensure that low or even middle income housing is not built in their town, because it will not "pay its way" in terms of taxes. The same financial motive that induces suburbs to keep low or moderately low income families out encourages them to bring clean, tax-paying industry in. An approach that combines both elements has been dubbed "fiscal zoning." It is a deliberate "beggar-my-neighbor" policy. The town that successfully practices it gets the industry while some other municipality is forced to bear the cost of public services for the factory's workers.[69]

A second motive for exclusionary practices is a desire to preserve neighborhood amenities. If a family moved into a suburb because they liked its "rural" character, they will probably want to keep it that way by prohibiting apartment house construction and perhaps even by slowing down further intrusion of single-family homes. In the late 1960s the desire to preserve suburban amenities received support from a new source, the environmental protection movement, which gave a certain legitimacy to what otherwise might have appeared a strictly self-interested policy. One result was a wave of suburban "growth control" or "development-timing" ordinances that sought, in a variety of ways, to limit the annual increase in the local housing stock.[70] These ordinances were justified as necessary

69. See Julius Margolis, "On Municipal Land Policy for Fiscal Gains," *National Tax Journal*, September 1956, pp. 247–57.

70. See Fred Bosselman, "Can the Town of Ramapo Pass a Law to Bind the Rights of the Entire World?" in David Listokin, ed., *Land Use Controls: Present Problems and Future Reform* (New Brunswick, N.J.: Center for Urban Policy Research, Rutgers University, 1974), pp. 241–72; Michelle J. White, "Self-Interest in the Suburbs: The Trend Toward No-Growth Zoning," *Policy Analysis*, Spring 1978, pp. 185–203; and Richard F. Babcock, "The Spatial Impact of Land-Use Controls," in Arthur P. Solomon, ed., *The Prospective City* (Cambridge, Mass.: MIT Press, 1980), pp. 267–70.

to achieve "orderly development." An unfriendly observer, however, might classify them as a form of exclusionary zoning. (Also see the section on Local Growth Control in Chapter 7.)

A final motive for exclusionary zoning is opposition to racial and/or socioeconomic integration. The distinction between feelings about race and about class is potentially significant since, if class prejudice plays an important part, we should expect opposition to integration to diminish as racial minorities converge toward the majority in socioeconomic characteristics.[71] Because race and class feelings are not freely expressed, it is difficult to know how much of the opposition to integration should be attributed to these antagonisms and how much to other motives. In recent years the situation has been further complicated by the growth of crime and delinquency as a major personal and social concern. Consider the case of the extraordinary local opposition that developed in 1972 to siting low income public housing in the middle class Forest Hills neighborhood of New York City. The housing project would not have affected neighborhood tax or expenditure levels, since these are established on a citywide basis. Hence, there was no financial motive for opposition. It might have affected the neighborhood's physical character in some degree, but certainly not enough to account for the ensuing uproar. Quite clearly, residents were expressing opposition to the entry of low income families they knew would be heavily black and Puerto Rican and they feared would bring an increase in crime and juvenile delinquency to what had been a relatively "safe" neighborhood.

What Would Be Gained by Opening Up the Suburbs?

A program that succeeded in opening up the suburbs to low and moderate income families might be expected to produce a variety of benefits. First of all, by encouraging the movement of blacks into the suburbs, it would obviously help to reduce the level of macrosegregation in metropolitan areas: increasingly black central cities surrounded by still largely white suburbs. If de facto integration is ever to be achieved in U.S. society, it is essential that the suburbs accept a substantially greater proportion of the metropolitan black population.

Second, it would promote freedom of choice in housing location for groups whose choices are now heavily restricted by exclusionary practices. Such freedom from imposed restrictions is a matter of right that also has practical economic consequences. The growth of suburban job opportunities was discussed in Chapter 11. It was argued that restraints on free-

71. Pascal, pp. 410–12.

dom of choice in housing systematically limit the access that minorities, now concentrated in the central cities, have to these attractive opportunities and also impose losses on them by limiting and distorting their consumption of housing itself. Those who do work in the new suburban plants and offices are likely to find themselves bearing unnecessarily heavy travel costs, since they cannot live near their jobs. The enforced separation of residence and job is one reason why reverse commuters—central city workers commuting to suburban jobs—are now such a rapidly growing segment of the metropolitan work force.[72]

Finally, removing housing restrictions in the wealthier suburbs would help to even up tax costs and service levels among different local governments. The well-to-do would no longer be able to use self-segregation as a means of escaping responsibility for sharing the cost of local public services provided to those with lower incomes. (It is a curious fact that one of the important consequences of the twentieth-century revolution in transport technology has been to facilitate this self-segregation.) Low and moderate income families moving into wealthy communities would benefit either by receiving a higher level of service or paying lower tax rates than before.

Policies to Encourage Racial and Economic Integration

Policies to encourage racial and economic integration within metropolitan areas can be divided, for purposes of analysis, into two groups: "permissive" policies and "active" policies. Permissive policies would remove the barriers of exclusionary zoning and discriminatory practice but would not bring housing costs down by means of subsidies. Active policies, on the other hand, would provide subsidies to bring suburban housing costs within the reach of low income groups.

We take up permissive policies first. Among those already in force is the Civil Rights Act of 1968, which prohibits racial discrimination in the sale or rental of housing. Numerous state laws do likewise. It is not easy to know how effective these statutes have been. However, we have already described a field survey by HUD which showed that significant discrimination in market practices still occurred in 1977.[73]

Whether or not the "retail" sort of discrimination that may occur in individual housing transactions can be curbed, it is certainly possible to do something about the exclusionary zoning regulations that now lend the color of legality to discrimination when it is practiced at "wholesale."

72. See Alex Anas and Leon N. Moses, "Transportation and Land Use in the Mature Metropolis," in Charles L. Leven, ed., *The Mature Metropolis* (Lexington, Mass.: D.C. Heath, Lexington Books, 1978), pp. 156–58.
73. See n. 65, above.

Local zoning ordinances are written under authority of state law. Consequently, the states have the power to require that they conform to nonexclusionary standards or even to a statewide plan. While local political interests have been strong enough to prevent radical revision of zoning standards by states, there have been a few instances of moderate reform.

Fair Shares. Suburban towns may well fear that "once we let down the barriers, a flood will follow." This fear can be alleviated by a state plan in which every jurisdiction is required to accept a "fair share" of low income housing so that none are asked to absorb very much. Along these lines, Massachusetts in 1969 adopted a zoning appeals law which placed an obligation on towns to accept a certain amount of low and moderate income housing and established a process under which an aggrieved developer could appeal to a state board for relief in case a town unreasonably refused permission to build.[74]

Fair share plans have also been developed voluntarily by municipalities in particular metropolitan areas. The best-known of these is the Housing Plan for the Miami Valley Region, adopted in 1970 by the counties and municipalities centered on Dayton, Ohio. The projected need for low and moderate income subsidized housing was allocated among the participating jurisdictions on criteria that took into account the capacity of each to provide schools and other necessary services. These allocations were also "ceilings," a feature that helped to make the plan politically acceptable.[75]

However, regional fair share plans are not likely to sweep the country unless municipalities are given some incentive to take cooperative action. For example, the federal and/or state governments could exert pressure by withholding various categories of grant funds from recalcitrant municipalities or by rewarding with special generosity those that cooperate.

Financial Reorganization. Because residents of the suburbs are genuinely concerned about the extra tax burden they would take on if they allowed an influx of low income households, appropriate public finance

74. This and other approaches to reform under state initiative are discussed in Robert W. Burchell and David Listokin, "The Impact of Local Government Regulations on Housing Costs and Potential Avenues for State Meliorative Measures," in George Sternlieb and James W. Hughes, *America's Housing, Prospects and Problems* (New Brunswick, N.J.: Center for Urban Policy Research, Rutgers University, 1980), pp. 313–58. On the Massachusetts zoning appeals law also see Leonard S. Rubinowitz, "A Question of Choice: Access of the Poor and the Black to Suburban Housing," in Louis H. Masotti and Jeffrey K. Hadden, eds., *The Urbanization of the Suburbs*, vol. 7, Urban Affairs Annual Reviews (Beverley Hills, Calif.: Sage Publications, 1973), pp. 341–43.

75. Rubinowitz, pp. 338–41.

reforms might help to weaken support for exclusionary policies. For example, if local school outlays were to be fixed at a statewide uniform level per pupil and financed entirely by a state property tax, and if all local welfare costs were to be absorbed by either the state or the federal government, then the financial motive for opposing low income in-migration would all but disappear. More generally, any form of grant or revenue sharing, or any reassignment of functions that shifts the responsibility for financing services to a higher level of government, would help to weaken the financial motive for exclusionary policies. (These issues in public finance are analyzed in detail in Chapter 15.)

Class Action Suits. Unable to overcome political opposition to reform through the legislative process, various groups have tried to halt exclusionary practices by bringing class action suits in both state and federal courts.[76] In state courts they have met with considerable, though not universal, success. For example in the case of *Oakwood at Madison v. Township of Madison,* a New Jersey court in October 1971 set aside the entire zoning ordinance of Madison Township. The court found that the ordinance dictated such high housing costs that it would automatically exclude 90 percent of the area's population from moving into the town and held that it therefore failed to meet the test of advancing the general welfare.[77] The next year in the same state a court, in the case of *Southern Burlington County NAACP v. Township of Mount Laurel,* invalidated a zoning ordinance that prohibited multifamily construction on the ground that it discriminated against the poor. Both decisions were later reaffirmed by New Jersey's Supreme Court.[78] On the other hand, in the case of *Golden v. Planning Board of Ramapo* the New York State Court of Appeals in 1972 upheld the Town of Ramapo's program of "planned sequential development" as not unreasonable or exclusionary.[79]

Attempts to overturn exclusionary zoning and growth controls have been less successful in federal than in state tribunals. For example, the federal courts have long recognized a constitutional right to travel. Plaintiffs in federal cases have argued that exclusionary zoning and growth controls are unreasonable restrictions of such a right. If that position were accepted, exclusionary zoning could be readily challenged in the federal courts. However, the Supreme Court in the case of *Boraas v. Village of*

76. A thorough review of these cases can be found in Richard P. Fishman, ed., *Housing for All Under Law,* Report of the American Bar Association Advisory Commission on Housing and Urban Growth (Cambridge, Mass.: Ballinger, 1978), chs. 2 and 3.
77. *The New York Times,* October 30, 1971.
78. Fishman, ed., pp. 104–13, 133–36.
79. Bosselman, pp. 248–49, 260–64.

Belle Terre in 1974 upheld a restrictive ordinance despite plaintiff's asser-
tion of a right to travel.[80] The Court's decisions during the 1970s have
been widely interpreted as showing a reluctance to have the federal courts
become involved in disputes over the housing effects of zoning.[81]

In any event, victories in court do not build low income housing
projects. With the exception of certain types of fair share plans, the
policies considered to this point are permissive only. They would help to
eliminate practices that now inhibit the free play of market forces in suburban housing, but they would do nothing to help the poor pay market
costs. Since the new private housing that might be constructed when the
barriers fell would remain beyond the reach of low income families, permissive policies would at most open the suburbs to the lower middle class.
The poor would be encouraged to move there only if they received support from active subsidy policies.

Active Subsidy Policies. Any really effective policy to move low income households into the suburbs would probably have to include subsidies directed specifically toward those areas. One approach would be to
establish metropolitan area housing authorities under state law, with the
power to build or lease subsidized, low rent public housing anywhere
within the region. The authority could make plans on the basis of regional
rather than purely local criteria and, if necessary, carry them out by overriding exclusionary local zoning ordinances. However, political resistance
by the suburbs currently makes the creation of metropolitan housing
agencies with coercive powers look highly unlikely. As a result of such
resistance, New York's Urban Development Corporation, which takes the
entire state as its field of operation, was deprived, in 1973, of its former
power to construct housing without conforming to local restrictions.[82]

At the federal level there are equally serious obstacles. The federal
government does not itself build low income housing, nor does it have the
power to dictate where localities shall build it, nor does it seem likely in
a nation devoted to the preservation of local autonomy that the Congress
would ever grant it such powers. However, a policy of rewards might be
acceptable where a policy of compulsion is not. For example, special
federal grants could be made to help defray the cost of municipal services
in towns that accept subsidized low income housing under a regional plan.
Morton Schussheim suggested funneling such aid through regional agen-

80. Kenneth Pearlman, "The Closing Door: The Supreme Court and Residential Segregation," *Journal of the American Institute of Planners*, April 1978, pp.
162–63.
81. Babcock, p. 278; Pearlman, *passim.*
82. For a brief history of UDC, including its later financial difficulties, see
Fishman, ed., pp. 505–08.

cies that have full authority to override local zoning, acquire land, and build low income housing, but there would seem to be no reason why it could not also be used in support of essentially voluntary regional efforts.[83]

Many analysts had thought that housing allowances, by making it possible for the poor to move into the nearer suburbs, where relatively inexpensive older housing is available, would also actively help to promote intrametropolitan racial and economic integration. However, results of the housing allowance experiments, described above, indicate that the benefits offered (at least in that case) were not large enough to induce significant changes in residential location.

The Consequences of Alternative Policies

Present housing and land-use policies, far from helping to promote racial and economic integration of city and suburb, have probably had just the opposite effect. The new construction strategy that has dominated our housing policy produces subsidized new construction in the cities and unsubsidized middle and upper class housing in the ring areas. Subsidized low income housing built in the cities tends to anchor the poor there. At the same time, the new construction strategy as a whole reinforces this effect, for it produces a substantial amount of filtering, and it is the older housing at the center that filters down to the lowest rent level. As Downs argues, the macrolocational outcome of a strategy based on new construction plus filtering is that the poor remain concentrated in the central city while the well-to-do settle in the outlying growth areas.[84] It goes without saying that these broad tendencies are further reinforced by the exclusionary land-use policies permitted under our system of local planning autonomy.

What would happen if exclusionary practices were now to be replaced by policies that permit but do not subsidize low and moderate income housing in the suburbs? The result would probably be an increase in the quantity of new moderate income housing built in the ring area and a more even distribution of such housing among localities of varying income levels. We have already cited the gains in the form of increased housing, job, and locality choice; reduced transportation costs; and improved public services that would accrue to those who could afford the

83. Morton J. Schussheim, "National Goals and Local Practices: Joining Ends and Means in Housing," papers submitted to the Subcommittee on Housing, Part 1, U.S. Congress, House Committee on Banking and Currency, June 1971, pp. 157–58. This and other possible federal initiatives are also discussed in Herbert M. Franklin, "Land Use Controls as a Barrier to Housing Assistance," in *Housing in the Seventies Working Papers*, vol. 1, pp. 551–60.

84. Anthony Downs, *Urban Problems and Prospects*, 2nd ed. (Chicago: Rand McNally, 1976), p. 83.

new housing. In a society dedicated to freedom of individual choice and equality of opportunity, such gains are ample justification for the necessary policy changes.

Ironically, however, policies that help only the middle or lower middle class to move to the suburbs may have the effect of aggravating social and economic conditions in the central city for those who remain behind. Consider, for example, the simple arithmetic of income levels. Suppose that a suburb that had used exclusionary zoning to keep out families with incomes below $25,000 a year now lowers the bars so that new housing becomes available to families with incomes as low as $20,000 a year. If the median family income in the central city is only $15,000 or $16,000 it is probable that the new out-migrants will have income levels below the median in the suburb to which they move but above the median in the city from which they came. In that case, their migration would lower the medians at both places and could well increase rather than narrow the difference between them. A reduction in the level of median family income in central cities would, in turn, exacerbate some of the most serious problems they now face, including the inadequacy of the local tax base and the deterioration of neighborhoods that is associated with housing abandonment. In short, opening up the suburbs only by means of permissive policies would help a substantial number of middle and lower middle class families—but very possibly at the expense of weakening the capacity of the core city for helping the poor who remained behind.

For the black population, a policy of opening up the suburbs only by means of permissive policies would aggravate the intraracial divergence in economic status already noted in Chapter 10 by increasing the spatial separation between black economic classes. The emerging black middle class would be increasingly attracted to the suburbs, while poor blacks remained within the increasingly impoverished inner city. This is certainly *not* an argument against opening up the suburbs. It *is* an argument for active policies to help move some of the poor into the suburban ring.

The Metropolitan Public Sector: Functions, Growth, Revenues

FOURTEEN

"My statistics come from the Census of Governments," announced the student describing his research to the members of a seminar in public finance. A visiting British scholar looked puzzled. "Census of Governments?" he asked, his voice rising in disbelief. "Whatever do you mean by that?" The student laughed and explained that in the United States there are so many governmental units that if the Census Bureau didn't count them every five years no one could be sure exactly how many there were or what they did.

It might be argued that in a nation devoted to competition in economics, democracy in politics, ethnicity in culture, and pluralism in social institutions, this multiplicity of governments should be counted a virtue: at once an indispensable means to, and an inevitable result of, the democratic diversity we prize. Yet we pay a price for it, too, especially in metropolitan areas, where the problems caused by an abundance of governments are frequently no laughing matter.

THE MULTILEVEL PUBLIC SECTOR

The structure of the public sector in the United States can best be described by a two-dimensional diagram, such as Figure 14.1. Along the vertical scale we mark off the three levels of government: federal, state, and local. It is conventional to treat local government as though it were a single level. In fact, the local sector in most places consists of many overlapping layers: cities, counties, school districts, water districts, and so forth. These are shown schematically in the

FIGURE 14.1
Structure of Government in the United States: A Two-dimensional View

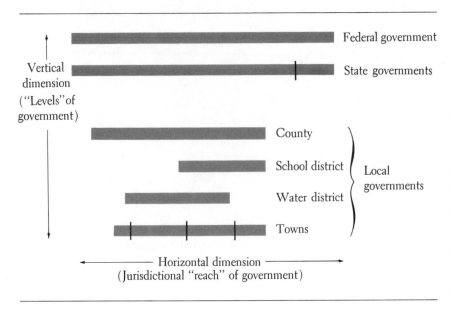

diagram. The degree of complexity at the local level is suggested by a few statistics: there were no less than 79,862 local governmental units in the United States in 1977, and only 18,862 of these were "municipalities." The 272 SMSA's then recognized by the Census alone contained 25,869 governmental units.[1]

The horizontal dimension of the diagram measures schematically the jurisdictional reach of the units of government in each of the layers. The pattern is clear enough at the federal and state levels. At the local level it becomes complex and unsystematic because the jurisdictions of the units vary in size both within layers and between them. A county may be larger or smaller than a city. A school district may take in one or more towns as well as unincorporated rural areas. A special district may overlap cities, counties, or towns. A single citizen may thus live under a bewildering array of local governments stacked one above the other.

Metropolitan Fiscal Problems

The vertical and horizontal dimensions of Figure 14.1 are useful in describing three problems of metropolitan public finance. The first is the

1. U.S. Bureau of the Census, *1977 Census of Governments*, vol. 5, *Local Government in Metropolitan Areas*, table 1.

"assignment problem." Both the functions of government and the power to finance them by various means are distributed along the vertical scale among the federal, state, and local governments and, within the local sector, among its many overlapping units. In an optimum multilevel structure, local governments would not be required, nor would they attempt, to perform functions that could be more effectively handled at a higher level. Arranging the most appropriate division of functions among the three levels of government as well as within the strata of the local level is the substance of the assignment problem.

Along the horizontal dimension of Figure 14.1 we can define two fiscal problems. The first is the notoriously haphazard arrangement of functions and boundaries within and across the local level. Because geographic boundaries for the provision of local services have not been drawn rationally, the local public sector is often unable to provide services at an optimum, or perhaps even acceptable, level of efficiency. A second, but related, problem in the horizontal dimension is the prevalence of geographic disparities in the distribution of needs and resources. The needs of the population for public services and the income and resources out of which to pay for them are not similarly distributed across governmental units at the local level. Serious inequities among individuals and between social classes arise from this geographic mismatch.

As we shall see, the local public sector has grown very rapidly in the United States since the 1950s. This growth, in combination with the difficulties resulting from inappropriate functional assignment, geographic disparities, and haphazard boundaries, has produced a fourth problem: a condition of severe fiscal stress in many of the older central cities that is often referred to loosely as the "urban fiscal crisis."

In the next section of this chapter we analyze the budgetary functions of government and the problem of assigning each function to the most appropriate level. That is followed by a section on the composition and growth of local public spending which concludes with an examination of the movement to limit that growth. We then study the sources and growth of local government revenue. The chapter closes with an examination of the property tax, by far the most important local levy and one about which there has recently been extended theoretical debate. The three remaining problems—haphazard arrangement of functions and boundaries, geographic disparities between needs and resources, and urban fiscal distress, together with some of the major policies and reforms that have been proposed to ameliorate them—are taken up in Chapter 15.

THE ASSIGNMENT OF FUNCTIONS
TO LEVELS OF GOVERNMENT

The essence of the assignment problem is to determine the most appropriate division of functions among the federal, state, and local governments. Let us begin by looking at broad categories of functions. Apart from regulatory action, government brings its influence to bear on the economy through the operation of its budget, which affects economic activity by means of both taxes and expenditures. In his highly influential treatise on public finance Richard A. Musgrave usefully divides the budgetary objectives of government in a market economy into three classes.[2] The first of these he calls "allocation," the second "distribution," and the third "stabilization." The task of allocation consists of providing those goods and services that, for a variety of reasons, the private sector cannot provide at all or cannot provide at prices and in quantities that are optimal. The task of distribution might better be labeled *redistribution*, since it consists of transferring income among individuals to correct the pattern of private market rewards in order to arrive at an ethically more desirable distribution of well-being. Last, the stabilization task involves using the fiscal powers of government to smooth out fluctuations in the level of aggregate economic activity.

In a unitary political system the three budgetary functions would be performed and, ideally, coordinated by a single government. Under the multilevel system of federal, state, and local governments adopted in the United States, matters become much more complicated. Lack of coordination among governments, overlapping of jurisdictions, the mismatch between a government's objectives and its resources all contribute—not haphazardly, but systematically—to preventing the public economy as a whole from functioning efficiently. To say this is not to argue that we should abandon multilevel government, which has indispensable virtues as well as characteristic defects, but rather to explain why the search for more effective forms of federalism is apparently an unending one.

Stabilization of Economic Activity

Under a multilevel system, state and local governments perform few stabilization functions. Quite rightly, they leave stabilization largely in the

2. R. A. Musgrave, *The Theory of Public Finance* (New York: McGraw-Hill, 1959), ch. 1. The normative approach to problems of public finance adopted in this and the following chapter is based largely on the work of Musgrave as applied to metropolitan areas by subsequent writers. See references below, and also Harvey E. Brazer, "Some Fiscal Implications of Metropolitanism," reprinted in William E. Mitchell and Ingo Walter, eds., *State and Local Finance* (New York: Ronald Press, 1970), pp. 331–45.

hands of the federal government. In this they really have no choice. The economies of states and localities are so wide open to the influence of the national economy, through trade, that it would be hopeless for them to attempt local stabilization by means of fiscal policy, even if they were permitted by their own constitutions to do so. As economic base analysis assumes, the level of local activity is influenced significantly by the strength of outside demand for local products. That demand depends largely on the behavior of the national economy, fluctuations in which would not be perceptibly influenced by stabilization efforts financed in a single locality.

Nor would local stabilization efforts be effective in stimulating the local economy directly. Recall in this connection the analysis of the foreign trade multiplier in Chapter 7. Because the marginal propensity to import is high in a local area, the local spending multiplier is very low. A large proportion of any increment to local spending "leaks out" into the national economy. Instead of recirculating to stimulate local activity, it is (from the local point of view) mostly wasted on the world at large. Any stimulus or restraint that local authorities might contrive to counteract outside forces would soon dissipate its effects nationwide. Thus locally financed stabilization measures are bound to be ineffective.[3]

Redistributing Income from Rich to Poor

In Musgrave's ideal scheme the tasks of allocation and distribution are logically separated, even though both may be performed by the same government. Under the heading of allocation, the government provides public goods and services to the extent that citizens want them and are willing to pay for them with taxes. If a redistribution of income is desired the most efficient way to carry it out is by making transfers in cash, rather than in services, from the rich to the poor. An income maintenance scheme of the sort described in Chapter 11 would be one way to carry out such transfers. The present federal welfare program makes use of other means such as Aid to Families with Dependent Children (AFDC) and Supplemental Security Income (SSI) that are also pure transfers, unconnected with the delivery of public services. The states, too, undertake a certain amount of pure income redistribution because they are required to share the cost of AFDC and may finance other forms of cash relief as well. Even localities may become involved, since some states require them to bear part of the welfare burden.

A clear distinction between allocation and distribution is not, however, maintained in practice by any of the three levels of government in

3. For further discussion, see Wallace E. Oates, *Fiscal Federalism* (New York: Harcourt Brace Jovanovich, 1972), pp. 4–6, 21–30.

the United States. Instead, they often adopt policies in which allocation and redistribution objectives are more or less deliberately joined. One might mention, for example, policies to encourage the wider distribution of services, such as medical and hospital care or education, that the majority of citizens regard as particularly meritorious, by providing them at less than full cost or perhaps entirely free. The redistributive effect of such policies can be seen clearly in the case of education: in a given community, benefits are received by rich and poor families in equal amounts per child, but the rich pay far higher school taxes than the poor. Even where redistribution is not an objective, however, the effect is the same: governments generally provide the poor with more service benefits than they pay for in taxes and the rich with less. Consequently real income is redistributed indirectly from the rich to the poor.

The extent of this redistribution cannot be observed directly. It can be approximated, however, by estimating separately the incidence of tax payments and the incidence of expenditure benefits by income class and then subtracting payments from benefits received within each class. Musgrave, Case, and Leonard carried out such estimates for the United States, using 1968 data. They found that, on average, families with incomes below about $8,000 received more in benefits than they paid in taxes to the federal government, while those with incomes above that level paid more in taxes than they received in benefits. The equivalent taxpayer "break-even point" vis-a-vis state-local government was about $10,000.[4] It bears repeating that the redistributive effect of government budgets results not only from deliberate income transfers and the provision of "poverty-connected" services, but also from the fact that the poor receive more in general service benefits than they pay for in taxes.

Economists usually argue that the function of redistributing income, like that of stabilization, should be left entirely to the federal government. They believe that the capacity of the lesser jurisdictions to redistribute income among their citizens is limited severely by the mobility of both taxpayers and expenditure beneficiaries. A city that taxes the rich to provide benefits for the poor to a greater extent than other cities do will tend to attract the poor and repel the rich. This response makes redistribution at the local level a self-defeating process. Nevertheless, as we have seen, local communities *do* engage in a degree of income distribution. Partly they can get away with it because not all resources are highly mobile. Partly they do not get away with it because mobile resources *do* often move when local fiscal pressure becomes sufficiently heavy. The self-defeating nature of locally financed income redistribution is among the

4. R. A. Musgrave, Karl E. Case, and Herman B. Leonard, "The Distribution of Fiscal Burdens and Benefits," *Public Finance Quarterly*, July 1974, table 8, p. 294.

strongest arguments for reexamining the assignment of fiscal responsibilities within our multilevel system of government. This difficult issue will be examined in greater detail in Chapter 15 when we analyze the problem of geographic disparities between needs and resources.

Providing Public Goods and Services

Having eliminated both stabilization and redistribution, we are left with allocation—the provision of public goods and services—as the only budgetary function that can appropriately be carried out by local government. Allocation activities are, in fact, the dominant concern of local government. Local citizens want and are willing to pay for services such as parks, sanitation, and police protection. One of the principal objectives of the local public sector is to provide such services, in accordance with citizen preferences, just as the private sector provides bread and shoes and washing machines in accordance with consumer preferences.

Stimulated by the work of Samuelson, Buchanan, and Musgrave,[5] economists have devoted much thought since the 1950s to the interrelated problems of finding an optimum division of functions between the public and private sectors and then satisfying the demand for those goods and services that are properly a public sector responsibility. One of the contributions of modern public expenditure theory has been the definition of a class of pure public goods or, as they are sometimes called, collective or joint-consumption goods. These goods and services have one or both of the following characteristics. First, they are subject to joint consumption, meaning that each consumer can enjoy such a good without diminishing the amount available to others. Examples would be national defense, the system of law and justice, public health programs, air pollution control, city planning, or police and fire services. By contrast, ordinary consumer goods are *not* subject to joint consumption: if Jones eats the loaf of bread it cannot also be consumed by Smith. Second, public goods are generally *not* subject to the exclusion process, meaning that it is not feasible to prevent anyone from consuming such a good once it is produced, whether or not he or she wishes to pay for it. Since most joint consumption goods also have the characteristic of nonexcludability, the same examples will again serve: how can any consumer be prevented from obtaining the benefit of a defense program or of local police or public health services once they exist?

5. In addition to Musgrave's *The Theory of Public Finance*, see Paul E. Samuelson, "The Pure Theory of Public Expenditure," *Review of Economics and Statistics*, November 1954, pp. 386–89, and "Diagrammatic Exposition of a Theory of Public Expenditure," ibid., November 1955, pp. 350–56; and James M. Buchanan, *The Demand and Supply of Public Goods* (Chicago: Rand McNally, 1968).

An important consequence of nonexcludability is this: if nonpurchasers cannot be prevented from benefiting, then the good cannot be sold in a market, and privately financed production is impossible. Public or joint-consumption goods thus form a core of activities for which financial responsibility *must* be assigned to the public sector. (Note that production may remain in private hands, as in the case of defense goods made under contract to the federal government or school buildings constructed by private contractors for the local school district.)

A very large question remains, however. How can society determine the optimum quantity of each public good to produce? The private sector makes use of prices to achieve an allocation of output that accords with consumer preferences. If perfect competition prevails in all markets and there are no externalities, price will equal marginal cost for every good, and the resulting allocation of resources in the market sector will be optimal. Samuelson, in his classic article on "The Pure Theory of Public Expenditure," showed that a different pricing rule would be optimal for goods subject to joint consumption.[6] This optimal solution is unattainable, however. Price systems cannot operate in the absence of excludability. Citizens will not voluntarily pay a price for defense services when they know they cannot be prevented from benefiting even if they do *not* pay. (This is often referred to as the "free-rider" problem.) To finance public goods we are therefore compelled to rely upon taxes levied in a political process. One must hope that a democratic voting procedure somehow succeeds in registering citizen preferences for public goods in the same way the market does for private ones.[7]

To be sure, the public sector in the United States also supplies many goods and services that do not have the character of pure collective goods, for example education, solid waste disposal, and hospital services. (Some of these will be further analyzed below.) In many such cases the public sector could make use of prices, in the form of user charges, more often than it has done to produce services in the quantities that its citizens want.[8] Yet even after all such opportunities have been exhausted, the bulk of public activity would still have to be paid for by taxes. It is therefore important to have an assignment of functions to the various levels of government that facilitates the most rational possible budgetary decision-making at each level.

6. See footnote 5.

7. Roland McKean explains how the political system responds to preferences in "The Unseen Hand in Government," *American Economic Review*, June 1965, pp. 496–505.

8. See the papers in Selma J. Mushkin, ed., *Public Prices for Public Products* (Washington, D.C.: The Urban Institute, 1972).

An Optimum Division of Responsibility:
The Principle of Fiscal Equivalence

Let us assume initially that all the services provided by the public sector are true joint-consumption goods and that each such good benefits a definable group of citizens who make up the entire population living within a perimeter that constitutes the "boundary" of that good. We want to know what division of responsibility for such goods among the levels of government will most efficiently satisfy consumer preferences. Mancur Olson's "principle of fiscal equivalence" gives us a good first approximation of the answer.[9] According to this principle, the provision of collective goods will be most efficient when the boundary of each collective good coincides with that of the government providing it. This proposition is intuitively plausible. Public goods must be provided through a budgetary rather than a market process. Supply is most likely to be optimal if the citizens who vote (or whose representatives vote) for provision are also those who will benefit. Consider two contrary cases. If the benefits of the collective good spill out beyond the boundaries of the providing government, we have the classic case of external benefits. Olson adopts the standard argument that too little of the good will then be provided. (See the discussion of externalities in Chapter 15.) In the opposite case, when the boundaries of the government reach farther than those of the collective good, Olson argues that provision is again likely to be suboptimal, though he recognizes possible exceptions. In any event, it is clear that when governmental boundaries do not coincide with public good boundaries "there are systematic forces which work against allocative efficiency."[10]

As Olson points out, the analysis yields a fundamental economic argument for a federal system. "Only if there are several levels of government and a large number of governments," Olson writes, "can immense disparities between the boundaries of jurisdictions and the boundaries of collective goods be avoided."[11] A three-tiered structure—federal, state, local—can radically reduce such disparities, thus contributing greatly to the achievement of allocative efficiency. Under a federal system each public good can be assigned to the level of government that has the most nearly equivalent boundaries. To a large extent this occurs in the United States. National defense is in the hands of the federal government, because the benefits of a defense system are necessarily nationwide in scope. Fire and police services are local responsibilities because the benefits of such

9. Mancur Olson, "The Principle of 'Fiscal Equivalence': the Division of Responsibilities among Different Levels of Government," *American Economic Review*, May 1969, pp. 479–87.
10. Olson, p. 483.
11. Ibid.

services are largely confined to the locality where they are produced. With local control, each town is free to choose the level of service its citizens want and are willing to pay for.

Complex Cases and Joint Responsibility

Most allocational activities in the public sector do not have the character of pure public goods. Consequently, other criteria in addition to fiscal equivalence must be brought to bear in deciding what level of government ought, ideally, to carry them out. When these more complex cases have been examined the best solution often appears to be some sharing of responsibility either with the private sector or between levels of government. Again, it is a virtue of the federal system, in contrast with a fully centralized one, that it can accommodate intergovernmental sharing when that is desirable. In a chapter devoted primarily to the metropolitan public sector it is not feasible to examine the ideal arrangement for carrying out every allocative function. However, it is instructive to review two general cases in which shared responsibility may be indicated.

Consider first the case of "merit goods." As explained in Chapter 12, a merit good is something that (the majority decides) is better for people than they realize. Society makes a judgment that, if left to themselves, consumers will buy less of such a good than would maximize their well-being within the constraint of their income. The government intervenes with a subsidy to reduce the price of the merit good in order to encourage greater consumption. This is an argument, though not the only one, that is often used to justify housing subsidies. The question is, who should finance the subsidy? Since the merit good argument relates mainly to the consumption habits of those with low or moderately low incomes, programs justified by it are likely to be redistributive from the relatively rich to the relatively poor, and since redistribution is not an appropriate function for local governments, or perhaps even for states, it follows that subsidies to encourage the consumption of merit goods should be financed by the federal government. Expenditure for housing would thus be a private function subsidized by the federal but not the state or local governments. The same conclusion applies in the case of health service subsidies or any others that are justified by the merit good argument.

Next, consider the case of a service that combines characteristics of the pure public good with those of an ordinary private good. Education is probably the most important example. It is a private good insofar as a benefit accrues directly to the person being educated, and exclusion is perfectly feasible. Yet over and above that, each individual's education also provides an external benefit that accrues to society as a whole. The nature of that externality can be explained as follows. In a democratic society we necessarily place great value on the existence of educated fellow voters. Moreover, we want the citizenry to be well-educated, not only in our own town, but in all localities, since those who have been poorly educated elsewhere may become a burden locally through migration or may affect events that have nationwide ramifications. The external part of the benefit of education has the character of a pure public good: each person benefits by it without diminishing the benefit available to others, nor can anyone be excluded from benefiting. Primary and secondary education have long been free, tax-supported services in the United States, not because exclusion and the collection of fees would be difficult, but because the public good aspect of schooling made it seem imperative that the whole population should be sufficiently educated.

Although this analysis suggests a valid national interest in the matter, public schools began and long continued as a strictly local enterprise. However, as Olson points out, we would expect improved transportation and communications and increased geographic mobility of the population to cause the external benefits of local services like education to rise, inducing an increase in subsidies from higher levels of government.[12] So it has been in education. State school aid developed gradually in this century and is now substantial. Large-scale federal aid began with the passage of the Elementary and Secondary Education Act of 1965. Thus all three levels of government now support this function. Whether the present division among them is satisfactory, however, remains an open question to which we return in Chapter 15.

LOCAL GOVERNMENT EXPENDITURES

The functional composition of local government general expenditures is shown in Table 14.1.[13] The totals shown include spending financed by aid from the federal and state governments. Such aid amounted to $95 billion in 1978–79, enough to pay for about 47 percent of expenditures. Since some intergovernmental aid is not restricted to specific functions, it is not usually possible to calculate exactly the portion of a particular function that is aid-supported. Thus, while Table 14.1 accurately depicts the size of programs and functions over which local governments have *administrative* control, it cannot be used as an indicator of *fiscal* responsibility.

As column 2 of the table shows, education is by far the leading

12. Ibid., p. 486.
13. General expenditure and general revenue are defined as all expenditure and all revenue except those of insurance trust funds and of government-owned utilities and liquor stores.

TABLE 14.1

Direct General Expenditure of Local Governments by Function[a]

| | FISCAL YEAR 1978–79 | |
	Millions of Dollars	Percentage Distribution
Total direct general expenditure	201,470	100.0
Education	87,931	43.6
Health and hospitals	14,432	7.2
Public welfare	11,676	5.8
Highways	11,361	5.6
Police protection	10,383	5.2
Sewerage	8,488	4.2
Interest	7,197	3.6
Fire protection	5,147	2.6
General control	5,133	2.5
Parks and recreation	4,742	2.4
Housing and urban renewal	4,510	2.2
Financial administration	3,379	1.7
Sanitation	2,992	1.5
Other	24,099	12.0

[a] Direct general expenditure includes all outlays except payments to other levels of government and expenditures by government enterprises including public utilities, liquor stores, and insurance trust funds.
Source: U.S. Bureau of the Census, Governmental Finances in 1978–79, table 10.

activity of local governments. Local schools account for 41 percent of their total outlays. Higher education adds almost 3 percent more. In this case, specific aid figures are available: in 1977–78, 8 percent of the revenue needed to support local schools was contributed by the federal government and 44 percent by the states.[14] Localities thus paid a little less than half the total cost.

The next largest functions are health and hospitals (7.2 percent) and public welfare (5.8 percent). These, together with housing and urban renewal (2.2 percent), make up a group of "poverty-connected" services that are either wholly or partly redistributive in intent. Fortunately federal and state aid do cover a large proportion of the costs shown here.

A third group of activities, sometimes called "common municipal functions," comprises those services performed by almost every general purpose local government. A list would include police, fire, and sanitation

14. Tax Foundation, Inc., Facts and Figures on Government Finance, 1979, table 208, p. 257.

services, sewerage, highways, parks and recreation, financial administration, and general control. These functions account for 25.7 percent of the outlays in Table 14.1. Here, with the recent exception of sewerage, the relative contribution of intergovernmental aid is undoubtedly lower than it is for education or the poverty-connected services. Accordingly the common functions make a greater relative claim on local governments' "own resources" than is suggested by the percentage distribution in the table. In that sense they remain the core responsibilities of local government. While most of these services, like police and fire protection, are in the public sector because they are true collective goods, not subject to exclusion, a few like solid waste disposal could be (and in many places are) performed by the private sector for a fee. As we shall see in the next chapter, a possible direction for reform is to pare away those functions in which the public sector enjoys no natural economic advantage.

Growth of Local Spending

The striking growth of the public sector in the United States is by now one of the familiar facts of twentieth century history. The thirty years following World War II were certainly no exception. Changes in the relative size of the public sector over time are best gauged by

TABLE 14.2

Growth of Local Expenditures and of Gross National Product

FISCAL YEAR	GROSS NATIONAL PRODUCT[a] (*Billions of Dollars*)	LOCAL EXPENDITURE[b] (*Billions of Dollars*)	EXPENDITURE AS % OF GNP
1954–55	399.3	22.5	5.6
1964–65	688.1	48.4	7.0
1974–75	1,528.8	144.1	9.4
1978–79	2,368.8	201.5	8.5
	COMPOUND ANNUAL RATE OF GROWTH		
1955 to 1965	5.6%	8.0%	—
1965 to 1975	8.3	11.5	—
1975 to 1979	11.6	8.7	—

[a] Gross national product is for calendar years 1955, 1965, 1975, and 1979.
[b] Direct general expenditures of local governments as defined in Table 14.1, note (a).
Sources: Gross national product: *Economic Report of the President,* January 1980, Table B–1, and *Survey of Current Business,* September 1980, table 1, p. 10. Local expenditure: U.S. Bureau of the Census, *Governmental Finances.*

comparing public expenditures with GNP. Table 14.2 shows that local expenditures rose from less than 6 percent of GNP in fiscal year 1954–55 to 7 percent ten years later and to 9.4 percent at their peak in 1974–75. The severe fiscal crisis in New York City during that year contributed to reversing the trend. From 1974–75 through 1978–79 local expenditures grew somewhat less rapidly than GNP; the proportion fell to 8.5 percent.

Recently adopted state taxing and spending limitations (to be discussed later in this chapter), and the mood of fiscal restraint that lies behind them, are likely to prevent the resumption of relative growth in the near future. Nevertheless, it is important to investigate the causes of past growth both to understand how we arrived at our present position and because some of the forces making for past growth will continue to press upon us whether or not we respond to them.

The reasons for local expenditure growth are many and complex. For analytical purposes public expenditures may be regarded as the product of two factors: the number of units of service provided and the average cost of providing a single unit. Increases in both factors have contributed to the growth of total local expenditure. Consider first the growth in quantity of services provided.

Urbanization and the Demand for Public Service

In a highly urbanized society it becomes necessary for government to provide some services such as sewage disposal, water supply, and recreation facilities that in a rural or village society individuals often provide for themselves. In addition urban society, because of its physical density and high level of socioeconomic interdependence, intensifies the need for such functions as police and fire protection, public health services, and public transportation. It is convenient to think of individual citizens as having demands for public service just as they have demands for such private goods as bread and shoes. Using the ordinary terminology of economic analysis we can then say that we would expect the per capita demand for units of local government service to increase rapidly simply as a result of the urbanization process itself.

Yet it seems likely that, quite apart from urbanization, rising living standards also have contributed to the relative growth in demand for public services. When living standards were low, as in the nineteenth century, people spent most of their incomes meeting the intense daily need for ordinary private goods such as food, clothing, and shelter. They held government spending to a bare minimum. As living standards rose, however, they chose to spend an increasing proportion of their income on the whole range of local government services, many of which were complementary to private spending. The increase can be viewed as a demand partly for a greater quantity of existing services, partly for better quality, and partly for the introduction of entirely new government functions. (In formal terms this amounts to arguing that the income elasticity of demand for government services—defined as the percentage change in demand for government services divided by the percentage change in income—has probably been greater than one.)

Rising Costs per Unit of Service

An increase in the per capita quantity of public services supplied undoubtedly accounts for much of the relative growth in local public expenditures during the twentieth century. However, in recent years the rising average cost of supplying each unit of service has also been a significant factor. Unit costs have been rising in the local public sector because public employees' wages and fringe benefits have gone up rapidly in recent years while output per employee has apparently risen little, if at all. Table 14.3 shows earnings in the municipal and private sectors, together with the consumer price index, at three dates. The data illustrate two trends. From 1965 to 1974 monthly earnings of city employees rose much faster than those of the average worker in manufacturing industry and also far outstripped the increase in the cost of living. During this period municipal sector earnings, which had long lagged behind, caught up with those in the private sector and in the largest cities, such as the four shown in the table, far surpassed them. After 1974, the urban fiscal crisis moderated the increase in municipal earnings. From 1974 through 1979 they rose less than earnings in manufacturing industry and less than the cost of living.

As any employer knows, the total cost of compensation includes not only wages but also fringe benefits such as pensions, health plans, paid holidays, and the like. A comparative study of fringe benefits in U.S. municipalities and in private industry shows that in 1975 benefits for police and fire personnel were considerably higher than the private sector average, while those for other municipal workers matched the level in private industry. Moreover, municipal fringe benefit costs in the period surveyed were rising considerably faster than either municipal wages or fringe costs in the private sector.[15]

City officials have been particularly inclined to offer generous retirement benefits to municipal workers, because financial arrangements allow them to take current credit for generosity while avoiding some of its cost

15. See Edward H. Friend and Albert Pike, III, *Third National Survey of Employee Benefits for Full-Time Personnel of U.S. Municipalities* (Washington, D.C.: Labor-Management Relations Service of the United States Conference of Mayors, 1977), pp. 3–9.

TABLE 14.3

Comparison of Monthly Earnings in Municipal Employment and in Manufacturing[a]

	1965	1974	1979	PERCENTAGE INCREASE 1965–74	PERCENTAGE INCREASE 1974–79
All cities	$ 480	$ 898	$1,219	87.1%	35.7%
Cities of 50,000 or more	527[b]	964[b]	1,315	82.9	36.4
New York City	585	1,064	1,313	81.9	23.4
Chicago	588	1,107	1,408	88.3	27.2
Los Angeles	712	1,261	1,814	77.1	43.9
Philadelphia	479	1,064	1,577	122.1	48.2
Average monthly earnings in U.S. manufacturing	532	904	1,341[c]	69.9	48.3
Consumer price index (1967 = 100)	94.5	147.7	195.4	56.3	47.4

[a] Average monthly earnings, all full-time municipal workers, excluding education.
[b] Common municipal functions, rather than all noneducational functions.
[c] Estimated from 1978 data.

Sources: Earnings in municipal employment: U.S. Bureau of the Census, *City Employment*, various years. Earnings in manufacturing: U.S. Department of Commerce, *Survey of Current Business*, National Income Issue (July), various years. Consumer price index: *Economic Report of the President*, January 1980, and *Survey of Current Business*, September 1980, p. S-6.

by not funding accruing obligations in full. Part of the cost of today's promises can thus be passed forward to future administrations. Although public awareness and state oversight may now have curbed this practice, the bills for past generosity are contractual obligations that will continue to mount rapidly in the future.[16]

The Effect of Productivity Lag

The impact of compensation expense on the cost of production is measured by unit labor cost, which is defined as compensation per labor hour divided by output per labor hour. For example, if a baker is paid $8.00 an hour and she produces 16 loaves of bread per hour, the unit labor cost of each loaf is 50¢. Increased output per worker allows wages to be increased *without* increasing unit labor cost: if the baker's output per hour rises 25 percent (to 20 loaves), then wages can also be increased 25 percent (to $10 an hour) without increasing unit labor costs at all ($10 ÷ 20 loaves = 50¢ per loaf). But if output per labor hour remains constant, then unit labor cost rises proportionately with wages.

How does this analysis help to explain the relative growth of local public expenditures? Except perhaps during the recent period of fiscal crisis, compensation costs have been rising faster in the local public sector than in private industry. Output per employee, on the other hand, is evidently rising faster in the latter. The result is that unit labor costs have probably gone up much faster in the public than in the private sector. This relative rise in the unit labor cost of public services may help to explain why local public expenditures have increased so much faster than the aggregate of public and private expenditures, as measured by GNP. To complete the argument, however, we must take account of demand as well as cost or supply conditions. This can best be accomplished by focusing on a single governmental function.

The Effect of Inelastic Demand

Figure 14.2 is a diagram of the supply and demand for police service in a hypothetical city. The number of units of service produced per time period is measured along the horizontal axis. The vertical axis measures not the absolute cost (or price) of a service unit but its cost (or price) relative to a composite of all other consumer goods. To simplify, we assume that police services can be produced at constant cost per unit (regardless of quantity), so that the supply curve is horizontal. Suppose

16. See Roy Bahl, Bernard Jump, Jr., and Larry Schroeder, "The Outlook for City Fiscal Performance in Declining Regions," in Roy Bahl, ed., *The Fiscal Outlook for Cities* (Syracuse, N.Y.: Syracuse University Press, 1978), p. 27 and table 15, p. 28.

FIGURE 14.2

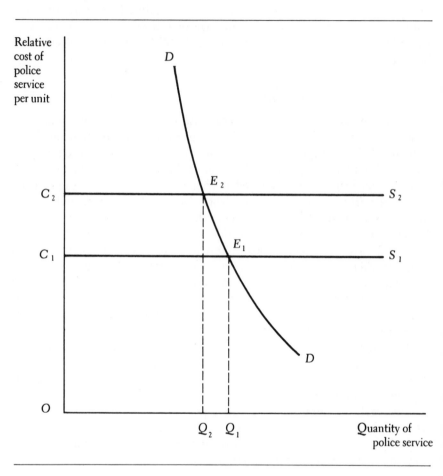

that in 1960 the relative cost of a unit is C_1, as shown by supply curve S_1. The demand for police services is represented by demand curve DD. The community provides itself with police services in the amount Q_1, as indicated by the intersection of the supply and demand curves at E_1. The total expenditure on such services equals the product of cost per unit (OC_1), and number of units produced (OQ_1), or the area of rectangle $OC_1E_1Q_1$. Now let us assume that by 1980, as a result of rising costs of compensation not offset by increased productivity, the relative cost per unit of police services rises to C_2 (supply curve S_2). At the higher price per unit the local citizenry demand fewer units, so quantity produced declines to Q_2, indicated by the new intersection at E_2. Total expenditure in 1980 therefore equals the area of rectangle $OC_2E_2Q_2$. Whether this is greater or less than the expenditure in 1960 $(OC_1E_1Q_1)$ depends entirely on the price elasticity of demand for police services. If demand is *in*elastic (elasticity < 1), the percentage decline in quantity is *less* than the percentage increase in unit cost, and expenditure on police service increases. On the other hand, if demand is elastic (elasticity > 1), quantity declines relatively *more* than price increases, and expenditure falls. The outcome thus hinges on the value of the elasticity of demand. What, in fact, is that likely to be?

Elasticity of demand depends on the availability of substitutes. If close substitutes are available, demand will be elastic: as price rises, consumers switch to the substitutes. If close substitutes are not available, demand will be *in*elastic: as price rises consumers to some extent may "do without," but they cannot obtain nearly equivalent benefits by purchasing something else. If an activity is in the public sector because it is a true collective consumption good with the property of nonexcludability, then we know that there cannot be a commercially marketed substitute. The demand for the public good is therefore likely to be highly price inelastic. In such cases—police service being one—when the unit cost of output rises, total expenditure is certain to increase.

Admittedly, broad statements about cost per unit of output in the local public sector are difficult to substantiate because in many cases we lack the measures of physical output needed to carry out precise unit cost calculations. Nevertheless, most analysts would agree with the conclusion reached by Bradford, Malt, and Oates, after a careful study of the available data, that "rising unit costs have been a major . . . source of recent increases in local public budgets."[17]

Local government activity is much more labor-intensive than is the output of the federal and state governments. Consequently, localities feel much more budgetary pressure when civil service wages rise than do the higher levels of government. Wage pressure in recent years has been greatly increased by the advent of municipal civil service unions. Wage demands by these unions are difficult to resist for two reasons. First, the unions typically control output of public services for which there are no ready substitutes and which cannot be stockpiled by consumers in anticipation of strikes. Second, they represent sizable blocs of local voters whom mayors are not eager to antagonize by taking a hard line against wage increases. However, as Table 14.3 shows, city governments became much more resistant to wage increases after the urban fiscal crisis seized national attention in 1975, and the movement for fiscal restraint that

17. D. F. Bradford, R. A. Malt, and W. E. Oates, "The Rising Cost of Local Public Services: Some Evidence and Reflections," *National Tax Journal*, June 1969, p. 201.

gained strength in the late 1970s is likely to support continued resistance to rapid municipal wage increases.

Yet it is important to remember that the cost pressure on local governments is the result not just of wage increases but of wage increases combined with productivity lag. If municipal wages do no more than keep up with wages in private firms while output per man-hour fails to increase as fast in municipal employment, then unit costs will continue to rise faster in the public than in the private sector.[18] Unfortunately, there is no easy solution to this problem. The very nature of public services such as education, the police, or hospitals and health makes it difficult to economize on the use of labor. Realistically, therefore, we must expect unit costs of local public services to continue to increase.

The Movement to Limit Spending and Taxing

We have seen that local government expenditures in the United States for many years grew faster than the economy as a whole, reaching a peak of 9.4 percent of GNP in 1974–75 (see Table 14.2). Since then the proportion has fallen slightly. The change in public attitudes toward spending and taxing—sometimes called the "taxpayers' revolt"—that became evident in the mid-1970s, probably means that growth relative to GNP will not resume in the near future.

The fiscal limitation movement captured headline attention when California voters in June 1978 overwhelmingly approved an amendment to the State Constitution known as Proposition 13.[19] By its provisions, property tax payments to local governments were cut back 57 percent, future increases in property tax revenue severely constrained, a two-thirds vote of qualified electors required to adopt new local taxes or increase rates of existing nonproperty levies, and a two-thirds vote in each house of the state legislature required to increase state tax rates. California thus combined a massive local tax cut with restraint of future tax rate increases at both the state and local levels.

While passage of Proposition 13 dramatized an apparent change in the public's attitude toward government, its provisions are not typical of

18. See William J. Baumol, "Macroeconomics of Unbalanced Growth: the Anatomy of Urban Crisis," *American Economic Review*, June 1967, pp. 415–26.

19. For a description and analysis of the fiscal limitation movement see Anthony H. Pascal, et al., *Fiscal Containment of Local and State Government*, doc. no. R-2494-FF/RC (Santa Monica, Calif.: The Rand Corporation, September 1979). A history of the events leading up to the passage of Proposition 13 is contained in Frank Levy, "On Understanding Proposition 13," *The Public Interest*, Summer 1979, pp. 66–89. A wide-ranging set of papers on fiscal limitation is presented in Proceedings of a Conference on Tax and Expenditure Limitations, *National Tax Journal* Supplement, June 1979.

other recently enacted fiscal limitations. These have taken a variety of forms.[20] Unlike Proposition 13 most of them involve limiting future growth rather than cutting back current magnitudes. Consider first the restraints placed on local governments. By the end of 1978, 24 states had enacted limitations on the property tax revenue that could be raised by localities. Only one of these (in addition to California) rolled back revenues in the manner of Proposition 13. The others aimed at restricting future growth. No state placed any limit on *total* local revenue. One adopted a limit on the rate of growth of local spending.

In addition, from 1976 through 1978, nine states adopted limitations on their own fiscal activity. Most of these (unlike limits applied to localities) affect expenditures rather than revenues. For example, New Jersey passed a law in 1976 that prohibits state expenditure from growing faster than state personal income. In most but not all cases, states that limited their own activity also enacted limits of some sort on localities.

Many of its supporters believe that tax and expenditure limitation is the only way to ensure that a democratic political system will not result in "overspending." Public officials, they argue, accede too readily to the pressure of concentrated interest groups who favor expanding particular programs at the expense of the general taxpayer. Supporters of fiscal restraints are convinced that only a binding legal limit on taxing or spending can prevent such behavior.[21]

Opinion surveys, however, indicate that the "taxpayers' revolt" reflects not only dissatisfaction with rising tax payments but also a growing conviction among voters that government is wasteful and inefficient. Many of those questioned express a willingness to forgo tax relief if waste can be eliminated.[22] Thus a vote for legal restraints can be interpreted as a way of trying to compel local government to operate more efficiently.[23] (We return to the issue of local government productivity at the end of Chapter 15.)

Like much other social legislation, fiscal restraint is likely to have unintended consequences at least as important as its intended results. In California, Proposition 13 immediately reduced local revenue by $7 billion. The amendment was adopted in the knowledge that a huge state surplus could be used to offset much of that loss, and so it was. The state provided $4.1 billion of emergency aid to localities. As the state "bailout" was institutionalized, Californians found that a major transfer of fiscal responsibility from local to state government had taken place. Liberals who

20. For a tabulation by type see Pascal, tables 4.1 and 4.2.
21. See Barry N. Siegel, *Thoughts on the Tax Revolt*, Original Paper 21 (Los Angeles: International Institute for Economic Research, 1979), pp. 4–5.
22. Pascal, pp. 3–5.
23. Siegel, pp. 12–13.

had long sought such a transfer, in order to reduce inequalities in spending between rich and poor municipalities and school districts, found their program suddenly adopted as the result of a victory by their long-time opponents. Conservatives, who generally support tax limitation out of a preference for "less government," may eventually regret the loss of local autonomy that will probably result as financial responsibility shifts toward the state capital.[24]

California represents an extreme case, since it sharply cut back local revenue instead of simply limiting its future growth. In the long run, however, the fiscal limitation movement could have a similar centralizing effect elsewhere. If restraints on local governments continue to outweigh those the states impose on themselves, fiscal limitation will probably accelerate the trend toward greater state responsibility for local services.

Finally, the combined effect of fiscal limitation and productivity lag should not be overlooked. If local spending is allowed to rise only as fast as GNP, while the unit cost of local public services is pushed upward by productivity lag, the value of local government output in real terms will be dropping rather than keeping pace with economic growth.

LOCAL GOVERNMENT REVENUE

The composition and growth of local government general revenue are displayed in Tables 14.4 and 14.5. Since local governments are normally required by state law to balance their current operating budgets, the rapid expenditure growth shown above in Table 14.2 is matched by the steep rise in revenues indicated in Table 14.5. In 1952 local general revenue amounted to only 4.9 percent of gross national product. By 1979 it had increased to 8.9 percent.

The three major revenue categories of local government are taxes, aid from the state and federal governments, and charges plus miscellaneous general revenue. The property tax has always been by far the most important local levy. In 1978–79 it accounted for 78 percent of tax revenues. However, Table 14.4 shows that its share is slowly declining, while sales and income taxes gradually assume greater importance.

The enormous increase in local government expenditures since the early 1950s has been financed by growth in all three major revenue categories. They did not all grow equally fast, however, so the composition of revenue changed over time. Especially significant is the growing importance of intergovernmental aid. In 1952 aid accounted for only 31 percent of general revenue, as compared with 56 percent derived from local taxes. By

24. Levy, p. 88.

TABLE 14.4
Local Government Revenues by Source
(fiscal years)

	1951–52 (Millions of Dollars)	1978–79 (Millions of Dollars)	DISTRIBUTION BY SOURCE			
			1951–52		1978–79	
			Total General Revenue	Tax Revenue	Total General Revenue	Tax Revenue
Total general revenue[a]	16,952	211,986	100.0%	—	100.0%	—
Tax revenue	9,466	80,606	55.8	100.0%	38.0	100.0%
Property tax	8,282	62,453	48.9	87.5	29.5	77.5
Sales and gross receipts taxes	627	10,579	3.7	6.6	5.0	13.1
Income taxes	93	4,309	0.6	1.0	2.0	5.4
Licenses and other taxes	465	3,264	2.7	4.9	1.5	4.1
Charges and miscellaneous general revenue	2,205	36,603	13.0	—	17.3	—
Intergovernmental revenue	5,281	94,777	31.2	—	44.7	—
From federal government	237	20,616	1.4	—	9.7	—
From state governments	5,044	74,162	29.8	—	35.0	—

[a] General revenue includes all receipts except those of government enterprises including public utilities, liquor stores, and insurance trust funds.

Sources: U.S. Bureau of Census, *Governmental Finances in 1978–79*, table 4, and 1977 *Census of Governments*, vol. 6, no. 4, table 6.

TABLE 14.5
Growth of Local Government Revenues and of Gross National Product

FISCAL YEAR	GROSS NATIONAL PRODUCT[a] (Billions of Dollars)	TAX REVENUE (Millions of Dollars)	OTHER GENERAL REVENUE[b] (Millions of Dollars)	INTERGOVERNMENTAL REVENUE[c] (Millions of Dollars)	TAX REVENUE AS PERCENTAGE OF GNP
1951–52	347.2	9,466	2,205	5,281	2.7
1961–62	563.8	20,993	5,711	11,641	3.7
1971–72	1,171.1	49,739	15,810	39,694	4.3
1978–79	2,368.8	80,606	36,603	94,777	3.4
COMPOUND ANNUAL RATE OF GROWTH					
1952 to 1962	5.0%	8.3%	10.0%	8.2%	
1962 to 1972	7.6	9.0	10.7	13.1	
1972 to 1979	10.6	7.1	12.7	13.2	

[a] Gross national product is for calendar years 1952, 1962, 1972, and 1979.
[b] Includes a variety of user charges and miscellaneous revenue.
[c] Includes all grants, shared taxes, or other payments from federal and state governments.

Sources: Gross national product: *Economic Report of the President*, January 1980, table B–1, and *Survey of Current Business*, September 1980, table 1, p. 10. Local revenues: U.S. Bureau of the Census, *Governmental Finances in 1978–79*, table 4, and 1977 *Census of Governments*, vol. 6, no. 4, table 6.

1979 aid was the source of 45 percent of local revenue, while taxes supplied only 38 percent. The various forms of intergovernmental aid will be analyzed in Chapter 15. At this point we take a closer look at the relationship between local tax revenues and economic growth, as measured by GNP.

Tax Revenue and Economic Growth: The Concept of Tax Base Elasticity

Each local tax has its own tax base: the financial aggregate to which the tax rate is applied. In the case of the property tax, the base is the assessed value of taxable local property. For a retail sales tax, the base is the annual value of taxable retail sales. The yield of any tax is the product of the base times the rate.

To facilitate analysis of the growth of local tax revenue, it is useful to define a GNP elasticity for each local tax. This measure, E_{LT}, indicates the relationship between changes in the revenue from a tax and changes in GNP, on the assumption that tax *rates* and the definition of the base are held constant. Thus,

$$E_{LT} = \frac{\text{percentage change in local tax revenue}}{\text{percentage change in GNP}}$$

The reason revenue from a particular tax changes when GNP changes, even though tax rates and definitions are held constant, is that economic growth usually causes growth in the tax base. Thus E_{LT} can be thought of as a measure of tax base elasticity as well as a measure of revenue elasticity with rates held constant. If a tax base has an elasticity greater than one, then as GNP increases, either through real growth or because of inflation, the revenue from that tax will increase faster than GNP, even if tax rates do not rise. On the other hand, if tax base elasticity is less than one, revenue will increase less rapidly than GNP when tax rates are held constant. Tax rates will have to be increased more or less regularly if revenue is to keep pace with the growth of GNP.

The value of E_{LT} for any tax is difficult to calculate because the objective is to measure changes over time not in tax revenue, which are easily observable, but rather in the size of the tax base, which may not be. Since the property tax accounts for almost 80 percent of local tax revenue, its elasticity obviously dominates the outcome for the local system as a whole. Unfortunately, estimates of its elasticity are particularly difficult to work out. First of all, the tax base of interest to the economist is the full market value of taxable property. The legal base for the property tax, however, is the assessed value of local property. This is intended to reflect market value, but, whatever the law may require, assessors do not usually assess property at its full market worth. In fact, the relationship between assessed value and market value varies widely between places and over time. Therefore it is necessary to adjust assessed value data systematically to arrive at estimates of market value from which tax base elasticity can be calculated. A second difficulty arises because there is reason to believe that the relation between changes in the market value of property and changes in a measure of aggregate income, such as GNP, is not constant but may fluctuate over time.

Estimates of the GNP elasticity of the property tax in the 1960s varied from a low of 0.8 to a high of 1.3, with the majority of estimates falling between 0.8 and 1.0.[25] This supported the conventional wisdom that the tax was inelastic: its yield would grow less rapidly than GNP if tax rates remained constant.

Sales and gross receipts taxes rank second in importance among local levies, accounting for 13 percent of tax revenues. The majority of statistical estimates put the GNP elasticity of this group at about 1.0.[26] The local income tax probably has an elasticity somewhat above unity, but accounts for only 5 percent of tax receipts. License fees and minor taxes, which account for the remaining 4 percent of local tax revenue, probably have an elasticity well below unity.

Putting these revenue sources together we could fairly estimate that the local tax system as a whole had a GNP elasticity of about 1.0 in the 20 years from 1952 to 1972. Using this elasticity figure we can then estimate the extent to which changes in tax rates apparently contributed to the growth of local revenues during that period. If the system as a whole had an elasticity of 1.0, tax rates had remained constant, and no new taxes had been adopted by local governments, local tax revenues would have increased at the same rate as GNP between 1952 and 1972. The latter increased by 237 percent. If local tax revenues had increased by the same percentage they would have amounted to $31.9 billion in 1972. In fact, they rose to $49.7 billion. This implies rate increases (plus new taxes adopted) of 56 percent, since $49.7 ÷ $31.9 = 1.56.

There is some direct evidence on property tax rates to support this estimate. Since every locality levies property taxes at a rate of its own choosing and since the ratio of assessed value to market value also varies from place to place it is difficult to calculate a meaningful national average rate. However, a compilation of data by the Advisory Commission on

25. See estimates compiled from a variety of sources by the Advisory Commission on Intergovernmental Relations in Report M–74, *State-Local Finances: Significant Features and Suggested Legislation, 1972 Edition*, table 134, p. 301; and discussion in Dick Netzer, *Economics of the Property Tax* (Washington, D.C.: The Brookings Institution, 1966), pp. 184–90.

26. Advisory Commission, 1972, table 134, p. 301.

Intergovernmental Relations shows that the nationwide average rate of tax, adjusted to full market value, on single family homes with FHA-insured mortgages rose from 1.34 percent in 1958 to 1.98 percent in 1971. (See Table 14.7 below.) That amounts to a 48 percent increase, and is roughly consistent with the 56 percent increase in *all* tax rates estimated above for a somewhat longer period.

Local tax rates would surely have risen even faster had it not been for the very rapid increase in aid from the state and federal governments indicated in Tables 14.4 and 14.5. This increase in turn was made possible by the fact that the tax systems of those governments have higher GNP elasticities than does the local tax system.

Because Washington relies so heavily on a progressive income tax for revenue, the GNP elasticity of the federal tax base as a whole is very high. As incomes rise either through real economic growth or simply because of inflation, families move into higher tax brackets and pay a larger percentage of their incomes in tax. Consequently, federal income tax receipts increase much more rapidly than family incomes do as the economy grows, and a 1 percent rise in GNP leads to much more than a 1 percent rise in total federal revenues. Historically the federal government has therefore been able to take care of its own needs, increase its grants to state and local governments and at the same time gradually reduce federal income and excise tax rates.

The tax base of the state governments is moderately elastic since they can and do make use of income taxes at mildly progressive rates. (In 1978–79 individual income taxes provided 26 percent of their tax revenue.) Nevertheless, the states have had to increase their tax rates markedly in order to finance their rapidly growing expenditures. These expenditures, of course, include the sharply increased state aid to localities shown in Table 14.4.

Local tax revenues as a percentage of GNP reached a peak in 1972. Since that date they have grown more slowly than GNP as local governments responded to the gathering strength of the "taxpayers' revolt." If we continue to assume that the local tax system has a GNP elasticity of unity, the decline in tax revenue relative to GNP from 1971–72 through 1978–79 implies that tax rates were reduced about 20 percent in seven years. However, it is likely that the size of the local tax base increased faster than GNP during the 1970s because taxable property values rose so rapidly. Purchasers were vigorously bidding up property prices apparently because they viewed real property as an excellent investment during a period of rapid inflation. If we assume that the local tax system as a whole had a GNP elasticity greater than unity during the 1970s, then the reduction in effective tax rates implied by the decline in local tax revenue relative to GNP after 1972 might be considerably greater than 20 percent.

Again, Table 14.7 provides some direct evidence: the average effective rate of tax on FHA-insured single family homes fell from 1.98 percent in 1971 to 1.34 percent in 1979, a rapid and substantial decline. Tax payments, of course, were increasing, not declining, but the market value of property was going up much faster than tax payments, so the effective rate of tax did fall sharply. The property market, however, has always been highly cyclical. The strong performance of property values during the 1970s should not be taken to indicate that they will continue to outstrip GNP in the long run. If their growth rate should again fall below that of GNP, upward pressure on property tax rates is likely to resume.

THE PROPERTY TAX

The property tax deserves special attention in a book on urban economics, not only because it is by far the most important tax levied by city governments, but also because its specific impact on building development and land use helps to shape the very structure of the city. For the same reasons the tax has traditionally been the subject of much debate, as economists have argued about its effects and about the probable consequences of proposed reforms.

The most important economic questions to be answered about any tax are: first, who pays it? Second, what effects does it have on economic activity? The first question is essentially one of income distribution, and therefore of equity, while the second is one of resource allocation, and therefore of efficiency. Although the answers to these questions are interconnected, it is convenient to separate them for purposes of analysis.

The question "Who pays the tax?" is the subject of tax incidence theory: the "incidence" of the tax is said to be on those persons who bear its burden. It is important to distinguish between "legal" incidence and "economic" incidence. For example, the Congress may enact a tax of so many dollars a pair on the production of leather shoes and command shoe manufacturers to pay it. The legal incidence is then on shoe manufacturers. But if, after the tax is imposed, these producers can raise their selling price sufficiently to cover the tax (or some part of it) they will have succeeded in "shifting" the tax (or a part of it) forward to retailers. Retailers in turn may succeed in raising prices enough to shift the tax forward to consumers. The incidence, or some part of it, then rests with consumers (who presumably can shift it no further).

When analyzing incidence, the economist tries first to establish which functional classes bear the burden of the tax and then what that implies about the distribution of the burden among income classes. A tax is said to be progressive if it takes an increasing proportion of income from an individual as income increases. It is called regressive if the proportion paid in taxes drops as income increases. If the proportion is constant over all income classes, the tax is termed proportional. In the case of the property tax, the functional classes to be considered would include such groups as landowners, building owners, tenants, owners of capital, and consumers. The distribution of the burden among income classes will obviously depend on its functional distribution, since functional classes differ systematically in the level and distribution of income among their members.

The question of how a tax affects economic activity concerns specifically its impact on the allocation of resources. Whenever a tax is imposed, those who are affected try to adjust their economic behavior to minimize its harmful effects. Such adjustment distorts prices in the marketplace away from what they would have been in the absence of a tax. These distortions cause a welfare loss as compared with the outcome if prices had been established under perfect competition with no taxes. This welfare loss is usually referred to as the "excess burden" of the tax because it is a loss in addition to the direct burden of paying the money cost of the levy. In the example of a tax on the production of leather shoes, suppose that manufacturers and retailers raise the price of leather shoes in an attempt to shift the tax. Some consumers will pay the higher price. Others will respond by purchasing canvas, rubber, or plastic shoes as substitutes. But the same consumers considered these to be inferior alternatives when *un*taxed leather shoes were available. Therefore, those who switch to avoid the tax are necessarily suffering a welfare loss. This is an example of "excess burden."

Upon reflection, it is clear that a tax cannot be shifted unless some participant in the system adjusts behavior to bring about the shift. But such adjustments distort prices and create excess burden. Therefore tax shifting always implies the creation of excess burden. Conversely, a tax that cannot be shifted distorts no prices and creates no excess burden.

Site Value Taxation

In the United States the property tax is almost always levied on the assessed value of land and improvements combined. It is conventional, however, to analyze the tax in two parts, since the portion that falls on land (or site) value has quite different effects than the part that is levied on improvements. Economists dream of taxes that cannot be shifted and therefore impose no excess burden. There are not many of them, but a tax on site value is generally acknowledged to be one. Consequently site

FIGURE 14.3

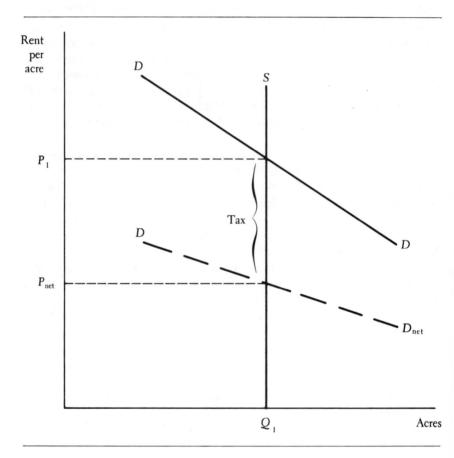

value—the value of unimproved land—has long been regarded by economists as a particularly fit object for taxation.

A tax on site value cannot be shifted by the landowner to any other party for one very simple reason: land is in fixed supply.[27] It is perpetually durable, and not reproducible, movable, or transformable. Consequently, if a city levies a tax on land value, there is no response by which the owner can reduce the burden. He or she simply pays the tax and goes on using the land in whatever way was most profitable before a tax was levied, for that will still be the most profitable use, net of tax.

This outcome is illustrated in Figure 14.3 which represents the

27. We here ignore the possibility of adding to the supply by extending landfill into waters adjacent to a city.

supply and demand for sites in a hypothetical city. It is convenient to use annual rent rather than capital value as the measure of price.[28] Site rent per acre is measured on the vertical axis, the number of acres supplied and demanded on the horizontal. In the interest of simplicity, the dimension of distance and the effect of accessibility on site rent are suppressed. All sites are therefore equally desirable to users. On the supply side, landowners are assumed to be perfect competitors.

The area of the city is Q_1 acres, no more, no less. Consequently, the supply of sites is represented as perfectly inelastic, a vertical straight line at Q_1. The demand curve DD is assumed to have the usual downward slope: if sites were cheaper, demanders would use more land in relation to other inputs. Since the supply is fixed, however, demanders in fact use Q_1 acres and pay P_1 rent per acre. Landowners accept P_1 as the highest obtainable rent. Their only alternative is inferior: withdraw land from the market and earn nothing.

Now suppose the city were to levy a tax of 50 percent on annual site rent. The amounts payable are shown in Figure 14.3 by the distance between DD and DD_{net}, which is 50 percent of the height of DD at every point. The price of land does not rise in response to the tax because it cannot pay any individual landowner to withdraw his supply. Consequently, users continue to pay P_1 per acre for the use of sites, landowners retain a net rent equal to P_{net} and return to the city a tax equal to $P_1 - P_{net}$ per acre. The tax is not shifted.

Because the supply of sites is not reduced by the tax, rent does not rise, and market prices are in no way distorted. Site value taxation thus has the virtue of being perfectly neutral in the sense of not disturbing an otherwise desirable allocation of resources. No tax better satisfies the criterion of economic efficiency.

It is sometimes argued that this tax also deserves unusually high marks on grounds of equity. Site value taxation taps what has been described as an "unearned increment" in wealth. The value of land is not created by the efforts of the landowner. Rather, it is the social and economic development of the entire community that gives particular sites their value. It follows that society would be perfectly justified in recapturing through taxation the unearned increment in value that would otherwise go to the landowner. Henry George and his followers have therefore advocated the imposition of very heavy taxes on land value. This argument, however, overlooks a pervasive complication. Since land frequently changes hands, there can be no presumption that present owners received any unearned increment. They may have paid anything up to the full current value for their parcels. Thus the unearned increment argu-

28. See discussion at the beginning of ch. 6.

ment supports the imposition of a heavy tax on *future* gains in land value
but cannot justify a tax that is levied *ex post*.[29]

The incidence of a tax on land value is clearly on those who own
land at the time the tax is imposed or its rate increased. Nor can owners
escape the tax by selling their holdings, since the expected future tax
burden is immediately capitalized into the present value of the land. Any
subsequent buyer pays a price that takes the tax into account and thus,
in effect, "buys free of tax." Since most land in the United States is owned
in common with improvements, we can assume as an approximation that
the tax on land is distributed among income classes in proportion to their
ownership of real property. On that basis its burden would probably be
distributed progressively in relation to income.

The Tax on Improvements: The Old View

The more important and analytically more controversial part of the
property tax is the portion levied on improvements, including rental and
owner-occupied housing and commercial and industrial property. While
there has always been some disagreement about the incidence of this tax,
most economists until recently concluded that in the long run the portion
of the tax falling on improvements would, with some exceptions, be
shifted forward from owners to users.[30] Thus the tax on department store
buildings would be passed forward to customers, the tax on factories to
consumers of their products, and the tax on rental housing to tenants.
This traditional conclusion we shall refer to as the "old" view. In recent
years it has been powerfully challenged by a "new" view, which holds that
a substantial share of the tax on improvements is borne by owners of
capital in general instead of being shifted to customers or tenants.[31]

The two views have radically different implications for the distribution of the property tax burden among income classes. Adherents of the
old view usually found the tax to be regressive, a serious deficiency in the
opinion of many observers. The new view reverses that verdict: the tax

29. In this discussion it is assumed that gains in land value are "real" rather
than the result of general price inflation.
30. See Herbert A. Simon, "The Incidence of a Tax on Urban Real Property,"
reprinted in Richard A. Musgrave and Carl S. Shoup, eds., *Readings in the Economics
of Taxation* (Homewood, Ill.: Richard D. Irwin, 1959), pp. 416–35 and references
cited therein; and Netzer, *Economics of the Property Tax*, ch. 3.
31. See Henry J. Aaron, *Who Pays the Property Tax?* (Washington, D.C.: The
Brookings Institution, 1975); Peter Mieszkowski, "The Property Tax: An Excise or a
Profits Tax?" *Journal of Public Economics*, April 1972, pp. 73–96; Dick Netzer, "The
Incidence of the Property Tax Revisited," *National Tax Journal*, December 1973, pp.
515–35. Harry Gunnison Brown is now recognized as an early (1924) proponent of
the new view whose work "has been generally neglected although known to many
economists." (Netzer, p. 516. Also see references to Brown in Aaron and Simon.)

turns out to be quite progressive, an important virtue in many eyes. In the following sections we explain both views in simplified form in order to capture the essence of each—but certainly without pretending to do full justice to the sophistication of the arguments on either side. To facilitate exposition we limit the analysis initially to the example of rental housing.

The old view is most easily explained by considering the impact of the property tax within a single locality. Assume initially that property taxes are levied at a rate *t* in all jurisdictions. Assume also that factors of production are geographically perfectly mobile, so developers of rental housing pay prices for their inputs, including capital, that are established competitively in national markets. If the locality under consideration is a very small part of the national whole, then we can assume that the supply of each input, including capital, to local developers is perfectly elastic at the going market price.

In Figure 14.4 the rental housing market is portrayed by means of a stock adjustment model. Quantity of housing available for rent is measured

FIGURE 14.4

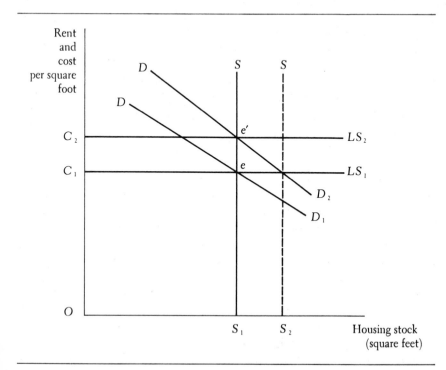

in square feet on the horizontal axis, rent and building cost per square foot on the vertical. As explained in Chapter 12, the housing market in the short run is dominated by the standing stock, since supply expansion is at best a very slow process. In Figure 14.4 supply in the short run is SS_1, the quantity of space in the standing stock. Consumer demand is given by DD_1, which can be thought of as showing the desired stock of housing at each price. The rent level per square foot that will yield investors in new construction the going rate of return on capital after paying property taxes at rate t is C_1. New construction leading to expansion of the standing stock will take place whenever rent exceeds C_1, which can therefore be called "the new construction rent level." Given the perfectly elastic supply of inputs, the horizontal straight line LS_1 at rent level C_1 is the long-run supply curve of housing stock. As long as tax rates remain geographically uniform, the new construction rent level is the same everywhere. In the locality depicted, SS_1 and DD_1 intersect at point e on the long-run supply curve. Hence the market is initially in long-run equilibrium with rent equal to long-run cost, C_1.

Now suppose that the local government decides to raise the rate of property tax to t'. The new construction rent level rises to C_2, the rent that developers of additional buildings must obtain to pay the higher tax rate and still earn the going rate of return on investment. The actual rent, however, remains at C_1. Thus in the short run, according to the old view, the burden of increased property taxes remains with the owner.

In the long run, however, the tax can be shifted by owners to tenants if market rent rises above C_1. This could occur because either demand increased or supply diminished. Demand would be expected to increase as a result of growing population or rising living standards. Supply could decrease because of demolition, fire, or conversion to nonresidential use. The case of increased demand is illustrated in Figure 14.4. As the population of the city grows, more housing space is required. The demand curve shifts to the right. As it does so, the market level of rent moves up along SS_1 because investors do not expand the housing stock while rent remains below C_2. When demand has increased to DD_2 rent reaches C_2, the new construction rent level that incorporates tax rate t'. The market is now in equilibrium at point e'. The tax increase has been fully shifted to tenants. Rents are now higher in this locality than elsewhere by the amount necessary to pay the higher rate of local tax, as indicated by long-run supply curve LS_2. If the tax rate had not risen, the stock of housing would have increased to SS_2 when demand increased. Instead, the stock remained at SS_1, and rents rose. (If demand should continue to increase, new construction would begin again, expanding the housing stock, and rents would rise no farther.) Thus the general conclusion under the old view is that, except in declining cities where the necessary market conditions may not occur, the burden of property taxes on rental housing is, in the long run, shifted by landlords to tenants.

The New View of the Property Tax

A crucial assumption of the old view is that a tax on real property does not affect the long-run rate of return to capital in general. The preceding analysis assumes, in effect, that there is a "going rate of return on capital" determined exogenously in activities and markets not reached by the property tax. This going rate is not affected by the imposition of a tax on property. Instead, when such a tax is levied, the gross rate of return on property rises sufficiently in the long run to leave the after-tax return in the taxed sectors still equal to the exogenously determined "going rate." It is precisely this assumption of an undisturbed "going rate of return" that the new view challenges.

The rate of return was treated as an exogenously determined variable by adherents of the old view because they employed "partial equilibrium analysis." Using this method, the analyst focuses on changes going on in one market or industry, while assuming that the broader economy is not affected in any relevant way by these changes. The analyst can then examine the particular industry while "all other things," including the economic environment in which the industry operates, are held constant. This is a useful simplification when the assumption of "all other things constant" is tenable. The method is clearly appropriate for such purposes as examining the incidence of a specific excise tax on, say, shoes. Such a tax might be expected to affect the market price of shoes, the rate of return on capital in shoe manufacturing, or the wages of laborers in that industry. But since shoe manufacturing is a very small segment of the economy, we would not expect the tax to have perceptible effects on the general price level, the rate of return on capital in general, or the average level of industrial wages. Adherents of the new view, however, argue that partial equilibrium analysis is not appropriate in the case of the property tax, which is imposed on a large proportion of the nation's tangible capital. Rather they see the property tax as a levy on broad categories of capital, and since capital is employed throughout the economy they argue that the tax should be analyzed in a general equilibrium setting.

The new view of the property tax actually has its origins in the work of Arnold Harberger, who published a general equilibrium analysis of the incidence of the corporation income tax in 1962.[32] Using arguments analogous to Harberger's, Peter Mieszkowski set forth the new view in

---

32. Arnold C. Harberger, "The Incidence of the Corporation Income Tax," *Journal of Political Economy,* June 1962, pp. 215–40.

1972.[33] Two assumptions, first employed by Harberger, are crucial to the analysis. First the rate of saving (i.e., capital accumulation) is assumed to be insensitive to changes in the rate of return on capital, allowing the analyst to treat the stock of capital as fixed in the face of property tax rate changes, even in the long run. This assumption may seem counter-intuitive. Wouldn't we expect the rate of saving to depend in part on the rate of return on capital? Harberger found no substantial evidence of such an effect in nearly a century of U.S. economic history.[34] Debate continues on this question, however. The second crucial assumption is that capital is perfectly mobile among regions and industries. This will probably strike most observers as reasonable. Capital markets in the United States are highly organized, market participants are well-informed and do regularly move funds between industries and regions.

Mieszkowski begins with the case in which all towns impose the same rate of property tax on all forms of reproducible capital. It can easily be shown that the burden of the tax then falls entirely on the owners of capital. We have already explained that a tax cannot be shifted unless it affects the supply of the taxed object. (Recall the case of land value taxation illustrated in Figure 14.3, above.) In the present case the supply of reproducible capital is assumed to be invariant to the rate of return. Property owners cannot shift the tax forward to tenants in their buildings or users of their products because the quantity of capital supplied is not reduced by the tax and hence its price to users cannot be raised. (Similarly, they cannot shift the burden backward to suppliers of labor or other services, because their own demand for these services is not reduced by the tax.[35]) Consequently, users continue to pay the same price for the services of capital as they paid before imposition of the tax and the net return received by owners falls by the full amount of the tax. This is just the opposite of the outcome according to the old view.

"Global" Effects and "Excise" Effects

Of course, all towns do *not* levy property taxes at the same rate, nor do they all tax every form of reproducible capital. There are substantial differences in both rates and coverage across jurisdictions. Mieszkowski is able to deal with both the generality of the tax and the particularity of these differences by distinguishing between the "global" and "excise" effects of the property tax system. Although the total supply of capital is treated as fixed in this analysis, the fact that capital is highly mobile means that differences in the rate or coverage of property taxes among

33. See note 26, above.
34. Harberger, p. 216.
35. Netzer, "Incidence of the Property Tax Revisited," p. 517.

jurisdictions will be compensated for by movements from high- to low-tax areas.

The process of adjustment is most easily explained by means of a numerical example. Table 14.6 gives hypothetical data for three groups of towns within a national system. Column one of the table indicates that before any property taxes are imposed the rate of return on reproducible capital in all towns is a uniform 6 percent. The three groups of towns are then assumed to impose taxes at the rates shown in column two: 3 percent in high-tax towns, 2 percent in those taxing at the average level, and 1 percent in low-tax towns. The immediate effect in all areas is to reduce the rate of return on local property by the amount of the tax. Hence the net rates of return at first fall to the levels shown in column three. Net returns are now lower in high-tax jurisdictions and higher in low-tax jurisdictions than elsewhere. Capital markets are therefore not in long-run equilibrium. Further adjustment occurs. Owners transfer capital out of high-tax and into low-tax areas or industries. This reduces the supply of capital in high-tax areas, thus tending to *raise* the before-tax return to capital there. It increases the supply of capital in low-tax areas, consequently reducing the before-tax return there. Migration of capital continues until after-tax returns are equal (with due allowance for risk) in all areas and industries, as indicated in column four. Capital markets are now in long-run equilibrium because net rates of return are everywhere equal. The local *cost* of capital, however, which equals the sum of the net return plus the rate of local tax, is not geographically uniform. As column five shows, capital services cost more in high-tax than in low-tax jurisdictions.

What Mieszkowski calls the global effect is shown in the table as the difference between the return that would be earned in the absence of all property taxes (6 percent, column one) and the net return earned after capital markets have adjusted to varying tax rates (4 percent, column four). It is the decline in the nationwide average return to owners that results from the imposition of property taxes at varying local rates.[36] If all towns imposed property taxes with identical rates and coverage there would be only a global effect. In fact, as we have already argued, there are significant local differences. These cause what Mieszkowski calls "excise" effects. The most obvious excise effect results from the difference between the cost of capital services in high- and low-tax communities that exists after the migration of capital has equalized net returns in all areas (column five of Table 14.6). These differences in the local cost of capital

36. There is no requirement in theory that this decline be precisely equal to the average rate of tax imposed, as it is in Table 14.6. It could exceed or fall short of that amount. (See Mieszkowski, p. 79).

TABLE 14.6
Two Views of Property Tax Incidence: Hypothetical Data

	(1) RATE OF RETURN ON CAPITAL BEFORE IMPOSITION OF TAX	(2) LOCAL PROPERTY TAX RATE	THE NEW VIEW			THE OLD VIEW		
			(3) NET RETURN AFTER TAX *Before Capital Migration* (1) − (2)	(4) NET RETURN AFTER TAX *After Capital Migration*	(5) COST OF CAPITAL SERVICES AFTER MIGRATION (2) + (4)	(6) NET RETURN AFTER TAX *Before Tax Shifting* (1) − (2)	(7) NET RETURN AFTER TAX *After Tax Shifting*	(8) COST OF CAPITAL SERVICES AFTER TAX SHIFTING (1) + (2)
High tax town	.06	.03	.03	.04	.07	.03	.06	.09
Towns taxing at national average rate	.06	.02	.04	.04	.06	.04	.06	.08
Low tax town	.06	.01	.05	.04	.05	.05	.06	.07

give rise to differences in the cost of production among localities, including differences in the cost of housing services.

Comparison of Results: New View Versus Old

How do the results to this point compare with those that would be predicted by the old view of the property tax? To facilitate comparison, results are worked out in columns six, seven, and eight of Table 14.6, starting again from the initial conditions given in columns one and two. According to the old view, property owners ultimately shift the entire burden of a tax on improvements to their customers. Consequently, their net return after shifting (column seven) is the same as it was before taxes were imposed, and two points higher than it would be according to the new view (column four), which asserts that net returns are depressed by the global effect. The old view holds that the cost of capital in all localities ultimately increases by the amount of the tax (column 8 = column 1 + column 2), whereas, according to the new view, much of the impact of the tax is absorbed by a reduction in net returns. As compared with the no-tax situation, the cost of capital, according to the new view, therefore rises in high-tax areas but actually falls in communities with low tax rates. Low-tax communities are seen as gainers in a nationwide property tax system: their cost of capital is reduced more by the global effect (column one − column four = .02) than it is increased by their own tax rate (.01). Intercommunity differences in the cost of capital, however, remain the same in the new view as in the old (compare columns five and eight).

Backward Shifting to Land and Labor

If excise effects consisted only of differences in the cost of capital among communities, we might argue (recalling Figure 14.4) that they will have more or less the same results as those attributed to the entire tax on improvements under the old view. Proponents of the new view, however, do not believe that excise effects are limited to differences in the cost of capital that are passed forward to tenants and customers in the form of higher prices. They argue that differences in the cost of local capital are bound to affect the level of local production, thereby impinging on the demand for inputs and consequently affecting the prices (i.e., incomes) of the other factors of production, land and labor. The possibility of such "backward" shifting of the property tax was generally (though not always) ignored in the partial equilibrium analysis of the old view. Unfortunately, the task of analysis becomes very complex once all these relationships are opened up for investigation. In what follows we examine, in a much simplified form, two possibilities: could differences in local tax rates on improvements be shifted backward either to land-owners or to workers?[37]

Consider, once more, the rental housing sector. In a high-tax community, the higher cost of capital obviously raises the cost of operating rental housing. In the long run the housing stock will therefore be smaller and rents higher than they would be if local taxes were no higher than the national average. That much has already been shown in Figure 14.4. But if the housing stock is smaller, then the demand for building sites is correspondingly reduced. Since land is not mobile, the supply of sites is perfectly inelastic. When demand falls, land prices must therefore be reduced below what they would otherwise have been. This reduction in cost stands as an offset to the higher cost of capital. One can even make a plausible case that it will fully offset the higher tax on improvements, leaving tenants as a class no worse off than if the property tax had been lower.[38] In short, because land is immobile it may be forced to absorb the impact of a tax on improvements.

What about labor? Again, the answer according to proponents of the new view depends on mobility. For example, if construction workers are perfectly mobile they will not, in the long run, accept lower wages or higher unemployment rates than exist elsewhere just because high taxes reduce local construction activity. Instead, they will move to places where taxes are lower and jobs more plentiful. On the other hand, if labor is not perfectly mobile, property taxes that reduce local economic activity might depress wages or employment. Lower wages would offset in part the higher local cost of capital, moderating its effect on housing rent or other local prices.[39]

Two points must now be emphasized. First, excise effects in towns with tax rates *below* the national average are mirror images of those in high-tax communities. In such towns the returns to immobile factors of production may be higher than they would have been if taxes had been higher. Taking a national perspective, it is plausible to argue that the excise-effect gains to factors of production in low-tax communities probably balance the analogous losses in high-tax areas. (The local perspective is quite another matter, to which we return below.) Second, it must be emphasized that changes in factor prices brought about by backward shifting of the property tax are offsets only to differences in local tax rates, not to the global effect, which they in no way mitigate.

37. For a fuller treatment see Mieszkowski, pp. 81–93, and Aaron, pp. 41–43.
38. Aaron, p. 42.
39. Aaron, pp. 41–42.

Incidence of the Tax on Other Sectors

Up to this point, in order to focus on differences between the old and new views of the property tax, we have limited the discussion of its incidence to the single example of the rental housing industry. Now very briefly we examine the incidence of the tax on owner-occupied housing and on commerce and industry generally.

Owner-occupied housing. The owner occupant stands in a double relation to housing, as the owner who produces housing services and, simultaneously, as the tenant who consumes them. According to the old view, the tax raises the cost of providing housing services because it must be added to the cost of capital used in housing. The owner occupant cannot escape this cost: as owner, he or she can pass it on to the tenant; as tenant, the same individual continues to bear it.

The new view reaches the same conclusion by a different route. The global effect of the tax is not thought to raise the cost of housing but, rather, to reduce the return to capital. The owner occupant bears the tax as an owner of capital. He or she cannot escape it, since the return is similarly reduced on all other forms of capital. However, positive differences between the local tax rate and the national average might be offset by lower prices for land, since higher taxes on improvements will reduce the demand for building sites. This will not help homeowners already in possession of sites at the time the tax rate rises above the average, but subsequent buyers will benefit.

Industrial and commercial property. Here the important distinction is between firms that produce strictly for the local market and those that produce for export to other communities. The former typically have little competition from producers based elsewhere. Consequently, according to the old view they would, in the long run, be able to shift a tax on plant and equipment of any reasonable magnitude forward to local customers. However, if a firm were competing in the national market with sellers based elsewhere who paid lower taxes, forward shifting would be possible only up to the rate paid by their competitors. In the long run one would expect such firms to relocate away from high-tax jurisdictions. However, if the town in which taxes were higher had locational advantages for the given firm's production at least equal in weight to the extra burden of the local tax, then the firm could, in effect, pay the tax out of its locational advantages without becoming noncompetitive or subnormally profitable. There would then be no advantage to relocating.[40] This explains why

40. Netzer, *Economics of the Property Tax*, p. 115, citing analysis by Harvey E. Brazer in "The Value of Industrial Property as a Subject of Taxation," *Canadian Public Administration*, June 1961, pp. 137–47.

cities may be tempted to assess very heavily the property of established local industries for which they think they have special locational advantages.

According to the new view, the global effect of the property tax is, of course, not shiftable. That much of the burden remains with the industrial or commercial firm in the form of a reduced return on capital. Local differences in tax rates are shiftable more or less as indicated by the old view. However, proponents of the new view would place greater emphasis on the possibility of backward shifting of local tax differentials to land and labor, whether or not part of such differentials is shifted forward to customers.

The Debate over Regressivity

As already indicated, the old and new views of the property tax imply radically different patterns of incidence by income class. Adherents of the old view generally believe the building (or "improvements") part of the tax to be regressive and reach policy conclusions on that basis. For example, they are likely to argue that the heavy reliance of local governments on the property tax is undesirable, since it imposes a greater relative burden on the poor than on the rich. Accordingly, they have often supported greater use of a local income or value-added tax or have urged that the tax rate on land be increased in order to allow reduction of the regressive tax on improvements.

According to the old view the tax on rental housing is ultimately passed forward to tenants in the form of higher rent, while the tax on owner-occupied housing is borne by the occupant in proportion to house value. In either case the incidence of the tax by income class depends on the relationship between housing expenditure and income. This is most easily illustrated in the case of renters.

Legally, the property tax is levied at a uniform rate on the assessed value rather than the market value of improvements. To simplify the illustration let us assume that assessed value always equals market value and that market value is a uniform multiple of rent in all classes of housing.[41] For each household, let Y = annual income, R = annual housing rent, and T = annual tax payment. The relationship between these variables can be written as

$$T/Y = T/R \times R/Y$$

Under the assumptions stated above, the ratio T/R will be equal for all families. The ratio of taxes to income (on the left-hand side of the equation) will therefore depend on how the ratio R/Y changes as Y varies. That, in turn, depends on the income elasticity of demand for housing. This elasticity can be expressed as percentage change in housing outlay divided by percentage change in household income. If the income elasticity has a value less than one, housing outlay increases by a smaller percentage than income as income rises, and the ratio R/Y therefore falls. In that case, T/Y also falls as income rises: the tax is regressive to income.

Adherents of the old view concluded that the incidence of the property tax on housing was regressive because numerous statistical studies had indicated that the income elasticity of demand for housing was well below unity. They believed that property taxes on business were also likely to be regressive because, in the long run, the part of the tax that fell on commercial and industrial property would be passed forward to consumers in higher prices. Since consumption is a declining fraction of income as income increases, that part of the tax, too, would be regressive to income. This conclusion was sometimes modified by assuming that as much as half the burden of the tax on business property remained with owners of capital and would therefore be distributed progressively to income. Even with this assumption, however, the aggregate burden of the tax on improvements (including both business and residential types) was thought to be moderately regressive.

Proponents of the new view, on the other hand, believe the tax on improvements to be progressive, perhaps even substantially so. This follows directly from their belief that the "global" effect of the tax is to depress the rate of return to capital by an amount equal to the average rate of tax across all localities. It will be recalled that the new view also describes a variety of "excise" effects resulting from differences between the local tax rate and the national average. In analyzing nationwide incidence, however, Mieszkowski suggests that excise effects can perhaps be ignored on the assumption that the opposite effects in high-tax and low-tax towns will cancel out for each income class in a national reckoning.[42] The primary burden of the property tax is therefore the global effect, which falls upon owners of capital in general. Since ownership of capital rises sharply with income, so does the burden of the tax. Consequently, adherents of the new view conclude that the tax does not deserve its reputation for burdening the poor and may, indeed, burden them less than any of the feasible alternatives.

In a market economy it is impossible actually to *observe* the incidence of a tax because the observed payer may have shifted the burden to someone else. Thus the landlord is observed to remit property tax payments to the city collector. But if the tax causes rents to rise sufficiently

42. Mieszkowski, pp. 79–80.

to cover the payment, the incidence is actually on tenants. What the tax analyst can do, however, is work out theoretical conclusions regarding the incidence of the tax (as we have done above) and then estimate in dollar terms what the burden of the tax *would* be on various income classes *if* those theoretical conclusions were correct. Musgrave, who pioneered this technique, has worked out estimates of the burden of the property tax for all income classes, using alternative incidence assumptions that correspond to the old and new views of the tax.[43] Two of these are compared in Figure 14.5.

The data in Figure 14.5 are estimates for the year 1968. If the old view is correct, property tax payments amounted to 6.7 percent of income for households in the lowest income bracket but only 3.3 percent of income for those in the highest bracket. By contrast, under the assumptions of the new view, the tax amounted to only 2.5 percent of income at the low end of the income distribution but took 9.9 percent of income in the top bracket.

Current Income Versus Permanent Income

Cutting across the debate between proponents of the old and new views of the property tax is another concerning the appropriate measure of income to be used in estimating its burden by income class. The income elasticity of demand for housing always turns out to be less than one when measured with respect to the current annual income of households. It is this result that led proponents of the old view to conclude that the tax on residential property was markedly regressive. However, when housing expenditures are compared with "permanent income"—that is, with a household's income averaged over a period of years—the income elasticity of demand for housing may turn out to equal, or even exceed, unity.[44] This has led critics to conclude that even if the old view were *correct* in assigning the burden of the residential property tax to tenants and owner occupants, it would be *incorrect* to conclude that the tax was therefore regressive.

Reverting to terms and assumptions defined above, if the income elasticity of demand for housing equals unity, housing outlay increases proportionately with income and the rent-income ratio (R/Y) does not change as income rises. In that case the tax-income ratio (T/Y) is also constant as income rises; the tax is thus proportional to income. If income

43. For a lucid explanation of the "heroic estimating procedures" such studies necessarily involve, see Richard A. Musgrave and Peggy B. Musgrave, *Public Finance In Theory and Practice*, 3rd ed. (New York: McGraw-Hill, 1980), pp. 265–71.

44. Aaron, pp. 27–32, explains how the choice of an income "accounting period" affects estimates of the relation between housing consumption and income.

FIGURE 14.5

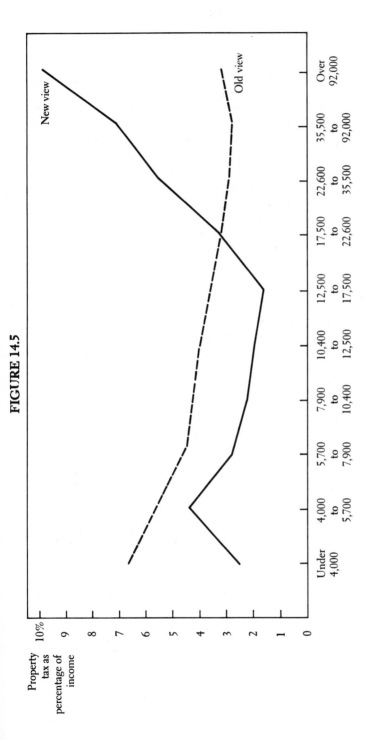

Income bracket (dollars)

Incidence assumptions—Old View: Residential property tax borne by renters and owner occupants; business property tax borne one-half by capital owners in general, one-half by consumers in general. New View: Tax on all classes of property borne by owners of capital in general.

Source: Richard A. Musgrave, Karl E. Case, and Herman Leonard, "The Distribution of Fiscal Burdens and Benefits," *Public Finance Quarterly,* July 1974, tables 1 and 2.

elasticity exceeds one, housing outlay increases *faster* than income and the rent-income ratio (R/Y) *rises* as income increases. In that case, the tax-income ratio (T/Y) also rises with income; the tax turns out to be progressive.

It is generally agreed that the income elasticity of demand for housing is greater when measured with respect to permanent rather than current income. However, not all analysts agree that permanent income is the correct base to use in measuring tax incidence. Furthermore, there is a wide range of variation in the estimated values of the income elasticity of housing demand with respect to permanent income. Some of the most recent estimates put its value well below one.[45] These issues, as well as the debate between proponents of the old and new views, would seem to insure that disagreement about the effects of the property tax will not soon be resolved.

The Property Tax from a Local Perspective

From a national perspective the new view would radically change our judgment about the incidence and effects of the property tax. Because the global effect of the tax is to reduce the net return to capital, the tax in the aggregate is seen as progressive instead of regressive. Yet it is important to recognize that, from a *local* perspective, the new view does not greatly alter the conclusions reached under the old. From the point of view of local voters or government officials the global effect stressed in the new view is of absolutely no consequence. It depends entirely on the national average tax rate, and no tax action by a single community can perceptibly affect the average rate in a large nation. From the local point of view, therefore, the national average rate is a "given." Consequently, changes in the local rate affect the local economy only through what the new view calls excise effects. The most important of these is that the local cost of capital will exceed its average cost in the nation by whatever margin the local rate of property tax exceeds the national average tax rate. But, as we have already pointed out, the old view leads to the same conclusion—compare columns five and eight of Table 14.6. Thus, according to both the new view and the old, if a town decides to raise the local rate of property tax, the primary effect will be to make local capital services more expensive.

The old view stressed the fact that by raising the cost of local capital, higher local property taxes have two effects that are likely to be considered undesirable. First, they raise the cost of housing, thus impeding progress toward improved housing standards. As we have already seen, in Chapter 12, the elimination of substandard housing has long been a major objective both of local and of national policy. Second, higher local property taxes increase local business costs, rendering the locality economically less attractive, especially to firms that must compete in outside markets with companies that may be located in lower tax jurisdictions. Business firms frequently enjoy a degree of freedom in the choice of location—not that one place is as good as another, but rather that there may be many almost as good as the best. Even businesses that serve a local market may be able to move within the metropolitan area to reduce tax costs. Consequently, if local governments impose tax burdens on business much above those prevailing in other places, they are likely to find some firms moving away and the tax base shrinking.

Leaving aside the possibility of backward shifting to land and labor (already discussed above), the new view reaches more or less the same conclusions. Thus the new view propounds a paradox. From a national perspective the property tax is made to look quite attractive—at any rate, not regressive and not a burden on housing consumption. Yet the tax is a local, not a national, one, and any locality that raises its property tax rates above the average is likely to bring on itself all the old evils.

In the United States variation in property tax rates—the source of excise effects—is, in fact, very large. Table 14.7 shows the average rate of tax, adjusted to full market value, on single family homes with FHA-insured mortgages. The nationwide average rate can be taken as an approximate measure of the "global effect." It stood at 1.34 percent in 1979. In that year taxes in the five states with the highest rates averaged 2.7 percent, or double the national average, while those in the five states with

TABLE 14.7
Property Tax Rates on Single Family Homes,
Adjusted to Full Market Value[a]

	1958	1971	1979
U.S. average	1.34%	1.98%	1.34%
Five states with highest rates	2.07	3.09	2.72
Five states with lowest rates	0.55	0.79	0.52

[a] Single family homes with FHA-insured mortgages.
Source: U.S. Advisory Commission on Intergovernmental Relations, *Significant Features of Fiscal Federalism, 1979–80, Edition,* Washington, D.C., U.S. Government Printing Office, October 1980, table 91.

the lowest rates averaged .52 percent, or less than 40 percent of the mean. Indeed, the figures in Table 14.7 suggest that inter-state variation in property tax rates has increased markedly since 1958. Moreover, since the table is based on statewide averages of local rates, the variation in local rates themselves must be considerably greater than these figures suggest. In the face of such data one cannot dismiss excise effects, and the burdens and distortions they imply, as unimportant.

The Unique Role of the Property Tax in Local Finance

When Benjamin Franklin wrote that "in this world nothing is certain but death and taxes," he was thinking, surely, of the property tax, which then, as now, was the fiscal mainstay of American local government. Especially since the late nineteenth century the tax has been subject to periodic storms of criticism. Not only have its incidence and effects been debated, but the adequacy of its administration has often been seriously questioned. There have been abundant proposals for both administrative and structural reform.[46] Reliance of local school districts on property tax revenues has been successfully challenged in state courts. Dissatisfaction with property taxes was crucial in making possible the passage in 1978 of Proposition 13 to limit local government levies in California. Yet despite the long history of such outcries, the property tax has survived as a major fiscal institution.

Its persistence is best explained by the unique function it performs in the local tax-expenditure system. The property tax has been designed, and is administered, to serve as the automatic balancer of the local budget. Schematically, this is how the system works. At the beginning of the budget year the local government decides what its total expenditures are going to be. Next, all revenues, except those from the property tax, are estimated. These are then subtracted from total expenditures. The difference, called the "levy," is then raised by a charge on the assessed value of all taxable property. The levy divided by the aggregate value of taxable property yields a tax rate that will necessarily provide enough revenue to balance the proposed budget. Each property owner is then billed for a payment equal to the tax rate times the assessed value of his or her property. The process can be summarized in three equations:

---

46. On the problem of administration see Netzer, *Economics of the Property Tax*, pp. 173–83, and Arthur D. Lynn, Jr., ed., *The Property Tax and Its Administration* (Madison, Wis.: University of Wisconsin Press, 1969). Proposals for administrative reform are examined critically in Aaron, ch. 4. Broad structural reforms are discussed in Aaron, ch. 5; Netzer, ch. 8; James Heilbrun, *Real Estate Taxes and Urban Housing* (New York: Columbia University Press, 1966); and George E. Peterson, ed., *Property Tax Reform* (Washington, D.C.: The Urban Institute, 1973).

proposed expenditures − other revenue = amount of levy

amount of levy ÷ aggregate assessed value of taxable property = tax rate

tax rate × assessed value of owner's property = owner's tax bill

With this arrangement, the local government can vary the tax rate each year (within possible state constitutional tax limits) to raise automatically whatever revenue is needed to cover expenditures. Other local taxes, where they exist, generally cannot be varied except by some sort of (probably difficult) legislative act.

This system is not only convenient but also facilitates a rational approach to making allocation decisions in the public sector. As Netzer points out,

> assessments and expenditure budgets are independently determined, and the tax rate is the result. Thus, the fiscal issue in local finance is apt to be joined on the question of expenditures rather than tax rates, which seems an appropriate arrangement. To the extent that expenditures and tax rates are simultaneously determined in the local political process, citizens are consciously relating the value of additional expenditures to their tax costs, which surely approaches the ideal prescription for the budget process with respect to the resource allocation "branch" of the public sector.[47]

By contrast, in the typical state budget process (and in the U.S. Congress until budgetary reform went into effect in 1976–77), proposals for additional expenditure are made with no reference at all to their tax implications, an approach that certainly doesn't encourage participants to make their decisions on the rational basis of willingness to pay for expected benefits.

Because it is so important in local budgets, the property tax becomes an issue in numerous questions of local public policy. In the next chapter, which is entitled "Problems of the Metropolitan Public Sector," we shall examine several of these, including the connection between the size of the property tax base and urban fiscal distress, the possibility of property tax base sharing between central cities and their suburbs, and the problem of attaining equity among school districts when school outlays depend heavily upon the value of local taxable property.

47. Netzer, *Economics of the Property Tax*, pp. 170–71.

Problems of the Metropolitan Public Sector: Inefficiency, Inequity, Insolvency

FIFTEEN

The problem of arranging the most appropriate division of budgetary functions among the three levels of government was discussed at the beginning of Chapter 14. It was concluded that local governments should not undertake either economic stabilization or the redistribution of income but should confine themselves to allocative functions —the provision of goods and services that for a variety of reasons are best paid for out of the public budget. Yet it must be recognized that serious problems arise for the metropolitan public sector even in carrying out the appropriate allocative functions. These problems can be summarized as "inefficiency," "inequity," and "insolvency." In this chapter we will analyze all three in detail and examine some of the major policies and reforms that have been proposed to ameliorate them.

HAPHAZARD BOUNDARIES: THE PROBLEM OF INEFFICIENCY

Within metropolitan areas the local public sector is notoriously fragmented. A single metropolis may contain hundreds of governmental units. Their boundaries and the division of functions among them are usually the result of long-gone historical forces and are rarely altered to reflect later circumstances. Because boundaries have not been drawn rationally in relation to current needs, it is often difficult for local governments to provide services efficiently.

The extent to which present arrangements interfere with efficient public sector operation can best be understood if we review the various goals of local government and see what criteria for drawing boundaries and assigning functions must be met in order to achieve each of them. It will become clear that there may be inescapable conflicts between the patterns that would maximize the fulfillment of each of the objectives taken separately. Any comprehensive "solution" is therefore likely to be a compromise involving only partial achievement of many desirable ends.

Providing the Optimum Level and Combination of Public Services

Producing the optimum level and combination of public services is the task of "allocation," described at the beginning of Chapter 14. For most public services there is not (nor could there be) a market through which individual demand would be more or less automatically registered and satisfied, as happens in the private sector. A political voting process must therefore be relied on to shape the provision of public goods and services in accordance with citizen preferences.

The "Tiebout Solution." It is tempting to argue that satisfaction of voters' preferences for public goods proceeds best when political jurisdictions are small and their populations are homogeneous in taste. As jurisdictions grow smaller, sensitivity of government to individual preferences is likely to increase because government and citizen are "closer." The possibility of homogeneity of tastes also increases as area size decreases, and the more homogeneous the desires of the population the more likely it is that citizens who fit the local norm will find all their wants nicely fulfilled. In fact, as Charles M. Tiebout argued, if there are enough minor jurisdictions within a metropolitan area and if individuals are not denied the choice of locality through discrimination, zoning, or lack of income, one might expect people with similar preferences to flock together in order to create communities congenial to their particular set of tastes.[1] Clearly the "Tiebout solution" to the problem of preference satisfaction could only work if governmental units within metropolitan areas remained small and very numerous.

Economists have by now offered a variety of criticisms of the Tiebout solution. One of these goes directly to the question of preference satisfaction. From the high degree of daily mobility in the metropolitan way of life—the fact that many people work, live, and shop in three or more different jurisdictions—it follows that metropolitan residents regularly consume public services in several places, while expressing their preferences

1. Charles M. Tiebout, "A Pure Theory of Local Expenditures," reprinted in William E. Mitchell and Ingo Walter, eds., *State and Local Finance* (New York: Ronald Press, 1970), pp. 21–29.

through voting in only one. In these circumstances it is not clear that small homogeneous communities maximize the possibility of preference satisfaction for their resident citizens.

One might go further, however, and question just how much importance we should concede to the objective of satisfying local differences in the "taste" for public services. If, as will be discussed below, we are moving toward acceptance of the idea that citizens are entitled as a matter of right to substantial equality in the level of public services no matter where they live, then we have already begun to chip away at differential preference satisfaction as a criterion. A community containing many retired couples may prefer to spend very little on schools, but if the state sets a standard, then the community cannot be allowed to express its preferences by violating the standard.

The wide variation in both the aggregate level and functional pattern of local expenditure is explained by a number of factors besides differences in local "tastes"—for example, by differences in per capita income, state and federal aid, and geographic and demographic characteristics. An upper middle class family may move from the central city to the suburbs because it finds public services there more suited to its "wants." But one suspects that a good deal of the improvement consists in being able to receive back as service benefit most of what it pays out to the local tax collector instead of seeing a substantial part of its tax payments go to provide services for the poorer families that do not "pay their way" in the tax-expenditure calculus, and who are found mostly in the central city. This is not an improvement that we can properly label as "better preference satisfaction," except to the extent that many people have a preference for not paying other people's bills.

Other things being equal, a maximum opportunity for satisfying individually different preferences for public services is, of course, desirable. But other things are not unaffected, if we maintain small jurisdictions for that purpose. For small jurisdictions within metropolitan areas certainly hamper effective area-wide planning, create demonstrable fiscal inequities, and may possibly prevent the realization of economies of scale in local government.

The problem of externalities. The process of satisfying local demand for public goods and services is seriously impeded by the existence of benefit and cost externalities, or spillovers. These occur when a service produced by one town for itself also yields benefits for or imposes costs on neighboring towns whose interests have not been taken systematically into account. Metropolitan areas are, by definition, densely settled, and the localities within them are systematically interdependent. In such a setting externalities are probably more the rule than the exception.

Consider a very simple case. Suppose that a town engages in mosquito abatement by means of chemical spraying within its own boundaries. The rational course of action for the single town would be to expand the program to the point where the marginal cost to the town of additional spraying just equals the marginal benefit to the town of the resulting additional abatement. The situation is depicted in Figure 15.1. The horizontal scale measures gallons of spray applied per year. The vertical scale shows marginal cost and marginal benefit (in dollars) for each additional gallon used. We assume that the cost of buying and spraying the chemical is constant per gallon. Hence the marginal cost curve is a horizontal straight line. The marginal benefit from incremental gallons of spray, however, declines over the relevant range because there are diminishing returns in mosquito abatement as more gallons are used. From the town's point of view optimum program size is OG gallons per year. To the left of G marginal town benefit exceeds marginal town cost: it pays to continue expanding the program. To the right of G marginal town benefit is less than marginal town cost: the program has been overexpanded. The optimum from the town's point of view is therefore at the point where the two curves intersect and marginal town benefit and cost are just equal.

If we consider the welfare of society, however, rather than of the single town, the optimum program is larger. Mosquito abatement in one town confers external benefits on neighboring localities. Regional benefit equals the sum of town benefit plus benefit external to the town. Therefore the curve showing marginal regional benefit must lie above and to the right of the town benefit curve. From the point of view of society as a whole it would be desirable for the town to expand the program to point H, where marginal cost just equals marginal regional benefit. This case illustrates the general rule that when externalities exist, ordinary decision-making processes usually lead to socially suboptimal outcomes.[2]

Benefit or cost spillovers probably exist for many urban public services. The subject of externalities has received a good deal of attention in recent years and will not be treated in detail here.[3] Suffice it to say that local education is now thought to produce nationwide external benefits, local pollution control clearly yields external benefits over a wide region,

2. Undersupply when external benefits exist, as in the text example, was once thought to be the general case. More recently it has been shown that with reciprocal externalities among suppliers, oversupply is also a possible outcome. See J. M. Buchanan and M. Z. Kafoglis, "A Note on Public Goods Supply," *American Economic Review,* June 1963, pp. 403–14; and Alan Williams, "The Optimal Provision of Public Goods in a System of Local Government," *Journal of Political Economy,* February 1966, pp. 18–33.

3. See for example the discussion in Werner Z. Hirsch, *Urban Economic Analysis* (New York: McGraw-Hill, 1973), pp. 22–26, 412–17, and the sources cited therein.

FIGURE 15.1

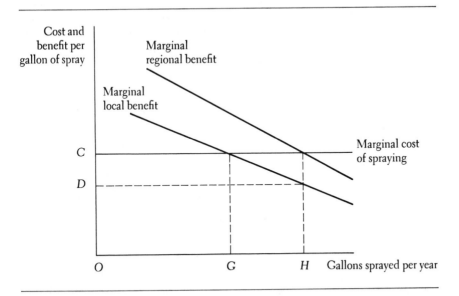

and even the activity of the local police force in suppressing crime probably confers benefits far outside the local jurisdiction.

There are two responses to the problem of externalities in the public sector, either of which would help to overcome distortions due to geographic spillovers and bring us closer to the optimum level of output for a given service. (1) Enlarge the jurisdiction providing the service until it takes in most of the area over which significant cost or benefit spillovers occur. In this way externalities are "internalized," and the interests of the jurisdiction become identical with those of society. Therefore the enlarged jurisdiction could be expected to make socially optimal output decisions. (2) In the case of external benefits, arrange for a higher level of government to subsidize the local agency providing the service by means of open-ended, matching, functional grants. In the case illustrated in Figure 15.1 it would be necessary to contrive a subsidy that would increase program size from OG to OH. (Intergovernmental grants for such purposes will be analyzed in detail below.)

Supplying Public Services at Minimum Unit Cost

Whatever services are to be supplied to satisfy citizens' preferences ought to be produced at the lowest possible unit cost. It is therefore important to discover how unit cost varies with the size of the jurisdiction in the output of particular local services. Although it is difficult to measure the output of a public-service-producing agency, economists have published some useful studies of unit costs in recent years, and the question continues to receive a good deal of attention.[4] If the technical conditions of production are such that a range of decreasing unit costs is followed by a range of increasing unit costs as the size of the jurisdiction increases, then the average cost curve is U-shaped, and unit cost is lowest for a jurisdiction whose size corresponds to the bottom of the U. Thus, if the average unit cost curve for a particular public service is U-shaped, the minimum unit cost criterion can indicate the best jurisdictional size for that service. Of course, if average unit cost curves are approximately horizontal, indicating that unit costs do not vary with the scale of output, then this criterion becomes irrelevant.

The situation is made more complicated if we allow for the fact that "producing unit" need not be synonymous with "jurisdiction." It is sometimes possible for smaller jurisdictions to purchase services from larger ones or from large private contractors. In that way governmental units can remain small without sacrificing the possible advantages of economies of scale in the production of local services. This sort of arrangement, sometimes called the Lakewood Plan, has been used successfully in Southern California.[5]

It is important to note that the minimum unit cost criterion can indicate when jurisdictions are too large to be efficient as well as when they are too small. Further study of public service costs may reveal, for example, that very large cities are now encountering *dis*economies of scale in public output, and that unit costs could be reduced by the decentralization of production, at least for some public services. This is only speculation, however, and the strong interest in the decentralization of urban services that began in the 1960s took its impetus less from considerations of economic cost than from a desire to increase democratic participation and to make government more accessible to the governed. These political objectives are the next category to be discussed.

Political Participation and Accessibility

Political as well as economic objectives must, of course, be taken into account in discussing the arrangement of metropolitan functions and boundaries. It is in the American tradition to favor small local governments on the ground that they encourage voter participation, are accessible to

4. See ibid., pp. 326–34 and studies cited therein.
5. See Robert Warren, "A Municipal Services Market Model of Metropolitan Organization," *Journal of the American Institute of Planners*, August 1964, pp. 193–204.

the citizen in the conduct of his or her daily business, and are sensitive to local needs. The influence of this very old tradition has been reinforced since the early 1960s by new demands within the larger cities for neighborhood government, community control, and administrative decentralization.[6] While there may be an element of romanticism in the notion that decentralization necessarily returns power to "the people" or "the community," no one who has lived in a large city is likely to dismiss the charge of excessive centralization or unresponsive bureaucracy as unfounded. Cautious as well as incautious observers are seeking ways to improve local government by redistributing functions and powers. As George F. Break has written:

> Among the major challenges to the U.S. federal system in the next few years, it now seems clear, will be the formation of more rational and effective systems of local government. While the solution of some of the most important urban problems requires integrated, areawide policy action, groups with special tastes and needs for public services are primarily concerned with local autonomy. What seems to be needed is some magic blend of centralizing and decentralizing changes that will create simultaneously both larger and smaller units of local government than any that now exist.[7]

It should be borne in mind, however, that public services differ greatly in the extent to which they involve politically sensitive issues. Voters by and large are not much interested in having access to the officials who operate the Fire Department, inspect meat markets, or distribute the water supply. On the other hand, they are most certainly concerned about access to the School Board and the Police Department. The criterion of political accessibility does not apply with equal force to all services.

Planning and Coordination

The metropolitan area is in its very nature an interconnected, organic whole. Consequently, many of its governmental functions ought to be planned on an area-wide scale. Transportation, recreation, and environmental protection are only the most obvious of these. A more ambitious reckoning would certainly include area-wide planning of land use densities and housing policy.

6. See, for example, Milton Kotler, *Neighborhood Government* (Indianapolis: Bobbs-Merrill, 1969); and Howard W. Hallman, *Neighborhood Government in a Metropolitan Setting* (Beverly Hills, Calif.: Sage Publications, 1974).

7. George F. Break, "Changing Roles of Different Levels of Government," in Universities-National Bureau Committee for Economic Research, *The Analysis of Public Output* (New York: Columbia University Press, 1970), p. 182.

The typically fragmented pattern of metropolitan jurisdictions makes such planning very difficult. Local units, sanctioned by the strong tradition favoring the right to local self-government, can often prevent effective action being taken on a metropolitan scale. Nevertheless, area-wide planning *is* on the increase. Partly this results from a growing recognition that in the long run planning and coordination can be in everyone's interest; partly it results from pressure applied by the federal government. Since the mid-1960s many federal grant programs have carried the stipulation that recipient local projects must be part of a comprehensive regional plan, and special grants have been made available to help finance new metropolitan planning agencies.

Meanwhile, within the larger cities, the neighborhood activism that has accompanied the movement for decentralization further complicates the process of planning and coordination. The neighborhood movement had its origins in opposition to the incursions of highway and urban renewal schemes. Its success in halting many of these projects has made both planners and politicians highly sensitive to the need for reconciling conflicting interests as part of the planning process. Of course, there is no technically "correct" way of doing that, if it can be done at all. This nicely illustrates the conflict between the various objectives of local government: if we increase the number of minor jurisdictions in order to maximize the formal representation of neighborhood interests we run the risk of seriously impeding large-scale urban planning.

GEOGRAPHIC DISPARITIES: THE PROBLEM OF INEQUITY

The problem of geographic disparities is easily summarized: the needs of the population for public services and the taxable resources out of which to pay for them are not similarly distributed across the map of local areas. Because local government plays such an important role in American life, geographic inequality in the distribution of local needs and resources is a serious issue. Rich towns can provide a higher level of service than poor ones. It may not matter *who* you are, but it does matter *where* you are. From the point of view of the individuals and social classes involved this appears to be an inequity, a denial of social justice. From the point of view of society it is more than that: the maldistribution of local resources impedes progress toward achieving major social goals such as better education, improved health, and reduced poverty.

Disparities in taxable resources give rise to differences between localities in the "tax-price" of a given bundle of services. For example, residents in a poor school district might have to pay a property tax rate of 3 percent to supply themselves with school services identical to those that a richer district could supply with a 2 percent tax. Such differences in tax-price are used by some analysts as an indicator of "fiscal disparity."[8] The term "geographic disparities," employed here, is broader, since it allows for inter-area differences in the cost of services as well as in the resources out of which to pay for them. We turn first to differences in resources.

Disparities in the Distribution of Taxable Resources

Within metropolitan areas the distribution of resources and population between central cities and suburban rings has been shifting rapidly. As we pointed out in Chapter 10, the influx of the poor to the central cities, combined with the outward migration of middle and upper income families to the suburbs, has reversed the earlier pattern in which income was higher in central cities than in the ring. Today income levels are distinctly higher in the suburbs, and the gap is widening steadily. At the same time, under the influence of forces described in earlier chapters, business as well as personal wealth has been dispersing to the suburbs.

Table 15.1 measures disparities in the distribution of taxable resources between central cities and the suburban areas of SMSA's. In 1959 median family income in central cities was already 11 percent below the suburban level. By 1979 the gap had widened to 21 percent. When income is measured per capita rather than per household, the disparity is somewhat reduced because suburban households are larger, and household income is therefore spread a little thinner. Even on this basis, however, central city income in 1976 was 12 percent below the level in the suburbs. Moreover, the trend toward increased disparity is clear under both income measures.

The per capita income measures in Table 15.1 are for the 37 largest SMSA's. When these are grouped geographically the table shows a marked difference in income disparity by region. The gap is widest in the large SMSA's of the Northeast, slightly narrower in the North Central (i.e., Midwest) region, and still narrower in the South. In the large SMSA's of the West, in 1976, per capita income was actually slightly higher in central cities than in suburban areas. In all regions, however, central city income declined markedly relative to suburban income between 1960 and 1976. The regional pattern of income disparities shown in Table 15.1 is strongly associated with differences in the average "age" of central cities in the

---

8. See, for example, William H. Oakland, "Central Cities: Fiscal Plight and Prospects for Reform," in Peter Mieszkowski and Mahlon Straszheim, eds., *Current Issues in Urban Economics* (Baltimore: The Johns Hopkins University Press, 1979), p. 330.

TABLE 15.1

Disparities in Taxable Resources Between Central Cities and Suburban Areas

		CENTRAL CITIES	OUTSIDE CENTRAL CITIES	RATIO: CC/OCC
I. Median family income (in 1979 dollars)				
	1959	14,681	16,529	.89
	1969	18,571	21,879	.85
	1979	18,089	22,942	.79
II. Income per capita (in current dollars)—37 largest SMSA's[a]				
All regions[b]	1960	2,054	2,170	.95
	1976	4,947	5,603	.88
Northeast	1960	1,999	2,309	.87
	1976	4,716	5,856	.81
North Central	1960	2,035	2,277	.89
	1976	4,773	5,584	.85
South	1960	1,848	1,868	.99
	1976	4,832	5,352	.90
West	1960	2,404	2,129	1.13
	1976	5,713	5,521	1.03
III. Average property value per capita (in current dollars)				
17 large older cities[c]	1961	6,223	6,074	1.02
	1971	9,419	11,282	.83
26 largest cities[d]	1971	8,088	9,585	.84
By region[b]				
Northeast	1971	6,844	8,732	.78
North Central	1971	6,947	9,652	.72
South	1971	7,534	8,692	.87
West	1971	11,504	11,083	1.04

[a] These are the 37 SMSA's for which systematic fiscal data are available back to 1957. See list in appendix table A-9 of Advisory Commission 1980 publication cited below.

[b] Regions are similar to Census definitions except that Washington and Baltimore are included in Northeast rather than South.

[c] A sample of large, older U.S. cities, chosen to illustrate central city fiscal problems. See William H. Oakland, "Central Cities: Fiscal Plight and Prospects for Reform," in Peter Mieszkowski and Mahlon Straszheim, eds., *Current Issues in Urban Economics* (Baltimore: The Johns Hopkins University Press, 1979), pp. 325, 327.

[d] All U.S. cities that had a population greater than 500,000 in either 1960 or 1970, except Washington, D.C. (omitted as not comparable), and Honolulu and Jacksonville (in which the city covered the entire SMSA in 1970). See George E. Peterson, "Finance," in William Gorham and Nathan Glazer, eds., *The Urban Predicament* (Washington, D.C.: The Urban Institute, 1976), pp. 47 and 76–77.

Sources: Median family income: U.S. Bureau of the Census, *Current Population Reports*, Series P-23 and P-60, various issues, and unpublished

four regions. As explained in Chapter 10, the older the central city, the lower its socioeconomic status is likely to be in comparison to its own suburbs.

Although income taxes account for only 5 percent of local tax revenues (see Table 14.4), it is indisputable that personal income underlies much of the local tax base. First of all, retail sales are heavily dependent on personal income, and sales and gross receipts taxes account for nearly 12 percent of local tax revenue. More important, there is a direct relationship between personal income and wealth in the form of residential property. Towns with wealthier families can therefore be expected to have more taxable residential property per capita than towns where the average income level is lower. Since residential property accounts for almost half of property tax payments, and the property tax produces 78 percent of local tax revenues, wealth in that form obviously makes up an important part of the local tax base.

Nevertheless, the casual observer may suppose that despite the dispersal of industry and middle and upper income population to the suburbs, the typical central city, with its towering CBD and dense development, must still have a larger property tax base per capita than the suburbs. In fact, such is not the case. Table 15.1 presents some evidence on this point. William H. Oakland's data for a sample of 17 SMSA's containing large, older central cities show that property value in 1961 averaged 2 percent higher in the central cities than in the suburbs. By 1971 the level in the same central cities averaged 17 percent below that in ring areas. Using a larger sample that included newer as well as older central cities, George E. Peterson of the Urban Institute found virtually the same level of disparity in 1971. When Peterson's sample is subdivided geographically, a pattern of regional differences emerges, which (not surprisingly) resembles the regional pattern of income differentials. The property tax base of central cities was lowest relative to that of suburbs in the Northeast and North Central regions. It was relatively higher, though still below the suburban average, in the South, while in the West it slightly exceeded the outside central city level.

The present situation of the older central cities contrasts strongly with their position forty or fifty years ago. Then as now the data suggest that residential property value per capita was higher in the suburbs than in the central cities. But this disparity was offset by the overwhelming

---

data. Income per capita: from two publications of the U.S. Advisory Commission on Intergovernmental Relations; 1960 data from *Trends in Metropolitan America*, February 1977, table 10; 1976 data from *Central City—Suburban Fiscal Disparity & City Distress*, 1977, 1980, appendix table A-7. Average property value per capita: 17 cities, from Oakland, table 10.3; 26 cities, Peterson, table 13 (see notes c and d above).

central city concentration of commercial and industrial property. Although the core cities then contained large populations of the immigrant poor, they were also centers of wealth that could be taxed for the support of local services. In recent decades, however, the evolving pattern of metropolitan settlement has inexorably turned the tables against them: the older central cities house an increasing proportion of the nation's poor whom they must service out of taxes on a decreasing proportion of the nation's wealth.

Disparities in the Cost of Services

The increasing concentration of the poor into the nation's inner cities has already been documented in Chapter 10. The rate of poverty in central cities as a whole is more than twice the rate in suburban areas. In SMSA's of a million or more the ratio is now 3 to 1, and the disparity continues to increase. Fiscally, this puts the central cities at a double disadvantage. The concentration of poverty not only reduces their tax base but also adds to their service costs.

Poverty affects the cost of public services in several ways. First, the higher the incidence of poverty the more a locality is likely to spend for poverty-connected services such as welfare, medical programs, housing assistance, and social services. While most of these functions are heavily subsidized by the state and federal governments, they are also likely to involve direct costs to the localities themselves.

Second, the presence of a poverty population raises the cost of providing services that are not ordinarily thought of as poverty-connected. As Peterson puts it, "population traits . . . help to determine how much it will cost to reach any given level of service quality."[9] Children from culturally and educationally deprived homes are more difficult to educate than are the daughters and sons of the middle class; crime rates are higher in poverty areas; street cleanliness is more difficult to maintain in slum neighborhoods because poor residents use the streets so heavily for recreation and social life.

In addition to paying the higher public service costs that result from the concentration of poverty, large inner cities also bear the burden of higher costs associated with their role as the center of a metropolitan economy. They must provide police and fire protection, traffic regulation,

---

9. George E. Peterson, "Finance," in William Gorham and Nathan Glazer, eds., *The Urban Predicament* (Washington, D.C.: The Urban Institute, 1976), p. 47. The effect of environmental factors, including population traits, on the cost of local public service outputs was first systematically analyzed by D. F. Bradford, R. A. Malt, and W. E. Oates in "The Rising Cost of Local Public Services: Some Evidence and Reflections," *National Tax Journal*, June 1969, pp. 185–202.

transportation facilities, and so on for a daytime work population much of which lives and pays the bulk of its taxes outside the city limits. These extra costs have sometimes been referred to as "municipal overburden."

To indicate the combined effect of population characteristics and "overburden" in raising the cost of providing common municipal services in central cities, Peterson calculated expenditure per capita on police protection in 1972–73 in the central cities and suburbs of his sample of 26 SMSA's. On the average, central cities spent $49 per capita, almost exactly double the $24 per capita spent by suburbs. In the older SMSA's of the Northeast and North Central regions, central cities spent 135 percent more per capita than did the suburbs.[10]

Fiscal disparities within SMSA's are summarized in Table 15.2, using data developed by Seymour Sacks for the Advisory Commission on Intergovernmental Relations. The table refers to the 37 largest SMSA's, a group for which systematic data are available back to 1957, which permits an examination of the trend in disparities over time. Reflecting the greater cost of providing public services in core cities, per capita expenditures there were 29 percent higher than in the suburbs in 1957 and 43 percent higher in 1977. In both years the per capita cost of noneducational expenditures was double the suburban level (the same ratio already noted for police outlays). Expenditures per capita on education are slightly lower in central cities than in suburbs, though they have been catching up.

Disparities in Tax Burden

Table 15.2 shows that to finance their higher level of expenditures, central cities collect substantially more tax dollars per capita than do the suburbs: 57 percent more in 1957, diminishing to a margin of 29 percent more by 1977. The disparity in tax receipts could decline while the difference in expenditures was growing because federal and state aid per capita to central cities increased more than did aid to suburban areas. In 1957 aid per capita was equal in the two parts of SMSA's. By 1977, central cities were receiving 67 percent more per capita.

Despite the sharp increase in federal and state aid and the decline in the intrametropolitan disparity in tax receipts, central cities continue to tax their citizens more heavily in relation to income than do the suburbs. A rough measure of tax effort can be obtained by dividing tax receipts per capita by income per capita. On that basis, the rate of tax in 1957 was 5.7 percent of income in central cities as compared with 3.7 percent in suburbs, a relative difference in excess of 50 percent (see Table 15.2). This difference resulted from the combination of higher tax receipts

10. Peterson, table 13, pp. 76–77.

TABLE 15.2

Local Government Tax and Expenditure Disparities Between Central Cities and Suburban Areas in the 37 Largest SMSA's[a]

	1957			1977		
	Central Cities	Outside Central Cities	Ratio CC/OCC	Central Cities	Outside Central Cities	Ratio CC/OCC
Expenditures per capita	$ 196	$ 154	1.29	$1,061	$ 761	1.43
Education	61	80	.80	346	372	.93
Noneducation	135	74	2.02	714	388	2.01
Federal and state aid per capita	40	40	1.01	490	306	1.67
Tax receipts per capita	117	80	1.57	453	364	1.29
Taxes as percentage of income[b]						
All regions	5.7%	3.7%	1.54	8.8%	6.5%	1.35
Northeast	6.8	4.4	1.54	11.3	7.7	1.47
North Central	5.7	3.5	1.63	8.7	5.6	1.55
South	4.8	2.8	1.71	7.0	4.8	1.46
West	5.2	3.7	1.41	9.1	7.8	1.17

[a] See Table 15.1, note (a).

[b] Average tax receipts per capita (1957 and 1977) divided by average income per capita (1960 and 1976). No allowance is made for possible tax exporting.

Sources: Fiscal data: U.S. Advisory Commission on Intergovernmental Relations, *Central City–Suburban Fiscal Disparity & City Distress, 1977*, table 4. Income data: Table 15.1 above.

and lower income in central cities. By 1977, the rate had increased to 8.8 percent in central cities and 6.5 percent in the suburbs. In absolute terms the disparity rose slightly. In relative terms it showed a moderate decline.

When SMSA's are grouped by region, the old central cities of the Northeast stand out as having by far the highest taxes in relation to income and the largest absolute margin above the suburban level. Relative disparities between central cities and suburbs, however, are about equal in the Northeast, North Central, and Southern regions. In the West, intra-metropolitan disparities are substantially smaller, again suggesting that the socioeconomic contrast between central cities and suburbs is less pronounced in the newer SMSA's of that region.

To be sure, these calculations do not allow for the possibility of "tax exporting" by local jurisdictions. This may occur, for example, when a tax is levied on local business property. If the taxed firm sells some of its output outside the local community it may, in effect, "export" some of the tax burden in the form of higher prices. Or, if the tax reduces profits and the firm is owned by nonresidents, some of the burden may be exported through lower dividends to outsiders. Netzer points out that the export percentage tends to be higher for central cities than for suburbs because a higher proportion of central city taxable property is commercial. In general, however, this difference in the capacity to export taxes is not large enough to eliminate the difference between local tax burdens in central cities and suburbs.[11]

The Effects of Redistributive Local Budgets

Up to this point the discussion of geographic disparities has concentrated on differences in the average level of taxes or the average level of expenditures between central cities and their suburbs. Average tax levels and average benefit levels within localities do not tell the whole story, however. It was shown in Chapter 14 that state and local budgets tend to redistribute income from rich to poor by giving the poor more benefits than they pay for and the rich less. We now wish to examine the process of income redistribution in greater detail and to show, in particular, how differences between communities in the average level of income interact with redistributive policies within localities both to create horizontal inequities—that is, violations of the ethical rule requiring equal treatment of equals—and to speed up the counterproductive process of tax base erosion.

11. Dick Netzer, "Impact of the Property Tax: Its Economic Implications for Urban Problems," in William E. Mitchell and Ingo Walter, eds., *State and Local Finance* (New York: Ronald Press, 1970), pp. 166–68.

TABLE 15.3

Taxes and Expenditure Benefits As a Function of Local Per Capita Wealth: A Hypothetical Example

	VALUE OF RESIDENTIAL PROPERTY	TAX PAYMENTS AT 2% OF PROPERTY VALUE	BENEFITS RECEIVED	FISCAL RESIDUAL OR NET GAIN
Wealthy Town				
Citizen W1	$100,000	$2,000	$1,400	−$ 600
W2	100,000	2,000	1,400	− 600
P1	10,000	200	1,400	+ 1,200
Total	$210,000	$4,200	$4,200	0
Poor Town				
Citizen P2	$ 10,000	$ 200	$ 800	+$ 600
P3	10,000	200	800	+ 600
W3	100,000	2,000	800	− 1,200
Total	$120,000	$2,400	$2,400	0

The estimates of budget incidence in the United States cited in Chapter 14 indicated that above an income level of about $10,000 (1968 prices) families paid more in state and local taxes than they received back in expenditure benefits, while below that level they received more in benefits than they paid in taxes. A part of this redistribution occurred because state and local governments *do* contribute funds to redistributive programs in the fields of health, welfare, and housing, even though an ideal division of budgetary functions would leave all such activities to the federal government. For the most part, however, redistribution occurs because even if state and local governments confined themselves entirely to allocative functions such as the provision of school, police, fire, and sanitation services, the manner in which these are typically financed would necessarily redistribute income from rich to poor. Let us see why this is so.

Following the argument of James M. Buchanan, we define fiscal pressure on the taxpayer as the difference between the sum paid in taxes and the value of benefits received.[12] Buchanan labels this difference the "fiscal residuum" of the individual. It is defined as positive if tax payments exceed benefits, negative if benefits exceed taxes, and zero if they are equal.

Table 15.3 presents a hypothetical comparison of the fiscal residuals received by taxpayers in two towns that differ in average level of income.

12. James M. Buchanan, "Federalism and Fiscal Equity," in R. A. Musgrave and C. S. Shoup, eds., American Economic Association, *Readings in the Economics of Taxation* (Homewood, Ill.: Richard D. Irwin, 1959), p. 99.

Each town has three citizens. Wealthy taxpayers, each of whom owns residential property worth $100,000, are denoted W1, W2, W3. Poor taxpayers, whose residential property is worth only $10,000, are denoted P1, P2, P3. The wealthy town consists of two wealthy taxpayers and one poor one; the poor town reverses these proportions. Each town raises all its revenue by a 2 percent tax on residential property.

In each of the hypothetical towns benefits are distributed on an equal per capita basis, as might well be the case with purely allocative functions. Since tax payments are proportional to wealth, while expenditure distribution is regressive to wealth, the rich in both towns pay more in taxes than they receive in benefits, while the poor receive more benefits than they pay for in taxes. Thus both towns redistribute real income from rich to poor. The right-hand column labeled "fiscal residual or net gain" shows the extent of the redistribution. It indicates that both rich and poor are better off in the wealthy town. Each individual pays the same amount of tax no matter where he or she lives, but the benefit level is higher in the rich town because the tax base there is larger. In the wealthy town the poor person enjoys a net gain of $1,200 via the public budget. In the poor town he or she would gain only $600. In the wealthy town the rich lose $600 on account of budgetary transactions. Their counterpart in the poor town loses $1,200.

Thus, differences in the fiscal resources of local communities, when coupled with redistributive tax-expenditure systems, create inequities: people of like income or wealth status are treated differently by the local government depending on whether they happen to live in a rich or a poor community. This is the equity problem in local public finance.

True, if localities were willing and able to charge for services on the benefit principle, that part of the local budget devoted to allocative functions would not be redistributive. Each resident would make payments equal in amount to the value of benefits individually received. There would be no fiscal residuum and, consequently, no redistribution of real income. Payment in proportion to benefit is, in fact, the theoretically preferred means of financing allocative functions. It was pointed out in Chapter 14, however, that citizens will not voluntarily pay prices based on benefits received when services are not subject to exclusion.[13] Nor can involuntary payments do the job, for there exists no general method of benefit taxation under which a government could collect compulsory payments that bear any close relation to individual benefits received.[14] As a

13. The point is developed in full in R. A. Musgrave, *The Theory of Public Finance* (New York: McGraw-Hill, 1959), ch. 4.
14. For a discussion of the rather limited possibilities that do exist for benefit taxation, see Richard A. Musgrave and Peggy B. Musgrave, *Public Finance in Theory and Practice*, 3rd ed. (New York: McGraw-Hill, 1980), pp. 239–40.

practical matter, therefore, local budgets are likely to remain redistributive from rich to poor, even if localities perform only allocative functions.[15]

Selective Migration and the Erosion of the Central City Tax Base

The fact that taxpayers of equal income are treated differently depending on where they live contributes to the problem of central city tax base erosion. Both rich and poor could improve their situation by moving from poorer to richer communities. The rich are able to do so at their own option. The poor can do so also, if the move involves migrating from relatively low income rural or nonmetropolitan areas or from outside the United States to the relatively more affluent U.S. central cities. But within a given metropolitan area the situation is different. The rich are able to improve their fiscal lot by moving from the central city to the suburbs, where the average income level is still higher. But the poor are effectively prevented from following them, not just by racial discrimination and large-lot zoning, but by the absence in the suburbs of a plentiful supply of the old, low rent housing on which they typically rely and by the high transportation costs required for suburban living. Selective migration consequently speeds the erosion of the central city tax base. Of course, this argument is not meant to suggest that the outward migration of the middle and upper classes is explained solely or even principally by calculations of tax-expenditure gain. But since we have sufficiently emphasized in earlier chapters the many other forces that are also at work, their repetition is not required here.

Thus far we have examined only the effects of differences in community income level. What happens if we also introduce differences in "redistributiveness"—that is, in the rate at which communities attempt to redistribute income via the local budget? It turns out that differences in redistributiveness affect the relative attractiveness of communities to rich and poor quite apart from differences in average community income level.

Obviously as between two localities where average income is the same, the poor will be better off in the one in which the budget is more redistributive and the rich in the one where it is less so. Differences in "redistributiveness" between any two towns, however, can offset the effects

15. For a statistical estimate of the net redistributive effect of school taxes and benefits in a suburban Philadelphia school district, see M. Brian McDonald, "Educational Equity and the Fiscal Incidence of Public Education," *National Tax Journal*, March 1980, pp. 45–54. McDonald finds a significant inverse relationship between net benefits (benefits — taxes) and family income for this purely "allocative" function.

of differences in average income level in generating fiscal gains for either the rich or the poor family, but not for both, and in so doing will necessarily have the opposite effect on the choice presented to the other income class. Thus the low income family will prefer the rich community unless the poor town offsets its disadvantage in wealth level by redistributing income more strenuously than does the rich; but in that case the poor town becomes even more repellent to the well-to-do. The latter will prefer the poor town if it is sufficiently less redistributive than the rich one; but in that event the poor town becomes even more repellent to families of low income.

Within our large metropolitan areas, the first case seems currently more relevant than the second. Since the 1960s the older central cities, with their concentrations of the impoverished and of ethnic minorities, have been under great pressure to direct public resources to the benefit of the lowest income classes. Thus they face a painful dilemma: if they spend more on the poor, they increase the fiscal pressure that encourages the rich to move out, thus eroding the tax base and undermining future prospects for those who remain; if they attempt to defend the tax base by choosing policies that are less redistributive, they can be accused of turning their backs on their poorest citizens.

These difficulties are compounded by the considerable mobility of business firms within metropolitan areas. Businesses are not likely to perceive much direct benefit to themselves from that part of the local budget that finances services to individuals. Thus if central cities in their effort to increase service levels for the poor raise tax rates on business much above those in the surrounding suburbs, they simply hasten the dispersion of industry that is already under way for other reasons, thereby further encouraging tax base erosion.

Do the Suburbs "Exploit" the Central City?

The fiscal-spatial relationship between central cities and suburbs has often been discussed in terms of "exploitation." As Julius Margolis has put it:

> The central cities argue that the suburbanite crowds their streets, demands police and fire protection while he shops and works, and then retreats outside the municipal boundaries into his valuable residential property, which the central cities believe should be taxed to pay for these public services. The suburban governments argue that they must educate the boom baby crop of the commuter; they must protect his family and his property, but the lucrative tax

base which should support these services—the factories and office buildings—is located in the central city.[16]

We have already noted that local public expenditures per capita are generally higher in central cities than in the surrounding ring areas. The initial evidence for "exploitation" was uncovered by Amos H. Hawley, who found a significant positive correlation between the proportion of ring population to central city population in metropolitan areas and the associated level of per capita central city expenditures.[17] This finding is consistent with the hypothesis that the daily "contact population" that enters from the suburbs caused an increase in the cost of "running" the central city.

Higher central city expenditures, however, do not suffice to support a finding of exploitation, since the daily contact population may add enough to central city taxable sales, income, and property to equal or even outweigh the extra service costs its presence imposes. To resolve this issue it is necessary to apportion central city costs, on a service-by-service basis, and central city revenues, tax-by-tax, between the contact and central city populations. Given the collective nature of so much public service consumption, the results are, at best, heroic estimates. Such studies as have been undertaken tend to show either no exploitation or exploitation so slight as to be trivial.[18]

The case for exploitation rests much more firmly on other grounds. The tax-benefit calculus in Table 15.3 shows that it is strongly in the interest of residents in the wealthy town to keep others out whose wealth level is below the town average, since such people will not "pay their way" vis-à-vis the local fisc. In Chapter 13 we described the exclusionary housing and land-use policies by which the suburbs have tried to prevent lower middle class and lower class families from moving in. This deliberate self-segregation by the suburban middle and upper classes reduces their own burdens at the expense of those remaining in the core cities. In that sense there is surely "exploitation."

Yet the word "exploitation" is itself inadequate. It has an almost

16. Julius Margolis, "Metropolitan Finance Problems: Territories, Functions, and Growth," in Universities-National Bureau Committee for Economic Research, *Public Finances: Needs, Sources, and Utilization* (Princeton, N.J.: Princeton University Press, 1961), p. 256.

17. Amos H. Hawley, "Metropolitan Government and Municipal Government Expenditures in Central Cities," in Paul K. Hatt and Albert J. Reiss, Jr., eds., *Cities and Society*, rev. ed. (New York: The Free Press, 1957), pp. 773–82.

18. See David F. Bradford and Wallace E. Oates, "Suburban Exploitation of Central Cities and Governmental Structure," in Harold M. Hochman and George E. Peterson, eds., *Redistribution Through Public Choice* (New York: Columbia University Press, 1974), pp. 43–90; William B. Neenan, "Suburban–Central City Exploitation Thesis: One City's Tale," *National Tax Journal*, June 1970, pp. 117–39.

exclusively ethical connotation, as of taking more or giving less than one ought to do. In fact, there is much more at stake than who pays the bills: the disparity between needs and tax-paying capacity at the local level is not only inequitable; it also reduces the commitment of resources we make toward meeting the national problems of inequality and poverty.

What can be done to overcome these disparities within metropolitan areas? Possible solutions to the major problems of metropolitan public finance will be taken up at length below. In addition, the reader should recall that in Chapter 13 we analyzed a variety of policies designed to open up the suburbs to poor and lower middle income families. One purpose of these policies is to give racial minorities the opportunity to exercise wider choice of residential location within metropolitan areas. There are sufficient arguments in favor of this as a matter of right, but, in addition, a relatively uniform geographic distribution of the poor (if one may speak in such crude terms) would also make it possible to use the entire metropolitan tax base in financing local services for that part of the population that does not "pay its own way." However, even the most active policies to open up the suburbs could hardly work fast enough to count as a solution to present metropolitan fiscal inequities.

To be sure, evolutionary forces, such as the aging of housing in the older suburbs, are already helping to bring about some movement of poor and lower middle income minority families into the suburbs and will continue to do so. But the dispersion of poverty that takes place as a result of natural evolutionary forces is already having its own unfortunate fiscal results. As low income families concentrate in a relatively small number of older suburban towns, those areas are beginning to face the same sort of fiscal squeeze already endured by the central cities. The natural processes of metropolitan development are not likely to eliminate intrametropolitan fiscal disparities in the foreseeable future.

URBAN FISCAL DISTRESS

The nation suddenly became conscious of an "urban fiscal crisis" when New York City teetered on the brink of bankruptcy in 1975. There had been earlier signs of trouble not only in New York but elsewhere. As early as 1971 the Advisory Commission on Intergovernmental Relations had initiated a study of City Financial Emergencies, which was published in 1973.[19] New York averted bankruptcy by means of sweeping budgetary reforms combined with emergency regulation and support by the state and

19. Advisory Commission on Intergovernmental Relations, *City Financial Emergencies*, July 1973.

federal governments.[20] In the years following that financial cataclysm other large cities have moved in and out of "crisis," as evidenced by temporary inability to meet payrolls, school years radically shortened to cut expenses, and even failure to meet debt obligations on time. Such events are the most dramatic signs of urban fiscal distress, but that problem itself is both more pervasive and less highly charged than these occasional symptoms would suggest.

Because the problem is many-sided, it is difficult to frame a concise definition of "urban fiscal distress." Perhaps an acceptable general statement would be that it involves an acutely painful imbalance between needs and resources.[21] Since localities are usually required by state law to balance their operating budgets, there cannot be an imbalance between expenditures and revenues. Fiscal distress therefore is measured not by budget deficits but by the pain generated in trying to avoid them.

We have already shown that central cities are under pressure to spend more per capita on public services than do the suburbs but have fewer resources per capita out of which to pay for them. If they are to meet the demand for services while balancing their budgets they must therefore tax themselves at higher rates than do the suburbs. Many of them have been doing so for some time. That kind of fiscal pain becomes fiscal distress when a gradually deteriorating central city tax base makes substantial cuts in service necessary while tax rates remain high or even increase.

Difficulty of Intercity Comparisons

Fiscal comparisons among U.S. cities are notoriously difficult to carry out. First of all, the division of functions between states and their localities varies widely from state to state. At one extreme lies the State of Hawaii, where local governments account for only 20 percent of combined state and local direct general expenditure. At the other is New

20. For a colorful description of New York's financial crisis and the events leading to it, see Ken Auletta, *The Streets Were Paved with Gold* (New York: Random House, 1979), especially chs. 2 and 3. A thorough, scholarly analysis of the causes and possible responses to the crisis is contained in *The City in Transition: Prospects and Policies for New York*, Final Report of the Temporary Commission on City Finances, Raymond D. Horton, Staff Director, June 1977 (New York: Arno Press, 1978).

21. This definition is borrowed from the title of ch. 9, "Fiscal Distress: An Imbalance Between Resources and Needs," in U.S. Department of Housing and Urban Development, *Occasional Papers*, vol. 4, July 1979, ed. by Robert Paul Boynton. Stephen M. Barro draws an interesting distinction between fiscal disadvantage, fiscal decline, and acute fiscal crisis in *The Urban Impacts of Federal Policies*, doc. no. R2114-KF/HEW vol. 3, *Fiscal Conditions* (Santa Monica, Calif.: The Rand Corporation, 1978), pp. 11–17.

York State, where localities are responsible for 74 percent of combined expenditure. In the United States as a whole, the local share averages 62 percent.[22] In states where localities bear a higher than average share of expenditure responsibilities, local taxes are also likely to be higher than elsewhere.

Second, functional arrangements at the local level vary widely.[23] For example, county governments carry out significant functions in most states, including functions within the boundaries of the cities they contain. However, a number of cities, including Baltimore, Denver, New York, Philadelphia, St. Louis, and San Francisco are either completely or substantially consolidated with their county governments. In general, these cities will be found to carry out a wider and more costly range of functions than such places as Chicago, Cleveland, Detroit, or Los Angeles, or indeed most smaller cities, which are serviced by a functioning county government.

At the height of the fiscal crisis it was pointed out that the City of New York annually spent about $1,500 per resident for public services, while Chicago managed quite nicely on only $300 per head. No wonder New York City was going broke! Such a bald comparison, however, was pointless, since New York supports many functions, including public schools, a public university, welfare, and a health and hospital system, services which in Chicago are left almost entirely in the hands of the state or of an independent (and not coterminous) county government. When such differences are overlooked, comparisons become meaningless. Yet the range of variation across the nation is so great that standardized comparisons are difficult to carry out. When it is necessary to compare individual cities, the best procedure is probably to examine data for those functions that are carried out by almost every city government. These "common municipal functions" include police and fire protection, streets and highways, sanitation, sewerage, libraries, parks and recreation, water supply, financial administration, and general control. We shall make use of this concept below.

The Causes of Urban Fiscal Distress

The underlying causes of urban fiscal distress can be quickly summarized. Fiscally distressed cities are likely to have experienced the following:

22. U.S. Bureau of the Census, *Governmental Finances in 1978–79*, series GF 79 no. 5, October 1980, table 12.

23. For a concise description of the variation in local functional responsibilities see U.S. Bureau of the Census, *City Employment in 1979*, series GE 79 no. 2, June 1980, pp. 2–3.

Population exchange. Massive out-migration of the middle class accompanied by a heavy influx of low income population weakens the city's tax base while simultaneously increasing the cost of providing public services.

Population and job decline. Decentralization of jobs and population into the suburbs leaves the central city with a smaller population and a shrinking economy.

The effect of population exchange on central city budgets was analyzed above under the heading of "Geographic Disparities." The budgetary "squeeze" it produces can obviously cause fiscal distress. That analysis need not be repeated here.

What *does* require further explanation is why job and population decline *per se* should also be troublesome. To be sure, such declines could be expected to reduce a city's tax base, thus generating pressure for higher tax rates, if service levels were to be maintained.[24] On the other hand, wouldn't a smaller population also reduce the need for services, thus matching on the expenditure side the decline taking place in revenues? In fact, however, the cost of providing services may not diminish in step with falling population. In that case, population and job decline would, indeed, add to the fiscal distress of central cities. There are two very different reasons why population loss may not lead to a proportionate reduction in public service costs. The first is structural, the second political.

Structural Problems of Declining Cities

The structural problem of decline is essentially one of excess capacity. As a city grows, its public infrastructure—streets, sewers, schools, transit systems, and so on—is expanded to serve the larger population. If the population then falls, the city is left with excess physical capacity. The per capita cost of running the infrastructure increases as the number of users declines.

To illustrate the effect of excess capacity, consider two kinds of public service. The first is provided over the whole area of the city through a network of physical structures: functions such as streets and highways, sewers, water supply, and rail mass transit. Once these systems are in place, there is little possibility of closing down portions of them to economize, should the population of the city begin to decline. Instead, each

24. Tax revenue per job (New York City, 1970) by industrial sector and type of tax, is estimated in Roy Bahl, Alan Campbell, and David Greytak, *Taxes, Expenditures and the Economic Base: Case Study of New York City* (New York: Praeger, 1974) table 2.45, p. 142.

system must be operated and maintained more or less in full. To the extent that part or all of these costs remain fixed, cost per person will increase as population falls. For example, the cost per passenger of operating a rail mass transit system rises markedly as the number of riders drops.

Next consider services such as education, police and fire protection, and hospital care that are provided on a district-by-district basis. As population declines, schools and hospitals become underutilized, which increases the cost per unit of service delivered. Likewise, the cost per resident of maintaining and operating a given number of fire and police facilities increases as population shrinks.

Some saving in operating costs might be achieved by closing schools, hospitals, and perhaps even police and fire houses. But there is typically strong neighborhood resistance to such moves. Moreover, if the population thins out haphazardly it may be difficult to find neighborhoods where facilities could plausibly be shut down.[25]

It must be noted, too, that closing down facilities does not reduce capital costs. Unless buildings can be sold back to the private sector (unlikely in a declining city) the capital embodied in them is a sunk cost and cannot be recovered. Debt service continues whether or not facilities are used. Indeed, the cost per taxpayer of servicing debt previously issued to finance the development of infrastructure increases as population declines.

Political Problems of Budgetmaking in Declining Cities

The second reason why service costs may not decline as rapidly as population can be labeled political. While the normative theory of public expenditure tells us that the economic objective of local government should be to supply those goods and services that cannot be provided efficiently by the private sector, it must be acknowledged that city governments, to use Peterson's phrase, also act as "suppliers of jobs."[26] There is, of course, a long tradition of city government "patronage" dating back to the nineteenth century, but it was only with the rapid growth of local spending after World War II that city governments became relatively substantial employers.

During the 1960s and early 1970s, when private sector employment

25. For a proposal to deal with the problem of population distribution and land use in declining cities, see James Heilbrun, "On the Theory and Policy of Neighborhood Consolidation," *Journal of the American Planning Association,* October 1979, pp. 417–27.
26. See discussion in Peterson, pp. 112–15.

in most of the older cities was dropping, the number of local government jobs frequently continued to expand.[27] These jobs were especially important to racial minorities for whom they often provided initial entry to white collar occupations. Public employee unions, potent for the first time during the 1960s, also exerted pressure to expand the number of jobs, and increased intergovernmental aid often made such expansion seem relatively inexpensive to local taxpayers. Under these circumstances it is not surprising that local politicians responded by "supplying" more jobs.

Once jobs were built into the local budget, the same political forces that helped put them there resisted their removal. Consequently, even after it became clear that massive economic and population decline was underway, the older central cities did not immediately move to reduce public employment and expenditure. Public employment per capita therefore rose rapidly until the mid-1970s. Although some cities began "belt tightening" earlier, it took the near bankruptcy of New York City in 1975 and the ensuing disruption of the municipal bond market to bring the era of municipal government expansion decisively to an end.

For the purpose of studying urban fiscal problems, Peterson and Muller constructed a sample of large cities grouped into three classes: growing throughout the study period; growing to 1970, declining thereafter; and declining all the way.[28] Peterson found that in 1964 there was relatively little difference in the level of local government employment per 1,000 residents in the three classes. By 1973, the "declining cities" and the "growing, then declining" group had reached per capita levels respectively 49 percent and 28 percent above the level of "growing" cities.[29] In the mid-1970s, however, a turning point occurred. The pattern reversed: employment in declining cities was curtailed, while in growing cities it continued to increase. Peterson hypothesizes that the period during which public employment and spending levels per capita were far higher in declining than in growing cities may have been "little more than an aberrant interval, during which the old cities temporarily refused to accept the fiscal implications of their economic decline."[30] Even if that turns out to be the case, however, it will not signal the end of "fiscal distress" as we have defined it. Resources will not have increased, nor needs, in any

27. See ibid., table 23, p. 112.
28. See Thomas Muller, Growing and Declining Urban Areas: A Fiscal Comparison (Washington, D.C.: The Urban Institute, 1975); and Peterson, "Finance," pp. 47–64 and 75–78. In both studies New York City is treated separately as a fourth category.
29. Peterson, table 6, p. 50.
30. Ibid., p. 51.

real sense, diminished. Declining cities will be living more frugally, but the painful imbalance between their needs and resources will remain.

Measuring Urban Distress

In analyzing geographic disparities in the distribution of resources between cities and suburbs (see Table 15.1) we pointed out the influence of city "age" and showed that the old cities of the North and East are much worse off in relation to their suburbs than are the relatively newer cities of the South and West. In the discussion of fiscal distress, following the lead of Peterson and Muller, we have emphasized the effects of growth and decline rather than age. In fact, however, declining cities are mostly "old" and growing cities mostly "new," so that the fiscal effects of age are difficult to disentangle from those of decline. In recent years a number of analysts have constructed indices intended to measure relative urban distress, and these indices usually include statistical factors measuring both age and growth. For example, the index developed by Richard P. Nathan and others at the Brookings Institution is the product of three components. The value of the index is larger—and the level of distress presumably higher—the lower the city's income, the greater its age, and the less its rate of population growth, each measured in relation to the mean of all cities in the sample.[31]

Such an index can be used in a number of ways. For example, the government might employ it to determine whether a city qualifies for a certain type of fiscal assistance. Or it might be used to classify cities by degree of hardship to see whether government grants are, in fact, going to the most distressed cities (a question we will return to below). Finally, such indexes can throw light on the question of whether disparities between fiscally distressed and fiscally healthy cities are growing or diminishing. However, their power to reveal the "true condition" of cities must not be exaggerated. They cannot do more than combine the ingredients put into them. Distressed cities are then simply those that rank high on

31. Richard P. Nathan and James W. Fossett, "Urban Conditions—The Future of the Federal Role," National Tax Association, Tax Institute of America, *Proceedings of the Seventy-first Annual Conference on Taxation,* November 12–16, 1978, table 1, pp. 32–35. The index is calculated from the following formula:

$$\frac{\dfrac{\text{mean per capita income}}{\text{city per capita income}} \times \dfrac{\text{city percent pre-1940 housing}}{\text{mean percent pre-1940 housing}}}{\dfrac{100 + \text{city rate of population change}}{100 + \text{median rate of population change}}}$$

The percentage of housing built before 1940 serves as a proxy for city age.

the particular measures chosen for the index. With that *caveat* in mind, let us see what an urban conditions index can tell us about trends in distress over time.

Regarding such trends, two hypotheses suggest themselves.[32] It might be argued on the one hand that in an economy where labor and capital are mobile we should expect disparities between cities eventually to be corrected by those equilibrating mechanisms that connect markets across the nation. For example, we explained in Chapter 3 how the migration of labor from poor to rich regions and of capital in the opposite direction could be expected to reduce interregional differences in wages and incomes.[33] On the other hand, one could argue that because of our fragmented system of local government, fiscal disparities will tend to be self-reinforcing. Cities with a growing poverty population will exhibit rising tax rates, probably combined with deteriorating public service quality. Middle and upper income families, including many of the more highly skilled members of the labor force, will move away, causing further fiscal deterioration. High tax rates, low service quality, and a decline in the average skill level of the population will render such cities increasingly unattractive to business. Economic decline will cause further fiscal distress in a cycle of self-reinforcing deterioration.

The Brookings index suggests that, at least for the period 1960–75, the second hypothesis is more nearly correct than the first: the most distressed cities tended to deteriorate further, while those better off remained relatively unchanged or improved slightly. The index was calculated for 1960 and 1975 for the 56 largest U.S. cities, excluding New York and Washington, D.C.[34] Scores in both years were standardized to an average of 100. Between 1960 and 1975 the range between the most and least distressed cities increased considerably, as did other measures of sample variation. The average score of cities in the worst-off quintile rose (indicating deterioration) from 180 in 1960 to 230 in 1975 while the scores of the three best-off quintiles either decreased or were approximately unchanged.[35]

Table 15.4 shows index scores for the central cities of the six largest

32. See U.S. Department of Housing and Urban Development, *Occasional Papers*, vol. 4, pp. 86–88.
33. For an interesting critique of this view, see the pages cited in preceding footnote.
34. New York City was excluded "because of the lack of readily available federal aid data comparable to other cities" (Nathan and Fossett, note 2, p. 41). Washington, D.C., was omitted presumably because it carries out functions elsewhere provided only by states.
35. Nashville and Jacksonville, two of eleven cities in the worst-off quintile in 1960, subsequently consolidated with the overlying county, making their 1975 scores not comparable with 1960. The averages cited therefore refer to the other nine cities.

TABLE 15.4

Urban Conditions in Large Central Cities

	URBAN CONDITIONS INDEX		PERCENTAGE CHANGE
	1960	*1975*	*1960–75*
North and East			
St. Louis	203.9	270.9	33
Pittsburgh	178.1	217.8	22
Boston	196.4	202.0	3
Detroit	149.0	180.9	21
Philadelphia	163.9	179.9	10
Chicago	137.3	167.5	22
Average, North and East	171.4	203.2	19
South and West			
San Francisco	112.3	125.8	12
Atlanta	69.6	75.8	9
Los Angeles	56.4	55.9	−1
San Diego	32.1	32.8	2
Dallas	38.1	28.6	−25
Houston	37.8	22.8	−40
Average, South and West	57.7	57.0	−1
Average, 56 cities	100	100	—

Source: Richard P. Nathan and James W. Fossett, "Urban Conditions—the Future of the Federal Role," National Tax Association, Tax Institute of America, *Proceedings of the Seventy-first Annual Conference on Taxation*, November 12–16, 1978, table 1, pp. 32–35.

SMSA's in the North and East and in the South and West.[36] These scores confirm earlier analysis which stressed the difference between the older cities of the former region and the predominantly newer cities of the latter. All the cities in the North and East group rank well above average on the index of distress. In the South and West category only San Francisco—by far the "oldest" in that class—is above the mean, and even San Francisco is far below any city in the North and East category. As in Nathan and Fossett's larger sample, the disparity between the better- and worse-off groups widened between 1960 and 1975. The average score of the six North and East cities deteriorated from 171 to 203, while the average for the six South and West cities was unchanged.

36. The cities were chosen to correspond as closely as possible with the two groups analyzed in ch. 3. Since New York, Washington, and Anaheim were not included in Nathan and Fossett's study, the central cities of the next biggest SMSA's, St. Louis and Pittsburgh in the North and East and San Diego in the South and West, were substituted.

It must not be assumed, however, that distressed cities are inevitably fated to suffer self-reinforcing deterioration. Nathan and Fossett point out that a number of cities that ranked above the average in hardship in 1960—including such major centers as Boston, Birmingham, and Baltimore—showed little or no further deterioration by 1975.

A SUMMARY OF PROBLEMS AND PROPOSALS

In this and the preceding chapter we have discussed four major problems of the metropolitan public sector: the inappropriate assignment of functions to levels of government; the haphazard arrangement of local functions and boundaries; the existence of geographic disparities between local needs and resources; and, finally, the pressure of urban fiscal distress.

What can or should be done about these problems? A number of programs already exist, and various additional reforms have been proposed. To discuss them, we will group them into four categories:

1. *Reassignment of functions:* proposals to transfer fiscal responsibility for certain functions from lower to higher levels of government
2. *Reorganization of the local public sector:* proposals to rationalize the arrangement of functions and boundaries at the local level
3. *Intergovernmental grants:* programs that transfer funds from higher to lower levels of government
4. *Economic self-help:* policies that cities themselves can adopt to improve their fiscal and economic performance

As we shall see, some of these reforms promise to mitigate several problems at once. There is no simple one-to-one correspondence between problems and proposed reforms. We have more than one stone to kill each bird, as well as some that may bring down more than one bird at a time.

THE REASSIGNMENT OF FUNCTIONS: PROPOSALS TO TRANSFER FISCAL RESPONSIBILITY

Revenue sharing, which we take up later in this chapter, is a form of fiscal assistance given by the federal government to states and localities with virtually no strings attached. Its proposal in the 1960s touched off an extended debate on the nature of American fiscal federalism between those reformers who favored increased intergovernmental assistance, such as revenue sharing, and others who argued for structural reorganization instead.

At that time it was an important argument in favor of revenue sharing that it would counteract "fiscal imbalance" in the American federal system. During the 1960s tax revenues from the federal government's highly elastic personal and corporate income taxes tended to increase faster than the need for federal expenditures. During the recovery phase of the business cycle, the federal government was in danger of running a budget surplus even before the economy reached full employment. Such a surplus would constitute a "fiscal drag," impeding the movement toward full employment and creating an argument for a federal tax cut.

The situation was just the opposite at the state-local level. Needs for expenditure—generated to a large extent by the population explosion of the 1950s and 1960s—were increasing faster than tax receipts from the relatively inelastic property and sales taxes. Consequently, as already shown in Chapter 14, these governments found themselves under continuous pressure to raise tax rates. Proponents of revenue sharing believed that transfering funds from the federal government, with its vast revenue-raising powers, to state and local governments, whose tax resources were far more limited, could not only prevent fiscal drag but improve the performance of the American federal system in other ways as well.[37]

Advocates of structural reform maintained that the major defects in the American system arose not from deficient revenue-raising powers at the lower levels but from an inappropriate division of functions among the federal, state, and local governments, which revenue sharing would paper over rather than correct. They took the position that instead of moving funds downward from higher to lower levels of government, the preferable reform would be to transfer fiscal responsibility for certain major functions from lower to higher levels. Both approaches, it might be noted, called for an increase in federal taxing and spending that would probably be offset only in part by a decline in the tax effort of states and localities.

Proposals To Increase the Functional Role of the Federal Government

Richard Ruggles made the case for radically altering the assignment of fiscal responsibilities by reviewing the strengths and weaknesses of each level of government. As he pointed out, "The federal government should

37. For a thorough statement of the case for revenue sharing, see Walter W. Heller, *New Dimensions of Political Economy* (New York: W. W. Norton, by arrangement with the Harvard University Press, 1967), ch. 3.

be the instrument for developing national policy."[38] It is also an efficient instrument for collecting taxes and disbursing funds. It is not well suited, however, to administering the details of complex public service programs at the point of delivery. If the public decides that as a matter of national policy every citizen is entitled to a first-rate education, good health care, and relief from poverty, then, according to this line of argument, it is the duty of the federal government to guarantee that this takes place by providing sufficient funds so that, despite geographic differences in wealth, every locality will be well served at equitable tax rates. In the language of economic theory, such services as health and education have nationwide externalities. Therefore decisions about the proper level of "output" must be reached nationally and made effective everywhere. Ruggles proposed that the federal government take over the costs, not only of welfare, but of providing a minimum standard level of education and health care.[39]

The strength of state and local government lies in the production, coordination, and delivery of public services at the regional and local levels. Therefore these governments should be entrusted with the administration even of those programs for which the federal government sets minimum standards and provides basic funds. If state and local governments wished to exceed the national standards, they could do so by adding revenue from their own sources. For services not charged with a national interest, such as police and fire protection, sanitation, and correctional institutions, state and local governments should have both financial and administrative responsibility. With some or most of the burden for "national" services lifted from their shoulders, they would have no difficulty financing the rest of their needs.

Much the same conclusions can be reached by applying to a multi-level system of government Musgrave's normative theory of budgetary functions. As explained in Chapter 14, the functions of stabilization and income redistribution are best left to the federal government. The only budgetary function appropriate to local governments is allocation—the provision of goods and services that cannot be supplied efficiently by the private sector. The allocative function, in turn, should be divided among the three levels of government according to the "reach" of the goods in question, so that Olson's "principle of fiscal equivalence" is as nearly as possible fulfilled. Each level of government should attempt to provide just that quantity of every public service that its citizens want and are willing to pay for. If the federal government has, indeed, done its job of

38. Richard Ruggles, "The Federal Government and Federalism," in Harvey S. Perloff and Richard P. Nathan, eds., *Revenue Sharing and the City* (Baltimore: The Johns Hopkins University Press, 1968), p. 70.
39. Ibid., pp. 62–68.

bringing about a desirable distribution of personal income, there will be no problem of individuals too poor to pay for their share.

On the basis of such arguments, Charles McClure advocated fiscal reorganization along the following lines.[40] In order to relieve lower level governments of any direct role in income redistribution, the federal government should enact an income guarantee to replace all existing welfare programs, some of which are now partially supported by state and local contributions (see Chapter 11). The federal role as redistributor of income should also be strengthened by reducing preferential treatment of certain kinds of income under the federal tax code. By rendering the federal income tax more progressive, such a reform would make it easier for state and local governments to adopt the possibly *non*progressive benefit taxes that are the most appropriate means of financing allocative functions. Finally, because education yields nationwide external benefits, the federal government should assume a greater share of its heavy financial burden.

Thus relieved of any obligation to redistribute income, and with the burden of financing education reduced, state and local governments could concentrate on those regional and local services of which they are the logical providers. For the most part they should pay for these services out of their own pockets, employing benefit taxes to the extent possible. Such taxes are desirable, both as a means to rational allocation decisions, and because they are unlikely to distort locational choices by inducing migration either of population or of business. (See discussion of "The Effects of Redistributive Local Budgets," above.) Since feasible benefit taxes are limited in scope, however, some financial gap would, no doubt, remain. This would be filled by using broad-based state and local sales and income taxes and/or by federal grants to support programs in which there is a specific, identifiable national interest. (The nature of such an interest and the kinds of grants it would justify will be discussed below.) In McClure's view, general assistance to state and local governments in the form of unrestricted revenue sharing funds would be justified, not as inherently desirable, but only as a stop-gap adopted "in lieu of a more sensible set of fiscal institutions."[41]

A variety of other plans have been offered for altering the assignment of functional responsibilities. The least sweeping calls only for the federal takeover of all welfare costs up to some acceptable national standard.

40. Charles E. McClure, Jr., "Revenue Sharing: Alternative to Rational Fiscal Federalism?" reprinted in R. C. Amacher, R. D. Tollison, and T. D. Willett, eds., *The Economic Approach to Public Policy* (Ithaca, N.Y.: Cornell University Press, 1976), pp. 225–43.
41. Ibid., p. 242.

Considerably more ambitious is the recommendation by the Advisory Commission on Intergovernmental Relations that the federal government assume all welfare costs and the state governments, thereby relieved of a heavy burden, in turn relieve localities of the major responsibility for the cost of elementary and secondary education.[42]

Effects on Geographic Disparities and Fiscal Distress

The principal objective of reorganizational proposals is to improve the functioning of our multilevel system by bringing the assignment of functions to levels of government more nearly in line with the ideal outlined at the beginning of Chapter 14. To what extent would they mitigate other problems as well? To begin with, it seems highly probable that they would help to counteract the effect of geographic disparities in taxable resources. In general, reorganizational proposals shift fiscal responsibilities upward to the federal government. The fraction of public expenditure supported by state and local taxes would fall. Therefore the level of public services (including the redistribution of income) would depend less than it now does on local income and wealth. Perhaps the effect can best be understood by considering the "polar case." If all public services were taken over by the federal government, distributed equally across the nation, and paid for out of federal taxes, geographic disparities in income and wealth would continue to exist but would have no effect on the level of public services or income redistribution in any locality. Reassigning functions to higher levels of government would move us—ever so slightly —in that direction.

Whether urban fiscal distress would also be relieved by such reforms is less certain; much would depend on details of the plans. For example, if the federal government were to take over the burden of paying for welfare programs, it would be unlikely to do so at anything like the level of support now provided in high benefit states such as California, Massachusetts, Michigan, or New York. Instead, benefits might be leveled up to, say, the 65th percentile of prevailing state levels. Taxpayers in high benefit states would probably find themselves paying additional federal income tax to support higher welfare payments in the formerly low benefit states. These added taxes might well outweigh the benefit of slightly higher federal contributions in their own states.[43]

42. Advisory Commission on Intergovernmental Relations, *Improving Urban America: A Challenge to Federalism* (Washington, D.C.: September 1976), pp. 16, 45–46, and 70–76.
43. For a more extended discussion see Peterson, pp. 93–96; and Alan Fechter, "The Fiscal Implications of Social Welfare Programs: Can They Help the Cities?" in L. Kenneth Hubbell, ed., *Fiscal Crisis in American Cities: The Federal Response* (Cambridge, Mass.: Ballinger, 1979), esp. pp. 139–47.

In any case, reorganizational proposals that require the outright assumption of additional responsibilities by the federal government have never been easy to bring about and seem especially unlikely during a period of fiscal restraint.

Increasing the Responsibilities of the States: The Case of Education

Regardless of whether the federal government eventually takes on additional functional responsibilities, there exists the possibility of important structural reorganization at the state level. If states were to take over fiscal responsibility for some functions now financed by local governments, they could greatly reduce the importance of income and wealth disparities at the local level. This issue has come to the fore in connection with education.[44]

In a series of lawsuits, residents of relatively poor school districts have alleged that the typical system of local public school finance deprives them of the right to an equal education. In the case of *Serrano v. Priest*, the California Supreme Court in August 1971 held that to finance education by a local property tax violated the "equal protection" clauses of both the federal and the California constitutions. The court based this finding on the fact that local property-tax financing of education leads inevitably to great disparities among districts in the level of spending on education. Thereafter, similar suits were brought by aggrieved families in federal or state courts in a majority of states. The first federal case to reach the United States Supreme Court came from the state of Texas. In March 1973 that tribunal overturned the lower court decision in the case of *Rodriguez v. San Antonio School District* and held that the Texas school finance system, though based on the local property tax and fraught with inequalities, was not in violation of the federal Constitution.

While the decision in *Rodriguez* effectively closed the federal courts to this issue, it has certainly not halted the drive for equalization at the state level. Suits brought under state law have already been successful and cannot be appealed to the federal courts. For example, the New Jersey Supreme Court in *Robinson v. Cahill* (April 1973) held that the state's system of educational finance failed to fulfill a mandate for equal educational opportunity in the state constitution. Furthermore, many states were already studying the possibility of full state assumption of all educational costs, or of strengthening the equalizing effect of their existing

44. For a thoroughgoing analysis of this complex question, see Robert D. Reischauer and Robert W. Hartman, with the assistance of Daniel J. Sullivan, *Reforming School Finance* (Washington, D.C.: The Brookings Institution, 1973).

school support payments, even before the recent flood of suits began. Under the pressure of court action, all are now pushed in that direction.

Aggregate data do indicate that the relative contribution of states to local public school revenue increased sharply after *Serrano*. For two decades prior to that decision, the state share was virtually stable at a level just under 40 percent. In 1971–1972 it was 38.3 percent. Thereafter it rose steadily, reaching 44.1 percent by 1977–1978.[45]

It is uncertain what effect the movement for tax and expenditure limitation will have on this trend. In California, where passage of Proposition 13 sharply cut back local tax revenue, the existence of a large state surplus made possible an immediate, massive increase in state funding of education. Elsewhere, as indicated in Chapter 14, tax and expenditure limitations tend only to restrict *future* fiscal growth. To the extent that these limitations are more numerous at the local than the state level, they are likely to put pressure on the states to assume a gradually increasing share of the financial responsibility for education.

In the longer run it is conceivable that the drive for equality in spending will extend beyond education. If citizens have a right to equal provision of education within the state, why not also to equality in the provision of other essential public services? If this view were to prevail, it would require far-reaching changes in state-local fiscal relations, as the states moved toward genuine equalization of the whole spectrum of local services.

REORGANIZING THE LOCAL PUBLIC SECTOR

The local level of government in the United States contains a bewildering set of overlapping layers of cities, counties, school districts, special purpose districts, and regional authorities. The geographic boundaries built into this system are often of ancient origin and may therefore not reflect current economic realities. Many of the problems of the metropolitan public sector could be ameliorated by reorganizing this governmental hodgepodge. Reform might involve altering the assignment of functions within the local sector, rationalizing local government boundaries, or a combination of both.[46]

Analysis of the problem of haphazard boundaries at the beginning of this chapter led to the conclusion that for each public service they should ideally be drawn so as to: (1) eliminate significant externalities; (2) minimize the unit cost of production; (3) provide political accessibility

45. Tax Foundation, Inc., *Facts and Figures on Government Finance*, 1979, table 208, p. 257.

46. For an institutionally detailed discussion of these issues, see Advisory Commission, *Improving Urban America* . . . , chs. 3 and 4.

for services where that is important; (4) facilitate area-wide planning and coordination. Even for a single service these criteria may well conflict. For example, political accessibility is important in the case of public housing, indicating the desirability of small jurisdictions. Yet housing policies ought to be planned on a regional basis, which indicates the need for a single metropolitan jurisdiction. For each service, therefore, even in an ideal system, it might be necessary to compromise among objectives in drawing boundaries. A second round of compromise is necessary in combining many functions under the jurisdiction of one or a few local governments. The alternative of setting up a separate "government" for each function in order to enjoy the optimum size jurisdiction for each one is obviously absurd, since it would make planning and coordination of services at the local level virtually impossible and, by dividing power among a multitude of elected officials, would seriously weaken political accountability.

Metropolitan Federation

In recent years, most advocates of metropolitan reorganization have rejected the notion of a monolithic, single-level regional government (even if that were possible), since such an arrangement would sacrifice too many values that are best realized under smaller local units. Instead, they have tended to favor establishing a less centralized form, such as metropolitan "federation." This is a two-tiered system, in which some functions are assigned to the metropolitan government to be conducted uniformly throughout the region, while others are left to be performed within the discretion of the constituent local governments. Ideally, functions would be divided between the two levels by applying the sort of criteria outlined above. Functions with important externalities or economies of scale or requirements for area-wide planning would be assigned to the "central government" of the federation. Functions that lacked those characteristics, or in which political access was an overriding consideration, would be left in the hands of the traditional, smaller local units. Reorganization could thus overcome many of the inefficiencies that arise under our present haphazard arrangements.

A two-tiered system could also go a long way toward eliminating the fiscal effects of intrametropolitan disparities in taxable resources. The higher tier government would finance whatever services it was designated to provide by means of uniform metropolitan-wide taxes. In addition, those services left for purposes of administration in the hands of the local governments could be financed in whole or in part by uniform federation-wide taxes. As a result, the weight of services dependent for financing upon the taxable resources of the lower tier governments would diminish. The fiscal impact of intercommunity differences in wealth and income within the metropolitan area would be reduced.

The best-known example of federation is the Municipality of Metropolitan Toronto. It was established in 1954 as a federation comprising the central city of Toronto and twelve suburbs. A reorganization in 1967 consolidated the twelve suburban municipalities into five Boroughs and increased the powers and responsibilities of the Metropolitan Government.[47] The success of Metropolitan Toronto has undoubtedly stimulated interest in federation in the United States.

Counties as Metropolitan Governments

In more than a third of all SMSA's, the entire metropolitan area lies within a single county. This coincidence can facilitate the creation of a metropolitan-wide government because it allows an already existing unit—the county—to be used as the major building block. In Florida, the Miami SMSA lies entirely within Dade County. A two-tiered metropolitan structure—the only example in the United States—was created in 1957, giving the county government greatly expanded powers to perform region-oriented services over the whole SMSA, while allowing the local governments within the county to retain control of other services such as police, fire, and education. A less tidy arrangement results from "city-county consolidation." In this scheme the central city government consolidates with that of the overlying county to form a new unit that provides one set of services over the entire county and an additional set within the smaller central city area. City-county consolidation along these lines took place during the 1960s in three cases: Nashville consolidated with Davidson County in 1962; Jacksonville, Florida, with Duval County in 1967; and Indianapolis with Marion County in 1969.[48]

Tax Base Sharing

The creation of a two-tiered structure of metropolitan government would mitigate the effects of geographical fiscal disparities by partially "regionalizing" both the metropolitan tax base and the provision of local services. A less ambitious plan, known as tax base sharing, calls for regionalizing a part of the tax base only. Supporters of this approach are

47. The Toronto experience, as well as other versions of the "two-level" approach, are described in John C. Bollens and Henry J. Schmandt, *The Metropolis*, 3rd ed., (New York: Harper & Row, 1975), ch. 12.

48. For further detail see Bollens and Schmandt, ch. 12; Demetrios Caraley, *City Government and Urban Problems* (Englewood Cliffs, N.J.: Prentice-Hall, 1977), ch. 5; and Melvin B. Mogulof, *Five Metropolitan Governments* (Washington, D.C.: The Urban Institute, 1972).

attracted by the fact that it can produce some equalization without interfering with local control over the provision of services.[49]

The only tax base sharing scheme in the United States has operated in the Minneapolis–St. Paul metropolitan area since 1974. Under this plan all municipalities within the area contribute 40 percent of the *increment* in the assessed value of their commercial and industrial property to a common pool. (Residential property is not involved.) Each then receives a share of revenue from taxes on the pooled value. An equalizing effect is built into the plan, since shares in the revenue are inversely related to the per capita market value of all property in each jurisdiction. An additional redistributive effect occurs to the extent that the growth out of which contributions are made is concentrated in jurisdictions that already have a strong property tax base. Studying the outcome in Minnesota after five years of operation, Andrew Reschovsky found that the plan did, indeed, tend to redistribute resources from high to low tax base communities within the suburban ring. It also benefited the two central cities.[50]

In general, however, the power of tax base sharing to overcome fiscal disparities between central cities and suburbs is limited by the fact that it operates on the revenue side and ignores differences in expenditure "need" (however defined). A central city's tax base per capita is not always weaker than the average for its suburbs, but its need for expenditure is almost always greater. In addition, as Reschovsky points out, if tax base sharing is limited to sharing the *growth* in property value, it is unlikely to have much effect in stagnant or declining metropolitan areas.[51] Yet, as we have pointed out (see Tables 15.1 and 15.2), it is precisely in those areas that city-suburban fiscal disparities are largest.

Netzer has written that "the income and wealth of the country is centralized within metropolitan areas and . . . despite regional differences in economic growth rates, whole metropolitan areas are viable fiscal entities for nearly all nonincome-redistributing public services."[52] Yet, however attractive schemes for regionalizing the metropolitan public

49. However, see the critical discussion in Roy Bahl and David Puryear, "Regional Tax Base Sharing: Possibilities and Implications," *National Tax Journal*, Symposium on Urban Fiscal Problems, September 1976, pp. 328–35.

50. Andrew Reschovsky, "An Evaluation of Metropolitan Area Tax Base Sharing," *National Tax Journal*, March 1980, pp. 55–66. Proponents of the Minnesota plan expect it also to induce a more efficient metropolitan land use pattern by reducing inter-local competition for development. See Katharine Lyall, "Tax Base-sharing: A Fiscal Assist for More Rational Land Use Planning," *Journal of the American Institute of Planners*, March 1975, pp. 90–100. Reschovsky also addresses this issue.

51. Reschovsky, p. 65.

52. Dick Netzer, "Public Sector Investment Strategies in the Mature Metropolis," in Charles L. Leven, ed., *The Mature Metropolis* (Lexington, Mass.: D. C. Heath, Lexington Books, 1978), p. 244.

sector through federation, city-county consolidation or tax base sharing may appear to civic reformers and to students of economics and public administration, they have not yet impressed American voters sufficiently to be adopted in more than a few places. Residents of the suburbs, given a choice, have understandably resisted sharing the fiscal burdens of the central cities. Their resistance is likely to increase the more distressed those cities become. Except for those instances in which the courts have been able to intervene on constitutional grounds, changes in the structure and performance of American local government occur more readily through gradual adaptation to new conditions than through sweeping reform. A less polite way of putting it would be that we are strongly committed to a policy of "muddling through."

Policies for "Muddling Through"

In practice, response to the problem of governmental fragmentation in metropolitan areas has taken three forms in recent years: the creation of metropolitan-wide special districts for selected functions, the formation of regional planning and coordinating councils of local governments, and the increasing reliance on the states as effective regional authorities. Let us consider these responses in order.

Most special district governments are set up to perform a single function, such as water supply, transportation, fire protection, sewerage, or housing and urban renewal. A few are empowered to perform multiple functions. To finance themselves special districts are given the power to levy taxes and/or charge fees, receive grants, and incur debt. The 272 SMSA's surveyed in the 1977 Census of Governments contained no less than 9,580 such units, which averages out to 35 per SMSA and provides ample evidence that most special districts are not metropolitan area-wide jurisdictions. However, 778 were multicounty districts dealing with such large-area functions as air pollution, airports, and mass transportation.[53] A well-known example is the Port Authority of New York and New Jersey, which owns and operates bridges, tunnels, bus terminals, part of the rail transit system, and numerous port facilities as well as the major airports in the bi-state (New York–New Jersey) port region.

Along such lines, special districts can and do perform functions across entire metropolitan regions that at the level of general purpose local government are almost hopelessly fragmented. But the horizontal coordination and planning that the special district may (but does not always) achieve for a single function is bought at the price of making

53. U.S. Bureau of the Census, *1977 Census of Governments*, vol. 5, *Local Government in Metropolitan Areas*, table 2.

coordination between functions more difficult than ever in the vertical direction, of fragmenting responsibility and accountability, and of weakening citizen influence in decision-making. Special districts continue to proliferate, but they are a far from satisfactory response to the problem of metropolitan jurisdictional fragmentation.

The need for area-wide planning and policy coordination among local governments within metropolitan areas has fostered the growth of various kinds of regional planning agencies in recent years. The federal government actively encouraged this trend, first, by making many of its grants conditional upon review of programs by an area-wide body with planning responsibilities and, second, by offering grants to defray the cost of planning itself. The Advisory Commission on Intergovernmental Relations estimates that by 1975 there were about 500 area-wide review bodies in operation (an average of almost two per SMSA.)[54] While such intergovernmental planning and coordination are better than nothing at all and may, indeed, be the most we can hope for at the present time, no one would suggest that they are an adequate substitute for more thoroughgoing structural reform of metropolitan government.

The vacuum left by the inability of metropolitan areas to cope with their own problems has to some extent been filled by state governmental action. As Netzer points out, "state governments under our constitutional system have very broad powers. . . . The states are the best regional governments we have, and they may be the best we are likely to get."[55] Since the 1960s state governments have played an increasingly active role in developing transportation, housing, open space, and other programs that require large-scale planning for metropolitan regions within their boundaries. There is good reason to believe this role will continue to grow.

INTERGOVERNMENTAL GRANTS

Grants are transfers of money from higher to lower levels of government. There would be a role for such transfers in even the most rationally organized federal society. In the less than perfectly rational American federal system, grants must do the additional job of compensating for the deficiencies in fiscal organization.

It was pointed out in Chapter 14 that intergovernmental transfers are a rapidly growing source of revenue to local governments. Their growth has been accompanied by an extensive literature on the economics of intergovernmental aid, including both theoretical analyses of their

54. Advisory Commission, *Improving Urban America* . . . , p. 235.
55. Dick Netzer, *Economics and Urban Problems*, 2nd ed., (New York: Basic Books, 1974), p. 237.

TABLE 15.5
Classification of Grants

	CONDITIONAL	UNCONDITIONAL
MATCHING	Open-ended: AFDC Medicaid Non–open-ended: "Categorical grants"	None
NONMATCHING	Block Grants Community Development CETA	General Revenue Sharing

likely effects on the spending and taxing decisions of recipient governments and attempts to measure empirically what those effects have actually been.

Table 15.5 presents in matrix form a useful classification of grants according to two important characteristics. If the grantor stipulates that the funds must be used for a specific purpose, such as housing rehabilitation, sewage treatment, or public schooling, the grant is said to be "conditional." If use of the funds is not restricted, it is called "unconditional." If the recipient government is required to put up some of its own funds as a condition of obtaining the grant—whether dollar for dollar or one dollar for ten—the grant is called "matching"; if not it is "nonmatching."

Three of the four spaces in the matrix correspond to existing grant types. In the upper left the category of conditional matching grants encompasses a wide variety of actual programs. These can be further subdivided. They are open-ended if the grantor is willing to provide funds without limit as long as the recipient government wishes to match them (e.g., federal aid to the states to support the AFDC and Medicaid programs). They are *non*–open-ended if the grantor limits the amount of available aid (e.g., when Congress authorizes a limited sum to be distributed to states or localities on a matching basis to support, say, mass transit improvement). Because matching grants usually apply to carefully defined categories of activity, they are often referred to as "categorical grants." They are by far the most numerous type, including, by one count, nearly 500 separate programs at the federal level alone.[56]

In the lower left space are conditional grants for which there are no

56. George F. Break, "Intergovernmental Fiscal Relations," in Joseph A. Pechman, ed., *Setting National Priorities: Agenda for the 1980's* (Washington, D.C.: The Brookings Institution, 1980), p. 251.

matching requirements. Examples would be the federal government's Community Development Block Grants and the Comprehensive Employment and Training Act (CETA) grants already discussed in earlier chapters. These programs provide funds that must be spent within broad functional categories but without matching requirements. The lower right space contains grants to which no conditions are attached: the funds can be spent on any object and have no matching requirements. General Revenue Sharing is such a program. On the upper right is an empty space: there exists no program in which funds are granted unconditionally but subject to a matching requirement.

Effects of Grants on Fiscal Behavior

The expected effects of grants on the taxing and spending behavior of local governments can be explained with the help of Figure 15.2. This diagram shows how a community chooses the optimum combination of public and private spending, given its level of income.[57] The horizontal axis of Figure 15.2 measures dollars spent by members of the community on private goods (P), its vertical axis, dollars spent on the public good (G), which is assumed to be the only output of the local government. The curves I_1, I_2, I_3 are members of a set of "community indifference curves."[58] Points on any one curve show combinations of public and private goods that yield equal satisfaction or utility to the community as a whole. For example, on indifference curve I_1 the community considers itself as well off with the combination at E_1 as with the combination at E_4. Well-being increases with movement to indifference curves farther from the origin. Thus the community is better off at E_2 than E_1 and at E_3 than E_2.

In the absence of grants from a higher level of government, the community's income is OA dollars and its budget constraint is the line AB. It can purchase OA of public goods, or OB of private goods, or any combination of the two along AB. Since the quantities of both goods are measured in dollar units, the distance $OA = OB$ and the budget line has a 45° slope. Given the income OA, the community would choose the combination P_1 of private goods and G_1 of public goods as indicated by

57. The diagram is a modification of Figure 6.1 in Werner Z. Hirsch, *The Economics of State and Local Government* (New York: McGraw-Hill, 1970), p. 129.
58. Hirsch (see n. 57) assumes that I_1, I_2, etc., represent "the preference function of the local government" rather than that of the community. The assumption that they are community indifference curves ("subject to all their acknowledged shortcomings") follows the treatment in Wallace E. Oates, *Fiscal Federalism* (New York: Harcourt Brace Jovanovich, 1972), p. 75. Students unfamiliar with the use of indifference curves can consult any textbook on microeconomic theory—for example, Jack Hirshleifer, *Price Theory and Applications*, 2nd ed. (Englewood Cliffs, N.J.: Prentice-Hall, 1980), chs. 3 and 4.

FIGURE 15.2

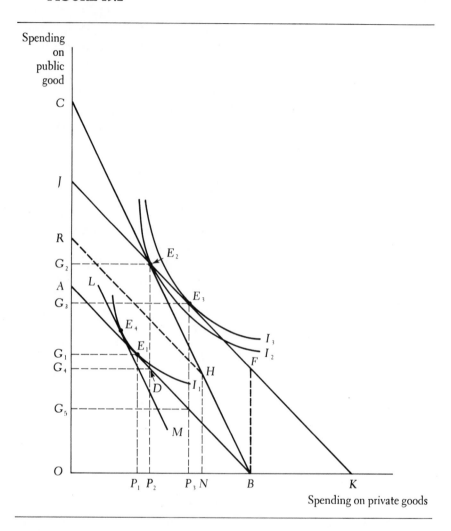

point E_1, since that point lies on the highest indifference curve attainable along budget line AB. Since E_1 is the position in the absence of outside aid, it becomes the reference point as we examine the effects of various types of grants on fiscal behavior.

Conditional Matching Grants

It was shown earlier in this chapter that when the benefit of a public service spills over local boundaries, the producing jurisdiction will generally provide less than the socially optimal quantity of the service. We can now show that an open-ended matching grant is an efficient instrument for correcting this misallocation of resources. Thus fiscal transfers can be used to overcome a problem that arises either because a function has been wrongly assigned to a lower level of government or because, within the local level, boundaries do not correspond closely to benefit areas.

As illustrated in Figure 15.1, a local government, left to its own devices, will ignore the external portion of a service benefit and produce up to the point where the internal benefit—the marginal local benefit in Figure 15.1—equals the marginal cost of production. In the presence of an externality the local government will produce the socially optimal quantity only if the cost of providing the service is reduced by means of a subsidy to the level of the marginal local benefit at the socially optimal level of output. In Figure 15.1 the optimal output is H gallons per year, and the subsidy needed to induce it would be $C - D$ dollars per unit of output.

Using Figure 15.2, we can show how an open-ended matching grant serves as the instrument for paying such a subsidy, and how it will affect fiscal behavior. Let us assume that the conditions of production and distribution of the service are such that the external benefit per unit is equal in value to the local benefit. In that case a grant that matches local expenditure on the public good dollar for dollar would cover the cost of producing the external portion of the benefit and induce the local government to produce the socially optimal quantity. Such a grant is indicated by the budget line CB in Figure 15.2. The one-for-one matching basis of the grant is indicated by the fact that from any point on AB the distance to the horizontal axis (which measures the community's contribution to paying for the public good), equals the vertical distance to CB (which measures the amount of grant support received). In the absence of a grant, the community consumes G_1 of the public good, as indicated by point E_1. The grant induces movement to E_2, on a higher indifference curve. Consumption of the public good rises to G_2, the socially optimal amount.

When indifference curves are used to analyze the behavior of individual consumers, the response to a change in price can be resolved into a substitution (or price) effect and an income effect. The same logic applies in this case. The matching grant has a substitution effect because it cuts the price of the public good, to the local community, in half. It has an income effect because the grant payment adds directly to the spendable income of the community. The substitution effect by itself induces the community to buy more of the public good and fewer private goods. The income effect by itself induces it to buy more of both goods, assuming that neither is an inferior good.

The income effect of the grant depicted by budget line CB, measured in real terms, is shown by movement of the community from indifference curve I_1 to the higher curve I_2. In order to show the pure price effect of the grant, we have to remove this income effect, while leaving intact the price change induced by the grant. We can do so by reducing the community's money income to the level indicated by budget line segment LM. Since LM is parallel to CB, it preserves the post-grant price ratio between public and private goods. Since it has a point of tangency with indifference curve I_1, it allows the community to enjoy the same real income as at E_1. Given the budget line LM, the community would choose to be at E_4. The pure price effect of the grant with no change in real income is then the movement from E_1 to E_4. The movement from E_4 to E_2 measures the pure income effect of the grant, after its price effect has been removed. The sum of the two movements is an increase in the consumption of the public good from G_1 to G_2 and of private goods from P_1 to P_2. Private goods consumption increases because the positive income effect (E_4 to E_2) more than offsets the negative substitution effect (E_1 to E_4). Since the two effects work in opposite directions for private goods, one cannot say a priori what the net outcome will be. With a different preference configuration, private goods consumption could have fallen instead of rising.

To pay for the increase in private goods consumption the local community has diverted funds that were formerly spent on the public good. In the absence of grants, the community spent OG_1 on the public good and the remainder of its income (G_1A) on private consumption. When the grant program is in effect, total spending on the public good rises to OG_2, but half of that is paid for by grant funds. As indicated by point D along budget line AB, the community now spends only OG_4 of its own funds on the public good. The difference, $G_1 - G_4$, is diverted to private consumption. Since the community's own spending on the public good is financed by local taxes, it follows that local tax payments are therefore reduced. When a grant program thus leads to a reduction in a community's own spending on public services, the effect of the grant is said to be "substitutive." When the community spends more of its own funds after receiving the grant, the effect is called "stimulative."[59]

Although the theoretical case is strong for using open-ended matching grants to subsidize the production of services that provide external benefits, they are not, in fact, widely used for that purpose. In the United States they serve a wholly different purpose—to reimburse state and local governments for a portion of their welfare and Medicaid expenditures. With

59. See George A. Bishop, "Stimulative versus Substitutive Effects of State School Aid in New England," *National Tax Journal*, June 1964, pp. 133–43.

TABLE 15.6

Federal Grants to State and Local Governments
(Fiscal years, millions of dollars)

	1972	1978	1981[c]
General revenue sharing	$ 0	$ 6,823	$ 6,857
Other general purpose grants	516	2,780	2,724
Broad-based grants[a]	2,855	11,533	9,997
Categorical grants[b]	31,001	56,753	76,735
Total	34,372	77,889	96,312
Exhibit: Economic stimulus programs	—	9,200	3,200

[a] Primarily nonmatching, within broadly defined categories.
[b] Primarily matching, with highly specific conditions.
[c] Estimated in source.
Source: Special Analyses, Budget of the United States Government, 1981,
tables H-1, H-8, H-11.

those few exceptions, the very numerous matching grant programs in the United States are closed rather than open-ended.[60] If they are intended to stimulate spending on particular services, the fact that they are not open-ended deprives them of much of their stimulative power. To illustrate, suppose that the matching grant depicted by budget line *BC* were subject to the limitation that aid activity cannot total more than *HN* per year in any locality. In that case, the post-grant budget line becomes *BHR*. To the left of the kink at *H*, matching ceases, and the grant no longer provides the stimulus of a substitution effect favorable to the consumption of the public good. Instead, it takes on the attributes of the conditional nonmatching grants to be discussed below.

The Debate over Categorical Grants

Table 15.6 shows federal outlays for grants to state and local governments, classified by type of grant. The fourth row, "Categorical grants," corresponds approximately to the class of matching, conditional grants discussed here. These now provide nearly $77 billion a year to state and local governments, or almost four-fifths of the $96 billion total. Even if we subtract Medicaid and public assistance grants, which are essentially reimbursement for welfare expenditures rather than typical categorical grant programs, we are left with more than $53 billion of other categorical aid.

60. For a description of the various formulas used in connection with matching grants, see Break, in Pechman, pp. 251–56.

In the Congress, political support for categorical grants is likely to be strong, since each program creates a set of highly involved beneficiaries, including its administrators, who exert pressure on its behalf. The proliferation of matching, conditional grants has been much debated since the 1960s. Advocates of this form of aid believe that the federal government has both a duty and a right to set national standards for the use of funds it supplies. They incline to the view that the federal government has promoted socially useful innovation more often than the state and local governments and contend that it is less subject to either outright corruption or manipulation by special interests. Consequently they believe that a considerable degree of federal oversight of grant programs is desirable.

Critics, on the other hand, have long claimed that categorical grants, each with its own narrowly defined objectives, its detailed federal performance standards, and its own matching formula, waste time and money at all levels of government by generating an almost impenetrable web of red tape. To meet this line of criticism a system of "block grants" has been gradually developed since the late 1960s. Within major functional areas such as community development, health, employment and training, social services, and criminal justice, grant programs have been combined, matching provisions dropped, requirements simplified, and objectives broadened. The federal government thus retains the power of directing its funds toward nationally defined and ordered objectives while leaving more responsibility in the detailed choice of means to state and local officials. The economics of these "conditional, nonmatching grants" will be taken up below. Their dollar value is indicated in Table 15.6, line 3.

Unconditional, Nonmatching Grants

As we have seen, open-ended matching grants derive much of their power to influence the behavior of recipient governments from the fact that they have a substitution as well as an income effect. The substitution effect is produced by the matching provision, which lowers the price of the subsidized activity relative to all other goods. As Oates aptly puts it, this alters "the terms of choice" facing the community and thus stimulates consumption of the subsidized good.[61]

Unconditional, nonmatching grants, such as those provided by General Revenue Sharing, stand in complete contrast to this. They are virtually free gifts of income, which the community can spend as it wishes. The "terms of choice" are not altered by the grant. The contrast between the two types is illustrated in Figure 15.2. The matching conditional grant

61. Oates, p. 77.

moved the community from E_1 to E_2. The amount of aid received at E_2 is $E_2 - D$ $(= K - B)$. If the higher level of government were to offer the same amount of aid in the form of an unconditional, nonmatching grant, the post-grant budget line would be JK. Since this line passes through E_2, we know that it offers aid equal in amount to the matching grant; since it is parallel to AB, we know that it augments the community's income by that amount no matter how the community arranges its spending.

Offered such a grant, the community would choose the combination of goods indicated by E_3, since that point lies on the highest attainable indifference curve. Since E_3 is on a higher curve than E_2, we see that the community is better off with an unrestricted grant than with a matching conditional grant yielding the same revenue. The reason, of course, is that the latter does not allow the community to select the combination of goods it would most prefer, given a free choice. This "distortion" of behavior, while not in the interest of the community itself, is the price that is paid to achieve the particular national objective implied in the conditional grant.

At E_3 the community buys more of both the public good and private goods than it would at E_1 (the "no-grant" position). However, payment for the public good out of its own resources drops from G_1 to G_5, and those funds are devoted to increasing private consumption from P_1 to P_3. Thus total spending for the public good rises by less than the amount of the grant. In this case, unlike the matching conditional grant, there is no substitution effect to introduce ambiguity about the effect on private consumption. Unambiguously, local private consumption rises, and local tax payments fall.

General Revenue Sharing

General Revenue Sharing, a system of unconditional, nonmatching federal grants to state and local governments, has been in effect since 1972. The concept was first developed by Walter W. Heller and Joseph A. Pechman in the mid-1960s as a way of using expected surplus federal tax revenues to relieve financial pressure on state and local units.[62] When the war in Vietnam eliminated the expected federal surplus, the proposal was temporarily shelved. It was revived later in a somewhat different form by President Nixon, under the title of "General Revenue Sharing." The State and Local Fiscal Assistance Act of 1972 authorized $30.6 billion of federal funds for General Revenue Sharing to be paid out in a series of five yearly installments. Thus the Act provided an average of just over

62. See citation in n. 37 above.

$6 billion per year in grant money to the states and localities, a significant increase in the level of assistance being provided at that time (see Table 15.6).

Funds allotted to General Revenue Sharing are granted to the states, and through them to all "general purpose" local governments. School districts and other special districts are thus not eligible for any part of the funds. The calculation of allotments has been summarized as follows:

> General Revenue Sharing funds are distributed among States on the basis of one of two formulas. The "three-factor" formula distributes the funds on the basis of population, tax effort, and per capita income. The "five-factor" formula includes two additional factors, urbanized population and State income tax collections. Each State amount is determined by the formula that maximizes its share. If the total of the shares is greater than the available authorization, all shares are reduced proportionally.
>
> Within the State one-third of all funds go to the State government, two-thirds to local governments. Distribution among local governments is based on the three-factor formula.[63]

It is an important feature of revenue sharing that it redistributes income from rich states to poor. In part this results from the fact that allotments are weighted inversely to per capita state income. But some redistribution would occur even if each state's share were strictly in proportion to population, with no special adjustment for income levels, since poor states contribute a much smaller amount per capita to federal tax revenues than do rich ones. However, the redistributive effect of revenue sharing at the local level is weakened by two limitations built into the allocation rules: first, every locality is guaranteed at least 20 percent of the average per capita distribution made to localities within its state, and, second, none may receive more than 145 percent of the average.

As originally conceived by Heller and Pechman, revenue sharing allotments were to have "no strings attached," a system of completely unconditional grants. The Congress did, however, attach a few strings in the Act of 1972. Predictably, these proved ineffective, owing to the fungibility of broad-based grants. If revenue sharing funds were applied to an approved purpose, then monies that otherwise would have gone for that purpose could be used for another that was not eligible for support. When the program was renewed in 1976, restrictions on use were dropped.

At the time of its adoption, General Revenue Sharing appealed to its proponents for a wide variety of reasons. As we indicated earlier, many

---

63. Office of Management and Budget, *The United States Budget in Brief, Fiscal Year 1974,* p. 55. A detailed explanation of General Revenue Sharing formulas and procedures can be found in U.S. Department of the Treasury, Office of Revenue Sharing, *What General Revenue Sharing Is All About,* undated.

supported it because it was regarded as a solution to the related problems of fiscal drag and fiscal imbalance. Although these problems faded rapidly in the 1970s, they were still under lively discussion in 1972. Revenue sharing was also endorsed as a way of protecting the progressivity of the U.S. tax system by substituting federal revenues, produced by a progressive income tax, for state and local funds that were apt to be raised by proportional or regressive taxes. Heller had always maintained that revenue sharing would stimulate state and local initiative and expertise by substituting unconditional aid for the highly restricted categorical grants that accounted for the bulk of federal assistance. This argument took on added weight by 1972 because of the proliferation of categorical grants enacted to support President Johnson's Great Society programs of the 1960s. Finally, many endorsed revenue sharing because they believed it was an effective way to redistribute funds from relatively rich to relatively poor states and regions.

Redistributive Effects

Certainly, from the perspective of the theory of public finance, redistribution is the principal justification for revenue sharing. In a multilevel system of government, no matter how rational the assignment of functions and arrangement of boundaries, there will still be geographic disparities in the distribution of taxable resources among communities. As we have shown earlier, citizens in poor jurisdictions will have to pay higher tax rates to finance a standard bundle of public services than citizens in a well-to-do locality. To many observers this will appear inequitable. On grounds of equity they might wish, as Oates puts it, "to ensure that every individual has access to a sound program of public works within his chosen locality at a cost in line with what he would pay elsewhere."[64] If that is the objective, then unconditional, nonmatching grants are the logical instrument to employ. In principle, then, revenue sharing provides a way of overcoming the geographic disparities in fiscal resources that we have cited as one of the major problems of the metropolitan public sector. (One must not assume, however, that redistribution from rich to poor localities is equivalent to redistribution from rich to poor individuals. Since wealthy communities usually contain some poor people and poor communities some who are rich, it is likely that an intergovernmental grant program that transfers income between areas will benefit some people who are rich at the expense of some who are poor.)[65]

In practice, General Revenue Sharing has, indeed, been redistribu-

64. Oates, p. 88.
65. See discussion in ibid., pp. 78–81.

tive, but on a very modest scale. Since this gift fund is not large by national standards and the rules of the game insure that every participant takes home a prize, that outcome should not be unexpected. In an ongoing study of the impact of revenue sharing, analysts at The Brookings Institution found the following pattern in the first round of payments.

Grants to states averaged $26 per capita and ranged from a high of $40 in Mississippi (lowest per capita income among the 50 states) to a low of $20 in Ohio (14th from the top in per capita income).[66] Not much redistribution there! However, the effect becomes much stronger if the distribution of benefits is compared with the presumed distribution of the cost of paying for the program. Subtracting each state's costs from its benefits yields an estimate of the net benefit (or loss) to each. One way of distributing the cost of the program among states is to assume that, in the absence of revenue sharing, each state's contribution to federal revenues could be proportionately reduced. These forgone reductions then constitute the presumed cost of revenue sharing to each state. When net benefits are estimated in this way there are losers as well as gainers and therefore a stronger redistributive effect. For example, Brookings found that Mississippi had the highest net gain, amounting to almost $26 per capita, while Connecticut registered the largest net loss, more than $17 per person.[67] The largest net gains tended to go to relatively poor states. The largest losers, however, were not necessarily the richest states, since some of those benefited by the fact that they ranked high on tax effort or degree of urbanization.

Revenue sharing grants to localities were also modestly redistributive. For example, per capita allocations to the 25 largest U.S. cities in 1972 averaged about twice the size of those to their suburbs, so the program does work to reduce central city–suburban fiscal disparities. However, the average amount received by these cities was only $23 per person, so the redistribution effect was small.[68] Within the 25-city group, the revenue sharing formula is somewhat more generous to the older, declining cities where fiscal stress has been greatest. A number of the older cities would have gained substantially more—St. Louis 78 percent more, Baltimore 51 percent, Philadelphia 47 percent—were it not for the limitation that no locality may receive more than 145 percent of the average local allotment within its state.[69]

66. Richard P. Nathan, Allen D. Manvel, and Susannah E. Calkins, *Monitoring Revenue Sharing* (Washington, D.C.: The Brookings Institution, 1974), table 4.1.

67. Ibid., table 4.2.

68. Ibid., table 5.3. Data are for allocations only, not for the net amount of allocations less estimated tax contributions. Allocations to overlying county governments, where such exist, were pro-rated to the city on the basis of population.

69. See analysis of the impact of the revenue sharing formula for cities in Peterson, pp. 87–88 and table 15.

Effects on Tax Effort

What effect has revenue sharing had on expenditure levels and tax effort in the receiving jurisdictions? According to the theory developed above (Figure 15.2), nonmatching, unconditional grants should be expected to finance less than a dollar-for-dollar increase in total spending by the recipient jurisdiction. Grant funds would be expected to substitute in part for public expenditure previously paid for out of a locality's own pocket. This, in turn, would allow local taxes to be reduced. Indeed, one of the purposes of General Revenue Sharing was to allow hard-pressed jurisdictions some tax relief, if that was the alternative they preferred.

Follow-up studies indicate that revenue sharing did, in fact, lead to tax reduction, but not to very much of it. Analysts at The Brookings Institution estimated the effects of revenue sharing on fiscal behavior by closely observing a sample of 65 jurisdictions, including eight states, 56 localities, and one Indian tribe. They found that localities, on the average, used about 50 percent of their first two revenue sharing allotments for various forms of new spending. An average of only 4.4 percent of allotments went for tax reduction. In addition, however, localities on average used 15.3 percent of their allotments to forestall tax increases that would otherwise have occurred. If these estimates are accurate, a total of about one-fifth of local allotments was substituted for tax effort.[70]

Economists have found these results puzzling. According to the standard theory presented above, nonmatching grants have only an income effect. The impact on local government spending should be the same as that of an ordinary change in private income. The marginal propensity to spend out of income on local public goods has been estimated at about 10 percent. Yet the evidence is that a dollar of unmatched aid raises local spending by something between 40 and 50 percent. A general explanation would be that "bureaucrats and politicians find it easier to avoid cutting taxes when the government receives revenue sharing monies than they do to raise taxes when some exogenous event raises the income of the community." Attempts are underway to modify the formal theory of grants so that it can account for these results.[71]

---

70. See Richard P. Nathan, et al., *Revenue Sharing: The Second Round* (Washington, D.C.: The Brookings Institution, 1977), table 2.1.

71. See papers in Peter Mieszkowski and William H. Oakland, eds., *Fiscal Federalism and Grants-in-Aid*, vol. 1 (Washington, D.C.: The Urban Institute, 1979). The quotation is from Paul N. Courant, Edward M. Gramlich, and Daniel L. Rubinfeld, "The Stimulative Effects of Intergovernmental Grants: or Why Money Sticks Where It Hits," ibid., p. 6.

Outlook for General Revenue Sharing

Political support for General Revenue Sharing grew weaker during the 1970s. Many interest groups came to believe that their particular concerns would be better served by old-fashioned categorical aid programs than by unconditional grants. In 1976 Congress extended General Revenue Sharing to the end of fiscal year 1980, providing payments at the rate of $6.85 billion a year, but inflation was now seriously eroding the program's real buying power. With Congress reflecting the national mood of fiscal restraint, renewal was only narrowly achieved in 1980. The program was extended through 1983, providing grants to localities at the rate of $4.6 billion per year. States, however, were made subject to new limitations: grants of $2.3 billion a year were authorized for 1982 and 1983, but only on condition that states give up an equivalent amount of categorical aid. Although the revenue sharing program had been conceived as a long-term commitment on which state and local governments could rely, its prospects for survival are now uncertain.

Conditional, Nonmatching Aid: Block Grants

In a sense, conditional, nonmatching grants stand halfway between the first two types we have discussed. They resemble categorical grants in stipulating what purposes the funds can be used for, but they resemble General Revenue Sharing in having no matching provisions.

Again, Figure 15.2 can illustrate the case. Suppose that the higher level of government wishes to encourage the production of the public good G, but without requiring that the recipient government match its contributions. Assume that the subsidy is to be equal in amount to the revenue sharing grant of BK ($= FB$) analyzed above. Since the grant "must" be spent on the public good, the post-grant budget line of the community becomes BFJ. The highest indifference curve that is attainable along this budget line is again I_3 at point E_3. But that is the same point that was chosen under revenue sharing. The conditional, nonmatching grant has precisely the same effect on local fiscal behavior as the unconditional grant had. The reason is this: as long as the community would *voluntarily* spend at least BF on the subsidized good out of its post-grant income, the formal *requirement* that it do so is without effect. This is obviously the case in Figure 15.2. In the region of E_3 the community freely chooses to spend far more on the public good than the amount BF. In practice, the fact that the grant is awarded for expenditure on G is defeated by the fungibility of money. In a budgetary context, no one can tell when a particular dollar of income is being spent on a particular object. Upon receiving the grant of BF, the community reduces its own contribution toward the purchase of the public good from G_1 to G_5 and diverts the difference to private spending. Yet the community *does* spend at least BF on the required object. Fungibility does the rest.

As we pointed out above, "block grants," a form of nonmatching conditional aid, have been introduced in recent years as a way of consolidating selected categorical grant programs into a simpler, more flexible system. However, if fungibility renders ineffective the requirement that block grants be spent on a particular activity, it remains to be explained why anyone should want to retain the pretense of a requirement. Why not go all the way to a system of unconditional aid instead of stopping at this halfway point? In part the answer is political. First, as Break points out, "grantors . . . may find it politically easier to justify appropriations of money presumably directed toward specific problems than those offered on an unrestricted basis."[72] Second, each block grant is distributed by means of a legislated formula that determines how much of the available fund goes to each state or locality. Participants in the political process readily become enthusiastic about a block grant program if its allocation formula is notably generous to their constituents. For these reasons, an economist might endorse conditional nonmatching grants as a practical way of achieving the fiscal objectives that pure theory ascribes to General Revenue Sharing. Finally, there is a minimum standards argument: block grants do insure that recipients spend at least the amount of the grant on a specific objective of national policy. For this last reason they might have a place in even the most rationally organized federal system.

Growth of Federal Aid to Cities

One of the striking developments of the last twenty years has been the rapid growth of direct federal aid to localities.[73] (See Tables 14.4 and 14.5.) The question of how this aid has been distributed deserves a closer look. Grants can be allotted to communities either by means of a formula or on a project-by-project basis.[74] We have already described the formula by which General Revenue Sharing allotments are determined. Formulas are also used to determine local shares of block grants, with the elements in the formula chosen to reflect the local incidence of the conditions the grant is intended to ameliorate. For example, the distribution of employment and training grants is related to the local unemployment rate. Many

72. Break, p. 258.
73. In addition to the references below, see the papers in Hubbell, ed., cited in n. 43, above.
74. See discussion in Break, pp. 251–69.

categorical grants, on the other hand, are distributed on a project-by-project basis, since there is often no way of designing a formula that will identify a set of eligible recipients for a narrowly focused program.

Trends in the distribution of federal aid to cities can be described in terms of two opposite tendencies: "targeting" and "spreading." In the jargon of public policy analysis, funds are "targeted" when their delivery is focused on population groups identified as having a particular problem. From the point of view of a policymaker trying to solve social problems, targeting is efficient since it means that each dollar of aid will have the largest possible effect. Spreading of grants, on the other hand, means that they are going to a larger proportion of localities; their distribution is becoming less concentrated.

During the 1960s federal aid, consisting almost entirely of categorical grants associated with President Johnson's urban-oriented Great Society Program, tended to be highly concentrated in the larger cities. In 1968 cities above 500,000 in population received 62.2 percent of direct federal-local aid, while cities below 100,000 received only 20.3 percent. By 1976 the share of the former had fallen to 44.4 percent, while that of the latter had risen to 30.3 percent.[75] This marked spreading of aid can be explained by the advent of General Revenue Sharing, under which thousands of local governments that had not previously received federal aid automatically began to do so, and by the growing importance of "broad-based" block grants, also widely distributed on a formula basis.

Of course, formulas can be devised that make for targeting rather than spreading. Important examples occurred during the severe recession that began in 1974–75. To combat unemployment the federal government adopted an Economic Stimulus Package consisting of Anti-Recession Fiscal Assistance, a Local Public Works program, and a program of Temporary Employment Assistance (under CETA). The first of these was a form of unconditional aid, while the last two were broad-based, conditional grant programs. As Table 15.6 indicates, their aggregate value was large, amounting to $9.2 billion in the peak year of 1978. The formulas for these programs targeted the funds effectively on cities with high levels of unemployment. Since these were also likely to be cities suffering fiscal distress, the Economic Stimulus programs are credited with an important role in preserving the fiscal health of the older central cities during the recession. Most elements in the program, however, expired automatically when the recession ended.

What impact has the sharp increase in aid to cities had? In the

75. Richard P. Nathan, "The Outlook for Federal Grants to Cities," in Roy Bahl, ed., *The Fiscal Outlook for Cities* (Syracuse, N.Y.: Syracuse University Press, 1978), p. 80.

earlier discussion of fiscal disparities (see Table 15.2) it was pointed out that aid has risen much faster for central cities than for suburban areas, but that the cities nevertheless continue to tax their citizens at a considerably higher rate in relation to income. One reason is that the twin problems of a rising poverty rate and a declining economic base grow worse even while budgetary aid is increasing. As a result, many of the older, declining cities remain under tremendous fiscal pressure despite the sharp increase in outside assistance.

By 1978, when the Economic Stimulus programs were at their peak, some of the older cities had become alarmingly dependent on federal aid. One study of a sample of cities took as a measure of dependence the ratio of direct federal aid to general revenue (taxes and fees) from each city's own sources. The ratio ranged as high as .69 to .70 in Buffalo, Detroit, and Cleveland, meaning that those cities were receiving about 69¢ in federal aid for every dollar raised locally.[76]

The extent to which federal aid will continue to be targeted on distressed cities obviously depends upon political factors. Each time a grant program incorporating distribution by formula comes up for renewal in the Congress a battle ensues over the terms of the formula, since that determines who ultimately gets the money. Population decline is steadily eroding the congressional representation of the older urban areas. As Robert Reischauer points out, distressed cities came out well under the countercyclical aid programs of the mid-1970s largely because the federal government had chosen them as the agents through which it would supply fiscal stimulation. Political support for targeted aid will be more difficult to marshal when the issue is relief for distressed cities rather than recovery from a nationwide recession.[77] In the usual case, the price of political support for a new aid program is a formula that spreads benefits well beyond the neediest cases. It is probably unrealistic to expect both targeting and long-run growth in federal aid.

WHAT CITIES CAN DO FOR THEMSELVES: IMPROVING ECONOMIC AND FISCAL PERFORMANCE

In this chapter we have described the causes of urban fiscal distress and examined three kinds of policies that could help to mitigate it: transfering functional responsibilities to higher levels of government, reorganizing the structure of the metropolitan public sector, and providing

76. Ibid., p. 77.
77. Robert Reischauer, "The Economy, the Federal Budget, and the Prospects for Urban Aid," in Bahl, ed., pp. 98, 108–10.

grants-in-aid. We come now to a fourth category, the things that cities can do for themselves to improve their economic and fiscal performance.

A Strategy of Private Development and Public Frugality

There is not much disagreement among economists about the appropriate strategy for cities in fiscal distress. Most would agree on two policies. First, fiscally distressed cities must work hard to slow or reverse the economic decline made evident in their loss of jobs. Second, they must not only hold down or reduce real aggregate spending but also manage the programs they *do* undertake more efficiently. (In discussing aggregate spending, the effect of general inflation must be borne in mind. The real value of expenditures will be falling as long as their money value does not rise as fast as the general price level.)

To hold onto their job base, declining cities must make themselves more attractive as places to do business. In the context of budget-making, that means choosing tax and expenditure policies with an eye to their effect on the business sector. Policies that hold or attract jobs will, in turn, generate tax revenue that can help to relieve fiscal distress. (Needless to say, they will also generate much-needed private income.)

A policy of budget restraint is obviously necessary in cities under fiscal stress simply to balance the current budget. In addition, it would be expected to help make the city more attractive as a business location, since lower expenditures allow lower tax rates.[78] Because the property tax is the residual balancer of the local budget, spending cuts translate into lower property tax rates, which, as was explained in Chapter 14, would be expected to stimulate local business investment (or at least discourage *dis*investment).

Some expenditures, however, provide benefits of direct interest to business: police, fire, transit, street and highway outlays, to name only the most obvious. Consequently, the reduction of spending does risk taking away benefits to business the loss of which would at least partially offset the gain from lower tax rates. This risk can be reduced to the extent that budget cuts are biased in the direction of human services rather than services of direct interest to business, but such a policy would be greatly to the disadvantage of the urban poor. Even budget cuts that affect all services equally will disproportionately hurt the low income population, since local budgets are redistributive in nature. As Table 15.3 demon-

78. Empirical studies, however, do not show conclusively that differences in tax rates affect industrial location decisions. See William H. Oakland, "Local Taxes and Intraurban Industrial Location: A Survey," in George F. Break, ed., *Metropolitan Financing and Growth Management Policies* (Madison, Wisc.: University of Wisconsin Press, 1978), pp. 13–30.

strated, the poor on average make net gains from the local budget, since they receive back more in expenditure benefits than they pay in taxes. General expenditure reductions work to their disadvantage by reducing the absolute size of the net gain.

Thus fiscally distressed cities are truly on the horns of a dilemma. Redistribution through city budgets cannot be maintained at its present level without risking insolvency. Yet society has been unable to agree on an alternative way of providing local services for the poor. The list of rejected alternatives need not be repeated here. In the recent past increased federal aid rescued most cities from the necessity of deep expenditure cuts. If such aid is cut back, or even levels off, while the situation of the cities continues to deteriorate, they will have no choice but to steadily reduce the output of public service, with all that implies for welfare, especially of their low income populations.

To this proposition the reader may quite properly respond that there is more than one way to reduce expenditures and that some may be less painful than others. We have already pointed out that central cities during the 1960s and early 1970s were to some extent acting as "suppliers of jobs." That implies a component of waste in city budgets. More than one politician has been elected on the promise of cutting out only the waste. We turn next to the question of "economizing."

Economizing

Arranged systematically, the possible methods of budget-cutting are these:[79]

Reduce the output of government services
    across the board
    selectively
Reduce the unit cost of output
    by reducing wages
    by increasing productivity

Let us examine these possibilities in turn.

When budget cuts are to be achieved by reducing the quantity of service offered, the question to be answered is whether the cuts be selective or across-the-board. Cutting across the board by a uniform fraction implies that all programs are equally beneficial at the margin. This is a proposition economists and public policy analysts find highly implausible. They would argue, instead, for selective or differential cuts that go deepest into pro-

---

79. The term "reduce" should be understood to mean "reduce or restrain increase in."

grams offering the lowest marginal benefits. An optimum set of selective cuts could be worked out, for example, through "zero base budgeting," a technique in which every program is systematically reviewed under the possibility of being cut back even to zero.[80]

Political realities, however, do not usually allow mayors to be very selective about reductions in spending. Every program has its constituency and, very likely, its organized body of municipal workers who resist energetically the prospect of becoming unemployed. Budget-cutting is never easy, but a plan to cut all departments or programs by about the same fraction, on the principle of sharing the misery, is likely to meet the least resistance. Consequently, the urban fiscal crisis has not been seized upon as an opportunity to rationalize the local public sector by selective pruning.

From the viewpoint of the public it is obviously preferable to economize by reducing the unit cost of public output rather than by simple budget-trimming, since lower unit cost allows expenditures to be reduced without cutting the level of public service. Unit cost can be lowered either by reducing wages or by increasing productivity, as measured by output per worker. The wage factor in local budget costs was analyzed in Chapter 14. From 1965 through 1974 public employee earnings rose much faster than either earnings in manufacturing or the cost of living. (See Table 14.3.) However, these relationships reversed after the onset of the urban fiscal crisis. From 1974 through 1979 municipal wages rose less than either private sector wages or the cost of living. Thus "real" public sector wages have, indeed, been reduced. Municipal employee unions have become less militant since their position was weakened first by the fiscal crisis and shortly afterward by the success of the tax limitation movement. Nevertheless, it is unrealistic to expect that they will continue to accept real wage cuts as deep as those registered after 1974. Hope for lower unit cost of public services therefore depends upon increasing the level of productivity in local government.

Improving Productivity in Local Government

As the size of the local sector has grown, so has interest in stimulating output per worker.[81] Most observers do not give municipal government high marks for productivity. Admittedly, aggregate comparisons between the public and private sectors of the economy may be unfair. Much of the

80. See David W. Singleton, Bruce A. Smith, and James R. Cleaveland, "Zero-Based Budgeting in Wilmington, Delaware," reprinted in Charles H. Levine, ed., *Managing Fiscal Stress* (Chatham, N.J.: Chatham House, 1980), pp. 179–93.

81. In addition to works cited below, see Harry P. Hatry, "Current State of the Art of State and Local Government Productivity Improvement . . ." in ibid., pp. 269–80; and Willis D. Hawley and David Rogers, eds., *Improving the Quality of Urban Management* (Beverly Hills, Calif.: Sage, 1974).

increase in output per worker in private industry is attributable to mechanization—the application of capital intensive methods of production. Some of the services for which local government is responsible—schooling, for example—are not easily mechanized, which accounts in part for the lack of productivity increase. Not all public sector functions are unique, however. A good many are also performed by the private sector—refuse collection, street paving, and bus transit, for example. In such cases it is possible to develop meaningful comparisons that provide a test of the relative efficiency of public production. Here are two examples.

Comparisons of public and private refuse collection in the United States have found costs to be lowest when a city contracts with a private supplier and highest when households deal with suppliers individually. Service by a municipal agency falls between the two, costing 15 to 25 percent more than collection under private contract, and this despite the fact that contractors' costs include excise and property taxes that municipal departments do not pay.[82]

A consulting firm hired by the City of Winnipeg, Manitoba, determined that private contractors' costs for constructing roads, sewers, and water mains were 14 to 35 percent less than the costs reported by the City's own public works force. On this basis, the consultants recommended that Winnipeg switch to private contracting for many of its construction requirements.[83]

It is not suggested that private provision of services is always less expensive. Studies have turned up contrary cases, as well. In addition, contracting brings its own set of problems, for example a potential for corruption and a need for regular monitoring of performance by a public agency. The Urban Institute concludes that because too little research has been done to date, the record so far is "essentially inconclusive."[84] At the very least, however, municipal governments should periodically compare their costs with the yardstick provided by the private sector to see where and how they could improve their own performance.

Attempts to increase productivity in municipal operations typically meet with resistance from workers and sometimes from their supervisors. In recent years a number of cities have experimented with monetary incentives as a way of overcoming such resistance. For example, in Flint, Michigan, the city agreed to share with its waste collection workers half

82. See E. S. Savas, "Policy Analysis for Local Government: Public vs. Private Refuse Collection," reprinted in Levine, ed., pp. 293–98; and Peter Kemper and John M. Quigley, *The Economics of Refuse Collection* (Cambridge, Mass.: Ballinger, 1976), ch. 6.

83. Donald Fisk, Herbert Kiesling, and Thomas Muller, *Private Provision of Public Services* (Washington, D.C.: Urban Institute, May 1978), pp. 29–30.

84. Ibid., p. 100.

532	*Urban Economics and Public Policy*

the savings that could be attributed to reduced overtime and improved productivity.[85] Studying this and two other monetary incentive programs, economists at The Urban Institute found that in each case "there were significant improvements in productivity . . . clearly attributable to the program." On the other hand, in two productivity experiments in which employees did not share in the benefits, "productivity improvements that could be attributed to the program were small, if any."[86] Despite the successes, however, monetary incentive plans are not likely to be widely adopted, in part because of opposition by union leaders who are traditionally suspicious of management "speed-ups."

Given the tremendous inertia of established institutions, it is not easy to be optimistic about the prospects for improving productivity in local government. Indeed, Netzer concludes that it is fruitless to urge upon local governments the application of "modern management methods." Instead, he argues for economizing by "stripping away functions and activities of marginal value, leaving them to private entrepreneurial initiatives or leaving them entirely undone."[87] Even that prescription, however, requires a radical shift away from the convention of economizing "across-the-board."

It may be that changing public attitudes will gradually force an improvement in municipal government performance. The rapid growth of intergovernmental aid during the 1960s and early 1970s led to a certain weakening of moral fiber at the lower levels of government. The more such aid became an accepted fact of life, the more local public officials were tempted to attribute all their troubles to its inadequacy. Blaming Washington or the state capital for insufficient aid became the all-purpose response to criticism. Urban voters tended to accept the explanation and failed to hold local officials responsible for keeping their own house in order. Now public sentiment has changed. As the movement to limit state and local taxes and expenditures indicates, voters have grown wary of solutions that require spending more money. This mood of restraint creates budgetary problems for distressed cities by limiting the availability of intergovernmental aid. In the long run perhaps it will also cause citizens to demand more efficient performance by local government and encourage public officials to risk trying to give it to them.[88]

85. John M. Greiner, et al., *Monetary Incentives and Work Standards in Five Cities* (Washington, D.C.: The Urban Institute, 1977), pp. 6, 47–52.
86. Ibid., p. 75.
87. Netzer, in Leven, ed., p. 249.
88. See Barry N. Siegel, *Thoughts on the Tax Revolt*, Original Paper 21 (Los Angeles: International Institute for Economic Research, 1979), pp. 11–14.

Postscript: The Future of Central Cities

SIXTEEN

Few things are more hazardous to predict than the future pattern of metropolitan settlement. The "City of the Future"—when we arrive at it—rarely resembles the drawings of the visionary artist or designer of an earlier age, and the projections of economists and sociologists are not likely to be much more reliable. Yet the developmental approach taken throughout this book, which has consistently focused attention on the process and direction of change, naturally raises the question of where current trends are carrying us.

OUTLOOK FOR THE OLDER CITIES

Discussion in earlier chapters emphasized the contrast between the central cities of the South and West and those of the North and East. The former are, for the most part, relatively young and prosperous. They are located in regions of rapid economic and population growth, which provides great buoyancy to their economies, even when their own populations are no longer increasing. In the near term at least, their continued prosperity is scarcely in doubt. It is in the older cities of the North and East, located in regions suffering relative economic decline, that one finds substantial population and job loss, housing abandonment, neighborhood deterioration and fiscal distress sometimes bordering on insolvency. No observer of these cities can escape some anxiety about their economic future. Their interrelated problems were amply documented in earlier chapters. What remains to be assessed is their future prospect. Are they likely to continue downward along their recent path, or do they have real prospects for achieving stability or even revival?

Heretofore we have stressed the self-reinforcing nature of central city decline. Several self-reinforcing processes were described in earlier chapters. First, the outward movement of the middle class and their replacement by the (until recently) in-migrating poor contributed to a cycle of deterioration that is linked to the spatially fragmented structure of metropolitan government. Middle class families leave the city in part to avoid paying taxes to support governmental services for its low income residents. But their exit further reduces the tax base, rendering the central city still more unpalatable for the well-to-do who remain behind. At the same time, the rising tax rates that accompany this process make the city less attractive as a business location, hasten the decline in jobs and economic activity, and thus further aggravate the city's fiscal situation. Second, it was pointed out in the preceding chapter that declining population may cause the unit cost of local public services to increase. This increase, in turn, would be expected to encourage further population and job loss in a self-reinforcing cycle. Third, population and job loss can lead to an additional self-reinforcing process of decline by reducing the positive economies of agglomeration offered by a city. Economies of agglomeration in the form of specialized services of production and consumption accrue as a city grows, attracting further growth. They are likely to diminish as it shrinks, encouraging further decline.[1]

That is not the end of the story, however. In general, economists expect processes of change in a market economy to generate counterforces that prevent either explosive growth or continuous decline and move the system, instead, toward a new equilibrium. It is certainly possible that such forces, operating naturally within the market system, could eventually halt the deterioration of the older central cities. The equilibrating factor in this case would probably be a relative decline in central city costs. As population and business activity fall off we would expect the prices (or rents) of housing, commercial and industrial space, and land all to decline relative to their levels elsewhere, including the surrounding suburbs. A reduction in relative costs would, in turn, make the city more competitive with other locations, thus slowing down its rate of decline. For example, it is probable that the low price of old inner city housing relative to accommodation in the suburbs was an important factor in initiating the

1. Concerning self-reinforcing versus self-correcting processes, see Katharine L. Bradbury, Anthony Downs, and Kenneth A. Small, "Some Dynamics of Central City–Suburban Interactions," *American Economic Review*, May 1980, pp. 410–14; Daniel Garnick and Vernon Renshaw, "Competing Hypotheses on the Outlook for Cities and Regions," *Papers* of the Regional Science Association, vol. 45, 1980, pp. 105–24; and John W. Pickering and Harold Bunce, "The Dynamics of Urban Distress," ch. 4 in U.S. Department of Housing and Urban Development, *Occasional Papers in Housing and Community Affairs*, vol. 4, July 1979, esp. pp. 86–88.

wave of housing renovation that improved many old inner city neighborhoods in the 1970s. (We return to the topic of housing renovation below.)

In theory, cost reduction in declining cities could eventually bring decline to a halt. There is no certainty of that, however. Conceivably, the cumulative forces making for decline could continue to overwhelm the effect of any offsetting reductions in local costs. In any case, cost reductions of the sort discussed here would at best bring stability at a reduced level of population and employment. They could not be expected to spark a recovery of growth, for if growth resumed, other things remaining the same, costs would again begin to rise.

Of course, other things need not remain the same. Fundamental economic forces may change in a way that is favorable to the prosperity of the inner city. Two major developments that have frequently been discussed in this connection are 1) the substantial rise in energy costs since the early 1970s; and 2) the radical shift in American life style reflected in demographic changes such as falling marriage and birth rates and the increased labor force participation of women.

The probable effect of rising fuel costs on the pattern of metropolitan settlement was discussed at the end of Chapter 9. We concluded, rather tentatively to be sure, that higher fuel prices may slow down "exurban" sprawl and encourage a denser pattern of suburban development but are unlikely to bring about a recentralization of population into the inner cities. On that question, no more need be said here. The possible effect of demographic change on urban structure, however, deserves a closer look.

Demographic Change and the Future of the Inner City

Alonso has coined the term "population factor" to describe the way people "arrange and rearrange themselves into families and households . . . their participation in the labor force, how they run their households and how they raise their children, if they have them."[2] Following World War II, the population factor strongly reinforced the growth of the suburbs. The postwar baby boom gave rise to a child-centered, family-oriented life style that for two decades became the American norm. Almost everyone got married and had children, and young families with kids to raise and send to school were strongly attracted to the suburbs.

With the end of the baby boom in the 1960s, however, the popula-

2. William Alonso, "The Population Factor and Urban Structure," in Arthur P. Solomon, ed., *The Prospective City* (Cambridge, Mass.: The MIT Press, 1980), p. 32.

tion factor began to change in a direction more favorable to the inner cities. Family size decreased as the birth rate fell from 23.7 per thousand of population in 1960 to 15.7 in 1979. The proportion of young married couples without children rose dramatically. An increasing number of women postponed marriage or chose not to marry, and the divorce rate steadily increased.[3]

These changes produced a marked shift in the composition of households during the 1970s. Those made up of married couples increased only 7 percent from 1970 to 1979, while the number of nonfamily households—consisting of single persons living alone or with nonrelatives—rose 66 percent.[4] When the number of married couples without children is combined with the number of nonfamily households, it is clear that there has been a rapidly growing population segment that is likely to be more favorably disposed toward living in the inner city than were the predominantly child-centered families of the baby boom decades.

Linked to these changes in attitudes toward marriage and child-bearing, both as cause and as effect, has been the rise of the working woman. In recent decades women have joined the labor force in unprecedented numbers: their overall labor force participation rate rose from 38 percent in 1960 to 51 percent in 1979. The increase was even sharper among younger women: for those aged 25 to 34, the rate went from 36 percent in 1960 to 64 percent in 1979. Well over 50 percent of all wives below the age of 55 are now in the labor force.[5]

It has been suggested that growth in the proportion of women who work outside the home will affect the pattern of metropolitan settlement over and above the effects associated with other changes in the "population factor." More specifically, two-worker families might be expected to choose residential locations different from those selected by otherwise similar families in which only one spouse works. For example, if husband and wife are both employed in the central city they would incur double commuting costs if they lived in the suburbs. In effect, they would pay twice as much in commuting costs for the benefits of a given suburban location as would a family with only one worker. From this argument, it seems plausible to expect members of a two-worker family to live closer to their places of work than would the employed member of a single-worker family.

To investigate this possibility, Janice Madden analyzed the extent of workplace-residence separation for a national sample that included several types of households: married with one earner; married with two

3. U.S. Bureau of the Census, *Current Population Reports*, series P-23 no. 350, May 1980, tables 2, 4, 7, and 8.
4. Ibid., table 10.
5. Ibid., table 19; and series P-23 no. 77, December 1978, table 20.

earners; and single, employed persons.[6] She found that when number of children and family income are controlled for, two-earner husband-wife households do *not* choose residential locations that are significantly different from those chosen by one-earner husband-wife families. Thus the hypothesis that labor force participation exerts an independent effect on residential location is not supported.

Madden's results, however, do not imply that the increase in female labor force participation fails to affect residential location choices. Rather, that effect appears indirectly through the influence of labor force participation on the other components of the "population factor," such as marital status and family size. When income is controlled for, Madden found that single working women and married working women with no children live closer to their place of work than do married women with children. To the extent that increased labor force participation leads to later marriage, smaller families, or higher rates of separation and divorce, it will, in Madden's view, "increase demand for smaller, more centrally located housing."[7] On the other hand, Madden's study confirms the tendency of households with higher incomes to live farther from their workplaces. Thus, the additional income provided by working wives encourages families to choose a more suburban residential location. (For theoretical analysis on this point, see Chapter 6.) The net effect of increased labor force participation by women on the pattern of metropolitan settlement will therefore depend on whether its impact on the "population factor" outweighs its income effects.

RENOVATION AND REVIVAL?

Theories of urban form descended from Burgess's concentric zone model (see Chapter 6) have always implied that the passage of time might bring a cycle of revival at the center of the oldest cities. In Burgess's original version, formulated in the 1920s, the middle and upper classes were driven from the urban center toward the suburbs by the combined forces of an expanding central business district that encroached on old inner city neighborhoods, and their own desire to live in new and better housing. Fifty or more years later the city has evolved to a very different stage. Central business districts have long since ceased to expand. Transportation improvements have moved heavy industry and blue collar jobs out of the inner city. The remaining employment is increasingly concen-

6. Janice F. Madden, "Urban Land Use and the Growth in Two-Earner Households," *American Economic Review*, May 1980, pp. 191–97.
7. Ibid., p. 197.

trated in the service sector, in professional, managerial, and white collar occupations that might be expected to attract the middle class. Finally, the decline in population in the older central cities has opened up a substantial amount of vacant land for potential re-use.

One might argue that these evolutionary changes, taken together, have prepared the way for a new era in metropolitan development. By building new or renovated housing near the center, cities could begin to attract the middle class back from the suburbs, sparking a self-sustaining revival that would carry them into a new era of prosperity. Such, at least, has been the perennial dream of inner city optimists. For many years there was little evidence of the projected revival. Then in the 1970s came some good news, a wave of housing renovation that moved a select number of inner city neighborhoods from the "run-down" to the "reviving" category. Is this interesting development the leading edge of the long-hoped-for general revival? A closer look suggests that it probably is not.

Studies of housing renovation conducted in a number of cities reveal a common set of characteristics of neighborhoods, of structures, and of the renovators themselves.[8] The neighborhoods are usually close to the center of the city and have well-defined boundaries. Some are historic districts. Most were run-down or shabby before renovation began but were not considered slums. The renovated units are usually owner-occupied, single-family structures, often row houses, generally dating from the nineteenth century (which lends a certain "period" charm to their architectural style) and often built originally for middle or upper class families. The renovators are predominantly young, highly educated, well-to-do households, often with two wage-earners, frequently childless, and rarely with more than two children. It is a consistent finding that the great majority of renovators were residents of the same city before undertaking renovation. Few came from the suburbs. Hence the new wave of renovation is not evidence of a back-to-the-city movement. It does, however, indicate that cities are now holding onto some middle class households that might formerly have moved to the ring area.

Changes in the "population factor" described above certainly help to explain the growth of that category of young adults who are doing most of the current renovation. The rise in suburban housing prices relative to those in central cities in the 1960s and early 1970s also stimulated the demand for inner city accommodation by young households seeking

8. See J. Thomas Black, Allan Borut, and Robert Dubinsky, *Private Market Housing Renovation in Older Urban Areas*, Research Report no. 26 (Washington, D.C.: The Urban Land Institute, 1977); Franklin J. James, "The Revitalization of Older Urban Housing and Neighborhoods," in Solomon, ed., pp. 130–60; and "Symposium on Neighborhood Revitalization," in *Journal of the American Planning Association*, October 1979, esp. papers by Shirley B. Laska and Daphne Spain and by Neil Smith.

more space.⁹ Thus the renovation movement does draw strength from several fundamental economic changes. Nevertheless it is not, and probably cannot be, of sufficient magnitude to make more than a small contribution to central city revival. If we look at the potential impact of the movement on housing, we see that the kinds of structures and neighborhoods that are amenable to renovation as it is now being done make up only a small fraction of the central city housing stock. The most deteriorated neighborhoods, occupied predominantly by low income families, are not being rehabilitated in this process and, if they were, their poor residents would be displaced, with the likely result of spreading deterioration elsewhere.¹⁰

The long-run significance of changes in the population factor is undeniable. Nevertheless, it may be insufficient to reverse or even to halt the self-reinforcing processes of urban decline. If we look at income data, we see that the central city poverty population actually increased during the 1970s. Against that background, a gradual rise in the number of middle class, nonfamily households is not going to keep the average income level in central cities from continuing to sink below the national mean, with all that implies for self-reinforcing decline. Nor are changes in the population factor by themselves likely to halt the decline in the total population of central cities, since their effects are constrained by the availability of jobs. The growth of nonfamily and childless-couple households may help central cities to hold on to some locally employed people who would have moved to the suburbs in an earlier period. But unless the older cities can stem the decline in the number of local jobs, they are not likely to succeed in stabilizing their populations. Thus despite fundamental changes in the population factor, it is not clear when, or if, the decline of the older central cities will be halted.

The Problem of Managing Decline

Unfortunately, we have not yet learned how to manage the process of decline. The United States has always been a growth-oriented society. Until very recently, city planning was understood to mean planning for growth, and growth is very much easier to cope with than decline. When a city is expanding, problems are not so much solved as they are outgrown. In the past, expanding central cities could often pay the cost of adjusting to the dictates of technological and other economic change by borrowing,

9. James, p. 131.
10. Concerning the problem of displacement, see Howard J. Sumka, "Neighborhood Revitalization and Displacement," *Journal of the American Planning Association*, October 1979, pp. 480–87; and "Comment . . ." by Chester Hartman and "Response to Hartman" by Sumka, Ibid., 488–94.

so to speak, against the present value of expected future growth. If the old infrastructure of streets, water supply, schools, and housing was becoming obsolete, it could readily be replaced by the new facilities that would, in any case, be needed to meet the requirements of rapidly rising demand. Old errors could be buried under new construction. Someone was always willing to pay for a second chance.

Today most of the older central cities are losing jobs and population. Expected future growth no longer attracts private and public capital resources out of which to pay for the replacement of obsolete structures and unsatisfactory neighborhoods. One might think that as its population declined a city's need for capital outlays would drop substantially, because additional capacity in schools, hospitals, and other expensive facilities would not be required. Budgetary relief from that source is minimized, however, by the facts of neighborhood change and the intra-urban redistribution of population. The old facilities, even if not obsolete, are often located in the wrong place to serve current demands.

In general, adjustment to change becomes more difficult when change is accompanied by decline. For example, widespread housing abandonment would seem to provide an opportunity for the creation of attractive parks and open spaces in old, formerly crowded slum areas. But the cities do not seem to know how to go about planning such change or how to pay for it even if they did.[11] It has been said, only half in jest, that our older cities now face insurmountable opportunities.[12] Perhaps we will yet learn how to turn them to advantage.

11. Regarding policies to cope with neighborhood decline, see section on "The Problem of Deteriorating Neighborhoods" in Chapter 13, references cited in Chapter 13, n. 58 and n. 61, and "Symposium on Neighborhood Revitalization," cited in n. 8, above.

12. Quoted in Norman Krumholz, "The Aging Central City: Some Modest Proposals," in U.S. Congress, House Committee on Banking, Finance and Urban Affairs, Subcommittee on the City, *How Cities Can Grow Old Gracefully*, December 1977, p. 100.

Index

Aaron, Henry J., 51n, 311n, 316n, 383n, 452n, 460n, 464n, 468n
Abandonment of housing. *See* Housing
Abrams, Charles, 390n
Advisory Commission on Intergovernmental Relations, 446n, 467n, 481n, 484n, 491, 504n, 511n
"Age" of cities
  and fiscal status, 479–481, 497–500
  and intrametropolitan income differentials, 280–281
  and population growth, 39–42
Agglomeration
  diseconomies of, 19–21, 64–66, 151
  of economic activity, 11–18
  economies of, 16–18, 65, 67, 79–80, 108–109, 110, 151, 323
  and Industrial Revolution, 2, 9
Agriculture, 7–8
  conversion of land to residential uses, 378
  rent of land, 119
  technological revolution in, 10, 11
  and urbanization of poverty, 276–277
Aid to families with dependent children (AFDC), 305–311, 315, 317, 318; table, 304
Allocation function. *See* Local government functions and boundaries
Alonso, William, 20n, 51n, 57n, 58, 59n, 69, 71n, 73n, 80n, 82n, 88n, 118n, 137–144, 146, 191, 535
Amacher, R.C., 503n
Amenity orientation, 79; table, 81
Anaheim, Calif., 38; tables, 40, 279, 499
Anas, Alex, 36, 48, 264, 265, 266, 415n
Andrews, Richard B., 155n

Antipoverty policies, 285–334. *See also* Employment policies; Housing policies; Income support policies; Poverty area policies
Apgar, William C., Jr., 184n, 342n
Ashenfelter, Orley, 296, 297n
Asher, Norman J., 227
Assignment of functions to levels of government. *See* Local government functions and boundaries
Atlanta, 25, 38; tables, 40, 244, 279, 499
Auletta, Ken, 492n
Automobile and truck
  and decentralization, 37, 42–51, 146
  and pollution, 19–20, 245–247
  See also Energy costs, rising

Babcock, Richard F., 135n, 191n, 413n, 418n
Bahl, Roy, 437n, 494n, 509n, 526n
Baily, Martin Ned, 301n
Baltimore, 24, 522; table, 244
Barnett, C. Lance, 404n
Barro, Stephen M., 492n
Barth, M. C., 306n
Basic-nonbasic theory, 154–160, 165–170
  compared with foreign trade multiplier model, 165–166
  critique of, 166–170, 184, 192–193
  location quotients and, 157–160
Baskin, Carlisle W., 87n
Bates, Timothy, 322n
Baumol, William J., 440n
Bay Area Rapid Transit system (BART). *See* Transportation
Beale, Calvin L., 59n, 60n, 63–64
Beesley, M. E., 203n, 232n, 248, 249

Bellusch, Jewel, 362n
Bendick, Marc, Jr., 400n, 401n, 402, 403n
Benefit-cost analysis
    and manpower training, 294–298
    and urban renewal, 381–382
    and urban transportation, 247–250
Benefits in kind, 285, 305
    housing, 359–361
Benefit taxation, 487–488. *See also*
    User charges
Berry, Brian J. L., 96–100, 105, 106n,
    116, 122n, 149, 150n
Bhatt, Kiran, 232n, 260n
Bid-rent curve. *See* Site rent
Birch, David L., 184n
Birth rate, 50–51, 58, 535–536. *See also*
    Demographic change
Bishop, George A., 516n
Black capitalism, 320–322
Blacks
    and discrimination in employment,
        288–289, 302, 330
    and human capital, 286–287, 302
    incomes of, 274–276, 299, 301–303;
        tables, 62, 274, 275, 328
        divergence in, 275–276
    and occupational status, 328–331;
        table, 330
    migration of, 55, 62, 281, 301–302,
        353; tables, 54, 282
    population, urban, 281–283
    poverty, 55, 272–276; table, 275
    and public housing, 370–371
    segregation of, 319–334, 408–420
    and substandard housing, 349–354;
        tables, 350, 352
    and tight labor markets, 298–299
    unemployment rates of, central cities
        versus suburbs, 327–328
    and urbanization of poverty, 281–283
Black, Thomas J., 538n
Blank, David M., 340
Bloom, Max R., 155n
Blue collar jobs, 325
Blumenfeld, Hans, 34, 192–193
Boeckh, E. H., and Associates, figure, 346
Bogue, Donald J., 30, 31, 32, 33n, 45,
    49n, 54n
Bollens, John C., 508n
Boraas v. Village of Belle Terre, 417–418
Borus, Michael E., 297, 298
Borut, Allan, 538n
Bosselman, Fred, 413n, 414n
Boston, 24, 38, 75, 79; tables, 40, 102,
    170, 244, 279, 499
    hinterland, 101–102; table, 102
Boundaries, jurisdictional. *See* Local gov-
    ernment functions and boundaries

Bowles, Gladys K., 54n
Bourne, L. S., 97n, 155n
Boyd, J. Hayden, 227
Boynton, Robert Paul, 492n
Bradbury, Katherine L., 534n
Bradford, D.F., 439
Bradford, William, 322n, 490n
Brazer, Harvey, 424n, 461n
Break, George F., 477, 512n, 517n, 525,
    528n
Brodsky, Harold, 127n
Brown, Harry Gunnison, 452n
Brown, H. James, 339n
Brown, James K., 320n
Brueggeman, William B., 388n, 389n
Buchanan, James M., 427, 474n, 486
Budgetary functions. *See* Local govern-
    mental functions
Buffalo, N.Y., 75, 527
Bulk-to-value ratios, and location of
    industry, 77–78; table, 81
Bunce, Harold, 534n
Burchell, Robert W., 356n, 416n
Burgess, Ernest W., 144–145, 537
Burns, Leland S., 338n, 363
Burright, Burke K., 264n

Calkins, Susannah E., 522n
Campbell, Alan, 494n
Caraley, Demetrios, 508n
Carcagno, G. J., 306n, 309n
Carlson, David B., 395n, 404n
Carter, Jimmy, 312, 317–318
Case, Karl E., 426, 466n
Casey, Stephen C., 351n
Catanese, Anthony J., 135n
Central business district (CBD)
    competing land uses in, 128–134
    and concentric zone theory, 144–145
    defined, 28
    effect of rising site rent, 151–152
Central cities
    definition, 23–24
    density patterns, 37–39
    disparities between needs and resources,
        423, 478–491; tables, 480, 484
    employment, decentralization of, 43–48,
        148–152, 325–326; table, 42
    exploitation by suburbs, 489–491
    fiscal distress, 491–500
    future of, 533–540
    migration, 52–55, 276–278, 281–283,
        353, 357, 407
    population change and decentralization,
        31–43, 48–52, 146–152; tables, 38,
        40–41
    poverty, 271–283; tables, 271, 273, 279

problems of decline, 493–497, 539–540
  self-reinforcing and self-correcting
    processes, 498, 534–535
  segregation and ghettos, 319–334,
    408–410
  See also Cities; Land-use patterns; and
    specific problems, e.g., Housing
Central office functions (corporate
  headquarters), 15, 18, 128–134,
  151–152; table, 81
Central place system, 87–116
  explanatory model, 87–92
  hierarchy of places, 93–96
    empirical evidence for, 96–100;
      tables, 98, 99
  hinterlands and, 100–101; table, 102
  and latent central services, 112–113
  and metropolitan areas, 116
  system of cities affected by change in
    economies of scale, 106–108, 113
    fuel prices, 111–112
    income, 105–106, 113–114
    population, 105–106, 113–114
    transportation costs, 108–112,
      113–114
  system of cities, empirical evidence,
    113–116; tables, 114, 115
  and urban economic base, 181
Chamberlin, E. H., 90
Cheslow, Melvyn D., 233n, 236, 237n,
  242, 252n, 253n
Chicago, 38, 75, 76, 144, 149–150, 196,
  367, 493; tables, 40, 170, 199, 244,
  279, 436, 499
  housing segregation, 409
  and job loss, 331–332
  land-value gradients, 149–150
Chinitz, Benjamin, 18, 184
Christaller, Walter, 87
Cipolla, Carlo, 12n
Cities
  definition, 23–24
  economic base of, 153–186, 192–193
  land-use patterns in, 116, 117–152
  location of, 67–86
  population growth before Industrial
    Revolution, 7–10
  system of cities, 87–116
  See also Central cities; Metropolitan
    areas; Suburban rings
City size
  advantages of, 16–18, 65
  disadvantages of, 19, 64–66
  income and, 64–66
  optimum, 20–21
Civil Rights Act (1964), 302
Civil Rights Act (1968), 409, 415
Clark, Colin, 122n

Clark, Kenneth B., 281n
Cleaveland, James R., 530n
Cleveland, 357, 527; tables, 199, 244
Coase, R.H., 248n
Codes, housing. *See* Housing
Cogan, John F., 316n
Communication oriented, 80; table, 81
Community control and decentralization of
  local government, 477, 478
Community development corporations,
  322–323
Commuting
  and concentric zone theory, 144–145
  and development of railroads, 35
  effect of rising living standards on,
    49–50, 139–149
  and job decentralization, 48
Comprehensive Employment and Training
  Act (CETA), 291–293, 300; table,
  292
Concentric zone theory (Burgess),
  144–145, 537
Corson, W.S., 309n
Cost-benefit analysis. *See* Benefit-cost
  analysis
Cost of living, by city size, 64
Costonis, John J., 125n, 126n
Courant, Paul N., 523n
Crecine, John P., 409n
Crime and delinquency, 19, 65, 338, 339,
  414
  and housing abandonment, 355, 356,
    377, 407
  in public housing, 369
  slum housing and, 361–363

Dallas–Fort Worth, 38; tables, 40, 244,
  279, 499
Davis, Kingsley, 1n, 10
Davis, Otto A., 373–377, 381
Dayton, Ohio, fair share housing, 416
Dean, John P., 362
Dean, Robert D., 87n
Decentralization. *See* Central cities;
  Metropolitan areas; Suburban rings
Delafons, John, 135n
De Leeuw, Frank, 344, 371n, 395n, 404n
Demand. *See* specific topics, e.g., Housing
Demand density and central place system,
  92, 102–110, 113
Demand, income elasticity of
  for housing, 343–345, 401–402
  for public services, 437–439
Demographic changes, effect on
  central city revival, 535–537, 538–539
  household composition, 535–536
  housing renovation, 538–539

Demographic changes (*continued*)
suburbanization, 50–51
See also Family structure
Density of urban-metropolitan population
and city "age", 39–40
and income levels, 49–50
land-use models and intraurban patterns,
122–128, 136–147
and population increase (overflow
effect), 37–42, 139, 146
and technology of transport, 34–36,
42–43, 137–138, 146
and transportation systems, 196,
265–266
De Salvo, Joseph S., 376n
Des Moines, Iowa, simulation model of,
182
Detroit, 38, 357, 527; tables, 40, 170, 244,
279, 499
housing segregation, 278, 409
and job loss, 331–332
Dewees, Donald, 202n, 203n
Dickinson, R. E., 101
Discrimination
antidiscrimination laws, 288, 302, 365,
409, 415
in employment, 288–290
in housing, 278, 340, 408–419
See also Segregation
Dispersion. *See* Central cities; SMSA's;
Suburban rings
Domencich, Thomas A., 210
Downs, Anthony, 319, 333, 408n, 419,
534n
Dubinsky, Robert, 538n
Duncan, Otis Dudley, 26, 95n

Earley, Joseph, figure, 123
Economic base studies, urban areas,
153–193. *See also* Basic-nonbasic
theory; Foreign trade multiplier
model; Input-Output analysis;
Simulation models
Economic policy for urban areas, 184–193
See also Growth policy
Economic rent, definition of, 121
Economies (and diseconomies) of
agglomeration. *See* Agglomeration
Economies of scale
and economies of agglomeration, 16
in freight handling, 75
market area size, effect on, 88–89,
106–108
in public services, 475–476
Edel, Matthew, 151n, 210n, 319n
Education
and antipoverty policies, 286–287,
288–289, 302

externalities in, 430–431
inequalities, financial, 505–506
local expenditure on, 431–432, 482–
483, 506; tables, 432, 484
and redistribution of income, 488n
See also Manpower training programs
Efficiency, as economic criterion, 4
Ekanem, Nkanta F., 404n
Elementary and Secondary Education Act,
431
Elevated trains, 35–36
Elevators, passenger, 35
Ellwood, D.T., 344n
Employment
and antipoverty programs, 285–302,
324–332
decentralization of, 43–48, 148,
151–152, 325–326, 331, 533–534,
539; table, 46
and economic base analysis, 153–166,
182, 186; table, 170
segregation and, 331–332
See also Employment policies;
Unemployment
Employment policies (antipoverty),
285–302
antidiscrimination policies, 288–289,
302, 330
and income maintenance policies, 286,
302–303
information and placement policies, 289,
296–297
job creation policies, 287–288, 290–294
evaluation of, 299–301
federally assisted programs for,
290–294; table, 292
maintaining tight labor markets,
290–291, 298–299
training programs, 286–287, 290–298
benefit-cost analyses of, 294–298
federally-assisted programs for,
290–294; table, 292
Energy costs
regional differences, 83–84; table, 84
and transportation systems, 262–263
rising, effects on
central city revival, 535
central place system, 111–112,
266–267
household location, 66
industrial location, 82–84
urban form, 147, 149, 263–266
Energy demand, price elasticity of, 264
Enns, John H., 264n
Entrepreneurship
and ghetto economic development, 321,
322
and urban economic growth, 184

Environmental protection
and area-wide planning, 477
and externalities, 191–192, 474–475
See also Pollution
Equity, as economic criterion, 4–5
Ervin, David E., 136n
Euclid v. Ambler Realty Co., 135
Evans, Alan, 19n, 64n
Expenditures on local public services,
431–442
central cities vs. suburbs, 482–483;
table, 484
and exploitation argument, 489–491
composition of, 431–433, 482–483;
tables, 432, 484
demand for, 434–435, 437–439
growth of, 423, 433–440
and rising unit cost, 435–440;
table, 436
limitation of, 440–442
and poverty, 482, 490–491
See also Fiscal limitation movement;
Geographic disparities; Local
governmental functions; Municipal
service costs; Urban fiscal distress
Experimental Housing Allowance Program,
399–406. *See also* Housing Policy
Exports
and economic base analysis, 154–166,
170–180
indirect, 160
location quotients as allocators, 157–160;
table, 159
local export promotion, 188–189
External economies of scale, and
agglomeration economies, 16–18, 76.
See also Agglomeration
External-economy orientation, 80; table, 81
Externalities (or "spillovers")
in housing, 360, 361–363
in land use, 134–136, 412
in public sector, 429–430, 473–475,
514–515
in transportation, 245–247
and urban renewal, 373–377, 382
and zoning, 134–136, 412
See also Pollution

Family assistance plan. *See* Income
maintenance
Family structure
and antipoverty programs, 305–306,
318; table, 303
and black poverty, 275–276; table, 275
See also Demographic change
Fauth, Gary R., 206
Fechter, Alan, 504n

Federal Housing Administration (FHA),
locational effects of policies, 52
Federal National Mortgage Association
(FNMA), 384
Federation within metropolitan areas,
507–508
Fiscal imbalance, 501, 519
Fiscal limitation movement, 434, 440–442,
468, 506, 530, 532. *See also*
Expenditures; Taxes
Fiscal zoning, 413
Fisher, Claude S., 363n
Fisher, I.N., 310n
Fisher, Peter, 244
Fisher, Robert Moore, 362n
Fishman, Richard P., 417n
Fisk, Donald, 531n
Fitch, Lyle, 252
Flint, Mich., municipal productivity,
531–532
Follain, James R., 404n
Food stamps, 285, 305, 306–307, 311,
317; table, 304
Foot-loose (foot-free) industries, 80
Foreign trade multiplier model, 154,
160–166
compared with basic-nonbasic theory,
165–166
Forrester, Jay, 189–190
Fossett, James W., 499, 500
Foster, C. D., 248, 249
Franklin, Herbert M., 419n
Freeman, A. Myrick, III, 339n
Freight absorption, and market areas, 96
Frieden, Bernard J., 330, 400n, 402n,
404n, 405
Friedly, Philip H., 356n
Friedman, John, 69n, 71n, 88n
Friedrich, Carl J., 71n
Friend, Edward H., 435n
Fuchs, Victor R., 64n
Fuel prices. *See* Energy costs
Furstenberg, George M. von, 319n

Garn, Harvey A., 323n
Garnick, Daniel, 534n
Garrison, William, 97–100
Gatewood, L.B., 79n
General assistance, 307; table, 304
Geographic disparities between needs and
resources of local governments, 423
478–491
disparities in cost, 482–483; table, 484
disparities in resources, 479–482; table,
480
disparities in tax burden, 483–485;
table, 484

Geographical disparities (*continued*)
  exploitation hypothesis, 489–491
  and redistributive local budgets, 485–
    489; table, 486
  reform proposals
    equalization within states, 505–506
    intergovernmental grants, 521–522
    metropolitan reorganization, 506–511
    reassignment of functions, 500–505
  See also Urban fiscal distress
Ghettos. *See* Poverty area policy
Gillingham, Robert F., 339*n*
Ginn, J. Royce, 184*n*
Ginzberg, Eli, 290*n*
Glazer, Nathan, 233*n*, 305*n*, 480*n*
Glickman, Norman J., 1*n*
Goedert, Jeanne E., 398*n*
Golden v. Planning Board of Ramapo, 417
Gorham, William, 233*n*, 305*n*, 480*n*
Government National Mortgage
    Association (GNMA), 384
Gramlich, Edward M., 523*n*
Grants. *See* Intergovernmental grants
Grebler, Leo, 338*n*, 363
Green Bay, Wisc., 400
Green, Christopher, 313*n*
Green, Howard L., 101; table, 102
Greenfield, Stuart, 330*n*
Greer, Scott, 8
Greiner, John M., 532*n*
Greytak, David, 494*n*
Grieson, Ronald E., 29*n*, 184*n*, 214*n*,
    233*n*
Grigsby, William, 347*n*, 372*n*
Growth policy
  growth as an objective, 185–186
  growth control, 191, 413–414, 417
Guaranteed minimum income. *See* income
  maintenance policies

Haddad, William F., 322*n*
Hadden, Jeffrey K., 416*n*
Haig, R.M., 13, 14–15, 43, 151, 155*n*
Hallman, Howard W., 477*n*
Hamer, Andrew Marshall, 239*n*, 259*n*
Harberger, Arnold C., 455, 456
Hardin, Einar, 295
Harlem, New York City, 324–325
Harris, Britton, 169
Harrison, Bennett, 289, 319, 330, 331
Hartman, Chester, 539*n*
Hartman, Robert W., 505*n*
Hatry, Harry P., 530*n*
Hatt, Paul K., 26, 100*n*, 490*n*
Hauser, Philip M., 139*n*, 281
Hausknecht, Murray, 362*n*
Haveman, Robert H., 290, 300, 306*n*
Hawley, Amos H., 490

Hawley, Willis D., 530*n*
Health
  and housing conditions, 362–363
  local expenditures for, 432, 518; table,
    432
Heilbrun, James, 321*n*, 322*n*, 325*n*, 342*n*,
    358*n*, 394*n*, 408*n*, 468*n*, 495*n*
Heinberg, John D., 395*n*, 404*n*
Heller, Walter W., 501*n*, 519, 520, 521
Highest and best use, doctrine of (land),
    134, 378–381
Highways. *See* Transportation
Hilton, George W., 258, 259
Hinterlands of cities, 100–102; table, 102
Hirsch, Werner Z., 474*n*, 476*n*, 513*n*
Hirshleifer, Jack, 513*n*
Hoachlander, Garreth E., 241*n*
Hoch, Irving, 19*n*, 64–66, 83, 84*n*
Hochman, Harold M., 490*n*
Hodge, Gerald, 99–100, 115, 116*n*
Hogan, William T., S.J., 78*n*
Home ownership
  favorable tax treatment of, 51–52
  federal home-ownership assistance
    (Section 235), 385–386, 387, 388,
    390; table, 383
  and renovation, 538
Hoover, Edgar M., 17, 18*n*, 44, 72*n*, 76,
    78*n*, 108–110, 127*n*, 196*n*, 278–279
Horowitz, Ann R., 319*n*
Horton, Frank E., 122*n*, 149, 150*n*
Horton, Raymond D., 492
Housing, 335–363
  abandonment, 355–358, 376–377, 391
    and filtering, 357, 407–408
  benefits, indirect, 361–363
  codes, 360–361, 365, 393–394
  condition of, 336–338, 349–355; tables,
    346, 352
  cost of new construction, 345–347
  externalities, 360, 361–363
  filtering process
    defined, 347–349
    and housing abandonment, 357
    and housing standards, 353–354,
      387–389
    and neighborhood deterioration,
      407–408
    and subsidized new construction,
      387–389, 419
    and urban renewal, 372
Housing Acts
    1937, 366
    1949, 335, 367, 372, 387
    1954, 372
    1961, 383
    1965, 384

1968, 385–387
1974, 397–399, 406
income and, 341, 343–345, 347, 349, 353, 354–355, 356, 357, 376, 391–393, 401–402
elasticity of demand, 343–345, 402
and land-use patterns, 117–149
maintenance of, 342, 348–349, 355, 356, 367, 369, 388–389, 393–394, 403
market model, adaptive, 339–345
competition, 340
demand, 343–345
supply, 341–343
and neighborhood quality, 338–339, 351–353, 358, 374–377, 413–414
renovation, 534–535, 537–539
subsidies, arguments for, 359–363
See also Housing policy; Discrimination; Home ownership; Segregation
Housing policy, 335–336, 365–420
housing allowances, 391–408
benefit formula, 392–393, 400
and code enforcement, 393–394
cost of, 395, 404–405
effects of, 401–404
and equity, 394–395
evaluation of, 405–406
and Experimental Housing Allowance Program, 399–406
and income, 401–402
"opening up" the suburbs, 410–420
class action suits, 417–418
exclusionary zoning, 411–414
integration policies, 415–420
public housing, 366–371; table, 368
cost of, 366–367
critique of, 368–371
leasing (Section 23), 371
strategies for, 335–336, 386–387, 389–391, 396–397, 405–406, 408, 419–420
subsidized supply: private housing, 382–391; table, 383
and filtering process, 387–389
and National Housing Goals, 386–387
rent supplements, 384–386
Section 8, 396–399, 405
Section 221(d)(3), 383–384, 388, 390
Sections 235 and 236, 385–388, 390
urban renewal, 372–377
benefit-cost analysis of, 381–382
See also Housing; Discrimination; Externalities; Home ownership; Neighborhood quality; Segregation
Houston, 38, 196; tables, 40, 199, 279, 499

Hoyt, Homer, 149, 155
Hubbell, L. Kenneth, 504n
Hughes, James W., 416n
Human capital, poverty and, 286–287

Ideal weight (Weber), 71–72
Immigration (foreign), 30, 53, 55. *See also* Migration
Imports, 154, 160–166
and basic-nonbasic theory, 164–166, 168–169
and foreign trade multiplier approach, 160–166
and input-output analysis, 171, 173, 176–179
Income, aggregate for an urban area
and economic base analysis, 153–186
basic-nonbasic multiplier, 154–157, 160, 165–170
input-output multiplier, 179–182
Keynesian foreign trade multiplier, 160–166, 168
and local economic policy, 186–193
Income, level of per family or per capita
and city "age", 280–281
and city size, 64–66
and discrimination, 288–289, 302, 330
geographic differentials in, 61–66, 271–281, 289, 328–331, 539; tables, 62, 271, 273, 279, 282, 328
and metropolitan fiscal disparities, 479–491; tables, 480, 484
and housing conditions, 341, 343, 345, 347, 349, 353, 354–358, 359, 391–394
and human capital, 286, 287, 302
and land-use patterns, 49–51, 52, 139–146, 537
and market areas of central places, 92, 103, 105–106
and migration, 61–66, 276–278
poverty
antipoverty policies, 285–334
defined, 269–271
urbanization of, 269–283
racial differentials, 62–63, 272–276; tables, 62, 273, 274, 275
redistribution of
by income support, 302–319
through local budgets, 425–427, 485–489
transportation and, 239–242
shift in, central cities versus suburbs, 278–279
See also Antipoverty policy; Housing policy

Income support policies, 286–287, 302–319
  and employment policies, 286, 302–303
  guaranteed income policies, 311–319
    and poverty gap, 314, 316
    structure of, 311–315; table, 313
    and work incentives, 310–311, 315–316, 318–319
  and housing allowances, 406
  public aid programs, existing, 304–311; table, 304
    criticism of, 309–311
    impact on poverty, 307–309; table, 308
    state-local burden of, 305
    welfare reform, 317–319
Income tax
  home-ownership bias, 51–52, 411
  at local level, 445; table, 444
  at state level, 447
Indianapolis, 24, 508
  export percentages, table, 159
Industrial Revolution, and urban agglomeration, 8–13, 29, 34
Inflation, and tight labor market policy, 300
Ingram, Gregory K., 184n, 190n
Input-output analysis, 154, 170–182
  advantages of, 176–179
  dynamic versions, 182
  final demand sector, 174–176, 179
  limitations of, 181–182
  multipliers, 179–182
  and simulation models, 182
Integration. See Segregation
Intergovernmental grants, 431–433, 483, 511–527; tables, 443, 444, 484, 517
  conditional grants
    matching (categorical), 514–518
    nonmatching, 524–525
  and externalities, 514–515
  federal aid to cities, 525–527
  revenue sharing (unconditional grants) 518–524
    effects on tax effort, 523
    redistributive effects, 521–522
Iron and steel industry, locational orientation of, 77–79, 95
  bulk-to-value ratio, 77
Isard, Walter, 67–68, 77, 78n, 109, 167n, 171n, 172

Jacksonville, Fla., 508
Japan, urbanization in, 1
James, Franklin J., 538n, 539n
Jenney, William LeBaron, 35

Job Corps, 293, 297; table, 292
Job training programs. See Employment policies
Johnson, Lyndon B., 521, 526
Joint-consumption goods ("pure public goods"), 427–428
Jones, Emrys, 1n
Jump, Bernard, Jr., 437n

Kadanoff, Leo P., 190n
Kafoglis, M.Z., 474n
Kain, J.F., 184, 185, 198n, 206, 225n, 227, 228, 259, 278, 281n, 319n, 331–332, 333n, 338, 339n, 342n
Kasvl, Stanislav V., 363n
Keeler, Theodore E., 226, 227, 230n, 232, 234, 245, 246
Kemper, Peter, 531n
Kemp, Michael A., 208, 210, 233n, 236, 237n, 242, 252n, 253n, 260n
Keynesian income determination model, 160–166
Kiesling, Herbert, 531n
Kirby, Ronald F., 260n
Kitigawa, Evelyn M., 45
Kohn, Clyde F., 97n
Kong, C.M., 344n
Kontuly, Thomas, 65, 66n
Kotler, Milton, 477n
Kouwenhoven, John A., 35n
Kraft, Gerald, 210
Kristof, Frank S., 355n, 356n, 358, 397n, 406n, 407n
Krumholz, Norman, 540n
Kulash, Damian J., 234n

Labor
  cost differentials and industrial location, 76–79; table, 81
  division of, and urban growth, 8, 9, 13–14
Labor markets
  and antipoverty policy, 286–289, 298–301
  and definition of metropolitan areas, 25
  queuing theory of, 288
Labor orientation, 79; table, 81
Labor unions, municipal civil service, 439
Ladies' garment industry, and agglomeration economies, 16
Lakewood Plan, 476
Landsberg, Hans H., 191n
Land use, 117–152
  Burgess's theory, 144–145, 537
  competing uses, 128–134
  explanatory models, 118–134, 136–145

externalities and zoning, 134–136, 365, 412
fuel costs, effects of, 147, 149, 263–266
growth and development, effects of
  empirical studies, 149–150
  income increase, 139–144, 146–147
  population increase, 139, 146–147
  site-rent increase, 150–152
  transportation improvement, 137–138, 146–147
highest and best use, 134, 378–381
mononuclearity, 118, 122, 128–129, 147–150
multinucleation, 264–266
succession of uses, 134, 378–381
transportation systems and, 152, 195–196
See also Site rent
Land value, empirical studies of, 121–122, 149–150
See also Land use; Site rent
Langford, T.W., 172n
Laska, Shirley B., 538n
Lav, Michael, 92n
Leahy, William H., 87n
Leaman, Sam H., 371n, 395n
Lee, T.H., 344n
Leonard, Herman B., 426, 466n
Leontief, Wassily W., 170
Leven, Charles L., 36n, 112n, 264n, 415n, 509n
Levine, Charles H., 530n
Levitan, Sar A., 286n, 322n
Levy, Frank, 440n, 442n
Listokin, David, 413n, 416n
Local government functions and boundaries, 423–431
  allocation function, 427–431, 471
    local variability of, 492–493
  "assignment problem," 423–424, 427
  fiscal equivalence, principle of, 429–430
  boundary criteria, optimal
    economies of scale, 475–476
    externalities, 473–475
    planning and coordination, 477–478
    political accessibility, 476–477
    preference satisfaction, 472–473
  "common municipal functions," 432–433, 493
  redistribution function (*See* Income, level of)
  reform proposals
    federation, 507–508
    regional planning agencies, 511
    special districts, 510–511
    tax base sharing, 508–510

states as regional units, 511
urban counties, 508
stabilization, 424–425
"Tiebout solution," 472–473
Localization economies, 17
Local-market activities, 14. *See also* Basic-nonbasic theory
Location of cities, 11, 67–68, 74–76, 85. *See also* Central place theory; Location of industry
Location of industry, 67–86
  changes in determinants of, 82–84
    energy costs, 82–84
  orientation, types of, 76–82; table, 81
  and production cost differentials, 76–82
  and subsidy policies, 188–189
  and terminal costs, 72–74, 76
  and transport costs, 68–76
  transshipment points, 75–76
  and urban growth, 74–76, 85–86
  See also Central place theory; Location of cities
Location quotient method, 157–160; table, 159
Long, Larry H., 277n, 283n, 310n
Los Angeles, 38, 196; tables, 40, 170, 199, 244, 279, 436, 499
Lösch, August, 87–88, 91
Low-income housing. *See* Housing; Housing policy; Income, level of
Lowry, Ira S., 184n, 355n, 358n, 376n, 392–395, 400n, 401, 403n, 404n
Lusterman, Seymour, 320n
Lyall, Katherine, 509n
Lynn, Arthur D., 468n
Lynn, Laurence E., Jr., 306n
Lyon, David W., 311n

McCarthy, Kevin F., 58, 59n, 60n, 61n, 64, 66n
McClure, Charles E., 503
McDonald, M. Brian, 488n
McDowell, James L., 402n
McGuire, Patrick, 180n
McKean, Roland, 428n
McKee, David L., 87n
McKenzie, Roderick D., 144n
Macrae, Norman, 112n
Madden, Janice F., 537
Mahoney, B.S., 316n
Mahoney, W.M., 316n
Maintenance of housing. *See* Housing, maintenance of
Malt, R.A., 439
Manpower training programs. *See* Employment policies, training

Mangum, Garth L., 322n
Manhattan, New York City, land-value
    gradient, 122–123
Manpower Development and Training
    Act, 290, 296
Manufacturing employment, in central
    cities and suburbs, table, 46–47
Manufacturing industries, location of
    decentralization, 43–46; table, 46
    type of orientation, 74–81; table, 81
    and urban hierarchy, 95
Manvel, Allen D., 522n
Marginal propensity
    to consume, 162–164
    to consume local goods, 162–166
    to import, 162–164, 168–169
Margolis, Julius, 28, 29n, 187n, 413n,
    490n
Market areas for central services, 87–92
    as hinterlands, 100–102; table, 102
    inside metropolitan areas, 116
    networks of, 90–92
    overlapping of, 100–102
    size of, 92, 102–110
        and increased economies of scale,
            106–108, 113
        and rising fuel prices, 111–112, 113
        and rising income, 105–106, 113
        and rising population, 105–106, 113
        and transport cost reduction,
            108–111, 113–114
    and societal scale, 110–111
    and urban hierarchy, 93–96
Market failure. See Externalities
Market orientation, 70–72, 78, 95; table,
    81
Marshall, Alfred, 127n
Mason, John M., 404n
Masotti, Louis H., 416n
Mass transit. See Transportation, public
Materials orientation, 70–72, 78, 95;
    table, 81
Mayer, Harold M., 97n
Medical assistance programs (Medicaid),
    285, 305–306, 307, 308, 311; table,
    304
Merit goods, 359–361, 430
Metropolitan areas
    definition, 24–26
    employment decentralization, 43–48;
        table, 46
    migration and, 52–64, 276–277,
        281–283; tables, 54, 56
    population decline and deconcentration,
        32, 55–64; tables, 56, 60
    population growth and decentralization,
        31–43, 48–52, 146–149; tables, 31,
        33, 40, 41

poverty in, 269–283; tables, 271, 273,
    279
public sector organization and finance,
    421–469, 471–532
See also specific problems, e.g., Housing
Meyer, John R., 198n, 225n, 227, 228,
    332n
Miami, Fla., 508
Miernyk, William H., 171n, 179n, 182n
Mieszkowski, Peter, 136n, 239n, 342n,
    370n, 452n, 455, 456, 457, 460n,
    463, 479n, 523n
Migration
    economics of, 61–64; table, 62
    and housing conditions, 353, 407
    low income, 189–191, 276–277
    and metropolitan-nonmetropolitan
        population change, 52–64; tables,
        54, 56, 60
    by race, 55, 62, 276–277, 281–282;
        table, 54
    selective to suburbs, 407, 411, 488–489
    and urbanization of poverty, 276–282
    and welfare benefits, 309–310
Miller, James C., III, 258n
Mills, Edwin S., 92n, 122n, 136, 149
Mingche, M. Li, 339n
Minneapolis-St. Paul, table, 244
    tax base sharing, 509
Minority Business Development Agency,
    321
Mitchell, William E., 424n, 485n
Mogulof, Melvin B., 508n
Mohring, Herbert, 213, 222, 227
Mononuclear city, 36, 37, 147–149
Monopolistic competition
    in rental housing market, 340
    of suppliers of central services, 90–92
Mooney, Joseph D., 332n
Morrison, Peter A., 58, 60n, 61n, 64, 66n
Mortgage policy, federal
    home-ownership bias of, 51–52
    and housing subsidies, 383–386
Moses, Leon N., 36, 48, 211, 264, 265,
    266, 415n
Mulford, John E., 402n
Mullendore, Walter, 182
Multipliers, in economic base analysis
    basic-nonbasic, 154–157, 159, 165–166,
        167–168
    foreign trade, 160–166
    input-output, 179–180
Municipal government. See Local
    government
Muller, Thomas, 496n, 497, 531n
Multinucleation, 264–266
Municipal service costs

labor costs, rise in, 435–437, 439,
    530; table, 436
  fringe benefits, 435–437
  productivity lag, 437, 530–532
  unionization, 439–440, 532
  "overburden," 482–483
  and population decline, 494–497
  and population traits, 482
Musgrave, Peggy B., 236n, 247n, 249n,
    464n, 487n
Musgrave, Richard A., 236n, 247n, 249n,
    359, 424, 426, 427, 452n, 464, 466n,
    486n, 487n, 502
Mushkin, Selma, 218n, 232n, 428n
Muth, Richard, 122n, 143–144, 342n,
    343, 344, 370n, 389

Nashville, Tenn., 508
Nathan, Richard P., 499, 500, 502n,
    522n, 523n, 526n, 527
National Advisory Commission on Civil
    Disorders, 334
National Commission on Urban Problems,
    369n
National Housing Goals, 386–387
National-market activities, 14. *See also*
    Economic base studies; Exports
Neels, Kevin, 232n
Neenan, William B., 490n
Negative income tax. *See* Income
    maintenance policy
Neighborhood government. *See*
    Community control
Neighborhood quality
  and abandonment, 355, 358, 377–378
  federal aid for, 406–408; table, 399
  measurement of, 338–339, 351–353;
    table, 352
  and urban renewal, 374–377
  and zoning, 413–414
Netzer, Dick, 446n, 452n, 456n, 461n,
    468n, 469, 485, 509n, 511n, 532n
Newcomb, C., 101
New construction strategy. *See* Housing
    policy
New York City, 35–36, 38, 75, 76, 79,
    152, 196, 367, 376, 395; tables, 40,
    170, 199, 244, 279, 436, 499
  fiscal crisis, 434, 491–492, 493, 496
  hinterland, 101–102; table, 102
New York State Urban Development
    Corporation, 418
Nixon, Richard M., 312, 317, 387n, 519
Nonmetropolitan areas
  growth of population, 31–32, 55–64;
    tables, 31, 33, 56, 60

migration and, 52–64; tables, 54, 56, 60
poverty in, 271–272; tables, 271, 273
Nourse, Hugh O., 2, 103n, 131n, 165,
    166n, 382n

Oakland, William H., 324n, 479n, 480n,
    523n, 528n
*Oakwood at Madison v. Township of
    Madison*, 417
Oates, Wallace E., 425n, 439, 490n,
    513n, 518, 521
Occupational earnings by area, 328–331;
    table, 329
Offner, Paul, 332n
Olsen, Edgar F., 342n
Olson, Mancur, 191n, 429, 431
Otis, Elisha Graves, 35
Overcrowding (housing), 336–338, 343,
    344, 349–354; table, 350
Overflow effect, 37–39, 146

Palmer, John L., 291n, 293n, 301n,
    306n, 318n
Park, Robert E., 101, 144n
Parsons, Talcott, 281n
Pascal, Anthony H., 296n, 409n, 414n,
    440n, 441n
Pearlman, Kenneth, 418n
Pechman, Joseph A., 291n, 315n, 318n,
    512n, 519, 520
Perloff, Harvey S., 122n, 502n
Persky, Joseph J., 278, 281n, 319n, 333n
Peterson, George E., 305n, 468n, 480n,
    481, 482, 483, 490n, 495n, 496, 497,
    504n, 522n
Pettigrew, Thomas F., 276n
Pfouts, R.W., 155n, 170n, 193n
Philadelphia, 25, 38, 172, 367, 522;
    tables, 40, 170, 199, 244, 279, 436,
    499
Philbrick, Allen K., 93–94
Phoenix, 400, 402
Pickering, John W., 534n
Pike, Albert, III, 435n
Pirenne, Henri, 9, 10
Pittsburgh, 74, 78, 95, 400, 401
Planning
  for decline, 494–495, 539–540
  and housing policy, 396
  and metropolitan regional problems,
    477–478, 511
  and neighborhood deterioration,
    407–408
  and transportation investment, 242–250
  See also Zoning

Police services, 432, 437–439, 477; table, 432
Polinsky, A.M., 344n
Pollution
and agglomeration, 19–20, 65
and automobiles, 19–20, 245–247
local policy toward, 191–192
Population. *See* Birth rate; Central cities; Cities; Demographic change; Density; Metropolitan areas; Rural areas; Suburban rings
Population size, effect on
land-use patterns, 139, 146, 151–152
market area size, 92, 105–106, 113
urban hierarchy, 105–106, 113, 114
Port of New York Authority, 510
Ports, and location of activity, 11, 75–76, 95
Poverty. *See* Income, level of
Poverty area policy, 289, 319–334
development policies
black capitalist approach, 320–322
branch plant strategy, 320
Community Development Corporations (CDC's), 322–323
evaluation of, 323–325
Harlem, 324–325
dispersal policies, 325–334
Power orientation, 79; table, 81
Preference satisfaction, in public sector, 427–431, 472–475
Prescott, James P., 182
Prest, A.R., 247n, 295n
Preston, Richard E., 97n
Production-cost orientation, 77–80; table, 81
Productivity in local governments. *See* Municipal service costs; Urban fiscal distress
Property tax, 445–469; tables, 443, 458, 467, 480
elasticity of, 445–448
and exclusionary policies, 413, 416–417
geographic disparities in, 481–482
incidence, 448–468
new view, 455–465
old view, 452–455, 459–465
on site value, 449–452
and redistribution of income, 486–488
regressivity, debate over, 462–465
revenue from, 442
role in budgetary process, 468–469
and school finance, 488n, 505–506
Proposition 13. *See* Fiscal limitation movement
Pruitt-Igoe housing project, 369
Public aid, 285, 302–309; tables, 304, 308
criticisms of, 309–311, 316–317

Public Employment Program (PEP), 291
Public finance, in metropolitan areas, 421–469, 471–532. *See also* specific topics, e.g., Urban fiscal distress
Public housing. *See* Housing policy
Public services. *See* Expenditures on local public services
Public Works Administration, 366
Puerto Rico, migration from, 276
Pugh, G. Douglas, 322n
Purnell, S.W., 310n
Puryear, David, 509n

Queuing theory, labor markets, 288
Quigley, John M., 332n, 338, 339n, 342n, 531n

Race. *See* Blacks; Discrimination; Segregation
Railroads
and metropolitan form, 34–37, 42–43
terminal costs of, 72
and urbanization, 11–12, 34–37
urban rail transit (*See* Transportation, urban)
Rapkin, Chester, 340
Rasmussen, David W., 407n
Redevelopment, urban. *See* Housing policy
Redistribution of income. *See* Income, level of
Regional economics, and urban economics, 2
Regional planning. *See* Planning
Regions
defined, 2
metropolitan area as, 24–25
Real estate tax. *See* Property tax
Redistribution of income. *See* Income, level of
Rees, Albert, 315n, 316n
Reid, Margaret G., 343, 344
Reischauer, Robert D., 505n, 527n
Reiss, Albert J., Jr., 26n, 100n, 490n
Renshaw, Vernon, 534n
Rent. *See* Site rent
Rental housing. *See* Housing
Rent certificates, 392
Rent gradient. *See* Site rent
Rent supplement program. *See* Housing policy
Reschovsky, Andrew, 509
Research and development, locational orientation of, 79
Retail employment, central cities and suburbs, table, 46–47

Retailing
  centralization of, 36–37, 43
  decentralization of, 44; tables, 46, 47
  and land-use patterns, 116, 148
  and urban hierarchy, 93–95, 95–96
    empirical studies, 96–100, 114–115
    market area size, 92, 102–110
Revenues of local governments, 442–448;
  tables, 443, 444. *See also* Taxes;
  Intergovernmental grants
Revenue-sharing. *See* Intergovernmental
  grants
Reversionary value of sites, 378
Ribich, Thomas I., 296*n*
Richardson, Harry W., 19, 20*n*
Robinson v. Cahill, 505
Rodriguez v. San Antonio School District,
  505
Rogers, David, 530*n*
Roman Empire, urbanization in, 8, 9
Romanoff, E., 172*n*
Roof, W.C., 408*n*
Rothenberg, Jerome, 210*n*, 319*n*, 363, 381
Rubinfeld, Daniel L., 523*n*
Rubinowitz, Leonard S., 416*n*
Ruggles, Richard, 501, 502*n*
Ruhr Valley, 74
Rural areas
  defined, 26–28
  housing conditions, compared with
    urban, 349–354; table, 350
  population change, 29–31; table, 31

St. Louis, 357, 522
  Pruitt-Igoe housing project, 369
Sacks, Seymour, 483
Sadacca, Robert, 370*n*
Saks, Daniel H., 332*n*
Salins, Peter D., 356*n*
Samuelson, Paul E., 427, 428
San Francisco, 38, 144; tables, 40, 244,
  279, 499
  BART (mass transit), 239–241
Santa Monica, 79
Saskatchewan, central place system of,
  99–100
Satellite cities, 28–29
Savas, E.S., 531*n*
Schafer, Robert, 410
Schechter, Henry B., 377*n*
Schlefer, Marion K., 377*n*
Schmandt, Henry J., 508*n*
Schnare, Ann B., 408*n*
Schnore, Leo F., 139*n*, 280*n*
School districts

financial inequality among, 505–506
  equalization cases, 505
  and increasing societal scale, 111
Schroeder, Larry, 437*n*
Schussheim, Morton J., 419*n*
Section 8 (housing), 396–399
Section 23 leasing program (public
  housing), 371
Section 221(d)(3)(housing), 383–386,
  388, 390
Section 235 (housing), 385–388, 390
Section 236 (housing), 385–388, 390
Segal, David, 339*n*
Segregation, 277–278, 281–283, 319–334,
  408–420
  and ghetto economic development,
    320–325
  in housing, 370–371, 408–420
  and jobs for blacks, 325–334
  opening up the suburbs, 410–420
  See also Discrimination
Serrano v. Priest, 505–506
Service employment, 9
  selected, central cities and suburbs,
    table, 46–47
  and urban growth, 9, 168–169, 181,
    192–193
  See also Basic-nonbasic theory
Sewell, David O., 295
Shackson, Richard H., 266*n*
Shannon, Fred A., 53
Shoup, C.S., 452*n*, 486*n*
Siegal, Barry N., 441*n*, 532*n*
Simmons, J.W., 97*n*, 155*n*
Simon, Herbert, 452*n*
Simulation models, urban and regional,
  182–184, 342*n*
Singleton, David W., 530*n*
Site assembly problem, 377–378
Site rent
  bid-rent curve, defined, 120
  definition of, 118
  economic character of, 121
  explanatory models, 118–134, 136–140
  gradient
    definition of, 120
    empirical studies of, 121–122,
      149–150
  and highest and best use, 134
  and marginal productivity theory,
    121–134
  and metropolitan growth and change,
    136–144, 150–152
  and succession of uses, 134, 378–381
Skala, Martin, 322*n*
Skyscrapers, and urban density, 35
Slum clearance, 366, 372–373, 390

Slum housing. *See* Housing; Housing policy
Small, Kenneth A., 226n, 227n, 230n, 232n, 234n, 246n, 534n
Small Business Administration, 321
Smith, Adam, 9
Smith, Bruce A., 530n
Smith, James P., 299, 302n
Smith, Neil, 538n
Smith, Sara, 100n
Smith, Wallace F., 379n
Sneed, Carl E., 323n
Snohomish County, Wash., central place system of, 97–98
Snyder, James C., 135n
Social Security Act (1935), 285, 305
Societal scale, 110–111
So, Frank S., 135n
Solomon, Arthur P., 191n, 276n, 535n
Solow, Robert M., 300n
Somers, G.G., 295n
South Bend, Ind., 400; table, 170
Southern Burlington County NAACP v. Township of Mount Laurel, 417
Spain, Daphne, 538n
Spanish origin population
    income and poverty level, 273–274; table, 274
    and poverty area development, 319
Sparrow, Frederick T., 324n
Special district governments, 510–511
Specialization
    and external economies of scale, 16
    and urban growth, 8–9, 12
    and urban hierarchy, 93–94
Standard Metropolitan Statistical Area (SMSA), definition of, 24–26. *See also* Metropolitan areas
State governments
    and equalization of local disparities, 505–506
    and federal revenue sharing, 519–522, 524
    and local zoning, 135, 416–417, 418
    as regional governments, 511
Stegman, Michael, 356n, 407n, 408
Sternlieb, George, 351n, 356–357, 358, 416n
Stettler, H. Louis, III, 324n
Stigler, George, 16
Stolper, W.F., 87n
Straszheim, Mahlon, 136n, 239n, 246n, 256n, 342n, 370n, 479n
Streetcars, 35–37, 42–43
Struyk, Raymond J., 367
Substandard housing. *See* Housing
Suburban rings
    definition, 26, 28–29

disparities between needs and resources, 423, 478–491; tables, 480, 484
and economic opportunity for blacks, 325–334; tables, 327, 328
employment decentralization, 43–48, 147–152, 325–326; table, 46–47
exploitation of central city, 489–491
migration, 52–55, 276–278, 281–283, 353, 407
opening up to minorities, 333–334, 366, 410–420
population change and decentralization, 31–43, 48–52, 146–150; tables, 33, 40, 41
poverty, 271–283; tables, 271, 273
See also Commuting; and specific problems, e.g., Housing
Subways, 35–37
See also Transportation, urban
Succession of land uses. *See* Land use
Sumka, Howard J., 539n
Supplementary Security Income Program (SSI), 305
Supply. *See* Employment policies; Housing; Housing policy
Supply side, of local economy, 184–186, 192–193
System of cities. *See* Central place system; Market areas

Tachi, M., 66n
Taeuber, Alma, 408n
Taeuber, Conrad, 53n
Taeuber, Irene B., 53n
Taeuber, Karl, 408n
Taggart, Robert, III, 322n
Targeted Jobs Tax Credit (TJTC), 294
Tarver, James D., 54n
Taxes
    elasticity of bases, 445–448
    federal, 447
    local, 442–448, 479–482, 483–485; tables, 443, 444, 480, 484
    fiscal limitation movement, 440–442
    property (*See* Property tax)
    and redistribution of income, 485–489
    sales, 446; table, 443
    state, 447
    tax base sharing, 508–510
    See also Geographic disparities; Urban fiscal distress
Tax Foundation, 432n, 506n
Technological innovation,
    and central place system, 102–105, 106–111, 112–113
    and city growth, 10–13, 34–37

and economic base analysis, 181–182
and land-use patterns, 136–139,
    146–147
and metropolitan decentralization,
    42–49
and transport-cost orientation, 82
and urban mass transit, 258–260
Tevis, Nancy L., 323n
Textile industry, locational orientation
    of, 78–79
Thompson, Wilbur R., 185n, 408n
Thurow, Lester C., 270, 287–288, 299,
    303
Tiebout, Charles M., 159, 160, 184, 185n,
    472
Timpane, Michael P., 315n, 316n
Tobin, James, 301n
Tollison, R.D., 503n
Toronto, Municipality of Metropolitan,
    508
Transit, public. *See* Transportation, urban
Transportation, urban, 34–37, 42–43,
    195–230, 231–267
  Bay Area Rapid Transit (BART),
    228–229, 242–244, 253–258; table
    254
  benefit-cost analysis of, 247–250
  congestion pricing, 212–219, 226–227,
    231–234
  costs
    automobile operating, 201–202;
      table, 202
    bus, 229, 242–245; table, 230
    congestion, 214–219, 226–227
    energy, 212, 261–267
    external, 245–247
    highway, 225–227, 242–247; table,
      227
    intermodal comparison, 201–206,
      227–230, 242, 245
    long-run, 219–230
    peak period, 218
    pollution, 245–247
    short-run, 212–219
    time and, 103–105, 111–112,
      133–143, 202–206, 208–212;
      tables, 204, 209
  demand, 201–212, 216
    elasticity of, 207–212, 216; table, 209
    and income, 206–207
    modal choice, 201–212
  energy use
    intermodal comparisons, 261–263
    price elasticity of, 264
    and system of cities, 266–267
    and urban form, 263–267
  federal policy and, 250–253, 258–259

Urban Mass Transportation
    Administration (UMTA),
    252–253, 258–259
  highway, 198–201, 207–209, 212,
    214–218, 219–227, 232–234,
    242–247, 251, 258–259
  investment
    and federal policy, 251–253, 258–259
    optimal, 219–224, 247–250
  and land use, 117–152, 195–196
  modes, use of, 197–201; tables, 199,
    200
  paratransit, 250, 259–261
  taxis, 260–261
  pricing
    actual, 231–236
    and income redistribution, 239–242
    optimal, 212–230
    public, 198–201, 207–212, 218–219,
      227–230, 242–245, 248–250,
      251–259
  innovations, 258–259
  mass transit financing, 236–242;
      table, 238
  Victoria Line (London), 248–250
Transport cost
  and central place system, 88–89, 92,
    102–105, 108–111
  and city growth, 10–13, 34–37
  and decentralization, 42–50
  declining importance of, 82–83
  and land-use patterns, 117–132,
    136–147
  and location
    of cities, 74–76, 85
    of industry, 68–76, 77–78, 82–83
  See also Transportation, urban
Transport-cost orientation, 77–79; table,
    81
Transshipment points, 75–76
Travel time, value of. *See* Transportation,
    urban (costs)
Truck. *See* Automobile and truck
Trutko, John W., 398n
Turvey, Ralph, 126n, 247n, 295n

Ullman, Edward, 87n
Unemployment, central cities vs. suburbs,
    327–328, 330–331; table, 327. *See
    also* Employment; Employment
    policies
Urban areas. *See* Central cities; Cities
Urban, definition of, 26–28
Urban economics
  definition of, 2
  spatial aspects of, 2–4

Urban fiscal distress, 423, 491–500;
     table, 499
  causes of, 493–497
  indexes of, 497–500
  political aspects, 495–497
  and population decline, 494–495
  reform proposals
     equalization within states, 505–506
     intergovernmental grants, 525–527
     metropolitan reorganization, 506–511
     reassignment of functions, 501–506
     self-help, 527–532
        economizing, 528–530
        increasing productivity, 530–532
  See also Geographic disparities; Local
     government functions and
     boundaries
Urban hierarchy, 93–100
  empirical verification of, 96–100;
     tables, 98, 99
  See also Central place system
Urbanization
  economics of, 7–21
  urban-metropolitan pattern in U.S.,
     23–66
Urban Mass Transportation Administration
  (UMTA). *See* Transportation,
     federal policy
Urban renewal. *See* Housing policy
User charges, 428. *See also* Benefit taxes

Vance, Rupert B., 100n
Vandalism, 355, 356, 369, 377
Van Valey, T.L., 408n
Vernon, Raymond, 14, 15, 44, 278–279
Vickrey, William S., 214n, 233, 252
Vining, Daniel R., 65, 66n
Viton, Philip, 244
Von Thunen, J.H., 88, 118n
Vrooman, John, 330n

Wages
  earnings of blacks, central cities vs.
     suburbs, 328–331; table, 329
  and economic growth, 186
  and migration, 276–278
  in public sector, 435–440, 529–532;
     table, 436
Wagner, Robert F. (Senator), 366
Wallace, James E., 390n
Walras, Leon, 170
Walter, Ingo, 424n, 485n

Walters, A.A., 214n, 216n, 219, 223n
War on Poverty, 286, 290
Warren, Robert, 476n
Washington, D.C., 38; tables, 40, 244,
     279, 499
Watts, Harold W., 315n, 316n
Webber, Melvin W., 253n, 254n, 255–258
Weber, Alfred, 71n, 75
Weicher, John C., 337n, 370n, 383n
Weiner, George D., 402n
Welch, Finis, 299, 302n
Welfare. *See* Public aid
Welfare criteria (economic)
  and equity, 4–5
  and local economic policy, 186–193
Wellisz, Stanislaw, 321n
Wetzler, Elliot S., 227
Wheaton, William C., 144, 145
Whinston, Andrew B., 373–377, 381
White, Michelle J., 413n
Wholesale employment, in central cities
     and suburbs, table, 46–47
Wilcox, J.E., 408n
Willett, T.D., 503n
Williams, Alan, 474n
Williamson, Harold F., Jr., 211
Wilner, Daniel M., 362n
Wilson, James Q., 373n
Wingo, Lowdon, Jr., 19n, 64n, 330n
Winnick, Louis, 340
Winnipeg, municipal productivity, 531
Woglom, W.H., 87n
Wohl, Martin, 198n, 218, 224n, 225n,
     227n, 228, 232, 260, 261, 332n
Women's labor force participation,
     535–536
  effect on location choices, 536–537
Wood, W.D., 295n, 296n
Woodfill, Barbara M., 376n
Work Incentive Program (WIN), 293
Work incentives, and antipoverty policy,
     309, 312, 314, 316, 317

Yinger, John, 410n

Zais, James P., 398n, 400n, 401n, 402,
     403n
Zoning, land use
  exclusionary, 411–414
     reform of, 415–420
  and externalities, 134–136, 412
  fiscal zoning, 411